'98 Champs:
The Greatest Season

A chronicle of the Yankees' amazing journey to the world championship

◆   ◆   ◆

From the first game of the regular season, to October's
grand finale, The Record's award-winning sports department
has brought readers the Yank's unprecedented season
through solid reports and columns.
This book is a complete game-by-game
compilation of those stories,
which first appeared in
The Record.

www.bergen.com

Published in 1998 by

The Record

150 River Street

Hackensack, New Jersey 07601

Cover design: Vivien Benvenuto

Cover photograph: Keith A. Muccilli

Content layout: Barbara Manning, Bill Merklee

Distributed by

The Record New Products Division

150 River Street

Hackensack, New Jersey 07601

All stories originally published in The Bergen Record.

For additional copies, contact
The Record New Products Division
150 River Street
Hackensack, New Jersey 07601-7172
(201) 678-3469

Table of Contents

1998 All-Staff
Record Roster

Bob Klapisch is the The Record's baseball columnist and former Yankee beat writer. Klapisch, of Teaneck, is a Leonia native and Columbia University graduate, where he pitched against the likes of major leaguers-to-be Ron Darling and Frank Viola. Klapisch is the author of several baseball books.

Adrian Wojnarowski joined The Record in 1997 as its lead sports columnist. A graduate of St. Bonaventure University, Wojnarowski is a Cliffside Park resident who formerly worked for The Fresno Bee in California. A winner of The Associated Press Sports Editors columnist of the year award, he covered the 1998 Winter Olympics in Japan for The Record.

Ken Davidoff is completing his first season as Yankees beat writer after serving in various roles covering high school, college, and pro sports for The Record since 1994. A New York City resident and University of Michigan graduate, Davidoff has been cited by The New Jersey Press Association for his work.

T.J. Quinn joined The Record in 1997 and his coverage of the World Series completed a season in which he was the Mets beat writer. Quinn, who previously worked in Salt Lake City and Chicago, is a University of Missouri graduate. He resides in Hackensack.

Gregory Schutta began his journalism career as a news reporter at the record in 1987. In 1991, he moved into sports writing. As a back-up baseball writer, his periodic reports on the Mets and Yankees landed him the steady Yankees back-up writer position this year.

Vinny Di Trani, the dean of The Record's sports writers, has been reporting on the Jets and the Giants for 30. Occasionally, Di Trani reports on hockey, basketball, and baseball. He also covered three Olympic games: 1980; 1984, and 1988. Di Trani can be heard on WFAN Radio's Giants pre-game shows during the 1998 season.

Mark Czerwinski, The Record's Devils reporter, took a break from his regular beat to report on a few Yankees games and among other stories looked at why David Wells was a better pitcher than a profit during this shining season.

Kevin T. Czerwinski has been a professional sportswriter for more than a decade. Currently he covers the PGA, Seton Hall basketball, Army football, and is a back-up baseball writer for Yankees and Mets home games. Before joining The Record in 1992, Czerwinski was a reporter for The Reporter Dispatch and The Patent Trader both of New York.

Tara Sullivan reported on the Yankees for The Record as a departure from her college sports beat specializing in football, basketball, and the Big East Conference. Sullivan co-wrote an upcoming book "Teresa Weatherspoon's Instructional Basketball Book for Girls," which is scheduled for release in the spring.

Tim Leonard is The Record's beat writer for the Metro Stars and fills in as needed to cover the Mets, Yankees, Rangers, Devils and college sports. Previously, he was a sports writer for The Troy Record, in Troy New York where he was recognized by The Associated Press for a series he wrote. Leonard began his sports writing career at Newsday.

Steve Adamek is a former Mets beat writer who has since moved to the NBA beat as the Knicks beat writer. He also had stints as a college reporter and columnist. A Syracuse University graduate who formerly worked in Columbus, Ga., Dover, Del., and the Herald & News in Passaic, Adamek, a Fair Lawn native lives in Oradell.

1998 Regular Season

Wednesday, April 1, 1998 — at Anaheim Angels

Angels 4, Yankees 1

Pettitte gets taste of facing ace
Tough start for Yankee

By KEN DAVIDOFF, Staff Writer

ANAHEIM, Calif. — Not that Andy Pettitte deserved to win Wednesday night's season-opener for the Yankees, but he'll probably win this year pitching worse.

Wednesday night, however, served as a reminder to the Yankees' new No. 1 starter: There's a price to pay for the honor of the opening day start.

"Obviously, starting in the No. 1 slot, it's going to take away a lot of wins," the southpaw said after the Bombers dropped a 4-1 decision to the Angels and ace Chuck Finley. "It's one of those things where you're going against the other team's No. 1 a lot. I know days off and stuff like that change matchups, but for the most part, when you look at it over a season, you're going to be against pretty much the No. 1 of the other team."

In his first opening day assignment, Pettitte, 25, pitched a shaky six innings, getting tagged for nine hits and walking three. Of the 18 outs he recorded, just six were on the ground. A man who majors in economy of pitches, he needed to wind up and throw 27 times in the first inning alone and tossed 17 pitches in the fourth.

Yet for all of that, he could've come away a winner if the vaunted Yankees offense had delivered on its great expectations. It didn't because, as Joe Torre noted before the game, "He [Finley] is a big-game pitcher, no question. He has pitched well against us. I guess it's been a big game every time he's faced the Yankees, because he's been great."

Indeed, the 35-year-old lefty may have entered Wednesday night with a 1-2 record and 8.36 ERA in three previous opening day starts, but he also boasted of 14-8, 3.87 ERA against the Yanks. On this night, Column B far outweighed Column A.

Although Finley walked six Yankees, he struck out seven and allowed just four hits and one run in seven innings.

"He had a good forkball," said Derek Jeter, who struck out twice against Finley and went 0-for-4 overall. "He was throwing it in good spots. To me, he hadn't thrown many forkballs in the past. He had it looking like a fastball. All you can do is pretty much tip your hat to him."

Which brings the conversation back to Pettitte. Being a No. 1 starter means having to tip your hat more often than any of your fellow rotation members.

Consider David Cone's 1997. On April 1, 1997, the veteran right-hander had the same line as Pettitte — six innings, four runs. He also took a loss, as Mariners lefty Jeff Fassero shut down the Bombers for a 4-2 triumph.

And it didn't end there. In his next two starts, both against Oakland, he totaled 14 shutout innings. He exited both times with a no-decision. In back-to-back June starts, one against Florida and Al Leiter, the next against the Mets and Rick Reed, he went 17 innings and permitted a composite of three runs. Again, both times, he came away without a decision.

"It can be difficult, it really can," Cone said. "You just hope it all evens out. Sometimes it doesn't."

Yet no one in the Yankees clubhouse doubts that Pettitte can handle that frustration.

"Will it be a little tougher this year? Probably," Pettitte said. "Will my runs per game support go down? Probably. But that had nothing to do with my ERA last year. You've just got to go out there and pitch. I'm not going to worry about anything else."

Reporter's Notebook:

In a Wednesday throwing session, Ramiro Mendoza worked with pitching coach Mel Stottlemyre and thinks he solved the problems with his mechanics that contributed to his poor spring training. He insists he will be a different pitcher tonight, when he starts against Oakland.

Mendoza acknowledged what Torre suspected the other day, that his young right-hander had trouble motivating himself for exhibition games, thus contributing to his lackluster numbers. Said Mendoza, "I threw hard in spring training. Now I'll throw harder."

Jorge Posada will catch Mendoza tonight.

Ricardo Aramboles, the 16-year-old Dominican right-hander whom the Yankees gave a $1.52 million signing bonus Feb. 26, arrived at the team's Tampa, Fla. complex Thursday. The Yanks plan to have Aramboles pitch in extended spring training, then pitch in the Gulf Coast League (Rookie class).

Four United States luge medal winners from the Olympic Games will be among the medalists honored by the Yankees at their home-opener in one week. Luge silver medal winners Chris Thorpe and Gordy Sheer will join teammates and bronze medalists Mark Grimmette and Brian Martin.

Thursday, April 2, 1998 — at Anaheim Angels

Angels 10, Yankees 2

Angels batters tee off Yanks

By KEN DAVIDOFF, Staff Writer

ANAHEIM, Calif. — Paging the Yankees offense. Come in, Yankees offense. Report your whereabouts immediately.

Two games down for this $72 million production, and this vaunted lineup — the one that was supposed to run circles around the rest of the American League — has produced a grand total of three runs. Chuck Knoblauch and Co. contributed two-thirds of that total Thursday night, as the Anaheim tandem of Ken Hill, Rich DeLucia, Mike Holtz, and Mike James combined for a seven-hitter to give the Angels a 10-2 victory and drop the Yankees' record to 0-2.

"All we need to do is score some runs," manager Joe Torre said before the first pitch was thrown at Edison Field. "Everybody was uptight [Wednesday] night."

They didn't seem much different Thursday. On the heels of their drab 4-1 loss to Angels ace Chuck Finley to start the season, the Yankees went 1-for-9 with two RBI with runners in scoring position. And the first RBI, Derek Jeter's sacrifice fly in the seventh, ended an RBI-less streak of 15 2/3 innings to start the season. The Yanks' one run Wednesday night came on a double play.

David Wells, meanwhile, had his good stuff and one bad inning. That frame, a three-run fourth, handed him an 0-1 record despite an overall respectable line of three runs and three hits in six

innings. Horrendous relief outings by Jeff Nelson (two runs) and Willie Banks (five runs) in the seventh and eighth put the game far out of reach in the seventh and eighth.

The Yankees put five runners on base against Hill in the first three innings but could do nothing with them. In the first, Jeter's bad baserunning made an inning-ending double play out of Bernie Williams' liner to center; in the second, Joe Girardi looked at a third strike to strand runners at first and second; and in the third, Knoblauch kept running on Paul O'Neill's flare and was doubled when Angels second baseman caught it rather easily.

And all of that eventually caught up to Wells, who cruised through the first three innings. With one out in the fourth, the southpaw went 0-2 on Dave Hollins and then got careless, laying a fastball right over the plate. Hollins smoked it over the left field fence for the 1-0 Anaheim lead.

As is Wells' way, he let the inning snowball. Tim Salmon beat out an infield single to deep short when Tino Martinez couldn't scoop Jeter's one-bounce throw. Former Yank Cecil Fielder drew a walk, and Garret Anderson's dribbler to short advanced the runners to second and third.

Wells got ahead of the next batter, Nevin, and then got sloppy again. This time, he hung a 1-2 curveball that Nevin lined to the left-center field gap for a two-run double. With the way the Yankees were executing on offense, the Angels' 3-0 lead looked secure.

After Garret Anderson came up with the play of the night, a sliding catch to nab a slicing Darryl Strawberry flare and kill a New York sixth-inning rally, the Yanks finally crossed the plate in the seventh. Angels reliever DeLucia issued a leadoff walk to Scott Brosius, and one out later, Knoblauch singled, moving Brosius to third. Jeter's deep fly to left drove home Brosius for the Yanks' first RBI of the season, and Knoblauch got away with tagging up and going to third when Anderson's throw was off-line.

With the lefty O'Neill up, Angels manager Terry Collins went to his southpaw Holtz, and it worked: O'Neill took a strike, then popped up harmlessly to shortstop to kill yet another rally. And Anaheim padded its lead with two runs in the bottom of the seventh off reliever Jeff Nelson.

Reporter's Notebook:

Ramiro Mendoza worked with pitching coach Mel Stottlemyre in a Wednesday throwing session and says he thinks he solved the problems with his mechanics that contributed to his poor spring training. He insists he will be a different pitcher tonight, when he starts against Oakland, than the shaky-looking Mendoza who compiled a 6.92 ERA in spring training.

"When I throw the ball up, that's bad," he said Thursday. "When I throw it down, that's good. I'm ready for [Friday]."

Mendoza acknowledged what Torre suspected earlier this week, that his young right-hander had trouble motivating himself for exhibition games, thus contributing to his lackluster numbers. Said the 25-year-old: "I threw hard in spring training. Now I'll throw harder." Stottlemyre lectured his charge on making sure he did just that.

Jorge Posada will catch Mendoza tonight. Torre told his backup catcher to expect a couple of starts a week this season.

Saturday, April 4, 1998 — at Oakland Athletics

Athletics 7, Yankees 3

Yankees winless and grinless

By KEN DAVIDOFF, Staff Writer

OAKLAND, Calif. — This had to be it. The breakthrough inning, the breakthrough moment of this destined-for-greatness Yankees season. Three two-out hits in that top of the third Saturday at Oakland Coliseum, a three-run lead, David Cone on the hill. Finally, these surprisingly inept 1998 Yankees would get in the win column.

As it turned out, the breakthrough inning happened about an hour later. Only, it was the home team A's who were breaking through against Cone and the Bombers.

And now there is just one remaining winless team in the American League: the Yankees. The Athletics' five-run sixth gave them a 7-3 victory and raised their record to 1-3. The lifeless Yanks, meanwhile, fell to 0-3, their worst season start since 1985.

"I had the lead, I was feeling good, I thought for sure I was going to put us in a position to win the game," Cone said. "It was just the opposite. I let the game get away."

"There's a lot of things going on right now," Paul O'Neill said. "There are people just not in sync.

There's no excuses. We're just not playing well."

The moment of reckoning arrived in the bottom of the sixth inning. With Oakland trailing 3-2, highly-touted rookie right fielder Ben Grieve led off with a liner to right field. O'Neill hesitated on it, then tried to make a diving catch. The ball slipped under O'Neill's glove, and Grieve made it to third for a triple.

Cone (0-1) got ahead 1-2 on the next batter, Kevin Mitchell, but lost him to a walk. Matt Stairs' hard grounder to first was snared by Tino Martinez, who whipped the ball home to nail Grieve. Mitchell made it to third on the play.

Jason Giambi walked on four pitches to jam the bases, and pitching coach Mel Stottlemyre went to the mound to talk strategy for the next batter, switch-hitter Scott Spiezio. Cone got a called strike to move ahead 0-1, and then he served up the doozy: A cut-fastball "right in his wheelhouse," as Cone said. It landed above the scoreboard that rests along the right field fence for a grand slam.

"I was trying to [set Spiezio up for] the next pitch," Cone said. "Obviously, I didn't get there."

Cone lasted one more batter, serving up rookie catcher A.J. Hinch's first big-league hit, and he departed with his worst regular-season line (5 1/3 innings, seven hits, seven runs, three walks, three strikeouts) since he allowed seven runs to Cleveland over five innings last June 29.

By this point, the Yanks' third inning was a faint memory. Scott Brosius, of all people, sparked the rally with a one-out double to right-center off winner Jimmy Haynes (1-0).

Joe Girardi fanned for the second out, but Chuck Knoblauch ripped a hard single to right, scoring Brosius easily, and went to second when Grieve threw weakly to home. For the Yanks, the 1-0 edge was their first lead of the season.

Derek Jeter's single to right brought Knoblauch home, and when Grieve threw weakly to the plate again, the Yanks shortstop took second. He scored on O'Neill's double to left-center. Finally, there was some life from this offense.

"It was a good inning," Knoblauch said. "The game opened up right there."

But there were still signs. Bad signs. As Cone mowed down the A's lineup, the Yanks loaded the bases in the fourth, only to see Girardi ground into an inning-ending double play. Knoblauch started the fifth taking a pitch to his left shoulder blade, and he got picked off by Haynes — for the second time — one out later.

The A's put a pair on the board in the fifth, with Rickey Henderson's single bringing home Hinch and Spiezio. Cone lucked out when Dave Magadan's bullet liner went right to Tino Martinez at first, who stepped on the bag to double off Henderson. The Yankees' 3-2 lead didn't seem safe, not with the way they were hitting and Cone was pitching. And, they found out one inning later, it wasn't.

It's definitely not too early to panic, not when the game is televised for George Steinbrenner's viewing displeasure. But the Yanks are trying their hardest to stay calm.

"We're still not scoring runs," manager Joe Torre said. "We will. It's just a matter of time."

Sunday, April 5, 1998 — at Oakland Athletics

Yankees 9, Athletics 7

Yanks win, might lose Rivera

By KEN DAVIDOFF, Staff Writer

OAKLAND, Calif. — By the time this ended, with Yankees temporary co-closer Jeff Nelson clumsily fielding a Rickey Henderson nubber and throwing to first, it was a miracle the Bombers didn't charge the Oakland Coliseum field.

Finally, the Yankees were in the win column Sunday, proud owners of a hellaciously ugly, 10-inning, 9-7 victory over the A's. Finally, they broke their homerless streak, ran the bases intelligently, and fielded in the clutch.

Finally, they could relax and avoid the terrifying possibility of still being winless entering their three-game Kingdome set against the powerful Mariners.

"We need champagne," Derek Jeter said. "That's what we should've gotten."

"Everything hurts," Joe Torre said. "My stomach hurts. My back hurts. So we only need to do this 95 more times."

Yet it wasn't all good news for the Yankees. During the ninth inning, closer Mariano Rivera aggravated the right groin injury that he suffered Monday, and he appears headed for the disabled list. Hence the co-closer title for Nelson, who probably will share duties with Mike Stanton.

The official diagnosis for the ailment is a strained right groin. It will be re-evaluated today

in Seattle, where rookie Mike Buddie will be waiting to take Rivera's spot on the roster barring a surprising recovery.

"It's soreness," said Rivera, who didn't think a trip to the DL will be necessary. "I don't think this is a pull."

This foreboding development barely tempered the Yankees' enthusiasm after their bizarre, four-hour 15-minute emergence from the land of the winless.

How difficult was it for these Yankees (1-3) to close out Win No. 1? Cliff Clavin had an easier time finding a date on "Cheers" than the Bombers did finding a victory.

They blew leads in the eighth and ninth innings. They stranded 10 runners, giving them 33 in four games.

Jorge Posada, getting his first start of the season behind the plate, lined a leadoff single to center off Mike Mohler (0-1) to set the table in the 10th. Scott Brosius lined a double to left field, putting runners on second and third. And Chuck Knoblauch lofted a fly ball to right, deep enough and far enough in the corner so that Posada tagged up easily for the winning run. Jeter's single past a drawn-in infield brought home Brosius for insurance.

Nelson (1-0), who relieved Graeme Lloyd in the ninth, closed the victory. Jeter made a great backhanded stab in the hole to rob leadoff batter Scott Spiezio of a single. Nelson allowed a two-out single to Dave Magadan, then came Henderson's dribbler. Nelson was so fired up, he jumped in the air and later said, "This is almost bigger than the World Series here."

Rivera entered the game with one out in the eighth, the Yanks up by a 5-4 margin, and runners on first and second. He got the second out but then surrendered a Magadan single to blow his first save opportunity of the year and tie the score. But Chad Curtis' ninth-inning, two-run homer to left off Mohler (who came in when Mike Fetters suffered a strained left calf while pitching to Tino Martinez) gave the Yanks closer a chance to get the "W."

The Panamanian righty was one strike away from that victory, a 1-2 count on Matt Stairs with two out, when Torre darted to the mound. Rivera was helped into the dugout by pitching coach Mel Stottlemyre and head trainer Gene Monahan.

In came Lloyd, needing that same one strike for the save. He threw a ball outside, got a foul tip, a ball low and outside, a foul ball, and a ball outside. Tying run, in Jason Giambi, at the plate. And the lefty-hitting

Giambi, who entered the at-bat a career 5-for-8 against Lloyd, blasted the second pitch to center field for a 407-foot homer.

"The way we kept coming back, we wanted it bad," Posada said.

They got it — but not without a price.

Monday, April 6, 1998 — at Seattle Mariners

Mariners 8, Yankees 0

Yanks take a beating

By KEN DAVIDOFF, Staff Writer

SEATTLE — On one hand, the Yankees had the positive momentum they generated with their first victory of the season Sunday. On the other, the negative momentum of leaving the site of that victory, Oakland, and flying to Seattle, home of the dreaded Kingdome.

That poor, puny one-game winning streak had no shot Monday night. It was the Kingdome, and starting pitcher Jamie Moyer, in a rout.

The southpaw Moyer used his off-speed repertoire to silence the Yankees bats for seven innings, and the Seattle bullpen closed the deal to continue the Mariners' recent dominance over the Bombers in this building. With its 8-0 victory in front of 27,445 loud fans, Seattle has now defeated the Yanks in 18 of the clubs' last 22 Kingdome meetings.

Moyer, 35, allowed just three hits in his seven innings and fanned 11 Yankees, his highest total since 1989 when he pitched for the Rangers. At one point, from the third inning through the sixth, he retired a total of 11 straight New York batters in evening his record at 1-1.

No. 1 starter Andy Pettitte (0-2) was the hard-luck loser for the Yanks. He kept his team in the game, but his only hope on this night was to blank the mighty Mariners. And that proved to be too large a task. He lasted seven innings, allowing four runs on nine hits, walking two, and striking out four.

The Mariners wasted no time making Pettitte feel unwelcome. Leadoff hitter Joey Cora got a hold of the southpaw's second pitch and ripped it to left-center, hitting the wall on a bounce for a double. Ken Griffey, Jr.'s one-out single to right brought Cora

home, Pettitte walked Edgar Martinez, then served up a line-drive single to former Met and current American League co-Player of the Week David Segui. Griffey scored easily for the 2-0 lead.

Pettitte calmed down after that and survived an Alex Rodriguez liner off what appeared to be his hip in the third inning. But he got careless in the fifth: Former Yankee farmhand Russ Davis lined a shot over Chad Curtis' glove in left for a double, Cora sacrificed him to third, and Rodriguez destroyed a 2-2 hanging cut fastball into the left field upper deck.

It was just the 14th ball to reach that area in the 22-year history of the Kingdome, and it ended an impressive run for Pettitte. The Yanks' southpaw had gone 12 starts, a total of 89 innings, without surrendering a round-tripper. The last player to go deep on Pettitte, was his current teammate Chuck Knoblauch, for the Twins on Aug. 1. It had also been 12 road starts (86 1/3 innings) since Cal Ripken, Jr. left the yard in Baltimore on June 4.

The Yankees, meanwhile, couldn't convert on the few early opportunities they had against Moyer. In the first, Derek Jeter caught a break when his one-out liner to left field was horribly misplayed by Glenallen Hill into a two-base error. The Yankees followed that with a Paul O'Neill strikeout and Bernie Williams bouncer to third.

With one out in the third, Knoblauch powered a ground-rule double to left-center. Jeter walked, and in a frightening play, O'Neill was hit in the left wrist when he blocked a ball thrown at his head. After a conversation with Yanks head trainer Gene Monahan, he stayed in the game, the caboose of the bases-loaded, one-out rally.

The cleanup hitter Williams stepped up against Moyer, and the at-bat went as such: Ball inside, ball low, swing and miss, swing and miss, swing and miss. Two outs. But there was still hope in the form of Tino Martinez.

On a 2-1 count, the Yankees' first baseman scalded a bullet to the left field corner. Considering Hill's weak defensive skills, the ball figured to drop. Only this time, Hill pursued, pursued, reached — and gloved the ball while falling down.

No Yankee would reach base again until the seventh, when they put runners on first and second with two outs. M's manager Lou Piniella approached the mound to boos; Seattle fans didn't want to see their horrendous bullpen. Sweet Lou obliged them, and Moyer induced Knoblauch to ground into an inning-ending fielder's choice.

Tuesday, April 7, 1998 — at Seattle Mariners

Yankees 13, Mariners 7

Yankees finally play like bombers

By KEN DAVIDOFF, Staff Writer

SEATTLE — Joe Torre called his second pregame meeting in two days Tuesday, and this one wasn't civil. The Yankees manager ripped into his players for their lifeless performance in the season's first five games, according to a team source, and told them to "Get angry and win."

Whether the players followed their manager's lead is up for debate. What is indisputable is that they won Tuesday night, outslugging the Mariners for a 13-7 victory at the Kingdome.

In lifting their 1998 record to 2-4, the Bombers found the perfect tonic in Seattle starter Jim Bullinger (0-1). The right-hander, making his first American League start after four years and change in the National League, seemed to specialize in fat fastballs right over the plate and hanging curveballs. The Yanks, who entered the game hitting .209 (second worst in the AL), pounded 18 hits off Mariners pitching.

And the most encouraging performance of all came from Darryl Strawberry. It had been a rough go so far this season for the 36-year-old. He had gone 0-for-10 and had looked bad doing it.

"I'm looking for a feeling," Strawberry said Tuesday afternoon. "I haven't quite had it yet. I'll get it. You never know what day it may be. Maybe tonight, maybe tomorrow."

"Tonight" was the proper response. The left fielder crushed two homers, drove home four runs, and scored three. He had last homered in the regular season Sept. 25, 1996 (he also had three homers in the American League Championship Series). It was his 29th multi-homer game, his first since Aug. 6, 1996.

Southpaw David Wells was the beneficiary of this downpour of hits. The veteran evened his record at 1-1 in going six-plus innings, allowing six runs and nine hits, walking three, and striking out three.

The Yankees wasted no time in escaping their funk. The first batter, Chuck Knoblauch, hit the first pitch he saw from Bullinger into the left-field seats. Derek Jeter needed just two pitches to rip a ground-rule double to left, and Paul O'Neill followed with a double to right, scoring Jeter.

Bernie Williams struck out, and Tino Martinez's bouncer ricocheted off the glove of Seattle's diving first baseman David Segui. Then Strawberry went deep for homer No. 1, a blast to the second deck in right-center.

To top the inning off, Jorge Posada went deep for his second homer. This one, also a mammoth shot, went into right for the 6-0 lead. The Yanks' three homers were the most in one inning since Williams, Charlie Hayes, and Andy Fox left the park in the ninth inning of a Sept. 12, 1996 game at Detroit.

Strawberry and Posada teamed for the Yanks' seventh run in the third when the left fielder doubled to left, moved to third on Tim Raines' single, and scored on Posada's sac fly to right. Four more runs, the last two on Strawberry's homer No. 2 to straightaway center, came in the fourth.

Wells had to raise some eyebrows when, handed a six-run lead before throwing his first pitch, he walked M's leadoff batter Joey Cora in the bottom of the first. Then he allowed a run-scoring double to Alex Rodriguez, and you had to wonder if the Yanks were in for yet another long night.

> **"**I'm looking for a feeling. I haven't quite had it yet. I'll get it. You never know what day it may be. Maybe tonight, maybe tomorrow.**"**
>
> *— Darryl Strawberry*

They weren't. Wells, who prepared for his start by playing air guitar to a heavy metal album, calmed down in the first. In the third, he shook off errors by Scott Brosius and Martinez and brilliantly worked his way out of a bases-loaded, one-out jam by striking out Edgar Martinez on a pair of nasty sinkers and inducing Segui to pop out to short.

He allowed a solo homer to Rodriguez in the fifth and a two-run dinger to Robert Perez in the sixth, and the M's added two more in the seventh, causing Torre to pull his starter. But on this night, the Yankees hitters made up for their past sins and gave their pitchers enough breathing room.

Wednesday, April 8, 1998
— at Seattle Mariners

Yankees 4, Mariners 3

Bombers pull off great escape

By KEN DAVIDOFF, Staff Writer

SEATTLE — It was all falling apart, right in front of Mariano Rivera's eyes. The game. The road trip. The season?

Maybe too drastic, but wow, this would have been a tough one to swallow.

Yet the Yankees' injured closer sat in the dugout Wednesday evening, calm as ever, he claimed, watching his replacement, Mike Stanton, create what seemed to be an inescapable jam.

"I've got confidence in my guys," he said. "You have to."

His guys came through, against the odds, and now they head home in relative tranquillity. Stanton's save of a 4-3 victory at the Kingdome capped an exhausting game, road trip, and, so far, season.

The Bombers own a two-game winning streak and 3-4 record, acceptable considering they started 0-3. There will be no need for a George Steinbrenner-mandated off-day workout today before Friday's home-opener.

"Resiliency is the word that comes to mind," Stanton said.

Stanton's adventurous ninth inning served as just part of the Yankees' story. Hideki Irabu excelled in his first start of 1998, keeping his team in the game for the first five frames. Chad Curtis delivered his second huge home run in four games. And thanks to all of these factors, the Yanks won a series in Seattle for the first time since they swept a four-game set in August 1994.

"When you start the road trip 0-3 and know that of the last four games, three are in this ballpark, and you come out 3-4, that, to me, is strong," manager Joe Torre said.

"It was big to go home 3-4 on the West Coast instead of 2-5," Chuck Knoblauch said. "It's a big difference, confidence-wise and record-wise."

How close it came to going that way. Stanton, who entered the game with two out and a 4-2 lead in the eighth, started the ninth by surrendering Russ Davis' second homer of the game.

So much for room for error.

Joey Cora followed with a ground ball single up the middle, and Alex Rodriguez's line-drive base hit to left made it first and second, none out. Up next: The intimidating duo of Ken Griffey Jr. and Edgar Martinez.

Griffey popped a 3-2 pitch to Curtis in left field. Then Martinez ripped the first pitch he saw to shortstop Derek Jeter, who flipped it to Knoblauch for the force at second. But Rodriguez had a good jump on the ball and was determined to prevent Knoblauch from doubling Martinez.

"I knew he was going to be coming," Knoblauch said. "It was just a matter of when he was going to get there."

Knoblauch got off a low throw that bounced on the lip of the artificial turf. Somehow, Tino Martinez swept it with his glove and held on for the game's final out. The Yankees dugout exited in ecstasy as Stanton notched save No. 1 in relief of Graeme Lloyd (1-0).

Curtis' two-run homer off Bobby Ayala (0-1) in the eighth, after he had failed to bunt over pinch-runner Homer Bush from first, gave the Yanks the 4-2 edge. Yet none of this would have been possible without the heroic, unexpected effort from Irabu, who still is working on his arm strength after his bout with right-elbow tendinitis.

The Japanese right-hander went five strong innings, allowing one run and four hits, walking two and fanning seven.

Relying almost solely on his fastball but throwing it at varying speeds, he tamed the team that leads all of baseball with 20 homers.

He topped out at 95 mph on the radar gun, and he thrived under pressure, stranding six runners. He caught his final batter, Edgar Martinez, looking at a 95-mph fastball with Griffey on second.

"I felt OK throwing out there," Irabu, who hadn't faced major-leaguers since a March 17 Grapefruit League game against Toronto, said through interpreter George Rose.

"There were a few different points and areas that I was able to do well with."

The Yankees are feeling better about all of their points and areas.

"Now," Tino Martinez said, "we're back to where we want to be."

Friday, April 10, 1998
— Oakland Athletics

Yankees 17, Athletics 13

Extreme game
Yankees win a wild one

By KEN DAVIDOFF, Staff Writer

NEW YORK — Everyone will have a story, a joke, a take on what transpired Friday at Yankee Stadium. Even in this age of expansion and the minuscule strike zone, it's not every day — or every year, even — that players, managers, and fans endure a contest like the Yanks' home-opening, 17-13 victory over Oakland in front of a record 56,717 fans.

Here is a sample, taken not exactly at random:

"I felt during the season that we were going to win some games [when] we didn't necessarily get good pitching," manager Joe Torre said.

"Some of our relievers have got to start showing ability," George Steinbrenner said. "We just can't turn to [Mike] Stanton and [Jeff] Nelson every game. We've got to have it from the young man from Colorado."

Attention, Yankees fans: If you come to a day game in the Bronx this season, don't make dinner plans. A night game? Tell your boss in advance that you'll be late the next day.

Attention, Darren Holmes, the young man from Colorado: Rent, don't buy.

Such was the fallout from the marathon, 4-hour, 6-minute affair that set the record for most total runs scored in the 75-year history of Yankee Stadium. In making such history, the game featured David Cone unable to secure a victory despite a seven-run lead, a 50-minute fifth inning, and Bernie Williams scoring four runs despite reaching the outfield just once.

"I'm working on my short game," said Williams, who had a legitimate single to center field, an infield nubber that he legged out for a hit, and three walks.

But enough of the one-liners. While the Bombers extended their winning streak to three games and evened their record at 4-4, this victory had more warning signs than a nuclear power plant.

"I think our pitching staff is great," said Tino Martinez, who slammed a three-run homer and drove home five runs. "I don't think we'll have to score that many runs too many times."

So far, however, they have had to. Only in their 4-3 victory over the Mariners on Wednesday did the Yanks receive nine innings of quality pitching. They surrendered seven runs in each of their first two victories, as the explosive offense masked the flaws with outputs of nine and 13.

And Friday served as Exhibit A of those pitching problems, especially evident with the home crowd condemning this football game of a baseball game. Cone put the Yanks in a huge 5-0 hole after 1 1/2 innings, and then after four, he had a 12-5 lead. But the A's, who entered the game having scored an American League low 25 runs in six games, knocked him silly, and with one out and a dwindling 12-7 lead, Torre had to turn to Holmes.

The 31-year-old right-hander, who signed a three-year, $4.6 million deal last winter as a free agent, promptly served up a Rickey Henderson single to right and a Jason McDonald two-run single up the middle, and hit Ben Grieve in the back. That was it for him. Rookie Mike Buddie allowed all three of those runners to score, giving Holmes a season ERA of 13.50.

"That young man was supposed to throw a 95-mph fastball," The Boss said of Holmes. "We've got to see it." He went on to point out that the signing of Holmes resulted from reports submitted by, yes, that's right, "my baseball people."

"I don't know," Torre said when asked what was wrong with Holmes. "He's up. He looks like he might be trying to overthrow the ball, since his breaking ball isn't as sharp as we know it can be."

Holmes, whose father, Bob, traveled from North Carolina to see his son's Yankee Stadium opener, was long gone from the ballpark by the time The Boss made him his first target of 1998.

After Buddie allowed the A's to make it an eight-inning fifth and a 13-12 advantage, the Yanks came back with four in the bottom of the inning off right-hander Jim Dougherty (0-1). Buddie picked up a couple of more outs to register his first major-league victory, and Graeme Lloyd and Jeff Nelson closed the game without further incident — leaving each Yankee to contemplate his long, long day and pick his own story, joke, or take.

"We'll be in some slugfests, but that's a little ridiculous," said Derek Jeter, who combined with Chuck Knoblauch, and Paul O'Neill to go 1-for-15. "That's going to the extreme a little bit. It seems like we played a doubleheader. It wasn't a sit-on-the-edge-of-your-seat kind of game."

The Yanks' seventh, eighth, and ninth hitters — Chad Curtis, Scott Brosius, and Joe Girardi — teamed for eight hits in 11 at-bats, four runs, and seven RBI.

Saturday, April 11, 1998
— Oakland Athletics

Yankees 3, Athletics 1

Andy dandy again

Yankee happy to snap slump

By BOB KLAPISCH, Staff Writer

NEW YORK — Andy Pettitte has won 40 games since 1996, which, according to the laws of logic, means the Yankee left-hander should have a limitless reservoir of self-confidence. But is Pettitte really anxiety-free? You'd be surprised.

"I wanted this one pretty bad," Pettitte said breathlessly after a 3-1 win over the A's on Saturday. "I was keyed up about it, really overthrowing. The thing is, I'm not used to losing."

Translate the pitcher-speak, and Pettitte is telling us he had panicked about an 0-2 start, during which righties were batting .432, and opponents with runners in scoring position were hitting .462.

The problem, according to one American League scout, was that Pettitte was missing precious miles per hour on his four-seam fastball, which made it impossible for him to work the inside corner on righties. Without that weapon, Pettitte's cut-fastball lost its deception, which explained the 5.54 ERA he brought into Saturday's game.

Maybe all these blemishes were due to the weather, or a still-weakened lower back, or — the theory that's too dark for the Yankees to consider — Pettitte's arm being taxed by too many cut-fastballs over the years.

At least this much is certain: Pettitte used up 118 pitches in just six innings — overthrowing, as he admitted, issuing four walks, throwing only one 1-2-3 inning — and had to be bailed out by Tino Martinez's over-the-shoulder catch in the sixth that snuffed out an A's threat.

The Yankees were already leading, 3-1, thanks primarily to Martinez's two-run single off Tom Candiotti in the third inning and the bases-loaded walk to Chad Curtis in the fifth. But Pettitte pitched himself into trouble a half-inning later, when, with one out, he walked Jason Giambi on four pitches, then walked Mike Blowers on a full count.

Yankees manager Joe Torre knew Pettitte was "really pushing the envelope at that point." Which meant the lefty had practically exhausted his pitch count, and was now being forced to deal with Scott Spiezio — who'd reached base twice in two previous at-bats.

But that's when Martinez rescued Pettitte. Spiezio lifted a massive foul ball behind first base, deep into the danger zone where the stands, the tarpaulin, and the photographers' booth all intersect. It's a first baseman's personal nightmare, trying to negotiate a pop-up, especially with his back turned away from the plate, against a high, cloudless sky like Saturday's.

Yet, Martinez said: "I knew all along, if the ball didn't drift into the stands, I was going to catch it. I liked making that play when I played in Seattle. It's a little different in the open air, but the big thing is getting a good jump."

It didn't hurt, either, that Martinez was straying into Yankee-friendly territory: Instead of obstructing Martinez, the fans "gave me room," he said, to catch the ball — a courtesy that would've never been extended to, say, Giambi or any opposing first baseman.

Incredibly, at the last moment, all Martinez had to do was extend his glove and wait for the ball to finish its descent. The catch was, in Pettitte's words, "huge," because it was the inning's second out. When Pettitte smothered rookie catcher A.J. Hinch with a 2-2, four-seam fastball that whispered over the inside corner, the crisis was over, and the Yankees were on a clear, unfettered path to their fourth straight win.

That's because the bullpen was so perfect: Jeff Nelson and Mike Stanton combined on three innings of one-hit ball. Still, it wasn't a day when the Yankees expected to ask for help so early — not with Petitte on the mound.

Sooner or later, he and Cone will have to return to their 1997 equations of ground balls and inside-corner strikes. Cone said he's still no wiser about his unraveling against the A's on Friday, saying: "My arm felt great when I woke up [Saturday] morning. It's all a complete mystery to me."

And as for Pettitte …well, if his arm doesn't need a better karma, his ego certainly does.

In fact, all you need to know about his state of mind was this exchange between the left-hander and his manager after the fourth inning, when Petitte got Hinch to bounce into an inning-ending double play.

Torre: "Smile, will you? Have a good time out there."

Pettitte: "I will, once this thing is over."

This — meaning the game, the losing streak, and the weird bout of insecurity that threatened to ruin Pettitte's April. Logic still can't explain that.

Sunday, April 12, 1998
— Oakland Athletics

Yankees 7, Athletics 5

Jeter's bunt lights bombers

By GREGORY SCHUTTA, Staff Writer

NEW YORK — The Yankees haven't been hitting homers with the frequency most people expect. But while the talk-show junkies fret and vent, the Bombers go about putting runs on the board any way the can.

Sunday, they used a key drag bunt to post a 7-5 victory over the Oakland A's and finish off a sweep of their three-game series.

Derek Jeter surprised everyone, including manager Joe Torre, with the bunt. It sparked a three-run sixth inning as the Yankees came from behind for the third time in three days.

It was the Yankees' fifth straight victory, tying their longest winning streak of the past two seasons, and their sixth in seven games since opening the season with three straight losses.

And after stealing six bases and the game Saturday, the Yankees have shown they don't need to rely on home runs to generate runs.

"Under normal conditions, he wouldn't do that, but he's been struggling lately," Torre said of his shortstop. "He knew that he had Paul O'Neill behind him, and that's never a bad play when you're batting second."

Instead, it turned out to be one of the two biggest plays in the game. The Yankees had already seen the Athletics plate three in the top of the sixth to take a 5-3 lead.

Chad Curtis, who reached base three out of four times up, led off the bottom of the sixth with a walk and stole his second base of the game. But Jorge Posada struck out and Scott Brosius flew to center, and it looked like the A's might get out of the jam.

Chuck Knoblauch was hit by a pitch, setting up Jeter with two out and the tying runs on base in a situation where many players would be looking for the homer.

"I was just trying to do something," said Jeter, who finished with three strikeouts in the game. "The third baseman [Dave Magadan] was back and didn't expect it. All I had to do was get it down and give O'Neill a chance to drive in the run."

O'Neill did just that, rocketing T.J. Matthews' first pitch off the reliever's ankle for a single and an RBI to cut the deficit to 5-4. Bernie Williams followed by bouncing a single through the box into center field off reliever Jim Dougherty for two more runs and a 6-5 lead.

"He doesn't do that very often," O'Neill said of Jeter. "But it turned out to get the tying run in scoring position where it could score on a base hit. It's a lot easier to score on a hit than to sit around and wait for the three-run homer."

Oakland wasn't dead yet, as Jason McDonald led off the seventh with a single, stole second, and went to third on a fly to right by Ben Grieve. That set up the second-biggest play of the game.

Mike Stairs popped a fly into short left-center field where Curtis flagged it and rifled a throw that was about 15 feet up the third base line. Posada repositioned himself to catch the ball in foul territory and dived back toward the plate to nab a sliding McDonald and end the inning.

Darryl Strawberry led off the bottom of the seventh with his team-high third homer of the season, and Mike Stanton came on to pitch a perfect ninth for his second save in two days.

"It feels good to win five straight," said Torre, whose team will host the Angels tonight in the start of a three-game series. "The biggest thing was winning those two games in Seattle. To know that we can beat that team two games in their own building did a lot for our confidence. You know, if you were to lose three straight at any other time of the season than at the beginning, nobody would really notice."

The players all agreed.

"It wasn't a big concern to us," Strawberry said.

"We were disappointed because we know we have a better club than that, but we knew it would come around. This club does whatever it takes to win. We know how to come from behind, and we're not afraid to come from behind. That's the sign of a good team."

"We got some big hits today," O'Neill said. "Tino [Martinez] got a big hit [a two-run double], Bernie got a big hit. That's how we're going to score runs — by getting big hits with runners in scoring position."

Wednesday, April 15, 1998
— Anaheim Angels — at Shea Stadium

Yankees 6, Angels 3

Yankees win, head to Detroit

By KEN DAVIDOFF, Staff Writer

NEW YORK — The Yankees may not have to worry about their aging ballpark for too many more years. As owner George Steinbrenner said Wednesday: "I think we will see a decision [on a new stadium] in 1998. All our options are still the same, but we should make a decision this year."

For right now, however, with Yankee Stadium in disarray, there's no place like the road.

The Yankees swapped weekend homestands with the Tigers on Wednesday. In a flip of the original schedule, the teams will play Friday through Sunday in Detroit and the following weekend at Yankee Stadium, if it is given a clean bill of health following Monday's accident.

"This is the right move," Steinbrenner said after his team beat the Angels, 6-3, in their unusual Shea Stadium matinee.

"I like it for a couple of reasons," Yanks manager Joe Torre said. "We get away from all the media here because there's so much extra media here, which could be a distraction. Plus, the next homestand will be a more meaningful homestand as far as the number of games [the Yanks will have a seven-game homestand, April 24-30, rather than the scheduled four-game stay].

"Whether it works remains to be seen. On the surface, it looks like something we want to do."

"Getting away from this right now is probably the best thing that can happen," right fielder Paul O'Neill said. "We won't have to answer all the questions about a steel beam."

The beam, or expansion joint, that fell through the left field upper deck of Yankee Stadium on Monday afternoon will cause the Bombers to play just three of their first 17 games at home. They opened the season with an eight-game West Coast trip, swept the A's at home in the Bronx last weekend, and played Wednesday at Shea after postponing the first two games of the Angels series. Tonight, they'll head to Detroit for the weekend series, then play Monday through Wednesday at SkyDome in Toronto.

"It's a little crazy, what's going on," catcher Jorge Posada said. "But if we keep playing, it's all going to be good with me."

The American League initiated the idea of swapping the series rather than shifting the site of this weekend's set to Shea. Said AL senior vice president Phyllis Merhige: "It seemed to us the fairest way to preserve the integrity of the schedule." The Tigers objected at first over concerns that switching dates would hurt attendance, according to a baseball source, but apparently were talked into it as doing something for the good of the sport.

"[Tigers owner] Mike Ilitch is one of the best owners in baseball," said Steinbrenner, who again shelled out praise to New York Mayor Rudolph Giuliani. The Tigers, who count on their annual weekend home series with the Yanks to draw some of their larger crowds, will be indemnified by Major League Baseball for any financial losses they suffer due to the flip-flop.

The trade gives New York City engineers another week to survey every nook and cranny of 75-year-old Yankee Stadium and make any necessary repairs. So far, with one more day of inspections expected, city workers have found nothing more serious than cosmetic flaws such as cracks in the outer facade and spalling caused by water that makes its way behind concrete and forces it out.

"This stadium will have gone through one of the most thorough inspections of any stadium in the country," Jerome Hauer, director of the New York City's office of emergency management, said Wednesday. Hauer said the city hopes to have all the repairs done by next Wednesday evening, leaving a one-day margin for error to tackle any final problems. He voiced strong optimism that the stadium could reopen a week from Friday.

Tickets for this weekend's series will be honored on the corresponding day next week — Friday for Friday, and so on. This weekend's scheduled promotional giveaways — 75th Anniversary Cap Day on Saturday and 75th Anniversary Key Ring Day on Sunday — also will be switched to corresponding days.

Friday, April 17, 1998 — at Detroit Tigers

Yankees 11, Tigers2

Yanks slam Tigers
Tino enjoys a grand night

By KEN DAVIDOFF, Staff Writer

DETROIT — It turned out the Yankees didn't have to worry about the Tigers getting mad at them Friday night. Or getting even. No, all the Tigers got Friday night was real bad, real early, showing no hunger for vengeance in what is being called "The Great Stadium Switch" here.

Like the playground bullies they are regarded as in this area, the Yankees disposed of the Tigers, 11-2. A Tiger Stadium crowd of about 6,000 — from an advance ticket sale of 12,348 for this game originally scheduled for next Friday — altered weekend plans to take in the ugly contest.

There were plenty of hard feelings — at least from the Detroit-area newspapers and Tigers fans — as a result of the schedule flip-flop in which the American League leaned heavily on the Tigers to agree to playing the Yanks this weekend at home and next weekend in the Bronx.

And it didn't help matters when George Steinbrenner made light of the trouble the Tigers went through to help the Yanks avoid playing at dreaded Shea Stadium this weekend while Yankee Stadium undergoes some repairs.

In a published report Friday, Steinbrenner was quoted as saying, "How is [Tigers owner Mike Ilitch] putting his fans at an inconvenience? We're trading one weekend for the other." When it was suggested to The Boss that a Detroit fan who planned on attending a game next weekend might have a wedding to attend this weekend, the Yankees principal owner responded, "Well, if you were going to a wedding next weekend, now you can come to the games. It works both ways."

Steinbrenner was livid with the way his comments looked in print. He scowled at New York reporters upon entering the Yankees' clubhouse Friday afternoon, and he released a six-paragraph written statement refuting his comments.

"I would never say that such a gracious act is no big deal," The Boss said in the statement. "It is a big deal! Mike Ilitch, the entire Tigers organization, and the fans have stepped forward to help us, and I am sincerely and deeply appreciative of this act of kindness."

In any case, with Steinbrenner cheering and shivering in the chilly Tiger Stadium stands, the Yankees (8-4) exposed the Tigers as an especially unemotional group, pounding out 12 hits and dismantling the home team for their seventh straight victory.

"We've got a pretty good offensive lineup," manager Joe Torre said. "One through nine are pretty good. Tino gave us the lead, and Jeter [padded it]."

Tino Martinez's monstrous, first-inning grand slam — the sixth of his career — off Tigers ace Justin Thompson (1-3) hit the facing of the third deck in right field and gave his team a 5-0 lead.

"It was a bad pitch," Martinez said of the hanging curveball. "I was looking for anything." The first baseman has 15 RBI in his past five games.

Jeter, who entered the game hitting .208, added a three-run blast in the fourth before being removed in the bottom of the inning as a precautionary measure to keep his sore left groin out of the cold. The Yankees poured on three more runs, with rookie designated hitter Shane Spencer notching his first career RBI and Tim Raines, batting third, tallying three hits.

Yankees starter Andy Pettitte (2-2), handed a five-run lead before he stepped on the mound, labored through 6 2/3 innings and 128 pitches on a 54-degree night.

He tied his career high with six walks while scattering six hits and fanning six. While he blanked the Tigers through the first six innings before tiring and allowing a two-run Bobby Higginson double in the seventh, he didn't execute a single 1-2-3 inning.

"I was battling and struggling with my command," said Pettitte, who lowered his ERA to 3.86. "I hate to make excuses, but the wind was blowing. It was really whipping out there …The guys got a lot of runs early, and that made it a lot easier."

"He had trouble feeling the ball in the cold, but he worked his tail off tonight," Torre said. "He was good."

Darren Holmes, who was singled out by Steinbrenner following a poor showing in the April 10 home opener, threw the final 2 1/3 innings in front of The Boss, permitting just one hit and one walk while striking out three.

Saturday, April 18, 1998 — at Detroit Tigers

Yankees 8, Tigers 3

Cone survives rough start

Yanks' bats tame Tigers

By KEN DAVIDOFF, Staff Writer

DETROIT — The expectations have fallen precipitously for David Cone in two short weeks. He used to be one of two pitchers the Yankees relied on to stop losing streaks. On Saturday, there was simply hope that he would not stop a winning streak.

He didn't. The veteran right-hander was an escape artist early and a pitching artist late, notching his first 'W' of 1998 with the Yankees' eighth straight victory, an 8-3 win over Detroit at Tiger Stadium.

"I just want to be a part of what's going on here," said Cone (1-1). "I don't want to be a detriment. I want to be a guy who can be reliable. Today was a first step."

It was a shaky one, to be sure. On a not-too-cold day, the 35-year-old lasted 5 2/3 innings and allowed seven hits, walked two, and hit one. Just two Tigers crossed home plate under his watch, but it could have been much, much worse if not for a superb play by Tino Martinez and some questionable baserunning by the Tigers.

"He's still finding it," manager Joe Torre said of his pitcher. "He's still going to get better arm strength. But I thought he made better pitches than last outing."

His first two outings of the season, both against American League West cellar-dweller Oakland, left him with a 14.90 ERA and a heap of frustration. There was nothing wrong physically, the man whose pitching shoulder went under the knife in 1996 and 1997 said repeatedly. It was all mechanical.

Things looked much the same in the first inning Saturday, the 75th anniversary of Yankee Stadium, which was closed for repairs following Monday's accident. Handed a 1-0 lead courtesy of a Paul O'Neill double and Bernie Williams single, Cone walked Tigers leadoff batter Brian Hunter. He induced Damion Easley to foul out to first, but while pitching to Bobby Higginson, Hunter stole second

and advanced to third on Joe Girardi's throwing error. One pitch later, Higginson drew ball four to make it first and third, one out.

Cleanup hitter Tony Clark smashed a hard grounder to the right of Martinez, who dove and backhanded the bullet, sprang to his feet, and whipped the ball to Derek Jeter for the force. Jeter threw it back to Martinez for the twin-killing.

"With a left-handed hitter, and a 0-2 count, they'll always try to hit the ball inside and drive it through the hole," Martinez said matter-of-factly.

"That was a huge play as far as David Cone went," Torre said.

It got worse for Cone before it got better. Luis Gonzalez started the second with a double to right-center, and Tigers designated hitter Frank Catalanotto followed with a flare single that fell in front of O'Neill in right. Joe Randa's single past a diving Chuck Knoblauch brought home Gonzalez to tie the game, and with first and second, Cone grazed catcher Raul Casanova's back on an 0-2 count to jam the bases with no outs.

But like the Cone of old, he got out of trouble. Bill Ripken hit a shallow fly to right, keeping Catalanotto at third, and Hunter knocked a "humpback," or a sinking line drive, to Knoblauch. For some reason, Casanova ran on the hit and was easily doubled off first.

"Maybe my luck's going to turn around," said Cone, who spoke of an improved slider and splitter. "I caught a break."

The Tigers took a 2-1 lead in the fourth, but by then Cone seemed more under control, and in the fifth he recorded his first 1-2-3 inning since the second inning of his first start on April 4 (a total of 13 innings in between). The Yanks scored two in the fifth and three in the sixth, and had his first win and an ERA that dropped to 10.57.

"There's no compensation for just going out there and struggling through a game, keeping your team close and coming out with a win," said Cone, who threw 113 pitches, 72 for strikes. "That's the best medicine of all."

The Yanks' eight-game winning streak is their best since they captured 10 straight from May 6-15 in 1994.

The Tigers announced a crowd of about 6,800, yet it seemed like more; the team is trying hard to be the victim in the schedule switch caused by Monday's Yankee Stadium accident.

Sunday, April 19, 1998 — at Detroit Tigers

Tigers 2, Yankees 1

Yanks let down Irabu

By KEN DAVIDOFF, Staff Writer

DETROIT — Disappointment and frustration filtered through the tiny visitors clubhouse at Tiger Stadium on Sunday afternoon. The Yankees' eight-game winning streak had run smack into obscure Detroit pitcher Brian Moehler, who shut down the Bombers for a crisp 2-1 victory.

Yet this malaise had a slightly different taste to it than your standard "We stunk" sensation. At least some of it came from the Yankees' regret they could not reward the strong pitching of their starter, the once-despised Hideki Irabu.

"He did a great job," Bernie Williams said of the Japanese right-hander. "It's unfortunate not to get him a win, the way he pitched today."

Irabu, making his first regular-season appearance in 11 days, made another giant leap in his maturation toward a legitimate, reliable big league pitcher. In six-plus innings, he allowed one run on three hits, walking two, and striking out seven. He left the game with stiffness in his right lower back, but it isn't considered serious.

His fastball hovered around 92 mph, below average for him, but he displayed a nasty curveball that continually baffled the Tigers and threw in his splitter as well. His 1.64 ERA leads Yankees starters.

"He can't be much better than that," catcher Joe Girardi said. "There aren't too many people who can be much better than that."

On this day, though, Moehler was. In the National League-esque affair that lasted 2 hours 47 minutes, Irabu and Moehler (1-2) had no-hitters through four innings. Moehler lost his chance for history first, when Chad Curtis knocked a controversial infield single in the fifth inning. Irabu followed suit in the bottom of the inning, giving up Frank Catalanotto's line drive to center.

With one out in the sixth, Brian Hunter drove a liner back to the mound. Irabu, who will never win a Gold Glove, turned away from the ball rather than try and grab it with his glove. The ball nailed him in the right lower back and ricocheted toward third base for an infield single.

The posse of manager Joe Torre and trainers Gene Monahan and Steve Donohue rushed to the mound, as is standard procedure in such plays, and within seconds they were all laughing heartily as though enjoying a screening of "Major League 3: Back To The Minors."

"He just kept saying, 'Back. Back. Back,'" Torre said. "We all knew that."

"In the sixth inning, when it happened, I was excited," Irabu said through interpreter George Rose. "I threw some practice pitches. As I went [on], it got tighter and tighter."

He looked strong through the sixth, then allowed a leadoff, tie-breaking home run to Tony Clark, a high, arching shot that grazed the Tiger Stadium overhang in right field. Irabu threw two more pitches, out of the strike zone to Luis Gonzalez, before exiting.

"It's a little bit tight right now," Irabu said after the game. "I can't quite turn as well as I'd like to."

The Yankees will monitor the injury, but they expect their No. 4 starter to pitch this weekend against the Tigers, a team against whom he holds a career 1.83 ERA in 19 2/3 innings.

The Yankees erased an "L" from Irabu's ledger in the eighth, when they tied the score at 1 on Curtis and Scott Brosius singles and a Jorge Posada fielder's choice. But reliever Darren Holmes, with some help from Williams, handed the lead right back in the bottom of the inning.

Holmes (0-1) allowed a leadoff single to Raul Casanova, walked Brian Hunter one out later, and threw a wild pitch that moved pinch-runner Kimera Bartee to third. Damion Easley lofted a pop to shallow center, and the speedy Bartee challenged Williams. It was no contest, as Williams' throw was well off to the first base side.

"He was too fast," Williams said. "I got a pretty good grip under the circumstances. I just didn't throw him out."

Todd Jones pitched a 1-2-3 ninth in relief of Moehler for his second save, and the home crowd of approximately 7,000 — of 12,568 tickets sold for the game switched due to the Yankee Stadium accident — cheered the end of their squad's seven-game losing streak.

The Yanks, meanwhile, headed to Toronto feeling better than ever about the guy whose turn in the rotation they used to dread.

Monday, April 20, 1998 — at Toronto Blue Jays

Yankees 3, Blue Jays 2

Yankees accept gift-wrapped win

By KEN DAVIDOFF, Staff Writer

TORONTO — Tony Fernandez is "one of the best fielders of all time," according to Derek Jeter. Yet when Jeter hit a bouncer to Fernandez in the 11th inning of Monday night's Yankees-Blue Jays marathon, he didn't concede the out.

"You never know," Jeter said afterward. "You never anticipate him missing a ball."

Those who watched last year's World Series know differently. With Chuck Knoblauch on third and two outs, the former Yankee bobbled the ball — just as he did when he played for Cleveland, to set up Florida's winning run in Game 7 of last year's Fall Classic. And so the Yankees pulled out perhaps their most satisfying victory of the season, 3-2, over the Blue Jays at SkyDome.

"It's definitely a big win for us to get that one," Knoblauch said.

Jersey City native Willie Banks, who hadn't pitched since April 2, pitched a roller-coaster bottom of the 10th to notch his first victory of the season. Mike Stanton pitched a perfect 11th inning for his fourth save.

With two outs in the 11th, Knoblauch — who had ended an 0-for-13 skid earlier in the game — ripped a two-out triple to deep right field off Toronto righty Bill Risley (0-2). That's when Fernandez committed his error, allowing Knoblauch to come home with the go-ahead run. Jeter celebrated his good fortune with a fist pump, and the Yankees had their lead.

The game looked like it would be over in the bottom of the 10th when Shawn Green blasted Banks' first pitch to deep center field for a double. Jose Canseco gave himself up, grounding to first to move Green to third.

Then, with the infield drawn in, former Bomber Mike Stanley knocked a bouncer to Jeter. The shortstop whipped the ball home, and the Yanks nailed Green in a rundown while Stanley made his way to second. Escape seemed feasible.

Until Banks (1-0) wild-pitched Stanley's pinch runner, Juan Samuel, to third. But after a pair of walks, one intentional, to load the bases, the righty sent the

game into the 11th when he got Fernandez to line out to Jeter.

"I didn't know what to expect" from Banks, manager Joe Torre said. "It's unfair to expect him to do a wonderful job, but he got them out."

"I was just thankful today," Banks said. "Now I can call my momma."

The Yanks were trailing, 2-0, until they scored a pair of runs off Jays' closer Randy Myers in the ninth. It was Myers' first blown save since May 3.

The game began as a pitchers' duel, until Toronto broke through in the sixth off Yankees starter David Wells. Jays rookie Kevin Brown led off with a hard liner that glanced the glove of a diving Jeter and headed toward left field. Brown made it to second for the double.

Shannon Stewart followed with a line-drive single to center, and Toronto third-base coach Eddie Rodriguez gave Bernie Williams' arm too much credit by holding Brown at third. It turned out not to matter, though, as Alex Gonzalez pounded a double off the base of the wall in left-center. Brown and Stewart scored easily for the 2-0 lead.

Wells avoided further trouble, inducing Shawn Green to ground out, walking the dangerous Canseco, and getting Stanley to ground into a 6-4-3 double play.

Throughout Wells' performance, he was harassed by a fan who constantly whistled while the southpaw went into his windup.

"The guy was a good whistler," said Wells, who lowered his ERA to 4.73 with 6 2/3 innings of two-run ball. "If there was a whistling contest, he'd win… Tomorrow, if he's there, I'll go into the stands. I'll pull a Tony Phillips [who attacked a fan a few years ago], but I won't hit the guy. I'll just whistle in his ear."

Tuesday, April 21, 1998 — at Toronto Blue Jays

Yankees 5, Blue Jays 3

Mendoza makes pitch to keep job

By KEN DAVIDOFF, Staff Writer

TORONTO — Ramiro Mendoza may not have notched the victory in Tuesday night's Yankees-Blue Jays game, but he could take something positive out of SkyDome: He outpitched Orlando Hernandez.

The Yankees fifth starter pitched superbly in a contest the Yankees went on to win, 5-3 in 10 innings, after Jeff Nelson blew the save for Mendoza in the eighth. Making his first start since April 12, the 25-year-old right-hander went seven-plus innings, allowing two runs on seven hits, walking two, and fanning two.

Meanwhile, Hernandez, pitching for Class A Tampa in Port St. Lucie, needed 85 pitches, just 44 of them strikes, to get through four innings. He allowed one hit and fanned eight, but walked three, hit two, and unleashed a wild pitch. The Yankees figure him to be a starter when he's ready for the majors, but on Tuesday, Mendoza's pitching spoke volumes about his desire to stay in the starting rotation.

"He pitched a wonderful game," Joe Torre said of Mendoza. "That'll always be in the bank."

Mendoza wasn't the only hero of the Yanks' 10th victory in 11 games, and their second straight in extra innings. Bernie Williams broke out of a slump with three hits, including the game-winner in the 10th, and Tino Martinez added three hits and two RBI. Jeff Nelson coughed up Mendoza's lead, the Yanks' first blown save since Mariano Rivera went on the 15-day disabled list, yet Nelson rebounded to keep the game a tie, and Mike Stanton pitched two perfect innings for the victory.

"This team has more angles than just being a big offensive team," Williams said.

The first seven innings, though, were all about Mendoza. Of the 21 outs he recorded, 17 came via the ground thanks to his sinker. Of the seven hits he permitted, three didn't leave the infield, and only one went for extra bases. Just one Blue Jay scored, Jose Cruz Jr. in the third, which neutralized Derek Jeter's solo blast in the top of the same inning.

"He was on top of his game," catcher Jorge Posada said. "He knew what he wanted to do. Change-up, curveball — he was on it all today. He was fun."

The second-year right-hander Mendoza used his limited English to call it his best start as a major-leaguer. He said he's not thinking about Hernandez, but he reiterated that he prefers starting.

Torre, for all his praise, indicated that he finds Mendoza just as valuable in the bullpen as the starting rotation, and his billiant start Tuesday wouldn't prevent a shift to relief.

"We tend to put vanity on the back burner here," Torre said.

Martinez's two-run, bases-loaded single off Jays starter and Kinnelon native Erik Hanson gave the Yanks a 3-1 lead in the top of the seventh, and Mendoza left the game after surrendering a Tony Fernandez double to start the bottom of the eighth.

Shawn Green flied to deep right off Graeme Lloyd, and Fernandez tagged up and advanced to third base. Nelson entered and struggled: Jose Canseco's double to left-center sent Fernandez home, former Yank Mike Stanley walked, and Ed Sprague — who entered the at-bat 1-for-8 lifetime with four strikeouts against Nelson — singled to center to score Canseco with the tying run.

Nelson salvaged the inning, and Martinez led off the 10th against Dan Plesac (0-2) with a simple grounder that Toronto first baseman Felipe Crespo botched. Then Williams — who had entered the night in a 2-for-19 funk — crushed a bullet over the head of the center fielder Cruz. Martinez scored for the go-ahead run, and Williams came home on Tim Raines' sacrifice fly for an insurance run.

"It felt pretty good," Williams said. "For some reason, I started to feel the ball better."

Before the game, Torre and Blue Jays management exchanged tense words as the Yanks manager spoke of his request during Monday night's game that Toronto baserunning instructor Maury Wills be removed from the dugout because he is not one of the Jays' six alloted coaches. Torre and Wills met before Tuesday's game, and Wills apparently agreed not to sit in the dugout again.

Wednesday, April 22, 1998
— at Toronto Blue Jays

Yankees 9, Blue Jays 1

Brosius is big in Yanks' rout

By KEN DAVIDOFF, Staff Writer

TORONTO — "I've been around some of the great ones — Spahn, Gibson, Seaver," Joe Torre said Wednesday afternoon. "They lose."

Sure enough, Roger Clemens lost Wednesday night to the Yankees and their ace Andy Pettitte (3-2). But there was no way the Yankees manager could have forecast which of his position players would lead the Bombers to victory over the great Clemens.

Scott Brosius, who entered the game with a

pedestrian .255 average and invisible .071 (1-for-14) lifetime mark against Clemens, knocked three hits off the Blue Jays' ace and tied his career high with five RBI, leading the the Yanks to a 9-1 dusting of Toronto, a series sweep, and a 5-1 road trip in preparation for Friday's Yankee Stadium "reopener."

"It's one of those things that happens every now and then," Brosius said. "He gets the best of me more than I get the best of him."

With Boston winning again in Detroit, the Yanks (12-5) remained a half game behind the Sox but in first place of the American League East by percentage points.

In what figured to be a low-scoring affair, with the Yanks' young Texan Pettitte taking on veteran Lone Star State native Clemens, Pettitte dominated to pick up his third straight victory, throwing the Yanks' first complete game of the season in the process.

Clemens (2-2) tied a career high of his own with the nine runs he allowed, although three were unearned. The Yanks, who finished with 10 hits, didn't really pound Clemens until the seventh, his final inning.

In the early going, it was all Brosius, whose five RBI accounted for the visitors' first five runs and all came with two outs.

His 3-for-5 evening lifted his average to .283, and while he has exhibited none of the power that he did two years ago when he hit 22 homers for Oakland, his two hits with runners in scoring position Wednesday night gave him a .389 (7-for-18) average in such clutch situations.

"Today was the Scott Brosius show," said Tim Raines, who added two doubles and three runs.

Brosius, who entered the game just 4-for-29 on the road trip, worked before the game with Yanks hitting coach Chris Chambliss.

"We worked on staying through [the pitch] and not pulling off," Brosius said. Before long, he had to test his new approach.

The first opportunity came in the second inning. With runners on second and third and two out, Brosius stood between a wasted inning and a productive one. He got a hold of Clemens' first pitch, a fastball, and went with it to right field, where it fell in front of Shawn Green for a single.

No one scored again until the sixth, when the Bombers capitalized on a pair of errors by Jays shortstop Alex Gonzalez to load the bases with one down. Chad Curtis hit into a force at home, putting Brosius in the hot seat again.

And he delivered again. He drilled an 0-1 Clemens splitter up the middle, and it somehow rolled past center fielder Jose Cruz Jr. to clear the bases for a double. This pitcher's duel had suddenly turned into a comfortable 5-0 Yankees advantage.

That's when it grew clear that this would be Pettitte's night. The tough southpaw lost his first two starts of the season, and he admitted Wednesday to being disgusted by his early incompetence. He gradually improved during his first two victories, and Wednesday he put it all together. In his nine innings, he allowed just the one unearned run on six hits, walked one, hit two batters, and struck out six. His ERA is now a very acceptable 2.86.

"That's the Andy that I'm used to," catcher Joe Girardi said.

"It wasn't anything about mechanics," Pettitte said of his prior troubles. "It's just about concentration and focus. ... I'm trying to go out there and be relaxed. I've been pitching way too uptight for me. I've been wearing myself down because I've been so frustrated with what I didn't have in a game. Worrying that my change-up wasn't there. Worrying that my curveball wasn't working.

"I've just got to go out there and figure out what I've got and don't come back [to the clubhouse] between innings and beat on myself, because by the fifth or sixth inning, I'm mentally drained."

Thanks to Pettitte and Brosius, the Yanks were anything but mentally drained Wednesday after playing 14 of their first 17 games away from their home park.

Friday, April 24, 1998
— Detroit Tigers

Yankees 8, Tigers 4

Yankees, stadium looking good

By KEVIN T. CZERWINSKI, Staff Writer

NEW YORK — There was more suspense in the stands than on the field Friday at Yankee Stadium.

While New York was busy toppling Detroit, 8-4, in what was billed as the Stadium's "reopener," the only real drama was waiting to see if any more of the 75-year-old building would come crashing down.

The Stadium held up, as did David Cone's arm in

his first night start of the season en route to the Yankees' fourth consecutive victory.

Owner George Steinbrenner was as entertaining in the stands as the Yankees were on the field. The Boss was sitting just four seats to the right of where a 500-pound support beam came crashing down two weeks ago, causing the Stadium to be closed for inspections and structural repairs.

Steinbrenner, decked out in a windbreaker and turtleneck, showed up 15 minutes before the game and took his seat in the loge section just past third base.

He schmoozed with fans wearing hard hats and thrust his arms in the air when Darryl Strawberry launched a two-run homer into the upper deck in right, highlighting New York's four-run first inning.

"It was like old times," Steinbrenner said. "It was like I was back in Cleveland when I was a kid, going to the stadium with a bunch of guys."

New York City mayor Rudy Giuliani, who earlier this week announced his initial plan for financing the construction of new ballparks for the Yankees and the Mets, chose to sit next to the New York dugout.

It all made for very good theater for the crowd of 26,173. But the real show was what took place on the field. Cone, who took a 10.57 ERA into the game, had a no-hitter going into the fourth.

And, even though the Tigers scored twice in the fourth, Cone was sharp. He allowed one run on an infield out by Tony Clark and another on a sacrifice fly by Luis Gonzalez. He struck out Damon Easley to end the threat.

Cone (2-1) pitched 6 1/3 innings before giving way to Mike Stanton, who was back in his role as setup man upon the return of Mariano Rivera from the disabled list.

Cone, who struck out four, walked two, and allowed three hits, left with runners on first and second after throwing 82 pitches. Stanton, however, got Bip Roberts to hit into an inning-ending, 4-6-3 double play.

"I still don't think I'm all the way back in terms of endurance," Cone said. "But the last two starts have been progressively better, which isn't saying much since the first two starts were awful. Tonight, I felt everything was there. It was nice to be in control.

"I had a real sharp slider. It was the first time I had it snapping all year. I've been searching for the right tempo and, for me, tempo is everything."

Strawberry was equally sharp. His first-inning homer, his fifth of the season, traveled 432 feet.

The blast was the highlight of a first inning from which Detroit starter Greg Keagle looked to be unable to escape. He allowed six hits in the inning, including a run-scoring double by Tino Martinez and an RBI single by Bernie Williams.

Strawberry also doubled off the base of the wall in the left-field corner in the third inning. He came around to score on Scott Brosius' two-out single.

Both benches and bullpens emptied in the eighth inning after Detroit's Bobby Higginson's bloop double scored two runs.

The bench-clearing non-brawl was a result of Mike Stanton plunking Detroit's previous batter, Joe Randa, with a pitch. After Randa and Raul Casanova scored on the double, Casanova exchanged words with Joe Girardi, and both benches emptied.

Detroit pitcher Sean Runyan hit Tino Martinez with a pitch in the bottom of the seventh to start the festivities.

Reporter's Notebook:

There was a unconfirmed report after the game that Darryl Strawberry's wife, Charisse, was punched in the stomach by a fan.

When asked about the incident, Strawberry said he didn't know anything and would check on it. Designated hitter Chili Davis made an appearance in the locker room before the game, sporting a cast on his right foot. He underwent successful surgery Monday to repair tendon and ligament damage. He expects the cast to be on for three weeks and anticipates being out of action until at least the end of June.

Saturday, April 25, 1998

Yankees 5, Tigers 4

Yanks' Wells keeps cool

Survives 'E' to gain win

By KEVIN T. CZERWINSKI, Staff Writer

NEW YORK — David Wells wouldn't have acted this way a year ago.

The Yankees southpaw wouldn't have been able to rebound from a fifth inning like the one he experienced Saturday if the calendar read 1997. But Wells displayed a new-found focus and was rewarded for his grit as the Yankees came back for a 5-4 victory against woeful Detroit.

The victory, which gives them a 6-0 home record, is their fifth in a row and 13th in their past 14 games. Detroit has dropped 10 consecutive road games.

Chad Curtis and Darryl Strawberry continued to make manager Joe Torre look like a genius with his platoon system.

They combined to account for the winning run in the eighth. Strawberry drew a two-out walk, stole second, and scored two pitches later as Curtis singled up the middle to make Wells (3-1) the winner. Mariano Rivera came on in the ninth to earn his first save.

But, the fact that Wells was still around in the eighth didn't appear possible in the fifth when he looked ready to unravel. The Tigers scored all of their runs in the inning, which was prolonged when Wells make a throwing error on a potential double-play grounder.

Wells gave up one-out singles to Luis Gonzalez and Joe Oliver. When weak-hitting Billy Ripken tapped one back to the mound, the inning looked to be over. After fielding the ball, Wells turned and fired it to the right of second base, past the glove of Derek Jeter.

The ball rolled into center as Gonzalez scored. Brian Hunter followed with a double, plating Oliver. Joe Randa then singled in two runs and the Tigers had a 4-3 lead.

Wells kept it together, getting Bobby Higginson and Tony Clark to fly out to right field to end the inning.

"I'm most impressed with the fact that Boomer [Wells] got it back," Torre said. "It was something last year that might not have happened. Last year, he wouldn't have retrieved it. When something went wrong, it stayed wrong last year."

Wells admits he goofed. But, he wasn't about to give in. He allowed just one baserunner — via a walk — over his final three innings.

"I had Derek on the play," Wells said. "When the ball was hit, he broke for second. I turned around and saw both of them [Jeter and second baseman Chuck Knoblauch] there and threw. It was my fault. It was pretty much a tailor-made double play if I knew how to field my position correctly.

"I'm not the type of person to give up though. I didn't feel I had my best stuff today and to give up

four runs in an inning is a bummer. But we have to go out there and fight. It shows good character and we're going to ride this."

Torre would also be wise to continue riding the Strawberry-Curtis-Tim Raines rotation. Raines had a hit Friday, and Saturday was Curtis' opportunity to shine. After the Yanks tied the game in the sixth on Ripken's error, he drove in Strawberry with the winning run.

"When I'm up there in that situation and the game is tied, I'm looking to drive one into the gap," Curtis said. "But when I see Darryl take off and get a good jump, I have to take the pitch.

"I think the rotation is working out. I think Joe knows every time he throws one of us out there, we're going to contribute. All three of us are good players, especially when we're hitting behind the guys we're hitting behind. Hitting seventh in this lineup is a real treat."

Monday, April 27, 1998
— Toronto Blue Jays

Yankees 1, Blue Jays 0

Pettitte takes Jays' best shot

By GREGORY SCHUTTA, Staff Writer

NEW YORK — Andy Pettitte may have been born in Louisiana, but he apparently has a bit of the great white north running through his veins as well. The Yankee left-hander took a comebacker off the leg for the second time this season, but managed to shake it off, outdueling Roger Clemens for the second time in five days and combining with three relievers to blank Toronto, 1-0, Monday night.

"Everybody's telling me to go out there and get some [goalie] gear on," Pettitte said after winning for the fourth straight time. "It's beginning to get a little aggravating."

Pettitte was nursing a one-run lead with one out and a runner on first in the top of the fourth inning when Toronto's Ed Sprague sent a line drive off Pettitte's right knee. The ball went straight up and landed in the glove of third baseman Scott Brosius, who threw to first base to double-up Carlos Delgado and end the inning.

Pettitte was limping slightly after the game. "I'm not worried about it," he said. "I can go my next start."

It was the second time this season that Pettitte was hit in the right leg. Alex Rodriguez bounced one off Pettette's thigh in Seattle earlier this season. Pettitte also took one off the thumb and cheek against Cal Ripken last year and got hit in the same knee against Toronto two years ago.

Pettitte got some help from Tino Martinez, who made a great pick to start an inning-ending 3-6-1 double play in the fifth, and appeared to get out of a first-and-third jam in the sixth with two strikeouts when manager Joe Torre said that's enough. Torre brought in right-hander Jeff Nelson, who struck out former Yankee Mike Stanley to end the inning.

"I just thought to myself there's no way he's going to pull me here," Pettitte said of Torre. "Not after I got two strikeouts. But that's why he's the manager."

"He gave me a bit of a cross-eyed look," Torre said. "I just tried not to look him in the eye when I do that."

Torre said that the sixth inning was going to be Pettitte's last anyway, and he wanted a right-hander to pitch to Stanley, who was hitting over .435 against left-handers this season.

Pettitte scattered seven hits and struck out seven before giving way to Nelson and then Mike Stanton. Mariano Rivera, who came off the disabled list Friday, made his third appearance, pitching a perfect ninth to notch his second save.

Monday brought the pitchers' duel that many people expected when Pettitte and Clemens hooked up in Toronto on Wednesday. Pettitte also won that duel, going the distance for the first time this season and allowing just one hit in a 9-1 victory.

Clemens, who gave up nine runs in 6 2/3 innings last week, was a different pitcher Monday but still came away the hard-luck loser, allowing one run on three hits and striking out eight in seven innings.

But it was two of his six walks that did him in as he sandwiched them around a Derek Jeter single to load the bases in the third, Tino Martinez's long sacrifice fly accounted for the game's only run.

"One run's got to be enough against a guy like Clemens," Torre said after the team stranded seven runners. "He gets tougher when he needs to get tough. He was tough against us last time out, but we managed to get a couple of two-out base hits against him when we needed them."

But Chad Curtis made it obvious from the outset that this was going to be a game of pitching and defense.

With a runner on second in the first inning, Curtis ran all the way to the left field line to snare Jose Canseco's sinking, slicing liner to save a run.

"That play was huge," Pettitte said. "I didn't think there was any way he would get it. I knew it wasn't out of the park, but I thought it was definitely a double down the line."

Instead, it was the first of several missed opportunities for the Blue Jays, who also left men in scoring position in the second and the seventh innings.

"When you don't score any runs, that's what happens," Toronto manager Tim Johnson said. "I thought that Clemens pitched better than Pettitte."

The win was the 14th in 15 games for the Yankees, who have only played seven games in Yankee Stadium this season. It helped them keep pace with the sizzling Red Sox, who won Monday night to remain percentage points behind the Yankees.

Tuesday, April 28, 1998
— Toronto Blue Jays

Blue Jays 5, Yankees 2

Yanks' streak is history

Blue Jays add to Mendoza woes

By GREGORY SCHUTTA, Staff Writer

NEW YORK — So far this spring the Yankees' Joe Torre hasn't had to make many of the major decisions that can plague a manager during a long season. When you've won 14 of 15 games, problems tend to work themselves out.

But Torre may have to decide very soon what to do with Ramiro Mendoza, who had his third tough outing in four starts Tuesday night against the Toronto Blue Jays and suffered his first loss of the season, 5-2, at Yankee Stadium. The loss is the first home defeat in eight games for the Yankees this season and also put a halt to their six-game winning streak.

But it was Mendoza's pitching that was on everybody's mind after the game. The 25-year-old right-hander gave up a bases-loaded double to Tony Fernandez in the first inning and a two-run homer to Ed Sprague on a 1-2 pitch in the sixth.

In 5 2/3 innings, Mendoza surrendered five runs, seven hits, and hit as many batters as he struck out (two). But if he's starting to hear the footsteps of Cuban defector Orlando Hernandez, who struck out 10 batters in five innings in his first start for Class AAA Columbus on Monday, he wasn't saying.

"I don't think about that," Mendoza said through interpreter Luis Sojo. "I just concentrate on my job. [Hernandez is] supposed to do his job and I'm supposed to do mine."

Torre said a decision on Mendoza and Hernandez is a long way off.

"Mendoza is on this club whether he's in the starting rotation or the bullpen," Torre said. "That's the most important thing to him. If I sense any doubt in his mind about that then we'll take care of it, but so far I haven't seen that."

The Yankees staked Mendoza to a 1-0 lead in the first inning on singles by Chuck Knoblauch, Derek Jeter, and Tino Martinez, who knocked in his team-leading 25th run. But the Yankees failed to capitalize any further against Toronto starter Woody Williams (2-1), who got Bernie Williams to pop to short and Darryl Strawberry on strikes.

Fernandez made the Yankees pay for that in the second. Jose Canseco and Darrin Fletcher singled to lead off the inning, and Ed Sprague was hit by a pitch to load the bases.

Then the ex-Yankee blasted a double into left-center field to clear the bases and give the Blue Jays a 3-1 lead.

The Yankees cut the deficit to 3-2 on a Bernie Williams triple and a Chad Curtis grounder in the fourth, but Mendoza got the ball up again in the sixth inning and Sprague took advantage by sending his third homer of the season into the left-field seats for two runs and a 5-2 lead.

"Mendoza had a bad second inning and then threw a bad pitch to Sprague with two strikes," Torre said. "When he keeps the ball down, he's fine. But when he gets the ball up, he's hittable. That's the thing with inexperience. It will bring inconsistency."

One of the bright spots for the Yankees was the play of Williams, who showed signs of breaking out of his slump with a double and a triple in four at-bats.

His fourth-inning triple hit high off the wall in center field. He also laced a double inside third base in the eighth inning and lined out sharply to the shortstop in the sixth. This comes one day after he blooped a double down the left-field line against Roger Clemens in the Yankees' 1-0 victory.

"I saw more life out of Bernie tonight," Torre said. "There was more movement in his body and he hit three balls on the screws. Hopefully this will get him untracked. You put a couple of days like this back to back and you're out of it."

Paul O'Neill continued to have his problems at the plate (0-for-4), but showed his value to the team by cutting down Fernandez at the plate on a short fly to right in the sixth and holding runners on third in the second and seventh innings.

Wednesday, April 29, 1998 — Seattle Mariners

Yankees 8, Mariners 5

Yanks roll behind an impressive Cone

By KEN DAVIDOFF, Staff Writer

NEW YORK — Joe Torre spoke like a nervous father Wednesday afternoon, one wary of letting his son ride his bike too far from home. David Cone would be given a short leash on this night, the Yankees manager said.

As the innings piled on, the veteran righty would have less and less room for error.

It turned out to be an unnecessary warning. Torre gladly let Cone ride like the ace of old. In his best start of the season, Cone overcame a difficult three-run first inning to dominate the mighty Mariners over six innings, striking out 11 en route to his third straight victory, 8-5, in front of 27,949 fans at Yankee Stadium.

"It's huge," said Cone, whose ERA, once four digits, dropped to 7.16. "It's nice to face a team that's as potent as Seattle and put it all together."

With the victory, their 15th in 18 games, the Yanks lifted their record to 16-6, the Bombers' best start after 22 games since the 1958 team jumped out to a 17-5 start.

With the Red Sox also winning, the Yanks remained atop the American League East by percentage points and a half-game behind.

And they couldn't have written a better script for such a historical victory. Cone (3-1), who was simply awful in his first two 1998 starts and showed gradual improvement over his next two, made No. 5 a keeper.

Displaying his best slider of the season and experimenting with a variety of windups and motions, he kept the M's off balance for the bulk of his stint. He allowed just three hits after the first inning for a total of six, and he did not walk a batter. Of his 112 pitches, 79 were strikes.

"He was great," catcher Joe Girardi said. "The control he had on his breaking stuff, and the deception. … I think this is the best he has thrown. He seems to get a little bit sharper each time."

His teammates practically abandoned him in the first, making three defensive miscues to help Seattle jump to a 3-0 lead.

But then the Yankees rallied to his defense. Derek Jeter, Chad Curtis, and Jorge Posada each homered, giving the Bombers only their third multihomer game of the season. After Cone departed, Mike Stanton, Jeff Nelson, and Mariano Rivera (third save) finished it off.

"When we beat Seattle, it's a huge lift — more than anyone except in our division," Cone said.

Misplays by Bernie Williams and Tim Raines and an error by Scott Brosius made the Mariners' first-inning 3-0 lead possible. But the Yanks came roaring back off Jeff Fassero (2-1), the tough lefty who went 3-0 against New York last year.

In the bottom of the first, Jeter ripped his third homer of the season, a solo job, before Raines singled and Williams walked. Tino Martinez then delivered a run-scoring single.

Martinez finished with two RBI, giving him 27 on the year.

In the third, the Yanks took the lead for good. With Jeter on second and one out, Williams knocked a pedestrian bouncer to Russ Davis, who unleashed a high throw to David Segui at first. Martinez moved the runners over on a bouncer to second, and Chad Curtis — who started in right field in place of the slumping Paul O'Neill — golfed a 2-1 Fassero outing into the left field stands for a sudden, 5-3 lead. Posada, starting at designated hitter, added his 417-foot solo blast in the fifth.

Reporter's Notebook:

Torre considered starting O'Neill (0-for-22) Wednesday night, but decided that he wanted to give his right fielder a day of rest. And why not do it against a left-hander? "It'll look so easy tonight on the bench," O'Neill said.

O'Neill entered the game in the eighth inning when Torre removed Raines as a precaution. When Raines was running toward third in the bottom of the seventh on Tino Martinez's single, "I just felt something [in my legs]," he said. "I didn't want to risk it. I felt like something might happen." Since nothing actually happened, Raines didn't think he would miss any playing time.

Graeme Lloyd, who hurt his left shoulder playing catch with Jeff Nelson on Sunday, underwent an MRI on Wednesday at Columbia Presbyterian Medical Center and was diagnosed with mild bursal inflammation. He is day-to-day.

Thursday, April 30, 1998 — Seattle Mariners

Yankees 9, Mariners 8

Yankees give a little extra

By KEN DAVIDOFF, Staff Writer

NEW YORK — The Yankees have no problem winning ugly, but Thursday night, they set a new standard for ugly drama.

Tino Martinez's line drive single in the 10th inning brought home Chuck Knoblauch to give the Yanks a 9-8 victory.

With their second straight victory and the Red Sox's 7-2 loss to Anaheim, the Bombers took full control of the American League East penthouse for the first time this season.

A Yankee Stadium crowd of 28,517 took in the crazy game, which featured six lead changes.

By the time the 4-hour 8-minute affair concluded, the exciting first three innings — in which Ken Griffey Jr. launched a pair of tape-measure solo homers and Darryl Strawberry, Martinez, and Alex Rodriguez each added highlight-film shots of their own — were as distant a memory as the "Miami Vice" craze.

Knoblauch led off the 10th by getting nailed in the back by a Bobby Ayala pitch — the second time in the game he was hit there. He keeled over in pain but stayed in the game.

Derek Jeter laid down a perfect sacrifice bunt, and he reached first when Ayala (0-2) unleashed a terrible throw.

Paul O'Neill's grounder just made it past the glove

of Rodriguez at shortstop, and Knoblauch held at third. That's when Martinez delivered the game-winner.

Mariano Rivera pitched a scoreless 10th to pick up his first victory and take some heat off bullpen predecessors Jeff Nelson, Mike Stanton, and Darren Holmes, who coughed up a three-run lead in the eighth.

The Yanks were rescued when Tim Raines started the ninth with a line drive homer to right field, sending the game into extra innings and setting up Martinez's final heroics.

Who better than Griffey to christen the evening's power barrage?

With two out in the first inning, he fouled off four straight offerings from David Wells before depositing a 2-2 pitch into the right field bleachers. The measurement: 420 feet.

The Yanks responded in the second with two mammoth blasts. First, Martinez got hold of a Ken Cloude fastball in his wheelhouse and sent it to the upper deck in right, where it hit the foul pole.

The measurement: 374 feet.

It was quite a shot, but it proved to be merely a warm-up act.

That's because Strawberry stepped to the plate one out later and tattooed a 1-1 pitch for his team-leading sixth home run. The majestic, arcing shot landed in Yankee Stadium's famous black seats, just the 15th ball to reach the sacred area since the new stadium opened in 1976.

The measurement: 442 feet.

And the Mariners, in turn, delivered two more solo taters off Wells in the third. Rodriguez went to left for 387 feet, and Griffey came through again, going 412 feet to right for his 11th of the season. He has a stunning 32 multihomer games in his 10-year career.

The Yanks tied the score at 3 in the fourth on a Bernie Williams single, a Strawberry walk, and Chad Curtis' single.

An inning later Curtis came through again.

Martinez drew a one-out walk, Strawberry added a two-out walk, and Curtis poked a 3-2 pitch to center for a soft, line drive single. Martinez scored easily to give the Yankees a 4-3 advantage.

The Bombers padded their lead to 7-3 in the sixth with O'Neill's bases-loaded, two-run double the key hit.

It was the second hit of the night for O'Neill, who entered the game in a 0-for-22 slump.

Reporter's Notebook:

Left-hander Graeme Lloyd (mild bursal inflammation, left shoulder) was placed on the 15-day disabled list after the game, retroactive to April 22. Right-hander Mike Buddie was recalled from Class AAA Columbus to take his roster spot. unavailable Thursday night.

Friday, May 1, 1998
— at Kansas City Royals

Yankees 2, Royals 1

Yankees' Irabu pulls it all together

By KEN DAVIDOFF, Staff Writer

KANSAS CITY, Mo. — The smile was wide and toothy, the head bobbing up and down like, well, one of those bobbin' head dolls.

Hideki Irabu had just been asked if he was happy to notch his first victory of 1998 on Friday night. The often-burdensome translation from American reporter to Irabu's interpreter George Rose to Irabu himself took place quicker than a Michael Johnson sprint.

"Yes," Irabu responded. "I'm very happy."

This was no cheapie, either. The Japanese right-hander recorded another landmark outing, going a career-long 7 1/3 innings in leading the Bombers to a 2-1 squeaker over the Royals at Kauffman Stadium.

"He's been very high on himself and how he's been pitching," Yanks pitching coach Mel Stottlemyre said. "Nevertheless, it's nice to get him that win."

With the victory — the 17th in their past 19 games — the Yankees (18-6) maintained their half-game lead over Boston in the American League East.

In lowering his microscopic ERA to 1.47, Irabu allowed the one run on two hits and two walks, striking out eight. He needed 89 pitches, 54 of them strikes, to achieve his new high-water mark.

"Irabu threw an outstanding game," said Mike Stanton, who aided his teammate in relief. "His fastball has been more than dominating. He's had a very good breaking ball and a very good split-finger. With the split, I think he learned it doesn't have to be a strike. It's a strikeout pitch. That's where it should be."

The splitter and fastball were primarily on display, with Irabu's heat averaging 93-94 mph and reaching

96 on the radar gun, and the nasty splitter registering 88 mph. And with this came the control that forced the Royals hitters to swing at the splitter, just in case it turned out to be a fastball in the strike zone.

"You've got to hand it to Irabu," Royals manager Tony Muser said. "I think he has a split-finger pitch you can't hit."

The only thing was, the Bombers couldn't do much with Muser's pitcher, either. Pat Rapp (1-3) had faced the Yanks once previously, when he was with the Marlins last year, and he struggled with his control, walking five in 3 1/3 innings.

It was a different Rapp this time, and when Johnny Damon hit a third-inning Irabu fastball that carried over the right-center-field fence for a 1-0 lead, one had to wonder if Irabu would be victimized again by a lack of run support.

He was, but he, Stanton, and Mariano Rivera (fourth save) made the two Yankees runs hold up. Bernie Williams picked up both RBI, on a sixth-inning single to score Paul O'Neill from second and an eighth-inning sacrifice fly to center, scoring Chuck Knoblauch from third.

The game's real drama arrived in the bottom of the eighth. Irabu created a second-and-third, none-out situation when he walked Ernie Young and threw wildly to first on a Mike Sweeney sacrifice. He induced pinch hitter Terry Pendleton to ground harmlessly to third before getting the hook from manager Joe Torre.

In came Stanton, and Damon ripped a line drive right to Scott Brosius at third. Brosius snared the ball and Young was trapped off the base, creating a lightning-quick, inning-ending double play.

Irabu called this his best start as a major-leaguer, but that's becoming old news. As Torre said, "He hasn't given up a whole lot."

Reporter's Notebook:

The Bombers' middle infield is ailing, but both Knoblauch and Derek Jeter opted to play Friday night. Knoblauch's left elbow was bandaged after he took a Bobby Ayala fastball there in the 10th inning Thursday night.

Jeter reaggravated his left groin in the eighth inning Thursday when he jumped to grab a high Knoblauch throw to second base.

Orlando Hernandez will pitch tonight for Class AAA Columbus in a home game against Indianapolis. It will be the second Columbus start for "El Duque.

The Yankees' two home games against Anaheim that were postponed due to the Yankee Stadium closure have been rescheduled. The April 13 game will be played Aug. 24, an off-day for both teams.

The April 14 contest will be made up as part of a separate-admission, day-night doubleheader Aug. 26. The day portion will start at 1:05, followed by the regularly scheduled game at 7:35.

Saturday, May 2, 1998
— at Kansas City Royals

Yankees 12, Royals 6

Yankees find the secrets to success

By KEN DAVIDOFF, Staff Writer

KANSAS CITY, Mo. — The pitching, hitting, speed, and defense have been there for the Yankees this season. Sometimes one of them at a time, sometimes all four working as a baseball symphony. Yet the Bombers are aware that another factor, one that you can't diagnose during your off-season, plays a key role in defining champions.

Luck.

"We've been getting a lot of breaks," Joe Torre said Saturday evening. "We may not be getting these breaks all of the time."

Then again, maybe they will. A trio of such lucky breaks helped the Yankees win their fourth straight game Saturday night, 12-6 over the Royals at Kauffman Stadium. The Bombers' good fortune is starting to become obnoxious: They've won 10 of 11 and 18 of 20, the latter for the first time since 1980. Their 19-6 record, the best in the major leagues, is the team's best start since it went 23-5 in 1958.

Saturday night could have been a night when this barrage of historical reflections reached an end, as starting pitcher Andy Pettitte simply didn't have it. But his teammates, the umpires, and fate helped the southpaw record his fifth straight victory after laboring through six innings of four-run, 10-hit, four-walk, three-strikeout ball.

Tino Martinez drilled a three-run homer, giving him 32 RBI, and Darryl Strawberry added his team-leading seventh homer, a majestic, 435-foot, pinch-hit grand slam in the ninth. But what stood out in this contest were three key plays:

• Paul O'Neill threw out Shane Mack at home in a bang-bang tag play in the bottom of the second.

• Bernie Williams' broken-bat grounder started a two-run rally in the top of the fourth, giving the Yanks a lead they never surrendered.

• The Royals' Mike Sweeney was out on a tag-up appeal call in the bottom of the sixth. Replays showed that Sweeney didn't leave early. Television broadcasts haven't always been able to synchronize shots of the ball and the runner, but in any case, the Yanks benefited from the fact that the play was close enough to contest.

That last play came after the Royals loaded the bases with one out, and Pettitte was clearly at the end of his rope. With Darren Holmes warming up in the bullpen, the Yanks starter induced Jose Offerman to loft a fly to medium right field. O'Neill delivered a good throw to home, but not good enough, and Sweeney scored from third to apparently make it a 6-5 game.

But wait, the Yanks said. Sweeney left third too early on the tag. Scott Brosius quickly moved to third, where he took the throw from Joe Girardi. And third base umpire Brian O'Nora punched Sweeney out for tagging up too early, meaning the inning was over and the Yanks still had a two-run lead.

The Royals went berserk, with manager Tony Muser arguing vehemently with O'Nora until he earned a boot. In the top of the seventh, when Derek Jeter tagged and scored on an O'Neill sacrifice fly, the Royals appealed the play, as well. To a chorus of boos, O'Nora signaled that Jeter had not left third too early.

In the Yankees' half of the fourth, Williams broke his bat while knocking an ordinary bouncer to third, but the bat's broken half sailed, boomerang-like, in the direction of Royals third baseman Jeff King. The veteran King focused on the bat rather than the ball, thus bobbling the ball for an error.

Martinez followed by ripping a double to right, sending Williams to third. Tim Raines' flare single to right scored Williams for the 2-1 lead. And Chad Curtis' sacrifice fly to center brought Martinez home for the insurance run.

King made up for his mistake with a pair of homers: a solo blast in the fourth and a two-run job in the fifth. In between King's power show, however, Martinez ripped a three-run blast to right following singles from O'Neill and Williams. Despite King's best efforts, his team was still in a 6-4 hole following his second homer.

Each team put together a big rally but scored just one run in a first inning that lasted 30 minutes. With one out in the bottom of the second, Shane Mack tagged up from third on a Shane Halter fly to medium right field. O'Neill's bullet to Girardi nailed Mack to keep the game tied. The replays showed that Mack had in fact slid safely into home in the bang-bang play.

Reporter's Notebook:

Orlando "El Duque" Hernandez pitched six innings for Class AAA Columbus on Saturday night, allowing four runs and seven hits, walking three and fanning 11. The Cuban refugee right-hander now has 21 strikeouts in 11 Class AAA innings over two starts.

Sunday, May 3, 1998 — at Kansas City Royals

Yankees 10, Royals 1

Yanks stay in groove

Thump Royals for fifth straight

By KEN DAVIDOFF, Staff Writer

KANSAS CITY, Mo. — This is paradise.

They are starting to blur into one another, these Yankees victories. The Bombers win pitchers' duels, they win slugfests, they win games they shouldn't win. They rarely celebrate, they rarely coast. And they rarely lose.

"We're just taking the field every night expecting to win," Paul O'Neill said after a 10-1 blowout of Kansas City on Sunday at Kauffman Stadium. "In spring training we got that attitude that we have a good team. We just keep plugging away."

Said manager Joe Torre, "I can't wait to get to the ballpark every day."

It's now five straight victories, 11 in the past 12 games, and 19 in the past 21, which is the best run for a Yankees team since the 1977 Bombers put together a 19-2 streak Aug. 14 to Sept. 4.

These Yankees are not riding one hot hitter, they make up for their mistakes, and they capitalize on the other team's mistakes.

"It's like it's contagious," Derek Jeter said. "Hitting

is contagious, pitching is contagious, winning is contagious."

On Sunday, the Yanks (20-6) got a little bit of everything. Ramiro Mendoza pitched seven innings of one-run, three-hit ball to pick up his first victory of the year. Homer Bush, getting his first start of the season in place of Chuck Knoblauch (sprained finger), stroked a pair of singles and scored twice. O'Neill poked his first homer of the season and 200th of his career, and Jorge Posada added his fourth dinger. Scott Brosius had three hits and Tino Martinez two as well as two more RBI to lift his total to 34.

"We feel like we've been doing everything right," Jeter said.

For the latest exhibit of Jeter's statement, consider the saga of Mendoza. The quiet right-hander didn't seem to have his good sinker in his first three innings.

Even though he didn't allow a hit, he walked two batters and recorded four of his nine outs in the air — an unusually high percentage for him. When Mendoza pitches like that, it's usually a matter of time before the hits and runs follow.

Posada knew something was wrong but couldn't quite put his finger on it. Until he went into the clubhouse during the top of the fourth, retrieved the videotape of the first three innings, and figured it out: Mendoza was aiming his pitches.

"I told him, 'Throw the ball and let it sink for you,'" Posada said.

Mendoza followed instructions, loosening his grip on the ball, and though the Royals' run and three hits came in Mendoza's final four innings, the fly balls and walks diminished.

Meanwhile, the Yankees offense did its usual work, pounding Tim Belcher (1-4) for eight hits over six innings and capitalizing on two errors. Of the six runs Belcher surrendered, four were earned.

"When you go on a good streak," Torre said, "you're more patient. You wait for your opportunity, and you try to seize it."

For all their early success and happiness, the Yanks know they must stay humble and keep things in perspective. After all, the stubborn Red Sox are 1 1/2 games behind in the American League East.

"We have confidence, but we know we've got to continue to play well," Jeter said. "It's not like we're blowing the rest of the league away."

Said Torre, "It's nice to look at the big picture and see where our record is and where we are and so on,

as long as we continue to concentrate on the little things."

Sunday seemed like a spring training game by the end. Dale Sveum was at first base, Luis Sojo at shortstop, and the rarely used Mike Buddie and Willie Banks pitched the eighth and ninth, respectively. But O'Neill's at-bat in the ninth spoke to the team's intensity.

The veteran crushed a Jeff Montgomery pitch to right, and it seemed a goner for certain. But the stadium wind held it in, and Larry Sutton caught it on the warning track.

"I didn't understand it," O'Neill said. "I hit that ball really well. It's kind of a sudden emotional thing, to hit the ball on the nose and it doesn't go out."

O'Neill seemed more frustrated with that out than he was satisfied with his earlier homer. The drought had reached the point where he and the slumping Bernie Williams had made a bet over who would go deep first. And now O'Neill, who said he felt little sentiment about notching career homer No. 200, is $1 richer.

But he cautioned reporters: "I'm not the story. The story is the Yankees playing really well. It's fun to be part of this team."

Tuesday, May 5, 1998 — at Texas Rangers

Yankees 7, Rangers 2

Yanks knock Rangers down a peg

By KEN DAVIDOFF, Staff Writer

ARLINGTON, Texas — Finally, some competition. After weeks of taking on the Detroits and Kansas Citys and struggling Seattles of the world, the Yankees faced a team almost as hot as they were Tuesday night in the Texas Rangers.

And the result looked eerily similar to when the Bombers took on the Detroits, Kansas Citys, and struggling Seattles of the world.

David Cone threw no-hit ball for 4 1/3 innings before sustaining a minor injury, and the Yanks pummeled Texas starter John Burkett to capture their sixth straight victory, 7-2.

Here come the nightly numbers: The Bombers (21-6) have won 12 of 13 and 20 of 22, the latter streak the best Yankees run since the 1953 team captured 21 of 23 from May 27 to June 19. No Yankees team has ever pulled off three six-game winning streaks so quickly; the 1928 Bombers accomplished this feat in 47 games.

"They're pumped," manager Joe Torre said. "We're going obviously really well right now. We're going to try to make this thing go as long as it can."

Besides the second night of the season, when the Yanks took on a 1-0 Angels club, the Bombers hadn't faced a division-leading team this season. Yet the prospect of facing the Rangers, who reside atop the AL West, didn't faze them.

Like any other game, Torre said beforehand, "It's a matter of whose pitcher does the job, who's more effective."

Cone won that battle over Burkett (2-4). The Yanks' veteran right-hander didn't really build on his two previous very good starts, but he pitched well enough (two runs, three hits, three walks, four strikeouts) to notch his fourth straight victory against one loss. He left after the fifth with a strain of his left knee and is considered day-to-day.

"I don't think it's serious," said Cone, who is leaving the team for a few days to be with his mother, who is having surgery. "But you don't really know until tomorrow or the next day."

Burkett, who entered the night having surrendered 31 earned runs, more than any other AL pitcher, was coming off his best start of the season: one run, four hits, no walks, and four strikeouts in seven innings April 29.

But that came against the Tigers, the AL's worst team. It didn't take long for the Yanks, baseball's best team, to remind Burkett he wasn't in Detroit anymore.

Chuck Knoblauch laced a double down the left-field line, and Derek Jeter laid a pretty bunt down the third-base line for a single. And Paul O'Neill ripped a high line drive into the right-field stands for a three-run jack.

Cone took this lead and stumbled out of the gate. He walked the second and third hitters, Mark McLemore and Rusty Greer, with one out, and cleanup man Juan Gonzalez's bouncer to third forced Greer at second. With the count 0-1 on Will Clark, Cone unleashed a pitch so wild it went to the non-home-plate side of Clark, allowing McLemore to trot home and Gonzalez to go to second. Cone composed himself and got Clark to ground to second for the third out.

The Yanks had taken the field for the second inning when plate umpire Mark Johnson stepped away and motioned to the rest of his umpiring crew. Johnson was too ill to continue, and since crew chief Jim Evans needed time to change into the home-plate gear, the Yankees departed the field for their dugout.

After a nine-minute delay, Evans returned to the field, ready to go. Johnson, who was suffering from dizziness, was taken to Arlington Memorial Hospital for further examination.

The Yanks knocked out Burkett when they added three runs in the fifth, with Joe Girardi and Jeter delivering RBI singles and a passed ball by Ivan Rodriguez allowing Girardi to score from third.

With one out in the bottom of the fifth and Cone's no-hitter still alive, Scott Brosius made a brilliant diving stop on a bullet by Kevin Elster. But when the Yankees third baseman jumped to his feet to make the throw to first, he dropped the ball. The close call was ruled a base hit.

The next batter, Luis Alicea, dropped a bunt down the first-base line, and that's when Cone hurt his left knee. He kneeled down in agony, causing Torre and assistant trainer Steve Donohue onto the field.

Cone talked his manager into letting him hang on for the rest of the inning. He allowed a soft line-drive single to left by McLemore that scored Elster, but he otherwise left unscathed. When the bottom of the sixth came around, Darren Holmes was on the mound for the Yanks.

Wednesday, May 6, 1998

Yankees 15, Rangers 13

Posada's hit plates winner in slugfest

By KEN DAVIDOFF, Staff Writer

ARLINGTON, Texas — Give the Yankees credit for their versatility. They can do action, drama, and, occasionally, comedy.

Jorge Posada's two-out single in the eighth inning sparked the Bombers to a 15-13 victory over the Rangers on Wednesday night in an absolutely absurd game that took 4 hours 6 minutes to complete at The Ballpark in Arlington.

"The guys are playing so good, we're going to win 2-1, 1-0 games, then when they see the pitcher's struggling, they're going to put up eight or nine runs," Andy Pettitte said earlier this week. And his words never rung more true than Wednesday, when the Yanks jumped to a 9-0 lead, only to allow the Rangers to tie the game at 13-13

The game also featured an amusing subplot involving Texas' star right fielder Juan Gonzalez and the Ballpark press box.

Mike Stanton picked up the win and Mariano Rivera his fifth save in the Yanks' seventh straight victory, their eighth consecutive road triumph, their 12th in 13 games, and their 21st in 23 (their best run since 1953).

Bernie Williams led off the eighth with a gapper to right-center field off loser Danny Patterson, and he legged it out for a triple. After Tim Raines struck out and Chad Curtis popped out to Texas first baseman Will Clark in foul territory, Posada broke the deadlock with his base hit off the glove of shortstop Kevin Elster. Derek Jeter added an insurance run with a solo homer in the ninth, giving him a career-high five RBI on the night.

The 28 combined runs marked the second most in a big-league game this season, the top total of 30 coming in the Yanks' 17-13 victory over Oakland in their home opener April 10. The Bombers' 18 hits tied their season high.

Ranger starter Bobby Witt entered the game having surrendered seven runs in each of his past two outings, and he got right to work on matching that figure. Leadoff hitter Chuck Knoblauch got hold of Witt's fifth pitch and deposited it in the left field seats. Two batters later, Paul O'Neill ripped his third homer in nine at-bats, a 409-foot blast to center. Before the Texas fans could even get settled, they were in a 2-0 hole.

And that proved to be just an appetizer. Witt walked the first two batters in the second, Curtis and Posada, and Scott Brosius sacrificed his teammates to second and third. Knoblauch walked, and Jeter cleared the bases with a triple to right-center. When O'Neill singled home Jeter for the 6-0 lead, Witt checked out with just 1 1/3 innings on his tab.

Tino Martinez's double plated O'Neill, and after Williams grounded to short, Raines went the opposite way and sent a high fly to left-center.

The ball carried, hit the top of the wall, and bounced over for a two-run dinger. The Yanks' seven-run second marked their best one-inning output of the season.

Just when you thought it was safe to put this one in the books, though, the Rangers showed why they've

been a pretty successful club themselves. Fernando Tatis started things innocently when he lined a single to left. Tom Goodwin singled to right and Wells walked Mark McLemore to load the bases.

Rusty Greer's groundout to first advanced everyone a base, breaking Wells' shutout, and then came the key play: Gonzalez ripped a line drive right at Knoblauch. Somehow, the second baseman — who has been coping with a sprained middle finger in his glove hand — let the ball go off his glove behind him. Goodwin and McLemore scored. Later, to express his dismay with the official scorer's ruling of a Knoblauch error, Gonzalez blew mock kisses at the press box.

Friday, May 8, 1998 — at Minnesota Twins

Yankees 5, Twins 1

Dome sweet dome

Happy return for Knoblauch

By KEN DAVIDOFF, Staff Writer

MINNEAPOLIS — There were boos. Huge boos. Bill Clinton-entering-a-National-Rifle-Association-convention boos. And only a smattering of cheers.

Each of the five times he stepped to the plate Friday night, each of the seven times he touched the ball in the field, Chuck Knoblauch was exposed to the resentment at his old home, the Metrodome.

The loudest and latest jeers, however, couldn't have been sweeter. First, the former Twins second baseman scored on a seventh-inning Derek Jeter single to give his new team a one-run lead. Then, he made a huge defensive play in the eighth to save the Yanks' eighth straight victory, 5-1 over Minnesota. The Bombers (23-6) have won 22 of their past 24 games, the most impressive run since the 1947 team captured 27 of 29.

"Nob-a-lak-ah stole the show today," said Jeter, pronouncing his double play partner's last name like only he can. "He just played the way he's capable of — good hitting, good running, good defense. Minnesota shouldn't have been surprised."

On Wednesday, Knoblauch said his goal would be to get booed at the end, since that would mean he had done something to beat his former team. And sure enough, the crowd of 22,612 — about 8,000 more than the Twins average — was angriest at game's end.

"We accomplished our goal, to win," he said. "Hopefully, we'll accomplish the same goal tomorrow night."

Hideki Irabu turned in another superb effort, going seven innings and allowing just one run and five hits to pick up his second straight victory. On this night, the right-hander didn't dominate the Twins, he simply shut them down. After averaging more than seven strikeouts for his first three starts, he fanned just three batters. He needed 79 pitches, 53 of them strikes, to pick up the win and lower his ERA to 1.42.

But this night, as Jeter said, was all about Knoblauch. The second baseman insisted he didn't hear the boos or the few cheers, and said he was "was very calm and relaxed.

"I didn't have to tell myself to tone it down," Knoblauch said.

He made infield outs his first two times up, then singled in the fifth inning and stole second base (although replays showed he was out). Irabu and Twins ace Brad Radke (3-3) were engaged in a crisp pitchers' duel, with Minnesota scoring once in the fourth and Jorge Posada's solo, fifth-inning blast to right evening things at 1-1.

With two outs in the seventh, the second baseman grounded a single into left field. On the first pitch to Jeter, he stole second. Jeter took a strike to even the count at 1-1, then golfed a low pitch into left for a single. Knoblauch scored easily for the 2-1 lead.

The real dramatics, however, came in the bottom of the eighth. After allowing a leadoff double to Pat Meares, Irabu was removed. Mike Stanton entered, induced Chris Latham to bunt a foul pop to Posada, walked pinch hitter and former Met Alex Ochoa, and he was gone. In came Jeff Nelson, who has been suffering all week from what may be strep throat.

Nelson went 3-0 on Paul Molitor, then threw a called strike that Posada let get away for a passed ball. Latham and Ochoa advanced. Nelson walked Molitor to jam the bases.

With the Yanks' infield drawn in, Matt Lawton punched a bouncer to Tino Martinez, who threw home for the second out. Ron Coomer drilled an 0-1 pitch back to the mound that glanced off Nelson's glove and bounced slowly toward second base.

"I thought I got it just enough that everyone was going to be safe," Nelson said.

But Knoblauch charged the ball and quickly stepped on second. In a bang-bang play, second base umpire Gary Cederstrom called Lawton out at second.

"It was just a reaction-type play," Knoblauch said. "A lot of bodies came together at second base."

The Yanks put the game away with three runs in the ninth, and Nelson pitched a scoreless ninth for his second save.

Reporter's Notebook:

Cuban right-hander Orlando "El Duque" Hernandez pitched 6 2/3 innings for Class AAA Columbus Friday night, allowing four runs and five hits while walking five and fanning nine. He has 30 strikeouts in 17 2/3 with the Clippers.

Saturday, May 9, 1998 — at Minnesota Twins

Twins 8, Yankees 1

Yankees' win streak halted

By KEN DAVIDOFF, Staff Writer

MINNEAPOLIS — Elephants forget. M&Ms melt in your hand. Movie sequels are better than the original.

And, occasionally, the Yankees lose.

Veteran journeyman Mike Morgan shut down the Yankees, Andy Pettitte was hammered by the American League's 12th-best hitting team, and the Bombers dropped their first game since April 28. The Twins rolled over the Yanks, 8-1, Saturday night at the Metrodome.

All of the ballyhooed streaks are over: the eight straight victories overall, the nine straight on the road.

"When you win as much as we've been winning, sometimes you forget what it's like to lose," said Yankees manager Joe Torre. "But once you do lose, it's a terrible taste in your mouth."

The streaks couldn't have ended in a more surprising fashion. After all, the Yanks had their ace going against a 38-year-old mediocre right-hander whose greatest claim to fame is playing for 10 different teams, including the 1982 Yanks.

But Torre has seen Morgan throughout his travels, and he warned reporters before the game: "You know, he's a good pitcher. He can crank up a game and shut you down. He has a good slider, keeps the ball down. He's been pretty durable. He keeps having injuries and bouncing back."

Sure enough, in scattering seven hits, walking one, hitting two, and striking out four over 8 2/3 innings, Morgan (1-1) made the Bombers look silly. The Yanks (23-7) didn't make it as far as third base until there were two outs in the ninth. For Morgan, it was his first career victory against the Yankees after seven losses.

Pettitte, meanwhile, let the Twins grab a 3-0 lead in the second, then allowed the first grand slam of his career to Matt Lawton, whom he had hit to start the game. In falling to 5-3, the southpaw surrendered seven runs, nine hits, and three walks in 5 2/3 innings.

"I just struggled from the get-go again," said Pettitte, who in his previous start allowed 10 hits over six innings but still got the victory. "I felt like I was real tentative at first. I was struggling to get in a rhythm again."

The drama began in the first inning, when Pettitte nailed Lawton in the back — after Derek Jeter had been nailed in the top of the frame. Lawton, clearly upset, walked toward the mound, picked up the ball, and threw it back to Pettitte.

David Ortiz started the bottom of the second by lining a single to second, and Brent Gates followed with a base hit up the middle. Pettitte went 1-1 on rookie catcher Javier Valentin, then served up a sinker that Valentin crushed to left field. Chad Curtis tried to make a leaping catch, but the ball evaded his glove and hit the left-center field wall. Ortiz and Gates scored for a 2-0 lead.

Valentin advanced to third on Lawton's grounder to first, then scored on Denny Hocking's sacrifice fly to center.

While the Yanks couldn't get anything going against Morgan, Pettitte kept the Twins quiet until the sixth. That's when he walked leadoff batter and former Met Alex Ochoa, and Pat Meares followed with a high bouncer to short that handcuffed Jeter. Ortiz singled to load the bases.

Pettitte retired the next two batters and it looked as if the Yanks would perform another of their magical escapes. But Lawton got hold of a Pettitte fastball over the plate and blistered it, high and deep over the right-center field wall.

The grand slam carried 420 feet and put the game out of reach, even for these Yankees, at 7-0. Lawton trotted slowly around the bases, glaring at the Bombers' southpaw.

Sunday, May 10, 1998
— at Minnesota Twins

Yankees 7, Twins 0

Yanks' Mendoza makes Twins go blank

By KEN DAVIDOFF, Staff Writer

MINNEAPOLIS — This could have been Ramiro Mendoza's home. Had things gone differently in early February, Mendoza could have been a Minnesota Twin as part of the package to land Chuck Knoblauch.

Joe Torre didn't want that to happen. The Yankees manager felt he couldn't afford to lose both prime prospect Eric Milton and Mendoza, who had been a valuable long reliever and No. 5 starter for the Bombers last year. So, he put in his two cents to George Steinbrenner and the Yankees' brain trust. Milton went, Mendoza stayed.

As fate would have it, Mendoza faced Milton Sunday in front of 12,444 fans at the Metrodome. And Mendoza made his manager look smart, throwing his first career shutout as the Yanks rebounded from a defeat Saturday with a 7-0 victory.

"He pitched really well," Torre said. "He was into it mentally. Especially the last three innings, he was like a locomotive."

The shy Mendoza, alternating between broken English and Spanish (with infielder Luis Sojo acting as an interpreter), said it was his best start as a major-leaguer. He needed just 96 pitches, 61 of them strikes, to complete the five-hitter. He walked none and struck out two in raising his record to 2-1.

"It feels great," the sinkerball specialist said after notching his second straight victory. "Hopefully, I'm going to keep doing it."

The Yanks pounded away at Milton (2-4) and four relievers, using 16 hits to slowly build their lead until Dale Sveum pinch hit for Tino Martinez in the top of the eighth. When that happens, the game is a blowout.

Along the way, however, the Twins had some opportunities to make it a contest. Every time, Mendoza worked out of trouble.

The Twins' biggest boondoggle surfaced in the

bottom of the sixth. With the Yanks holding a 5-0 lead, Twins shortstop Pat Meares led off with a flare single to right, then was forced at second on a Chris Latham grounder. Todd Walker singled to right, moving Latham to second.

Brent Gates ripped a comebacker that Mendoza calmly grabbed and whipped to second for what figured to be an inning-ending, 1-6-3 double play. Except Derek Jeter dropped the ball.

"Easiest play of the year," Jeter later said, shaking his head.

Bases loaded, one out, future Hall of Famer Paul Molitor at the plate. Molitor swung at the first pitch and delivered a hard bouncer to third. Scott Brosius gloved it and started the inning-ending, 5-4-3 twin-killing, the third of four double plays the Yankees would tally.

After that, Mendoza sat in the dugout and said to Sojo he was starting to feel tired.

"Come on, man," Sojo said. "You've got to go for it. Get your first shutout."

No, Mendoza corrected him, he had four last year. Nevertheless, he stayed in there, ignored the sight of Darren Holmes and Graeme Lloyd warming up in the bullpen, and dominated the final three innings. It wasn't until after the game that Sojo realized Mendoza was teasing him. This was indeed his first career shutout.

"He pitched the best game of his life," catcher Jorge Posada said. "He didn't want to strike out anybody. He just tried to get ground balls. It was very easy to catch him."

It was somewhat easy to hit Milton, who allowed four runs and nine hits in five innings. Said Milton: "I didn't have anything. I finished the game with just my fastball and my change-up."

"I thought he threw better than that," Posada said. "I caught him in spring training [in 1997], and he was an overpowering left-hander. He wasn't overpowering today."

"It's normal to pitch against your old club and get pumped up," Torre said. "He looked uncomfortable. He's going to be a good one."

Torre and the Yankees return home for 11 days after wrapping up their 7-1 road swing. They haven't lost two straight since losing the first three games of the season.

"We take the same approach every day," Martinez said. "We don't think about streaks or anything like that. We have a lot of confidence. We feel in order for them to beat us, they've got to put in their best."

Tuesday, May 12, 1998
— Kansas City Royals

Yankees 3, Royals 2

Bernie's homer powers Yanks

By KEVIN CZERWINSKI, Staff Writer

NEW YORK — Bernie Williams had a great weight lifted from his shoulders Tuesday, and David Wells may have finally put a weighty issue to rest.

Williams, who has averaged 25 homers a year over the past two seasons, belted his first homer of '98 in the Yankees' 3-2 victory over the Royals, ending a 119-at-bat drought.

Williams launched a Glendon Rusch (3-5) fastball into the right field seats in the first inning.

"It's good to finally be able to get that one," Williams said. "Hopefully, it will be the start of something good happening. The most important thing is that I don't have to hear it anymore about not hitting a home run."

"I think not hitting that first home run was just working on Bernie too much," said Yankee manager Joe Torre. "I think everyone telling him it wasn't important just made it worse."

His two-run homer in the first inning gave Wells some breathing room.

Wells (4-1) pitched eight innings, getting stronger as the game went on. He allowed five hits, only one after the third inning. He struck out nine and walked one.

His performance comes on the heels of his last outing — a week ago in Texas — in which he gave up seven runs in 2 2/3 innings. Torre questioned Wells' conditioning — or lack thereof — following that game. Wells responded after a shaky start Tuesday to improve to 12-3 lifetime against the Royals.

"As for David, the first four innings he was just OK," said Torre. "The last four innings, he was great. He was throwing the ball by people with pop. I think after that last outing he felt a little cheated because he had a big lead and then got no decision out of it."

Torre and Wells discussed the pitcher's conditioning between starts, clearing the air after Torre said, "Maybe he's not in shape."

But, Wells had kept mum about the talk he had with Torre. He finally spoke Tuesday.

"The fact that you guys [the media] are stirring something up that doesn't need to be stirred up doesn't mean that I'm going to get caught in a quarrel. It's none of your business what goes on between Joe and I behind closed doors.

"I think certain situations are better left unsaid. We want to keep turmoil to a minimum and concentrate on the main goal and that's winning ballgames."

Wells will be winning quite a few games if he continues to pitch the way he did in the second half of Tuesday's game. Of his nine strikeouts, eight came after the third inning. He struck out two in the fourth, sixth, and seventh innings.

"It was nothing specific I was doing late, I was just in a groove," Wells said. "You get that way and you just try to stay ahead of the hitter and keep him off-stride."

Despite Williams' bat and Well's arm, the Yankees needed Joe Girardi's savvy to win the game. The catchers' sacrifice bunt in the bottom of the fifth scored Chad Curtis with what proved to be the winning run.

The Yankees held on as Mariano Rivera came on to pitch a perfect ninth for his sixth save of the season.

Wednesday, May 13, 1998 — Texas Rangers

Yankees 8, Rangers 6

Bernie's slam lifts Bombers

By T.J. QUINN, Staff Writer

NEW YORK — For a moment on the field, Bernie Williams whooped and shouted like a warrior, watching his grand slam soar to the bleachers in right.

He composed himself after that fifth-inning shot, and was almost apologetic in the clubhouse afterward.

"I'm not trying [to be a home run hitter], to tell you the truth," Williams said. "I'm just trying to keep my same approach."

Same approach, vastly different results.

After going 31 games without a home run, Williams had his second in two nights Wednesday, providing a crucial cushion in an 8-6 Yankees win over the Texas Rangers.

Before a crowd of 23,142 that George Steinbrenner is sure to find fault with, Williams, Chuck Knoblauch, and David Cone finally became part of the fun that has become the 1998 Yankees season.

Different approach, same results.

That's a 26-7 record — best in the majors — 25 wins in 28 games, and another game put between the Yanks and the surprising Boston Red Sox, who lost to the Minnesota Twins, giving Joe Torre's crew a 4 1/2-game lead in the AL East.

"Can't explain it," Derek Jeter said of the Yanks' success. "We've got a long way to go."

But surely Jeter can understand why fans and even some Yankees feel that this season is already something special.

The Yankees ran to their current record largely without Williams' power, Knoblauch's hitting ability, or Cone's stamina. They got all three Wednesday, plus a critical three-run home run by Jeter in the third that erased back-to-back Texas home runs in the second.

Knoblauch was 4-for-5 with a double, a run scored, and two RBI, while Cone (5-1) went 6 1/3 innings and gave up four runs to earn his fifth straight win.

"I had a Catfish Hunter night, giving up three solo shots and getting away with it," Cone said. "This is the best I've felt yet. I'm not quite there, but I'm getting to the point where I can go deeper into games."

Cone, who faced Texas a week ago, said he regretted only three pitches, the three that ended up leaving the yard. This time around, he said, Texas changed its strategy. Juan Gonzalez did when he hit an inside fastball into left-center.

"I thought he was going to spot me a fastball like he usually does, and he spotted it out by the monuments," Cone said. "Other than [the home runs], I felt good."

Good as he felt, Cone needed Jeter's three-run shot off Rick Helling (6-1) and Williams' slam to earn the win.

With the scored 3-3 in the fifth, Jeter led off with a walk, then almost ran himself out of the inning when Paul O'Neill doubled to right. Jeter rounded third and seemed determined to run home before he saw third base coach Willie Randolph's "stop" sign. Jeter slipped as he tried to go back to third and was saved only by shortstop Kevin Elster's wild relay.

With Jeter at third and O'Neill at second, Texas manager Johnny Oates had the choice of having Helling face Tino Martinez with first base open or Williams with the bags loaded. Helling had never faced either, but Martinez is 18-44 (.409) this season with runners in scoring position, and Williams was 9-for-39 (.231).

Martinez was walked and Williams made the Rangers pay for the botched throw and the walk with a 410-foot blast to right-center.

Cone left the game with a 7-4 lead, but reliever Jeff Nelson gave up two runs in the seventh to put the game at risk. Torre didn't want to bring closer Mariano Rivera in the game so early, so he relied on Mike Stanton and Darren Holmes to get him to two outs in the eighth, when AL batting leader Ivan Rodriguez came to bat.

Rivera came in and gave up a double to Rodriguez before closing out the eighth, and allowed a double and a single in the ninth before earning his seventh save in seven opportunities.

"You hate to lose a game with a three-run homer and a grand slam," Torre said. "In this day and age of high-scoring games, you never know what's enough."

Thursday, May 14, 1998 — Texas Rangers

Rangers 7, Yankees 5

Yanks edged in 13
Irabu sharp, bullpen isn't

By T.J. QUINN, Staff Writer

NEW YORK — Before the bullpen burst into flames and the offense fell asleep, Hideki Irabu was king of the Bronx on Thursday night.

He took his hot streak up against the hottest hitters in the American League, the Texas Rangers and their .303 average.

For seven innings, the Yankees looked unbeatable, as Irabu held the Rangers scoreless on three hits.

Then the bullpen that Irabu once seemed destined to join let their starter down one man at a time in a 7-5 loss in 13 innings.

Rusty Greer's two-run home run off Willie Banks (1-1), the sixth Yankees pitcher and the worst member of the staff, gave the Bombers their eighth loss of the year.

Before Greer's shot just skimmed past the right field foul pole, relievers Mike Stanton and Jeff Nelson combined for a four-run Texas eighth. Mariano Rivera then blew his first save by giving up his first run of the season in the ninth.

All the while, the Yankees offense that had built a five-run lead after six innings managed a single and a walk after the eighth, never seriously threatening.

Irabu's steady progress still leaves him short of recognition. He has one inning too few to be officially considered among the league's leaders. His Thursday night outing left him with an ERA of 1.11, well ahead of Boston ace Pedro Martinez and his official league-leading 1.79. To qualify after his next start, Irabu will have to pitch at least 6 2/3 innings, assuming five days pass before he takes the mound again.

Irabu threatened to come apart in the second inning, loading the bases with two walks and a single with two out. During a 14-pitch stretch in the second, he threw 12 balls, including a wild pitch.

Before Texas was able to take advantage, though, Irabu struck out Tom Goodwin swinging to end the inning.

Irabu led off the third inning with a walk to Mark McLemore, but that was the end of the Rangers' free rides. McLemore tried to steal second and was killed by a perfect throw from catcher Jorge Posada. Irabu retired the next 12 batters before giving up a single to Ivan Rodriguez in the seventh.

The Yankees offense didn't exactly explode against Texas starter Darren Oliver, but it showed the same ability to squeeze out runs that has guided the Bombers all season.

In the third inning, Scott Brosius got things going with a one-out single past third baseman Fernando Tatis. Chuck Knoblauch took a pitch on the arm, and Derek Jeter singled to load the bases and give himself a 10-game hitting streak.

Paul O'Neill, who had grounded into a double play in his first at-bat, singled to left, bringing in Brosius and Knoblauch.

Jeter kept another streak alive: For the second night in a row, he survived a baserunning mistake.

When O'Neill hit his single to left, Jeter tried for third, possibly assuming the Rangers would try for a play at the plate. Left fielder Greer's throw was cut off by Tatis at third, however, and he missed tagging Jeter out by inches. Wednesday night Jeter overran third despite a stop sign from third base coach Willie Randolph and slipped trying to get back, but he made it because of a poor throw.

With runners at first and third and one out, though, the Yankees were unable to take advantage. Bernie Williams walked to load the bases but Tino Martinez struck out swinging and Tim Raines grounded to third.

Chad Curtis hit a leadoff home run in the fourth to make it 3-0, and another big inning in the sixth gave Irabu a comfortable cushion.

Martinez led off with a single to center, Curtis drew a one-out walk, knocking Oliver out of the game in favor of reliever Al Levine, who gave up a single to Posada to load the bases.

Brosius followed with his second hit of the night, driving in Martinez and Curtis before Knoblauch grounded into a double play.

Friday, May 15, 1998 — Minnesota Twins

Twins 7, Yankees 6

Twins topple Pettitte

Yankees lose second in row

By VINNY DiTRANI, Staff Writer

NEW YORK — Andy Pettitte was cuffed for his second straight start Friday night by the Minnesota Twins, and the pitcher and his manager appeared to have different reasons for his mini-slump.

Pettitte gave up seven runs in seven innings, including four runs in the third, as the Twins recorded a 7-6 victory over the Yankees.

It marked the first time since they dropped their first three games that the Bombers have suffered consecutive losses.

"I just think he was trying to be too careful, too perfect," manager Joe Torre said of Pettitte. "And as a result he was running the count. He'd get up on a guy, 1-2, and the next thing you know he was behind, 3-2.

"His stuff was all right. He was just trying to do too much with it."

Pettitte (5-4) had won five consecutive games before dropping a 7-1 decision to the Twins on May 9 in Minnesota.

In the last two starts against the Twins, Pettitte has allowed 21 hits and 14 earned runs in 12 2/3 innings (9.95 ERA).

Twelve of those hits came Friday night, with Marty Cordova driving in three runs with a single and a double, and Ron Coomer knocking in two more with a home run.

"I just left a lot of pitches over the middle of the plate, and that to me says my mechanics were out of

whack," Pettitte said of his performance. "I think I was just rushing things.

"It's frustrating when your teammates go out and bust their butts and score six runs and you give up seven. It's a joke."

Torre left Pettitte in for seven innings because the pitcher had six days' rest before this start and will have five more before he pitches against Baltimore on Thursday. Pettitte got better as he went along, and wanted to stay in the game past the seventh and his pitch count of 131.

"I slowed down a little bit and got in a little groove," he said.

Former Yankees prospect Eric Milton was the beneficiary of the hitting, and avenged a defeat to the Yankees on Sunday. The left-hander did not pitch that well, however, giving up five runs and eight hits in five innings.

Onetime Met Rick Aguilera retired the Yankees 1-2-3 in the ninth for his eighth save, dropping the Yanks' home record to 11-3.

The Twins started off quickly against Pettitte with three hits and two runs in the first inning. Shortstop Pat Meares, who ended Thursday's contest with a game-winning hit against Boston, started Friday's with a single to center. He took third when Matt Lawton hooked a double down the left field line.

Paul Molitor knocked home the first run with a sacrifice fly to center. Cordova's line-drive single to right brought home Lawton to make it 2-0 before Coomer banged into an inning-ending double play.

The Yankees retaliated against Milton with three runs in the second. Tino Martinez led off with a double, and after Tim Raines popped out, Chad Curtis drew a walk. Scott Brosius delivered both runners with a double to left, then scored on Derek Jeter's two-out single to right.

But Pettitte was knocked around again in the third. He got off to a rocky start by walking Denny Hocking, a .103 hitter. Then, after two outs, he walked Molitor.

Cordova, who entered the game hitting .417 against left-handers, got his second hit, a double that drove in two to put the Twins back on top. Coomer followed with a 405-foot homer to left-center, his seventh of the season, and Pettitte was behind, 6-3.

The Twins added a run in the fourth after Jon Shave singled — his first big-league hit since 1993. Shave stole second, took third on Meares' infield hit, and scored on a fielder's choice. Lawton got the RBI when his chopper was fielded by Martinez, who could not make the throw to the plate because Pettitte had drifted into his line of fire.

Curtis cut the margin to 7-5 with his fifth home run, a two-run shot in the sixth that chased Milton and brought in Mike Trombley. Jeter made it 7-6 in the seventh when he led off with his seventh homer of the year into the left field stands.

Reporter's Notebook:

A moment of silence was observed prior to the game in honor of Frank Sinatra. The Yankees will continue to play Sinatra's song "New York, New York" at the end of all home games. Torre said he is a big Sinatra fan and had met the singer on several occasions. Torre said he was not aware of the Marlins-Dodgers trade talks Friday because he spent the whole day listening to Sinatra's music.

Evander Holyfield threw out the first pitch …Designated hitter Chili Davis, on the disabled list with tendon and ligament damage in his right ankle since the first week of the season, visited teammates in the locker room before the game. He leaves today for rehabilitation in Tampa, Fla.

Saturday, May 16, 1998 — Minnesota Twins

Yankees 5, Twins 2

Yankees gaining faith in Mendoza

By GREGORY SCHUTTA, Staff Writer

NEW YORK — The shadow of "El Duque" is not looming as large in Ramiro Mendoza's Yankee future as it once was.

The Yankees' No. 5 starter continues to pitch like an ace, holding the Minnesota Twins to four hits and two runs over eight innings Saturday in a 5-2 victory at the Stadium. It was the third straight victory for the 25-year-old right-hander, who's allowed just 12 hits and three runs in 24 innings while beating Kansas City once and Minnesota twice.

"I think he's pitching like this because he wants to help us, he wants to prove to us that he's a good pitcher, and he wants to make our decisions tough," manager Joe Torre said after the Yankees ended a two-game losing streak, their longest since the first week of the season. "And I really don't mind that."

After watching the bullpen blow a big lead

Thursday and Andy Pettitte post one of his worst outings of the year Friday, Yankee fans had plenty to cheer about Saturday as the Bombers battered Twins starter Bob Tewksbury for five runs and 10 hits in five-plus innings. Derek Jeter did most of the damage, going 4-for-5 with three runs scored, including a key two-run single in the sixth.

"Bob Tewksbury throws a lot of strikes and a lot of first-pitch strikes," Jeter said. "I think Mel [Stottlemyre] said he threw first-pitch strikes to each of the first nine batters. So you've got to take advantage of that. You've got to be aggressive."

And Jeter was that, extending his hitting streak to 12 games, the longest by a Yankee this season, and matching his career high with four hits in a game. He singled and scored in each of his first three at-bats as the Yankees took a 3-1 lead.

Then with the bases loaded and one out in the sixth, Jeter lined a single between short and third to score Jorge Posada and Scott Brosius and give the Yankees a 5-1 lead. That was all for Tewksbury.

"It was a change-up that I was able to get around on," Jeter said. "When the ball's inside, I've been working on pulling the ball rather than trying to go to right field."

But the rest of Jeter's hits were up the middle or to right field, which was fine with Torre.

"With him, taking the ball the other way is the way to handle Tewksbury," Torre said. "He's been hacking the ball real well lately."

And Mendoza, who threw his first career shutout a week ago in Minnesota, has been throwing the ball well. He was perfect through the first four innings before giving up a hit and an unearned run in the fifth inning on the first of two Chuck Knoblauch throwing errors.

Mendoza's only real trouble came in the seventh when he gave up back-to-back singles to Matt Lawton and Marty Cordova to start the inning. Orlando Merced followed with a double-play grounder to Jeter as Lawton scored to cut the Yankees lead to 5-2.

Mariano Rivera, who blew his first save opportunity of the season Thursday against Texas, pitched a perfect ninth for his eighth save of the season.

"I wanted to complete the game," Mendoza said through an interpreter, "but I don't mind that Mariano Rivera came into the game."

"I did that because there's a guy out there who throws 100 miles per hour and is paid to do that," Torre said of bringing in Rivera. "But I think that

Mendoza is in a real good groove right now. In the inning where he gave up the back-to-back base hits, he just got the ball up. Mel went out and reminded him of that. A sinkerballer is a sinkerballer."

And Mendoza was a sinkerballer, getting 14 ground ball outs to eight outs on fly balls.

"I've been working on my mechanics and keeping my arm up," Mendoza said. "It's not easy. I struggle sometimes to keep the ball low, but I've been successful."

And that's what Torre was hoping for when he made Mendoza his fifth starter.

"I knew from the day I met him that he's a pitcher," Torre said. "And with Kenny Rogers leaving and Dwight [Gooden] gone over the off-season, you knew we were going to need pitching with the question marks like [David] Cone and [Hideki] Irabu. The question with Mendoza as a starter is whether he will hold onto the focus for the entire game."

"I'm more confident now," Mendoza said. "I want to play well to stay in the rotation. If they send me to the bullpen, I'll do the job there."

Sunday, May 18, 1998 — Minnesota Twins

Yankees 4, Twins 0

Mr. Perfect

Wells in the record books

By GREGORY SCHUTTA, Staff Writer

NEW YORK — You sensed by the seventh inning that Sunday might be special at Yankee Stadium, where the large crowd started booing every ball called by plate umpire Tim McClelland. By the ninth inning, the fans were on their feet roaring with every strike and dying a little bit more with every ball.

The 49,820 fans on hand in search of those elusive Beanie Babies went home as part of baseball history after left-hander David Wells threw the first perfect game at Yankee Stadium since Don Larsen in Game 5 of the 1956 World Series.

"This is something I'll cherish for the rest of my life," Wells said. "Nobody can take it away from me. And to do it here with the tradition that they have here makes it even more special. There could have been 16,000 people here and it would have sounded like 50,000. That's how special this is."

When right fielder Paul O'Neill squeezed Pat Meares' fly ball to clinch the 4-0 victory over the Minnesota Twins and Wells' first perfect game since high school, the fans sounded like 100,000 and the Yankees had a celebration that was surpassed only by a certain October night in 1996.

"As soon as he caught it, I turned around to look for Jorge [Posada] and there's Luis Sojo," said Wells, who pumped his fist twice when he knew he had pitched the 13th perfect game in modern major league history.

"I thought, 'Wow, he got off the bench fast.' That was probably the finest moment in my life, getting mauled by every single player on the team. It was even better than the World Series."

Wells was carried off the field on the shoulders of Darryl Strawberry, Bernie Williams, and Wille Banks, an honor last given to Dwight Gooden after his no-hitter against the Seattle Mariners on May 14, 1996. Wells then made one more emphatic wave of his cap to the fans, who hadn't moved from the moment he stepped on the mound to begin the ninth inning.

"After the pitchers warm up in the bullpen, I always ask [pitching coach] Mel [Stottlemyre] how it went," manager Joe Torre said. "He just said 'Wow.' He was terrific. He had everything working."

Three days shy of his 35th birthday, Wells struck out 11. Only four batters managed to get to three-ball counts, and two of them struck out.

The key came in the seventh inning with the Yankees protecting a 2-0 lead. Wells went to 3-1 on veteran designated hitter Paul Molitor but came back to strike him out on a vicious sinker.

"I threw a sinker over the outside part of the plate," Wells said. "It was the best pitch I threw all day, and he just swung over it."

"That was the one batter that scared me," Torre said. "You don't go 3-1 on a guy like Molitor and get away with it."

The only other scare came with one out in the eighth inning, when Ron Coomer lined a shot to the right side of second base that Chuck Knoblauch backhanded, knocked down on the short hop, and threw to first to get the out.

"Any time you get a ball like that that's hit on a low liner or that you're going to have to short-hop, you just try to stay low so you can react if it hops up," said Knoblauch, who had two throwing errors Saturday. "It's a reaction play, and luckily I reacted to it."

Williams was the hitting star with two doubles and a solo home run, his third homer of the year and third in less than a week. Strawberry also had an RBI triple in a two-run seventh inning, when the Yankees gave Wells a little breathing room.

And he did the rest, with incredible command of his fastball, curve, and change-up.

"About the seventh inning I started getting nervous," Wells said. "I was kind of hoping the crowd would shush a little. It's something you're afraid to get caught up in because then your nerves start to go and you hang a pitch and boom, it's gone. If you pitch a perfect game, you're a hero. If you don't, you've still pitched a great game."

"I was just praying we'd get a couple more runs," Torre said. "I didn't want to do anything that would mess it up."

Although Wells wouldn't say it directly, Sunday's performance was a measure of vindication. He was ripped by Torre and Stottlemyre after blowing a 9-0 lead May 6 in Texas. Sunday was the second straight victory by Wells, who allowed five hits and two runs in eight innings in a 3-2 win over Kansas City on Tuesday.

"I wasn't mad at him personally," Stottlemyre said of that night in Texas. "I was disappointed. Whenever you give a pitcher that kind of lead and you feel he short-changed himself, you get disappointed. But David is the type of guy who whenever he's challenged, or he thinks he's challenged, he goes out and dominates."

Said Torre: "Boomer can pitch, there's no doubt about it. He may have been more determined after letting that one go in Texas, but now he's got an accomplishment that he can take with him and that's very special."

Tuesday, May 19, 1998 — Baltimore Orioles

Yankees 9, Orioles 5

Fighting back

By KEN DAVIDOFF, Staff Writer

NEW YORK — Any concerns George Steinbrenner had about a team hangover following David Wells' perfect game were erased late Tuesday night.

In a game featuring one of the most vicious brawls in recent baseball history, the Yankees erased a four-run deficit to defeat the Orioles, 9-5, for their third straight victory.

The score and the plays on the field were very, very secondary on this night, one in which 31,311 Yankee Stadium patrons took in a sight as ugly as Wells' Sunday perfect game was pretty.

"It's not a very good state of affairs when two major league teams go at it like that," said Yankees pitcher Graeme Lloyd, who played a large role in the fight.

The brawl was sparked by Baltimore reliever Armando Benitez, who hit Tino Martinez with a fastball in the back with two outs in the bottom of the eighth inning, right after Bernie Williams had crushed a 408-foot three-run home run into the right field upper deck that proved to be the game-winner. It was as blatant a purpose pitch as there can be in baseball.

"That's the dumbest thing I've ever seen," Derek Jeter said. "You go ask [the Orioles]. They'll tell you it's dumb."

"The guy was classless," Steinbrenner said. "He should be suspended for a month."

"I think it's the most chicken[bleep] thing I've seen in my life," general manager Brian Cashman said. "I'm sure [the Orioles] are as embarrassed about Benitez as anybody."

Benitez claimed the pitch was an accident, that he was just trying to throw inside to Martinez.

This wasn't the first time that Benitez nailed Martinez. In 1995, after Benitez surrendered a grand slam to Seattle's Edgar Martinez, he beaned Tino Martinez, who was then on the Mariners. For that reason, Yanks pitcher Jeff Nelson — who was also on the Mariners — knew a fight was coming as soon as Williams went deep.

Home plate umpire Drew Coble immediately threw Benitez out of the game. Martinez took a couple of steps toward the mound and Benitez dropped his glove, making a "come and get me" gesture with his hands. With Darryl Strawberry leading the way, the Yankees' bench cleared, and the bullpens headed toward the mound.

At first, there were just words exchanged, and it looked as though it might be a standard bench-clearing incident. But then Lloyd, usually the most mild-mannered of players, tackled Benitez and the fisticuffs began.

As manager Joe Torre would say later, "Every time you stopped a leak out there, a new one would open somewhere else."

"All I know is, I was pushed from behind," an emotional Lloyd said.

"All the rest is on tape."

Scott Brosius appeared to throw a couple of punches, as did Strawberry, who landed a left hook to Benitez's face, then fell into the dugout, where he was pummeled by an unidentified Oriole.

Martinez had to be held back by his teammates,

and Strawberry was escorted back to the Yankees' dugout by Torre. Ejections were issued to Lloyd, Nelson, Strawberry, and Baltimore pitcher Allan Mills, in addition to Benitez.

Strawberry, who sported a swollen left cheek after the game, declined to comment, saying, "I don't know what's going to happen." At first glance, Strawberry and Martinez seemed to be all right, although Martinez — who also did not speak to the media — was said to have a large welt in the middle of his back.

The melee lasted about 10 minutes. And on the first pitch from new Baltimore pitcher Bobby Munoz, Tim Raines cranked a 408-foot, two-run blast to right. The entire Yankees team came out of the dugout to welcome Raines.

"By no means was I thinking, 'Hit a homer here,'" Raines said.

In the next few days, there are sure to be some suspensions issued by the American League. Those suspensions, Steinbrenner said, should all come down to one thing: "Who started it?"

The teams must still play two more games in this series, and as Torre said, "What went on tonight is going to be a very tough thing to forget."

"I think [AL President] Dr. [Gene] Budig will react," Steinbrenner said. "He may react by saying that [Orioles owner] Peter Angelos and I have to go three rounds. I'm ready. I'm working out three days a week."

Wednesday, May 20, 1998 — Baltimore Orioles

Yankees 9, Orioles 6

Bombers keep pouring it on

By KEN DAVIDOFF, Staff Writer

NEW YORK — Yankees held a short meeting Wednesday afternoon so Joe Torre could remind his players that victory, not revenge, was the goal on this night, just like every other.

As has been the case throughout this season, the Bombers made their manager look smart, pounding the Orioles, 9-6, behind Hideki Irabu's shaky yet effective pitching and Derek Jeter's and Tim Raines' solid hitting. The Yanks' fourth straight victory and the Orioles' seventh straight loss satisfied the 32,449 Yankee Stadium fans who mostly seemed to have

revenge on their minds in the wake of Tuesday night's vicious bench-clearing brawl.

"We don't worry about what happened yesterday," said Jeter, who extended his hitting streak to 15 games with a single, double, and triple. "I think you just take it day by day."

"Our concern," Torre said, "is winning games." Nowhere in this contest, he felt, were there signs of continuing tension.

At least on the field. In the stands, there was undoubtedly a unique electricity, justifying the Yankees' deployment of extra uniformed and undercover police officers throughout the ballpark. The game was only minutes old when the crowd began chanting, "Tino! Tino!" a tip of the hat to Tino Martinez, who took the Armando Benitez pitch in the back Tuesday night, precipitating the brawl.

And the game's biggest cheer had everything to do with Tuesday and nothing with Wednesday. When Graeme Lloyd, who received a three-game suspension Wednesday for his role in the fight, relieved Irabu in the top of the seventh, he received the loudest ovation he has ever received as a Yankee.

"I looked up and made sure we brought in the right guy," joked Torre, who called his left-handed specialist "a cult hero."

"It was very nice," Lloyd said. "It's great to be appreciated for the things you do. I want to be appreciated mostly for my pitching, but it's nice."

The two teams had agreed beforehand to play nice. George Steinbrenner said he spoke amicably with O's owner Peter Angelos on Wednesday, and Baltimore manager Ray Miller issued a public apology before the game. Besides, Torre said, this was an individual complaint about Benitez, not the whole Baltimore team.

"I think we just want to get this behind us," Steinbrenner said.

When Miller took his lineup card to home plate umpire Dale Ford, he implored the ump to give both teams the benefit of the doubt regarding pitchers throwing inside.

Sure enough, when Jimmy Key's first pitch to Chuck Knoblauch was inside, the players and umpires ignored the loud boos. Said Knoblauch: "I didn't have any other thoughts other than 'Ball one.'"

Key would proceed to hit Chad Curtis in the left foot, and Irabu would later hit two Orioles batters. None of them appeared intentional, and none drew the ire of either team.

Irabu labored through 6 1/3 innings, allowing two

runs and six hits, walking three, and striking out two. But he held the O's to 1-for-8 with runners in scoring position in lifting his record to 3-0.

"He had no command today," Torre said of his right-hander.

"When I let up the first run, I just concentrated on not letting them get a second run," Irabu said through his interpreter, George Rose. "When they got a second run, I concentrated on not letting them get a third run."

His offensive teammates gave him plenty of breathing room, pounding 15 hits off Key (4-3) and two relievers. Jeter fell a homer short of a cycle and drove home two runs, while Raines had three singles and drove home three runs.

"Right now, I feel good," said Jeter, who lifted his average to .341. "But I don't even try to think about it."

Raines, meanwhile, increased his average to .326, showing he can thrive despite not playing every day. "I don't think it's surprising to me," said Raines, 38. "I think it's surprising to most baseball people."

The Yanks' victory gave them an overwhelming 13-game lead over the O's, but they refused to write off the defending American League East champs.

"We'd like to think they are [finished]," Torre said, "but we know better than that. You never get to that point where you can peek at the finish line."

Thursday, May 21, 1998 — Baltimore Orioles
Yankees 3, Orioles 1

Yanks finish clean sweep

By KEN DAVIDOFF, Staff Writer

NEW YORK — To a week that already featured redemption and retaliation, the Yankees added rehabilitation Thursday night.

Andy Pettitte looked like his old self at Yankee Stadium, outpitching a brilliant Scott Erickson to give the Bombers their fifth straight victory, a 3-1 decision over the Baltimore Orioles.

Pettitte (6-4) pushed away the memories of three previous bad starts.

"I told the guys in here, 'I feel like I had lost 20 in a row,'" he said after scattering eight hits over eight innings, walking two, and fanning six. "And I had

only lost two. I was in unfamiliar territory. I had had three bad starts in a row, and I don't know if I had had three bad starts [previously] up here in the big leagues. It was definitely a big start for me."

Said manager Joe Torre: "He's an intense young man. He matched [Erickson] and pitched a hell of a game."

To the delight of the 34,588 fans who chanted, "Sweep! Sweep! Sweep!" as Mariano Rivera pitched a perfect ninth for his ninth save, the Bombers (31-9) overcame Erickson's dominance to knock the defending American League East champs 14 games out of the division penthouse. They did so thanks to the contribution of the previously invisible Dale Sveum and the hustle of Paul O'Neill, who ensured earlier Thursday that he will be a Yankee in 1999.

In other words, it was just another day at the office for these 1998 Bombers, who have put together the second-best 40-game start in franchise history. Only the 1928 Yankees, at 33-7, started quicker.

On this night, Pettitte played the most important role. In his previous three appearances, two of them losses, he allowed 18 runs in 18 2/3 innings for an 8.68 ERA. His wife, Laura, is at the Pettittes' home in Deer Park, Texas, close to delivering their second child, and Dad has admitted that it hasn't been easy living alone.

Yet he used five days of rest constructively, working with pitching coach Mel Stottlemyre to slow his pace.

"I was muscling up," he said. "When you muscle up, your ball goes flat."

He cruised through the first 3 2/3 innings, then hung an 0-2 curveball that Rafael Palmeiro tattooed, knocking it off the facing of the right field upper deck for a 1-0 Baltimore lead. With Erickson dominating the Bombers, retiring 13 straight batters after Chuck Knoblauch's leadoff single, the homer looked like it might hold up.

"Erickson was unhittable early," Torre said.

Joe Girardi began the sixth with a single off Roberto Alomar's glove, and Sveum followed with a sharp grounder up the middle. Alomar made an impressive backhanded stab, then chose a behind-the-back toss to double play partner Mike Bordick. Bad decision. Bordick couldn't handle it, putting runners on first and second.

Knoblauch went up thinking sacrifice, and he laid a perfect bunt down the third base line. Cal Ripken gloved it, paused, and threw the ball wildly, allowing Girardi to score the tying run.

When Alomar and Palmeiro started the eighth with singles, Pettitte looked to be in serious trouble. But Torre said, "I wouldn't let [Pettitte] pitch that deep into the game, then bring in someone else."

As he does when he's at his best, Pettitte thrived under the heat. He induced Joe Carter to pop harmlessly to second, then struck out Ripken and B.J. Surhoff to kill the threat. In all, the left-hander stranded nine runners.

"I was just trying to make quality pitches," Pettitte said. "I was pounding [Carter] in with some fastballs, and I got him to fly out. Same with Cal, threw him a good curveball to strike him out. Then I threw B.J. four straight sinkers."

On the heels of that, the Yanks took the lead in the bottom of the inning. Sveum — who started for the injured Tino Martinez, who is day-to-day with a bone bruise in his right chest wall — lined a one-out single to left, his first hit of the season, and went to second on Knoblauch's single. Derek Jeter's walk loaded the bases, and O'Neill hit a bouncer to second. Alomar tried to end the inning with a 4-6-3 double play, but O'Neill beat Bordick's relay throw by a step as Sveum scored.

Bernie Williams' single plated Knoblauch for an insurance run.

Friday, May 22, 1998 — at Boston Red Sox

Red Sox 5, Yankees 4

Red Sox cool down Yankees

By KEN DAVIDOFF, Staff Writer

BOSTON — Maybe Friday night will prove to be nothing more than a speed bump. Maybe it will be a turning point. Either way, if anyone thought that the Red Sox would yield meekly to the Yankees juggernaut, Boston put forth a convincing argument at Fenway Park.

In a rare, late-inning collapse, the Bombers blew a four-run lead to fall to the Red Sox, 5-4, in the teams' first meeting of 1998. The game's entire tone changed in what seemed like a blink of the lightning-quick 2 hours 30 minutes it took to complete this one as the Yankees' American League East lead fell to four games.

"We just didn't get the job done out of the bullpen," manager Joe Torre said.

For all the talk about this being just another game and just another series, the Yanks (31-10) — who became the last team in the majors to reach double digits in the loss column — took the Bosox seriously enough to make sure they had all 25 players. Darryl Strawberry, Graeme Lloyd, and Jeff Nelson appealed their suspensions resulting from Tuesday night's brawl with the Orioles to make themselves eligible for the whole weekend.

But Nelson turned out to be one of the primary perpetrators. Starter Ramiro Mendoza entered the seventh with a 4-1 lead and promptly gave up a leadoff homer to Troy O'Leary.

John Valentin followed with a fly ball to left that Tim Raines couldn't see through the lights, and it fell for a single. Valentin advanced to second on a Mike Benjamin groundout and moved to third on a wild pitch.

Jason Varitek doubled down the left field line, scoring Valentin, and Torre lifted Mendoza for Nelson. The right-hander allowed a single to Lou Merloni, putting the tying run on third and the winning run on first, then walked Darren Lewis to load the bases.

> **"**I got it in my mind that I don't want the tying run to score. That took me away from being aggressive with the guy. I let that get to me too much.**"**
>
> — *Jeff Nelson*

"I got it in my mind that I don't want the tying run to score," Nelson said. "That took me away from being aggressive with the guy. I let that get to me too much."

Lefty Mike Stanton came in to face Darren Bragg, threw a fastball too much over the plate, and had it pounded for a two-run single up the middle.

In the Yankees' eighth, Chuck Knoblauch and Derek Jeter drew leadoff walks, but southpaw Ron Mahay retired Paul O'Neill (strikeout) and Tino Martinez (popup), then closer Tom Gordon induced Bernie Williams to fly to left.

The Yankees went down meekly in the ninth, much to the dismay of George Steinbrenner, who expressed his frustration through the final innings with animated gestures.

The appeal deal has had more twists and turns than a mystery novel since the American League announced the suspensions Wednesday. Strawberry said he wanted to get his sentence over with and sat out games on Wednesday and Thursday.

Steinbrenner said he'd rather have his players serve their terms so the team could close the door on the entire incident.

Then, the maneuvering began. On Thursday, Lloyd said he would appeal his suspension, and Nelson said he would serve his.

The Yanks wanted Lloyd to be available for the Red Sox and their tough lefties Mo Vaughn and Troy O'Leary, and they wanted Nelson — who was scheduled to sit out upon the completion of Lloyd's suspension — to move up and sit out against Boston rather than the White Sox and their tough right-handers Frank Thomas and Albert Belle.

Strawberry, meanwhile, said that he was waiting for marching orders from the players' union regarding an appeal of his third game out.

The Yankees must have realized that their designated hitter held a lifetime .385 (5-for-13) average against Friday night's starter Tim Wakefield with two homers and six RBI. Strawberry went 0-for-3 against the knuckleballer.

Finally, on Friday, the team said that all three players were appealing. AL President Gene Budig offered to come to Boston on Sunday, or to meet the Bombers in Chicago next week, to rule on the appeals.

Yet as of late Friday, the players' union had not approved a hearing date. Thus, all three players are active until further notice.

"The process allows you to do certain things," Torre said with a grin.

The sinkerballer Mendoza and the knuckleballer Wakefield relied on their respective strengths to cruise through the first three innings. Wakefield got two quick outs in the fourth, then allowed two quick singles to O'Neill and Martinez, with O'Neill going to third on Martinez's rope to the right-field corner. Williams stepped to the plate right-handed, something the switch-hitter does against Wakefield.

Wakefield served up a knuckler that didn't knuckle, and Williams sent it over the Green Monster for a 3-0 Yankees lead.

Saturday, May 23, 1998 — at Boston Red Sox

Yankees 12, Red Sox 3

Not perfect, but still darn good

Yanks show Red Sox, they can bounce back

By KEN DAVIDOFF, Staff Writer

BOSTON — Yesterday and tomorrow don't matter. Every game is independent of the rest. One day at a time.

They are words that form one of sport's most cliched philosophies — and, usually, one of its most unrealistic. But the 1998 Yankees have put forth a convincing presentation that this mentality can work if adhered to religiously. Saturday, the Bombers again displayed their resiliency, shaking off a dramatic Friday night loss to pound Boston with a 12-3 victory at Fenway Park.

"We gave away a game [Friday night] which we know we should have won," Darryl Strawberry said. "We live with it, but one thing we do is we tell ourselves to come back the next day and go after them again."

> **❝** That's been kind of our approach all year, to not get real up after a win and not get real down after a loss. **❞**
>
> — *Scott Brosius*

"That's been kind of our approach all year, to not get real up after a win and not get real down after a loss," Scott Brosius said.

"There are a lot of games in the season, and we're going to win a lot and lose some. You take it and move on to the next day."

And so it has been. Of the Yankees' 10 losses, half have come in clusters: They lost the first three games of the season, then dropped a May 14 series closer to Texas and a May 15 series opener to Minnesota. The other five were one-game skids.

The first four of the one-game skids were followed

by winning streaks of at least three games. Now, the Bombers are 1-0 following their most recent defeat, one featuring a blown four-run lead that may have lingered for a few days on another team.

"We're a confident club," Yankees manager Joe Torre said. "The reason we're confident is we've gone out and won so many ballgames. We're very confident, very calm, very productive."

Saturday was about one individual, David Wells, until Darren Bragg's first-inning flare landed between a sun-blinded Derek Jeter and Chad Curtis for a base hit. That ended the southpaw's chance at two straight perfect games and left him short of the major league record for consecutive retired batters. Suddenly life in the Yankees universe returned to normal.

Strawberry began the second inning with a ground single up the middle, then stole second and went to third on a wild pitch by Bosox starter Derek Lowe (0-3). Jorge Posada drew a walk, and Curtis lined a single to left to score Strawberry.

Brosius laid down a bunt single to load the bases, and Dale Sveum hit into a force at home plate. Chuck Knoblauch stepped up, worked the count full, fouled off a couple of pitches, and went with Lowe's outside fastball, sending it into right field.

"I knew I hit it hard," Knoblauch said. Right place, right time. With the Fenway winds blowing toward right field, the ball carried and carried until it landed over the right field wall for a grand slam, tying Knoblauch's career high of four RBI.

In his last five games, the Yankees leadoff hitter has looked as advertised, hitting at a 7-for-16 clip with six runs scored, lifting his batting average from .238 to .257. "I've lowered my hands [on the bat] and flattened out the bat," he said. "My hands are where they should be."

The Yanks added two more in the third and another in the fourth, meaning Wells had an 8-0 cushion to work with when he was tagged for two homers and three runs in the bottom of the fourth.

While he cruised through the seventh, his teammates put the finishing touches on yet another offensive masterpiece. By game's end, the Bombers had compiled 15 hits, and everyone in the starting lineup had scored at least one run. Strawberry, Brosius, and Curtis each had three hits. Friday seemed as distant as that 1-4 record the Yankees owned during the season's first week.

"It's nice that there's still a certain calm after a loss," Torre said. "You don't feel the urgency to have to do something. That's what winning does for you."

Sunday, May 24, 1998 — at Boston Red Sox

Yankees 14, Red Sox 4

Knoblauch gives Cone a boost

By KEN DAVIDOFF, Staff Writer

BOSTON — The Yankees have constructed their magical 1998 largely without typical contributions from two veteran All-Stars. And while Chuck Knoblauch struggled to find his stroke and David Cone made like Dr. Frankenstein with his experiments in pitching mechanics, everyone in the organization preached the same mantra: patience.

Both the second baseman and the right-handed pitcher played prominent roles Sunday afternoon in the Yanks' 14-4 shellacking of the Red Sox at Fenway Park. With his second homer in two days, Knoblauch rewarded his manager's and teammates' patience. With his shaky yet ultimately successful six-inning outing, Cone asked his fellow Yankees for a little more.

"Baseball's about 'What have you done for me lately?'" Knoblauch said. "It felt good to be able to contribute a little bit and start swinging the bat in a way like I feel I'm capable of swinging it. Hopefully it's a week I can continue to build on."

"I know I'm going to get better," Cone said. "I know I'm going to get stronger. The fact of the matter is I don't feel like I'm all the way there yet. I'm very confident I will get there, though."

The Yankees can afford to trust Cone's self-confidence, just as they could Knoblauch's. Sunday's victory, their second straight, increased their American League East lead to six games over the Red Sox, a new high for the season. It also gives the Bombers a 5-1 record in a week that had been targeted as a litmus test: three games at home against the Orioles, three games here against the Bosox.

Whether it was fortunate timing or a sign of his mettle, Knoblauch contributed his best week in pinstripes, going 8-for-19 with eight runs scored and eight RBI. On Sunday, with the Yanks in a 2-0 hole, eighth and ninth hitters Dale Sveum and Joe Girardi started the third with back-to-back singles. Knoblauch stepped to the plate against Bret Saberhagen (5-3), saw a 2-1 fastball that he liked, and whacked it.

"When you put a good swing on the ball and you

hit it solid, sometimes you can get it to carry," the Yanks' leadoff hitter said. "It wasn't like I took an uppercut swing. It was a nice, level swing. Solid contact on the fat of the ball. It goes up."

Up and over the Green Monster, the first time in his career that Knoblauch cleared Fenway's legendary left-field wall.

That gave the Yanks a 3-2 edge and set off yet another explosion of runs (four more in the third, six in the fifth, one in the ninth) for a club that has reached the double-digit mark five times this month. Knoblauch drove home another run in the fifth when he was hit by a Ron Mahay pitch with the bases loaded, thus tying his career high of four RBI for the second straight game.

"Everyone knows Chuck can play," said Derek Jeter, one of three Yankees (along with Scott Brosius and Joe Girardi) to tally three hits. "It's no secret. He's been playing like that for the last six or seven years. You don't expect anything less of him."

The same expectations exist for Cone. He permitted five Red Sox to reach base in the first five innings, yet held them to two runs.

In the fourth, he hit two consecutive batters, Mike Benjamin and John Varitek, with one out. He looked livid, but managed to escape without letting a run cross home.

"He was out of tune," manager Joe Torre said. "A Mercedes is a great car, but if it's out of tune, then it's not going to ride smoothly. He's finding it. He's trying to find it."

Monday, May 25, 1998 — at Chicago White Sox

Yankees 12, White Sox 0

Irabu, Yanks breeze

By KEN DAVIDOFF, Staff Writer

CHICAGO — The game's last batter, Jeff Abbott, tapped a soft bouncer to the mound. Hideki Irabu snatched it, paused, and threw to first. Game over. Yanks win, 12-0, over the White Sox. Irabu gets his first career shutout and takes over the major league lead in ERA with a sparkling 1.13.

And yet, the right-hander's milestone performance couldn't have left the most indelible impression on the minds of the 19,812 fans who went to Comiskey Park on Monday night. That right would have to belong to the Godzilla-like scoring behemoth that is the Yankees' offense.

"Wow," manager Joe Torre said after his team put double-digits on the scoreboard for the third straight day. "I don't know what I can say. Right now, we're guessing right, we're taking advantage of every situation. We're very aggressive. The last three days, it's been incredible."

Aggressive, persistent, most certainly annoying if you're rooting for the other team. The Yanks, coming off their weekend massacre of the Red Sox at Fenway Park and knowing they have Boston again this weekend in the Bronx, showed no signs of an emotional letdown against lowly Chicago. In the last three games, the Bombers have compiled 38 runs and 46 hits.

"We took today as a new challenge, a new team," said Bernie Williams, who hit his sixth homer, a three-run job in the sixth, in his last 13 games.

And with the victories, now three straight, the historical comparisons keep coming. The Bombers' 34-10 start is tied for the fifth-best jump out of the gate in American League history. The 18-7 road record is the best by a Yankees team since the 1976 club started 19-6.

On a present-day note, the Yanks' AL East lead grew to seven games with the Red Sox' 7-5 loss to the Blue Jays.

"I'm going to have a tough time cracking this lineup," joked team RBI leader Tino Martinez, who has missed the last three games with a sprained right shoulder.

Chisox starter Jaime Navarro lasted just one-third of an inning — or 20 minutes, depending on how you track these things. Seven of the first eight Yankees batters reached base safely as six runners crossed the plate. Jorge Posada and Scott Brosius each drove home two runs in a half-inning that ended 23 minutes after it began.

So before Irabu took the mound, he already had as many runs from his teammates as he had surrendered in 38 2/3 innings. But he started the game looking very shaky. After Chad Curtis ran down a missile to left from first batter Ray Durham, Wil Cordero lined a single to right, and Irabu walked the intimidating duo of Frank Thomas and Albert Belle to jam the bases. Suddenly that 6-0 lead didn't seem very comfortable.

"I didn't know where the ball was going to go," Irabu said through his interpreter, George Rose.

Yet as he has done consistently this season, the 29-year-old right-hander escaped danger with a James Bond-like panache. He caught Robin Ventura looking at a different-looking fastball for a strikeout, and he induced rookie outfielder Magglio Ordonez to tap a comebacker to the mound. Irabu pounced on it and softly tossed to Posada for the force at home.

He needed 23 pitches to escape the first inning. For the final eight innings, he needed just 87 pitches, or fewer than 11 per. While his fastball didn't top 93 mph on the radar gun, he successfully integrated his curveball and split-fingered fastball into the mix. And it didn't hurt that the White Sox seemed to put up the white flag, swinging at a ton of first pitches.

"Once he got rolling, he was terrific," Torre said of Irabu.

Tuesday, May 26, 1998 — at Chicago White Sox

Yankees 7, White Sox 5

Yanks win ugly
O'Neill's HR erases miscue

By KEN DAVIDOFF, Staff Writer

CHICAGO — The Yankees did not play their usual crisp baseball Tuesday night. They made enough pitching, fielding, and hitting mistakes to resemble the team across the Comiskey Park field, the lowly White Sox.

Yet the Bombers played well enough to win. Paul O'Neill's three-run homer in the eighth inning proved to be the difference in his team's fourth straight victory, 7-5. The Yanks' 35-10 record is tied for the fifth best in American League history through 45 games.

Andy Pettitte started and struggled mightily with his command, setting a career high with seven walks. Thanks to his teammates, though, he avoided his fifth loss of the season.

O'Neill's 376-foot bomb to right field off Keith Foulke followed a Chuck Knoblauch single and Derek Jeter hit-by-pitch, and neutralized what could have been a bad memory of an ugly bottom of the seventh.

"We made some mistakes and got away with them," said manager Joe Torre. "Hopefully we'll learn from them."

Jeff Nelson picked up the victory, and Mariano Rivera notched his 10th save with a scoreless final 1 2/3 innings.

The Yanks had a scare in the bottom of the ninth, though. After Rivera recorded two outs, Albert Belle

singled to center. Then Robin Ventura drove a long shot to right field that was only a few feet foul from being a game-tying homer. Ventura eventually walked, though, and Rivera got Magglio Ordonez to ground to first to end the night.

The White Sox capitalized on a number of fielding mistakes in the seventh to score two runs for a 4-3 lead. Luis Sojo made two bad plays at first base, while Bernie Williams made a poor throwing decision on Frank Thomas' sacrifice fly. But O'Neill's homer erased his teammates' sins.

"Today wasn't one of our better efforts," said Yankees catcher Joe Girardi, "but we managed to get the win."

The Yanks took a 3-2 lead in the top of the seventh inning when Tim Raines led off with a double to the right field corner, advanced to third on Chad Curtis' deep lineout to right, and scored on Scott Brosius' bouncer to short.

White Sox starter Jim Parque had quite an assignment for his major league debut. When the Yankees defeated the Red Sox twice and the White Sox once by scores of 12-3, 14-4, and 12-0 in their previous three games, they became the sixth team this century to win three straight games by nine or more runs — and the first team to do so on the road. Their 12 or more runs in those three games tied the American League record.

> **❝**We made some mistakes and got away with them. Hopefully we'll learn from them. **❞**
>
> *— Joe Torre*

Parque, a southpaw, made it through his first big league inning unscathed, working around a pair of walks, to put a zero on the scoreboard. He wasn't as successful in his second inning, allowing a Curtis leadoff single, hitting Brosius in the hip, letting Girardi sacrifice the runners over to second and third, and allowing Sojo to hit into a fielder's choice, scoring Curtis for the 1-0 Yankees lead.

After cruising through the first inning, Pettitte opened the second by issuing a free pass to Belle. He worked the count to 2-1 on Ventura, then unleashed a fastball "right over the dish," as the Texan southpaw always calls the heart of the plate. Ventura smoked it over the right field wall for a two-run dinger and a 2-1 Chicago lead.

Pettitte, who is leaving the club to be with his wife for her induced labor Thursday in Texas, looked to be in more trouble when he started the fourth with consecutive walks to Ventura and Ordonez.

Brosius went to the mound to talk with Pettitte — maybe it was just to discuss coverage of a sacrifice bunt, maybe it was just to give the pitcher a moment's breather.

Whatever its purpose, it worked. Thanks to strong defensive plays by Pettitte, Knoblauch, and Jeter, the Yanks escaped without any damage.

The Yanks KO'd Parque in the fifth, or, more appropriately, the rookie KO'd himself by walking Tim Raines with the bases loaded and none out to force home the tying run. In very un-Yankee-like fashion, though, Curtis, Brosius, and Girardi went down against Chicago reliever Carlos Castillo, stranding three teammates.

Wednesday, May 27, 1998
— at Chicago White Sox

White Sox 12, Yankees 9

Yanks drop slugfest
White Sox pound staff

By KEN DAVIDOFF, Staff Writer

CHICAGO — The Yankees finally ran out of gas Wednesday night.

Four Yankees pitchers combined to allow a season-high 17 hits as the Bombers offense couldn't keep up with the White Sox at Comiskey Park. Lowly Chicago toughed it out in a seesaw game to pick up a 12-9 victory, ending the Yankees' most recent winning streak at four games.

"We kept fighting back," manager Joe Torre said. "We couldn't get the guys to put a Band-Aid on it."

Jeff Nelson took the loss for New York (35-11), and it was an "L" much deserved. After all, the righty reliever was pounded for four runs and four hits and walked three (one intentional) in 1 2/3 innings.

It was Nelson's third straight blown save, and he will have two days to think about what he's doing wrong, as he begins to serve his suspension for his role in last week's brawl with the Orioles.

"I'm very concerned about Nelson," Torre said. "He's leaving a lot of balls in the middle of the plate. He will be OK."

"It's just tough when you go through something like this," Nelson said. "I don't think I've had an outing like this in I don't know how long."

But Nelson was not the only mound culprit on this night, which raised the team ERA from 4.05 to 4.23. Starter Ramiro Mendoza brought nothing to the table, lasting just three innings, and reliever Willie Banks continued his descent toward ex-Yankeedom by allowing three runs and three hits in two innings.

And finally, after the White Sox' three-run seventh off Nelson, the Yankees offense petered out. With Tino Martinez and Scott Brosius nursing minor injuries, the short-handed Bombers couldn't keep up with the suddenly explosive Chisox.

Bernie Williams homered, tripled, and singled and drove in four runs in the losing effort. After going through his first 31 games homerless, the Yankees center fielder has seven in his past 15 games, tying him for the team lead with Derek Jeter and Darryl Strawberry.

With one out in the White Sox seventh, Mike Cameron ripped a triple to right field. Nelson walked Chad Kreuter, and on a 1-1 count to Ray Durham, the reliever unleashed a vicious slider that Jorge Posada couldn't handle.

The ball skipped toward the backstop as Cameron scored the lead run. Kreuter, who advanced to second on the passed ball, came home on Durham's double to left for an 11-9 edge. Durham scored the inning's third run on a Nelson wild pitch.

After scoring one run in the fifth, the Yanks regained the lead in the sixth off reliever James

> **❝ I want to go out there and do so well. I'm gripping the ball and I feel like I'm going to put my fingers right through it. ❞**
>
> *— Willie Banks*

Baldwin. Luis Sojo started the three-run rally with a hard grounder off the glove of shortstop Mike Caruso, and Chuck Knoblauch walked after Dale Sveum struck out. Jeter hit into a fielder's choice at third, and Paul O'Neill sent Knoblauch home with a double to left field.

With an 0-1 count, Williams sent what seemed to be a pedestrian fly to center. But the ball kept carrying, over Cameron's glove, and came inches from clearing the wall. Jeter and O'Neill scored for a 9-8 Yankees lead.

That lasted a few minutes. With Nelson relieving Banks in the bottom of the sixth, Durham led off with a long triple to right-center that Williams almost tracked down before crashing into the fence. Caruso's single through the left-side hole scored Durham for the 9-9 tie.

Banks took the mound to start the fourth, retired Kreuter on a fly to deep center, and then got into quick, big trouble: Walk to Durham. Single to Caruso. Groundout to Frank Thomas, advancing the runners. And a 422-foot, mammoth homer to straightaway center to Albert Belle, who had just two hits in 11 previous at-bats against Banks. With that, the White Sox had an 8-5 lead.

"Willie, he's trying so damn hard," Torre said. "He has no command when he does that. You can't get behind Albert Belle 3-1 and try to throw a fastball by him."

"I want to go out there and do so well," Banks agreed. "I'm gripping the ball and I feel like I'm going to put my fingers right through it."

Mendoza didn't have his sinker working and lasted just three innings, getting pounded for five runs and nine hits. The Sox jumped out to a 2-0 lead in the second.

In a blink, the Yankees took those two runs back and then some, with Williams' 410-foot, two-run blast to center highlighting a five-run third.

And in another blink, there was a tie game. With one White Sox run on the board in the bottom of the third and runners on second and third, Robin Ventura smacked a liner back to the mound that hit Mendoza's right thigh and flew behind the pitcher. Mendoza dove at it in an effort to catch it on the fly, but the ball fell for a single, bringing home Thomas from third.

The Yankees starter stayed in the game after an examination by team head trainer Gene Monahan and surrendered the tying run on Greg Norton's sacrifice fly.

Thursday, May 29, 1998 — Boston Red Sox

Yankees 8, Red Sox3

Worn-out Sox

Boston bounced by Wells Yanks widen gap in East

By VINNY DiTRANI, Staff Writer

NEW YORK — Many of the Yankees didn't get to sleep until 5 a.m. Thursday after flying home from an ugly loss the night before in Chicago.

Left-hander David Wells went to the Yankee Stadium mound Thursday night with less-than-perfect stuff against a Boston team that usually knocks the tar out of him.

Slugging first baseman Tino Martinez, originally in the lineup, was scratched when he experienced pain in his sore shoulder.

So what happened? Ho-hum, just another Yankee win, an 8-3 decision over the Red Sox in what more and more looks like it could become a classic season.

"We try not to look at the big picture," said manager Joe Torre, whose team is 36-11 with an 8 1/2-game lead over Boston in the AL East. "If you look at the big picture, the law of averages says this and that. So we're trying to deal with it one game at a time and ride this streak as long as we can."

Even Torre, however, conceded this team might accomplish some great things before the season is over.

"We are good, we can do a lot of things," he said. "What helped us tonight was we stole a few bases and forced them into some mistakes. We're not the home run hitting team like some other Yankee clubs, although we do have some ability to do that, too."

The Yankees did that twice Thursday night, including a mammoth poke by Darryl Strawberry that gave them a 3-0 lead in the third inning.

Getting that early lead was key, said Paul O'Neill, who chipped in with two hits, two RBI, and a super defensive play to help kill a Boston rally in the eighth.

"Getting in after a night like that," he said, referring to a 12-9 loss to the White Sox, "made it pretty tough, guys were dragging. But getting that lead early lifts everyone up, gets the crowd into it, and gets everyone going."

O'Neill doubled home the Yankees' first run in the first inning, then scored the second when he stole third and continued home on an error. That gave Wells, who struggled through the night, a nice cushion.

Wells (7-1), making his first Stadium appearance since his May 17 perfect game against Minnesota, was tagged for 10 hits, including two homers, in seven innings of work.

"There's something about that team," Wells said of the Red Sox. "No matter how many times I face them in a season I think I'm going to go 0-for against them. I try to challenge them, but they always seem to get the best of me."

Wells is 8-16 in his career against the Sox with a 5.25 ERA, but he's 2-0 this season.

"It was our offense and defense that kept us in the game tonight," he said. "My control wasn't the best. I was up in the zone. I didn't have my best stuff, but I did make some good pitches at crucial times. And I relied on the guys behind me to make the outs."

> **"** Getting in after a night like that made it pretty tough, guys were dragging. But getting that lead early lifts everyone up, gets the crowd into it, and gets everyone going. **"**
>
> *— Paul O'Neill*

In addition to O'Neill's sliding catch that kept reliever Mike Stanton, who got his fifth save, from an eighth-inning problem, shortstop Derek Jeter made a fine play on a ground ball in the sixth.

Catcher Jorge Posada gunned down a runner to end that inning as the Yankees had another strong defensive game.

Offensively they took advantage of some wildness by knuckleballer Tim Wakefield (6-2) and some butchering of the flutterball by catcher Jason Varitek to grab a 5-1 lead.

Mo Vaughn's two-run homer cut it to 5-3 in the fifth, but Posada poked a solo shot in the bottom of the inning to make it 6-3.

"We're trying not to think about the long term, because you can look up and lose four or five in a row very quickly," Torre said.

Friday, May 29, 1998 — Boston Red Sox

Yankees 6, Red Sox 2

Worth the wait

Rain doesn't slow bombers Cone, Yanks foil Red Sox

By KEN DAVIDOFF, Staff Writer

NEW YORK — Call it The Late Show at Yankee Stadium. The bulk of 47,160 fans stuck around through a 2-hour 13-minute rain delay Friday night, and, at least for those rooting for the Yankees, it proved worth the wait.

While the person who generated the most pregame buzz, Tino Martinez, proved to be a dud, David Cone and the rest of the Yankees easily picked up the slack and ran over the Red Sox, 6-2, for their second straight victory and fourth straight over the Bosox. The Yanks (37-11), whose start is tied for the fifth best in American League history, lead Boston by 9 1/2 games in the AL East.

Best of all for the fans, they received a lovely parting gift. As a reward for their patience through the driving rain and winds, the Yankees announced that customers could exchange ticket stubs from Friday night's game for a free ticket to one of six August games (two against Minnesota, four against Anaheim).

Ticket stubs should be mailed, along with a first and second choice of the desired game and a self-addressed stamped envelope, to New York Yankees Ticket Office, Dept. B, Yankee Stadium, Bronx, N.Y., 10451.

Martinez, making his first start in a week, looked rusty, going 0-for-4 with two grounders to second and two popouts. But that was to be expected. He admitted before the game that his right shoulder blade (still aching and swollen from the Armando Benitez beaning) wasn't perfect, but that it was good enough to play and stop the idea that he needed to go on the disabled list.

"I think if I could play, I want to play as long as I don't hurt myself," the first baseman said. "There's no chance of that from the injuries I have."

From Cone, on the other hand, it has been difficult to know what to expect. The Yankees' onetime ace has struggled greatly this season, with his now 7-1 record more a sign of the 8.8 runs per game of support he has received than his pitching. His last two starts, in particular, were ugly, with opponents totaling 15 hits in 12 innings.

"He tells me, 'Don't give up on me, I'll get there,'" manager Joe Torre said before the game.

From words came action. In his between-start mound work this past week, the 35-year-old right-hander moved from the extreme left side of the pitching rubber to the right, and it clearly paid dividends. He lasted seven innings, his longest outing this season, and made just 84 pitches, 54 for strikes — an extremely low number for Cone.

His split-fingered fastball seemed much improved as he allowed just two runs, on a pair of Reggie Jefferson homers, and four hits while walking just one and fanning seven.

Cone stepped on the mound after the long delay, retired Darren Lewis on a bouncer to third, and served up a first-pitch, 406-foot blast to Jefferson. It looked as if it could be a long night, in what was already a long night, for Cone.

With one out in the second, John Valentin smoked a shot to left-center, and it looked to be a goner as well. But this one somehow stayed in the park, hitting the top of the wall, and Valentin was stranded at second when Cone retired the next two batters.

The Yankees offense put together a typical rally, one that gave Cone some breathing room, in the third. Chad Curtis started it with a single to left-center, and he moved to second on a Scott Brosius grounder to third. Joe Girardi walked, putting Yankees on first and second, and Chuck Knoblauch's base hit through the left-side hole scored Curtis for the tie.

Derek Jeter hit a single so hard to right field that Girardi had no chance to score from second. With the bases jammed, Paul O'Neill swung at Lowe's first pitch and knocked a flare to left.

It fell in front of Troy O'Leary, bringing home Girardi and Knoblauch, but O'Leary nailed Jeter trying for third on the play. Still, the inning had achieved its purpose.

As did the next inning. A Bernie Williams single, Curtis walk, Brosius single, Girardi single, and Knoblauch single brought home another three runs and knocked out Lowe.

Jefferson hit another first-pitch, solo round-tripper, this one to right, in the sixth to cut the Yankees' lead to 6-2.

Saturday, May 30, 1998
— Boston Red Sox

Red Sox 3, Yankees 2

Yankees lose pitchers' duel

Saberhagen, Gordon end Red Sox' slide

By KEN DAVIDOFF, Staff Writer

NEW YORK — Lately, on those rare occasions when the Yankees have lost, they have lost to themselves. There have been breakdowns in specific areas: Relief pitching. Hitting in the clutch. Fielding.

Saturday, the Yankees lost to the Red Sox. The Bombers' two-game winning streak crashed into the impressive right arms of Bret Saberhagen and Tom Gordon, as Boston halted a six-game losing funk and a four-game drought against the Yankees with a 3-2 squeaker in front of a full house of 55,191.

> **❝I hit it pretty hard. This is probably the only park in the league where it stays in. ❞**
>
> *— Scott Brosius*

Not that the Yanks (37-12) ever suffer defeat gladly, but this was one where all they could do was shrug. There were no blown opportunities for which they could curse themselves, no lousy plays that would cause them to lose sleep.

"It was a good game," manager Joe Torre said. "It was none of our shortcomings today. They pitched very well."

"There just weren't a lot of hits out there today," Scott Brosius said.

The loss was the Yanks' third in their past nine games, which means that the Bombers are actually falling back to earth a tad. Those other two defeats, however, came in games that they would have won had they executed properly. On May 22, the Yanks' first game against the Red Sox at Fenway Park, the offense fell asleep after building an early 4-0 lead, and Jeff Nelson pitched poorly in relief, suffering the "L" in a 5-4 loss. On Wednesday at Comiskey Park, Ramiro Mendoza, Willie Banks, and Nelson served up 12 runs to the White Sox, neutralizing the nine runs the Yanks scored.

While Saturday's loss came by just one run, Torre couldn't find fault with anyone. Not starting pitcher Hideki Irabu (4-1), who was tagged with his first loss of the season despite limiting the Red Sox to three runs and three hits in seven innings. Not his batters, who managed just seven hits off Saberhagen, middle reliever Jim Corsi, and Gordon. It was just one of those days.

"You have to tip your hat to them," Derek Jeter said.

The Yankees manufactured a run in the third when Chad Curtis walked, went to second on Saberhagen's errant pickoff attempt, and scored on Jorge Posada's broken-bat single to center. Mo Vaughn's two-run dinger in the fourth ruined Irabu's no-hitter, and the Bosox added a run in the seventh when Lou Merloni singled home Scott Hatteberg.

The Yanks put runners on first and third in the seventh against Saberhagen, and Sox manager Jimy Williams lifted his starter, inserting Corsi to face his former Oakland teammate Brosius with two outs. Brosius connected for a healthy rip to left-center.

"I hit it pretty hard," the third baseman said. "This is probably the only park in the league where it stays in."

It landed, and stayed in, the glove of Red Sox center fielder Darren Lewis.

"That's just one of those things," Brosius said.

When Chuck Knoblauch started the eighth with a base hit, Williams went for his closer Gordon, who eventually allowed Knoblauch to come around for the home team's second run but stranded Paul O'Neill at third base.

Curtis drew a one-out walk in the ninth. Posada whiffed for the second out, and Curtis stole second with the count 0-1 on Brosius, putting the tying run in scoring position. But Brosius again sent the ball to Lewis, this time a pedestrian fly ball. Game over. A relatively painless defeat.

"We've been playing so well," said Tino Martinez, who went 0-for-4 in his second game back from his right shoulder blade injury. "We'll keep going. We'll put it behind us and come back tomorrow."

The loss ended the Yanks' home winning streak at seven games, which tied a season high.

Sunday, May 31, 1998 — Boston Red Sox

Red Sox 13, Yankees 7

Boston cream
11-run inning foils Bombers

By KEN DAVIDOFF, Staff Writer

NEW YORK — When there are worries about Andy Pettitte, the southpaw usually tops the list of critics.

And right now, there is reason to be worried. In what was billed as a pitchers' duel with Boston ace Pedro Martinez on Sunday, the Yankees ace lasted just 2 2/3 innings (including the bulk of a 42-minute, 11-run third) to lose a dramatic 13-7 game at Yankee Stadium. He has lost three of his last five starts and has a 6.88 ERA (27 earned runs in 35 1/3 innings) in that span.

But the pitcher is coming off an emotional week in which his wife Laura struggled to deliver their second child. So on this day, a day in which the 25-year-old was booed by a full house of 55,711 fans, there would be no self-flogging.

"He almost didn't make it through the birth," Pettitte said of his son, Jared, who was born Thursday. "It made me realize what was important and helped me relax even more. I felt really relaxed and realized this isn't that important. It's important because it's your job, but your family's the most important."

Pettitte did not get a decision in Tuesday's 7-5 victory over the White Sox. He left Chicago on Wednesday morning for his Deer Park, Texas, home. Early Thursday morning, Jared's birth was induced.

It went fine at first; the doctor even joked Andy could do the delivery, it was so easy. But suddenly, there were complications.

"The umbilical cord was wrapped around his throat," Pettitte said. "We had to cut the cord before he was delivered. He lost a lot of blood, and because the blood has oxygen, he had trouble breathing. He turned blue, but they gave him oxygen for a couple of hours."

Jared Pettitte is still hospitalized, but the parents have been told he'll be fine. Andy Pettitte flew to New York on Saturday and arrived right as the Yanks were starting their game against the Red Sox.

He started off well Sunday, cruising through the first two innings with only a walk to John Valentin. He struck out leadoff batter Darren Bragg in the third. And then it fell apart quicker than the plot to "Spice World."

Jason Varitek singled to right. Darren Lewis walked. Valentin singled to left. Nomar Garciaparra doubled down the left field line, scoring two.

With the infield in, Mo Vaughn hit a screaming grounder to Chuck Knoblauch. The second baseman whipped the ball home, but the Red Sox were running on contact, and Valentin scored the third run.

Former Yankee Jim Leyritz bounced to third, and Scott Brosius looked home for the force. But catcher Joe Girardi figured Brosius would try to turn the 5-4-3 double play, so he had broken to back up first base. As a result, Brosius could only get the force at second, and the Bosox upped their lead to 4-0.

From there, it was a dizzying array of hits — nine, all told — and runs. A total of 76 pitches were thrown in the inning, 43 from Pettitte (who left when the score was 6-0 and was charged with eight runs) and 33 from Darren Holmes. The 11 runs were the most by a Yankees opponent in an inning since July 2, 1943, when 12 Indians scored in the fourth inning of a 12-0 New York loss.

That the Yanks still made a game of it was testament to their tenacity, but second baseman Lou Merloni's brilliant diving stop of Jorge Posada's hard grounder up the middle in the seventh — resulting in an inning-ending double play to kill a bases-loaded rally — cut the Yanks' run supply at seven. Meaning that Pettitte never quite got off the hook.

"That's the frustrating part, to see how the guys kept fighting," Pettitte said. "If I just go out there [and pitch decently], I get the win."

Manager Joe Torre admitted concern for the first time, but reiterated he didn't think it was a physical problem. "To me, he has good stuff, if he'd just make people hit the ball as opposed to trying to keep them from hitting the ball," the former catcher said.

Reporter's Notebook:

Brian Cashman didn't speak to Seattle general manager Woody Woodward on Sunday, as the Randy Johnson auction seems to have quieted down. The Yankees GM has been entertaining offers for Jersey City native Willie Banks, who was designated for assignment Thursday. He hopes to trade Banks so the team can receive something in return.

The full house gave the Yanks a four-game series total of 200,244 fans, an average of 50,016 per game. It marked the largest four-game total at Yankee Stadium since Sept. 12-15, 1985, when 215,510 people poured in to see the Bombers take on Toronto.

Ramiro Mendoza, who starts tonight, has been undergoing treatment for a bruise on his right thigh, which absorbed a Robin Ventura line drive last Wednesday in Chicago.

Monday, June 1, 1998 — Chicago White Sox

Yankees 5, White Sox 4

Raines shows son a thing or two

By GREGORY SCHUTTA, Staff Writer

NEW YORK — Tim Raines Jr. is expected to go high in today's major league draft. But on Monday night, dad showed Junior how it's done.

Tim Raines scored from first base on a two-out double by Chad Curtis in the 10th inning to give the Yankees a 5-4 victory over the Chicago White Sox and put an end to their two-game losing streak.

It also got closer Mariano Rivera off the hook after he blew his third save in 13 opportunities this season after he gave up a two-run, game-tying single to Robin Ventura in the eighth.

Jeff Nelson pitched the 10th inning to pick up his third win.

"I saw the replay of him watching it all, and he didn't show any emotion until the umpire signaled safe," Raines said of his 18-year-old son, who was at the Stadium on Monday. "I think he just wanted to make sure I was alive for tomorrow."

Raines, who walked with two out, showed he was alive and kicking with his mad dash from first. Curtis, who had already homered in the game, lined a shot off reliever Matt Karchner into the left field corner, and Raines just kept on going, as the relay throw from shortstop Mike Caruso got past catcher Chad Kreuter.

"I saw Tim cross the plate and the ball go by, and it was just such a great feeling," Curtis said. "When I hit it, I figured if [left fielder Albert] Belle bobbled it, then we might have a shot. But he picked it clean and I figured that they'd hold him up."

But with two out and the No. 9 hitter coming up,

third base coach Willie Randolph went for it.

"I knew coming around third base that it would be a close play or a play at the plate," Raines said. "Before I got there, I could see the ball go by. He had me blocked off the plate, so if he had caught the ball, I would have been out by a mile."

Manager Joe Torre said that was a play that had to be made.

"I was happy it was a bang-bang play," Torre said. "I've been in situations like that as a catcher and it's a tough play to make. The catcher has to watch two things. I think the ball beat him, but Tim was so close that it might have distracted him."

"When you're at home, you've got to take chances like that and make something happen," Raines said.

The Yankees were making a lot of things happen as they banged out three home runs in the first five innings. Tino Martinez, who was carrying an 0-for-12 collar into the game since rejoining the Yankees lineup Friday, broke out in a big way with two singles and a two-run blast into the right field seats, his seventh of the season, in the fifth for a 4-1 lead.

Jorge Posada and Curtis got things going with solo homers in the second and third respectively. It was Posada's seventh and Curtis' sixth.

Chicago battled back as Belle blasted his 11th homer over the fence in left-center in the sixth to cut the lead to 4-2.

Then with Frank Thomas, Belle, and Ventura coming up with no out and the tying runs on in the eighth, Torre called for Rivera. It was the first time in the right-hander's career he had been asked to go six outs for the save.

"He hadn't pitched since Chicago [last week]," Torre said. "We thought that he was so well rested that we could do that."

And in the beginning it worked as Thomas struck out and Belle flied out to center. But Ventura pulled a 1-2 fastball into the right field corner to tie the game, 4-4.

"I don't think he got it away enough," Torre said of Rivera. "He was trying to get it away and he was wild in the middle of the plate."

The Yankees had a chance to win it in the ninth as Posada led off with a walk and rookie Homer Bush, making his 11th appearance and sixth as a pinch hitter, stole second and continued on to third on Kreuter's throwing error with one out. But with the infield in, Derek Jeter grounded to short, and Paul O'Neill lined out to center to end that threat.

Tuesday, June 2, 1998
— Chicago White Sox

Yankees 6, White Sox 3

Yanks show bite
Wells wins; dog nips Cone
'El Duque' gets surprise start tonight in N.Y.

By GREGORY SCHUTTA, Staff Writer

NEW YORK — "El Duque" will be making his first start as a Yankee tonight. And he's got a little dog named Veronica to thank for it.

Cuban defector Orlando Hernandez, who was called up as insurance in case David Wells couldn't take his start against the Chicago White Sox on Tuesday night, will make his debut tonight against the expansion Tampa Bay Devil Rays after David Cone was scratched — literally — from his scheduled start by a dog bite to his right index finger. Reliever Todd Erdos was optioned to Class AAA Columbus to make room on the roster for Hernandez.

"It's kind of embarrassing," Cone said sheepishly after the Yankees downed the White Sox, 6-3, to complete a two-game sweep. "I thought about lying [to manager Joe Torre] but was afraid I'd forget the lie. It's always better to tell the truth."

And the truth is that on a visit with his mother Sunday night, Cone tried to push her Jack Russell terrier away and got bitten, opening up a cut that hadn't healed to Torre's satisfaction by Tuesday night.

"I thought I could have pitched through it," said Cone, who also invoked the name of Yankee first baseman Wally Pipp, who was replaced by Lou Gehrig after complaining of a headache and never returned. "But Joe wanted to play it safe. He thought it could open more during the course of the game. I don't expect it to affect another start."

"I think David would have had trouble throwing all his pitches," Torre said. "It's really a freak thing. David is so conscious of not doing things with his right hand for just that reason."

And for just that reason, the second foreign phenom in two years will be making his debut at Yankee Stadium. But the Yankees have gone to great pains to avoid the circus that accompanied ki Irabu to the Bronx last year.

Hernandez, 28, the older half-brother of 1997 World Series and National League Championship Series MVP Livan Hernandez of the Florida Marlins, was 6-0 with 59 strikeouts in 42 1/3 innings at Columbus this year.

He was signed as a free agent by the Yankees in March after defecting from Cuba in an open fishing boat with his wife and five other people the day after Christmas.

"I think he is a very brave man," said first base coach Jose Cardenal, who came to the United States from Cuba on a visa in 1961 and didn't return until 1984. "He told me that they spent three days in the water with no food, no water, no nothing. I don't think I could have jumped into a little fishing boat like that and risked my life like that."

"It's a great story," Cone said. "He's been through a lot and everybody seems to want to see him."

More than 22,000 fans came out Tuesday to see the Yankees and Wells sweep the White Sox after dropping two straight to the Boston Red Sox over the weekend.

Wells, who said that the twinge he felt Monday morning was gone by Tuesday, scattered seven hits over eight innings while striking out eight to pick up his eighth victory in his past eight decisions.

Mariano Rivera, who blew his third save in 13 tries Monday night, tossed a perfect ninth for his 11th save.

Wells got a lot of support from the offense, which banged out 11 hits, including home runs from Paul O'Neill and Derek Jeter. Jeter's shot, a three-run opposite-field blast on a 3-0 pitch, was the big hit as the Yankees scored four runs in the fifth inning to take a 5-2 lead.

Tim Raines led off with a single and scored on a two-out single by Scott Brosius to tie the score, 2-2. Chuck Knoblauch then reached when second baseman Ray Durham bobbled an easy grounder trying to toss the ball to second base for the force.

Jeter made the Sox pay four pitches later with his eighth homer of the season.

"The big thing is that they gave us more than three outs today, and you can't do that with this team," Jeter said.

Wednesday, June 3, 1998
— Tampa Bay Devil Rays
Yankees 7, Devil Rays 1

Cool customer
'El Duque' takes control

by BOB KLAPSICH, Staff Writer

NEW YORK — Brian Cashman eased his Isuzu Trooper into the right lane of the Major Deegan Expressway, less than a mile before the Yankee Stadium exit. This was 9:45 a.m. Wednesday, still too early for the general manager to experience an anxiety attack.

But that was before Cashman saw the marquee, which brightly announced: El Duque's Debut. Cashman's eyes widened in disbelief, which is why he pressured the gas pedal and powered the truck into a final sprint to the Stadium.

The moment he walked into his office, Cashman ordered the sign rewritten. Within minutes, workers were substituting a wiser, more subtle proclamation: Tampa, 7:30. Which should tell you the Yankees, who watched Hernandez beat the Devil Rays, 7-1, finally understand the difference between marketing and mindless Nineties hype.

"The message I wanted to send was that Orlando Hernandez is no different than any other Yankee," said Cashman, who knows that's not quite true. None of his players had ever been banned from playing baseball in their native country, just because a brother — the Marlins' Livan Hernandez — had defected two years earlier.

No Yankee had ever been separated from his children because of a political defection. And certainly none had ever spent three days without food and water on a Caribbean island last December, awaiting rescue from the Coast Guard after escaping Fidel Castro.

Hernandez's bravery would've made him an easy gimmick for Cashman — news conferences, a pregame welcome from Mayor Rudolph Guiliani, who is, after all, the Yankees' personal cheerleader, and the requisite macho pep talk from George Steinbrenner.

Instead, The Boss remained in Tampa, Fla., and a group of fans who hung the letters "D-U" on the upper level railing — preparing to add a string of K's — were told to remove the "D-U." A simple K-corner, which is all the right-hander ever wanted. Hernandez introduced the Bronx to his funky, high leg kick, and an arsenal of weapons which, if it didn't blow away hitters, at least kept them uncomfortable.

Through the first five innings against Tampa Bay on Wednesday, it became obvious why Hernandez was the ace of the Cuban national team in 1996, and why he was 129-47 representing his country. He threw a fastball no better than 91 mph, but always on a corner, and strengthened by a sidearm slider and slow, looping curveball.

By the time Hernandez had finished seven innings, — one run, five hits, two walks, seven strikeouts — he was given a standing ovation from the fans, which he said "made my eyes watery." Speaking through a translator, Hernandez made it clear that wearing pinstripes represented the last word in a long-distance war with Castro.

In fact, when someone asked what he'd say to the Cuban leader, given the chance for a face-to-face meeting, Hernandez smirked and said, "I wouldn't waste my time standing in front of him."

Clearly, this man is unafraid, but then again, the Devil Rays knew that, since he defeated them without an unhittable fastball.

But is that really a deficit? In a sense, Hernandez is lucky, because without a 98-mph heater, he can escape the comparisons to Hideki Irabu, who only now is recovering from a last year's turbo-hype. Remember it? A high-90's fastball, an inhuman splitter as quick as 93 mph, and an unrelenting desire to be a Yankee, only a Yankee.

With that kind of advertising campaign, Torre said, opposing hitters "were best off not leaving the hotel." The manager was being sarcastic, of course, because American League hitters turned into carnivores, batting .311 against Irabu and banishing him to long relief.

It sure didn't help Irabu that he didn't speak English and that no one in the clubhouse spoke Japanese. So the gulf between the pitcher and his teammates widened by the week. The Yankees mistook Irabu's insecurity for arrogance — which created a clubhouse backlash so severe, pitching coach Mel Stottlemyre estimated "10 or 11" players were openly opposed to Irabu's presence on the team.

But there's no such cancer threatening to take down Hernandez now. This is true for several reasons. First, Hernandez made a point of befriending many of the Yankees in spring training, so he's no stranger to them now.

Second, Hernandez's language barrier is far less restrictive than Irabu's, since six Yankees — Mariano Rivera, Luis Sojo, Jorge Posada, Ramiro Mendoza, and first base coach Jose Cardenal — speak Spanish. And finally, Hernandez's personal history has created a built-in reservoir of respect from the Yankees, who, in Posada's words, "showed what kind of man he is by what he went through to get here."

Of course, Torre still says "the time isn't right" to give Hernandez permanent residence in the rotation. But that's just the Yankees trying to make the pitcher comfortable.

It's the right approach, but it's already obvious Hernandez will survive the American League. Somehow, you sense Castro was a tougher opponent than Wade Boggs.

Thursday, June 4, 1998
— Tampa Bay Devil Rays

Yankees 6, Devil Rays 1

Irabu show the way
Solid outing for win No. 5

By MARK J. CZERWINSKI, Staff Writer

NEW YORK — Hideki Irabu looked genuinely surprised Thursday night when someone asked the Yankees right-hander if he had started thinking about a trip to next month's All-Star Game in Colorado.

"No, not at all," Irabu said through his interpreter, shaking his head for emphasis.

Irabu's numbers, however, say otherwise. His 6-1 victory over the expansion Tampa Bay Devil Rays at Yankee Stadium proved to be another typical night at the office for Irabu, who lowered his major league-leading earned run average to 1.45.

"He had good stuff again," said manager Joe Torre after Irabu scattered six hits and struck out six in 7 1/3 innings to improve his record to 5-1.

"He had better command after the first couple of innings. Then he kicked into gear. He just needs something to ruffle his feathers a little bit."

That ruffle came in the second and third innings, the only time Irabu seemed to labor. Despite a sharp curveball, Irabu's control was off and it got him into a bit of trouble.

Irabu opened the second inning with a walk and

a hit batsman, but got out of that jam when Bobby Smith bounced into a double play. He also gave up two hits in the third inning as the Devil Rays scored their only run.

"There were a couple of dangerous points in the game where it could've gotten away from us, but we were able to turn it around," Irabu said. "I think up to there, I wasn't really in my rhythm."

"It just took him a little while to get going," said catcher Joe Girardi. "Sometimes you don't go out with your best stuff, and you've got to find it."

Irabu already had a 4-1 lead when he began to settle down. He struck out the side in the fourth inning and got off the hook in the fifth thanks to some shoddy base running by the Devil Rays.

"We helped him get out of trouble early," said Tampa Bay manager Larry Rothschild. "He turned it up a little bit once he got the lead, but I don't think he was especially sharp tonight."

Perhaps, but Irabu was as sharp as he had to be on a night that the Bombers continued to make mincemeat of the Tampa Bay pitching staff. They had little trouble getting a handle on the wobbly junk served up by knuckleballer Dennis Springer, especially early in the game.

"I don't ever look forward to a knuckleball pitcher," said right fielder Paul O'Neill, who homered in the seventh inning and extended his hitting streak to 12 games. "We might get five or six straight hits, and then he'll throw a good one to you."

That, however, became a mere subplot on a night in which Irabu added another page to his potential All-Star resume. Irabu hasn't allowed more than three earned runs in any of his nine starts, allowing two or less eight times.

"I expect a quality outing every time out," Torre said.

"The biggest factor is that he's relaxed," Girardi said. "We know him better this season, so we have an idea of how he wants to pitch and what he has to do to be more effective. That's as opposed to last year when we had to more feel our way through."

That's a big difference. And right now, that's the difference between a multimillion dollar bust and a would-be All Star.

Reporter's Notebook:

Luis Sojo had a strong game in his first start in place of the injured Derek Jeter. He handled seven chances flawlessly, and seemed to click well with second baseman Chuck Knoblauch.

"I go back to 1996 and remember the key plays he made for us at second base and shortstop," Torre said. "His range is limited, but he has great hands and knows how to play shortstop."

Friday, June 5, 1998 — Florida Marlins
Yankees 5, Marlins 1

What problem? Pettitte goes distance

By GREGORY SCHUTTA, Staff Writer

NEW YORK — The questions have been nagging for the last month. What's wrong with Andy Pettitte?

While the rest of the Yankees' rotation was making a shambles of the American League, Pettitte suffered through a stretch during which he went 1-3 in five starts and saw his ERA balloon to 4.88.

On Friday, the left-hander found the cure for what ailed him in the form of the Florida Marlins, holding the gutted fish to five hits and pitching his second complete game of the season as the Yankees dumped the world champions, 5-1, on the opening night of interleague play.

"Tonight was very important," said Pettitte (7-5). "You sit here and watch everybody else doing so good, and you want to do good. I've had so much success here. I was in unfamiliar territory with this."

Pettitte, who went 51-24 his first three years with the Yankees, has been suffering through his worst stretch as a Yankee. He lasted only 2 2/3 innings against Boston on Sunday, the shortest outing of his career.

While he seemed to get a gift from the baseball gods in the form of the Marlins, a shadow of their world championship selves, Pettitte refused to take anything for granted.

"The way I've been pitching, I knew I could make them look like a great team," he said. "It doesn't matter who they are."

Except for former Dodger Todd Zeile, who went 3-for-3 with a double and a run scored, Pettitte made the Marlins look like the youngsters they are. He struck out four while walking one and was rarely in trouble.

"He was challenging people, something he hasn't been doing in a while," manager Joe Torre said. "He went into the game with the attitude that I dare you to hit it. He has movement on his ball. If he'll just let it go and trust it, he'll be alright."

"I worked hard in between starts looking for my release point," Pettitte said. "Once I did that, that was the difference. I had my two-seamer working so when I was in trouble, I never worried about sending up a little sinker and letting them beat it into the ground."

A lot of balls were beaten into the ground as Pettitte and rookie Joe Fontenot of the Marlins hooked up in an unlikely pitcher's duel. Fontenot, making his third major league appearance, brought in an 0-2 record and 12.27 ERA in seven innings of work.

He looked like a major league pitcher for the first five innings, holding the Bombers to a double by Paul O'Neill and a bloop single by Chuck Knoblauch.

The Yankees finally broke through with a run in the sixth on an RBI single by Tino Martinez, driving in O'Neill. O'Neill extended his hitting streak to 13 games with two hits in four trips.

Florida tied the game, 1-1, when Knoblauch threw the ball away on what appeared to be an inning-ending double play in the seventh. It was his sixth error of the year.

Darryl Strawberry came to the rescue in the bottom of the seventh by blasting his team-high ninth homer of the season, a solo shot to left-center field, as the Yankees scored two runs for a 3-1 lead. They added two more in the eighth on four walks and a hit batsman, a cushion that allowed Pettitte to remain in the game instead of being removed for closer Mariano Rivera.

"I didn't want him to go through Zeile again," Torre said. "But with the four-run lead, I figured I'd keep him in there."

The game was closer than most people, except for the Yankees, thought it would be.

"They're still a professional team, and you have to go out there and play the game," Strawberry said.

"We're not a high school team," Marlins manager Jim Leyland said. "We're a professional team. We weren't intimidated."

Torre didn't think they would be.

"I don't care if the Yankees are in first place or in last place, it's always a feather in a team's cap to come in here and beat the Yankees," he said. "We're not going to take anybody for granted."

Saturday, June 6, 1998 — Florida Marlins

Yankees 4, Marlins 2

Mendoza states his case

By GREGORY SCHUTTA, Staff Writer

NEW YORK — The battle lines have been drawn. Three days after Orlando "El Duque" Hernandez scattered five hits over seven innings in a victory over Tampa Bay, Ramiro Mendoza came back to allow just three hits over 7 1/3 innings in a 4-2 victory over the Florida Marlins on Saturday.

The next move goes to El Duque, who will make his second start of the season Tuesday in Montreal — not as a replacement for dog-bite victim David Cone, but for David Wells. Cone will take today's start against Florida for Wells, who has tendinitis in his shoulder.

> **❝** That was about the same stuff I had against Minnesota. I just go out and try to do my job the best I can. Joe and Mel have a decision to make. If I have to go back to the bullpen, then I'll do that job the best that I can. **❞**
>
> *— Ramiro Mendoza*

"I have nothing against El Duque," Mendoza said through interpreter Jose Cardenal. "He's got a job to do, and so do I."

Mendoza has been in the eye of the El Duque hurricane for more than a month, because he's the most likely candidate to lose his place in the starting rotation to the Cuban defector. And although Mendoza pitched well in two of his previous three starts, he came away with three no-decisions.

Saturday was different, as he mowed down the "defending" World Champions in front of 36,419 fans on the way to his fourth win of the season. The 25-year-old right-hander didn't allow a hit over the first three innings, pitching to the minimum number of batters.

Meanwhile, the Bombers were staking him to a

4-0 lead against former Met farmhand Jesus Sanchez. The 23-year-old left-hander, part of the trade that sent Al Leiter to the Mets over the winter, came into the game as one of only two Marlin pitchers with a winning record.

But the Yankees had him on the ropes by putting men in scoring position in each of the first two innings, and put him down with a four-spot in the third. Chuck Knoblauch led off with a single, stole second, and scored on a Luis Sojo single.

Then after a Paul O'Neill single, Bernie Williams sent a three-run blast inside the left field foul pole for his eighth homer of the year and a 4-0 lead.

"Bernie's just been in a real groove," manager Joe Torre said of the center fielder, who is batting .485 (16-for-33) on the homestand. "He was the difference in the game today."

Mendoza got the ball up in the fourth as Todd Dunwoody led off by sending Mendoza's 1-2 offering over the fence in right-center to cut the lead to 4-1. Edgar Renteria followed with a single. But Mendoza retired 10 of the next 11 batters, eight of whom failed to get the ball out of the infield.

After putting two men on with one out in the eighth, Mendoza was replaced by Graeme Lloyd, who promptly gave up an RBI double to pinch-hitter Dave Berg to cut the lead to 4-2.

But Lloyd and Jeff Nelson got out of that inning and Mariano Rivera pitched a perfect ninth for his 12th save.

"That was just a great performance," Torre said of Mendoza, who threw 62 strikes in 93 pitches. "But that's the way he's been. I think there's been one start in the last seven that he hasn't pitched well."

That was a three-inning stint at Chicago where he gave up five runs on nine hits in a 12-9 Yankees loss. Otherwise, Mendoza has gone at least six innings in each of his last seven starts without a loss.

"That was about the same stuff I had against Minnesota," Mendoza said, referring to his only complete game of the season, a five-hit, 7-0 shutout at Minnesota on May 10. "I just go out and try to do my job the best I can. Joe and Mel [Stottlemyre] have a decision to make. If I have to go back to the bullpen, then I'll do that job the best that I can."

"It's a nice situation to be in," Torre said of having six quality starters for five spots. "Naturally, if you have anybody pitching like him [Mendoza], you want to make sure he stays comfortable."

And for Mendoza, that means taking his regular turn next weekend against Cleveland.

Sunday, June 7, 1998 — Florida Marlins

Yankees 4, Marlins 1

Cone doggone good for yanks

Allows two hits, fans 14 in first start since canine bite

By GREGORY SCHUTTA, Staff Writer

NEW YORK — Yankee pitching coach Mel Stottlemyre walked up to David Cone after the eighth inning, shook his hand, and told him that was it. Cone tried to talk him out of it.

It's kind of hard to argue with a guy who is throwing a two-hitter with 13 strikeouts. It's even harder when it's David Cone.

The 35-year-old right-hander went out, added one more strikeout, and retired the side in order as the Yankees beat the Florida Marlins, 4-1, to complete a three-game sweep of the gutted Fish Sunday.

"Mel looked at [manager] Joe [Torre], and Joe looked at Mel, and then Joe said, 'OK, but you put one man on and you're out of there," Cone said. "They seemed to read that I needed it more for my confidence than for anything else."

"The fact that it was a player with the veteran status that David Cone has earned did figure in the decision," Torre said after the Yankees' seventh straight victory. "And we're trying to get him to a point in his arm strength, and the only way to do that is to pitch him. He really went after people in the ninth."

The complete game is the first for Cone since May 1997, and the first complete-game victory since he beat the Chicago White Sox in May 1996. That was his last start before undergoing surgery for an aneurysm in his pitching shoulder.

"I knew going into this year that retaining my best stuff late in the game was the last hurdle I would have to cross," said Cone, who took the start for the injured David Wells after sitting out eight days with a dog bite on the index finger of his pitching hand. "I told Joe and Mel that we couldn't keep me at 100 pitches forever."

Cone threw 122 pitches, 84 of them for strikes, in winning his eighth game without a loss in his last nine starts. He went a season-high seven innings in his last start, allowing four hits and two runs in a 6-2 victory over Boston on May 29.

"It was his best yet," catcher Joe Girardi said. "He's close to what we saw in spring training, where he was smooth and everything was going [well]. He made things easy for me."

But he made things tough on the Marlins, who suffered their 11th straight loss. Cone struck out the first four batters and retired the first seven before catcher Gregg Zaun broke through with a single through the hole between third and short. Cone followed that by retiring the next 10 before hitting one batter and walking another in the sixth.

He lost the shutout in the eighth inning when Craig Counsell walked on a 3-2 pitch with two out and Todd Dunwoody banged a double off the center field wall to drive him in.

"The only time I got worried about him was in the sixth when he walked a couple of people," Torre said. "He got a little out of sync but then found himself."

By then, the Yankees had found their hitting shoes against Marlins rookie Ryan Dempster, who entered the game with just 3 1/3 innings of major league experience.

Paul O'Neill belted his seventh homer of the season in the first, and Tino Martinez and Bernie Williams hit back-to-back homers in the third — the first time the Yanks have done so this year — as they built a 3-0 lead. Williams' homer was a 418-foot-shot into the blackened center field bleachers, the 16th to reach that section in the history of the remodeled Yankee Stadium and the second in Williams' career.

"It's always a big deal, especially when you think of all great the players who've played in this stadium and played for the Yankees," Williams said, after joining Reggie Jackson and Danny Tartabull (three times) as the only players to reach that area more than once. "You never take something like that for granted."

But the performance of the day came from Cone, who threw his repertoire of pitches despite the cut on his index finger.

"He went strictly with fastballs and breaking balls early on," Girardi said. "My idea in calling the game was not to throw the splitter if we didn't have to because I didn't want to irritate the cut or open it up. [Cone] wanted to throw the splitter in the seventh, so I knew he was all right."

"I featured everything I had today, and I was very encouraged by that," Cone said. "I felt I was consis-

tently ahead of the batters and attacked them all day. Before my last start, I moved from the left side of the rubber to the right side, and that's really helped me. It's given me a little more leverage in throwing my pitches and give my pitches a little more bite."

And with the Yankees, now 44-13, another bulldog in the rotation can only help.

Tuesday, June 9, 1998
— at Montreal Expos

Yankees 11, Expos 1

Valuable imports

Mixed results from mound help

Orlando magic: El Duque wins again

By KEN DAVIDOFF, Staff Writer

MONTREAL — The ridiculous could be found Tuesday night in Orlando Hernandez's first trip to the plate, bat in hands. The man known as "El Duque" looked more like a 14-year-old at his first high school dance, scared out of his wits. He actually made contact with Carlos Perez's third pitch, weakly fouling it, before waving at a bouncing curveball for strike three.

The sublime could be found everywhere else at Olympic Stadium.

In his second major league start, El Duque mowed down the Expos on a four-hitter, and the Yankees pounded Perez and a succession of relievers for an 11-1 beheading.

A crowd of 16,238, the most vocal of whom were Yankees fans, took in the impressive performance.

"This was very important for me, my first complete game in the big leagues," said Hernandez, with catcher Jorge Posada serving as his interpreter. "It was good to give some rest to the other guys on the staff."

In lowering his ERA to a microscopic 1.13, Hernandez needed 125 pitches (82 strikes) to complete his masterpiece. He walked just one and struck out nine. Until the ninth, no Montreal player made it as far as third base.

And now the Yankees cannot possibly lift El Duque from their starting rotation. The inflammation in David Wells' left shoulder gave Ramiro Mendoza a reprieve this time around. But once everyone is healthy, it's hard to believe that George Steinbrenner will stand for the removal of the electric Hernandez (2-0).

"He definitely deserves to do it again, no question," manager Joe Torre said. "We just have to figure out how it's going to happen. He'll get another start." That will most likely take place Sunday against the Indians or Monday at Baltimore, depending on how Wells feels after he throws today.

Meanwhile, the juggernaut that is the 1998 Yankees won its eighth straight game, tying its best streak of the season, and lifted its record to a stunning 45-13, a .776 winning percentage. Only the 1939 Bombers had a better 58-game start, with a 46-12 mark. The 1928 and 1953 clubs also jumped out of the gate at 45-13.

This one figured to be a pitchers' duel, with the Expos ace Perez going for the home team. Instead, the Bombers put up a total of 17 hits. Bernie Williams homered for the third straight game, Scott Brosius homered twice, Luis Sojo pounded four hits, and Paul O'Neill extended his hitting streak to 16 games, tying a career best and setting the high-water mark for a Yankee this season.

That mouthful being said, Tuesday was really all about El Duque. Showing the same command, ability to change speeds, and variety of release points as he did in his debut against Tampa Bay on Wednesday, the Cuban right-hander mastered the Expos. Only a ninth-inning rally prevented him from notching his first shutout.

"He makes it seem so easy when he lets the ball go," said Torre, who compared Hernandez's style to Juan Marichal's. "I'm very relaxed sitting on the bench, watching him."

"His command is what's impressive, especially after sitting out for so long," said Joe Girardi, who caught Hernandez for the first time and thought him similar to teammate David Cone. "He must have had somebody to throw to [in Cuba].

Hernandez appeared to have slightly better velocity than he did in his previous start, but with him, it's all about ball placement and deception. His first K came on a first-inning backdoor slider to Brad Fullmer that dropped like a split-fingered fastball. The next one, in the second, occurred when Mark Grudzielanek went fishing for a curveball that bounced. And so it went all night, with the Expos never really having a clue.

The alleged 28-year-old refused to contemplate what this start meant for his Yankees future, saying, "I'm only pitching to win. I'm not thinking about what's up next." He added, "It doesn't matter what level I'm in. I'm trying to do well."

As for his hitting, as he put it, "Oaf!" He finished 0-for-5 with three strikeouts, but his fourth-inning grounder almost sneaked through the right-side hole, and he executed perfectly a sixth-inning sacrifice bunt. Just another sign of Hernandez's athleticism, which has so delighted the Yankees.

But then again, there's nothing El Duque has done that hasn't thrilled everyone in the organization. "It's kind of neat to see," Girardi said. "The guy brings a glove and a pair of shoes, and you see how spoiled we are. A lot of times, I think we take things for granted."

Unlike Hernandez. "I'm grateful to Joe Torre for letting me pitch," the right-hander said. "Hopefully I can keep coming along."

Wednesday, June 10, 1998
— at Montreal Expos

Yankees 6, Expos 2

Bombers level Expos

By KEN DAVIDOFF, Staff Writer

MONTREAL — The 1998 Yankees have been challenging history every night they play, what with their being on pace to tally the best regular-season record this century.

But Wednesday night was one for history to be made, not challenged. On a night when much good and bad happened for the Bombers (the bad being an injury to Bernie Williams), Tim Raines stole the show by swiping the 800th base of his career en route to the Yanks' season-best ninth straight victory, a 6-2 win over Raines' old team, the Expos.

It was a busy, busy night at Olympic Stadium, as the 14,335 who showed up certainly got their money's worth. They witnessed Hideki Irabu get the first regular-season hit by a Yankees pitcher since the advent of the designated hitter; they saw Williams go down with an injury that looked bad at first and now may be only a sprained right knee; they saw Paul

O'Neill rip three hits, extending his hitting streak to a career-high 17 games.

And before a heavy rain shower in the seventh inning caused a 36-minute delay, they saw Irabu pitch and pick up his sixth victory, further fortifying his All-Star campaign.

But considering that Raines became just the fourth player this century to reach the 800-steal mark (joining Ty Cobb, Lou Brock, and Rickey Henderson), he earned top billing. Especially because this milestone came during his first game in Montreal since 1990.

"For them to remember me the way they have, to me, it was only fitting that it happened here," said the 38-year-old Raines, who spent his first 10 seasons with the Expos.

"That was nice," manager Joe Torre said. "It only seemed appropriate. This is where he started."

Raines made a dash for third base in the fourth inning, but Irabu fouled a ball off. He drew a walk to lead off the eighth, and said he figured, "This is it. Either throw me out, or I'll get my 800th stolen base."

He let one pitch, a ball, pass by Scott Brosius, and then he took off. The throw from catcher Chris Widger arrived much too late, and Raines had No. 800, his fifth of this season. He was promised the actual base, although after the game the Expos staff was still cleaning it.

"It's important," he said. "It's nothing I sought out to do when my career started. … I've been fortunate enough to play as long as I've played. I've gotten the opportunity to continue to get them."

Before the celebration, the Yankees had a scare with Williams. The center fielder cranked a double off the wall in left-center to start the sixth. After Raines whiffed, Williams went for third on an 0-1 pitch to Brosius. Coming into third he got his spikes caught, though, and slid awkwardly for the last 10 feet or so, where he said he hyperextended the right knee. He laid on the bag for a moment, causing Torre and assistant trainer Steve Donohue to dart out of the dugout.

"It was ugly," Williams said.

He tested the knee by walking a few steps and stayed in the game, scoring on Brosius' single to right. Williams played center field in the sixth, then the knee started to stiffen, prompting his removal for Chad Curtis.

Williams will return to New York today for a full slate of tests, so the Yankees will know much more by today or Friday. He said he had no feel for the injury's severity, offering only, "It hurts right now."

Finally, there was Irabu. The right-hander offered a mix of heat and curveballs in limiting the Expos to five hits and two runs over six-plus innings. His league-leading ERA rose to 1.59, even though Torre said, "This was probably the best in his last few starts."

The real fun for him, though, came from his trips to the plate. In pregame batting practice, Irabu — who is easily the Bombers' worst hitting pitcher — hit a homer that drew a huge cheer from the fans. And in his first at-bat, he lined a single to center.

"I was surprised," a smiling Irabu said through his interpreter George Rose. His last hit came for his alma mater Tinsei High School in Japan — with an aluminum bat, of course.

The last Yankee pitcher to record a hit in the regular season was Larry Gowell, who doubled off Milwaukee's Jim Lonborg on Oct. 4, 1972.

"I would've bet the house," David Cone said, "that he would not have gotten a hit."

Thursday, June 11, 1998 — at Montreal Expos

Expos 7, Yankees 5

Yankees come apart after Pettitte exits

By KEN DAVIDOFF, Staff Writer

MONTREAL — Andy Pettitte couldn't believe it. Here he was cruising to victory Thursday night at Olympic Stadium, when who should come to the mound but manager Joe Torre, a most unwelcome visitor. And after a few seconds of back-and-forth debating, the left-hander was out of the game in the seventh inning, history, eight letters in a box score. It was as though Torre were the father catching his son out after curfew and dragging him home.

The reason for this sudden, unexpected departure: Torre saw something in Pettitte's delivery that he didn't like, something in the left leg the manager believed was caused by the "catch" the pitcher complained of in his left buttock an inning earlier. Whether Torre's caution saved Pettitte from aggravating the ailment isn't known. What is known is that the Yankees bullpen proceeded to blow a four-run lead to the Expos, giving the Bombers their first loss of June, 7-5, and snapping a nine-game winning streak.

"I don't feel anything," Pettitte said after the game.

"I just felt like I needed to stretch it out. But Joe said it's better to be safe than sorry."

Said Torre: "I didn't want him to alter his delivery. I thought he was maybe a little out of whack."

Torre and the Yankees can afford to utilize such caution, of course. In fact, it's encouraged because it's so evident so early that they're going to reach the postseason and no injury has proven insurmountable. Earlier Thursday, the Bombers had placed perhaps their best player, Bernie Williams, on the 15-day disabled list with a sprained right knee.

In the past 10 days alone, the Yanks have dealt with a slew of minor injuries to their starting pitchers, making room for Orlando Hernandez and subsequently preventing Ramiro Mendoza from being demoted to the bullpen. First, David Cone missed a turn when his mother's dog bit the pitcher's right index finger. Then David Wells sat out when he experienced inflammation in his left shoulder.

But this nick to Pettitte doesn't look like it will buy Mendoza time. Though Torre said he'd wait and see how his lefty felt, Pettitte said the "catch" had been caught, that this was not related to his back troubles of last year, and that there was no way he will miss a turn.

Pettitte allowed a Vladimir Guerrero double to center to start the seventh, then surrendered a Rondell White line drive on which Chad Curtis just missed making a diving catch. He threw the ball to second baseman Chuck Knoblauch, who let the ball get away from him, permitting Guerrero to score and break the shutout.

And then, suddenly, Torre was at the mound speaking to Pettitte. Just as suddenly, Pettitte was on his way back to the dugout, his day done. Mike Stanton was summoned from the pen.

He walked Chris Widger and allowed a single to Mark Grudzielanek to load the bases. Jose Vidro's sacrifice fly to left scored White, and Stanton walked Ryan McGuire to reload the bases.

Torre went for righty Jeff Nelson, and Montreal manager Felipe Alou countered by pinch hitting lefty Brad Fullmer. Alou prevailed when Fullmer lined a two-run double into the right field corner, cutting the Yanks' lead to 5-4.

Nelson issued an intentional walk to F.P. Santangelo, loading the bases again, and after Graeme Lloyd struck out Scott Livingstone for the second out, Darren Holmes entered to face Guerrero. The right fielder ripped a gapper to right-center, scoring all three runners for a 7-5 lead. The inning final-

ly ended when Guerrero was nailed at third trying for a triple.

Before that half-inning, the Yanks seemed well on their way to victory. Expos rookie starter Carl Pavano made the Yankees look foolish for four innings, pitching to the minimum 12 batters and allowing just one hit. But a fifth-inning error by McGuire at first base opened the floodgates and allowed four runs to score, with Scott Brosius and Joe Girardi each tallying two-run singles. Tino Martinez's homer the next inning made it 5-0.

Sunday, June 14, 1998 — Cleveland Indians

Yankees 4, Indians 2

Newest Yankee picks up the slack

By MARK J. CZERWINSKI, Staff Writer

NEW YORK — No Derek Jeter. No Bernie Williams. No problem.

It was business as usual for the Yankees on a damp and drizzly Sunday at Yankee Stadium, even against a top-flight team such as the Cleveland Indians. And if there's any lesson to be learned from the Yankees' 4-2 victory, it's that this team will not have any problem digging up replacement heroes.

Case in point, rookie left fielder Ricky Ledee. David Cone's latest gem might have been the difference in the game, but the major league debut of the Yankees' top prospect stole some of the spotlight.

> **"** I don't know how other guys feel, but I was nervous.
> You dream about being here, and all of a sudden it happens. **"**
>
> *— Ricky Ledee*

Ledee, who waited nine years and two rainouts for his big moment, singled in his first at-bat on the first pitch he saw.

He also picked up a stolen base and made a nice catch against the left-center field wall.

And though the kid might not be here for the long

run, he should make life without Williams rather interesting.

"I don't know how other guys feel, but I was nervous," Ledee said. "You dream about being here, and all of a sudden it happens."

Ledee got a nice ovation from the crowd of 42,949 when he was announced in the starting lineup, and another when he slapped a Jaret Wright pitch into right field with one out in the second inning.

The left-handed hitting Ledee also seemed to make an instant impression on the Indians. Cleveland manager Mike Hargrove replaced left-hander Ron Villone of Bergenfield with veteran Paul Assenmacher when Ledee came to the plate with runners on second and third in the seventh inning.

"That's a great deal of respect they showed him when they took out a left-hander to bring in Assenmacher," Yankees manager Joe Torre said. "I guess Mike Hargrove knows he's going to be a pretty good hitter."

Despite his potential, Ledee is not going to be the one to fill the offensive void until Williams returns later this month. That's the job of players such as first baseman Tino Martinez, who drove home three runs, including a two-run single in the fifth inning off Wright that gave the Yankees a 3-0 lead.

And that was plenty of offense, considering the way Cone, who had 12 strikeouts in eight innings, was throwing.

"Cone was very good," said Hargrove, whose team lost its third straight game. "I don't think he threw 10 fastballs all day. He threw a lot of breaking balls and sliders."

"He had the same consistency with all his pitches," Yankees catcher Joe Girardi said. "He was making quality pitches, and he had everything working. That's as good as he's been, and his last two games put together are as good as it gets."

Even without Jeter and Williams.

Reporter's Notebook:

Mariano Rivera made his first appearance since June 6, giving up two hits and a run in the ninth inning but earning his 13th save. "He was probably a little rusty as far as command," Torre said. "But his stuff looked good." ...Ledee said his catch on a Mark Whiten drive in the second inning helped ease his nerves. "He looked comfortable out there," Torre said. "That first play out at the wall was not easy, but he made it look easy." ... The Yankees tied the 1912 Boston Red Sox and 1970 Cincinnati Reds for most consecutive non-losing series in a season (24).

Monday, June 15, 1998
— at Baltimore Orioles

Orioles 7, Yankees 4

This time Yankees go kerplunk

By KEN DAVIDOFF, Staff Writer

BALTIMORE — You just can't get these teams together without an incident anymore.

The bad blood from the ugly May 19 Yankees-Orioles brawl at Yankee Stadium resurfaced at Camden Yards on Monday night — only with the Yankees playing the role of instigators this time. No benches cleared and no punches were thrown, but Mike Stanton's seventh-inning drilling of Eric Davis superseded the pitches, hits, and runs of the O's 7-4 victory.

If it was truly an accident, as Stanton and the Yankees maintained, it at least earned a deja vu award for nearly mirroring Armando Benitez's actions of last month in the Bronx.

"Absolutely not," said Stanton, who was immediately thrown out of the game by home plate umpire John Hirschbeck. "It was a ball that got away from me. I respect Eric Davis. He's done a lot in the game and been through a lot in his life. No way."

Shortly after he hit Davis, Stanton called him to apologize. "Hopefully," Davis said, "he means what he said."

"As far as the incident, I'll defer my comments and see what the Yankees say," O's manager Ray Miller said. "The only thing that stands out a little bit in my mind is that I said with Benitez, the guilt, or truth, lies within the ball, the guy that threw the ball. As apparent as it was with Benitez, I think that was as apparent [with Stanton], and I guess we'll just have to wait and see if justice and swiftness is as severe in the state of Maryland as it is in New York."

Benitez's actions resulted in an eight-game suspension, but he sabotaged his own case when he urged the Yankees to "bring it on" after he hit Tino Martinez following Bernie Williams' three-run homer. It appears unlikely Stanton will be disciplined any further.

All of this obscured a game that featured David Wells' first start since June 2 (and his first loss since April 2) — a shaky one in which he pitched through the stiffness in his left shoulder — and Ricky Ledee's first major league home run.

With two outs in the seventh inning, Rafael Palmeiro ripped a Stanton pitch 378 feet into the stands in right-center, padding Baltimore's lead to 6-4. Up stepped Davis — who, as coincidence had it, wears uniform No. 24 for the Orioles, just as Martinez does for the Yankees.

Martinez took a Benitez first-pitch fastball to the back, right between the 2 and the 4 on his jersey. Monday night, Stanton threw a first-pitch fastball at Davis' back — right between the 2 and the 4. Before there could be any reaction, Hirschbeck ejected Stanton.

While Davis winced in pain, Yankees manager Joe Torre — who claimed no bad feelings toward the O's before the game — argued with Hirschbeck, pleading that the HBP was unintentional. The crowd of 48,022, which had seemed significantly Yankees-heavy earlier in the night, unleashed a torrential wave of boos. An obscene cheer began seconds after. Davis had to leave the game for pinch runner Jesus Tavarez.

"I don't think he threw at him intentionally," Torre said of his pitcher. "The ball sailed, and Eric stands on top of the plate. ... But I can understand where the umpires are coming from."

After the Yankees had erased two deficits, the Orioles took the lead for good in the sixth. B.J. Surhoff lined a first-pitch single up the middle. Cal Ripken Jr. placed a ball in the same spot, except that Wells managed to stop it with his right foot and retired Ripken at first. Lenny Webster lofted a seemingly harmless fly to left, but Ledee moved back, not forward, and couldn't get to the ball in time. First and third, one out.

After trying to bunt, Mike Bordick lifted a fly ball to medium left field. Ledee positioned himself, caught it, and unleashed a solid throw to home. It beat Surhoff, who had tagged up, but Yanks catcher Jorge Posada failed to block the plate. Surhoff therefore was able to touch safely with his right leg before Posada's tag.

"I thought I had him, but when I saw the replay, he was clearly safe," said Posada, who tied a career high with three hits.

The game's start was delayed by 12 minutes due to rain, and Wells threw just all right in his first start back from inflammation in his pitching shoulder. After allowing five runs and 10 hits in six-plus innings, he was lifted when a 27-minute rain delay interrupted the bottom of the seventh.

"Overall, it felt good," the veteran southpaw said. "During the game, I got very loose. The humidity helped a lot."

Tuesday, June 16, 1998 — at Baltimore Orioles

Orioles 2, Yankees 0

Yankees sunk by Ponson

By KEN DAVIDOFF, Staff Writer

BALTIMORE — The Yankees spend more money on international scouting than any other major league team, and that's reflected on their big-league roster, which features players from Japan, Cuba, Puerto Rico, and Panama (not to mention Australian Graeme Lloyd and Venezuelan Luis Sojo, who came via trades). But they have not yet established a presence in the Caribbean area.

Expect that to change as soon as this morning, assuming George Steinbrenner caught Tuesday night's Yankees-Orioles game on the television. If he did (and he misses Yankees games about as often as Cal Ripken Jr. misses a start), he saw the Orioles' Aruban rookie Sidney Ponson dominate the Yankees for 6 2/3 innings and pick up his first career victory over the Bombers and Hideki Irabu, 2-0, at Camden Yards.

"The guy threw great," Scott Brosius said. "He was throwing in the mid-90s and had command. It was one of those nights where you tip your cap to the guy and don't make anything more of it."

In losing the second straight of this three-game set, the Yankees (47-16) suffered their first series defeat since they were swept by the Angels in two games to open the season. Their streak of 24 straight non-losing series ties the 1970 Reds and 1912 Red Sox for the best in baseball history.

Ponson entered the evening with a very humble resume: With three previous starts and 14 appearances to his name, he owned a career record of 0-4 with a 6.21 ERA. In a 2 1/3-inning relief outing against the Yankees on May 19, he was rocked for four runs and three hits while walking three.

But this night, he looked like an entirely different pitcher. With a fastball that actually was clocked consistently in the high 90s and a nasty change-up, he retired 17 of the first 18 batters he faced before letting up in the seventh.

In all, the 21-year-old allowed two hits while walking one and striking out four. Reliever Arthur Rhodes pitched the final 2 1/3 innings for his third save to complete the shutout.

"I was throwing the ball over the plate," said Ponson, who helped blank the Yanks for the first time since Seattle's Jamie Moyer and Paul Spoljaric teamed for an 8-0 victory April 6. "I'm just happy to be here. It's a great ballpark and great fans. The team supported me tonight, and I was pretty confident. That's why I was throwing strikes."

Irabu (6-2) pitched well enough to win, as he has in each of his 11 starts this season, but the O's nipped him for individual runs in the fifth and sixth. In permitting two runs over seven innings, his ERA rose to 1.68 — still the best in the American League.

After 4 1/2 scoreless frames, Lenny Webster started the bottom of the fifth with a short bouncer down the third-base line that Brosius tried to rush to first base.

His throw was much too low. Mike Bordick followed by lining a first-pitch single to center, putting men on first and second with none out.

Irabu continued to persevere, retiring Brady Anderson on a foul pop to first and Joe Carter on a soft liner to center. But Harold Baines grounded an 0-1 splitter up the middle, bringing Webster home for a 1-0 lead. Roberto Alomar started the sixth with a solo homer to right-center, extending Baltimore's lead to 2-0.

The Yanks finally put together a rally in the seventh, putting men on first and second with two outs. Ponson threw two balls to Chad Curtis and O's manager Ray Miller had seen enough. He lifted the rookie for Rhodes.

The southpaw threw three straight strikes, the last one about a foot over the strike zone, to make Curtis look bad.

"Instead of seeing the pitch, I just swung," said Curtis, who is in a 6-for-25 funk.

> ❝I was throwing the ball over the plate. I'm just happy to be here. It's a great ballpark and great fans. The team supported me tonight, and I was pretty confident. That's why I was throwing strikes.❞
>
> — *Sidney Ponson*

Wednesday, June 17, 1998
— at Baltimore Orioles

Yankees 5, Orioles 3

Strawberry, Yankees pop Orioles

By KEN DAVIDOFF, Staff Writer

BALTIMORE — Darryl Strawberry put on a batting practice show for the ages Wednesday evening, becoming the first player in the seven-year history of Camden Yards to reach the video screen in right-center field. The crowd went nuts, but the man who hit it didn't even notice. He never watches his BP hits, he insisted.

But Tino Martinez watched, and felt compelled to reach out to his teammate upon his return to the dugout.

"I can tell when he's swinging well and when he isn't," the first baseman said. "He's got so much power, when he waits on the ball, he can hit it anywhere. I told him, 'Stay right there.'"

Good advice. Strawberry followed his mammoth pregame blast with an equally impressive homer that counted, sparking the Yanks to a 5-3 victory over the Orioles.

It was a much-needed victory, considering the Bombers had lost two straight and three of four and were starting to show the strain of playing without the injured Bernie Williams and Derek Jeter.

It also eased the pain of the afternoon's startling news of Mike Stanton's five-game suspension and $1,000 fine for his drilling of Eric Davis in Monday night's game. And while Andy Pettitte pitched his third straight effective game to lift his record to 8-5 and Mariano Rivera threw the final 1 2/3 innings for his 14th save, it was Strawberry who set the tone for the night.

"Straw had a lot of fire tonight," David Cone said. "It was almost as if he thought he had something to prove."

Consider it proven. His 465-foot three-run jack to straightaway center field in the first inning, the longest ever in Camden Yards, has earned him a steady spot in the lineup until his bat cools off.

The 36-year-old tried to play the humble route. When asked if he knew his first-inning bomb set a record, he responded, "I know now. I really didn't think about it. I think the most important thing I thought about was it gave us a 3-0 lead. We wanted to get off to a good start."

But when pressed on where this blast ranks in his storied career of tape-measure dingers, including the 1988 shot off the top of Olympic Stadium and the 1985 round-tripper off the Busch Stadium clock, he conceded, "That fits at the top. I can't say that me or anybody could hit a ball like that again."

Luis Sojo started the first-inning rally with a one-out walk, and Paul O'Neill followed with a grounder that eluded third baseman Cal Ripken Jr. Martinez whiffed, and Strawberry followed with his piece of history. For the first time in the series, the Yanks had the lead, 3-0.

"It was a big start for us after getting shut out [Tuesday]," manager Joe Torre said. "To jump-start with three runs was big for Andy."

Pettitte took it from there, checking in with 7 2/3 innings, two runs, and six hits while lowering his ERA to 4.13. He allowed a pair of solo homers, to Rafael Palmeiro and Joe Carter, and he escaped his worst jam when he won a 10-pitch, sixth-inning battle with Palmeiro, inducing him to ground into a double play.

"I feel good," said Pettitte, who suffered no relapse of the left-buttock twinge that caused Torre to lift him prematurely in his last start. "I just want to keep it going."

Thanks to Pettitte and Strawberry, the Yanks are back on the track toward keeping their magical season going.

Thursday, June 18, 1998
— at Cleveland Indians

Indians 5, Yankees 2

El Duque helps cuff Tribe

By BOB KLAPISCH, Staff Writer

CLEVELAND — This time it was the Indians' turn to experience the Orlando magic — a steady blur of fastballs and change-ups and sliders, all feathering the corners with the precision of laser surgery. Which is exactly what it feels like to be dissected by El Duque: precise and painless, one soft at-bat after another.

"Obviously, this guy knows how to pitch. Everything he throws, it's to a spot," said Kenny Lofton.

That's no small endorsement, considering Lofton was the only Indian who was able to solve Hernandez, going 3-for-4. Otherwise, the Tribe could've easily been the Expos or the Devil Rays, melting away in a 5-2 loss to the Yankees on Thursday.

Actually, Hernandez, who, in 7 2/3 innings, allowed two runs, scattered seven hits, and struck out seven, wasn't around by the time the Bombers rallied in the ninth inning against Mike Jackson. Joe Torre had removed El Duque with two out in the eighth inning, the bases empty, the score tied at 2, moments after Manny Ramirez had tapped a weak roller up the first base line.

It was a typical moment of triumph for Hernandez, whose up-and-in two-seam fastball smothered Ramirez. And that's exactly why El Duque's eyes widened in disbelief when he saw Torre leaving the dugout, summoning lefty Graeme Lloyd to face the left-handed-hitting Jim Thome.

Asked if he was startled by the unprovoked hook, Hernandez said, "In Cuba I would've been surprised. But we have such a great bullpen here, I wasn't surprised."

Not at all?

Hernandez paused a moment, then smiled so broadly his eyes were reduced to slits.

"Well, maybe," El Duque said with a laugh. "But with the lefty coming up, maybe that's what [Torre] wanted."

Lloyd and Jeff Nelson subdued the Indians, setting the stage for the Yankees' bizarre three-run rally in the ninth. It began with Tino Martinez's single to center, after which Tim Raines chopped a double over third baseman Travis Fryman's head.

With runners on second and third, Jackson struck out Darryl Strawberry, intentionally walked Jorge Posada to load the bases, then blew away Chad Curtis on three pitches. Which brought this confrontation to the eleventh hour: Jackson against Scott Brosius.

At 0-1, Brosius bounced a slow roller up the third base line — so weakly, in fact, that he beat Fryman's throw to first base. And that appeared to give the Yankees the go-ahead run.

But that was before home plate umpire Tim Tschida ruled the ball had bounced off Brosius' foot — a foul ball. This, despite replays that clearly showed the ball hit off the plate.

Torre, of course, argued hotly in Tschida's face, and Brosius said, "I knew the ball didn't hit me. But once [Tschida] made the call, I tried to get myself together for the rest of the at-bat."

Their dance stretched all the way to a full count, at which point Jackson dared Brosius with pure heat. How close was it? So near to the outside corner that for a moment, Brosius froze, as did Tschida. But the gap between the ball's path and the corner was enough to force in a run, giving the Yankees a 3-2 lead, and when second baseman David Bell committed a throwing error on Chuck Knoblauch's infield single, the Yankees were ahead, 5-2.

And that made it easier for the Yankees to exhale and appreciate Hernandez, who, in David Cone's estimation, is already beyond the tentacles of the American League's scouting system.

"I don't know what else [scouts] can learn about him, because he hides the ball so well," Cone said. "His leg kick is so high, and he hides the ball behind the leg. There's no way he's tipping his pitches."

Paul O'Neill added, "He worked out some jams today like he's been in the league for 10 years. We're still learning about him, but of his three starts, this was by far the most impressive."

Hernandez was so dominant, the Indians only got the ball out of the infield four times in the first six innings. But O'Neill was right: The Indians forced Hernandez to sweat at times, since he had only one 1-2-3 inning.

In fact, Lofton's two-out, two-run single in the seventh inning came after El Duque had been ahead 0-2, and he said, "I made a bad pitch," referring to a change-up he left over the plate. Had Lofton not been thrown out trying to take second on O'Neill's throw to the plate ...well, who knows?

"I'm not taking anything away from Hernandez, because he pitched a great game," said Thome. "But I think next time we'll have a better plan."

Fine, said Hernandez, who smiled again and reminded everyone, "It's a war out there."

Reporter's Notebook:

In the first inning, Indians manager Mike Hargrove alerted umpires that Hernandez was moving his right hand in his glove from the stretch position, which, technically, constitutes a balk. Hernandez said, "I've always done that," and added Hargrove's protest couldn't possibly have distracted him.

"If I wasn't distracted by jumping into a little boat and going four days without food," Hernandez said, "this wasn't going to, either."

Friday, June 19, 1998 — at Cleveland Indians

Indians 7, Yankees 4

Inside stuff

O'Neill the most recent victim

Hit batters anger Yanks

By BOB KLAPISCH, Staff Writer

CLEVELAND — If the Yankees are already at war with the Orioles, it may not be long before a second front is opened with the Indians. And when the simmering hostilities with the Tribe finally explode, the Yankees say make no mistake: It'll be Jaret Wright who will have acted as the provocateur.

Wright, who broke Luis Sojo's left wrist in spring training with an errant fastball, hit Paul O'Neill above the right elbow Friday night. Although both benches remained calm — and the incident had no bearing on the Yankees' 7-4 loss to the Indians — O'Neill was still angry afterward, openly suggesting Wright had purposely thrown at him.

"After what [Wright] did to Luis, there's not a lot of good feeling about him in here," O'Neill said. "The guy throws hard, and a lot of guys think he threw at Luis on purpose."

O'Neill was struck in the first inning, with two out, and the bases empty. Instantly, he glared at Wright and even though he didn't approach the mound, home plate umpire John Shulock acted as a potential buffer, walking O'Neill up the first base line.

Even with Shulock as an in-his-face escort, O'Neill still shouted at Wright.

"I didn't hear what he said," said Wright. "I'm sure he didn't like [being struck], but that's baseball."

Little by little, the Yankees and Indians come closer to what'll certainly be an October collision. Whether or not their dislike for Wright will be resolved by then is an open question, but the Yankees are aware Cleveland represents, in Andy Pettitte's words, "the best measuring stick of how good" the Yankees are.

"There's no question the Indians are going to give us trouble, now and in the playoffs, too," Pettitte said before the game. "They're a good team and they show it every time we play them."

The Tribe certainly exposed all of David Cone's flaws Friday, pummeling him for five runs in 5 2/3 innings — including home runs by Jim Thome and Kenny Lofton. Cone had relied heavily on his four-seam fastball and slider in registering 26 strikeouts in his past 17 innings, but against the Tribe he "made a lot of mistakes and they took advantage of every one of them."

Cone allowed Thome a solo home run in the second inning, and practically melted down for good in the fourth, when five of the seven batters he faced reached base. There were three hits, a walk, two wild pitches, and a hit batter that gave the Indians a 3-1 lead.

In fact, you'll be able to find the following account in the Recipe for Disaster cookbook: Singles by Omar Vizquel and David Justice. A wild pitch. A walk to Thome, loading the bases. An RBI single by Manny Ramirez. A slider that hit Mark Whiten on the foot, again loading the bases. Another wild pitch, scoring another run.

Cone shook his head in disbelief.

"As good as I've been in my last few starts, I was just as bad tonight," said Cone. "My command was that off."

Yet, incredibly, the Yankees returned fire on Wright in the fifth inning, scoring three runs on Scott Brosius' two-run single and Derek Jeter's run-producing fielder's choice. That gave the Yankees a 4-3 lead, and even though Cone was losing the fight with an obviously flat slider, all he had to do was get six more outs.

Instead, Cone gave up a two-run homer to Lofton in the bottom of the fifth. The right-hander admitted it was "the key to the game. We'd just gotten a lead, and I turned around and gave it right back. I have to believe that pretty much demoralized us."

Cone allowed David Bell a leadoff single in the inning, but refused to forgive himself for the slider he said "just sat there" for Lofton to crush. One swing, and Cone's nine-game winning streak was over. But, to be fair, the Yankees weren't quite history until the seventh, when Thome punished a curveball that Graeme Lloyd carelessly left up in the strike zone, giving the Indians their 7-4 margin.

The Yanks learned several lessons Friday night. For one, Cone's mechanics still aren't perfect. He tinkered endlessly between rushing and slowing down his delivery, trying too hard to throw what he called "the really nasty slider."

"It was one of those nights you just have to chalk up as a bad game," said manager Joe Torre.

And as for Wright …well, this subplot doesn't have an ending. Not yet, anyway.

Reporter's Notebook:

Jeter reported no problems in his first game since returning from the disabled list. He was 0-for-3 with a walk.

"I wasn't comfortable at the plate until that walk [in his fourth plate appearance]. The other at-bats, I had fastballs that were right there. I just couldn't do anything with them."

Saturday, June 20, 1998
— at Cleveland Indians

Yankees 5, Indians 3

Wells rumbles, humbles Thome

By BOB KLAPISCH, Staff Writer

CLEVELAND — David Wells may or may not deserve to be an All-Star, and it's contestable whether he is even the Yankees' best pitcher. But is there any doubt this big, sloppy man is unafraid of a late-inning street fight?

"He lives on the edge, and then …it's like something clicks in," said Indians manager Mike Hargrove, his words a mixture of regret and respect. That's understandable, since Wells' smothering of Jim Thome in the eighth inning was the crossroads in the Yankees' 5-3 win over Cleveland on Saturday.

Every time Wells pitches, he challenges the modern notion of pitching, where arsenals have to be deep and varied. In fact, it still doesn't seem possible that Wells — who throws only a straight fastball, an old-fashioned top-to-bottom curveball, and a cameo change-up — can be so unhittable with runners in scoring position.

Yet, Thome was frozen by a 2-2, outside-corner heater that ended an eighth-inning rally and reinforced the unspoken belief among the Yankees that Wells — not Hideki Irabu, not Andy Pettitte, not even David Cone — will be the bridge between a near-perfect regular season and a long October.

If nothing else, Wells seems to have survived the recent, miniature crisis in his left shoulder. With the biceps tendinitis now under control, Wells said, "I had no worries in the world out there. It was like a blessing for me."

Suddenly, the numbers are mounting a campaign for an All-Star selection: Wells is 9-2 and hasn't issued a walk in his past 20 innings. An All-Star? Yanks manager Joe Torre said, "You have to consider him. He's got a good thing going right now, and I think that perfect game gives him an extra check mark."

Wells wasn't blemish-free against the Indians, allowing eight hits, but he did strike out nine, none more important than the eighth-inning punch-out of Thome. Talk about damage control: The Tribe had already scored a run in the inning, thanks to Manny Ramirez' RBI single. And, with Thome at the plate, they were one swing away from a 5-5 tie.

If the stakes weren't already steep enough, Wells fell behind 2-0, threw an inside-corner fastball for a strike, then delivered what he called "the key pitch" in the at-bat— a 2-1 curveball that dropped angrily below Thome's bat.

"I know he's their best hitter," Wells said of Thome. "That kind of situation just brings out the best in me."

Thome, now guessing, managed to foul off another curveball, but was helpless with the 2-2 fastball Wells threw over the black on the outside corner. Thome never moved, never even twitched, as the Indians drew their last breath of the afternoon. Not even a so-so ninth inning from Mariano Rivera could spoil Wells' work.

The Yankees have now won 23-of-31 on the road this year, and are 17-6 at Jacobs Field. Not bad, considering that only 24 hours earlier David Cone surrendered a 4-3 lead in his worst outing since April.

But as soon as Wells blew through the first six Indians, it was obvious that Darryl Strawberry was right when he said, "We might lose a game here and there, but we always, always managed to bounce back."

All it took were RBI doubles from Tino Martinez and Strawberry in the fourth, followed by Scott Brosius' solo home run off Dave Burba in the fifth.

When Paul O'Neill added an RBI later in the fifth, the Yankees had a 4-1 lead. And with Wells throwing those small, hissing fastballs, you could almost sense the Indians turning their hopeful gaze to rookie Bartolo Colon, who faces Irabu tonight.

Colon's mission? To make the Yankees look human. Somehow.

Reporter's Notebook:

The Yankees continued their verbal war against Jaret Wright. Torre said the fact that Wright hit O'Neill on Friday night "angers you when you see it, because Wright sort of stared at Paul. It sure [ticks] you off." …Torre has agreed to serve as one of the American League coaches at the All-Star Game …Derek Jeter committed his first throwing error of the season and is 1-for-8 since returning from the DL. "It's like spring training for me. I'm totally lost up there," Jeter said.

Sunday, June 21, 1998 — at Cleveland Indians

Indians 11, Yankees 0

Irabu, Yankees get roughed up

By BOB KLAPISCH, Staff Writer

CLEVELAND — From the very first inning, with his first sub-90 mph fastball, Hideki Irabu knew he was naked before the Indians. Within moments, Irabu's worst-case scenario had become a reality: no heat, no location, no chance of matching Bartolo Colon, the Tribe's right-hander who was throwing 99 mph.

Actually, there's no way for a box score to truly paint the portrait of the Yankees' 11-0 loss to the Indians on Sunday night, when Irabu was so awful, he lasted only three innings. The Japanese right-hander, who was leading the American League with a 1.68 ERA, allowed five runs, including three home runs, and in a rare moment of humility, admitted he needed to "take a step back" to find the reason for his suddenly anemic fastball.

By contrast, Colon blistered the Yankees with a fastball that bordered on inhuman, striking out 10 in eight innings. Of the Yankees' three hits, only one — Darryl Strawberry's opposite-field line drive in the fourth — was hit with any authority.

Otherwise, the night belonged to Colon, who, at 23, has already become the Tribe's best pitcher, even more dominating than Jaret Wright. Strawberry flatly said: "The guy can deal, man. He's a much better pitcher than Wright. Better command, and he throws a lot harder, too."

Incredibly, Colon averaged 95 mph, and made it clear early on how easy it would be. With one out in the second inning and the bases loaded — the result of back-to-back walks to Strawberry and Jorge

Posada, and Chad Curtis' bloop single — Colon blew away Ricky Ledee with a fastball that hissed over the outside corner at 96 mph.

Colon then ended the inning by reducing Scott Brosius to jelly, rearing back for a 2-2 fastball that rose from the belt to the neck before the Yankee third baseman was halfway through his swing. Brosius looked at Colon in disbelief, then slammed his bat to the ground, the universal gesture of defeat.

Later, Indians manager Mike Hargrove recounted a conversation between Brosius and Tribe third base coach Jeff Newman. According to Hargrove, Brosius said: "It's bad enough that he [Colon] throws so hard. What's not fair is nothing he throws is straight."

As for Irabu …well, once it was obvious that Colon owned the strike zone, the best the Yankee could hope for was to stay even. Actually, it was reasonable for the Yankees to expect that, since Irabu had been close to unhittable lately. But that's only because Irabu's fastball was reaching as high as 94-95 mph.

Not on this night, though. The mysterious dropoff in Irabu's heater allowed Manny Ramirez to go deep twice Former Yankee Mark Whiten went yard, as well. Irabu spoke of a "subtle" mechanical problem he intends to fix in the next five days, although he wouldn't specify what was wrong.

It could be a tired arm. It could be a hitch in his delivery. It might even be the 5-7 pounds Irabu appears to have gained in the last week. Whatever the theory, this much was certain: "He didn't have location, and he didn't have velocity," Posada said.

The Yankees saw that in the second inning, when Ramirez rocketed a 3-1 fastball — which was clocked at 89 mph — 421 feet over the center field wall. Whiten followed that with another homer to center, and down 2-0, Irabu knew he was at a crossroads.

"Obviously, I wasn't throwing the ball where I wanted," he said after the game. "My control wasn't very good, and as a result, that affected my mechanics."

The third inning wasn't any prettier than the second. With one out, Irabu walked David Justice, then watched helplessly as Jim Thome bounced a single off Derek Jeter's glove behind second base.

With runners on first and second, the Indians were about to bury Irabu. All they needed was one more listless fastball, which Irabu delivered over the middle of the plate. This was one was clocked at a mere 88 mph and Ramirez again cleared the center field wall.

That was all Yankees manager Joe Torre needed to see, replacing Irabu with Darren Holmes in the fourth, and effectively turning the last five innings into an exhibition match. With Colon throwing so hard, the outs were fast and merciless, and not even the proud Bombers were ashamed to admit they'd fallen victim to an iron axiom: There's no human antidote to the perfectly placed 97 mph heater.

"The guy pretty much dominated us," said Jeter, knowing no one in the room would argue.

Monday, June 22, 1998 — Atlanta Braves

Yankees 6, Braves 4

Yanks' pen proves mightier

By KEN DAVIDOFF, Staff Writer

NEW YORK — The marquee match, the one pitting Andy Pettitte against Greg Maddux, didn't resolve much Monday night. Like the 1996 World Series, Monday night's Yankees-Braves matchup came down to a case of whose bullpen was better. And, like the 1996 World Series, the Yankees won in a landslide.

While the unimposing trio of Dennis Martinez, John Rocker, and Mike Cather cast doubt on whether the Braves can add a second world championship to their 1990s resume, Jeff Nelson, Mike Stanton, and Mariano Rivera pitched like old times in helping the Bombers win Round One of this four-day, interleague bonanza, a 6-4 thriller. A loud Yankee Stadium crowd of 53,316 created a playoff-like setting.

"I'm very comfortable with our bullpen because we've got balance," manager Joe Torre said. "I think our bullpen right now is better than it's ever been."

Lately, though, due to a combination of strong starting pitching and explosive offense, it had been more invisible than it had ever been since Torre took over in 1996. On this night, with Pettitte taking on pitcher of the decade Maddux, it figured to be another one where the starters took the spotlight.

Instead, Tim Raines took the spotlight, clubbing a two-out, two-run double in the seventh off the 43-year-old Martinez (2-4) to give the Yanks (51-18) the lead. Nelson (5-3), Stanton, and Rivera (17th save) combined to allow just one hit over the final 2 1/3 innings.

"The opportunities for us here have been far and few between, with the starters going so well," said

Nelson, whose stiff back has contributed to his sub-par 4.59 ERA this season. "But we've done it in the past. Everybody should know that we're going to get the job done."

The cases of anyone on this team not getting the job done this season have been few and far between. The latest example of the Yankees' excellence came in the way they dealt with Maddux.

The Bombers solved Maddux about as well as a team can, using the combination of patience and aggressiveness that Torre mentioned before the game (yes, he knows that's a contradiction) to knock the four-time Cy Young winner for three runs and nine hits. Perhaps most impressive, they worked him for 87 pitches over just six innings. Last year, when Maddux crafted a 2-0 shutout over the Bombers in the Bronx, he made just 86 pitches over nine innings.

"The one thing we talked about was the quality of our at-bats," Torre said. "[Maddux] doesn't give you many pitches per at-bat."

Maddux revealed after the game he was hindered by a sore neck all night, and even thought about skipping his start.

Yet the Yanks erased two deficits against the right-hander. Pettitte fell into 2-0 and 3-2 holes, the first coming in the third when Raines got his glove on a double by former Yankee Gerald Williams, the second in the sixth. Both times, the home team came right back in the bottom of the same inning.

Danny Bautista started the seventh with a grounder that hit third base and skipped into left field for a single. Ozzie Guillen sacrificed him to second, then Pettitte caught Tony Graffanino looking at a third strike and walked Williams.

Chipper Jones battled Pettitte to a 2-2 count before pulling a grounder through the hole between short and third. Scott Brosius reached for it, then Derek Jeter, but neither could stop it as Bautista scored the lead run. Pettitte was immediately lifted for Nelson, who got out of the inning without further damage.

Maddux didn't appear for the bottom of the seventh, with the veteran Martinez in his place. Martinez walked the first batter he faced, Chuck Knoblauch. A Jeter bunt that forced Knoblauch at second was called back when the umpires decided the ball hit Jeter in the batter's box, and Braves skipper Bobby Cox was ejected for arguing. After the commotion, Jeter flied to center.

For what happened next, maybe Cox was better off in the safety of the visitors' clubhouse. Paul O'Neill walked, and Tino Martinez popped out to second. Up

stepped Raines. He worked the count to 2-2, then blasted a double over center fielder Andruw Jones' head, scoring Knoblauch and O'Neill for the 5-4 lead.

"It's a good feeling to get a hit like that, with the big crowd and all," Raines said.

The veteran went to third on a wild pitch by Rocker and scored an insurance run on Chad Curtis' single. The bullpen took care of the rest.

Tuesday, June 23, 1998 — Atlanta Braves

Braves 7, Yankees 2

Duque of hazard

Braves hammer Yankees rookie

Hernandez loses first

By KEN DAVIDOFF, Staff Writer

NEW YORK — It had to happen sometime. That it happened Tuesday night, against the Braves, in a packed Yankee Stadium, with George Steinbrenner witnessing him for the first time — well, just say that Orlando Hernandez's timing for his first bad start could have been better.

"El Duque" looked more like a Duque of hazard, suffering his first major league loss as the Bombers dropped the second game of their interleague series with Atlanta, 7-2. A crowd of 54,775 watched Tom Glavine and the Braves even the four-game set at 1-1, with the final two contests at Turner Field tonight and Thursday.

"My pitches weren't strikes," Hernandez said through interpreter Leo Astacio. "They went that far [motioning a small amount with his fingers] out of the strike zone. The batters just didn't swing at borderline pitches as they have in the past."

"He wasn't sharp tonight," manager Joe Torre said." He was missing pitches, but that's going to happen. If you're going to have a problem with him, that's where the problem is going to be."

After three excellent starts that produced a 2-0 record and 1.52 ERA, Hernandez lasted just 3 2/3 innings Tuesday, allowing six runs (three earned) and six hits. He walked four, the most free passes he has distributed as a Yankee, and fanned five. His ERA rose to a still-impressive 2.30.

And in his opinion, he should have fared better. "They're very good hitters," he said of the patient Braves lineup, "but today was their lucky day." Lucky, El Duque said, because home plate umpire John Hirschbeck squeezed his strike zone just enough to be rendered ineffective.

"A few calls didn't go his way," catcher Jorge Posada seconded. But he added: "He was wild. He didn't seem to have the control he had before," primarily with his fastball.

The Braves — who tied the Yanks' 51 victories for the most in baseball, although the Bombers have played seven fewer games — tallied individual runs in the second and third, then broke the game open in the fourth. Ryan Klesko lined a 3-0 pitch for a single to left-center. Javy Lopez walked. Michael Tucker struck out, then Andruw Jones knocked a pedestrian grounder to third. Scott Brosius simply couldn't glove it, jamming the bases with one out.

Hernandez got ahead of Ozzie Guillen, 1-2, then threw three straight close balls, forcing Klesko home. Curtis Pride followed with a walk on a close full-count pitch, bringing Lopez across the plate. El Duque fanned Keith Lockhart for the second out, but when Chipper Jones ripped a single to center for two more runs and a 6-1 lead, the right-hander's day finished early.

"We watched films of him, and we saw that he struck out a lot of guys swinging out of the zone," Chipper Jones said. "We knew we had to be patient with him."

None of this fazed El Duque after the game. Looking as relaxed as if he had just gone for a leisurely walk, Hernandez said, "I'm not happy because the team lost, but I am happy because my curveball was good, my slider was good, my fastball had a lot of velocity, and my change-up was good." Later, he added "I learn from my losses, not my wins. It's my way of thinking. I'm not at all disappointed."

His lesson of the night: "Try not to walk so many people."

Glavine (10-3), meanwhile, limited the Yanks to two runs — on solo homers by Derek Jeter and Paul O'Neill — and seven hits to win his eighth straight decision on the road (dating back to last season). Rookie Kerry Ligtenberg pitched an uneventful ninth to wrap it up.

Reporter's Notebook:

According to a report, a movie based on Hernandez's escape from Cuba is in the works, with Cuba Gooding Jr. and Antonio Banderas set to star.

The Braves rearranged their starting rotation so that Denny Neagle (8-5, 3.25) will pitch Thursday against David Wells. John Smoltz, originally scheduled for the series closer, has been shifted to Friday against Toronto.

Wednesday, June 24, 1998 — at Atlanta Braves

Yankees 10, Braves 6

Yankee bats turn up heat

By KEN DAVIDOFF, Staff Writer

ATLANTA — "Hey, Bu-Bu, what's going on?" Chuck Knoblauch asked a sweaty Hideki Irabu on Wednesday afternoon in the Turner Field visitors clubhouse.

The pitcher grinned and declared, in his broken English, "Hot-lanta!"

"Yeah, it sure is," the second baseman replied with a laugh.

Laugh off the heat. The Yanks did just that, using the 92-degree game-time temperature to their advantage as they pounded the Braves, 10-6, to take a 2-1 lead in this much-hyped, four-game, home-and-home interleague series. A Yankee-heavy crowd of 48,980 sweated and cheered through three hours and 19 minutes of baseball.

"I kind of like the heat," David Cone said. "I'm older, so the heat helps me get loose. I'd rather pitch in the heat than the cold."

That was a good thing for the Yankees (52-19), since the 35-year-old Cone (10-2, tied for the second-most victories in the American League) was the starting and winning pitcher. He fell into a 2-0 hole, but the Bombers wore down Braves starter Kevin Millwood and knocked him out in 3 2/3 innings. Braves fielders were sluggish as well, committing three errors that contributed to eight Yankees runs.

To succeed through such heat, "It's just a mindset," manager Joe Torre said. "You don't even think about it."

After three innings, the Yanks were down, 2-1, and yet there was a feeling that they were in the driver's seat. While the Braves struck quickly against Cone — with Ozzie Guillen's first-inning homer and

Andruw Jones' second-inning double (scoring Curtis Pride) accounting for the two runs — the Yanks worked Millwood for 72 pitches, or a little more than five per batter, in those three frames.

"[Millwood] was getting into a lot of three-ball counts," said Tino Martinez, who broke out of his 14-for-83 slump with two of the Yanks' 13 hits and two RBI. "We knew we were eventually going to get him."

They did in the fourth. It began innocently enough with Chad Curtis drawing a leadoff walk. Scott Brosius fisted a single to right-center, and Joe Girardi doubled over the head of Jones in center field, scoring Curtis to knot the score at 2-2.

Up came Cone, who prides himself on being a pretty good hitter for a pitcher. This time he produced what looked like a harmless bouncer to first. But with Brosius barreling home, Ryan Klesko, playing in place of the injured Andres Galarraga (sore back), threw the ball slightly off-line to the plate. Javy Lopez caught it, with no chance at tagging Brosius, and whipped it significantly off-line to first. So off-line that it went into right field, allowing Girardi to score for the 4-2 lead. Cone, who went to second on the play, picked up the first regular-season RBI by a Yankees pitcher since Lindy McDaniel homered off Detroit's Mickey Lolich on Sept. 28, 1972.

Homer Bush's sacrifice bunt moved Cone to third, and the pitcher came home on Derek Jeter's single up the middle for the fourth run of the inning.

Cone took over from there. He escaped a first-and-third, no-out jam in the fourth, allowing one run, and breezed through his last three innings. In all, he needed just 99 pitches, 72 of them strikes, to complete his seven frames. He issued no walks, hit one batter, and struck out seven in one of his better showings of the season.

"He was pretty flushed, but I think he pitched the seventh inning as well as he pitched any other," Torre said.

And now Cone, who started the season with two awful starts, finds himself with a nifty 10-2 record and a getting-there 4.64 ERA and a chance to make the AL's All-Star team.

Torre thinks Cone deserves it.

As for Cone, "I don't know," he said, thinking about the question. "I think there's a lot of pitchers who are as deserving or more deserving. I was the beneficiary of a lot of runs early on."

He'll have another start before the pitchers are announced. Meanwhile, the Yanks' 10 runs marked their highest total since they lost Bernie Williams to a sprained right knee. Girardi contributed three hits, and Darryl Strawberry, making a rare start in left field and batting cleanup for the first time since September 1996, extended his hitting streak to 10 games. It's his best run since a 13-gamer in 1991.

Thursday, June 25, 1998 — at Atlanta Braves

Yankees 6, Braves 0

Wells shows Braves his best stuff

By KEN DAVIDOFF, Staff Writer

ATLANTA — Like a dog at a mail carrier's convention, David Wells felt very much out of place Thursday night in the severe humidity of Turner Field. After all, "Boomer" is much more into air conditioning and cold beer than sweat and dehydration.

But the veteran southpaw is on a heck of a roll, his best as a Yankee, and he wasn't going to let the elements stop him on this night. In temperatures that hit 93 degrees on the first pitch, Wells, 35, outpitched Braves southpaw Denny Neagle to give the Bombers a convincing 6-0 shutout and a 3-1 series victory between the best teams in baseball.

"I'm dead," Wells said afterward. "It's hot out there. Every inning was a battle for me."

And every battle was won. In lifting his record to 10-2 and lowering his ERA to 3.92 — numbers that make him a shoo-in for the American League All-Star team — Wells recorded his second shutout of the season, tying four other pitchers for the league lead.

"He pitched as good as you can late in the game when you're tired," pitching coach Mel Stottlemyre said.

He did this in 117 pitches, 86 of them strikes. He has not walked a batter in his last 30 innings. He did this, also, under National League rules, which meant he batted four times. The highlights: He grounded a single into left and crushed a flyout to the right field warning track.

"I was getting really lightheaded out there," Wells said. "But I had a shutout out there." So he kept going. When Stottlemyre started to go to the mound in the sixth, just to give him a breather, Wells waved him back. No need to mess with his groove.

And what a groove it has been. Wells' worst start

this year came on May 6 in Texas, when he lasted just 2 2/3 innings in the 94-degree weather, and afterward manager Joe Torre questioned the southpaw's fitness. Since then, Wells has lost just once, won seven times, and tossed in a perfect game for good measure.

"Send that dude to Colorado [site of the All-Star Game]," said David Cone. "He's been our best pitcher. I've never seen Boomer so confident."

And so the Yankees left Atlanta confident, having convincingly beaten the Braves. "It makes you feel better because you beat the best club in the National League," Torre said. "It's a feather in your cap."

After five scoreless innings from both sides, the Yanks (53-19) broke the game open with a five-run sixth. Paul O'Neill's two-run triple and Chad Curtis' two-run homer were the highlights.

Reporter's Notebook:

In a freak eighth-inning play, Tino Martinez took a John Rocker pitch in the back, practically the same spot where he was hit by Armando Benitez on May 19 that caused him to miss eight games. This one was a breaking ball and clearly unintentional, but, as Torre said, "It still hurts." Martinez could sit tonight against Mets lefty Al Leiter, with Jorge Posada likely to get the nod at first.

Torre declared Jeff Nelson unavailable Thursday night and said it was likely that the team doctors would examine the reliever's aching lower back today. A stint on the disabled list is possible. Nelson, who pitched poorly Wednesday night, admitted that his back felt a little worse Thursday, but reiterated that he wanted to pitch through his soreness and stiffness.

Friday, June 26, 1998 — at New York Mets

Yankees 8, Mets 4

Bombers baffle Mets relievers

By T.J. QUINN, Staff Writer

NEW YORK — Mel Rojas watched all night as the vaunted Yankees lineup took pitch after pitch, showing discipline that he rarely had seen from other teams.

Then he saw Al Leiter wrench his knee on a ground ball in the seventh inning, and the bullpen phone rang.

Leiter exited, and the right-handed Rojas came out and warmed up, ready to face the left-handed Paul O'Neill with two runners on base, runners who could give the Yankees the lead.

Rojas threw fastballs and split-fingered pitches as he warmed up and decided on a course of action.

"I was going to throw the split-finger," he said. "I felt good. I wanted to get it in the dirt."

It wasn't in the dirt. Instead, he threw a low strike, and O'Neill reached to get it. The ball exploded off the bat, landing over the left-center field wall and giving the Yankees a 6-4 lead.

"He's a strong guy," Rojas said.

People used to describe the Mets bullpen that way, but lately the relief corps has been having a rough go of things. After Rojas' neck-twister, John Hudek and Brian Bohanon also gave up runs en route to an 8-4 loss.

For most of the season, the Mets have tried to get games to the bullpen, where they almost always outlast the other team. Friday was one of those increasingly more common nights when they were outpitched from the seventh inning on.

> **"**I was going to throw the split-finger," he said. "I felt good. I wanted to get it in the dirt.**"**
>
> *— Mel Rojas*

All but Rojas chastised themselves for making bad pitches (Rojas said it was a good hit and not a bad pitch), but all three agreed that they rarely have seen a team with the discipline and power of the Yankees.

"Pitches that other teams swing at, they're not touching," said Bohanon, who gave up two hits, a walk, and a run in his third of an inning. "We just didn't make our pitches."

Hudek said he was surprised at the Yankees' aggressiveness against the relievers.

"Mel: first pitch. Bo: first pitch. Me: first pitch," he said.

Leiter's problem came from the other side of the spectrum. The Yankees just wouldn't chase what he wanted them to and hit pitches he was sure they would take.

"It was frustrating. Very frustrating," he said. "I watched a lot of tape on Chuck Knoblauch, and he almost never swings at the first pitch. Then I throw him a strike [in the fifth inning] and he hits it. Why did he do that? I really want to ask him.

"[Scott] Brosius — how the hell does a guy look

for a curveball that's down and that's away and hit it? What can you do?"

Rojas said that was the way that he felt about his pitch to O'Neill.

His fateful split-fingered pitch wasn't in the dirt, as he had hoped, but he said it wasn't a bad pitch.

"I went up to Mike [Piazza] and asked, 'Was it up?' And he said, 'No.' Then I went inside and looked at the tape and it wasn't up. He's really, really strong," Rojas said.

The first question for manager Bobby Valentine, though, was why Rojas was in there in the first place. Why have the right-hander face a dangerous lefty such as O'Neill when the Mets have three left-handed set-up men and a left-handed closer.

Valentine, who stopped short of getting testy, said there was no other choice. He also didn't agree with Rojas' analysis of the pitch.

"[Dennis] Cook wasn't available, Bohanon hasn't had success against left-handers, [Bill] Pulsipher has been in the majors for two days," Valentine said. "[Rojas] made a bad pitch to a very good hitter, and he hit it out. I could easily go with a left-hander and not get second-guessed, but that's not a baseball play."

A blast for Yanks
O'Neill HR crushing blow in victory

By KEN DAVIDOFF, Staff Writer

NEW YORK — This opening game of the 1998 Subway Series had pitchers' duel written all over it. In one corner stood Hideki Irabu of Chiba, Japan, the American League's ERA leader. In the other, New Jersey native Al Leiter, the owner of the best ERA in the majors.

Instead, between Yogi Berra and alternating chants of "Let's Go Yankees" and "Yankees [stink]," Shea Stadium had somewhat of a slugfest on its hands. Leiter outpitched Irabu, but Leiter's possibly serious injury begot the unimpressive Mets bullpen, and so the Yanks prevailed, 8-4, in front of 53,404 fans.

"We're a patient ballclub," Yankees manager Joe Torre said. "Our pitchers keep us in the game, plus we have good at-bats."

Irabu kept his team in the game, but he continued his fade toward mediocrity, earning a no-decision in

5 2/3 innings of work. He allowed four runs, six hits, three walks, and struck out five. But at least he apparently has his health.

Leiter pitched much better than Irabu until the fateful seventh inning. That's when he suffered a strain of his left knee that is labeled day-to-day. He will undergo an MRI today.

The teams exchanged leads through the first six innings, with the Mets holding a precarious 4-3 edge with two-thirds of the game completed. Then, with the top of the order up in the seventh, the Yankees took control.

Chuck Knoblauch drew a leadoff walk, and Derek Jeter followed with a nubber between the mound and first base. John Olerud pursued it, Leiter headed to first, and Jeter, realizing that he had a chance to beat this one out, booked for first base. He dove, easily beating Leiter to the bag.

That's when Leiter (9-4) sustained the injury." There was no pop," the Mets' ace said. "It was right at the end there."

He left the game limping, and in came Mel Rojas to pitch to Paul O'Neill. The right-hander hung his first pitch, a splitter, and O'Neill sent it the other way, 387 feet into the left-field seats. Yanks lead, 6-4. Major boos for Rojas.

"I'm glad we played here tonight, because that ball doesn't go out in Yankee Stadium," O'Neill said.

The Yanks added two runs in the eighth. Ramiro Mendoza (5-1), who relieved Irabu in the sixth, left the game with one out in the ninth, after creating a save situation for Mariano Rivera. The Yanks' closer strolled in, facing a first-and-second, one-out situation, and strolled to his 19th save.

All of this covered up for Irabu's subpar outing. Torre credited the right-hander for getting out of a bases-loaded, none-out jam in the first, allowing just one run. But this is clearly not the same guy who blazed out of this 1998 campaign. He still holds the league lead in ERA, 2.47 to the 2.51 posted by Cleveland's Bartolo Colon, but he noted, "I'm going to need to look back and think about the thing that made me successful. Today didn't go well. My last start didn't, either. At this point, I'm satisfied just to be in the starting rotation."

The Yankees have to be satisfied overall, though, considering the starting lineup they posted. For all the pomp and circumstance surrounding this modern-day Subway Series, the Yankees came to Friday's series opener like the guy who wears a sweatsuit to his own wedding. Their starting lineup was more fitting for a spring training, split-squad contest than for a regular season affair that means so much to George Steinbrenner, despite his denials.

But as The Boss always says, it's not where you start, it's where you finish.

"It doesn't matter who we throw out there," Derek Jeter said. "When we put them out there, we find a way to win."

On Friday night, Joe Torre put out Jorge Posada at first base, the first time the second-year player manned that position. He put out Tim Raines in the cleanup spot, the first time the 38-year-old hit there since Aug. 29, 1989, when he was with the Expos.

Tino Martinez, benched due to his slump and the fact that the Yankees were facing a tough left-hander, wound up playing the last four innings. Posada made a couple of miscues at first, but he was overall satisfactory. Raines went 1-for-3 before being lifted for defensive substitute Ricky Ledee.

One down, two to go in this supposedly ordinary weekend. "If you win this series, you say it's a good series," Jeter said. "If you lose, it's just another three games."

Saturday, June 27, 1998 — at New York Mets

Yankees 7, Mets 2

Shea Miserables

Bombers cause havoc in Flushing

By TARA SULLIVAN, Staff Writer

NEW YORK — One swing and the Subway Series became just another three-game set won by the Yankees. The blow was struck by Tino Martinez, and three runs later, after Bobby Jones' hanging curveball landed 364 feet away over the right field fence, the Yankees had erased another deficit and any hope the Mets had of grabbing Big Apple supremacy.

With a 7-2 victory at Shea Stadium, the Yankees displayed again to the 53,587 in attendance how wide the current chasm between the Bronx and Flushing is, guaranteeing themselves of being on the plus-side of this three-game intracity equation.

Not that the Yankees didn't get plenty of help from the Mets. First baseman John Olerud dropped a sure out on Paul O'Neill's fourth-inning ground ball to shortstop Rey Ordonez, creating a one-on, one-out situation rather than two outs with the bases empty. Darryl Strawberry followed with a single through the right side of the infield, and Martinez cleared the bases with his 11th home run. After playing only the late innings in the first game of the series, Martinez made his return to the starting lineup memorable, finishing with two hits, the second a double to ignite a four-run seventh.

"With two left-handers in a row [Atlanta's Denny Neagle on Thursday night and Al Leiter on Friday], I didn't want to play Tino against both," Yankees manager Joe Torre said. "He was struggling a little [five hits is his previous 44 at-bats]. That was a big day for him. He also had a two-hit night in Atlanta, so hopefully it's the start of something for him."

Martinez has been out of sorts since he was hit in the back by an Armando Benitez pitch May 19 and is hitting .189 since returning to the lineup. But his timely homer Saturday was a salve both for Yankees starter Andy Pettitte and for his teammates, who bounded out of the dugout to congratulate their first baseman.

"That was big," said Pettitte, who improved to 9-5 after going 6 1/3 innings, giving up four hits and striking out nine. "I was able to relax. I was already in a groove, but that was definitely a big hit to get us up by two [3-1]."

Pettitte spotted the Mets a one-run lead in the second inning, started by Butch Huskey's single. He went to second on a wild pitch, and Pettitte walked Brian McRae. Ordonez then grounded to third baseman Scott Brosius, whose attempt at a 5-4-3 double play was thwarted when second baseman Chuck Knoblauch threw wild to Martinez, allowing Huskey to score.

"Definitely, I was struggling through the first three innings," Pettitte said. "I was struggling with the mound, getting used to it. There was a hole in the mound, and it sloped more than usual. But I just kept battling and quit thinking so much."

That is music to the ears of Torre, who delivered that exact message to Pettitte in the dugout.

"He just gets so out of sorts sometimes," Torre said. "He had a bad rhythm when the game started. He thinks too much sometimes. I don't usually talk to him during the game, but I talked to him in the fourth inning and said, 'Andy, you're complicating it for yourself. Just go out and don't think too much.'"

The advice was a lot easier to follow thanks to Martinez's home run, and now, the Yankees have a sweep clearly in view.

"These games are not any bigger than any other games, but the fans create such excitement," Martinez said. "It's fun for the players because the fans create such an atmosphere."

The barometer rose loudly in the Yankees' favor as the game inched toward its inevitable conclusion. Scoring in the four-run seventh started with a sacrifice fly by Chad Curtis and was stretched by Derek Jeter's two-run, two-out single to right, the final insult Jones (6-5) would suffer. O'Neill then drove in the Yanks' final run with a first-pitch single off reliever Bill Pulsipher.

But really the Yankees should thank Ordonez, who inexplicably tried to get Jorge Posada — moving from second to third base on Brosius' one-out grounder. With Pettitte on deck, Ordonez should have gone for the sure out, but instead he hit Posada in the back with his throw, and everyone was safe. Pettitte did indeed strike out, but the Yankees, given an extra out, made it count.

"They capitalize on mistakes very well, and that's the sign of a great team," Mets manager Bobby Valentine said of the group that has yet to lose 20 games and stands at 55-19.

It was a team that brought the Bronx to Queens on Saturday. About half of the crowd was in their corner when the game started, but nearly all of the fans that remained after it started to rain in the ninth inning wore pinstripes.

> **"** Andy, you're complicating it for yourself. Just go out and don't think too much. **"**
>
> — *Joe Torre*

As Bernard Gilkey began what would be the Mets' final at-bat, chants of "Let's go Yankees" easily swallowed chants of "Let's go Gilkey." And when Mike Stanton ran the count to 0-2, Yankees fans clapped in earnest and were rewarded with a called third strike. Only the Yankee Stadium strains of "New York, New York" were missing.

"There's still one more game to go," Torre said." "We don't think in terms of series, we think in terms of games."

The crowd of 53,587 pushed the two-day total to 106,991, the first time the Mets have drawn consecutive 50,000-plus crowds since 1970. The Mets never have drawn three straight crowds of more than 50,000.

Sunday, June 28, 1998 — at New York Mets

Mets 2, Yankees 1

Met-amorphosis
Amazins turn tables on Bombers

By KEN DAVIDOFF, Staff Writer

NEW YORK — Once again they saved the best for last. The Yankees might have clinched bragging rights the day before, but the intensity in Sunday night's Subway Series finale soared to the same exciting levels as last year's decisive Game 3.

In a tight contest featuring some final-play controversy, the Mets salvaged the final game, winning a 2-1 pitcher's duel. Nearly all of the Shea Stadium crowd of 53,749, the largest of the series, stuck around for the nail-biter finish.

And those who cheered "Let's Go Mets" were rewarded and saved the humiliation of being swept by their crosstown rivals.

"The whole team wanted this win today," Mets starter Masato Yoshii said.

"To have lost three in a row, period, would have been bad enough," catcher Mike Piazza agreed.

Though Yoshii went to bed Sunday night with a no-decision, he could take primary responsibility for the Mets' triumph. The Japanese right-hander matched his better-known Cuban counterpart, Orlando "El Duque" Hernandez, for seven innings as each allowed a run. Yoshii had a no-hitter for 4 2/3 innings, Hernandez for 5 2/3.

Dennis Cook threw the final two innings for the victory, while Ramiro Mendoza relieved Hernandez in the ninth and suffered the loss. A crazy play, prompted by a Luis Lopez sacrifice fly, ended the game in wild fashion. But in the end, the momentary confusion simply prolonged the Mets' malaise before they could finally feel good about themselves.

In Yoshii's seven innings, he allowed the one run and two hits. His four walks set a career high, but so did his 10 strikeouts. It was his best performance since May 21, when he pitched a complete-game victory over the Reds.

"I don't think that Yoshii could have pitched better," Mets manager Bobby Valentine said. "Ask the Yankees hitters if they liked what they saw … or if they didn't like what they saw."

"I'll tell you what: I thought he had more pitches — slider, sinker," Yanks catcher Jorge Posada said. "He came right at us with the fastball and splitter. He had a really good splitter."

Though Hernandez started slow and improved as the game went on, Yoshii dominated from the beginning. Edgardo Alfonzo muffed a hard-hit Paul O'Neill ball in the fourth and was charged with an error. Tino Martinez and Posada drew walks in the second, and Posada was given an intentional pass in the fourth. Never in that time did a Yankee get as far as third base, and the hits column still read "0."

With two out in the fifth, Derek Jeter hit a humpback liner into right that fell in front of Butch Huskey for a clean single. One no-hitter down, one still alive.

El Duque's fall from history began with a two-out, sixth-inning strikeout. Piazza flailed at a pitch that was so outside it was beyond Posada's reach. Piazza easily reached first on the wild pitch.

John Olerud worked the count full, then knocked a shot to right similar to Jeter's single in the fifth. O'Neill got a good jump, though, and tried a shoestring catch. If he had one more step on the ball, he would have caught it. Instead, he trapped it, and both no-hitters were now gone.

> **❝To have lost three in a row, period, would have been bad enough.❞**
>
> *— Mike Piazza*

With runners on first and second, Carlos Baerga knocked a liner back toward the box. Hernandez started to stick his glove out toward it, then held back, and the ball landed in center field. Piazza scored easily for a 1-0 lead as the crowd went wild.

The Yanks came right back in the seventh when Scott Brosius pulverized a 1-0 Yoshii offering into the visitors' bullpen. The estimated 404-foot shot knotted the score at 1.

That set up the wild ending, which set up the Mets to go on for the rest of the season. If they had to win just one out of the three, perhaps it was best to win the last.

"I wish all three games were as exciting as this one," Valentine said. "I was saying from the dugout that this was a fun game. I think there was an appreciation of that on both sides of the field."

Nevertheless, he and his players will have to move on from a series that provided more bad than good for the home-team supporters.

Tuesday, June 30, 1998 — Philadelphia Phillies
Yankees 9, Phillies 2

Cone reaches back
Vintage effort in Yanks win

By KEVIN T. CZERWINSKI, Staff Writer

NEW YORK — It was hard to tell whether it was 1998 or 1988 Tuesday night at Yankee Stadium.

It was New York and David Cone was on the mound, but if you didn't know better, you would have sworn it was the Cone of the late Eighties — the one who wore blue and orange for the team across town — that was mowing down the Phillies. The veteran right-hander withstood a 50-minute rain delay and what proved to be a feeble attack in pitching the Yankees to a 9-2 victory in the opening game of New York's last interleague series of the season.

Cone pitched his second complete game of the season, improving to 11-2. It matches his best start since '88, a year in which he also started 11-2 en route to a 20-3 season with the Mets. He struck out 11, the 51st time in his career he has fanned 10 or more, and didn't issue a walk for the second consecutive game.

Cone had a perfect game through two outs in the fifth inning and allowed just five hits. The only blemish that kept him from picking up his first shutout as a Yank was a ninth-inning homer by Jon Zuber.

"I know I'm a lot better at what I'm doing now than I was 10 years ago," Cone said. "I know how to make adjustments. I think I've really made a lot of progress in my last four or five starts. I always figured that if my arm held up, I'd be all right.

"I know I don't throw the ball as hard as I used to throw it, but I've been fairly consistent since my first two starts."

Considering Cone's recent history of arm problems, it appeared his chances of finishing the game were spotty when the skies opened up for a 50-minute rain delay that began in the second inning. But Cone came back after the layoff and actually looked stronger. He was particularly sharp in the seventh and eighth innings, striking out five consecutive batters.

"I was a little worried about the rain," Cone said. "But ironically, I was a little better after the rain. I was a lot smoother after the delay."

Gregg Jefferies, Cone's teammate with the Mets in

the '80's, had this take after going hitless in four at-bats.

"I think he threw faster back then [with the Mets] but everything else is the same," Jefferies said. "The control, the angles, it was all there. He's such a competitor. It doesn't matter if it's 2-0 or 9-0, he will battle you like it was the seventh game of the World Series."

That fact was evident in the sixth inning. Mark Lewis and Desi Relaford led off with back-to-back hits, giving the Phils runners on second and third. Cone stepped up, though, and struck out Teaneck's Doug Glanville, got Jefferies to ground out, and struck out Scott Rolen to get out of the jam.

"He was very determined in that sixth inning," New York manager Joe Torre said. "I think that was vintage David Cone right there. We played some poor defense in that inning, and for him to pick everyone up like that was a throwback for him.

"I think he's better now than he has been in the three years that I've been with him. He's been great. He's been as good as he's going to be in terms of arm strength. Except for the game against Baltimore [a no-decision April 19] he's done great. He's got great command."

Darryl Strawberry, Tim Raines, and Chad Curtis led New York's nine-hit attack, picking up two hits apiece. Strawberry looked like a Texas golfer cutting a shot under the wind in the second inning when he lined his 11th home run of the season into the left field bleachers just before the rains came. He had two RBI on the night, as did Raines and Curtis.

Wednesday, July 1, 1998
— Philadelphia Phillies

Yankees 5, Phillies 2

Wells doesn't run dry

Overcomes middle-inning bumps to bounce Phils

By KEVIN T. CZERWINSKI, Staff Writer

NEW YORK —As evident early that David Wells didn't have command of all his pitches. His curveball wasn't, well, curving, and his breaking ball wasn't breaking.

But Wells, who was named to the American League All-Star team Wednesday, has thrived on such situations this season. So it wasn't surprising to see him gut his way through seven innings en route to picking up his 11th win as the Yankees topped Philadelphia, 5-2, before 28,919 fans at Yankee Stadium.

The Yankees matched the best start in franchise history after 77 games (57-20), tying the start by the 1928 squad.

Wells was the catalyst, pitching out of tight spots in the fourth and seventh innings, bending a little but never breaking when the Phillies threatened to knock him out. Wells (11-2) scattered seven hits, struck out four, and walked none while lowering his ERA to 3.75. He has not walked a batter in his past four starts, a stretch that has reached 36 innings.

"I had no breaking ball at all," he said. "I knew in the first inning that I didn't have a curve. I had to rely on my fastball and my sinker. My mechanics were off, and I was rushing my pitches. As a result, I got them up at times.

"But, you have to battle like I battled tonight. If you don't have your best stuff, you have to be able to pull a rabbit out of your hat. You have to keep the hitter on his front foot and come up with something that works. That's been my philosophy since I learned how to pitch. You have to keep fighting in that situation."

That strategy never has produced a first half of a season like the one Wells is experiencing this year. By his own admission, this is the best start he has had, and he has impressed manager Joe Torre with his resolve.

"He didn't have his curveball, and he ran out of gas in the seventh," Torre said. "Maybe it was the excitement of being named to the All-Star team. I don't know. But he battled. And that's the difference between him now and last year. He is battling through those situations.

"I like to think its maturity. I think he's a different pitcher. He may not think so. But when he doesn't have the stuff he normally has, he battled through. In these situations last year, he was a thrower. Now he's a pitcher, and whatever he's doing is sure working in my mind."

Wells' first brush with collapse came in the fourth inning. He threw 10 pitches to Scott Rolen before the slugging third baseman sent a rocket into the black seats in center field. It was just the 17th time a ball has landed in the black since the Stadium was remodeled.

Wells then gave up hits to Rico Brogna and Kevin Jordan before Brogna scored on Mark Lieberthal's groundout to tie the score at 2.

The Yankees broke the game open in the fifth inning, sending eight men to the plate. They tatooed Matt Beech (3-6), with first baseman Tino Martinez picking up the big hit in the inning — a two-run single. Martinez also belted a two-run homer in the second inning and began showing signs that he might be breaking out of the slump he has been in since being hit with an Armando Benitez pitch May 19.

The outburst gave Wells a little breathing room. He did, however, get into trouble again in the seventh. Base hits by Mark Lewis and Desi Relaford gave the Phillies two men on with two out, prompting a visit to the mound from Torre. Wells remained in the game and got Teaneck's Doug Glanville to fly out to left to end the threat.

"Joe asked me if I was getting a little bit tired," Wells said. "I told him yes but that I still had something left. I said give me one more batter and if I don't get this guy out then get me out of here.

"This has been the absolutely best first half I've ever had. I think a lot of it has to do with the guys I have behind me and the way they've played. They've come through in the clutch and I think that keeps you in a good frame of mind."

Mike Stanton's status regarding his impending suspension remains unclear. The American League has yet to render a decision on his appeal, and the delay has led Torre to speculate that the league is waiting for interleague play to conclude so Stanton can serve his suspension against American League teams…. Chili Davis has the cast off his right foot and is rehabbing his ankle after April surgery. Torre said Davis has lost some weight since spring but is moving around well and should rejoin the team next month.

Thursday, July 2, 1998 — Philadelphia Phillies

Yankees 9, Phillies 8

Tino makes it extra special

By KEVIN T. CZERWINSKI, Staff Writer

NEW YORK — Don't let the euphoria of the Yankees' monstrous come-from-behind victory Thursday night over the Philadelphia Phillies hide the fact that there might be trouble brewing.

Rookie Ricky Ledee's bases-loaded single in the 11th inning scored Paul O'Neill with the winning run in a 9-8 victory before a crowd of 31,259 at Yankee Stadium. The victory wouldn't have been possible without the heroics of Tino Martinez.

The first baseman cracked two home runs, including a two-out, three-run shot in the ninth to tie the score at 8 and erase a five-run Phillies' lead.

The Yanks have the best record in franchise history after 78 games (58-20) and matched the most wins by a major league club in the first 81 games of a 162-game season (the 1970 Reds were 58-23 after 81 games).

But there is a red flag that's signaling caution concerning starting pitcher Hideki Irabu. Only the combined heroics of Martinez and Ledee were able to prevent Irabu from picking up his third consecutive loss.

The Japanese import was roughed up by the Phils, surrendering three home runs before getting pulled with none out in the fourth inning and the Yanks down, 5-0.

> **❝The bat is just flying for him now. It's like a pitcher throwing 95 miles per hour.❞**
>
> *— Joe Torre*
> *on Tino Martinez*

"The last couple of starts, Irabu has not been like he was earlier in the year," Yankees manager Joe Torre said. "His location and velocity aren't consistent now. I don't think there's anything wrong physically, because on his workout days he still has good pop on his pitches.

"But too many pitches he makes now are up in the zone. I'm concerned. He's throwing too many good pitches to hit."

Irabu is equally concerned about his performance, saying after the game that he's fine physically but that he knows he is hurting the team.

In three-plus innings he gave up five hits and three walks with no strikeouts. He has looked horrible in his past three starts and hasn't won a game since June 10.

It's a far cry from his performance in April and May, when he was 4-1 with a 1.49 ERA. Since then he is 2-2 with a 5.29 ERA. He also has given up eight home runs in his past three starts.

Martinez, meanwhile, seems to have snapped out of the slump he has been suffering through since getting hit by an Armando Benitez pitch May 19. He had two hits and four RBI Wednesday and came back with three hits and four RBI Thursday.

"I was glad to come through in that situation," Martinez said. "[Derek] Jeter and O'Neill got on, and I just tried to hit the ball hard to keep the rally going.

I've hit home runs before to win games, but I'm glad about this one.

"He threw a 2-1 fastball that I sat on. I didn't think he wanted to go 3-1 on me and risk loading the bases in that situation. It was a good ball to hit. I know I said I was looking forward to the All-Star break and I still am, but I was kidding with [Chuck Knoblauch] the other day that we'd both get hot right before the break, and we are. I feel that this is the way I'm capable of swinging the bat. That's how I look at it."

Torre also thinks Martinez has put his struggles behind him.

"The bat is just flying for him now," Torre said. "It's like a pitcher throwing 95 miles per hour. He's not forcing the bat through the zone anymore.

"I think possibly the first home run tonight really got him going. It just jumped out of here. Before the last two games, he was pressing, squeezing the bat. I think it may have even started with that second base hit [Wednesday] night."

Friday, July 3, 1998 — Baltimore Orioles

Yankees 3, Orioles 2

Yanks steal a win
Curtis helps foil O's in 9th

By TIM LEONARD, Staff Writer

NEW YORK — The timing was either going to be perfect or deadly. Chad Curtis knew that as he stood on second base, plotting how to get to third with one out in the bottom of the ninth inning against the Baltimore Orioles.

Curtis' logic was simple: There are a lot more ways to score from third base than from second base with one out. With the score tied and extra innings looming, he decided he needed to do something to help the Yankees win. So on an 0-1 pitch to Scott Brosius, Curtis put his head down and took off for third. He made it a split-second before Jeff Reboulet applied the tag.

The stolen base accomplished Curtis' purpose when Brosius stroked Jesse Orosco's next pitch into the gap in right-center field to bring home the Yankees' most daring player with the winning run in a 3-2 victory over the Orioles on Friday night at the Stadium. The victory raised the Yankees record to

59-20 and allowed them to maintain their 10-game lead over second-place Boston.

"My thinking there is 'Let's take a shot,'" said Curtis, who made the decision to go on his own. "If I get thrown out, we get to hit after them."

Neither team was doing much hitting, which made the play all the more daring. Tim Raines led off the ninth and reached when Orosco hit him with a 3-2 pitch. Curtis followed with a single to put runners on first and second.

Pinch-hitter Dale Sveum botched a bunt attempt, which resulted in Raines being forced at third. That's when the wheels in Curtis' mind began to turn. It wasn't an easy decision.

"There's one out. Whether it's Scott hitting or Joe [Girardi] hitting, a fly ball right there scores me," said Curtis, who hit a solo home run in the fourth inning to tie the game at 2-2. "I have to weigh the pitcher's time, how close the infield is holding me, the score, whether we're at home or on the road. If we're on the road, I might not go there."

Curtis' stolen base was reminiscent of a play last season against the Minnesota Twins, when he tried to steal second in the ninth inning and was thrown out, thwarting a potential rally in a game the Yankees lost.

"There's no fear in him," Brosius said. "If he sees an opportunity, he goes for it. It turned out to be a great play. The thought of a stolen base didn't enter my mind until he got in there. Then I thought it was a great idea."

Curtis' derring-do and Brosius' clutch hitting brought an end to an as-advertised pitching duel between the Yankees' Andy Pettitte and Orioles starter Mike Mussina. Runs, hits, and rallies were not part of the deal for either team. Mussina went 7 1/3 innings, striking out nine. Pettitte pitched a complete game, battling his control much of the time. He gave up just four hits, but walked six, allowing two third-inning runs.

After a shaky start that including yielding a run in the first, Mussina sailed through the middle innings, but got into trouble when Derek Jeter became the first Yankee to reach second base since the fourth inning with a double to lead off the eighth. Luis Sojo failed to sacrifice and eventually grounded to shortstop. Orosco relieved Mussina and got Paul O'Neill to ground to short with the infield drawn in. Tino Martinez followed with a smash to second that Roberto Alomar fielded cleanly to snuff out the scoring chance.

With the crowd of 43,328 roaring, Pettitte escaped a jam in the ninth, getting Mike Bordick to ground to Brosius with runners on first and second. Pettitte got out of an identical situation in the seventh, when he struck out Bordick with runners on first and second. All four of his strikeouts came in the seventh and eighth innings.

"With Mike on the mound, he's one of the quality pitchers in this league. You don't go in against him expecting to blow a team out," Brosius said. "It's just been one of the qualities of our team to grind it out and play nine hard innings and 10 if it takes 10."

Friday night, that wasn't necessary.

Saturday, July 4, 1998 — Baltimore Orioles
Yankees 4, Orioles 3

Call Yanks lucky
Ump thwarts O's late rally

By TIM LEONARD, Staff Writer

NEW YORK — Miller sat behind his desk in the visiting manager's office, his graying hair looking like someone had just dragged a rake through it. The Orioles manager lit a cigarette and motioned to the baseball rule book, open to a page that he wanted someone to read.

Miller had highlighted a section that read, in part, that an umpire's requisite job is to make sure a play is called correctly. In Miller's mind, that didn't happen in the ninth inning Saturday at Yankee Stadium. Because of that, the Yankees were able to defeat the Orioles, 4-3, for their 60th victory of the season.

The key play came with runners on first and second and no outs. Chris Hoiles attempted to sacrifice, but his bunt was fielded by Yankees closer Mariano Rivera, who spun and fired to Scott Brosius at third.

That's where judgment and interpretation came into play. Brosius appeared to hold the ball for about as long as Jeffrey Maier did, when the Old Tappan youth helped Derek Jeter's fly ball become a home run in the 1996 playoffs against these same Orioles. In the blink of an eye, the ball was in and out of Brosius' glove. Third base umpire Marty Foster had his right arm in the air to call pinch runner Jeff Reboulet out. Seconds later, he was using it to eject third-base coach Sam Perlozzo.

"I tried to be real quick with the exchange and it never got to my hand," said Brosius, who was trying to double Hoiles at first. "It was definitely one of those calls that could go either way."

Miller rushed onto the field and argued that Foster was behind Brosius and not in position to make the call. He asked crew chief Ken Kaiser to intervene, but Kaiser would not because, according to that same rule book, the umpire making the call has to ask for help. Home plate umpire Fieldin Culbreth could not help because, Miller said, he had been hit with Hoiles' bat and did not see the play.

"We don't look to see if we're right or wrong. That's not our job," said Kaiser, who ejected Miller. "The umpire said the ball was dropped in transition."

"It's a shame. …He was out of position," Miller said. "To me, that's not judgment. To me, that's incompetence. No one is trying to show you up. Someone is just asking for common sense. The last quote in this book is 'Get it right.'"

Common sense, of course, was predicated by what side of the field you were sitting on. The Yankees and a Fourth of July crowd of 37,390 obviously agreed with what transpired, no matter how atrocious the call looked on replays.

"It was a judgment call. I'm glad it went the way it did," Yankees manager Joe Torre said. "I thought he was out."

Right or wrong, the call went the Yankees' way, as did the game. Rivera got Rich Becker to ground into a 4-6-3 double play to finish a shaky inning and a game that was symbolic of how the season has gone for both teams. Chad Curtis singled home Tino Martinez and Tim Raines in the sixth as the Yankees overcame a 3-2 deficit.

The controversial ending upstaged an outstanding effort by Orlando Hernandez, which, appropriately enough came on Independence Day, a holiday Hernandez says he has been celebrating every day since defecting from Cuba with seven others.

"Today for me is a very special day. Since Dec. 26 I have been free. I have my liberty, that in itself makes it special," said Hernandez, who also noted that it was the birthday of his youngest daughter, Steffi. "In Cuba, we know about Independence Day and we learn about it. For me, my first experience with the Fourth of July is today. Since Dec. 26, every day has been Independence Day."

Hernandez went eight innings, allowing six hits and three runs, two earned. After allowing two runs in the first — the third straight start he has struggled in the first inning — El Duque blazed through the Orioles lineup. He retired nine of the last 10 hitters he faced.

"As the game progressed, I tried to work ahead in the count, stay ahead of hitters, and throw strikes. The tricks of pitching you don't really share," Hernandez said. "It's not as important to have a good first inning as it is to be victorious at the end."

No matter how it happens.

Sunday, July 5, 1998 — Baltimore Orioles

Yankees 1, Orioles 0

Yanks find a way

Victory comes on hit-by-pitch

By TIM LEONARD, Staff Writer

NEW YORK — After the game the topic was history — all different kinds. There is the continuing saga of the 1998 Yankees' attempt to make history by establishing themselves as one of baseball's all-time great teams. There was the kind of performance from David Cone that made the 52,506 fans at Yankee Stadium flash back a decade or so. There also is "history," which can be used to describe the Baltimore Orioles' chances of making the postseason.

Though the Yankees routinely win, rarely are their victories routine. Such was the case Sunday, when Cone was masterful and the only run scored when Orioles starter Scott Erickson hit center fielder Chad Curtis with a 3-2 pitch with the bases loaded in the third inning. Cone made the run stand up, helping the Yankees raise their record to 61-20, which ties the 1902 Pittsburgh Pirates and 1907 Chicago Cubs for the best record after 81 games.

"The record means something to me. It means we've had a dominant first half. But we have to play a second half," manager Joe Torre said. "We get a chance here for a day or so to look back and see what we've done. We have three days to enjoy the hell out of it, then we get back into it Thursday."

The Yankees were 6-0 in their last homestand before the All-Star break and won their third straight one-run victory over the Orioles (38-50). Cone improved to 12-2, the most wins he has had

before the break in his career.

"This is a great way to end the first half, considering the support I've been getting," Cone said. "It's about time I picked us up. I've gotten a lot of runs this season."

The Yankees go into the All-Star break having occupied first place for 76 days. If they can duplicate a first half that has turned more heads than Cindy Crawford, they would finish the season with 122 victories and a .753 winning percentage. The 1906 Chicago Cubs went 116-36 (.763) to set records for most wins and highest winning percentage in a season. The 1954 Cleveland Indians (111 wins and a .721 winning percentage) hold the AL records.

"I don't think we think too much about it. We just go out and play and send out a quality starter," catcher Joe Girardi said. "The guys in here love to play. There's so much pride in this room as far as how we play the game."

Once again, they played well enough to win, as pitching and defense helped an offense that squandered a couple of early chances. Curtis struck out with the bases loaded in the first inning and Ricky Ledee did the same in the third. But the Yankees found a way to scratch out a run in the third.

Luis Sojo and Paul O'Neill stroked one-out singles to put runners on the corners. Erickson struck out Tino Martinez but walked Tim Raines to load the bases. He got ahead 0-2 before Curtis worked a full count. Then came the pitch that glanced off Curtis' left shoulder, forcing in Sojo.

"One-nothing on a hit batter. That's nuts," Torre said. "It was a strange game, but it was a hell of a game."

Cone made it so, allowing seven hits with four strikeouts and no walks in eight innings. He threw 110 pitches, 74 for strikes in an outing that was more efficient than overpowering. Cone utilized several arm angles in his delivery and a sinking fastball to keep the Orioles off-balance.

"This is the best I've ever been in my career in terms of being consistently ahead of hitters," Cone said.

Cone survived a few scary moments. Rafael Palmeiro hit a first-inning blast that landed less than 10 feet foul in the upper deck. In the fourth, Palmeiro sliced a drive into the left field corner, where Ledee ran over and appeared to make a leaping catch at the wall but lost the ball on the way down. Ledee picked up the ball and threw out Eric Davis at third. Curtis also made a strong throw home on Mike Bordick's fly in the fifth to prevent Cal Ripken from scoring.

When it was over, players scrambled out of the clubhouse to catch flights home for the three-day break. All had a message from Torre waiting at their lockers. It was brief and to the point:

"Enjoy the All-Star Break."

"Be careful."

"We have a lot of work to do in the second half and a long way to go."

Bring your history books.

Thursday, July 9, 1998
— at Tampa Bay Devil Rays

Yankees 2, Devil Rays 0

Pettitte rescues sluggish bombers

By KEN DAVIDOFF, Staff Writer

ST. PETERSBURG, Fla. — Yankees looked like a team coming off a three-day break Thursday night. They didn't hit much. The fielding was erratic. Mariano Rivera looked more like Mitch "Wild Thing" Williams at time. In short, this was no greatest team in baseball history.

But that has been the essence of these Yankees, especially since they lost Bernie Williams to injury: They don't always make it look easy. Yet they almost always win, and Andy Pettitte made sure that happened again Thursday night. Pettitte pitched eight scoreless innings, leading the Yankees to their seventh straight victory, 2-0 over the Devil Rays.

"We'll take whatever we can get," manager Joe Torre said, "but it's usually based on how we pitch."

They have pitched extremely well, especially their starters, and that's why their 62-20 record equals the 1902 Pirates for the best start in history. With David Cone and Rivera having shut out the Orioles on Sunday, 1-0, the Yankees have recorded back-to-back shutouts for the first time since July 4-5, 1989. They have not given up a run in 22 innings.

In their first regular-season game in the area George Steinbrenner calls home, the Yanks needed Pettitte's best start of the season and Joe Girardi's second-inning, two-run homer, one of just four Yankees hits. While raising his record to 11-5, the 26-year-old allowed five hits over eight innings, walked one, and struck out eight. He has a 5-0 record with a 2.24 ERA in his last seven starts, lowering his overall ERA to 3.66.

"He just didn't miss," Girardi said. "Good breaking ball, good change-up. That's the best his cutter has been all year."

Pettitte's cut-fastball runs in against right-handers, so it helped that Tampa Bay manager Larry Rothschild started eight righty batters (including switch-hitters). Pettitte didn't allow a Tampa Bay runner to reach third base until the eighth inning.

And what a bottom of the eighth inning it was. The first two Devil Rays went down without difficulty, then No. 9 hitter Miguel Cairo lined a single to center. Randy Winn hit a routine grounder to third that Scott Brosius bobbled for an error. Quinton McCracken battled his way to a walk, loading the bases with two outs.

Torre went out to talk to Pettitte and when Torre goes to the mound rather than pitching coach Mel Stottlemyre, that usually means a pitching change. This time, though, Torre asked Pettitte how he felt, the pitcher said he was fine, and Torre returned to the dugout.

"For three years, I've been waiting for him to do that, to not pull me," Pettitte said. "I wanted to say something funny, but it was a little too critical right there."

Third baseman Bobby Smith fouled Pettitte's first pitch meekly toward the visitors' dugout, then missed the next, a cutter, for strike two. He stroked the next pitch hard to second. Knoblauch fielded it and threw high to first base. Tino Martinez leaped for the ball and reached out to tag Smith, who was called out by first-base ump Al Clark for going out of the baseline.

"My heart stopped," Pettitte said. "Tino made a great play."

As for Knoblauch, who has had problems with routine throws all season long, he joked, "I knew [Martinez] could catch it."

Rivera struggled in the ninth, walking the first two batters — equaling his season total for 31 2/3 innings. He escaped, retiring pinch hitter and former Yankee Wade Boggs for the final out and his 23rd save, and the Yankees and Pettitte were free to celebrate.

Pettitte's last seven starts are all the more appreciated because in his previous six, he was 2-3 with a 7.64 ERA. Now that he is better, he thinks he knows the reason for his struggles: His wife Laura was home in Deer Park, Texas, giving birth to their second child. He hated being without his family.

"I wasn't even paying attention to what I was doing," Pettitte said. "I was coming out of the game not even knowing what I did to hitters. I was in a Twilight Zone."

Now, he's back to being himself. Even if the Yankees weren't quite themselves Thursday.

Saturday, July 10, 1998
— at Tampa Bay Devil Rays

Yankees 8, Devil Rays 4

Yanks, Irabu survive
Errors, walks mar victory

By KEN DAVIDOFF, Staff Writer

ST. PETERSBURG, Fla. —They could have called it Ugly Night at Tropicana Field on Friday, although it probably wouldn't have been a real hot ticket if they promoted it that way. The Yankees-Devil Rays game featured enough ugly baseball to fill two or three "Major League" movies. Ugly fielding, ugly pitching, ugly baserunning. Ugly ballpark, for that matter.

In the midst of all this ugliness, Hideki Irabu wasn't quite as ugly. The right-hander, facing a possible demotion from the starting rotation, pitched effectively enough to pick up his first victory in five starts and save his job, as the Yanks defeated Tampa Bay, 8-4.

"I liked what I saw today, no question," manager Joe Torre said of his starting pitcher. "I didn't expect it all back in one time, but I thought he pitched well tonight."

And so the beat goes on for this team's run at immortality. With their eighth straight win and their 12th of 13, the Bombers lifted their record to 63-20 and kept pace with the 1902 Pirates for the best start in baseball history.

For his fourth straight start, Irabu (7-3) couldn't make it through the sixth inning — this after having reached that mark in 10 straight.

But he showed grit by not allowing more than one run in any inning and escaping a jam in the bottom of the fifth. In 5 1/3 innings, he allowed three runs and seven hits, walked four, and struck out five. He allowed two homers, although one was an inside-the-park job by Tampa Bay's Dave Martinez.

The 29-year-old insisted he didn't feel the pressure to save his spot in the starting five. "More than that, I felt pressure to keep the ball down and throw hard strikes down in the strike zone," he said through his interpreter George Rose. "That's what a major league pitcher is supposed to be able to do, and that's the kind of pressure I put on myself today."

He looked like a man under pressure. His control was still off. He unleashed one wild pitch in the second inning that Joe Girardi described as "a hook that didn't break until it hit the back wall." His splitter was still not helpful, and his curveball was erratic.

But he brought the gas, a fastball that sailed between 91 and 94 mph, as opposed to the 88-91 of his previous three starts, which produced a 10.79 ERA. That proved to be enough against the worst team in the AL.

In the second, two walks and a wild pitch contributed to the run. In the third, Fred McGriff smoked a two-out, 1-0 pitch to the left field stands for a solo homer. And in the fourth, Chad Curtis misplayed Martinez's line drive to short center into the inside-the-park round-tripper.

Chuck Knoblauch's three-run homer knotted the score, 3-3, in the fifth, and then came the critical bottom of the fifth. Quinton McCracken knocked a hard grounder to Knoblauch, and the second baseman let the ball skip off of his glove for an error. Wade Boggs hit a grounder into the hole between short and third that Derek Jeter snared. Since McCracken was running on the pitch, Jeter had to go to first, and his short throw couldn't be picked up by Tino Martinez at first. Jeter was charged with an error.

When McGriff walked, Irabu had himself bases loaded, no out, and — with Darren Holmes warming up in the bullpen — no margin for error. First up, Paul Sorrento. Irabu worked the count full, then struck out Sorrento on a nasty outside fastball.

Next came Dave Martinez. The count went to 2-2 before the right fielder drilled a grounder right at Jeter. The shortstop started what should have been a routine 6-4-3 double play, but only Tino Martinez's scoop of yet another low Knoblauch relay prevented disaster and ended the inning.

"He actually gave us five outs to get out of the inning without giving up a run," pitching coach Mel Stottlemyre said. "I thought that was awesome."

The Yanks capitalized on two Tampa Bay errors in the sixth to take a 5-3 lead, and Irabu notched one more out before Graeme Lloyd took his place and rescued the Yanks from a first-and-third, one-out jam.

Scott Brosius' three-run dinger in the eighth assured that everyone in the road grays would leave this ugly domed stadium feeling good.

Reporter's Notebook:

Jeff Nelson (fractured right pinky toe) threw from a mound Friday for about 10 minutes and looked fine, Torre said. He could come off the 15-day disabled list as early as Tuesday.

Saturday, July 11, 1998

— at Tampa Bay Devil Rays

Yankees 2, Devil Rays 0

Cone wins No. 13

Yanks make it nine in a row

By KEN DAVIDOFF, Staff Writer

ST. PETERSBURG, Fla. — David Cone knows he's supposed to maintain his focus, see the forest through the trees and all that. He knows that's one of the reasons why the Yankees are on pace to post the best record in baseball history.

But he couldn't help himself Saturday night. Not after checking in with another superb outing, outpitching All-Star Rolando Arrojo to help the Yankees maintain their record pace. When he tossed eight shutout innings to give the Bombers their ninth straight victory, 2-0 over the Devil Rays at Tropicana Field, he lifted his record to 13-2 — the best start of his career.

"I'm thrilled," he said. "Considering what happened to me the last two years and earlier this year, I couldn't be happier."

Said catcher Joe Girardi: "That's the best stuff he's had all year. Same thing — everything worked."

In throwing the bulk of the Yanks' third shutout in their past four games, Cone helped the Bombers lift their record to 64-20, tying the 1902 Pirates for baseball's best start ever. The nine-game streak ties the Yanks' best of the season. The last time a Bombers team had two nine-game runs in the same season was 1961.

In lowering his ERA to 3.77, Cone threw 110 pitches, 64 of them for strikes. Manager Joe Torre never really considered letting his ace stick around for the ninth, saying, "We want him here all year."

Cone, of course, wanted to try to become the fourth different Yankees starting pitcher to notch a shutout, but he understood his manager's reasoning.

"It's tough to second-guess Joe Torre," he said. "He's protecting me, and I appreciate that."

Cone's first two starts of the season, in which he compiled a grisly 14.90 ERA over 9 2/3 innings, are too close in his mind to fret over not getting a shutout. So are the 1996 and 1997 operations to repair his pitching arm.

He struggled in the first inning Saturday, allowing a leadoff single to Randy Winn, who was caught stealing by Girardi. He gave up the first of his three walks to Wade Boggs but got out of the inning and rarely faced a crisis the rest of the way. He did so by contradicting conventional wisdom and starting hitters with off-speed stuff, then finishing them off with fastballs and a nasty back-door slider.

Arrojo got a two-strike count on the game's first batter, Chuck Knoblauch, then nailed him in the back for Knoblauch's American League-leading 12th hit-by-pitch. After Derek Jeter struck out looking (Knoblauch stole second during the at-bat), Paul O'Neill lofted a fly the other way. Tampa Bay left fielder Quinton McCracken went back resembling more a child dancing under the sun than a professional baseball player. He got a piece of it, but the ball went off his glove.

Knoblauch scored, and O'Neill slid in safely for a double after second baseman Miguel Cairo dropped the in-time relay throw.

Cone and Arrojo conspired to keep zeroes on the scoreboard for the next 5 1/2 frames, and the Yanks extended their lead to 2-0 in the seventh. Scott Brosius and Girardi had back-to-back singles, and Knoblauch's fly to center scored Brosius from third.

Mariano Rivera entered the game in the ninth and added some excitement by surrendering singles to Boggs and Paul Sorrento. But Rivera retired Dave Martinez on a comebacker and struck out pinch-hitter Bobby Smith to pick up his 24th save.

The Yankees offense has suffered since Bernie Williams went down with a sprained right knee last month, but the team has continued to dominate because of Cone and his fellow starters.

"Their guy pitched great," Girardi said Arrojo.

"But two was enough."

A crowd of 44,859, just the second sellout in Devil Rays history, took in the contest.

Reporter's Notebook:

Knoblauch's steal of second in the second inning gave the Yankees 99 stolen bases for the season, surpassing the 1997 Yankees' season total of 98.

Tuesday, July 12, 1998
— at Tampa Bay Devil Rays

Yankees 9, Devil rays 2

Bats finally come to life for Yankees

By KEN DAVIDOFF, Staff Writer

ST. PETERSBURG, Fla. — the 1998 Yankees could complain that they've been slumping — in the middle of their longest winning streak.

It's true, though. And they're not paranoid or whiny; they have been playing below their lofty expectations. The Concorde-like offense of the first two months had slowed to tricycle speed since Bernie Williams went down with a sprained right knee. That they continued to dominate was a tribute to their pitching.

Two early runs wouldn't be enough to support the arms in the road grays Sunday, though. Either the bats would wake up at Tropicana Field or a loss in front of Bay Area resident George Steinbrenner would take place.

The Yankees met the challenge, as they most always do, and once again the depth of this club showed itself. Homer Bush's aggressive baserunning lit the fuse for a seven-run ninth inning, sparking a 9-2 victory over the Devil Rays. The Bombers' 10-game winning streak is the best of the season and their longest since May 1994.

"Hopefully," manager Joe Torre said, "this is the start of something for us."

As if everything accomplished to this point was …what? Nothing? But what do you expect from a team that lifted its record to 65-20, tying those pesky 1902 Pirates for the best start in baseball history? From a team boasting a 15-game AL East lead over Boston, the largest by a Yankees club since 1958?

"We were winning games," Tino Martinez said, "but we weren't playing real well."

Particularly following the All-Star break. The Devil Rays, the worst team in the AL, had the winning run at the plate in the the ninth inning Thursday and Saturday before the Yankees emerged with a pair of 2-0 victories. Friday's 8-4 victory was a one-run game until the eighth.

Fast forward to Sunday, 2-2 in the ninth. David Wells had to leave after five innings, up 2-1, suffering from an ailing right big toe that he bruised Thursday. Ramiro Mendoza allowed the tying run in the sixth. The Yanks, after tallying runs in the second and third, could do nothing against the 1-9 Tony Saunders and reliever Albie Lopez.

With Devil Rays closer Roberto Hernandez on the hill, Darryl Strawberry looked at four straight balls for a leadoff walk in the ninth. That's when Torre inserted Bush to run for the veteran designated hitter. It was Bush's first appearance since June 30.

As Bush stepped on first base, he immediately took a daring 4 1/2-step lead off the bag — about as far as he goes when he's ready to steal. Torre signaled for Chad Curtis to bunt, and the center fielder put one down too hard, between the mound and first base.

"Once I saw the ball bunted down, I took off," Bush said. He beat Hernandez's throw to shortstop Aaron Ledesma in a close play, making it first and second. Scott Brosius did the same thing — a too-hard bunt, this one to Hernandez's right. The reliever could have had Bush, but he hesitated and his off-line throw to third was late.

After Ricky Ledee struck out, Chuck Knoblauch stepped into this bases-loaded, one-out situation and fell into an 0-2 hole. He looked at a 99-mph pitch for a ball outside, fouled off a 96-mph offering, then took an 85-mph splitter to the back of his left shoulder. He shook off the pitch and trotted to first, and Bush came home for the 3-2 lead.

From there, the floodgates opened: Derek Jeter hit a two-run single, Martinez clubbed a three-run double, and Jorge Posada stroked an RBI single. The sweep of the Devil Rays was complete, and a fan seated near the stadium organist requested — unsuccessfully — "New York, New York."

The rookie Bush has made it here, with this team, in his limited role. "Even in blowout games, I feel like I have to get a hit, just to make an impression on Joe," he said. Torre has noticed. Now, the manager hopes, his pinch runner will inspire his team to reach its potential.

Monday, July 13, 1998 — at Cleveland Indians

Indians 4, Yankees 1

Yankee-killer

Indians righty looks mighty Wright foils N.Y. again

By KEN DAVIDOFF, Staff Writer

CLEVELAND — Yankees, of course, insisted there was nothing special about playing the Indians on a Monday night in July. None of that playoff preview nonsense for this focused, one-game-at-a-time group. "Not yet," George Steinbrenner said. "I'm thinking about getting my team back together. Williams, Davis, and the rest of them playing."

Monday night, however, may have served as a peek into the more distant future, after the return of Bernie Williams and Chili Davis, and it was a hazy view. The Indians, who bounced the Yankees from last year's postseason, showed once again that they have the potential to do the same thing this October.

With a full house, including The Boss, taking in the action at modern, luxury-box-heavy Jacobs Field, Cleveland got the better of a Jaret Wright-Orlando Hernandez matchup, 4-1, to end the Bombers' 10-game winning streak.

The Yankees continued their offensive slump without Williams (sprained right knee).

"They're going to score some runs. We need to score runs to win here," said Paul O'Neill. "This is putting too much pressure on our pitchers."

The Yankees, whose 65-21 record ties them with the 1902 Pirates and 1912 Giants for the best start in baseball history, suffered their first loss since that memorable 2-1 squeaker to the Mets on June 28. That's 15 days without a defeat, for those scoring at home.

Nevertheless, this wasn't an "Oh well, we'll get 'em next time" kind of loss. Not with Steinbrenner in the house. Not against the Indians, who — if the season ended today — would have the second seed in the American League, setting up a possible New York-Cleveland AL Championship Series. Not against Wright (9-5), who has enemies in the Yankees' clubhouse due to his hit-by-pitches of Luis Sojo (in spring training) and O'Neill (on June 19 at The Jake), and who became the first pitcher this season to record two victories against the Yanks.

Wright, who has dyed his hair platinum blond since beating the Yanks in that June 19 game, lasted seven innings, allowing a run and eight hits, walking two, and fanning four. The Bombers left seven men on base.

"He didn't have as good stuff as the last time," Scott Brosius said of the powerful Wright, who beat the Yanks twice in last year's AL Division Series. "But he was able to move the ball around."

Wright surrendered the game's first run Monday night. With two outs in the fourth, Darryl Strawberry sent a long, high blast to the ballpark's deepest environs — the area in left-center field where the fence shoots out from a height of eight feet to 19. The ball hit a ledge just above the high wall, 419 feet from its liftoff point, and bounced back on the field. Second-base umpire Mark Johnson ruled it a homer, which prompted an unsuccessful argument from Indians manager Mike Hargrove.

Hernandez held onto that 1-0 lead for one entire batter. With one out in the bottom of the fourth, El Duque served up a juicy fastball away. Jim Thome, the Indians' top home run hitter, devoured it, slamming it 408 feet the other way into the left field bleachers. Tie game.

The next batter, Manny Ramirez, drew a walk, and Brian Giles ripped a double off the left-field wall, putting runners on second and third. Sandy Alomar's flare single to right drove Ramirez home for the 2-1 Cleveland lead. It snapped a string of 56 innings in which the Yankees had not allowed more than one run in an inning.

Thome ripped a triple off the left-center field wall in the sixth and scored on Ramirez's sacrifice fly, and Kenny Lofton — who is 5-for-8 lifetime against Hernandez — added a solo homer in the seventh.

El Duque lasted 6 2/3 innings in suffering the first loss by a Yankees starter since he dropped one to the Braves on June 23. He allowed eight hits, walked two, and fanned five, and the two home runs he gave up doubled the amount he had surrendered in 43 1/3 previous innings.

"I thought I pitched good," Hernandez said, with his catcher Jorge Posada interpreting. "I wasn't lucky. I pitched where I wanted the ball to go, and they got to it."

They, of course, are a pretty good team. Which is partly why Yanks general manager Brian Cashman, when asked if he's satisfied with his team, responded, "I'm comfortable. Am I satisfied? I can't say that right now."

Tuesday, July 14, 1998 — at Cleveland Indians

Yankees 7, Indians 1

Pettitte silencing his critics

By KEN DAVIDOFF, Staff Writer

CLEVELAND — When queried last week, Andy Pettitte confessed, somewhat apologetically, that he was not a student of baseball history. Ever heard of Honus Wagner, he was asked. The star of the 1902 Pirates, the team the Yankees have been racing for the best-ever start in baseball? Nope, he responded.

But he does know his own history rather well. He remembers his poor showing in last year's American League Division Series against the Indians. He needed to pitch well, for his own psyche, Tuesday night, in his first game against the defending AL champs since October.

And so he recorded some good history, good for himself and the Yankees. Pettitte, 26, pitched a complete-game nine-hitter, giving the Bombers a split of this two-game Jacobs Field series with a 7-1 victory.

"He wants to know that he's comfortable pitching in this ballpark," Joe Girardi said of Pettitte, "that he can win in this ballpark."

"It's nice to come in here and be on a roll, stay focused, and throw the ball good," said Pettitte, who acknowledged that the 0-2 record and 8.49 ERA he put up in October was on his mind.

In winning their 15th of 17 games, the Yankees lifted their record to 66-21, tying those 1902 Pirates for the best 87-game beginning stretch. They have not lost two straight games since June 15-16.

Pettitte (12-5), who had such a miserable May, is now on a roll worthy of his team. Since May concluded and his wife, Laura, 3-year-old son Josh, and newborn son, Jared, returned to New York from the family's Deer Park, Texas, home, the southpaw has put up a 6-0 record with a 1.76 ERA. In his past three starts, he is 3-0 with a 1.04 ERA.

"The season runs 162 games. There are slumps for pitchers and slumps for hitters," manager Joe Torre said. "The good ones are going to do what they're supposed to do. And that's what he's on his way to right now."

There was concern early that Pettitte was on his way back to trouble. Omar Vizquel knocked a flare single to right in the first, went to second on Manny Ramirez's hit to left, and advanced to third when Pettitte hit Jim Thome on the right forearm. That loaded the bases with one out, not a good situation considering the Yanks and Orlando Hernandez had been beaten the previous night by the Tribe and Jaret Wright.

But Pettitte escaped with minimal damage: Travis Fryman flied out to medium center field, scoring Vizquel on the tag-up, and former Yankee Mark Whiten hit into an inning-ending fielder's choice.

Chad Curtis, who signed a three-year, $6 million contract extension following the game, walked with one out in the second and Ricky Ledee followed with a blast to the right field wall. Curtis scored the tying run and Ledee made it to third for his first career triple.

> **"** The good ones are going to do what they're supposed to do. ... **"**
>
> *— Joe Torre*

The Yankees took a 2-1 lead in the third when Girardi walked, moved to third on Chuck Knoblauch's flare single to right, and, after Derek Jeter and Paul O'Neill struck out, scored on Tino Martinez's base hit to center.

Martinez added a double to left-center in the sixth, and Whiten gave his former teammates a gift when he misplayed Darryl Strawberry's short liner to left, missing on a sliding, backhanded catch and allowing the ball to go past him for a run-scoring double. Strawberry came out of the game for Tim Raines, and after the game Strawberry said the team is considering putting him on the 15-day disabled list so that he can rest his ailing left knee.

As the Yankees added insurance runs for Pettitte, the lefty cruised the rest of the way. He didn't strike out anyone, but he walked only two and hit one batter. Girardi said his batterymate had his best stuff of the season.

Reporter's Notebook:

Bernie Williams (sprained right knee) went 1-for-3 in his first game for Class AA Norwich at Portland, Maine, clubbing a double off the right-center field wall, hitting a sacrifice fly to left field, and drawing a walk. In seven innings, Williams made two putouts and cleanly fielded a single. The switch-hitter batted lefty and righty. He plans to play for Norwich today and Thursday and return to the Yankees on Friday in Toronto.

Wednesday, July 15, 1998 — at Detroit Tigers

Yankees 11, Tigers 0

Yankees show Tigers their entire arsenal

By KEN DAVIDOFF, Staff Writer

DETROIT — Perhaps the dingiest stop on their climb toward baseball history, the Yankees experienced a revival of sorts Wednesday night in Tiger Stadium.

Sure, they have been rolling since the second week of the season, but lately, all the wheels on this magic bus haven't been spinning just right. In the past month, Hideki Irabu had looked like a shadow of the pitcher who led the galaxy in ERA for a while. At the same time, the Yankees offense had not been the same since Bernie Williams went down last month with a sprained right knee.

Both components showed new life at one of baseball's oldest stadiums. Irabu continued his incredible dominance against the Tigers, and the offense gave him more than enough run support in an 11-0 thrashing of helpless Detroit.

The Yanks, at 67-21, kept pace with the 1902 Pirates for the best start in baseball history.

"These last four games, I've been working on getting it back," said Irabu through his interpreter George Rose, the "it" being the quality pitches that worked for him earlier in the season. "Tonight, I was able to get my stuff back."

Irabu entered the game out of the danger zone, thanks to his decent showing (5 1/3 innings, three runs) last week at Tampa Bay. But the Yankees wanted to see their right-hander continue his climb and not fall back to the 10.79 ERA he had put up in his final three starts of the first half.

Before the game, Jorge Posada told his pitcher to have fun. Against the Tigers, his favorite playmates, Irabu did just that. In winning his second straight start, Irabu (8-3) pitched eight innings, his longest outing since his first career shutout May 25. He allowed five hits and three walks while striking out one. His ERA dropped to 2.79.

"Overall, he was much more aggressive," pitching coach Mel Stottlemyre said. "That's what I wanted him to be."

His fastball showed movement and reached as high as 97 mph on the radar gun. His curveball was his best in months, and his splitter had its moments. He still had difficulty getting ahead of batters, but no one was complaining. He even picked Damion Easley off first base in the third inning.

"I could tell that he had fun today," Posada said.

"That's the best I've seen him throw since the last time we faced Detroit," said Dale Sveum, who had two hits, a run, and an RBI in a rare start at third base.

Irabu is now 3-0 with a 1.30 ERA in four career starts against Detroit. While manager Joe Torre downplayed the idea that his pitcher owns the Tigers, Irabu offered a playful laugh and said, "It's nothing like that. They're major-leaguers."

Not very good ones, though. While Irabu shut down the Tigers, the Yanks bided their time against 22-year-old Seth Greisinger for four innings before busting out with a three-run fifth. They added a pair in the sixth, and made it a laugher with a six-run eighth. The 11 runs were the Yankees' highest output since they beat the Expos, 11-1, on June 9, and the 13 hits their best of the second half.

"I think we're capable of scoring runs," said Paul O'Neill, who went 3-for-5 and hit one of the Yankees' three eighth-inning home runs. "When you have good pitching and you're going to score runs, you're going to be a good team."

"When O'Neill starts hitting the ball, it makes things easier for everyone else," Torre said. "It was a good night for us."

"I think they have a very good team," Tigers manager Buddy Bell said. "It was pretty evident that they were on a roll and we couldn't stop them."

Posada and Chuck Knoblauch added home runs in the eighth. Knoblauch now has three homers and 10 RBI since the All-Star break. Mike Buddie pitched a scoreless ninth for the Yankees' ninth shutout of the season, and the Yanks departed this dark place with a brighter-than-ever outlook.

Thursday, July 16, 1998 - at Detroit Tigers

Tigers 3, Yankees 1

Tigers show teeth

By KEN DAVIDOFF, Staff Writer

DETROIT — Warning: Too many pitchers' duels can be hazardous to a baseball team's health.

The Yankees haven't had a really bad showing by a starting pitcher since Hideki Irabu was pummeled two weeks ago, but they suffered their second loss of the week Thursday night, falling to the Tigers and Brian Moehler, 3-1, at Tiger Stadium.

"We should have saved a few runs from the night before, and we would have been all right," catcher Joe Girardi said, referring to an 11-0 victory Wednesday night.

Despite falling to 67-22, the Yanks kept pace with the 1902 Pirates, who also lost game No. 89, for the best start in baseball history. Their offense, despite what manager Joe Torre called a night of good swings, continued its recent pattern of hot-and-cold outings.

David Cone served as prey to the predator Moehler on this night. In a 2-hour 27-minute affair — maybe the players were trying to escape the smoke from a nearby fire that hovered over the ballpark — the veteran right-hander went the distance, allowing seven hits, walking three, and fanning seven. One of three runs he gave up was unearned. His ERA dropped to 3.66 and his record to 13-3.

Moehler, a 26-year-old right-hander, became the second pitcher to defeat the Yankees twice this season. Cleveland's Jaret Wright founded that list Monday night when he recorded a 4-1 victory.

"I don't throw against David Cone," said Moehler, who held the Bombers to a run in eight innings in a 2-1 victory here April 19.

"I throw against the hitters. I knew I couldn't give up a lot of runs."

He obviously listened to himself. On his second pitch, Moehler surrendered a Chuck Knoblauch homer to left field, the second baseman's third in three games.

Moehler wouldn't give up much of anything else through the eighth inning. Mixing sinkers and curveballs and using all of the strike zone, he let one Yankee get as far as second base. He scattered his seven hits over eight innings, didn't walk anybody, and fanned five.

"He pitched very well," Torre said. "Maybe not as well as when we faced him earlier this year here. He moved the ball around a lot. ...Starting in the fifth inning, I thought he started to settle in and make some better pitches."

Said center fielder Chad Curtis: "He's just a guy who, you see his stuff and you say, 'Oh, as soon as he makes a mistake, I'm going to get him.' He didn't make too many mistakes."

Neither did Cone, really. Through seven innings he cruised, allowing a fifth-inning solo homer to catcher Raul Casanova, recalled from Class AAA Toledo

earlier in the day.

Cone's slider, splitter, curveball — they all looked nasty.

Damion Easley, who had whiffed in his three previous at-bats, rocked a slider for a double off the left field wall with one out in the eighth, and Yanks pitching coach Mel Stottlemyre went out to the mound to lecture his charge. Mike Stanton continued warming up in the bullpen, but as Torre said, "I had to give David the chance to lose there."

Cone battled Bobby Higginson to a full count, then got him swinging on a beauty of a backdoor slider. One to go.

Up came cleanup hitter Tony Clark, and Cone didn't give him much to hit, walking him on five pitches. Outfielder Luis Gonzalez, who had three hits in his previous 28 at-bats, grounded the first pitch he saw, a splitter, to right field for a single. Paul O'Neill charged the ball, and in his zealousness to get Easley at home — which would have been nearly impossible — he threw it well over Girardi's head. That allowed Clark to score, and Gonzalez went to third. Cone struck out Geronimo Berroa for the final out, but the damage was done.

Derek Jeter led off the ninth with a bunt single off of Moehler, then relievers Sean Runyan and Todd Jones peacefully recorded the next three outs.

Friday, July 17, 1998 — at Toronto Blue Jays

Blue Jays 9, Yankees 6

Yanks get no relief

Jays explode in big seventh

By KEN DAVIDOFF, Staff Writer

TORONTO — Yankees were hoping they could compensate for the loss of Jeff Nelson internally. After Friday night, such a course of action is oh-for-one.

Darren Holmes got the Yankees into trouble at SkyDome, and Mike Stanton compounded the problem as the Yanks suffered their second straight loss, 9-6 to the Blue Jays. The Yanks, who hadn't lost consecutive games since June 15-16, fell to 67-23 but kept even with the 1902 Pirates for the best start in baseball history.

"Jeff Nelson's a big part of this club," said Holmes, who fell to 0-2 after retiring just one of the three batters he faced in Toronto's five-run seventh inning. "But we've got a whole bullpen full of guys who have had a lot of experience in late-inning roles."

Indeed, in Holmes, Stanton, and Mariano Rívera, the Yankees have three pitchers who have served as their team's primary closers. However, the current closer Rivera, who last pitched July 11, is useless if the setup men can't get the game into the ninth.

And that's what happened Friday night. What started as a pitchers' duel between Yanks surprise starter Ramiro Mendoza and Blue Jays legend Roger Clemens turned into an embarrassing forum for Holmes and Stanton. Holmes certainly didn't help his cause in taking over for Nelson, who is out for at least another four weeks with a lower back sprain and pinched nerve.

"It's time for Darren Holmes to shine," general manager Brian Cashman said Friday afternoon. Instead, the 32-year-old's already dull light dimmed, as he dropped to 0-2 and his ERA rose to 4.88. Now, Cashman will probably feel the heat from his boss to acquire a more reliable righty setup man. After making phone calls to fellow GMs on Friday, he found the market somewhat bare.

The lefty Stanton, meanwhile, was pummeled for six runs — including a game-breaking grand slam by Shawn Green — lifting his ERA to a ghastly 6.43. Toss in a few Joe Torre decisions that backfired, and it made for a grisly night in front of 39,172 fans at SkyDome, the Blue Jays' second largest home crowd of the season.

"It just didn't work out tonight," Torre said. "It's frustrating, but it's not aggravating."

About two hours before the first pitch, starter David Wells was scratched and pushed back to the first game of Monday's doubleheader against the

> **"Jeff Nelson's a big part of this club. But we've got a whole bullpen full of guys who have had a lot of experience in late-inning roles."**
>
> — *Darren Holmes*

Tigers, giving him three more days to rest his bruised and infected right big toe. During the game, Wells had the nail extracted from the toe by area podiatrist Glen Copeland.

Mendoza pitched well for 5 2/3 innings, allowing just a Shawn Green solo homer in the fourth to match the Yanks' one run in the fourth off of Clemens. Graeme Lloyd bailed him out of a sixth-inning jam.

Holmes came out of the bullpen to start the seventh and, on the first pitch of his audition, surrendered a single to left by former Yankee Mike Stanley. Pinch-runner Juan Samuel stole second, and another former Yankee, Tony Fernandez, poked a base hit through the left side, advancing Samuel to third.

Holmes struck out Ed Sprague, and his day was done. Stanton came in to face Darrin Fletcher and Toronto manager Tim Johnson countered with right-handed pinch-hitter Shannon Stewart, who struck out. Stanton needed just one out to keep Holmes' ledger clean and preserve the tie, but couldn't get it.

Alex Gonzalez drilled a 1-1 pitch over Chad Curtis' head for a ground-rule double, scoring Samuel for the 2-1 lead. Tony Phillips, making his first major-league appearance of the year after being purchased from Class AAA Syracuse earlier in the day, was walked intentionally after Stanton fell behind, 2-0, loading the bases for Green.

Torre pointed to the fact that lefties were hitting .167 against Stanton and Green was batting .192 against lefties.

In this case, the numbers were inconsequential.

Green hit a grand slam to straight-away center on a 3-2 pitch, his second homer of the night. The Jays held a comfortable 6-1 lead, SkyDome rocked, and somewhere in Tampa, Fla., the earth under George Steinbrenner shook.

Stanton allowed three more runs in the eighth, and there was some late-inning hullabaloo when home-plate umpire Ed Hickox issued a warning to Toronto pitcher Paul Quantrill after he hit Tim Raines with a pitch in the ninth inning — this after the always moody Phillips had nearly gone off when he took a Mike Buddie pitch to the back in the eighth.

But that was small-picture ugliness. The Yankees have to concern themselves with the big-picture ugliness, as in, their bullpen better shape up quickly.

"We get so many innings out of our starters right now that we're just not getting innings," Holmes said.

Saturday, July 18, 1998 — at Toronto Blue Jays

Yankees 10, Blue Jays 3

Bernie gets back with a bang

By KEN DAVIDOFF, Staff Writer

TORONTO — Like magic, Bernie Williams reappeared in the Yankees lineup Saturday afternoon, and all of their problems — problems 29 other teams would kill for — disappeared.

The Yanks' shaky bullpen didn't matter on this beautiful SkyDome day. That's because the club's other Achilles' heel, a struggling offense, came to life with the return of its cleanup hitter as the Bombers pounded the Blue Jays, 10-3, to end a two-game losing streak.

Starting at designated hitter to avoid straining his rehabilitated right knee on the artificial turf, Williams went 3-for-5 with a homer, two RBI, and three runs. He hit left-handed in all six plate appearances.

"It's like having all of your family here," Paul O'Neill said. "It's what this team is. We like each other, we've got a good team, and it's good to have everybody here playing, instead of a couple of guys in Tampa and one guy somewhere else. I think everybody relaxes when you get everybody back in the lineup."

"It feels good," said Williams, who spent much of the past month healing the sprained knee at the Yankees complex in Tampa, Fla. "It feels real good. Especially with the win."

The victory lifted the Yanks to 68-23, as they kept pace with the 1902 Pirates for the best start in baseball history.

Orlando Hernandez improved from his last outing, a loss at Cleveland, and held the Jays to one run and six hits in seven innings. Tim Raines went 3-for-4 and clubbed his sixth career grand slam, giving manager Joe Torre an enjoyable 58th birthday. He had been winless in his first two birthday games as the Yankee skipper.

"You see how important it was," he joked. "I brought in my closer."

Mariano Rivera did pitch, only because the right-hander hadn't made an appearance in a week. He yielded two solo homers in the ninth.

Williams woke up Saturday morning with no anxiety about returning to the team. He laughed when told of a Toronto newspaper column that stated a) that Williams' Puerto Rican heritage prevented him from being more popular in New York, thereby keeping the Yankees from meeting his contract demands; and b) that the Yankees had a five-year, $50 million offer on the table. Yanks general manager Brian Cashman called the first allegation "irresponsible," the second "inaccurate."

When Williams suffered his injury June 10, he was on a roll, having gone 30-for-65 (.462). His .353 batting average became the American League's best when Ivan Rodriguez hit a slump. But recently, Williams dropped from the leaderboard because he didn't have enough plate appearances.

"[Don] Mattingly always told me that he thought when he went on the DL, he always came back the way he was swinging when he went on," O'Neill said. "It might be a mental thing."

Might be. With a protective brace securing his knee, Williams first stepped to the plate with two out and O'Neill on first. He worked the count full before knocking a slow bouncer to second. As Williams sped down the baseline, former Yankee Tony Fernandez gloved the ball, then couldn't switch it to his right hand. It was the first of five Blue Jays errors, creating a bevy of Yankee scoring opportunities.

Blue Jays starter Juan Guzman struck out Williams in the third, but Williams knocked a soft line-drive single to right in the fifth. The homer came on the first pitch Williams saw from ex-Met Robert Person in the seventh. Williams walked in the eighth and finished with a hard single up the middle.

"In the first two at-bats, I was kind of anxious," Williams said. "Then I said to myself, 'Go out and have some fun.'" He has a .358 average, and should be back on top of the batting leaders in a few days.

El Duque, who had been knocked around Monday by Cleveland's left-handed hitters, was tagged for five hits in 14 at-bats by the Jays' lefties Saturday, so there's still some work to be done on that front. But in his most important confrontation of the day, he struck out lefty Shawn Green — whose two homers killed the Yanks on Friday — on a hard breaking ball with runners on second and third and two outs in the fifth. He totaled seven strikeouts while walking three.

"Every game, every inning, every hitter is an experience for me," said, Hernandez, with first base coach Jose Cardenal interpreting. "I approach each game like it was the last game in the World Series."

Saturday, getting to the World Series again seemed a very doable goal.

<u>Reporter's Notebook:</u>

In another bizarre news report, Fox Sports stated that the Yankees were interested in signing Mike Piazza should he enter free agency after the season. The Yanks always monitor the big-money free agents, but they're quite satisfied with Jorge Posada as their catcher of the future.

Sunday, July 19, 1998 — at Toronto Blue Jays

Blue Jays 9, Yankees 3

Yanks turn ugly
Pettitte gets hammered

By KEN DAVIDOFF, Staff Writer

TORONTO — On July 5, Derek Jeter played the Yankees' final game of the first half of the season and went straight from the Bronx to a plane bound for Denver, where he played in the All-Star Game. From the Rocky Mountains he headed southeast to Tampa, Fla., to meet his teammates for the start of the second half. Then came Cleveland, and Detroit, and finally Toronto.

With the final contest of this 11-game, four-city odyssey behind the Yankees late Sunday afternoon, Jeter — who endured 12 games and five cities — had his itinerary planned.

"I'm going to New York City," the Manhattan resident joked, speaking as though he were making his initial visit to the Big Apple. "I'm going to see the Statue of Liberty, the Empire State Building. I don't even know where I live."

That pretty much summarized Sunday's sloppy 9-3 defeat at the hands of the Blue Jays at SkyDome, the Bombers' third loss in four games and just the third time this season they have dropped a series. In falling to 68-24, the Yanks dropped behind the pace of the 1902 Pirates, whose 69-23 mark is the best all-time start after 92 games.

"I can't wait to get home," said Andy Pettitte, who was pounded for 1,316 feet worth of homers in suffering his first loss since May 31. "Three starts on the road, that's a long road trip."

The Yankees finished the trip 7-4, inconsequential in

the big picture, but as manager Joe Torre said, "When you win six of the first seven, it's not a good trip."

Sunday was not a good game for the best team in baseball. In addition to Pettitte's struggles, the Yanks were 3-for-12 with runners in scoring position and had two men picked off second base by Woody Williams (9-4).

"There's no excuses," catcher Joe Girardi said, dismissing the last-game-of-the-road-trip angle. "We just played bad."

Pettitte (12-6) was perfect through two innings and fanned Kevin Brown to start the third. At that point, with the Yanks up, 1-0, things fell apart. Craig Grebeck ripped a ground-rule double to left-center and Alex Gonzalez walked.

When Pettitte fanned Tony Phillips, Girardi's throw appeared to nail Grebeck trying to steal third, so much so that Pettitte started to head toward the dugout. But third base umpire Mark Johnson called Grebeck safe, and Gonzalez swiped second on the back-end of the double steal. The replay appeared to confirm the call, as third baseman Scott Brosius tripped while dealing with the throw and tagged Grebeck high.

"I think it probably looked funny to him because I was stumbling and bumbling," Brosius said.

Pettitte fell behind Shannon Stewart, then decided to walk him to load the bases. Pettitte knew he had enjoyed his share of success against the next batter, Jose Canseco, having held him to 5-for-22, a .227 average.

Canseco looked at two inside pitches, then ripped an over-the-plate fastball into the second deck in left field for a 389-foot grand slam.

"I made a mistake to Jose, and Jose can hit mistakes," Pettitte said. "It was just one of those games. I wasn't locating my fastball."

In the fourth and fifth innings, respectively, Chad Curtis and Paul O'Neill were picked off second base when Gonzalez sneaked behind the bag both times and took quick throws from Williams. More opportunities blown.

"There are not too many pitchers in the league who can wheel around like that to second," Curtis said. "I wasn't expecting that good a move."

A run in the fifth cut the deficit to 4-2, and Pettitte walked Stewart to start the bottom of the inning. One out later, Carlos Delgado cranked a Herculean blast to the fifth deck in right field, measured at 467 feet. Never before in SkyDome's 10-year history had a hitter reached that point.

"I knew I hit it pretty good, but I didn't think it would go as far as it did," Delgado said of his shot that cleared the Hard Rock Cafe.

In the seventh, Canseco did it again, ripping one 460 feet off the facing of the fifth deck in left field. That made it 7-3, and the Yanks packed it in after that.

"That was a bomb," Canseco said.

"I kind of lost my focus out there for a bit," said Pettitte, who tied his career high with seven walks. "You can't do that. It kind of got me out of my game plan."

He might as well have been speaking for all his teammates.

Monday, July 20, 1998 — Detroit Tigers

Game 1: Tigers 4, Yankees 3

Game 2: Yankees 4, Tigers 3

Yanks earn split of twi-nightmare

By KEN DAVIDOFF, Staff Writer

NEW YORK — Let's play three!

Apparently, a doubleheader on their first day home — after a grueling, four-city, 11-game road trip to start the season's second half — wasn't enough to whet the Yankees' baseball appetite. Their Monday twi-night doubleheader with the Tigers turned into an all-night, 26-inning affair.

Nine hours 11 minutes after David Wells threw the first pitch of Game 1, Brian Hunter made the last out of Game 2, as the Yankees gained a split with a 4-3 squeaker. Hideki Irabu (9-3) lifted his career record against Detroit to 4-0 and recorded his third straight victory, as he allowed three runs in seven-plus innings. Mariano Rivera notched his 25th save with a scoreless ninth.

Game 2, however, was the night's sprint. The Tigers outlasted the Yankees in the Game 1 marathon, 4-3, in 17 innings.

By the time the night's action had concluded, just a tiny fraction of the original 36,285 Yankee Stadium fans remained.

With his final out of the night, Hunter set a major league record with 13 hitless at-bats in a doubleheader.

Game 2 started at 10:32 p.m., and the American League lifted its 1 a.m. curfew because this is the Tigers last visit to New York this season.

"It was a hell of a game," said manager Joe Torre after the Yankees' Game 1 loss. "I'm just sorry we were on the short end."

Wells threw the Game 1 first pitch at 4:06 p.m., and Luis Gonzalez caught Bernie Williams' hard liner to left 5 hours 50 minutes later to end that contest, making it the longest Yankees game since the Bombers and Tigers played 18 innings in six hours on Sept. 11, 1988.

At least the Yankees won that one, riding Claudell Washington's homer to a 5-4 victory. In Game 1, however, they didn't score after the third inning and stranded 22 runners, 17 from the eighth inning on — falling one short of the 23 runners the 1927 Yankees stranded. Or, as Torre put it, "We left 326 guys on base."

Both teams used up their bullpens, and Torre admitted that he was asking remaining bench players Joe Girardi and Luis Sojo about their pitching arms. Williams, playing center field for the first time since returning from his sprained right knee, entered the game needing 11 plate appearances to requalify for the American League batting leaders. He tallied nine, although his long outing prompted Torre to bench him for Game 2.

The Tigers finally prevailed in the first game when Luis Gonzalez lined a single to center against the Yanks' seventh pitcher, Darren Holmes (0-3), to start the 17th. Gabe Alvarez flied out to right, and Paul Bako grounded one through the hole into left, moving Gonzalez to second. Joe Randa followed with a single to center, scoring Gonzalez for the lead.

Derek Jeter singled to lead off the bottom of the inning, but Paul O'Neill hit into a hard 6-4-3 double play, and Williams' flyout ended it.

Despite enough stranded runners to staff both sides of a football game, Torre expressed no disappointment with his team, saying, "I'm very proud of my ballclub.

They played hard." They turned five double plays, and Williams and Curtis each made excellent running catches in the outfield.

The Bombers loaded the bases in the eighth, 10th, 12th, and 15th innings and couldn't get a run home. The culprits were too many to list, but in defense of the Yankees, the Tigers helped themselves with several good defensive plays.

Tuesday, July 21, 1998 — Detroit Tigers

Yankees 5, Tigers 1

Jeter, Cone lift weary Yanks

By KEN DAVIDOFF, Staff Writer

NEW YORK — Derek Jeter was one of three Yankees to play all 26 innings in Monday night's marathon doubleheader. David Cone was one of three to play zero.

Together, they ensured that their team would log just nine innings Tuesday night. Cone regained the major league lead in victories with another excellent outing, and Jeter set a personal career high for homers in a season as the Bombers disposed of the Tigers, 5-1, for their 70th victory of this history-chasing campaign. A Yankee Stadium crowd of 35,980, including Old Timers Day invitee Jim Bouton, took in the action.

"I slept all day today," said Jeter. "I felt kind of [sluggish] at home, but once the game got going, once Coney kept us in the game, everything was all right."

As almost everything has tended to be with the Yankees this year. Yet again, coming off the long Monday night and the grueling, four-city, 11-game trip before that, the Bombers (70-25) showed off their resilience in winning their second straight and becoming the fastest Yankees team to reach the 70-win mark. The 1927 club started its World Series season 70-26.

"It's so important to handle bad things well," manager Joe Torre said. "That, to me, is important if you expect to get into the playoffs, because you can't let anything get off the focus on what you're doing."

Torre let his players sleep in Tuesday, canceling batting practice and requiring them to report by 6 p.m., merely an hour and a half before first pitch. At first it didn't look like the brightest move, as the Tigers scored thanks to a Damion Easley double, a cheap Bobby Higginson infield single (Cone was late in covering first), and a Scott Brosius error on a Tony Clark grounder.

First and third, one out, one run in, and another long night looked possible for the Yankees. But Cone bore down to fan Luis Gonzalez and induce Geronimo Berroa to pop to second.

"It's nice to pick up your defense," Cone said. "Scottie has played so well. It was nice to pick him up for a change."

From there, Jeter took over the game's second act. The shortstop went 6-for-12 during Monday night's virtual triple feature, pounding out two more hits than anyone else. Paul O'Neill went a respectable 4-for-12 and Chad Curtis 3-for-10.

When the team reported for work Tuesday, Torre told O'Neill he would be getting the night off. No, O'Neill told the skipper, Curtis needed the rest more than he did. Curtis, who had started every game since Bernie Williams' June 10 injury, said no, give Paul a rest. Torre chose to bench Curtis, although he would enter the game in the seventh as a defensive substitute.

Through all this, Torre never considered benching Jeter, and he was right not to do so. The 24-year-old showed no strain, pounding homer No. 11 to right to tie the game in the first. After the Yanks took a 3-1 lead in the second courtesy of four singles and a double play, Jeter walked to start the third, stole second and third, and came home on Tino Martinez's sacrifice fly. In the fifth, he made an excellent defensive play when he lunged to his left to grab an Easley grounder, spun, and threw him out.

"It's nice to be young," Torre said.

Cone was not going to lose his four-run lead, not with what he called "the best curveball of my career" and what Torre called the best stuff he's seen from the pitcher since he became the Yankees manager. The veteran righty went eight innings in lifting his record to 14-3, scattering eight hits, walking one, and fanning 10. He threw 134 pitches (89 for strikes), tying his Yankees high set Aug. 5, 1995.

He escaped a second-and-third, two-out jam in the seventh by catching Higginson looking at a fastball, and the Yanks cruised the rest of the way, having won the battle between Cone and Brian Moehler (10-7), a matchup they lost last week.

Wednesday, July 22, 1998 — Detroit Tigers

Yankees 13, Tigers 2

Yanks find nothing can deter El Duque

By KEN DAVIDOFF, Staff Writer

NEW YORK — Orlando Hernandez faced an obstacle course of energy-sappers Wednesday afternoon at Yankee Stadium. Never before had he started in the big leagues on just three days' rest. Never before had he pitched in such humidity at a major league ballpark.

Never before had he balked in a big league game.

Only the balk call, in the third inning by home plate umpire John Shulock, inspired El Duque to throw a tantrum worthy of John McEnroe. But the rookie right-hander managed to leap all of his hurdles, both natural and self-created, and last six innings to pick up the 13-2 victory over the Tigers. The Yanks have won three straight games since their 17-inning, 4-3 defeat in Game 1 of Monday's doubleheader.

"Anything that happens on the field, I'm not going to lose my focus," Hernandez said through his interpreter, Leo Astacio, after raising his record to 5-2. "If the sharks couldn't deter me, then I'm not going to let anything on the baseball field deter me from what I have to do."

The sharks to which he referred are those he battled on his raft ride to freedom, when he defected from Cuba late last year. If he dealt with them in a manner similar to how he dealt with his teammates and Shulock, have pity on the sharks.

The Yankees were up, 5-0, when El Duque walked Trey Beamon leading off the third. Damion Easley struck out, then Bobby Higginson lined a single to right. Tony Clark hit a grounder down the third base line that reserve Dale Sveum missed, and a fan touched it to make it a ground-rule double. Beamon scored, and Higginson advanced to third.

On his first pitch to Luis Gonzalez, Hernandez stepped off the mound improperly, resulting in the balk. Higginson came home, and El Duque became enraged, yelling at everyone around him, from Shulock to manager Joe Torre to catcher Jorge Posada to first baseman Tino Martinez.

"He was stubborn," Torre said. "Whether it's right or wrong, or whatever, we can't do anything about it. He was fine, but he was still disturbed by the fact that he didn't [balk]. He's very set in what he wants. Luckily, I had some support from my Spanish-speaking first baseman and catcher."

"After the balk, there was a lot of frustration," said Posada. "He was frustrated. I was frustrated because he wasn't listening to me."

"We just wanted to tell him that we had a lead there, to forget about it and get the next guy out," said Martinez.

When the hullabaloo finally ceased, after Torre used an official mound visit to calm his starter, Hernandez took charge. Gonzalez popped out to Derek Jeter, and Gabe Alvarez

flied out to left field to end the inning.

Paul Bako and Deivi Cruz started the fourth with singles, but Hernandez retired nine of the next 10 batters. By that time, the Yankees had a comfortable 10-2 advantage and El Duque had thrown 94 pitches. So Torre inserted Darren Holmes to start the seventh.

"I consider myself a pitcher who has to be aggressive," Hernandez said.

That's how he persevered through the heat, short rest, and emotional roller coaster to scatter seven hits, fan seven, and walk two. Throw in 12 hits of support, including homers by Chuck Knoblauch, Darryl Strawberry, and Posada, and it was just another American learning experience for El Duque.

Friday, July 24, 1998 — Chicago White Sox

Yankees 5, White Sox 4

Straw's two HRs lift Yanks to win

By GREGORY SCHUTTA, Staff Writer

NEW YORK — The stance is still there — bat held high, legs spread wide, and the menacing stare in from atop his 6-foot-6 frame. But the days of Darryl Strawberry sending moonshots into the New York air 35 times a season are long gone.

New York fans, however, never forget, and 44,264 of them called the 36-year-old slugger out for one of his patented curtain calls Friday night after his 422-foot blast over the center field fence gave the Yankees the lead for good in a 5-4 victory over the Chicago White Sox. The win was the fourth straight for the Yankees and 72nd of the season, leaving the Bombers one game behind the pace of the 1902 Pittsburgh Pirates for the best record in major league history.

"There's no greater feeling in the world than to be able to do that in front of a New York crowd," Strawberry said. "It's always a thrill and always will be one."

Especially considering Strawberry has been hobbling around on bad knees since spring training. But when he gets hold of a pitch, it ignites a crowd like nothing short of a Mark McGwire homer has in 1998.

Strawberry blasted two round-trippers Friday night. The first, a solo shot into the second deck in right field in the fourth inning tied the game, 3-3.

In the sixth, after the White Sox, had taken a 4-3

lead, Strawberry again showed off the bat speed that terrorized the National League for 11 years by sending left-hander Bryan Ward's 3-2 pitch into center field, just missing the black bleachers, for a 5-4 lead. It was his third homer in two games, his second multihomer game of the season, and the 30th of his career.

"That's Darryl," manager Joe Torre said. "I don't get awed by his shots any more. He did it enough times against me. It's nice that he's doing it for me."

It's nice that he's doing it for anybody. Strawberry has been struggling physically since undergoing arthroscopic surgery on his left knee last June. It's been worse lately since the Yankees opened the second half of the season on the hard artificial turf in Tampa Bay.

"Before spring training, I wasn't hopeful of getting much out of him because of what I saw him go through last year," Torre said. "But Darryl at half-speed still scares people. He's still a threat. He still helps the batter in front of him because pitchers don't want to face him."

And he still leads the Yankees with 15 homers, one more than Paul O'Neill, who had a two-run blast in the first inning.

"The knee is feeling better lately," Strawberry said. "I've been able to keep my back leg planted. Before I wasn't able to dig in like I want to and I've been bringing the leg up and reaching for balls."

"Darryl works hard," Torre said. "He knows that there are times that he needs a day off and that there are times that we can't give him a day off. Some days when I don't put him in the lineup, he'll come in here and thank me for the day off. But every time I ask him how he feels, he says, 'Whatever you want to do.'"

It was the second straight game the Yankees hit three homers. The homers made a winner out of Andy Pettitte, even though the left-hander pitched with less than his best stuff.

Pettitte, coming off a tough outing in a 9-3 loss at Toronto on Sunday, gave up four runs, two of them earned, on eight hits while striking out six in seven innings. But when the White Sox had a chance to break the game open with the bases loaded and one out in the fifth inning, Pettitte slammed the door by striking out Robin Ventura and Magglio Ordonez.

"I'm happy," Pettitte said. "I felt like I scuffled even though I was never able to get in a groove. But I got some big outs when I needed them. But I'm still falling behind a lot of guys, and I can't do that."

Reporter's Notebook:

A developer wants to build a new stadium for the Yankees next to a $1.2 billion office, hotel, and rail station he is building in Secaucus.

William McCann, president of Allied Junction Corp., said he has spoken with "high-level" officials in Governor Whitman's administration about his proposal.

But a spokeswoman for the governor said discussions about a possible site for the Yankees in New Jersey are pointless because owner George Steinbrenner has not committed to moving the team.

This article contains material from The Associated Press.

Saturday, July 25, 1998 — Chicago White Sox

White Sox 6, Yankees 2

Irabu, Yankees get socked around

By GREGORY SCHUTTA, Staff Writer

NEW YORK — History was on parade Saturday as the Yankees welcomed back some of their all-time greats for the 52nd annual Old Timers Day. But when the pitching and swinging started for real, the current Yankees didn't exactly have a day for the record books.

Hideki Irabu gave up eight hits and six runs over six-plus innings as the Yankees fell to the Chicago White Sox, 6-2, in front of a crowd of 55,638 at Yankee Stadium. The loss brought their four-game winning streak to an end and put the Yankees (72-26) two games off the pace of the 1902 Pittsburgh Pirates for the best start in major league history.

"We just didn't pitch well enough to win," said manager Joe Torre. "When you give up six runs, you can't expect to win a game like that."

Irabu, who had won three straight games following the All-Star break, breezed through the order the first time around, retiring 11 of the first 12 and facing the minimum through four innings. But his luck wasn't as good the second and third times.

Albert Belle, who has been on fire since the All-Star break, Robin Ventura, and Greg Norton erupted for consecutive singles against Irabu to start the fifth and seventh innings and ignite rallies that resulted in two and four runs against the right-hander.

"Around the cleanup area I had a lot of trouble," Irabu said after tying his career high as a starter by allowing six runs. "There was one guy I was able to keep at bay [Frank Thomas, who went 0-3] but the other guys got a lot of opportunities."

And they took advantage. In the fifth inning, Norton rapped the third straight single against Irabu to drive in Belle and tie the score, 1-1. Paul O'Neill then snagged a fly off the bat of Magglio Ordonez and sent a strike to Jorge Posada at home, but the catcher failed to block the plate and Ventura slid in behind him for a 2-1 White Sox lead.

"On a thing like that everything happens so fast," Posada said. "You just have to learn to wait for the ball instead of trying to go out and get it."

The Yankees tied the score in the sixth on singles by Bernie Williams and Tino Martinez and a sacrifice fly by Posada, but the White Sox put it away with four more runs in the seventh.

This time they erupted for four straight singles against Irabu with Norton driving in Belle and Ordonez singling in Ventura for a 4-2 lead. That was it for Irabu (9-4), but not for the White Sox.

Darren Holmes relieved, but didn't have much luck. Mike Cameron sent a slow bouncer to first and Norton slid in just ahead of Martinez's throw to Posada at home for a 5-2 lead. Chad Kreuter struck out, but Ray Durham singled in Ordonez for a 6-2 lead.

Mike Buddie eventually stopped the bleeding, but not before walking Thomas to load the bases and getting Belle to pop to second to end the inning. Buddie retired the final seven batters to face him.

"I thought he had good stuff," Torre said of Irabu. "He just couldn't get past that part of the order."

"I didn't think I was bad today," Irabu said. "But near the end, I think I got the ball up and that hurt me."

"He just ran out of gas," Posada said.

But the manager said it was more than that.

"I think the key was that he got behind on a lot of guys. When you get behind, they can do a lot of things like sending the runner," Torre said. "We lucked out a little bit last night when Andy Pettitte was getting behind, but not today."

The Yankees got on the board first when Homer Bush led off the third inning by stretching a shot into left field into a double and eventually scored on a Derek Jeter single. But they wasted a leadoff double by Scott Brosius in the fifth as Bush grounded out, Chuck Knoblauch, playing his first game of the sea-son at designated hitter, was caught stealing after a walk, and Jeter flew out to center.

Trailing by four runs in the bottom of the seventh, Bush singled with one out and Knoblauch walked. But Jeter struck out and Paul O'Neill hit into a force play to end that threat.

Mike Sirotka scattered eight hits over six innings and allowed just two runs to earn his 10th win of the season. The Yankees were their own worst enemies, leaving nine men on base.

Sunday, July 26, 1998 — Chicago White Sox

Yankees 6, White Sox 3

Bernie ball
Hot bat carries Yankees

By GREGORY SCHUTTA, Staff Writer

NEW YORK — When the Yankees won 24 of 31 games while Bernie Williams was on the disabled list with a sprained knee, some people wondered how much the Bombers missed the switch-hitting center fielder. If you ask manager Joe Torre, the answer is, "a lot."

Barely a week off the disabled list, Williams smoked a Jaime Navarro slider into the right field stands to snap a tie in the sixth inning as the Yankees dumped the Chicago White Sox, 6-3, Sunday. The victory was No. 73 for the Yankees and capped a 5-2 homestand.

"It's a matter of having the whole team together," Torre said as his team prepared for its second and final trip to the West Coast. "It takes the pressure off of one guy to try to do it all. A guy like Paul O'Neill can go hitless, but I still like having him in the line-up every day."

David Wells (12-2), who was bumped back a day from his scheduled start because of gout in his right foot, pitched into the eighth inning and struck out 10 batters despite having less than his best stuff. He made two big mistakes, both of which left the park.

Albert Belle hit the first one, sending his 31st homer of the season and 12th since the All-Star break over the fence in left field to lead off the second. And Ray Durham sent a two-run blast over the 408-foot sign in center field with two out in the fifth.

So it was Williams to the rescue. He doubled to the

base of the wall 399 feet away in left-center field to lead off the second and scored on Jorge Posada's 11th homer two outs later.

Williams stroked a two-out single in the third to drive in Chuck Knoblauch for a 3-1 lead.

But the big hit came in the sixth, when Williams ripped Navarro's first pitch of the inning into the stands in right to give the Yankees the lead for good, 4-3. Right fielder Magglio Ordonez barely had time to turn and watch it.

> **❝He's a different pitcher from the guy I saw last year. He finds ways to adjust and get back in sync when he struggles.❞**
>
> — *Joe Torre*
> *on pitcher David Wells*

"I've really been seeing the ball well," Williams said. "It started when I came back in Toronto [July 18]. I spent a couple of days on rehab in Portland [with Class AA Norwich] and got my timing down. It just went from there."

And it hasn't stopped. Williams blasted a homer in his first game back against Toronto and is batting .371 (13-for-35) since his return. He's also leading the American League in batting with a .355 average.

"Every time I come back from an injury, it's a struggle to get back to action," he said. "The physical part of the game isn't always there right away. But as long as I prepare like I always do and get the mental part of the game down, I'm OK."

In the past, the mental part of the game has sometimes been a problem for Wells. But Torre and his teammates have seen a slight change this season.

"He's a different pitcher from the guy I saw last year," Torre said. "He finds ways to adjust and get back in sync when he struggles."

And he struggled in the fifth inning, walking two batters before Durham's home run and committing an error at first base on the next batter after the homer. But he struck out Frank Thomas for the second time to end the inning.

In the seventh, with runners on first and second, Wells induced a pop-up from Thomas on an inside fastball to end that threat. Thomas went 0-for-4 against Wells with two strikeouts. Wells also fanned Belle, Wil Cordero, Mike Cameron, and Robert Machado twice each.

"He didn't have his best stuff out there, but he battled," Posada said. "He definitely had a good curveball working, but he was really only a two-pitch pitcher out there instead of having all four of his pitches. But he came out and battled. It was a good outing."

And it makes the long ride to the West Coast an easier trip. The Yankees opened the season there, going 1-4 in their first five games and prompting the question "What's wrong with the Yankees?"

The won their next two games to return home 3-4 and have gone 70-22 since.

"It's just another road trip for us," Torre said. "I don't think there's any baggage out there that we have to take care of. We're at a point now where we just want to go out every day, play our game, and hold our own."

"We had a meeting after the fourth game of the season," Williams said. "We all knew that this team was better than it played those first four games. That meeting is what turned the season around for us. We just have to continue to play with the same attitude we had after that meeting."

Tuesday, July 28, 1998 — at Anaheim Angels
Yankees 9, Angels 3

Sky-high Yanks ground Angels

By KEN DAVIDOFF, Staff Writer

ANAHEIM, Calif. — Like the class loser who has since become a multimillionaire, the Yankees made their return to Edison Field a triumphant one Tuesday night, pounding the Angels, 9-3.

David Cone pitched seven strong innings to become the major league's first 15-game winner, and Derek Jeter, Darryl Strawberry, and Bernie Williams homered to pace a 14-hit New York attack. In short, the Bombers, who are now 74-26 after the 100-game mark, did everything Tuesday night that they didn't do the first time they were in Anaheim.

It's hard to believe that this history-chasing juggernaut began its memorable 1998 campaign with a flat 0-2 record here. "That seems like April of three years ago," Mike Stanton said. Then, the sky seemed to be falling. Now, with the team's biggest concern whether to pursue a trade for Randy Johnson, the sky is the limit.

Anaheim has turned out to be a pretty good team,

currently holding a one-game lead over the Rangers in the American League West, and if the season ended now, the Yanks and Angels would face off in the playoff's first round. But behind the inept starting pitching of Jason Dickson (9-8) and three errors, the Angels didn't do themselves proud in front of 36,241 fans, many of whom rooted for the visitors.

The last time the Yanks were here, they had no idea of the roller coaster that Cone (15-3) would ride. His first two starts went so poorly that the veteran right-hander contemplated retirement after this season.

Since then, of course, he has remade himself as the wiser, more economical pitcher he strived to be in spring training. Tuesday night was not one of his sharper performances of late, but that's more a reflection of how dominant he has been than of any shakiness he displayed Tuesday. The righty allowed three runs (one earned) and six hits in seven innings, fanning six and walking two. His ERA is now 3.33, low enough to merit the Cy Young Award talk that has been directed toward him.

He has not allowed more than two earned runs in his past seven starts, and his 135 1/3 innings pitched for the season means that barring injury, he can cruise to the 200 he needs to activate his option for 1999.

The Yankees quickly showed that they have no aversion to Edison Field, as their second batter Jeter blasted a homer to straight-away center.

That proved to be an appetizer for the main course, served by Dickson in the second inning. Tino Martinez started it with a nubber between the mound and third base that Dickson couldn't handle, creating the cheapest of singles. Strawberry balanced that one by powering an outside offering over the left field fence for his team-leading 16th homer.

Chad Curtis singled off the glove of Angels third baseman Dave Hollins, and Scott Brosius knocked another infield single, this one fielded by shortstop Gary DiSarcina after Hollins started to pursue it in the hole, then backed off.

Curtis then beat Dickson's throw to third on Joe Girardi's bunt back to the mound. With the bases loaded, Chuck Knoblauch checked his swing on a 3-2 pitch, according to first base ump Jim McKean. That scored Curtis for the 4-0 lead, and Paul O'Neill's sacrifice fly to center sent Brosius home.

The Angels chipped away at the Yanks' lead, as Tim Salmon ripped a solo homer in the second and Williams misplayed Darrin Erstad's base hit to center for an error, allowing Jim Edmonds to score from first. Williams made up for his miscue with an oppo-

site field dinger to left in the fifth, giving the Bombers a 6-2 advantage.

Two Angels errors in the sixth led to three more Yankees runs, and the game was officially a blowout.

Wednesday, July 29, 1998 — at Anaheim Angels
Angels 10, Yankees 5

Angels give Yankees taste of their own

By KEN DAVIDOFF, Staff Writer

ANAHEIM, Calif. — They wanted to make a movie about him. That, reportedly, was the Angels' pitch to Orlando Hernandez when he was a free agent back in spring training

El Duque, of course, went with the Yankees' green over the Angels' celluloid — and he reportedly still has a deal for a film biography. Fortunately for the Cuban refugee, there will be no movie based on the way he pitched Wednesday night.

In his first start against the team he could have joined — and what could have been his last start this season, should the Yanks acquire Randy Johnson or another starter this week — Hernandez pitched the worst game of his young major league career, suffering a 10-5 defeat at Edison Field. The Cuban refugee lasted just 3 1/3 innings and was shellacked for 10 runs and 13 hits, more than any Yankee starter has allowed this season. Overall, the Angels' 19 hits were the most by a Yankees opponent this year.

Angels manager Terry Collins inserted five lefty hitters into his lineup, and that proved to be a bright move, as the quintet went 9-for-13. Left-handers are now batting .348 (48-for-138) against El Duque. His ERA rose from 2.43 to 3.84 while he fell to 5-3.

The fourth inning ranked as one of the 1998 Yankees' ugliest, right up there with the 11-run third inning they allowed to Boston on May 31 and the 8-run Oakland fifth in the memorable April 10 home opener.

Among the lowlights: Garret Anderson started the madness with a liner to right that tipped off Paul O'Neill's glove after the right fielder appeared to react late to it. Dave Hollins followed with an ordinary grounder to right, and when O'Neill took his time fielding it, Hollins hustled for a double.

Two runs later, Orlando Palmeiro crushed a two-run double to right-center, then got caught between second and third. But the Yankees weren't positioned properly for the rundown, and Jorge Posada had to run to cover third. In his haste, he dropped a throw from Derek Jeter.

Tim Salmon's two-run homer to left made it a 10-2 game, and El Duque was through. He took off his cap, exposing his shaven head to the crowd, and jogged back to the Yankees dugout.

From the beginning, the Angels seemed to have little difficulty solving the mystery of El Duque. They hit the ball hard consistently in the first and scored two runs in the second on three straight hits and a Justin Baughman bullet that went off Hernandez's left leg to Jeter for a run-scoring, 1-6-3 groundout.

Darryl Strawberry slammed his fifth homer in his past 25 at-bats to give the Yanks a 1-0 lead in the top of the second, and Jeter's rocket over the right field wall tied the game at 2-2 in the third.

Thursday, July 30, 1998 — at Anaheim Angels

Yankees 3, Angels 0

Yanks leave Disneyland happy

By KEN DAVIDOFF, Staff Writer

ANAHEIM, Calif. — The 1998 Yankees started the season with an Andy Pettitte-Chuck Finley matchup at Edison Field and have undergone minimal changes since. Only Willie Banks and Dale Sveum are no longer members of the team, while Chili Davis has been hurt since departing Disneyland's hometown.

How fitting, then, that on what could have been the last night before the Bombers undergo dramatic alterations, Pettitte and Finley faced each other once again. This time, they both lived up to their billing, throwing zeroes on the scoreboard and posting no-decisions. And this time, the Yankees won, 3-0 in 10 innings.

In lifting their record to 75-27, the Yankees showed once again that the Randy Johnson rumors may intrigue them, but they don't distract them.

Derek Jeter drew a walk from Rich DeLucia (1-4) to start the 10th and stole second. DeLucia then issued free passes to Paul O'Neill and Bernie Williams, and that was the end of his night.

Southpaw Mike Holtz entered, and the Angels moved their infielders in. Holtz jumped ahead of Tino Martinez, 0-2, and allowed a grounder to first

that may have been an out under normal circumstances. But the drawn-in ex-Yankee Cecil Fielder couldn't get to it. The ball rolled by the diving Big Daddy and scored Jeter and O'Neill for the game's first runs. Williams scored from third on Chad Curtis' flyout to right for a 3-0 lead.

Ramiro Mendoza lifted his record to 6-2 with two scoreless innings in relief of Pettitte, and Mariano Rivera notched his 28th save.

Earlier this week, Joe Torre said that a victory against Finley would be meaningful, to have that confidence against him should these two teams cross paths in the playoffs. Now, Finley will have the mental edge. In 15 innings against the Yanks, he has an 0.60 ERA.

It hasn't been an easy ride for the Angels' platinum blond southpaw. In a span of 10 days, he suffered three unusual injuries. First, on July 15, he lacerated his knee while sliding across the base path on a tag attempt. That required eight stitches.

Three days later, he was hit on the right forearm by a line drive off the bat of Joe Carter while sitting in the Angels dugout at Edison Field. And six days after that, he was sitting in the visitors dugout in Kansas City when Jeff King's liner struck him in the pitching arm. That caused his start against the Yankees to be pushed back from Wednesday to Thursday.

On this night, though, he showed no wear and tear. While Pettitte lasted seven innings, scattering seven hits, walking three, and fanning four, Finley made it through eight frames, allowing just four hits, issuing four bases on balls, striking out nine.

Just because it was a pitchers' duel in the early going didn't mean there weren't opportunities. In the third, the Yankees loaded the bases with two outs, then Finley caught Martinez looking at a third strike. The Angels put runners on first and second with one out in the fifth, only to see leadoff batter Justin Baughman hit into an inning-ending, 1-6-3 double play.

The Bombers looked to have something going in the sixth when Williams led off with a walk and Martinez knocked a single to left. But their aggressive style, which has led to so many victories this season, backfired: Williams ran on a 1-2 pitch in the dirt that Tim Raines waved at, and Angels catcher Matt Walbeck nailed the center fielder for a strike 'em out, throw 'em out double play. Shane Spencer walked to keep the rally alive, and Scott Brosius put the rally to rest a moment later when he couldn't beat out a nubber to second.

Dave Hollins' two-out bunt in the bottom of the sixth caught the Yankees by surprise and gave the Angels first and second. No problem for Pettitte: He retired the red-hot Garret Anderson on a grounder to first.

Pettitte recorded the first two outs of the seventh without difficulty, then Gary DiSarcina reached first when he knocked a sky-high bouncer to third that he easily beat out for an infield single. Baughman followed with a line-drive single to right-center, moving DiSarcina to third, and Baughman advanced to second when Pettitte's first pitch to Darin Erstad bounced for a wild pitch.

Erstad swung at that pitch, took the next one for a strike, and took the next three for balls. With the count full, he offered a slow grounder to third that Brosius grabbed and threw to first in time.

Friday, July 31, 1998 — at Seattle Mariners

Yankees 5, Mariners 3

Irabu overcomes anxiety

By KEN DAVIDOFF, Staff Writer

SEATTLE — You looked at Hideki Irabu's facial gestures and body language Friday afternoon and you thought you had traveled back in time to 1997, when the man known then as the "Japanese Nolan Ryan" alienated teammates, umpires, and interpreters with his icy personality.

You watched Irabu pitch Friday night at the Kingdome and you knew you were safely based in 1998.

With trade rumors swirling around the right-hander, Irabu worked through his stress and checked in with a solid outing, leading the Bombers to a 5-3 victory over the Mariners. All of the Mariners' runs came on solo homers, and the Yanks hit three of their own, two catcher Jorge Posada.

Irabu (10-4) lasted seven-plus innings, allowing six hits, striking out five, and walking one. Mariano Rivera pitched the ninth for his 29th save.

Considering how Irabu looked before he threw his first pitch, an observer would have predicted disaster. When he first learned that he was on the trading block, he was in good spirits, according to friends. But by Friday, he was testy, rarely speaking.

And word got to Joe Torre. "Probably," the manager said when asked if Irabu was upset. "But we can't do anything about it. Some people are more on edge than other people.

"You don't trade somebody like Randy Johnson for someone you don't use," Torre continued, explaining that Irabu should be flattered. "For every team that trades somebody, there's the other team that wants him."

The Yankees struck first in the second with a pair of long doubles. Chad Curtis started the inning with a blast to center field that hit the base of the wall. After Posada whiffed, Shane Spencer drilled a liner to right-center that hit the wall just above the glove of the diving Ken Griffey Jr. Curtis scored easily for the 1-0 lead.

Posada and Scott Brosius each delivered solo homers in the fourth, and Seattle's Alex Rodriguez cut his team's deficit to 3-1 in the fourth with his 32nd round-tripper. Curtis singled home Tim Raines in the fifth to give the Yanks a 4-1 advantage.

Edgar Martinez and David Segui went deep on consecutive pitches in the seventh to make it 4-3 game, and Posada's second dinger, in the eighth, pushed the Yanks' lead back to two runs.

Irabu allowed a leadoff single to Shane Monahan in the eighth, and that was it for him. Mike Stanton entered and promptly gave up a walk to Joey Cora, putting himself in a first-and-second-none-out situation with Rodriguez, Griffey, and Martinez due up.

Stanton escaped. Brosius made a leaping catch of a Rodriguez liner, Griffey looked at a third strike, and Martinez hit a blast that Spencer caught up against the right field wall.

<u>Reporter's Notebook:</u>

Chili Davis (surgically reconstructed right ankle) went 1-for-4 with a single Friday for Class AA Norwich …Darren Holmes, suffering from back stiffness, was unavailable Friday night.

Saturday, August 1, 1998 — at Seattle Mariners

Yankees 5, Mariners 2

Yanks feeling their oats

By KEN DAVIDOFF, Staff Writer

SEATTLE — This one was a masterpiece, which was appropriate considering its historical significance. When they combined superb starting pitching with timely power and defense to defeat the Mariners on

Saturday, 5-2, the Yankees raised their record to 77-27.

Fifty games over .500. On Aug. 1. No team in baseball history has put together a better record after 104 games. Only the 1902 Pirates did as well.

"I always base what we do on being five games over .500, then 10 games over … increments of five," manager Joe Torre said. "I remember last year how excited I was to finish the season 30 games over. This is pretty rarefied air here."

"This team has tremendous perspective," David Cone said. "We know that anything can happen. That being said, it's a significant achievement."

Against the Mariners' Jamie Moyer, the pitcher who dropped the Yankees to new lows back in April, the Bombers reached new heights. David Wells provided the mound heroics, Derek Jeter and Tino Martinez fronted the offensive attack, and Martinez made the defensive play of the game. In all, the first day of life without the Randy Johnson rumors couldn't have gone much better.

The calendar read April 6 when the Yankees entered the Kingdome and proceeded to get pummeled, 8-0. Moyer, who succeeds with off-speed trickery, limited the Bombers to three hits and a walk in seven innings, dropping them to a humbling 1-4 record.

"We were not happy," Cone recalled. "Top to bottom, everybody here was miserable. We were thoroughly embarrassed."

The season turned around the next day, and the Yanks hadn't faced Moyer since. They almost scored in the first, but Derek Jeter was called out at home by umpire Tim Welke despite replays showing Jeter was safe. Then Wells started his day by serving up a single to Joey Cora and a two-run homer to Alex Rodriguez.

Any thoughts of deja vu diminished as the day progressed. Jorge Posada singled home Martinez in the second for one run. Martinez crushed a solo homer into the right field upper deck to tie the game in the fourth. Jeter's dinger to left gave the Yanks a 3-2 lead in the fifth. Run-scoring doubles by Bernie Williams and Tim Raines in the eighth gave Wells a three-run cushion.

By the time Moyer left in the eighth, he had been knocked around for 11 hits and had yielded two walks. He struck out seven.

"He wasn't hitting his spots," Torre said of Moyer, whose personal five-game winning streak against the Yanks ended. "He can make you crazy with his fastball, change-up, fastball, change-up. Today, he just wasn't as sharp as he was the last time."

"The last time we faced him, he pretty much stuck it to us," Jeter said. "We tried to take advantage of every opportunity we could. He's the type of pitcher where you have to be patient and wait for his mistakes."

After his first two batters, Wells was mistake-free, with some help from his teammates. Rodriguez singled to start the sixth, and Ken Griffey Jr. followed by smoking a grounder toward first base. Martinez somehow snared the ball, touched first, and tagged Rodriguez for the double play.

"Tino was lucky," Jeter said. "He didn't even see that ball. He stuck out his glove and caught it. That's a big play, though."

Martinez agreed, saying, "The ball just found my glove."

> **❝The last time we faced him, he pretty much stuck it to us. We tried to take advantage of every opportunity we could. He's the type of pitcher where you have to be patient and wait for his mistakes ❞**
>
> *— Derek Jeter*
> *on the Mariners' Jamie Moyer*

When Rich Amaral and Cora singled to start the eighth, Wells had to retire Rodriguez, Griffey, and Edgar Martinez if he wanted his complete game. In eight pitches, all of them strikes, he completed his goal: Rodriguez whiffed on a curveball in the dirt, Griffey advanced the runners to second and third, and Martinez offered a harmless foul pop to first. The Mariners went down in order in the ninth, and Wells had himself a 13-2 record. The Yanks have won four straight here after losing 18 of the previous 22.

"Boomer did his best pitching at that point in the game," Cone said. "He made some great pitches in that sequence."

Wells, who provided highlight-reel material in the fifth when his hat fell off during a pitch to Joey Cora, wouldn't discuss his performance. He told team director of media relations Rick Cerrone that he had to go somewhere, but he was seen in the Kingdome 30 minutes after leaving the clubhouse.

Sunday, August 2, 1998 — at Seattle Mariners

Mariners 6, Yankees 3

Yanks' lapses costly
Cone denied 16th victory

By KEN DAVIDOFF, Staff Writer

SEATTLE — It all seemed a little off, as if the Yankees' compass that points them toward history had been sabotaged Sunday night.

There was a certain out-of-focus feel to the Yanks' 6-3 defeat to the Mariners. David Cone, pitching to catcher Jorge Posada for the first time, walked a season-high four batters, even though he struck out 11. Rookie Shane Spencer, making his major league debut at first base, made some beginner mistakes. The Yankees offense hit into three double plays.

If you're looking for a theory, try this one: This probably was the Bombers' final game at the Kingdome, this beautiful city's dank building that will be abandoned by the Mariners in 11 months for a new outdoor ballpark, Safeco Field. If the preliminary schedule for 1999 holds, the Yanks will not visit the Pacific Northwest until the second half of the season, when the new park is open.

The Bombers finished with a 67-62 record here, but the memories will mostly be bad and bizarre. Especially the three heartbreaking games they lost in the 1995 American League Division Series.

"I have no desire to come back to this place," said Cone, who started Game 5 of that memorable series.

By dropping to 77-28, the Yankees fell behind the pace of the 1902 Pirates, who started that long-ago campaign with a 78-27 mark.

Cone, who admits to being a high-maintenance batterymate, has enjoyed a strong working relationship with Joe Girardi since Girardi joined the team in 1995. When the veteran receiver was scratched with muscle spasms in his back, Posada was penciled in behind the plate.

Spencer, meanwhile, made his first major league start at first base while Tino Martinez rested against Mariners emergency starter Paul Spoljaric. Normally a reliever, Spoljaric got the nod after scheduled starter Randy Johnson was traded to the Astros late Friday night. With Martinez holding a career 1-for-9 mark with seven strikeouts against the left-handed Spoljaric, Bombers manager Joe Torre planned to substitute Martinez after Spoljaric departed.

Posada, it should be noted, did nothing technically wrong in his handling of Cone. But the Yankees ace admitted to feeling "a little out of sync" in the early going, attributing it to "the human element."

"I enjoyed working with Jorge," said Cone, who allowed all six Mariners runs and nine hits. "There's a little bit of an adjustment when I shake him off. He doesn't know exactly what I want to throw. Sometimes I don't know what I want to throw when I'm out there."

"It was fun," Posada said. "He's got the nastiest slider that I've ever caught."

Paul O'Neill's homer gave Cone and the Yankees a 1-0 lead in the first, but the Bombers offense was otherwise dormant in the early going. And in the second, Cone's long, strange trip began in earnest: Edgar Martinez lined a leadoff single to right, and Jay Buhner walked one out later. After Cone struck out former Yankees farmhand Russ Davis, Joe Oliver grounded a single to left field.

Mariners third base coach Steve Smith waved home Martinez, and Chad Curtis charged the ball and unleashed a nice throw. It landed in Posada's glove on a short hop and beat Martinez to the plate, but the catcher couldn't hang on. Tie score, 1-1.

"The ball skipped," Posada said. "It hit me right in the chest."

With one out in the third, Alex Rodriguez ripped a double to left-center. Cone got ahead of Ken Griffey Jr., 0-1, then threw a high but catchable pitch that glanced off Posada's glove. Rodriguez went to third on the passed ball, and Cone proceeded to issue free passes to Griffey and Martinez, loading the bases with one out.

David Segui drilled a bullet to first base that Spencer caught and then dropped, and a double play seemed a given. The rookie could have tagged Martinez, who was just a few feet away, then touched first. He could have thrown home for a 3-2-3 double play. Instead, he paused and threw to second, and Derek Jeter's relay to first was too late to nail Segui. Rodriguez scored for the 2-1 lead, and Spencer's mistake was magnified when Buhner singled home Griffey.

Martinez actually shielded the ball, Spencer explained, and he thought he did the right thing going for two.

"I couldn't believe he [Segui] got down the line that fast," he said. "He sniffed it. He wanted that RBI."

The Mariners added another run in the fourth, the Yanks cut it to 4-3, and Buhner's mammoth two-run dinger off a Cone laredo slider in the seventh gave the home team enough of a cushion.

Monday, August 3, 1998 — at Oakland A's

Yankees 14, A's 1

Yanks have a blast
Four homers back El Duque

By KEN DAVIDOFF, Staff Writer

OAKLAND, Calif. — Either A's pitcher Mike Oquist lost a bet to his manager Art Howe, or the A's bullpen was emptier than the Montreal Expos' savings account. Whatever the true story is, the Yankees took part in an ambush Monday night at Oakland Coliseum.

Chuck Knoblauch's two homers and five RBI led the Bombers' offensive charge as Oquist suffered the worst beating by a major league pitcher in over two decades, 14-1. Oquist, the 30-year-old right-hander, was pummeled for 14 runs and 16 hits in five innings. Included in that carnage was a seven-run second inning (tying the Yanks' season high) and a five-run third. The Yanks' four homers tied a season high.

On Aug. 14, 1977, in the second game of a double-header at Cleveland's Municipal Stadium, Milwaukee's Bill Travers was racked by the Indians for 14 runs and 18 hits in seven innings. No pitcher had matched Travers' travesty until Oquist.

Yankees starter Orlando Hernandez was coming off a doozy of a start himself. Against the Angels at Edison Field on Wednesday, El Duque endured a 10-run, 13-hit assault in 3 1/3 innings. On this night, given runs by the handful, he cruised for his sixth victory and second complete game. He limited the A's to three hits and held left-handed hitters to a 1-for-15 night (.067) after struggling so much against them this season. His long effort was especially appreciated, considering that today the Yanks will start two relievers, Ramiro Mendoza and Mike Buddie, in a doubleheader and will probably need what's left of the bullpen to finish the games.

So maybe Hernandez could feel for Oquist, whose grisly line set a team mark for incompetence in runs. With no outs in the fourth inning, each of the Yankees' starting nine had recorded a base hit.

And Knoblauch had three by that time. The second baseman and leadoff hitter had been mired in a horrendous slump lately, 2 for his last 27 and 8 for his last 63 heading into Tuesday night, and his average stood at .246. Worse, the All-Star swing which seemed to be returning to him about two weeks ago had disappeared. He stopped waiting out pitchers and started hitting many more fly balls than usual.

"I think he's going to get anxious if he keeps on looking up at the scoreboard and sees his batting average at about .250," Joe Torre said recently of Knoblauch. The manager had reminded his second baseman that he was a line-drive hitter, that he shouldn't let his recent home run splurge affect his swing.

Monday night didn't necessarily cure what ails Knoblauch; he has now gone 30 at-bats without drawing a walk. But at least he hit the stuffing out of the ball, setting a career high with five RBI, and perhaps that can boost his confidence and point him in the right direction, if it's still possible for him to find it this late in the season.

Knoblauch started the game with a double and came home immediately on a Derek Jeter double. But that first inning, like a garage band that warms up for a Grateful Dead show, would be long forgotten by the time the night was over.

The second inning was a merciless attack on Oquist and the A's: Chad Curtis singled to center. Jorge Posada walked. Scott Brosius knocked an infield single that shortstop Miguel Tejada threw away when he tried to get Curtis at third. Curtis scored. Knoblauch homered to left-center for three more runs.

Tejada couldn't hold on to Jeter's flare to shallow left. Paul O'Neill homered to left, plating two more runs. Bernie Williams doubled to right. Tino Martinez singled to left, scoring Williams for the inning's seventh and final run.

Matt Stairs ripped a solo homer off El Duque in the second, but the Cuban right-hander struck out the next three batters: Jason Giambi, Scott Spiezio, and Ed Sprague. In the third, the assault continued. Knoblauch's second homer, a two-run job, went to left. Darryl Strawberry joined the party with a two-run blast to left for the fourth and fifth runs of the inning. Through all of this, Howe never put a call into his bullpen.

Oquist allowed one more run in the fifth, before he was finally lifted for southpaw Mike Mohler.

Reporter's Notebook:

Chili Davis, rehabilitating his surgically reconstructed right ankle, went 0-for-5 with three walks in a double header for Class AA Norwich on Monday. The designated hitter could be back in pinstripes as soon as Friday, when the team returns home.

Tuesday, August 4, 1998 — at Oakland A's

Game 1: Yankees 10, A's 4

Game 2: Yankees 10, A's 5

Crash! Pow! Boom! Yanks sweep A's

By KEN DAVIDOFF, Staff Writer

OAKLAND, Calif. — No one wearing pinstripes is involved in the Roger Maris hunt. No one wearing pinstripes has even half of Mark McGwire's home run total.

Lately, however, the Yankees have been imitating the Bronx Bombers of old. This team that prides itself on such subtleties as working the pitch count and moving the runners hit the stuffing out of five more baseballs in Tuesday night's doubleheader, coming from behind in both contests to post an incredibly dramatic 10-5 victory in Game 2 and a more routine 10-4 triumph in Game 1.

Darryl Strawberry homered once in each game, including a grand slam in Game 2, Tino Martinez and Paul O'Neill left the yard in the nightcap, and Chuck Knoblauch went deep in Game 1, giving the Yanks 22 homers in the first nine games of their West Coast jaunt. In 27 games since the All-Star break, they have left the yard 44 times, an average of more than 1.5 per game. In the 81 games before the three-day rest, the Yanks had slugged 90 homers, about 1.1 per contest.

"I have no clue what that's all about," Joe Torre said after Game 1, of his team's power surge. "But that's what I like about our club. We're capable of hitting [homers], but we don't wait for them. We don't have to rely on them."

"I don't think we're a team that tries to go up there and hit home runs," Strawberry said. "I guess it's just a stretch where we're all going through it. But the timing couldn't be better."

He was referring to this West Coast stretch, where the team has often struggled. Their sweep lifted their record on this trip to 7-2, and their season record to 80-28, with the 52 games over .500 a new high-water mark for the year. Torre, not one for hyperbole, said that this team would beat the 1976 Reds.

Former Yankee Kenny Rogers started the ninth inning of Game 2 owning a 5-1 lead and on the verge of revenge, redemption, respect, or whatever he

wanted. But he surrendered leadoff singles to Martinez and Tim Raines, and A's manager Art Howe felt that his starter had enough. Closer Billy Taylor entered the game.

Chad Curtis hit a hard grounder to third that Mike Blowers couldn't handle, loading the bases. That's when Torre decided to pinch hit Strawberry for Joe Girardi.

The count went to 2-2 before Strawberry grabbed hold of a Taylor offering and stroked it to straight-away center. The ball carried, carried, carried — and landed over the 400-foot sign in center field. Tie game, 5-5. It was Strawberry's second pinch hit grand slam of the season; he is the first player in American League history to accomplish such a feat. Strawberry's former Mets manager Davey Johnson and Mike Ivie did so in the National League.

The Bombers weren't done. After Jorge Posada hit a comebacker to the mound for the inning's first out, Chuck Knoblauch grounded a single up the middle and moved to second on a Taylor balk. Derek Jeter hit a bullet to second that Scott Spiezio snared on a bounce, practically with his eyes closed. His throw to first was shaky, and Jason Giambi had to stretch to make the catch.

As first-base umpire John Shulock called Jeter out, Giambi tried to rise, and Jeter's knee smacked into Giambi's head. As Giambi lay on the ground motionless and Jeter flew down the first-base line, Knoblauch rounded third and scored the lead run. The A's later reported that Giambi suffered from a mild concussion and was taken to a local hospital for tests.

O'Neill and Martinez added two-run homers and Chad Curtis chipped in with a run-scoring double, making for an nine-run inning, a season high. That the Yankees built their lead to 10-5 meant they robbed Mariano Rivera of another save opportunity, just as they did when they increased their advantage from 7-4 to 10-4 in the ninth inning of Game 1. Graeme Lloyd earned the victory with two shutout innings in relief of Mike Buddie, who was rocked in the first inning of his first major league start but stuck around for six.

In the first game, the Yanks overcame a season-high four errors, three by Scott Brosius, to reward Ramiro Mendoza for his solid effort. In his first start since July 17, the spot starter went 6 1/3 innings, allowing four runs (two earned) on seven hits. He walked two and struck out one. Mike Stanton picked up his sixth save in relief of Mendoza.

Wednesday, August 5, 1998 — at Oakland A's

A's 3, Yankees 1

Yanks knuckle under

A's Candiotti bests Irabu

By KEN DAVIDOFF, Staff Writer

OAKLAND, Calif. — This West Coast trip of trade rumors and pinch-hit grand slams ended with a whimper Wednesday night, with the Yankees at the mercy of a 40-year-old knuckleballer.

Hideki Irabu pitched a complete-game two-hitter and still lost, thanks to the mastery of A's veteran Tom Candiotti. The home team salvaged a 3-1 victory and left the Bombers (80-29), who were looking to clinch a .500 record for the season with 53 games remaining, with a very acceptable 7-3 record on this physically and mentally exhausting trip.

It has been a torturous stretch for the Yankees, in fact, since the end of the All-Star break. In 28 days, they have played 28 games, 21 of them on the road, scattered about seven different cities (and two countries). They recorded a 19-8 record in that time, the .704 winning percentage trailing their season percentage of .734.

And now, the path to the playoffs seems as smooth as a Harlem Globetrotters' schedule. Of their 53 remaining games starting Friday, just 18 are on the road. Less than half, 25, come against teams that currently have winning records.

Few Yankees have sweated through this portion of the schedule more than the right-hander Irabu. In the second game following the break, he found himself pitching for his spot in the starting rotation. He did so, continued to pitch well for the most part, and then last week, he found himself in the eye of the Randy Johnson storm. He started Friday's game at the Kingdome not knowing if he would still be a Yankee by night's end.

He was, and on Wednesday night his two-hitter was a career best, even if his record fell to 10-5. He walked two, hit one, and struck out five.

Besides a Tino Martinez homer, the Yanks were helpless against Candiotti (7-13), who limited the visitors to four hits and fanned six while walking two.

With the Yanks down by just one run in the bottom of the eighth and Irabu looking to keep the deficit small, former Bomber and future Hall of Famer Rickey Henderson snapped an 0-for-21 slump by slamming a 1-1 pitch over the left field fence. Martinez walked with two outs in the ninth, bringing up Tuesday night's hero Darryl Strawberry. But the veteran designated hitter struck out on four pitches, ending the game in a brisk 2 hours 16 minutes.

So often, it seems, Irabu can't get his curveball and split-fingered fastball working and must rely solely on his fastball. Wednesday was not one of those nights. He had it all going early. The A's first batter, Henderson, whiffed on a splitter. Matt Stairs, the first batter of the second inning, hit a curveball to short for a groundout. Mike Blowers ended the second by looking at a fastball for a third strike. Irabu revved his heat up to 95 mph.

The Yankees, meanwhile, were having a devil of a time against Candiotti and his crazy, floating pitch. In one hilarious fourth-inning sequence, Paul O'Neill flailed and missed a knuckler. Candiotti came back with the same pitch, and O'Neill, as if he were playing in a weekend softball league, had time to take two steps toward the ball and hit it to left field for a flyout.

In the fifth, the Yanks salvaged some self-respect when Martinez drove a homer over the right field fence for a 1-0 lead.

Irabu lost his perfect game in the fourth, when he issued a two-out walk to Ben Grieve, and he put himself in serious trouble by hitting Ed Sprague and walking Blowers to start the fifth. Miguel Tejada sacrificed the runners to second and third, and Rafael Bournigal lined the first pitch he saw to right field for a single, ending the no-hitter and shutout as Sprague came home to tie the game.

A.J. Hinch followed Bournigal with a fly to medium right field, upon which Blowers easily tagged up from third base and scored for a 2-1 Oakland lead.

When O'Neill and Bernie Williams started the seventh with consecutive singles, the Yanks seemed to have solved Candiotti. Martinez struck out, then Darryl Strawberry walked to load the bases. Here was their big chance, with Chad Curtis the first contestant. His fly to center was way too shallow for O'Neill to tag up.

Jorge Posada battled to a 2-2 count, then knocked a hard but catchable ball to center. End of inning, three men stranded.

Friday, August 7, 1998 — Kansas City Royals

Yankees 14, Royals 2

Yanks make a sweeping return

By GREGORY SCHUTTA, Staff Writer

NEW YORK — When Shane Spencer's first career homer barely cleared the fence in the left-field corner at Yankee Stadium on Friday night, he returned to the dugout expecting to reap the rewards that have been coming to Yankee heroes for 81 wins so far this season.

"Instead, they were ragging on me to go out and hit a real one," he said.

So the 26-year-old rookie from California obliged one inning later, sending a 370-foot shot off the upper deck facade in left to cap a 5-for-5 night and give the Yankees a 14-2 victory over the Kansas City Royals and a sweep of the first of three day-night doubleheaders the Yankees will play in the next six weeks. David Wells pitched his second consecutive complete game and didn't walk a batter for his 14th win of the season. David Cone struggled early in the day game but settled down to go 6 2/3 innings for his major-league-leading 16th win in an 8-2 victory.

"I haven't stopped smiling yet," said Spencer, who had his career day in front of 37,988 fans, including his mother, Althea, and his girlfriend, Heidi. "I'm sure [my mother is] crying right now. It's the first time she's watched me play up here."

And she picked a perfect time to do it. Spencer, starting the second game in right field as manager Joe Torre gave most of his starters a rest, hit his first two career homers, posted his first career five-hit game, and made his first career curtain call at Yankee Stadium.

"That first one was a tough call," Torre said. "But that second one removed all doubt. He couldn't get that smile off his face. Everybody was very happy for him."

"I didn't want to think about it," Spencer said of the curtain call. "I went down the steps and I could still hear them cheering, and I'm thinking maybe, just maybe."

The season has been filled with maybes for Spencer, who before Friday had just three hits in 17 at-bats in three stints with the Yankees.

"It's tough," he said. "You know you sit on the bench and watch these guys go out and whup everybody day in and day out, and you just hope that some day you can be part of it."

Spencer was a major part of it Friday, as were a number of part-time Yankees as Torre got creative with his lineup for the nightcap. Luis Sojo gave Tino Martinez a night off at first and had three hits and two RBI.

""That's just the way this team is," said Wells, who scattered six hits. "These guys are mentally and physically ready every time to go out. They sit seven or eight or nine ballgames without playing and are still ready to go when they get the call. It adds character to this team."

So do performances like Friday. The Yankees, who didn't get into New York until late Thursday morning after flying all night from Oakland, roughed up Kansas City pitching for 22 runs and 30 hits while four pitchers did not walk a batter.

> **❝I haven't stopped smiling yet. …❞**
>
> *— Shane Spencer*

The hitting was the story as the Yankees banged out five homers in the two games, giving them 28 homers in the past 12 games. Darryl Strawberry lead the charge, banging a solo shot 400 feet into the upper deck in right in the opener for his ninth homer in his last 32 at-bats.

The Royals took a 1-0 lead against Wells in the third inning of the nightcap on back-to-back doubles by Johnny Damon and Jermaine Allensworth. But Chuck Knoblauch hit his 14th homer, a career high, in the bottom of the inning for a 1-1 tie.

The Yankees took the lead with two runs in the fourth and then broke it open with five in the fifth. Bernie Williams hit a two-run home run to left-center for a 5-1 lead.

"That's what makes this team so special," Strawberry said. "We've got a group of guys. It's not just one guy. In '96 and '97, we had a few bad apples on the team who would gripe about at-bats. But we don't need that on this team. Everybody wants to stay on the same page."

And each page is coming together to form a best-seller of a season.

Saturday, August 8, 1998 — Kansas City Royals

Yankees 14, Royals 1

Yanks make life easy for 'El Duque'

By GREGORY SCHUTTA, Staff Writer

NEW YORK — Orlando Hernandez appears to have it all. He's living in a new country with a $3 million per year salary and pitching every fifth day for the best team in baseball.

What the right-hander doesn't have is the two daughters he left behind in December when he defected from Cuba on a rickety boat.

So you would think Yankees' Family Day would be tough for him. But instead, "El Duque" celebrated the day in front of 45,975 of his nearest and dearest friends at Yankee Stadium on Saturday, scattering four hits in eight innings and striking out seven as the Yankees manhandled the Royals for the third straight game, 14-1.

"To tell you the truth, I didn't even know it was Family Day," Hernandez said with a smile after winning his seventh game. "In all forms, I feel like my teammates are my family and …those kids running around today are my kids."

Kids and parents alike watched as the Yankees dismantled the Royals for the third game in two days. They erupted for 12 of their 14 runs in the final three innings on the heels of their 22-run, 30-hit performance in Friday's day-night doubleheader sweep.

Jorge Posada swung the big bat, driving in a career-high six runs with a two-run single in the six-run sixth and a two-run doubles in the seventh and eighth.

"It's very special because I had my dad in the stands today," Posada said. "It's nice to have a big day with him watching."

Chuck Knoblauch, who has more home runs since the All-Star break than Mark McGwire (11 vs. 9), hit his second in two days to give the Yankees a 2-0 lead in the fifth.

The Royals, who had managed just one bloop single against El Duque over the first five innings, got one back in the sixth on singles by Mike Sweeney, Johnny Damon, and Hal Morris. Hernandez then walked Jose Offerman to load the bases but got cleanup hitter Dean Palmer to hit into an inning-ending 6-4-3 double play on the next pitch.

"That's the way it is with El Duque," Knoblauch said. "Whenever he gets guys in scoring position, he seems to turn it up a notch and get the pitch he needs in that situation. At the time, it was 2-1, so that was a big play right there."

"He doesn't scare," manager Joe Torre said. "He doesn't panic. He keeps his head about him, which means he's putting his experience to work for him. He's very confident, which I think is half the battle."

The Yankees then broke the game open with six runs in the bottom of the sixth, capped by a three-run homer by Scott Brosius. The Yankees have hit 29 homers in the past 13 games.

"They can turn a game around quickly," Kansas City manager Tony Muser said. "They are a very good team."

"Hitting is contagious," Knoblauch said. "A couple of guys will get things rolling and others will follow suit. It's nice to score some runs and take some of the pressure off of our pitchers."

El Duque cannot say he has been starving for runs. The Yankees have scored in double digits in five of his seven wins, including a complete-game 14-1 victory over Oakland on Monday. That came on the heels of his worst loss when he gave up 10 runs on 13 hits in little more than three innings in a 10-5 loss to Anaheim.

That loss also brought to light El Duque's weight-loss problems, which he joked about Saturday.

"I gained four pounds this week," he said proudly. "The entire road trip, all I ate is Burger King and McDonald's. I'd like to think it was the Burger King and McDonald's."

Torre and Posada pointed more to Hernandez's ability to pitch inside.

"That's got to be the best game I've seen him throw since he's been here," Posada said. "He was getting left-handers out, coming inside on them. He was moving the ball in and out on both lefties and righties."

"It was nice to see him jam a lot of left-handers which shows that he was coming in off the plate real well," Torre said. "That was one of the things I wanted him to work on."

Reporter's Notebook:

Andy Pettitte threw for the second day in a row without any pain and will take his regular start today against the Royals. … Queens native Mike Jerzembeck made his major league debut, pitching a perfect ninth with one strikeout. … El Duque and

Jerzembeck combined to halt Offerman's hitting streak at 27 games. Offerman's last gasp came in the ninth inning when he hit a dribbler in front of the plate. Jerzembeck got off the mound quickly and threw him out to end the streak. ... The Yankees are a season-high 54 games over .500 (83-29). They could lose their 50 remaining games and still finish four games over .500.

Sunday, August 9, 1998 — Kansas City Royals

Yankees 5, Royals 4

Royal flush

Mendoza puts up zeros as Yanks sweep K.C.

By GREGORY SCHUTTA, Staff Writer

NEW YORK — David Cone rarely has come out of the bullpen in his long major league career, but still he knows the mentality of a relief pitcher.

"It's an uncertain life," he said. "You never know when you're going to get called in or when you're going to have to sit."

It's that uncertainty that has kept Ramiro Mendoza from embracing his role as the swingman in the Yankee bullpen for the past two months. But performances such as Sunday's are what will most likely keep him out there for the rest of the season.

Mendoza came in for an ineffective Andy Pettitte with a man on third and the Yankees trailing the Royals by three runs. He retired seven of the eight men to face him and picked up his eighth victory as the Yankees came back for a 5-4 victory in front of a sold-out Yankee Stadium on Beanie Baby Day II.

"Usually when a player gets sent to the bullpen, it's a punishment," said manager Joe Torre, who pulled Mendoza from the rotation in June, when Orlando Hernandez came to the Yankees. "We tried to convince him that it wasn't a punishment but that we had too many starters and we felt he was the best-equipped to go out there. He wasn't happy about it at first, but you can see that he understands his role. You can see it in his body language, the way he comes in games and shuts people down."

Mendoza (8-2) shut down the Royals, who were enjoying a fine afternoon in the Bronx after getting pummeled by the Yankees, 36-5, in three games over the previous two days. Pettitte, who skipped his previous start because of a strained trapezius muscle, was touched for four runs and eight hits in 5 2/3 innings and left trailing, 4-1, with two out and a man on third in the sixth inning.

Mendoza, who would have gotten the start if Pettitte couldn't go, came in and got catcher Sal Fasano to fly to center on his first pitch to end the threat. He went 2 1/3 innings, hitting one batter for his lone runner and striking out one before giving way to Mariano Rivera, who pitched a perfect ninth for his 30th save of the season.

"I'm glad with the job I have," Mendoza said. "It is important. I come in with guys on base and I have to get them out."

"It's a different job than he's used to," Torre said. "He has to be ready on a moment's notice, and he's got to get that first guy out."

And that first guy, plus the run he could have allowed, turned out to be very big in the bottom of the inning, when the Yankees broke through against Hipolito Pichardo for three runs to tie the score at 4. Up until that point, the Yankees had managed just three hits, including Scott Brosius' 12th homer of the season in the third inning.

Paul O'Neill doubled into the gap in left-center, scoring Chuck Knoblauch and Derek Jeter to cut the deficit to 4-3. O'Neill went to third on a wild pitch and scored the tying run when Bernie Williams sent a blast deep to right that Johnny Damon caught leaping against the fence.

Williams then came through in the eighth thanks to some heads-up baserunning from Jeter, who went from first to third on a stolen-base attempt when the pitch sailed over Fasano's head. Williams blooped a single into no man's land in center field to score Jeter and give the Yankees the the margin of victory.

"Some games are easy, and some games are hard," said Williams, summing up the Yankees' four-game sweep of the Royals in nine words. "To be a good team, you have to be able to win every way you can. If it's not the defense, it's the offense. Good pitching and good baserunning. We knew it was too early in the game to get down."

And Torre said it's too early in the season for Mendoza to get down in the bullpen.

"He's done the job all year, both as a starter and a reliever," Torre said. "We appreciate him and what he's done, which I think is most important. Every time he comes in, the game is in the balance. That should show just how important we think Ramiro Mendoza is."

"I'd rather be a starter than a reliever, but I'll accept the decision of the manager," Mendoza said. "I just want to do what I can to help the team."

Monday, August 10, 1998 — Minnesota Twins

Yankees 7, Twins 3

Yankees amaze even themselves

By GREGORY SCHUTTA, Staff Writer

NEW YORK — How good is this Yankees team? Everything about them is now the "biggest," the "longest," or the "best."

Even the calm, understated Joe Torre, who's had a front-row seat for the last four months, allowed himself a moment to marvel at the accomplishments of his team.

"All I can say is 'Wow,'" he said.

The Yankees put another notch in their gun Monday, downing the Minnesota Twins, 7-3, to go 56 games over .500 (85-29) for the first time since the 1961 Yankees of Mantle and Maris finished the season 109-53. They also homered for the 12th straight game, their longest streak since going 16 straight in 1994, and extended their AL East lead over Boston to 17 1/2 games, their biggest lead since going 18 1/2 games up on Boston in 1941.

"I think maybe we'll look back at the end of the season and say, 'Wow, look what we did,'" Paul O'Neill said. "But right now we just want to go out and get a win."

"I think the reason we are where we're at is because we've kept the ability to focus on the game we're playing," said Scott Brosius. "Yesterday's game doesn't mean anything today and tomorrow's game doesn't mean anything yet. Maybe when everything's said and done and the season is over, we can look back and appreciate it more."

The Yankees have certainly appreciated the most recent performances of Brosius and starter Hideki Irabu. Brosius homered for the third straight game, sending his 13th homer of the season 407 feet over the fence in left-center for two runs in the Yankees' three-run fourth inning.

The Twins, were making their first appearance at

Yankee Stadium since David Wells pitched a perfect game against them May 17. The right-hander, coming off one of his best outings of the season in a tough 3-1 loss to Oakland last week, held the Twins hitless over the first four innings and allowed just two hits over seven shutout innings.

Marty Cordova's clean single up the middle leading off the fifth broke a string of 14 1/3 hitless innings by the Twins against Yankees pitching, dating to a two-out single by Todd Walker in the eighth inning against Ramiro Mendoza on May 16. Mariano Rivera threw a perfect ninth to save the 5-2 victory for the Yankees, and Wells was perfect the next day.

Irabu wasn't perfect, hitting Otis Nixon with the first pitch of the game and walking two while striking out four, but he was close enough. Torre lifted him for Mike Stanton to start the eighth and the left-hander, who hadn't pitched since Friday night, promptly put two men on and gave up a three-run homer to Matt Lawton to cut the lead to 7-3.

"I just thought he had had enough," Torre said of his decision to lift Irabu, who threw 103 pitches, 63 for strikes. "The main reason is because I don't want to go too far with anybody at this point in the season."

> **"** … right now we just want to go out and get a win. **"**
>
> *— Paul O'Neill*

"I wanted to go another inning, but I wasn't sure if I would make it," said Irabu (11-5).

Irabu has gone 5-2 in his last seven starts after going 0-2 with two no-decisions in his previous four.

"Actually, I think his last three games have been outstanding," Torre said. "He's pitching better than he was earlier in the season. His fastball is working, his splitter, his curve. He mixes in a change once in a while. It makes it tough to sit on any one pitch."

"I'm really just trying to keep the ball down and throw the batters' timing off," Irabu said.

That's something opposing pitchers have failed to do recently against Yankees batters. The Bombers continued to earn their nickname with two homers Monday night, giving them 27 in their last 12 games and 35 in their last 16.

Bernie Williams added his 15th of the season, a solo shot to right, to give the Yankees a 7-0 lead.

With three homers in the last three games, Brosius has made his two-week funk at the end of July a distant memory.

Tuesday, August 11, 1998 — Minnesota Twins

Yankees 7, Twins 0

Torre gets even — thanks to Wells' shutout

By KEN DAVIDOFF, Staff Writer

NEW YORK — Chasing ghosts has become a sport of necessity with these 1998 Yankees, what with their pursuit of baseball's long-held record for most victories in a season. Tuesday night, though, the 1906 Cubs took a back seat to names such as Alex Trevino, Kelvin Chapman, and Roy Staiger. And David Wells.

When Wells and the Yankees blanked the Twins, 7-0, at Yankee Stadium, the southpaw extended his scoreless streak against Minnesota to 25 innings overall and 18 this season. The first nine innings he threw against them this year, of course, came in his May 17 perfect game here.

The victory, the Yankees' sixth straight, extended the Bombers' record to 86-29, meaning they need to go 31-16 in their final 47 games to establish the modern-day record with 117 victories. It also marked the first time the franchise has been 57 games over .500 since Sept. 10, 1939.

But on this night, at least one Yankee was thinking in more modest terms. Joe Torre's career managerial record now stands at 1,168-1,168. "When you consider where I came from recordwise, I'm proud of it," Torre said. "Now I don't want to get to .500 anymore in my career."

> **❝** ... Every time he goes out there, he wants to throw a game like that. **❞**
>
> *— Jorge Posada*
>
> *on pitcher David Wells*

Torre became the Mets' player-manager May 31, 1977. He recalls winning three of his first four games until the reality of his subpar team — featuring the likes of Trevino, Chapman, and Staiger — sank in. When Torre was fired following the 1981 season, he carried a 286-420 record out the door.

His three seasons with the Braves and five with the Cardinals inched the overall mark toward a clean slate. When he took the Yankees' job in November 1995, he was at 894-1,003.

It was last year when Torre's brother, Frank, said to him, "I want to get your record to .500." Joe replied by saying, "Don't even think about it." Now, thanks to this incredible team, he is there.

There today, rather than later this week, thanks to Wells. Pitching on three days' rest, the 35-year-old tossed his third shutout of the year, tying Detroit's Brian Moehler for the American League lead, and his third straight complete game. He needed just 101 pitches, 72 of them strikes, to record the masterpiece. He issued no walks and fanned four while permitting four hits.

Wells' perfect game ended after one batter this time, when Brent Gates punched a double down the third base line past Scott Brosius. While the Yanks pounded their former prospect, Eric Milton (6-9), for five runs and nine hits in four innings, Wells improved as the game progressed, allowing some fly balls early, then settling down and recording more groundouts.

"It's just a matter of adjusting out there," said Wells (15-2, 3.28 ERA). "When you find yourself lunging, you tell yourself to stay back, get the ball out in front. That way you can locate your curveball, getting it down in the dirt, as well as your fastball."

Adjustments such as that are what Torre believes his pitcher wouldn't have made before May 17. Including his memorable day of 27 up, 27 down, Wells is 11-1 with a 2.35 ERA in his last 14 starts.

"You [pitch a perfect game] in this ballpark, as a member of the Yankees, that's a very proud thing that you're able to accomplish," the manager said. "When you think of all the history involved, and you're the only one to pitch one here in the regular season, and you think how far back the Yankees' tradition goes, obviously his being so involved with the Yankees to begin with ...I think he's taken on more responsibility."

"It only helps somebody after a game like that," Jorge Posada agreed. "He was perfect that day, so it's got to help your confidence. Every time he goes out there, he wants to throw a game like that. It's not going to happen again, but it's like he wants to throw one again."

Wells disagreed, calling May 17 "just another game. ... I don't even want one of those again. It's too much. It changes your life drastically. Let [one of the other Yankees pitchers] get it."

The southpaw joined Jim Bunning as the only pitchers this century to have a perfect game against a team, then shut that team out the next time. Bunning did so against the Mets in 1964.

Wednesday, August 12, 1998

— Minnesota Twins

Yankees 11, Twins 2

Girardi takes turn as Yankees' star

By KEN DAVIDOFF, Staff Writer

NEW YORK — You could see it unfold, each man going in motion as if it were a football play: LaTroy Hawkins unleashing the pitch. Tim Raines dashing for third base. Scott Brosius trailing him, going to second. Ron Coomer bolting for third to cover the bag, Todd Walker preparing for a play at second.

When Joe Girardi knocks Hawkins' pitch into the gap in left-center field, Raines scores easily, Brosius is waved home by third base coach Willie Randolph and makes it without a play. The Yankees take a one-run lead over the Twins in the fourth inning.

The hit-and-run executed to perfection. By the man who excels in the little things for this team that is accomplishing ridiculously big things.

"I don't hit a lot of home runs, so you have to be able to do the other things," Girardi said Wednesday after the Yanks proceeded to thrash the Twins, 11-2, at Yankee Stadium. "It's important to me."

Which means it is to the Yankees. Now 87-29 and back at a .750 winning percentage for the first time since July 16, their seven-game winning streak is their fifth of such length. The other 13 teams in the American League have combined for five. Girardi's double gave the team a lead for its 41st straight game, a major league record. The old mark, according to the Elias Sports Bureau, was 40 by the 1932 Yankees.

But such numbers are as meaningful to the Yankees' day-to-day universe as the Dow Jones average — less meaningful, on second thought. No, they can better appreciate a day at the office such as the one Girardi contributed Wednesday: the game-winning RBI and another successful stint behind the plate catching David Cone, who overcame early troubles to post his major league-leading 17th victory.

"Joe's great," Cone said. "He probably knows me better than anyone I've had catching me. He never gives up on me. He knows that from inning to inning I can change and there might be one adjustment that'll get me back."

Said manager Joe Torre: "I think Girardi has a role in settling [Cone] down. He's been there before. He understands David, he watches every move, he watches body language. He tries to create as much as David does."

Girardi, as is his nature, plays down such high praise.

"He knows what he has to do," the 33-year-old said of Cone. "For the most part, I don't say much. All I try and do is slow him down a little bit so he can think about what he's doing. He knows the adjustments that he has to make, and he always finds a way to get it done."

Cone did not look himself early, putting his team in a 2-0 hole through three innings courtesy of four singles, a double, two walks, and a hit batter. He struggled in navigating his way through a hole on the pitchers' mound.

The 35-year-old right-hander confesses to requiring high maintenance when he steps on the field, and he can sometimes be seen shouting angrily at Girardi, who insists such give-and-take doesn't bother him.

> **"**I don't hit a lot of home runs, so you have to be able to do the other things,**"**
>
> *— Joe Girardi*

"I usually take a step back," he said. "I let him blow off steam. He's a feisty pitcher. You have to understand that's his personality. It's his competitive nature. So you don't take it personally."

By the fourth, Cone had adjusted to the hole on the mound, and that's when the Yanks began teeing off on Hawkins (7-11).

The game would become silly. The Yanks' 18 hits tied their season high. Brosius, who homered for the fourth time in five games, matched his career high with five RBI.

Girardi, like many of these Yankees, was here in 1996, when the Bombers won the World Series, but unlike many of these Yankees, his role has lessened in the interim. Jorge Posada now gets about 60 percent of the starts behind the plate. He is the catcher of the future. Girardi has a $2.7 million option for 1999, or the team can buy him out for $300,000.

Yet there is no question in the catcher's mind as to which season has been more enjoyable. "[1996] was fun," he said. "The type of team we had was a lot of fun. But from the standpoint of approaching this great atmosphere every day, I don't think you can beat this."

Thursday, August 13, 1998 — Texas Rangers

Yankees 2, Texas 0

Hernandez fans 13 in spurring Yanks

By GREGORY SCHUTTA, Staff Writer

NEW YORK — Tino Martinez could only stand at first base and marvel as the noise level grew to thunderous proportions. It was the noise that could only come from more than 50,000 fans packed into Yankee Stadium.

And it's noise you almost never hear on a midweek night in August in the Bronx.

But Thursday night the Yankees faced the Texas Rangers on a night with all the electricity of a Game 7 in October and came out with a stirring 2-0 victory behind a 13-strikeout performance from Orlando Hernandez. It was the first salvo in what many people, including the fans who have sold out the stadium for the rest of the weekend series, feel is a preview of the first round of the American League playoffs.

"During the postseason it's like that through the entire game," Martinez said of the almost constant roar that filled the stadium. "It's that loud. It's that intense. It's a very exciting night. When the place is packed like that, it's more exciting for us and more difficult for the other team."

Hernandez also had a little something to do with making things difficult on the Western Division leaders, holding the Rangers to just two hits over 8 1/3 innings while breaking Stan Bahnsen's 30-year-old record of 12 strikeouts for a Yankees rookie. Juan Gonzalez, the major leagues' RBI leader with 119, was a three-time victim of El Duque's dancing breaking ball, going down on three pitches with men on first and second and one out in the fourth inning to help defuse the Rangers' only threat in the game.

"I threw him three sliders," said Hernandez, who won for the fifth time in six starts and raised his record to 8-3. "I worked him inside then outside. I didn't want to give him anything over the plate."

That was also the recipe for the rest of the Rangers as he got Mike Simms (.341) three times, and Ivan Rodriguez (.323) and Mark McLemore (.271) twice each.

"It was remarkable to watch his approach to the right-handed hitters like Juan Gonzalez and Ivan Rodriguez," said Bernie Williams. "He had so many angles from where he threw the ball that they had a lot of trouble picking it up. It was just amazing to see the right-handers not have a clue out there."

Hernandez got the fans behind him early with 10 strikeouts in the first five innings. He struck out the side twice, including getting Gonzalez, Will Clark, and Rodriguez in the second.

His only trouble came in the fourth when he gave up a one-out double to McLemore and a walk to Rusty Greer. But he got Rodriguez on three pitches and, after a walk to Clark, got Rodriguez looking at a down-and-out curveball for strike three with the bases loaded.

From that moment on he brought the crowd to a deafening roar with every two-strike count. He left to a thunderous ovation with one out and a man on in the ninth, and Mariano Rivera came in to get Clark and Rodriguez for his 31st save of the season.

"It's good support," Hernandez said of the chanting with two strikes and the standing ovation. "But to tell the truth I don't listen to it. I try to concentrate on what I have to do."

"Every time we've played on this homestand it seems to have been like that," manager Joe Torre said. "The fans don't need Texas to come in here to get excited."

And apparently the Yankees don't need the 66 runs they scored in beating up the hapless Kansas City Royals and Minnesota Twins in the first seven games of this homestand. The Bombers managed to get just three hits off hard-luck loser Rick Helling (15-7), none after the third inning, and saw their streak of consecutive games with a home run come to and end at 14.

Paul O'Neill walked and eventually scored on a Tino Martinez single in the first inning. Scott Brosius singled in the third, went to second on a wild pitch and third on a Chuck Knoblauch groundout before scoring on a Derek Jeter sacrifice fly for the Bombers' second run.

"It's been a few days since we've had the bats taken out of our hands like that," said Brosius, who had been one of the hottest Yankees with four homers in his previous five games. "But we managed to scratch out a couple of runs early and just left the rest to El Duque."

And El Duque delivered, making a strong case for being part of the rotation when the Yankees open the five-game Divisional Series in October. It's a decision Torre is not looking forward to making.

"As late as possible," he laughed when asked when he expects to make that decision. "It's the kind of decision you don't make until your back's to the wall."

"I cannot predict the future," Hernandez said. "It's better that everybody win so that the team wins."

"From what I can see, it's a friendly competition," Torre said. "They're making my decision a lot harder, but as long as they're winning, it's a nice problem to have."

Friday, August 14, 1998 — Texas Rangers

Yankees 6, Rangers 4

Andy regains form
Solid effort tops Rangers

By GREGORY SCHUTTA, Staff Writer

NEW YORK — You won't find a psychiatrist's couch in the Yankees' clubhouse. But after Andy Pettitte's shaky outing against the Kansas City Royals on Sunday, manager Joe Torre said he and Mel Stottlemyre spent more time working on the left-hander's mind than his arm.

And Friday night it appeared to pay off as Pettitte pitched seven strong innings for his 14th win of the season as the Yankees held on for a 6-4 victory over the Western Division leading Texas Rangers. It was the ninth straight win for the Yankees, coming on the day that the two millionth customer this season walked through the turnstiles.

The Yankees broke the 2,000,000 mark for the third straight year, drawing 46,547 in Yankee Stadium Friday night to increase their attendance to 2,005,583 in 54 home dates. If the Yankees, who were averaging 36,963 fans per game going into Friday, average 38,247 in their final 26 dates, they would break the 3,000,000 threshold that George Steinbrenner has claimed is necessary for him to consider keeping the Yankees in the Bronx. Their all-time attendance record of 2,633,701 in 1988 seems certain to fall.

"I thought he seemed more relaxed tonight," Torre said of Pettitte. "He expected too much of himself against Kansas City after missing a start [strained trapezius muscle], and when it wasn't exactly what he wanted it to be he fought himself and got out of sorts."

On Friday, the only fighting was against the Rangers as Pettitte scattered five hits over the first seven innings as the Yankees took a 3-1 lead.

"I was much more uptight my last start because of missing the start before," Pettitte said. "I was nice and relaxed tonight. I threw a lot more strikes. I was getting my curveball over and my first-pitch fastball over for strikes. I think that was the difference."

His lone mistake went over the wall in left field off the bat of Todd Zeile in the fifth inning to cut the Yankee lead to 2-1. Zeile was hitting .378 against Pettitte entering the game.

In the seventh, Pettitte got some help from his defense after walking Juan Gonzalez to lead off the inning. Will Clark's pop fly fell among centerfielder Bernie Williams, second baseman Chuck Knoblauch, and shortstop Derek Jeter.

But Williams scooped up the ball and threw to Tino Martinez covering second to get a rare 8-3 force at second on Gonzalez, who had to hold up to see if the ball would be caught. The play cost the Rangers a run as Ivan Rodriguez followed with a single.

"That's just instinct," Torre said. "Tino followed the play and it worked for us, and of course Bernie coming up throwing like he did."

The Yankees took the lead on an RBI double by Joe Girardi in the third and solo homers in the fourth and fifth by Williams and Knoblauch, respectively. Williams' line shot into the rightfield stands was his 17th of the season and extended his hitting streak to 16 games.

They looked like they put it away with three more runs in the seventh on an RBI single from Knoblauch and a two-run single from Jeter. But the Rangers battered a tired Pettitte and ineffective Ramiro Mendoza for two runs on four hits before Mariano Rivera put out the flames by getting Rodriguez to ground into a forceout.

Rivera earned his second straight save and 32nd of the season despite giving up a solo homer to Mike Simms in the ninth.

But everybody's mind was on Pettitte, who was 4-0 at the Stadium against the Rangers. He wasn't dominating, allowing three runs on seven hits with three strikeouts, but he pitched well enough to win.

"He was a lot more consistent down in the zone," Torre said. "He had some trouble in the eighth, but I think that was more because of the long seventh inning where he had to sit."

Darryl Strawberry didn't have much time to sit as he made his first start in left field since June 28, making one error and one putout in his only two chances. The error came in the second inning when

Strawberry took three steps in on a low liner by Juan Gonzalez and then tried to cradle the ball as he fell to his knees.

It was the first trial run of the Chili Davis contingency plan that calls for Strawberry, who's surgically repaired knees haven't kept him from leading the team with 21 homers this season, will most likely have to spend more time in the outfield when Davis returns as early as Monday in Kansas City.

Saturday, August 15, 1998 — Texas Rangers

Texas 16, Yankees 5

Yanks can't win them all

By GREGORY SCHUTTA, Staff Writer

NEW YORK — Hideki Irabu couldn't believe what he was seeing. There was Rusty Greer, reaching out for one of Irabu's split-fingered fastballs, and sending a high drive into left field.

"When he hit it, I said, 'This isn't going to be a home run, '" Irabu said. "There's no way. It's going to go outside the foul pole."

Instead the ball settled into the left field stands, just beyond the 318-foot sign by the foul pole for a grand slam, capping the Texas Rangers' six-run second inning en route to a 16-5 victory Saturday that snapped the Yankees' nine-game winning streak. More importantly, it may have taken away any chance of Irabu starting against the Rangers should the clubs meet in the playoffs.

"It definitely goes into the hopper," manager Joe Torre said after watching the Rangers batter Yankee pitching for 16 runs on 18 hits. "What you do is try to get all the information you can and hope to make the right decision later."

"I don't think about that right now," said Irabu (11-6), who lasted just 2 1/3 innings and was tagged for six hits and seven earned runs. "The Yankees are going to get into the playoffs, but I don't think about that just yet."

Todd Stottlemyre, pitching for the first time against a team on which his father, Mel, serves as pitching coach, settled down after a shaky two innings to throw four strong innings and beat the Yankees for the 12th time in his career. He gave up five runs on nine hits over six innings to raise his record to 2-1 since joining the Rangers in a trading-deadline deal. Stottlemyre is 11-10 overall.

"They got to me early," said Stottlemyre, who gave up five runs in the first two innings but left in the sixth with a 7-5 lead. "Pudge [catcher Ivan Rodriguez] was wearing a path to the mound. But a lot of the guys understood the pressure I was under."

Torre, trying to determine what his pitching rotation will be in October, got enough information Saturday to fill an encyclopedia. Tops on the list was learning that Yankees pitchers cannot get behind in the count against the Rangers, who are hitting .286 as a team, just one percentage point behind the Yankees and Red Sox.

Greer's homer, his 10th of the season, erased the 4-0 lead that the Yankees took in the first inning when they sent eight men to the plate. The Rangers added another run in the third, before breaking the game open with nine runs in the eighth and ninth innings.

Mike Simms put the game out of reach with a three-run, eighth-inning blast off Ramiro Mendoza that traveled 438 feet into the visiting bullpen in left-center field for a 10-5 Rangers lead. It was Simms' 14th of the season.

The 16 runs were the most the Yankees have yielded since dropping a 16-4 decision in Milwaukee in 1996 and the most at the Stadium since losing 16-3 to Toronto in 1992.

"Sometimes you feel like you have it coming to you," said Torre, who's seen the Yankees do the same thing to the opposition several times this season. "The unusual thing was having the four-run lead in the first and then seeing it just disappear so quickly. We've been spoiled because our starting pitching has been excellent."

And Irabu has been a major part of that, coming off two of his best outings of the season against Oakland and Minnesota. But the big right-hander, who had allowed just four hits over 15 innings in his previous two starts, didn't have it against the Rangers.

"I wish I knew where I was bad, too," he said. "Overall I don't think I was able to mix my pitches well."

Irabu, in his shortest outing of the season and second shortest as a starter, threw just 36 of his 63 pitches for strikes. He walked four.

"He just didn't have good command today," Torre said. "He walked people, and when you get behind [in the count] against this ballclub, they can hurt you."

If there's one weakness on this Yankees ballclub, the Rangers may have finally found it by getting to the bullpen early.

Sunday, August 16, 1998 — Texas Rangers

Yankees 6, Texas 5

Bernie bash

Homer in ninth invokes spirit of Bambino

By TARA SULLIVAN, Staff Writer

NEW YORK — The spirit of Babe Ruth has swirled within the soul of these Yankees all season. David Wells fashions himself a modern-day Ruth. The title of greatest Yankee team ever is up for grabs, perhaps to be taken from Ruth's 1927 edition. Around the majors, Ruth's prowess is remembered daily as Mark McGwire, Sammy Sosa, and Ken Griffey Jr. chase the single-season home run mark once held by Ruth.

Sunday, on the 50th anniversary of the Babe's death, the Yankees heeded his ghost in a most honorable way. Bernie Williams crushed an 0-1 fastball into the upper deck in right field in the bottom of the ninth inning, earning New York a 6-5 win over Texas to cap a 10-1 homestand. Williams, an anti-Ruthian figure with a low-key, modest personality, nevertheless performed the most Bambino-like act in a player's arsenal.

"It's what baseball is all about. You have dreams of things like this," Williams said. "It was a great way to end the game. It's a great tribute to his [Ruth's] memory."

Williams' game-winning shot was New York's third home run of the day, a total Texas matched against Wells. While the Yankees' left-handed starter was quick to explain Texas' power by crediting a wind blowing out to right field, the Yanks' Darryl Strawberry (solo shot in the second) and Derek Jeter (two-run homer in the first) needed no such assistance. Jeter credited something entirely different for an upper-deck, opposite-field blast that left teammates with their mouths agape.

"I think Babe Ruth was up there blowing it out," Jeter said. "I've never hit one that far, even in batting practice. It went a long way."

"That was about the longest home run the opposite way by a right-handed hitter that you'll see," pitcher David Cone said. Manager Joe Torre shared the same view. "How about Jeter?" he smiled. "Guys who've played here don't remember a righty hitting the upper deck. When he came back, he even said, 'Wow.'"

It's been a season full of such exclamations for New York, 90-30. The Yanks tied the 1944 Cardinals as the quickest team to reach 90 wins, though this one was hard-fought.

Jeter's homer gave the Yankees a 2-0 first-inning lead, which seemed like a quick antidote for Saturday's 16-5 shellacking from the Rangers. The advantage was up to 3-0 after Strawberry's homer, but Wells struggled to keep the ball down, battled with location, and gave up two home runs to Roberto Kelly (three RBI) and a solo homer to Royce Clayton. Wells left the game tied at 5-5 after six innings, unable to deliver a win on a day when a pregame moment of silence was held for his all-time favorite player and idol, Ruth.

The Yankees, who got an RBI single from Tino Martinez in the third and added another run in the fifth when Martinez grounded into a 6-4-3 double play to score Paul O'Neill, had every chance to take the lead in the seventh and eighth innings. But Martinez ended the seventh-inning, two-on, one-out threat with a 4-6-3 double play, and Jeter ended a bases-loaded, two-out eighth with a sharp grounder to third. It was all forgotten with Williams' homer, for which he was awarded a curtain call by the 50,304 fans.

"I was disappointed because we had a chance to wrap it up in the eighth and get Mo [Mariano Rivera] in there with a save situation," Cone said. "We were looking at another long game, but all of a sudden, one swing of the bat and it's over."

Williams' bat continues to smoke opposing pitching — he went 4-for-5 Sunday and leads the league with a .355 average — as the value of the potential free agent grows each day. "Bernie has a great deal of dignity," Torre said. "He understands what he means to these players and understands [the contract issue is] different. I've never been involved, especially in New York, with such a lack of carping or trying to posture yourself."

Yet, that quiet style has found its niche on Ruth's hallowed ground.

"Ruth built this place," said Torre, who recalled sitting in his Brooklyn home as an 8-year-old as the news of Ruth's passing interrupted a television program. "He brought the home run into the game. To have won with a home run — that's what you talk about when you think of Babe Ruth."

Monday, August 17, 1998
— at Kansas City Royals

Yankees 7, Royals 1

Yanks add Chili to the menu

By KEN DAVIDOFF, Staff Writer

KANSAS CITY, Mo. — He arrived at the ballpark late Monday afternoon, having been up for some 13 hours, but he insisted on playing. Chili Davis had 118 games to heal his surgically reconstructed right ankle. He didn't need any more time off.

And while he looked rusty during his first major league game in 136 days, the Yankees designated hitter made an impact, delivering a key fifth-inning RBI single to help the Bombers coast to a 7-1 victory over the Royals and Jersey City native Jose Rosado (6-9) at Kauffman Stadium.

Davis, who was reinstated from the 60-day disabled list before the game, went 1-for-4. In addition to his single, he struck out twice, walked, and bounced back to the mound. He is 2-for-8 (.250) as a Yankee, with his first RBI coming Monday night.

"Tonight I thought I'd be a little nervous, and I really wasn't," said Davis. "I have to feel that's pretty much because of the ballclub I'm on. I just figured it wasn't up to me to come out here and do everything. The guys have been doing it all year. It's just a matter of me getting in and trying to get some quality at-bats."

The ballclub he's on compiled some more amazing statistics Monday as it won its 11th game in 12 tries. The Yankees (91-30) have a 20-game lead over the Red Sox in the American League East.

Their biggest-ever lead is 21 1/2 games, accomplished four different times in 1941. And another thing: Tonight, the Bombers have a chance to sweep the Royals in the season series; so far, the Yanks are 9-0. Not counting interleague play and strike-shortened years, the Yankees have never swept a season series in their 96-year history.

Oh, and by the way, David Cone won again. On the one-year anniversary of the day he walked off the Yankee Stadium mound in the top of the second inning of a game against Texas (he would wind up needing surgery on his right shoulder after the playoffs), he became the first major league pitcher to notch 18 victories in 1998. He struggled with his command early, walking four in the first three innings, but allowed just one run on five hits over seven innings.

In lowering his ERA to 3.37, he increased his inning count to 163, meaning he needs just 37 more to reach 200, which will give him the right to activate a $5.5 million option for 1999.

"I'm still leery of what happened last year," Cone said. "Until I get through the whole year, I'm not going to relax."

Davis had little time to relax Monday. His day started at 5 a.m. in Norfolk, Va., where he was staying with Class AAA Columbus. He didn't know whether he would be flying back to Columbus with the Clippers or meeting the big league team in Kansas City.

The Clippers left without him, and he received a message to call Brian Cashman. The Yankees general manager told him that he was going to Kansas City, but first, George Steinbrenner had to rubber-stamp the move.

That kept Davis twiddling his thumbs in Norfolk until 11:30, when Cashman called and asked, "Can you make a 12:30 plane?" He did, hopping on a puddle-jumper to Washington, then switching to a direct flight to Kansas City. He arrived at the ballpark just as the team was stretching and told manager Joe Torre he was ready to play.

He struck out his first two times, then came up with runners on first and second and two outs in the fifth. Rosado offered a fastball down in the zone that Davis smacked into left for a single. Girardi scored to give the Yanks a 2-0 lead, and four more runs would come across, three on Tino Martinez's blast over the right field fence.

Cone (18-4) protected the lead, and yet another successful day at the office was in the books for the Yankees.

Tuesday, August 18, 1998 — at Kansas City Royals

Yankees 3, Royals 2

Curtis carries Yanks
Sheds slump to plate winner

By KEN DAVIDOFF, Staff Writer

KANSAS CITY, Mo. — Chad Curtis was supposed to get the night off. Mired in slumps numbering 0-for-13 and 1-for-20, he was, Yankee manager Joe Torre said, a mess.

"We need to get the Hoover vacuum in there and

clean [Curtis] out, then start all over again," Torre said early Tuesday evening.

Of course, so fittingly for this magical Yankees' season, Curtis went from bench rider to hero in less than four hours. With Mariano Rivera having blown his first save in 23 chances and the Yankees bullpen burning itself for days to come, Curtis singled home Bernie Williams in the 13th inning to give the Bombers a 3-2 victory.

"I've really been trying to back off the ball and get back to basics," said Curtis. "It hasn't been working out lately. Hopefully I can build off this one and get back to helping the team."

As they do with every triumph, the Yanks made some more obnoxious, "Aren't they great?" type history on this night. In lifting their record to 92-30, matching the 1996 Yankees regular season win total, they set yet another high-water mark for 1998. They were last 62 games over .500 on Sept. 28, 1939. Moreover, they swept the season series with the Royals, 10-0, outscoring them 78-22. Never in their 96-year history, besides strike-shortened seasons and interleague play, had the Yanks done that to anyone.

Williams started the 13th by lining a first-pitch single to left off Matt Whisenant (1-1). After Paul O'Neill whiffed and Chili Davis popped out to right, up came Curtis, who had entered the game as a pinch runner for Darryl Strawberry in the sixth and made outs in his first two at-bats. Whisenant's 0-1 pitch was way outside and went all the way to the backstop. Williams easily advanced to second.

Curtis lined the next pitch to center, and Williams came home with the game-winner.

"Sometimes you just bottom out, and there you are," said Torre. "You get a pitch to hit, and there it is."

Bayonne native Joe Borowski pitched a scoreless 13th, his second shutout inning, to pick up his first victory as a Yankee.

Mariano Rivera notched the first out of the ninth, then walked Luis Rivera to start the rally. Terry Pendleton stroked a single to left, moving Luis Rivera to second, and with Larry Sutton up, the two runners advanced to second and third on a Jorge Posada passed ball. The Yanks elected to intentionally walk Sutton, loading the bases and creating a force at any base.

Mike Sweeney launched a fly to deep center field, and Luis Rivera easily tagged up and came home with the tying run. The potential winning run, Pendleton, made it to third.

With the 26,259 fans in attendance loudly encouraging their Royals to salvage this final game of the season series, Jermaine Dye looked at an inside pitch for a called third strike, sending the game into extra frames. Considering Hideki Irabu and Ramiro Mendoza are temporarily out of commission and reliever Mike Buddie is slated to start Thursday's game, the extra-inning affair was the last thing the Yanks needed.

Until Mariano Rivera's ninth-inning hiccup, Orlando Hernandez was poised to win his fourth straight start. He has now put together these remarkable numbers over his last four starts: 33 innings, three runs, 14 hits, eight walks, and 33 strikeouts. His ERA is down to 2.72.

The Royals sent Pat Rapp against him Tuesday. When Rapp faced the Yankees 12 days ago in the first game of a day-night doubleheader, he couldn't find the plate, walking seven en route to an 8-2 defeat. On Tuesday night, the free passes hurt him again. With one out in the sixth, he walked Tino Martinez, then Davis, setting himself up for a meeting with Darryl Strawberry.

As if he were scripting an educational film on the dangers of throwing pitches out of the strike zone, Rapp proceeded to fall behind Strawberry, 3-1. By that point, he had little choice but to serve up a fastball down in the zone, which the Straw Man knocked to the right side. Kansas City second baseman Jose Offerman may have stopped it if he had jumped for it a half-second sooner. Instead, the ball skipped into right for a single, scoring Martinez for the 2-1 lead.

After the Bombers went down 1-2-3 in the first, Williams started the second with his 20th homer, a 417-foot missile to left-center.

The game went on cruise control from there, with both teams nipping but neither finding any success. An odd moment in the top of the fifth temporarily put the breaks on the pace. With Martinez getting ready to lead off, Royals' third baseman Dean Palmer was thrown out of the game, probably for complaining about the calls of home plate ump Jim McKean.

The Yanks put runners on first and second with two outs that inning but couldn't cash in, and that hurt a bit when Sutton got hold of a 2-2 El Duque offering in the bottom of the fifth and sent it over the wall in right-center, knotting the game at 1-1.

Wednesday, August 19, 1998

— at Minnesota Twins

Twins 5, Yankees 3

Yankees waste their opportunities

By KEN DAVIDOFF, Staff Writer

MINNEAPOLIS — The Yankees have a bottomless well of confidence that they lug around the country in their pursuit of baseball history. Always, they feel, they are due for an outburst, or a key out, or a bounce to go their way. The game will be theirs. They know it.

Wednesday night's game at the Metrodome featured several such moments, junctures that fans watching at home probably pointed to and said, "Here we go. This is it." But each time, the window of opportunity shut, and the Twins halted the most recent Yankees winning streak at three with a 5-3 victory.

"We weren't supposed to win the game, evidently," said manager Joe Torre. "We've had a good run, had lots of breaks. Tonight they didn't go our way."

The New York hitters went 1-for-13 with runners in scoring position, often failing in spectacular fashion. The seventh inning, in which Minnesota reliever Mike Trombley escaped a bases-loaded, none-out situation by fanning Paul O'Neill, Bernie Williams, and Tino Martinez, is a sure bet to make the Twins' highlight video.

Maybe the Bombers — whose 92-31 record ties the 1906 Cubs for the best-ever record after 123 games — were out of sync after the harrowing plane ride they survived early Wednesday morning from Kansas City, Mo., to Minneapolis. Maybe the Twins pitchers were juiced by the opportunity to knock the Yankees off their perch. In any case, this was not your ordinary 1998 Yankees game.

"It's so easy to get comfortable and say, 'What the heck, we're 60 games over .500,'" O'Neill said. "Bull. We've got to win games."

The Yanks entered the night with a tired bullpen after Tuesday's 3-2, 13-inning victory over the Royals. With minor injuries to Hideki Irabu and Ramiro Mendoza requiring reliever Mike Buddie to start tonight's game, manager Joe Torre had little flexibility with his relievers. Therefore, the manager

had little choice but to stick with Andy Pettitte for a while, no matter what happened.

Pettitte (14-7) wasn't terrible, but he wasn't very good, either. He went eight innings, thus sparing his relievers, and allowed five runs on nine hits. The southpaw walked three and struck out five.

"I was just inconsistent," Pettitte said. "I can't walk guys."

The Twins, meanwhile, used five pitchers to escape with their third victory against the Bombers in 10 tries. Reliever Dan Serafini was rewarded with the victory.

Down 5-2, Joe Girardi and Chuck Knoblauch started the seventh with singles, and after Trombley replaced Serafini, Derek Jeter walked to create a bases-loaded, none-out scenario, with 3-4-5 hitters O'Neill, Williams, and Martinez due up.

And so followed the game's most incredible sequence: O'Neill tried to check his swing on a 1-2 forkball in the dirt, but third base ump Rick Reed punched him out. O'Neill is in an 0-for-13 funk.

"The only word I can possibly think of is embarrassing," O'Neill said. "I was always in the middle of it. I feel bad."

Williams flailed and missed at an off-speed pitch. Martinez swung through two change-ups for strikes two and three. No runs, two hits, no errors, three men left on base.

"It was just one of those days," Martinez said. "You've got to give them credit."

The Yanks took a lead for the 48th straight game in the second, as Morgan issued successive walks to Williams, Martinez, and Chili Davis.

Tim Raines, boasting a career .338 average (49-for-145) with the bases loaded, could hit only an easy bouncer to second baseman Denny Hocking, who tagged Davis and threw to first for the twin-killing. Williams, whose steal of second ended a streak of nine games in which the Bombers didn't swipe a base, scored for the 1-0 edge.

The Twins quickly erased that deficit, scoring twice in the second. Former Met Alex Ochoa started the rally with an infield single and David Ortiz walked. The two men pulled off a double steal when the third strike to Terry Steinbach (swinging) went under Girardi's glove, and Ochoa came home on Hocking's grounder to shortstop. Pat Meares' two-out single to left on an 0-2 count scored Ortiz for the 2-1 lead.

Another Twins run in the third made it 3-1, and the Yanks responded with a run in the fourth.

Thursday, August 20, 1998 — at Minnesota Twins

Twins 9, Yankees 4

Yanks turn sloppy
Five errors lead to loss

By KEN DAVIDOFF, Staff Writer

MINNEAPOLIS — The previous time this happened to the Yankees, they literally hadn't won anything yet. Chili Davis was still healthy, Willie Banks got hit hard, and Joe Torre described his team's performance as "everything that's horse [bleep]."

One hundred twenty-two games later, deja vu visited the Metrodome (except for the Willie Banks part). Remember where you were: The Yankees were roughed up by the Twins on Thursday night, 9-4, to suffer just their second series sweep of the season. The first, as you probably remember, came in the first two games of the season against the Angels.

In setting a season high with five errors and producing just two runs and five hits off Twins starter Frank Rodriguez (3-2), who entered Thursday night with a 6.57 ERA, the Yanks lost two straight for the first time since July 19-20. This was just their fourth series defeat of the year, their first since they dropped two of three games to Toronto on July 17-19.

"We played the ugliest game we've played all year," Paul O'Neill said.

"Today, we were awful," Torre said. "Lots of errors, and we didn't pitch well. What you have to take out of these last two games is you can have a couple of bad games in a row. You have to deal with it."

The blowout defeat also ended the Yanks' major league record of consecutive games in which they held a lead at 48. In falling to 92-32, they fell off the pace of the 1906 Cubs, who were 93-31.

Quick quiz: What team is responsible for the most Yankees defeats in this season of so few defeats? The answer is these 56-70 Twins, who ended the season series a respectable 4-7. The Red Sox, Blue Jays, Indians, Tigers, and Angels have each taken three games from the Bombers.

Before the game, Torre praised Minnesota for its offensive approach.

"They're not going to swing at bad balls," the Yankees manager said. "They don't try to do too much. They don't give you part of the plate."

Rookie Mike Buddie learned that lesson firsthand,

as he was thumped for six runs (four earned) and seven hits in 4 1/3 innings to suffer his first major league loss. He deserved the defeat, but he probably should have shared it with the defense. Joe Girardi, Tino Martinez, Scott Brosius, Graeme Lloyd, and O'Neill were the five culprits. The previous time a Yankees team made five errors was April 19 of last year in a 3-2 victory over the White Sox.

"He did all right," Girardi said of Buddie. "We didn't play well behind him. We stunk."

The only bright spot Thursday night, and it was a dim bright spot, was that O'Neill ended his funk at 0-for-15 with a flare single to right-center in the eighth. He singled again in the ninth.

Matt Lawton knocked a single up the middle to start the fourth, and Marty Cordova swung at Buddie's next pitch, fouling it off. Cordova's bat hit Girardi's glove, however, and plate umpire Fieldin Culbreth immediately raised his hand to signal catcher's interference. Girardi argued passionately to no avail.

"I was just arguing for the sake of arguing," Girardi said. The fact that Girardi, perhaps the team's most even-tempered player, resorted to such quibbling reflected the team's frustration.

David Ortiz lofted a flyout to center, but that proved to be a tease for the Yankees. Ron Coomer lined an 0-2 pitch to right-center for a single, scoring Lawton and sending Cordova to third, and Todd Walker singled home Cordova for the 3-1 lead.

The bottom fell out in the fifth. Buddie issued a one-out walk to Brent Gates, Lawton singled up the middle, and Cordova singled to center. That scored Gates and ended Buddie's day. In came Lloyd, who promptly walked Ortiz to load the bases before Coomer lofted a sacrifice fly. A Walker grounder evaded a drawn-in Martinez for the inning's third run, and Terry Steinbach singled home Ortiz to make it 7-1.

The Bombers further humiliated themselves in the sixth, committing two errors (one when the ball slipped from Lloyd's hand on a pickoff attempt, making it look as though he were executing a spike after a touchdown) to push across an eighth Minnesota run. It became 9-2 in the seventh.

In his first career start Aug. 4, Buddie endured a terrible first inning, getting pounded for five runs. This time, the first inning was much smoother. After allowing a leadoff single to Otis Nixon, Buddie induced two grounders that moved the leadoff hitter to third. He then caught Cordova looking at a third strike.

Buddie got careless in the second, though, serving up a fastball at the belt to Coomer that the first baseman sent over the fence.

Friday, August 21, 1998 — at Texas Rangers

Yankees 5, Rangers 0

Wells hurls blanks

Four solo shots support shutout

By KEN DAVIDOFF, Staff Writer

ARLINGTON, Texas — This was where the old David Wells last appeared, the one who refused to make adjustments when he didn't have his best stuff. The one who drove Yankees manager Joe Torre batty.

So Friday night presented the 35-year-old the opportunity to prove conclusively he was a changed man, at least on the mound. That he had come full circle, in effect, from the pitcher he was on May 6.

On a night when the Yankees were looking to avoid just their second three-game losing streak of the season and give their bullpen a rest, Wells couldn't have presented a better argument in his defense. The southpaw went the distance, blanking the Rangers on six hits for a 5-0 victory at The Ballpark in Arlington.

"Toward the end, I turned to [pitching coach] Mel [Stottlemyre] and said to him, 'This is a little bit different than the last time he pitched here,'" Torre said.

Wells said he had done his best to forget about that May 6 start. Instead, he focused on his poor showing against the Rangers last Sunday at Yankee Stadium. "I wanted to redeem myself," Wells said. "I tried to make better pitches, and I did."

The Yankees, 93-32, tortured Texas starter Esteban Loaiza (1-3) with four solo homers. Tino Martinez went deep twice. His first blast gave him 100 RBI for the season, making him the first Yankee to pass the century mark in three straight seasons since Martinez's first base predecessor, Don Mattingly, did so from 1984-87.

In going the distance, The Boomer — whose 16th victory tied his career best set in 1995 and '97 — walked just one and fanned seven. Texas hitters had two opportunities all night with a runner in scoring position (no Ranger made it past second). Both times, Wells struck the batter out to end the inning. It couldn't have been any more of a contrast from the last time he took the mound at The Ballpark.

On May 6, Wells was given a 9-0 lead after two innings. He never made it out of the third, getting racked for seven runs in 2 2/3 innings. Torre was so upset, he publicly questioned whether Wells was out of shape.

The manager and the pitcher didn't speak for three days, until Wells asked Torre and Stottlemyre for a closed-door meeting. There, each man got everything off his chest, and Wells has been brilliant since. The May 17 perfect game came two starts later. He has put together a remarkable 12-2 record — including eight straight wins — and 2.42 ERA in 17 starts. His four shutouts lead the American League.

"I think he believes in himself more now," Martinez said. "In the past, when he got hit around early, I don't want to say he gave up, but he would just lose. Now, he goes six or seven innings even if he doesn't have his good stuff,"

Ironically, Wells and his perfect game were in the news Friday, as a published report said Major League Baseball was investigating American League umpire Al Clark for allegedly selling baseballs that were said to be from the May 17 game. Wells, who reportedly alerted baseball officials to Clark's actions, didn't comment on the report, and he obviously wasn't fazed by it.

> **❝I think he believes in himself more now.❞**
>
> *— Tino Martinez*
> *on pitcher David Wells*

He entered the night with a 12.46 ERA against the Rangers in two starts. In addition to the May 6 game, he was pummeled for five runs and 10 hits in six innings last Sunday. That Texas could be a playoff opponent made Wells' performance all the more important and impressive.

"After the second or third inning, I settled down and starting pitching my game," Wells said. "I am very aggressive and move my pitches in and out. You've got to keep them on their toes. When you've got knock them off the plate, you do it. I just tried to battle them. They have the poitential to gap you or hit the ball out of the park."

The Yankees have played three games in Texas this year, and Chuck Knoblauch has started two of them with homers. Friday night's leadoff dinger, on a 1-1 Loaiza fastball down the middle, went 407 feet into the left field stands.

Saturday, August 22, 1998 — at Texas Rangers

Yankees 12, Rangers 9

Brosius, Yanks skewer Rangers in Texas

By KEN DAVIDOFF, Staff Writer

ARLINGTON, Texas — Mark down another classic on your 1998 Yankees calendar.

In a marathon shootout featuring five lead changes, five homers, five errors, and nine pitchers, the Yankees outlasted the Rangers, 12-9, Saturday night at The Ballpark in Arlington. Scott Brosius delivered the key blow, an eighth-inning, three-run homer off former Yankee John Wetteland, to give blue-chip Bombers rookie Ryan Bradley a victory in his major league debut.

David Cone pitched poorly (5 2/3 innings, six runs), but still left the game with the victory his until Mike Stanton blew it, setting up Bradley for his memorable moment. Bernie Williams increased his major-league leading batting average to .353 with three singles and a double, and he drove in four runs.

This was a crazy one, this second straight victory which made the Yanks 94-32. It will likely be thought of as one of the best, along with David Wells' May 17 perfect game; the Aug. 4, 10-5 victory over Oakland featuring Darryl Strawberry's pinch hit grand slam; and the July 2, 9-8 victory against the Phillies with the two-out, three-run rally in the bottom of the ninth.

Onetime Yankees flop Xavier Hernandez (5-3) — who allowed Williams' game-winning, bottom-of-the-ninth homer last Sunday — took the mound to start the eighth, and he surrendered a one-out single to Tino Martinez. Chad Curtis laced a single to right-center one out later, putting men on first and third. Rangers skipper Johnny Oates, taking no chances, junked Hernandez for his closer Wetteland to face Brosius.

The Yanks' No. 8 hitter fouled the first pitch back, then took a ball outside. Wetteland offered a low fastball, and Brosius hit it on the head. It carried, carried — and just cleared the right field fence. The Yankees' bench erupted, as Martinez, Curtis, and Brosius rounded the bases for the 11-9 lead.

Mike Stanton never had a chance in the seventh. Lefty Rusty Greer singled to right-center, then Juan Gonzalez launched a blast well over the left field seats, knotting the game at 8. Will Clark sent the very next pitch for a solo homer to right. That was it for Stanton, as Bradley was summoned for his debut.

Joe Girardi started the sixth by ripping a triple over the head of Greer in left field. Chuck Knoblauch walked, and Derek Jeter lined a single to center. Girardi scored for the 5-4 lead, and when Tom Goodwin bobbled the ball, Jeter and Knoblauch moved to second and third.

Paul O'Neill ripped a sacrifice fly to right, scoring Knoblauch, and Jeter came home when Bernie Williams singled to right for his third RBI of the day.

Armed with a 7-4 lead, Cone couldn't make it through the sixth. Warren Newsom drilled a two-out single to center, Royce Clayton walked, and Goodwin lashed a double to the right-center gap, sending both runners home. Stanton replaced Cone and caught Mark McLemore looking at a third strike to preserve the one-run advantage. It became a two-run advantage in the seventh when Brosius singled, stole second, and scored on a McLemore error on a Knoblauch grounder.

McLemore beat out an infield single with one out in the first, and Greer drew a walk. After Cone fanned Gonzalez on a nasty slider, he unleashed a 2-1 pitch (with Clark at bat) that never touched Girardi's glove. Instead, it hit the catcher in the left arm and skipped behind him. Greer and McLemore advanced to second and third. Clark drove the next pitch to deep right, but O'Neill gloved it at the warning track.

And by the next time he took the mound, Cone had a 2-0 lead. Chili Davis and Brosius singled, Davis scored on Girardi's base hit to right, and Jeter singled home Brosius.

Clayton started the third with a beauty of a bunt single and then stole second. After Cone retired the next two batters, he walked Greer for the second time; entering the game, Cone had held Greer to a 5-for-29 showing (.172).

To pour some more lighter fluid on the fire, Cone threw three straight balls to Gonzalez. The American League's RBI leader took strike one, then ripped the next pitch into the second deck in left field. The homer, the sixth of Gonzalez's career against Cone, traveled 449 feet — tying it for the third longest in The Ballpark's five years.

A pair of Rangers errors allowed the Yanks to put up two runs and take a 4-3 lead in the fourth, as Williams singled home beneficiaries Knoblauch and Jeter. That lead lasted for exactly one pitch in the bottom of the fourth; Cone's first offering to leadoff batter Ivan Rodriguez was clobbered into the left field seats.

Sunday, August 23, 1998 — at Texas Rangers

Rangers 12, Yankees 3

Yankees can't keep up with Rangers

By KEN DAVIDOFF, Staff Writer

ARLINGTON, Texas — There's something about the Yankees and Rangers that brings out the worst in each. The worst baseball, that is.

The final game of the season series was an appropriately ugly one Sunday night at The Ballpark in Arlington, where the Yanks fell short, 12-10, in yet another slugfest.

Orlando Hernandez (8-4) was rocked for seven runs in five innings — this after he fanned 13 Texas batters Aug. 13. Mike Stanton again failed to pitch effectively. Rookie Ryan Bradley was pummeled a night after he picked up a "W" in his major league debut. All of this made moot 13 Yankees hits, including four homers.

The Yanks battled back from 6-0 and 12-6 deficits only to be denied in the ninth when John Wetteland earned his 34th save.

"If you don't pitch, [the Rangers] let you know about it," Yankees manager Joe Torre said. "You don't squeak by against these guys. But overall, I'm happy with the way my guys kept coming back. The way we kept battling back made the whole night worthwhile."

The Bombers fell to 94-33 and finished their weeklong road trip 4-3. They have 35 games remaining in their history-chasing season, and 24 are at home, where they are 48-9.

For the most part, this Yankees year has been as dominant as those numbers: Their starting pitchers tame the opponents, and the offense usually produces more than enough runs. But with a couple of notable exceptions, defeating the Rangers has been a major chore. The Yanks won the season series, 8-3, but you

> **❝**I didn't have good control of my pitches [in the first inning], and I think that's what cost us the game.**❞**
>
> *— Orlando Hernandez*

can bet they'll be rooting against Texas to surpass the Angels in the American League West.

The first 10 games of the series averaged a draining 3 hours 28 minutes, with the Yankees scoring 75 runs to the Rangers' 62. And Rangers right fielder Rusty Greer, who had a single, home run, and four RBI Sunday night is 18-for-47 (.383) with three homers, 16 RBI, and nine runs against the Bombers this season.

Jorge Posada's solo homer in the eighth cut the Yanks' deficit to 12-10 and marked the first time in his career that he homered from both sides. Five other Yankees have done it — Mickey Mantle, Roy White, Tom Tresh, Bernie Williams, and Roy Smalley.

El Duque had a chance to force Torre to start him in the postseason, especially if the Rangers are the opponent, but instead he won points only for sticking it out after a six-run Texas first. His ERA swelled from 2.72 to 3.19.

"When you get behind in the count, that's what happens," Hernandez said through interpreter. "I didn't have good control of my pitches [in the first inning], and I think that's what cost us the game."

The bottom appeared to fall out of this seesaw when the Rangers poured on five runs in the sixth off Stanton and Bradley. Greer's three-run homer to right ranked as the lowlight.

Of course, that turned out not to be a turning point, because the Yankees answered with three runs in the seventh to make it 12-9.

Hernandez didn't have as much trouble throwing inside to left-handers as he did during his previous struggles. This time he just couldn't get anyone out, period, in the first — although all but one of the five hits he surrendered were singles.

After Hernandez walked Tom Goodwin to start the Rangers first, it all went downhill. Luis Alicea drove a ground-rule double to right-center. Greer knocked an infield single off El Duque's glove, scoring Goodwin.

Juan Gonzalez grounded a single to left, scoring Alicea. Will Clark walked. Ivan Rodriguez hit into a fielder's choice at third, scoring Greer. Todd Zeile knocked a single to right, scoring Clark. Warren Newson sent a single to right, scoring Rodriguez. Finally, Royce Clayton's sacrifice fly to right scored Zeile for the 6-0 lead.

In all, the half-inning lasted 28 minutes and required 41 Hernandez pitches.

Monday, August 24, 1998 — Anaheim Angels

Angels 7, Yankees 3

Angels solve Pettitte, Yankees

By TIM LEONARD, Staff Writer

NEW YORK — Andy Pettitte has no problem tipping in a restaurant or for good service. On the field, though, is another story.

That's why the Yankees starter seemed a bit incredulous after being told by Chili Davis that he might be tipping his pitches to the Anaheim Angels. By then — after a five-run seventh inning — it was too late.

Whether the Angels had a clue as to what Pettitte was throwing, they sent 11 batters to the plate in the seventh to erase the Yankees' lead on the way to a 7-3 victory Monday night before 22,203 at the Stadium.

"My reaction was that I can't do anything about that in the middle of a game. I'm trying to get guys out," Pettitte said. "I felt good. Mechanically, I was as sound as I have been in a long time."

The Yankees dropped to 94-34 and, with the second-place Red Sox idle, their American League East lead fell to 18 games. The Yankees are 2-4 in their last six games, which for most teams would constitute a slump. For the Yankees, it represents a couple weeks' worth of losses.

The loss was the Yankees' 10th in 58 home games and was due in part to their travel schedule as much as their ineffective hitting against Angels starter Jack McDowell, who allowed six hits and two runs in seven innings.

"I hate to lose. We don't like to lose, whether it's one in a row or four of six," Yankees manager Joe Torre said. "We're not concerned, but we don't like to lose."

The buzz after the game was as much about whether Pettitte was tipping his pitches as it was about another big inning sabotaging an otherwise fine outing. MSG Network analyst and former major-leaguer Jim Kaat raised the point that Angels hitting coach Rod Carew may have picked up something in Pettitte's delivery that was causing him to tip his pitches.

"It's amazing to me how many people are geniuses in the TV booth. It [ticks] me off," said Yankees catcher Joe Girardi, whose run-scoring single in the fifth gave the Yankees a 2-0 lead. "They didn't see him [tip off pitches] in the first, second, third, fourth, fifth, sixth, or eighth? What do you think?"

Pettitte handled the Angels easily through six innings, allowing three hits. No Anaheim runner advanced as far as second base. If the Angels knew what was coming, they certainly disguised it very well.

Of course, in the seventh inning the Angels circled the bases as if on a carousel. Garret Anderson dealt the early blow, crushing a home run off the facing of the upper deck in right field. The blast, Anderson's 13th, also scored Tim Salmon, who led off the inning by lining a double off the wall in right-center.

After Troy Glaus singled, Phil Nevin and Gary DiSarcina whacked back-to-back doubles, the latter of which scored two runs to give the Angels a 4-2 lead. Darin Erstad later singled to score DiSarcina and was one of three Angels left on base when Pettitte struck out Todd Greene to end the inning.

"I heard some unbelievable stuff on TV while I was laying down on the trainer's table," injured Angels center fielder Jim Edmonds said. "I don't know what they were talking about. I was pretty amazed at what they were saying."

The idea seems far-fetched. After all, Pettitte didn't face more than four batters in any of the other seven innings he pitched. He threw 114 pitches, 77 for strikes, in what would have been a dominant performance without the seventh inning.

"I stayed in a real good rhythm," Pettitte said. "It's frustrating when you feel you've got it together and they seem to hit it anyway."

Tuesday, August 25, 1998 — Anaheim Angels

Angels 7, Yankees 6

Torched by an Angel

Yanks bullpen crumbles in loss

By TIM LEONARD, Staff Writer

NEW YORK — There aren't many options in the bullpen these days. And with Ramiro Mendoza starting the first game of a day-night doubleheader today, there was one less. That's why the Yankees haven't looked so invincible recently.

Mike Stanton and Mike Buddie combined to waste a gritty effort by Hideki Irabu, who had missed his last start after being hit with a line drive in the left foot. Stanton allowed hits to three of the four batters he faced and Buddie gave up a two-run single to rookie third baseman Troy Glaus as the Angels scored four runs in the seventh and handed the Yankees their third straight loss, 7-6, Tuesday night in front of 35,881 at Yankee Stadium.

"Obviously it's [the fans'] right and prerogative to voice their opinion," said Stanton, who left to a chorus of boos and saw his ERA rise to 6.41. "I'd be the first to say I don't blame them. I've stunk lately."

It was the second straight game the Yankees had taken a lead, only to watch as the Angels came back to win as the bullpen continues to struggle. The three-game losing streak matches the Yankees' longest of the season.

"I hate to think that people are giving up on Mike Stanton after what he did in the first half," said Yankees manager Joe Torre. "You go out there [to make a pitching change] and you have to have confidence. You have to feel like the guy you're bringing in is going to do the job."

The loss was the Yankees' fifth in seven games and dropped their record to 94-35. The Bombers, who are 3-5 against the Angels this season, must win their next six games to become the first team in baseball history to win 100 games before Sept. 1.

"I don't think we're alarmed, but we don't like losing," Torre said. "We've become pretty spoiled and we become a little bit angry when we lose."

Allen Watson showed the Yankees what they have been missing recently when he came in for starter Omar Olivares in the fourth inning. Watson neutralized the Yankees, striking out five in three innings. The only run he was charged with came after he had left the game, as pinch-hitter Chili Davis crushed a line drive off the wall in left field. The single off reliever Pep Harris allowed Bernie Williams to score from second and cut the Angels' lead to 7-5.

Harris injected some pep into the Yankees offense. Scott Brosius led off the eighth with a bloop single and went to second when Harris and catcher Matt Walbeck got crossed up on Derek Jeter's nubber in front of the plate. Paul O'Neill got his third RBI of the game when he singled to score Brosius and cut the Anaheim lead to 7-6.

Troy Percival relieved Harris and avoided any further damage by striking out Williams and getting Tino Martinez on a grounder to second.

"During the course of a season you're going to lose some games. We haven't done it much," said Jeter, whose baserunning gaffe short-circuited a potential fourth-inning rally. "We left some guys on base but they made some good pitches."

The Yankees powered their way to a 4-1 lead with a pair of runs in the first and third innings off Olivares. Williams singled home Chuck Knoblauch and then scored when Martinez smashed a double to center field for his team-leading 103rd RBI.

O'Neill didn't hit the ball as well as Martinez, but his slicing line drive down the left field line cleared the fence for a two-run home run in the third. The homer, measured at 360 feet, was O'Neill's 19th of the season.

It appeared to be all the support Irabu would need. Irabu hadn't pitched since an Aug. 15 disaster against the Texas Rangers in which he allowed seven runs in two innings before leaving the game after being hit on the left instep by a shot off the bat of Tom Goodwin.

Irabu struck out three in the first two innings, but struggled with his location and seemed to tire quickly. He managed to get through six innings, but was relieved by Stanton after walking Randy Velarde to open the seventh. Stanton promptly threw away a pickoff attempt and Velarde scored from second when Darin Erstad doubled just inside the bag at first to tie the score at 4.

Down 4-1, the Angels had made it a one-run game in the sixth with three consecutive singles after Irabu hit Garret Anderson. Glaus and Walbeck both lined run-scoring singles to close the gap to 4-3 before Irabu struck out Gary DiSarcina and got leadoff hitter Orlando Palmeiro to ground out to Martinez.

A pair of one-out walks got Irabu in trouble in the fourth, and Jeter ranged far to his left only to boot a potential double play grounder to load the bases. But Irabu struck out Walbeck on a nasty splitter and retired DiSarcina on a comebacker to escape the jam.

The Angels scratched out a run in the third after DiSarcina led off with a double. Palmeiro then sacrificed DiSarcina to third and he scored on Velarde's groundout to cut the lead to 2-1.

Reporter's Notebook:

Only bleacher-seat tickets remain for Saturday's game against the Seattle Mariners. The tickets are available at the Yankee Stadium advance ticket windows and local TicketMaster outlets.

Wednesday, August 26, 1998 — Anaheim Angels

Game 1: Angels 6, Yankees 4

Game 2: Yankees 7, Angels 6

Paradise lost?

All not well as Yankees get a split

By TIM LEONARD, Staff Writer

NEW YORK — If ever an injury summed up a week for a team, the one that kept Ramiro Mendoza from starting the first game of Wednesday's day-night doubleheader against the Anaheim Angels was it. Recently recovered from tendinitis in his right shoulder, Mendoza was a late scratch after having a cyst on his posterior drained.

That he didn't start was a pain in the butt. So was the reason he didn't.

That was just part of the week that has become painful for the Yankees. The team that doesn't seem to lose had its losing streak extended to a season-high four games in the afternoon after the Angels handed rookie right-hander Ryan Bradley a 6-4 loss in his first major league start.

A ninth-inning rally in the nightcap prevented things from getting worse as the Bombers pulled out a 7-6 victory after Mariano Rivera blew a save in the top of the inning.

Derek Jeter delivered a two-out single that brought home Jorge Posada with the winning run. Posada walked, went to second on Scott Brosius' sacrifice, and took third on a groundout by Homer Bush before Jeter slapped a single past the dive of first baseman Darin Erstad.

"It's sort of a wake-up call for us," Jeter said.

This was after Rivera was unable to avoid the recent pitfalls of the bullpen. He allowed a two-out single down the right field line by Erstad that scored Norberto Martin from first base with the tying run.

"Relief. There's no question," Yankees manager Joe Torre said. "When you have your closer in the game and you're one out away, the air's out of the balloon.

"You hate losing, and you look at the standings and we're in pretty good shape. But when you're in the game you don't think about the standings."

Pitching is a big reason why the Yankees have been struggling lately. When they have gotten a strong effort from a starter, the leads have been squandered by the bullpen.

"You never want anything to spiral," Torre said. "Any time you start losing games two, three, four in a row, a little piece is chipped off your confidence."

Mendoza is not expected to pitch until Friday at the earliest.

"As soon as his [butt] feels better he's going to pitch," Torre said. "He's uncomfortable. It's just a matter of when he can do what he can do."

Bradley didn't have much time to get nervous. He found out he was starting about 90 minutes before the game. He did a credible job under the circumstances, allowing seven hits, six runs — five earned — and striking out eight in five-plus innings.

"He did all right. He was up at the 100-pitch count and was running on empty," Torre said. "He gutted it out."

Bradley looked more nervous facing the media after the game than he did against the Angels lineup, especially after he sailed through the first four innings, striking out five and allowing one hit. The Angels got to him in the fifth, when Gary DiSarcina doubled home a run and Reggie Williams followed with a home run on an 0-2 slider that gave Anaheim a 3-2 lead.

Erstad and Tim Salmon led off the sixth with back-to-back doubles, and Garret Anderson followed with a run-scoring single before Bradley was replaced by Graeme Lloyd.

"I did pretty well in the first four innings, and then I hit a wall," Bradley said. "I just want to learn from the mistakes I made. If I get another chance, I don't want to make those mistakes."

That next chance will come in Columbus. Bradley was optioned to the Yankees' Class AAA team after the game as the Bombers purchased the contract of right-hander Jay Tessmer from the Clippers. To make room for Tessmer on the 40-man roster, the Yankees designated first baseman Ivan Cruz for assignment.

Bradley has had a meteoric rise through the Yankees system this season after starting at Class A Tampa, where he went 7-4 with a 2.38 ERA. He spent about two weeks at Class AA Norwich before another promotion to Columbus on Aug. 14. He earned his first major league victory in his Yankees debut, a 12-9 victory over Texas on Saturday. The previous pitcher to move so quickly through the Yankees system was Andy Pettitte.

But Bradley was unable to stop a streak that quickly has changed the feel-good attitude that has surrounded this team all season. The party line in the clubhouse is that losing is part of baseball. Well, for the 1998 Yankees it hasn't been. Until now.

"Now the questions aren't who are we going to play in the World Series, now the questions are will we get there," Torre said.

It certainly has been a weak week. A pain in the butt, too.

Thursday, August 27, 1998 — Anaheim Angels

Yankees 6, Angels 5

Off the wall

Bernie's shot lifts Yankees

By STEVE ADAMEK, Staff Writer

NEW YORK — It began as David Cone vs. Chuck Finley, Cy Young Award candidate vs. Yankee-killer, a showcase pitching matchup, one that could be reprised in the postseason.

It ended long after they were gone Thursday night — actually this morning — after the Yankees had thrown away so many opportunities, when Bernie Williams rattled a one-out, run-scoring double off the wall in left-center to give the Yankees a 6-5, 11-inning victory over the Angels.

And maybe, just maybe, if only in a whisper after this less than classic game, the Yankees issued this statement with their victory, only their fourth in the past 10 games: The Angels don't own us.

True, the Halos leave town having won the season series, 6-5 — including the first three of five meetings this week — something Yankees manager Joe Torre said before the game "should give them confidence" if the teams meet in the postseason.

But this night, Finley — who had won eight of his past nine decisions against the pinstripers and 15-of-23 overall — was ordinary. So was Cone, seeking his 19th victory.

In the end, though, both pitchers were bit players as the Yankees, who squandered first-and-second, none-out opportunities in the first and sixth innings, got only one run with the bases loaded and one out in the seventh, and gassed 3-1 and 5-4 leads, prevailed on Williams' drive on a 1-0 pitch from Mike Fetters.

A leadoff walk to Derek Jeter and a hit-and-run groundout by Tim Raines preceded Williams' hit.

Rookie right-hander Jay Tessmer, picked up the victory in his major league debut with a 1-2-3 11th that included two strikeouts.

The Yankees' sixth-inning opportunity was the most conspicuously missed, for it seemed Angels manager Terry Collins played right into the Yankees' hands. With those runners on first and second and the left-handed Finley about to face the right-hitting Luis Sojo, who was certain to bunt, Collins yanked Finley for right-hander Pep Harris.

That made Torre's move obvious, exit Sojo, enter Tino Martinez. Exit Martinez three strikes later, however, the first two called, the third a splitter Martinez missed by a mile.

Then Torre let righties Girardi and Homer Bush, his eighth and ninth hitters, bat, rather than pinch-hit for them from among Paul O'Neill, Jorge Posada, and Darryl Strawberry. Both failed and although O'Neill later tied the game with a sacrifice fly and Chuck Knoblauch produced a 5-4 lead in the eighth with another, Ramiro Medoza couldn't hold that lead in the ninth, sending the game into extra innings and eventually past midnight.

Cone, seeking his first 20-victory season in 10 years, lost the plate in the sixth, walking three straight batters, and departed one out into that inning after allowing four runs on three hits and four walks.

Finley, winner of eight of his last nine decisions against the Yankees, lasted only five-plus innings, surrendering three runs on seven hits and five walks.

To rest some of his regulars and stack the lineup with right-handed hitters against Finley, Torre sat down lefty hitters Martinez and Paul O'Neill, plus righty Scott Brosius, and started Sojo at first, Chad Curtis in right (with Tim Raines in left), and Homer Bush at third base. He also wavered before starting Chili Davis as his designated hitter after Davis pulled a rib cage muscle Wednesday that will limit him to right-handed hitting.

Thus, it wasn't exactly Murderer's Row the Yankees threw at Finley, with Raines batting third, and a bottom four of Curtis, Sojo, Joe Girardi, and Bush.

But in the fourth, after Cone allowed a two-out run in the third on Randy Velarde's run-scoring single, Davis took the direct route to wipe out that 1-0 deficit after a two-out walk to Bernie Williams. He smoked a 2-1 belt-high fastball from Finley well into the right-center field bleachers for the fourth homer of his career off Finley.

Against Finley, however, it's feast or famine for Davis, for in 22 other at-bats against the Angels left-hander, he has only two hits, including a sixth-inning double Thursday.

Then in the fifth, Raines salvaged a run out of a situation the Yankees threatened to squander as they did a first-and-second, none-out opportunity in the first. After Girardi's ringing double to left-center opened the inning, Bush failed to move him over, bunting foul twice, then striking out on a horrendous pitch trying to produce a right-side grounder. A walk and an out later, however, Raines plated Girardi by bouncing a single up the middle to make it 3-1, Yankees.

Cone promptly squandered that and called it a night when he lost the plate in the sixth, walking three straight before allowing Tim Salmon's sacrifice fly and Jim Edmonds' two-run double.

Friday, August 28, 1998 — Seattle Mariners

Yankees 10, Mariners 3

Yanks return to form
Rip Mariners for El Duque

By KEVIN T. CZERWINSKI, Staff Writer

NEW YORK — Sometimes you just need a good laugh.

Seattle provided one for the Yankees Friday. The underachieving Mariners looked very much like a team content to play out the season in losing, 10-3, before 49,789 fans at Yankee Stadium.

It's hard to imagine a team having the kind of season the Yankees have had needing a laugher. Chasing a major league record for victories and possibly clinching a playoff spot before the NFL season starts can make for some boring baseball after a while.

But, after the grueling week the Yankees endured, losing three-of-five in a difficult series with Anaheim, a sledgehammer of a victory was certainly welcome.

Everything went right for the Yankees, who won their third straight and evened their record on the current homestand at 3-3. With 97 wins, the Yanks have surpassed last year's total with 29 games to play. It's the most wins by a Yankees team since the 1980 team went 103-59.

Orlando Hernandez (9-4) pitched seven strong innings for his first win since Aug. 13. He scattered

three hits and struck out eight.

The Yanks, who scored five times in the first inning, had 12 hits and were never threatened.

"Having a laugher definitely helped," manager Joe Torre said. "It was nice to have a big lead like that where we would relax a little and not continue the tension that we had in the Angel series.

"It's just been a tough week all the way around. That Texas series was difficult, too. This whole week reminded me of when we went to Cleveland and then came back here to play Atlanta and the Mets."

Second baseman Chuck Knoblauch proved to be the catalyst at the plate with four hits and two runs scored.

"It seems like this week has just been one long day for me since we were standing on the tarmac at 6 o'clock Monday morning," said Knoblauch of a stretch that began with a Sunday night game in Texas and the Yankees arriving back in New York as dawn broke Monday. "It was good to jump out to this kind of lead and get a little breathing room."

And El Duque made the lead stick. When last we saw Hernandez, he was surrendering seven runs on eight hits in five innings to the Rangers on Sunday night. He had been struggling against left-handers, so Seattle's powerful left-handed hitters presented a potentially dangerous situation.

Hernandez, though, cut through the Mariners line-up, including slugger Ken Griffey Jr., with relative ease while making few mistakes. In the process, he upped his record in night games to 5-4. In contrast, his record in the daylight is 4-0 with a 1.86 ERA.

"I've been working very hard with the catchers and the pitching coach on going inside against lefties and it's been working out," Hernandez said. "I had trouble with the mound in Texas and I think that was part of the problem there. Today, though, I was able to throw strikes and work ahead in the count.

"The big lead was nice, but as I've said in the past, it could also be pretty dangerous. There is always the chance you let up with a big lead. My teammates kept coming over to me in the dugout and saying 'Duque, keep your head in the game, it's still 0-0.'"

While the Yanks were telling Hernandez the score was 0-0, the scoreboard told a different tale. The Yanks batted around in the first inning for the 29th time this season. They scored five runs on five hits, the 23rd time they have scored five or more runs in an inning.

Chili Davis had the big blow, a two-run double off Paul Spoljaric (4-3). The Yankees added two more in the third on Scott Brosius' two-run homer into the upper deck in left field, his 17th of the season.

By the time Tim Raines drove in two more runs with a fourth-inning double, all that was left was to see if Griffey would hit a homer. He did not. He went 0-3 with a walk, flying out twice.

Saturday, August 29, 1998 — Seattle Mariners

Yankees 11, Mariners 6

Jeter Meter: .334 and rising

By KEVIN T. CZERWINSKI, Staff Writer

NEW YORK — It's not a debate that rivals the Willie, Mickey, and the Duke wars of the Fifties. But, the argument about who the best shortstop is in the American League gets more heated every day.

New York's Derek Jeter is regarded by many as the third-best player among the trio that includes Seattle's Alex Rodriguez and Boston's Nomar Garciaparra. Jeter, however, continued Saturday to make a case for being placed a little higher on that list.

He collected three of New York's season-high 19 hits in the Yankees' 11-6 victory over Seattle before 55,146 fans at the Stadium in a game that wasn't nearly as close as the score indicated.

Jeter shares the league lead in hits with Rodriguez at 175. Jeter also scored four runs, upping his league-leading total to 110. But wait, there's more. He collected his 17th home run of the season, breaking the single-season mark for Yankee shortstops that was set by Roy Smalley in 1982.

And, if that isn't enough, his batting average jumped to .334 as he continues to chase teammate Bernie Williams (.343) for the American League batting title.

"I'm trying to remember what it was like when I was 24," New York manager Joe Torre said. "He's like kid dynamite, he's got so much going for him, the least of which is his confidence. It's the type of confidence that's not offensive.

"He feels he can get a hit off anyone, anytime. It's very rare for someone to feel that way with the limited amount of experience he has. He's very different from anyone I've ever seen. It's not fair to project what he'll do over the course of his career, but he's

sure off to a hell of a start."

Jeter sure helped the Yanks, who have won four straight, to a great start Saturday. He picked up hits in three of his first four at-bats, including a two-run homer in the fourth.

It helped stake Andy Pettitte to an 11-0 lead, allowing the Yanks to proceed on cruise control from the fourth inning on.

"The home run record is nice, but I'm not trying to go out there and set any kind of record," Jeter said. "I just want to go out and have good at-bats, and in that regard it's been a great season so far. I think you appreciate it because you look at past teams here and the great players they had. Now, though, it's over with. You move on."

Jeter's performance also had some of his teammates and Torre talking about a batting title. Williams also collected three hits.

Entering Saturday night's action, Williams led the AL, Mo Vaughn (.335) was second, and Jeter was third.

"Sure I think Derek has a chance to win a batting title," Torre said. "But I'm still going to have to go with Bernie because he's a switch-hitter. If Derek did it, though, I would not be surprised.

"I'm not sure if there's any ceiling for him. He's leading the league in runs scored and he missed three weeks. He's a tough kid, both physically and mentally. That will enable him to do a lot of things."

Including continuing to draw comparisons to A-Rod, who belted his 38th home run of the season off Pettitte in Seattle's five-run seventh inning.

The Mariners, however, came back with too little, too late.

Sunday, August 30, 1998 — Seattle Mariners

Mariners 13, Yankees 3

Nobody's perfect

Irabu's spirit sinking more than his splitter

By KEVIN T. CZERWINSKI, Staff Writer

NEW YORK — Hideki Irabu might have to start worrying whether he'll have a spot in the Yankees' starting rotation come October.

He looked horrible Sunday as the Yanks were trounced by Seattle, 13-3, in the series finale at the Stadium. Irabu lasted just 3 1/3 innings, allowing a career-high eight earned runs and 10 hits in absorbing his fourth loss in his past six decisions. He also gave up one of Ken Griffey Jr.'s two home runs.

The 55,341 fans booed Irabu, whose splitter didn't split and whose fastball found wood more often than Jorge Posada's glove. The poor outing leaves Irabu winless since Aug. 10, and it's difficult to envision manager Joe Torre giving Irabu the nod over Orlando Hernandez in the playoffs.

"It was a bad pitching performance," Torre said. "Hopefully he will straighten himself out. He didn't have good command of his stuff today, there were too many pitches in the middle of the strike zone. [Pitching coach] Mel [Stottlemyre] said he had a good splitter in the bullpen before the game. It just didn't work in the game.

"Everything we see from here on will go into the hopper as far as making decisions. He missed a start with the bad foot, and his last few games haven't been good. It all comes down to pitching, and if you don't pitch well you're going to get your butt kicked."

The Mariners jumped all over Irabu in the first inning, collecting four runs and four hits. All were hit hard. It didn't get any better in the second, when Griffey rocked a three-run homer, his 46th of the season.

"I'm thinking about what's going wrong now, too," Irabu, who before the game spoke with the Japanese Little League team that lost the title game to Toms River on Saturday, said through interpreter George Rose. "I think today when I got hit, I got hit hard. Even when I made good pitches, I got hit.

"When I'm throwing my splitter, I try to throw it low. But if I throw it too low, the batters won't swing at it. So I tried to get it up just a little and I got it up too high. If I keep throwing like this, I'm going to be worried about the playoffs."

Posada, who hit his 16th home run of the season in the fifth inning, couldn't offer much of an explanation for Irabu's poor performance, either. He said that between innings he told Irabu, through Rose, that he should just keep the ball low. Irabu didn't comply.

"It was just a matter of location," Posada said. "His splitter was getting too high. At the end, you could sense he was getting frustrated. He just didn't have it. I'm just hoping he'll get it back for his next start."

Because the game got out of hand early, most of the fans didn't hang around to see things heat up in the late

innings. Seattle's Jose Paniagua plunked Scott Brosius in the back in the seventh inning, causing Brosius to leave the game. Brosius later said he was fine.

Griffey came up in the eighth and hit his 47th homer, this one off Mike Buddie. After a David Segui single, Buddie threw a wild pitch past the feet of Rob Ducey. On the next pitch Buddie plunked Ducey in the leg. Ducey took exception and walked toward the mound.

Both benches cleared, and Ducey and Buddie exchanged words. Buddie was ejected. Graeme Lloyd then came in and hit John Marzano, but nothing came of it and he was not ejected.

"The umpire [crew chief Drew Coble] gave Buddie the benefit of the doubt on the first pitch and then threw him out after he hit him," Torre said. "That was fair."

It was the second time in the game the teams exchanged words. In the third, Chad Curtis touched things off when he failed to slide as the Mariners turned an inning-ending double play. Curtis veered off as he approached second base, and shortstop Alex Rodriguez took exception. Players from both sides milled around, but there was no trouble.

Tuesday, September 1, 1998 — Oakland A's

Yankees 7, A's 0

David like Goliath

Shuts out A's in two-hit gem

By MARK J. CZERWINSKI, Staff Writer

NEW YORK — David Wells had a feeling warming up in the bullpen Tuesday night at Yankee Stadium, and it wasn't a good one.

"It was a pitiful warm-up," Wells said. "Pitiful. I didn't think I would last three innings out there. It was a bizarre night. I didn't think things would happen the way it turned out."

The feeling was still there during the national anthem, as Wells confided to Casey Gaynor, a pitcher for the Little League World Series champion Toms River East team.

"I have nothing tonight," Wells told Gaynor. "Be ready to come in."

It turns out that Wells is a much better pitcher than prophet. Not only was the big guy sharp as nails in his 7-0 victory over the Oakland A's, but he came within seven outs of becoming the first pitcher to throw two perfect games in one season.

"Perfect," said manager Joe Torre. "That explains it all. It means you're not allowed to breathe or do anything wrong. But he was pretty terrific."

And that's putting it mildly. Wells' two-hit, 13-strikeout performance improved his record to 17-2, and may have pushed him one step closer to his first Cy Young Award.

Besides, Wells is still perfect at Yankee Stadium this season. He's 11-0 in 15 starts at home, allowing 37 runs in 115 2/3 innings.

Wells lost his shot at immortality with two out in the seventh inning. He got two quick strikes on Jason Giambi before he smacked a hanging curveball into center field for a clean single.

"I had a different grip in my glove," said Wells, who was happy with the pitch. "I had a good curveball working, but I wanted to throw a cutter to him. But I went with what Jorge Posada called."

"He made a good pitch," Torre said. "[Giambi] just hit it off the end of the bat."

Wells, however, seemed more relieved than annoyed by Giambi's spoiler. As he took the mound in the eighth, the southpaw made sure he said a few words to the Oakland first baseman.

"I thanked him," Wells said. "I said, 'Thank you, man, you took a lot of pressure off me.'

"Like I said a while back, I didn't want to throw another perfect game. That's why I thanked him."

To hear the A's tell it, Wells also should have thanked home plate umpire Jim McKean. Manager Art Howe wasn't happy with McKean's strike zone, covering home plate with dirt following his ejection at the end of the sixth inning, when Wells struck out the side.

"I've been in the big leagues a long time," said former Yankee Rickey Henderson, who was caught looking twice. "I have a great eye and know the difference between a ball and a strike. Wells had an advantage, and he didn't even need it."

Wells knew early on that he had the stuff to throw another no-hitter. The crowd also picked up on it early, roaring their approval every time he threw a strike.

"About the third inning, I said 'Hey man, this can't be happening again,'" Wells said. "The way I was striking guys out, the way my pitches were going, you couldn't help but think about it."

The Yankees did their part to turn the spotlight on Wells, scoring six runs in the first two innings off veteran knuckleballer Tom Candiotti. They batted around in a four-run first inning, and Bernie Williams made it 6-0 with a two-run home run in the second. Tino Martinez added his 24th homer in the seventh.

And, as usual at Yankee Stadium, Wells didn't disappoint.

"I'm not disappointed," Wells said. "Hey, we won the damn game."

Reporter's Notebook:

The Yankees have 99 wins in 136 games. The 1954 Cleveland Indians hold the American League record for the fewest games to reach 100 victories (140).

Derek Jeter was named American League Player of the Month for August.

Wednesday, September 2, 1998 — Oakland A's

A's 2, Yankees 0

Silent night

A's Heredia quiets Yanks, denies Cone

By KEN DAVIDOFF, Staff Writer

NEW YORK — That the Yankees didn't win their 100th game Wednesday night at Yankee Stadium most likely didn't cause anyone in pinstripes to lose a wink of sleep. That David Cone looked like his old self most likely caused those in pinstripes to sleep even better.

Veteran journeyman Gil Heredia shut down the Yankees' bats, 2-0, to disappoint a crowd of 30,332 that sat through a 2-hour 14-minute rain delay before the first pitch in the hopes of seeing the home team notch its 100th victory earlier than any team in American League history.

"We wanted to [get No. 100 at home]," said manager Joe Torre, whose team will start a six-game road trip Friday at Chicago. "But I hope we don't get it at home now."

Heredia, a 32-year-old who has lived at 11 minor league addresses and pitched for four major league teams in his 12-year career, tossed 7 2/3 innings of five-hit ball, striking out five and walking none.

For this night, though, the Yanks could tolerate an opponent outpitching Cone, because the right-handed veteran did so little wrong in having his record fall to 18-5.

It was not a crucial start for Cone, not after he overcame two Armageddon-esque starts of the season to put together a candidacy for the AL Cy Young Award. Nevertheless, he had been conclusively unimpressive his previous two times out, failing to get through the sixth inning both times for two no-decisions.

That's why the Yankees had to be encouraged by Wednesday's start. In showing both velocity and good ball movement, the 35-year-old lasted seven innings, allowing a run and four hits, walking two, and striking out 10. His ERA dropped from 3.67 to 3.58.

"Tonight was as good as I've been in a few starts," Cone said. "I had one point in my last few starts where I wasn't sharp. Tonight I was able to avoid that."

Cone has pitched 181 innings on the season, meaning he needs 19 to reach the mark that will activate an option to return to the Yankees next year for a $5.5 million salary.

So while hometown fans might be disappointed that win No. 100 almost certainly will come away from the Bronx, they can at least take solace in Cone's success.

"I was very pleased with his outing," Torre said. "Hopefully, he's where he was earlier, before he got out of whack."

The only troubling note came in the form of Mike Stanton, who permitted the A's second run on a Ryan Christenson homer to left in the eighth. The left-handed reliever has given up 12 homers. Last year he surrendered just three.

Whenever that 100th win does come — the 1954 Indians hit the century mark in their 140th game, meaning the Bombers have two more tries to rewrite the AL record — it probably won't get a much larger reaction from the players than did victory No. 7, or 42, or 86.

"It's one of those round numbers that sounds good, but I don't think it has any more meaning," Scott Brosius said before the game Wednesday. "This year, we've been so good about not focusing on things like that. It's hard to focus on that now."

Still, some felt an appreciation for the milestone.

"It's always special to win 100 ballgames," said Darryl Strawberry, whose 1986 Mets won 108 in the regular season. "It's a hard thing to accomplish. It

means this is a team that's really played at a level where nobody else is playing at."

"It's great," Torre agreed. "For a manager that never won more than 96 before this year, it's something you can never imagine in spring training. Unless somebody puts your feet into the fire and says, 'Guess how many games you're going to win,' you're always going to think 95, 96, and it doesn't mean you don't think you're a good club."

At 99-38, this better-than-good club must go 18-7 in its remaining 25 contests to break the 1906 Cubs' record of 116 victories.

The fans who stuck around had barely shaken off the rain when the A's jumped on the scoreboard. Christenson lined a single to left and moved to third when Jason Giambi — who took the plate to boos thanks to breaking up David Wells' perfect game Tuesday night — ripped a bullet that skipped past Tino Martinez. Matt Stairs drove home Christenson on a hard grounder to second.

While Cone regained his composure and frustrated the A's with his usual choice of poisons, the Yankees were helpless against Heredia. Two Yankees made it as far as second base in the first seven innings.

Friday, September 4, 1998
— at Chicago White Sox

Yankees 11, White Sox 6

Yanks: Happy 100th

Bernie socks pair of homers

By KEN DAVIDOFF, Staff Writer

CHICAGO — This one felt scripted: down early, up late, and a touching, injury-recovery story in between.

Victory No. 100 arrived for the Yankees on Friday night in the form of an 11-6 triumph over the White Sox at Comiskey Park. Bernie Williams hit two homers, including the game-winner in a four-run eighth inning, and Jeff Nelson pitched well in his first outing after a 70-day absence with a bulging disk in his lower back.

In all, it was typical of this remarkable team, which set the American League record by notching its 100th win in its 138th game, sooner than any other team in history. The 1954 Indians held the former mark at 140. The Yankees' magic number to clinch the AL East is five.

"Any time you talk about the best record at this time, that's pretty special," manager Joe Torre said. "Baseball's been around a long time."

Nelson, who along with Darren Holmes was activated before the game, pitched a quick but very encouraging two-thirds of an inning in the seventh, retiring the dangerous Frank Thomas and Albert Belle. Graeme Lloyd relieved him and wound up picking up the victory.

"I went from [Class] A ball to facing the best hitters in the league," Nelson said. "I'm kind of glad I got it over with."

Referring to Nelson's performance, Torre added: "That was good. I was happy to get Nellie in that situation."

Chuck Knoblauch began the game-turning eighth against loser Chad Bradford with a nubber between first base and the pitcher's mound. Its location was perfect, and the White Sox couldn't even make a clean play on it. Infield single.

The Yankees second baseman stole second on a 1-1 pitch to Derek Jeter, who then singled home his teammate to knot the score at 4.

Paul O'Neill made the first out of the inning, a fly to center, but on the first pitch to Williams, Jeter stole second and went to third when Chad Kreuter's throw eluded shortstop Mike Caruso. With the count 3-1, Williams crushed his second homer into the right-field stands. It was the fifth time in Williams' career (third time in the regular season) that he went deep from both sides in a game. He is hitting a league-leading .344.

Tino Martinez made it back-to-back round-trippers, sending a blast to right to give the Bombers a 7-4 lead. Four more runs crossed in the ninth.

Whether that half-inning or the one that preceded it ranked as the night's highlight was up for debate. Orlando Hernandez had pitched six mediocre innings (four runs, six hits, a career-high six walks, three strikeouts) when Torre decided to throw Nelson into the fire with Thomas, Belle, and Robin Ventura due up.

Thomas took a strike, fouled a pitch into the right field stands, and knocked a liner to center that Chad Curtis charged and grabbed on a slide. Belle popped a 1-0 pitch toward the third base line, where Jeter planted himself and caught it.

And that was it. Torre decided to quit while he was ahead and brought in the left-handed Lloyd to face

the lefty-hitting Ventura. That left Nelson with a line of two-thirds of an inning, no runs, and no hits. He threw just five pitches, all strikes.

While Nelson is a cinch to make the playoff roster if he's healthy, Holmes will have to conquer long odds to do the same.

Hernandez simply lost control in the fifth inning, issuing free passes to Thomas, Ventura, and Greg Norton. That Chicago could get only one run out of it, with Jeff Abbott's sacrifice fly giving the home team a 4-3 edge, was quite a break for the Yankees.

The White Sox jumped out to a quick 2-0 lead courtesy of the meat of their lineup. Thomas crushed a two-out double to the left field corner in the first, and Belle followed with a 400-foot dinger to left.

Shane Spencer slugged a solo homer in the third, but the Sox added a run in the bottom of the inning when Caruso singled, stole second, went to third on a Hernandez wild pitch, and came home on Belle's sac fly to center.

With one out in the fourth, O'Neill lofted a pedestrian pop that fell in no-man's land in short center field. Caruso at shortstop made a run for the ball, but it glanced off his glove. O'Neill hustled for a double. Two pitches later, the score was tied, with Williams having jacked a 1-0 offering deep into the left field stands.

Saturday, September 5, 1998
— at Chicago White Sox

White Sox 9, Yankees 5

Pettitte gives Yankees cause for concern

By KEN DAVIDOFF, Staff Writer

CHICAGO — Normally, baseball players hold court with the media at their lockers. But with his teammates trying to dress quickly and avoid the Saturday night postgame traffic, Andy Pettitte searched for a less intrusive location to answer questions. Finally, he settled on a tall garbage can in the middle of the Comiskey Park visitors clubhouse.

"I'll stand right here in the trash," he said with a laugh.

Which was fitting after his lousy performance in

the Yankees' 9-5 defeat. The left-hander lasted just two innings, his shortest outing of the season, getting pounded for five runs and six hits. A slip on a second-inning follow-through prompted a visit by manager Joe Torre, pitching coach Mel Stottlemyre, and head trainer Gene Monahan, but Pettitte finished the inning and said after the game that he felt fine.

As for his pitching, Pettitte said, "I felt good. I felt pretty good. I really don't know. I felt like I made a couple of bad pitches. I didn't think I made that many real bad pitches to give up five funs in two innings, but I guess I did."

Yes, his manager and catcher confirmed, he did.

"He didn't have good stuff," Torre said. "It looked like he was cutting it off a little bit. He wasn't finishing."

"His stuff in his last two starts was outstanding," catcher Joe Girardi said. "His stuff tonight, it wasn't too good."

Jim Abbott made his return to the major leagues success, notching his first victory since Sept. 8, 1996, in front of 33,092 fans, the White Sox' best draw of the season. Even though the Yanks fell to 100-39, their magic number to clinch the AL East fell to four courtesy of the Blue Jays' 4-3 victory over the Red Sox.

Had Abbott bested his former team in a pitcher's duel, the Yanks could have shrugged it off and tipped their hat to the left-hander. Instead, they have to wonder if their own left-hander can right himself with the postseason looming.

Pettitte's 4.12 ERA has increased with each of his past six starts, a foreboding sign from someone being counted on in the postseason. In those six starts, the 26-year-old has allowed 27 runs and 47 hits in 36 2/3 innings for a 6.64 ERA.

"I felt like I was getting it together my last two starts," said Pettitte, who was hit hard in one inning in each of those outings. "I guess it's the story of the season. I put together a couple of good ones, and then I struggle. I kind of get right back to where I was before."

"I think Andy thinks it's bigger than we think it is," Torre said. "The last two outings were good. But Andy is such a perfectionist that one bad inning out of seven isn't good enough. He wants to fix that one inning. We always assure him, saying, 'You're fine, you're fine. Everything will be OK.'"

After the Yanks scored two runs off Abbott in the first, the White Sox got one back in the bottom of the inning. While Abbott calmed down, Pettitte went the other way. His first pitch of the second was jacked over the fence in right-center by Magglio Ordonez, knotting the score at 2. Greg Norton walked, Mike Cameron popped to shortstop, and No. 9 hitter Robert Machado, owner of a .205 average, drilled a run-scoring double to right-center, giving Chicago the lead.

Pettitte's ineffectiveness allowed Torre to get a look at two pitchers he wanted to see: recently acquired Jim Bruske and rehabilitated Darren Holmes. In his first appearance as a Yankee, Bruske got lit up for two homers — including Albert Belle's 44th — in the third inning. Holmes, who missed more than a month with a bulging disk in his lower back, looked good, allowing a run in three innings.

"Holmes did well," Torre said. "He had a good curveball tonight. That's as good a curveball as he's had all year as far as location."

"My breaking stuff is a lot better," agreed Holmes, who said his back felt fine.

On the other side, there was Abbott, protecting his large lead through 6 1/3 innings and providing the lowly White Sox with some cheer.

"It hasn't really sunk in," he said. "I never thought I'd be back, so the significance of tonight for me personally is a little overwhelming."

Sunday, September 6, 1998
— at Chicago White Sox

White Sox 6, Yankees 5

Irabu, Yanks continue slide

Righty surrenders six runs in 2 1/3 innings

By KEN DAVIDOFF, Staff Writer

CHICAGO — At one point in this season, Hideki Irabu was arguably the ace of the best team in baseball. Blazing fastball, nasty splitter, perfectly placed curveball — he was on top of the his game, owner of a microscopic ERA, and candidate for a spot on the American League All-Star team.

Now, there is no one on the Yankees who better represents this club's fall to earth than Irabu. On a sweltering Sunday afternoon in Comiskey Park — the same stadium where the right-hander pitched his first big league shutout on Memorial Day — Irabu was torched again, lasting just 2 1/3 innings and allowing all of the White Sox' runs in a 6-5 defeat.

At 100-40, the Bombers have dropped two straight and four of six and are 8-10 in their last 18 games. Those 1906 Cubs have to be feeling pretty good about themselves; it would take a 17-5 record in the final 22 games for New York to set the all-time record for victories.

But that hardly ranks as a concern in the Yankees clubhouse. Instead, someone needs to solve the mystery of what has happened to Irabu, or else he may not be joining his teammates in the playoffs.

"I feel really good," he said through his interpreter, George Rose. "My conditioning is fine, my arm is fine, my shoulder is fine. I warmed up very well in the bullpen. I'm asking myself [what's wrong], too."

George Steinbrenner arrived in town Saturday night, watched the game Sunday with White Sox owner and good buddy Jerry Reinsdorf, and even joked around with his players after the loss. But when asked what plagued his $12.8 million investment, the Yankees owner frowned and said softly, "I don't know."

The line for Irabu read six runs, eight hits, two walks, and one strikeout. He threw 53 pitches, 27 for strikes. In his last four starts, he has lasted a total of 14 innings and has been torn apart for 25 runs (all earned) for a 16.07 ERA. He has allowed 29 hits, walked 13, and fanned 10.

Earlier in the season, the right-hander said, he would throw similar pitches and they would be fouled off or hit for outs. Now, he lamented, "I'm just not able to do that."

After the Yanks went down 1-2-3 in the first, Irabu took the mound and went 1-2-3-4-5 — that is, five straight balls. After leadoff hitter Ray Durham walked, Craig Wilson did the same, setting the table for Frank Thomas, Albert Belle, and Robin Ventura. The Yanks were fortunate to head into the second down only 1-0.

The second, though, went much worse, with four runs coming across as the White Sox batted around. An error by shortstop Luis Sojo pushed the first run home, then five more Chicago players would get hits before the frame ended. Robin Ventura led off the third with a homer for the sixth and final run.

"[Irabu] was throwing hard," Jorge Posada said, "but everything was up in the zone."

The Yanks aren't sure what they'll do with Irabu. They'll probably keep him in the starting rotation, manager Joe Torre said. Pitching coach Mel Stottlemyre said he'd like to see "a little more fire" on the mound.

But with the playoffs inching closer — the Yanks can clinch the American League East with two victories in the next three days against the Red Sox — time is ticking. And right now, Irabu simply can't be trusted on the mound.

"No question, when you get to playing a five-game series, seven-game series, you have very little room for error to get it polished up," Torre said.

Reporter's Notebook:

Shortstop Derek Jeter didn't start for the first time since June 18, his last day on the 15-day disabled list with a strained abdominal muscle. He pinch hit for Sojo with two outs in the ninth and was called out by home plate umpire Larry Barnett on a very suspect third strike.

Both Andy Pettitte (slipped on the mound in his Saturday night start) and Darren Holmes (made his first appearance Saturday since being activated off the 15-day disabled list with a bulging disk in his lower back) reported to work Sunday feeling fine.

Monday, September 7, 1998
— at Boston Red Sox
Red Sox 4, Yankees 3

Yanks catch bad break

Fan's glove aids Bosox

By KEN DAVIDOFF, Staff Writer

BOSTON — While they were talking about Ruth and Maris in St. Louis, here at Fenway Park the talk was of Jeffrey Maier.

Yes, it was another one of those nights, the kind when a fan goes from observer to participant. And this time, that concept worked against the Yankees, as a controversial homer by Seton Hall alumnus John Valentin gave the Red Sox an exciting, come-from-behind 4-3 victory.

"If someone is going to reach out over the fence

and catch a ball, let it happen when we're 19 games up," said George Steinbrenner, who sat in the stands and watched the Bombers drop their third straight contest. "I seem to recall that happening other times."

In addition to the legendary exploits of Maier, who aided a Derek Jeter homer in Game 1 of the 1996 American League Championship Series against the Orioles, there was a play Aug. 30 of last year in which a Yankee Stadium fan reached over the right field wall and grabbed a Darrin Fletcher fly ball from a jumping Paul O'Neill.

That incident sparked the near-fight between The Boss and David Wells (who allowed the Fletcher hit), when Wells castigated Steinbrenner for not having better security in the stands. And as fate would have it, Wells was on the wrong end of Valentin's homer, suffering his first defeat since June 15 after pitching brilliant, one-hit ball for the first six innings.

In all, this one hurt. "We had a good game, and we let it get away," Jorge Posada said. "That's upsetting for me."

The Yanks, losers of 11 of their last 19, need to defeat the Red Sox in the next two games here in order to clinch the American League East before returning home. For Boston, this could prove to be a crucial victory, as it halted a four-game losing snide and staved off the red-hot Blue Jays, who have closed within five games of the AL wild card.

After Boston scored three times in the seventh to knot the score at 3, Valentin came to bat with two outs and no one on in the eighth, took ball one, then smoked a high fastball to straightaway center. As Bernie Williams prepared to grab the rebound off the high wall and throw it back in, the unidentified fan reached out and the ball bounced off his glove and into the stands.

"I thought he went out and reached for it," Williams said.

"There's no doubt in my mind it was going to hit the wall," said Chad Curtis, who was in left field. "I've got a good angle, and it was a bad call, but I'm not going to get on him [second base ump Chuck Merriwether] for making that call. When in doubt on that play, you've got to call a home run."

"Those are the evils in ballparks like this, where fans have access to [the ball]," manager Joe Torre said. "I think the umpires have to be aware and position themselves better."

Apparently, a Yankee fan in the stands wound up with the ball, and he threw it back on the field, earning an ejection by stadium security.

Torre said he didn't come out and contest the call because his players didn't. At the end of the inning, Williams approached Merriwether and asked him about the play. Merriwether told Williams that he thought the ball hit the fan in the chest. Curtis said there was no way that took place.

Red Sox closer Tom Gordon mowed down the Yanks in order in the ninth for his 39th save, leaving the Bombers frustrated about the strange ending to this game and their recent subpar play.

But it was The Boss, of all people, who chose to look on the bright side. "If you've got to lose these one-run games the way we lost this one," Steinbrenner said, "now's the time to do it."

Tuesday, September 8, 1998
— at Boston Red Sox

Yankees 3, Red Sox 2

Cone's 19th clinches East tie

By KEN DAVIDOFF, Staff Writer

BOSTON — Nothing that happened in Fenway Park on Tuesday night was going to upstage Mark McGwire, but the Yankees and Red Sox put on quite a show of their own. The players and 33,409 fans shouldn't have a hard time remembering where they were the night McGwire topped Roger Maris.

David Cone outpitched Pedro Martinez in a duel of American League Cy Young Award candidates to become the major leagues' first 19-game winner, and Mariano Rivera survived a nerve-wracking bottom of the ninth to give the Yanks a 3-2 victory over the Bosox. The Bombers clinched a tie for the AL East and with one more victory or Boston loss, the division is officially theirs. They also snapped a three-game losing streak.

"It was like a playoff atmosphere out there," manager Joe Torre said. "There's no question, with Martinez and Coney out there, it was the way it was supposed to be."

Throw in McGwire's homer and its timing within this game, and it made for an incredibly exciting show. For seven innings, Cone and Martinez matched each other in a 1-1 tie. There was no disputing, however, that Cone was the superior pitcher. He faced 22 batters, one over the minimum in those seven innings, allowing two hits (one of them a Nomar Garciaparra solo homer in the second, walked none, and struck out 11.

"This is as good as I've felt all year," Cone said. With 188 innings on the season, the veteran is 12 frames away from the 200 mark, which will activate a $5.5 million player option for 1999.

Joe Girardi began the game-turning eighth with a bullet to shortstop that Garciaparra stopped but could not glove. His throw to first wasn't even close and the official scorer ruled it a single.

With the count 1-0 on Chuck Knoblauch, it happened: McGwire went deep off Steve Trachsel for his history-making homer. A significant portion of the crowd cheered. Martinez's next pitch bounced in front of catcher Scott Hatteberg and got away, with Girardi going to second.

When Knoblauch won a long at-bat by singling up the middle and moving Girardi to third, the Red Sox played McGwire's homer on the large screen. The fans gave a standing ovation, Derek Jeter stepped away from the plate, and Bosox pitching coach Joe Kerrigan came to the mound to calm his pitcher.

After Jeter walked to load the bases, the Yankees broke the tie on a slow Paul O'Neill grounder to second, an intentional walk to Bernie Williams, and a bases-loaded walk to Tino Martinez.

Graeme Lloyd, Jeff Nelson, and Mike Stanton pitched to one batter apiece in the eighth, with only Nelson doing his job. That prompted Torre to ask Rivera to get the final five outs. Rivera stranded two runners in the eighth, then retired Darren Lewis to start the ninth before the real drama began.

John Valentin walked and Mo Vaughn and Garciaparra singled to load the bases. Troy O'Leary drove home Valentin with a sacrifice fly to center, and Williams' throw to third evaded Jeter at the base and backup Scott Brosius, allowing Garciaparra and Vaughn's pinch runner Donnie Sadler to advance to second and third.

Former Yankee Mike Stanley worked a walk to jam the bases, and up came Darren Bragg: Called strike, called strike, check-swing strike. Yankees win, Rivera gets his 34th save.

The struggling Yankees needed a victory like this. "Maybe," Jeter said, "this is a wake-up call for us."

WELLS DIGS A HOLE: Among David Wells' many improvements this season has been his ability to overcome adversity.

On Monday night, the veteran southpaw admitted,

he regressed in that department. A ball call by home plate umpire Larry McCoy in the seventh inning upset him so much that he wound up suffering the loss in the Yanks' 4-3 defeat to the Red Sox.

"It was terrible back there," Wells said Tuesday. "I threw a pitch right down the middle in the seventh inning…. That kind of flustered me a little bit, and then the inning happened."

The 1-2 fastball to leadoff batter John Valentin was ruled high by McCoy. Valentin lined out to left, but the next three batters reached base. And Valentin wound up hitting the game-winning homer in the eighth.

Wednesday, September 9, 1998
— at Boston Red Sox

Yankees 7, Red Sox 5

AL East Champs!
Champagne flows after Yankees win

By KEN DAVIDOFF, Staff Writer

BOSTON — After Derek Jeter threw out John Valentin at 10:21 p.m. Wednesday, after the Yankees did their polite little on-field celebration for the Fenway Park fans, they returned to the sanctity of their clubhouse and expressed their true feelings.

Foregone conclusion, shmoregone conclusion. That this American League East title was a long time coming made no difference when Tino Martinez caught Jeter's throw to secure the 7-5 victory over the Red Sox and clinch the division crown. These players were thrilled, and they weren't ashamed to show it.

"Winning the division championship is a big step," said Paul O'Neill, who slugged two insurance solo homers in the fifth and eighth innings. "We've played hard all year to wrap this up early."

"To win the division, we're not going to take it for granted," agreed Martinez. "You have to enjoy these days."

This day, as O'Neill noted, came quite early, quicker than any of the Bombers' six previous division titles. The last team to clinch first place so soon was the 1975 Reds, who got it done Sept. 7. The 1941 Yankees hold the team record, having won the pennant Sept. 4. The victory also gave New York

(102-41) a 20 1/2-game division lead, tying the franchise mark also set in 1941.

And the partying lasted late. The visiting clubhouse rained champagne and beer, cigar smoke was more plentiful than oxygen, and Jeff Nelson raised the stakes when he began rubbing chocolate pudding in his teammates' hair. As the standard plastic covering protected the players' belongings, they hooted and chanted and basically acted very silly.

"I thought it was just right," David Cone said of his team's jubilation level. "There's nothing wrong with displaying emotion."

Before the game, manager Joe Torre held a brief meeting with his team, issuing this single instruction: "Don't hurt each other." The order was followed, after an exciting game that closed an exciting three-game series.

Jeter knocked a pair of early solo homers, and Ramiro Mendoza picked up the victory by pitching three strong innings in relief of Orlando Hernandez. Scott Brosius and Chuck Knoblauch made Mendoza's win possible by each making a strong defensive play that initiated the Bombers' two double plays.

Thanks to Jeter's two moonshots, each to center field, and a three-run fourth against knuckleballer Tim Wakefield (15-8), the Yanks had a 5-0 lead, and it looked as if they would cruise to their 102nd victory.

Not! El Duque had not allowed a three-run homer, let alone a grand slam, in his first 120 2/3 major league innings. But with one out and the bases jammed in the fourth, Scott Hatteberg sent a bullet well into the right field seats to close the gap to 5-4.

When Hernandez loaded the bases again, notching the second out in the midst, he was lifted for Mendoza, who had to face none other than Mo Vaughn.

With no room for error, Mendoza went to work: Ball inside. Ball inside that got away from Jorge Posada, but not enough for Trot Nixon to score from third. Hard grounder to second, where Knoblauch picked it up and tossed to first for the inning's final out.

The teams exchanged runs in the fifth, with Brosius making a great grab of a Mike Stanley missile to start a 5-4-3 double play and limit the damage. Knoblauch made an improbable stab of a Vaughn scorcher in the seventh to begin a 4-6-3 double play, and O'Neill's second dinger made it 7-5.

Mike Stanton threw a perfect 1 1/3 innings to build

the bridge from Mendoza to Mariano Rivera, who took over to start the ninth. Rivera's 35th save couldn't have been easier: Mike Benjamin bounced back to the mound. Darren Bragg struck out. Then Valentin's bouncer to short, marking the first Yankees division clinching on the road since the Oct. 2, 1978 playoff game at Fenway Park.

"It's great to see the guys from the bullpen getting together," Rivera said. "We needed this."

Really, the whole team came together for this victory, which has been standard procedure. "This ballclub has been together all year," Torre said. "We'll be together until there's no more baseball for us."

Thursday, Sepember 10, 1998
— Toronto Blue Jays

Yankees 8, Blue Jays 5

Pettitte's struggles go on

Yanks win despite his shaky outing

By GREGORY SCHUTTA, Staff Writer

NEW YORK — During the 25 years that George Steinbrenner has owned the Yankees, a talk with The Boss has been characterized as a lot of things. "Relaxing" is rarely one of them.

But for Andy Pettitte, votes of confidence from Steinbrenner and manager Joe Torre could be the difference in the final three weeks to the playoffs.

Reeling from three losses in his past four starts, the Yankee left-hander battled back from a five-run second inning Thursday to throw four shutout innings and notch his 16th win of the season, 8-5, over the Toronto Blue Jays.

"He just told me to relax, you're going to be all right," Pettitte said of his talk with Steinbrenner, who followed the Yankees recently as they marched to the Eastern Division title. "It makes you feel good to know that you can give up five runs in an inning and still have Mr. Steinbrenner and [manager Joe Torre] and everybody else on this team behind you 100 percent."

Pettitte certainly had the Yankee bats behind him as the Bombers battered former Cy Young Award winner Pat Hentgen and three other pitchers for eight runs and 13 hits. Paul O'Neill, who had two homers in the division-clinching win over Boston on Wednesday night, picked up where he left off with two more Thursday. His two-run blast in the first inning was his third in as many at-bats and gave the Yankees a 2-0 lead.

"We could have had a letdown," said O'Neill, who also had a solo shot against Dave Stieb leading off the fourth inning. "But we were coming home to our own building and we had to liven up our fans."

"That's just the character of this team," said catcher Joe Girardi, who had two doubles and an RBI. "We don't take any nights off. We have too much pride for that."

Pride could be what has caused Pettitte's recent troubles, according to Torre, who said before the game that the lefty may be putting too much pressure on himself to be perfect.

"Instead of trusting what you do, you think about things that you don't usually think about," the manager said. "I went through that as a hitter, and pitchers go through the same thing."

That could be the explanation for Pettitte's second inning. Staked to a 2-0 lead by O'Neill, Pettitte failed to keep the Blue Jays down, giving up four singles and a two-out, three-run bomb by Jose Canseco into the left field stands for a 5-2 Toronto lead.

"I was kind of feeling my way through it, aiming my way through it," Pettitte said of the first two innings. "That kind of flattens the ball out. I gave up a big three-run homer to Canseco. It was a cutter that I left out over the dish."

The saving grace for Pettitte was that Hentgen, who beat him out for the Cy Young Award in 1996, couldn't get anybody out either. Handed a three-run lead, Hentgen promptly gave one run back in the second on a Chuck Knoblauch RBI single.

It was the Toronto outfield that opened up the gates in the fourth as the Yankees took the lead back with four runs on five hits. With one out and men on first and second, Darryl Strawberry lifted a catchable fly ball into the gap that center fielder Jose Cruz Jr. and right fielder Shawn Green let drop between them for an RBI single.

Rookie Ricky Ledee followed by dropping a fly into the left field corner that went for a ground-rule double to tie the score at 5. Scott Brosius then drove in Strawberry with a sacrifice fly to right and Girardi gave the Yankees a 7-5 lead with the first of his two doubles.

Handed the lead for the second time, Pettitte, who

had allowed the five runs on seven hits in the first three innings, held on with both hands. He retired eight of the final 10 men to face him before giving way to Jeff Nelson to start the seventh inning.

"After he got further along, he got better," Torre said. "I thought he was pretty good tonight, except the second inning stunk. But he straightened himself out. His problem was he got behind people and threw balls down the middle."

"It's been a real weird season for me," Pettitte said. "It's embarrassing for me to say I've been struggling with 16 wins."

Friday, September 11, 1998
— Toronto Blue Jays

Blue Jays 5, Yankees 4

Yankees go down fighting

By KEN DAVIDOFF, Staff Writer

NEW YORK — Friday night at Yankee Stadium was supposed to be about Hideki Irabu's campaign to make the Yankees' playoff roster and Roger Clemens' campaign to win the American League Cy Young Award. Instead, it turned into a night about old grudges revisited, pitches thrown inside, and defending one's teammates.

An exchange of hit batters sparked a fifth-inning brawl between the Yankees and Blue Jays that lasted more than 10 minutes, resulted in five ejections, and overshadowed the outcome of the game, which Toronto won, 5-4, in front of 35,856 fans. The American League will not make any rulings until Monday at the earliest, but suspensions could be given to the Bombers' Darryl Strawberry (who earned a three-game sentence for his role in the memorable May 19 fight with the Orioles) and bench coach Don Zimmer.

The Yankees' anger was pointed directly at Clemens, who hit Scott Brosius with a pitch in the fourth inning that set off the extracurricular activity. A brawl that could have injured someone, with the playoffs looming, made the situation more infuriating.

"He threw at him. I don't think it could have been any more obvious," Derek Jeter said. "It's not like he has control problems."

"Roger Clemens gets away with things that gets other people thrown out of games, and that's a perfect example of it," said manager Joe Torre, who was ejected in the bottom of the fourth. "As long as [the umpires] don't do anything, why should he stop?"

"Richie Garcia [who umpired third base] is a good friend and a good umpire," George Steinbrenner said. "But [the umps] weren't consistent. We'll see what [AL president] Dr. [Gene] Budig does about this. It'll be interesting."

It should be noted that The Boss purposely mispronounced Budig's name as "BUD-ig" rather than the proper "BU-dig," a sign of his lack of respect for him.

Clemens hit Brosius in the back right after Ricky Ledee's sacrifice fly scored Tino Martinez for the Yanks' third run of the inning, tying the game at 3.

"It was my first two-seamer, and I was coming in on Scott," Clemens said. "It had nothing to do with the inning I was having."

As the fans booed, Brosius glared, took a step toward the mound, and walked to first. From the dugout, Chad Curtis yelled at Clemens, as did Jeter, and Strawberry stood on the top step of the dugout. Someone threw a cup from the dugout onto the field.

Torre emerged from the dugout furious, obviously wanting at least a warning given to Clemens. What angered Torre even more was that this was the same umpiring crew that ejected Mike Stanton on June 15 when he hit Eric Davis immediately after a Rafael Palmeiro homer.

When home plate umpire Mike Reilly refused his request, Torre became more irate and earned himself the hook. Zimmer took over the manager's duties.

Shannon Stewart led off the the fifth, and Irabu didn't hesitate to retaliate. His first pitch nailed the left fielder in the back of his shoulder. Stewart pointed to the mound, and Irabu charged the plate. The benches and bullpens emptied, and as Stanton pulled Irabu away from the fracas, a mass of players formed to the right of the Blue Jays' dugout. Strawberry threw at least one punch, and Stewart was pinned to the ground. Zimmer, meanwhile, argued furiously with the umps, bumping Reilly in the process.

When the chaos ended, Zimmer, Strawberry, Homer Bush, and Toronto pitcher Bill Risley had been ejected. Jays manager Tim Johnson joined the list a moment later. Incredibly, Irabu was allowed to stay in the game

Afterward, Irabu denied throwing at Stewart, and said that Stewart provoked him by giving a "come and get me" type gesture.

"I think [Irabu's] pitch was every bit as unintentional as Roger's was," said Brosius, speaking sarcastically.

In a March 17 exhibition game between these teams at Legends Field in Tampa, Fla., Clemens beaned Jeter after Irabu had hit Jose Canseco and Alex Gonzalez. Clemens faced the Yanks twice in April without incident, then nailed Jeter again in a July 17 meeting at SkyDome.

As for the game, Clemens got a no-decision and suffered a contusion of his right palm, below the pinkie, when he tried to barehand two consecutive Yankees hits in the third. Irabu, who suffered his fourth straight loss, lasted six innings and struck out eight, but set a career high by allowing four homers.

Saturday, September 12, 1998
— Toronto Blue Jays

Blue Jays 5, Yankees 3

Yanks fight the blahs

Fall to Blue Jays in ho-hum affair

By TIM LEONARD, Staff Writer

NEW YORK — There is no sense of panic. That the Yankees have lost 11 of their last 20 games seems like a mere bump in the road to the postseason. Until then, serenity seems to have overtaken the Bronx.

So concern wasn't the emotion of the day Saturday after the Yankees fell to the Toronto Blue Jays and a pitcher named Chris Carpenter, 5-3, before a matinee crowd of 48,752 at Yankee Stadium.

The Yankees looked like a team on auto pilot in dropping their second straight to the Blue Jays, who moved to within four games of the Boston Red Sox in the race for the American League wild card.

"I think we can rise to the occasion. We're playing well, but you lack a certain amount of intensity after you clinch," Yankees manager Joe Torre said. "It's not a matter of coasting, but I think we're a couple of octaves from where we want to be."

Another bevy of low notes left the Yankees at

103-43, meaning they must go 14-2 in their final 16 games to eclipse the major league record of 116 wins in a season by the 1906 Chicago Cubs. More realistic are the franchise-record 110 wins by the 1927 Yankees or the American League-record 111 wins by the 1954 Cleveland Indians.

Even Yankees owner George Steinbrenner refused to become flustered about his team's recent fortunes, or lack thereof. Steinbrenner was as placid as his team as he discussed their recent stretch.

"There's a balance as to when you can give them rest and not be concerned, and when you tighten it down," Steinbrenner said after a brief postgame meeting with Torre. "We've got to see some more young players because we have to see who's got it and who doesn't for next year."

The here and now wasn't very attractive as David Wells struggled through six innings and the Yankee bats could do little against Carpenter. After scoring twice in the first inning, the Yankees got just three hits the rest of the way. Two of their four hits came from leadoff man Homer Bush, who started in place of Chuck Knoblauch.

Bush doubled inside the bag at third and scored on a groundout by Paul O'Neill in the first. Tino Martinez got his team-leading 115th RBI when he drove in Derek Jeter with a sacrifice fly to give the Yankees a 2-1 lead.

After that, Carpenter confounded the Yankees for seven innings with a treacherous curveball and a sneaky fastball. He set down 18 of the last 20 hitters he faced, 11 of those on ground balls. The only bit of offense from the Yankees came when Bush singled to lead off the sixth, stole second, went to third on a groundout by Jeter, and scored on a wild pitch to cut the Blue Jays lead to two runs.

"I don't think you can really identify it or read anything into it because of the need," Torre said of the recent stretch. "It's not like they come in and yawn and go out and play."

Wells' command took a nap around the fifth inning, when the Jays took the lead for good. Tony Fernandez led off with a single and scored on a long double to center by Benito Santiago, who went to third on the throw home. When Wells cut off that throw, he made an off-balance throw to third that skipped into the outfield, allowing Santiago to score.

It was that kind of day. Fernandez tripled home two runs in the sixth to make it 5-2, as the Blue Jays looked like the only team on the field playing with something on the line.

Meanwhile, the Yankees only seem to have history to pursue.

"Records don't mean anything. What means something is getting to the Series," Steinbrenner said. "This is a quote from Reggie, 'You're nothing 'til you get there.'"

The Boss quoting Mr. October. How much more serene can things get?

Sunday, September 13, 1998
— Toronto Blue Jays

Blue Jays 5, Yankees 3

Cone deprived of 20th victory

Yanks Pen fails to bail him out

By GREGORY SCHUTTA, Staff Writer

NEW YORK — It was a performance fit for Harry Houdini, but even the great escape artist eventually failed.

For David Cone, who found ways to wiggle out of jam after jam in the first five innings Sunday, his water torture came in the sixth inning. That's when he loaded the bases after three straight singles and then watched helplessly as three pitchers allowed all three runners to score, lifting the Toronto Blue Jays to a 5-3 victory over the Yankees.

It was the Yankees' third straight loss to the streaking Blue Jays, who have won 14 of their past 16 games to pull within three games of Boston in the AL wild-card race. But more important in Yankeeland, it was a missed opportunity to give Cone (19-6) his 20th win, a plateau he hasn't reached since 1988, when he went 20-3 for the Mets.

"I feel bad that we lost the game, but I feel even worse for David," said Graeme Lloyd, who relieved Cone with two out in the sixth inning and promptly gave up a two-run single to Shawn Green to tie the score at 3. "He pitched his heart out for us all year, and we've got to back him up. I feel like it was my loss, because I didn't go in there and do my job."

Neither did Jeff Nelson, who followed Lloyd by plunking Jose Canseco on the left elbow, or Mike

Stanton, who gave up an 0-2 RBI single to Carlos Delgado to give the Jays the lead for good, 4-3. All three runs were charged to Cone, who gave up a homer to Shannon Stewart on his third pitch. Cone pitched with men in scoring position in each of the next four innings despite striking out 11 over 5 2/3 innings.

"I was flirting with disaster all day, and it finally caught up to me in the sixth," Cone said. "I left a mess out there, and they scored the runs."

Cone went into the sixth leading, 3-1, thanks in large part to Derek Jeter, who drove in two runs, with a sacrifice fly in the first and a triple in the third. He has 79 RBI on the season, breaking his career high of 78 in his rookie season of 1996.

But the Blue Jays, playing with their backs to the wall in the wild-card race for the past three weeks, battled back against Cone in the sixth as Darrin Fletcher and Craig Grebeck singled with one out. The Jays loaded the bases when Cone and rookie third baseman Mike Lowell, making his first major league appearance, collided trying to field a bunt by Alex Gonzalez.

Cone struck out Stewart for the second out, but manager Joe Torre said that was enough, pulling Cone after 123 pitches.

"David didn't have the same command that he had last time," Torre said of Cone's seven-inning, two-hit performance against the Red Sox. "But I think last time could have been right up there with the best two or three outings of the year. It might have been different if he had better command, but the way he was pitching today, I would have gone out and gotten him anyway."

"When you get this close [to 20 wins], you certainly want to get it," a disappointed Cone said. "But I've still got a chance at it, and that's all you can ask. If you'd told me after my first two starts [16 runs, 18 hits, nine innings] that I would have a chance to win 20, I would have jumped at it."

Cone is expected to make two more starts, beginning Saturday in Baltimore on five days' rest. Torre will insert rookie Mike Jerzembeck into the rotation Tuesday against Boston to give each of his starters an extra day of rest in preparation for the playoffs.

And Torre is at the top of the list of people who hopes Cone reaches the milestone after battling back from career-threatening shoulder surgery for an aneurysm two years ago.

"I don't think the number 20 is as significant for David as his coming back from where he's come from to reach 20," Torre said.

Reporter's Notebook:

Paul O'Neill's legendary intensity might have come back to haunt the Yankees on Sunday when he was ejected for throwing his equipment at the plate after being called out on strikes with the tying runs on base to end the seventh inning. Chuck Knoblauch and Jeter walked with two out in the ninth inning, but rookie Shane Spencer, replacing O'Neill, lined out hard to left field to end the game.

"I feel umpires should try to keep players in the game as much as they can," Torre said. "If they issue some kind of warning, fine. Paulie shouldn't have done what he did, but in the heat of battle you sometimes say and do something you regret later. I feel umpires should understand that."

Lowell, one of the jewels of the Yankee farm system, took advantage of the flu bug going around the locker room to start his first major league game. He got his first hit in his first at-bat with a broken-bat single into short center field against Kelvim Escobar in the second inning. ...Regular third baseman Scott Brosius played first base for the first time this year in place of Tino Martinez, who with Tim Raines was ill.

The attendance of 47,471 on Backpack Day gave the Yankees a season attendance of 2,615,050, just 18,651 short of their all-time high of 2,633,701 in 1988.

Monday, September 14, 1998
— Boston Red Sox

Yankees 3, Red Sox 0

El Duque makes blank-et statement

By KEN DAVIDOFF, Staff Writer

NEW YORK — Joe Torre needed to get a message to Orlando Hernandez this past week, and even though El Duque has learned a good deal of English in the past six months, there wasn't much room for subtlety.

So the Yankees manager grabbed his rookie right-hander by the head and pretended to throw it against a wall. "We need to clear this head out," Torre explained.

Hernandez got the message, and followed it. And the dividends were on display Monday night at Yankee Stadium. In front of a crowd of 42,735 that helped the Yanks establish a single-season attendance record, El Duque outdueled Cy Young Award candidate Pedro Martinez, blanking the flailing Red Sox on three hits, 3-0, for his first shutout.

"I want to thank him," Hernandez said, through interpreter Leo Astacio, of his manager. "I was in the process of trying to clear my head, and he gave me the confidence to go ahead and clear it. I've been thinking about past games and how I had to come back strong."

His past games had indeed been troubling, though they were sort of lost in the incompetence of his fellow starters Hideki Irabu and Andy Pettitte and the overall flatness of the team, which had lost three straight and 14 of 25. In his past two starts, El Duque lasted a total of 9 2/3 innings and allowed eight runs, earning two no-decisions.

In addition to benefiting from his manager's lecture, Hernandez learned a new change-up grip from Irabu, of all people. Armed with new physical and mental weapons, he pitched what Bernie Williams called, "The best game he has pitched so far." He struck out nine, didn't walk a batter, and hit two men.

"He just mixed it up tonight," Torre said. "They were off-balance, didn't take a lot of good swings, and that's what he's capable of."

"I learned to pitch to my strengths," Hernandez said. "I have to work ahead of hitters. I tried not to throw as many as balls as before. When I was behind, I didn't nibble as much."

The Yanks (104-44) scored a run in the fifth, courtesy of a Darryl Strawberry single, a Jorge Posada single to right that advanced Strawberry to third, and Luis Sojo's sacrifice fly. Two more runs came home in the seventh, with Scott Brosius knocking an RBI single and later scoring on a Martinez wild pitch.

After eight innings, El Duque figured he was done. "They're probably going to bring in Mo," he told Posada, referring to closer Mariano Rivera.

Posada shook his head. "You're going to finish this game," he told his batterymate. "Keep going."

If it had been a 1-0 game, Torre said, he may have brought in Rivera. Since it wasn't, and Hernandez's pitch count was under 100, he let his starter go for the shutout.

"We put a lot of our plans on the back burner," said Torre, who wanted to get Jeff Nelson in to see how he did in consecutive days.

Speaking of plans, it's clear El Duque is the favorite to be the fourth starter in the playoffs should Torre opt for four over three. "It's nice to have tough decisions to make," Torre said. "He put his hat in the ring, there's no question."

The crowd gave the Yanks a season attendance of 2,657,785, breaking the 1988 record of 2,633,701. There are still 10 home dates remaining.

Red Sox 9, Yankees 4

Bosox whip Yanks
Jerzembeck pummeled

By GREGORY SCHUTTA, Staff Writer

NEW YORK — Wakefield says that he doesn't watch the scoreboard. But the warm breath of the Toronto Blue Jays breathing down the necks of the Boston Red Sox was unmistakable Tuesday night at Yankee Stadium.

Why else would manager Jimy Williams go against his own book, starting his right-handed lineup against Yankee right-hander Mike Jerzembeck? And why else would he bring in All-Star closer Tom "Flash" Gordon in the ninth inning of a blowout?

Because after losing nine games in their past 11 and seeing their wild-card lead dwindle from 12 games to a measly three in the last three weeks, the Red Sox were desperate for a win. And they finally got one, handing the Yankees their fourth loss in the past five games, 9-4, and at the same time stretching their lead back to four games over the Blue Jays, who lost 7-5 in Cleveland.

Knuckleballer Tim Wakefield, who had given up 18 runs in 14 innings in losing his previous three starts, allowed just three hits over six innings to earn his 16th win of the season.

"We've been playing this way all year," said catcher Jason Varitek, who got a rare start against a right-hander and rewarded Williams with a pair of homers in his first two at-bats. "It was just a matter of time before our hitting and pitching came together at the same time."

And it came at a time when the Yankees are more interested in Sept. 29 when the playoffs open, than Sept. 15.

In a move that could do nothing less than infuriate the Blue Jays, manager Joe Torre gave Jerzembeck his first start. Unfortunately, it wasn't the debut the rookie probably dreamed about growing up in Queens.

Pitching with 20 family and friends among the 43,218 at Yankee Stadium, the Archbishop Molloy graduate lasted just 2 1/3 innings, allowing five runs and four hits. And it was his former Georgia Tech teammate Varitek who did the damage.

Jerzembeck, who played one year with Varitek before transferring to North Carolina, gave up a two-out, three-run homer to the rookie catcher to give the Red Sox a 3-0 lead after three. The switch-hitting Varitek, who was hitting just .208 batting left-handed going into the game, also had a two-run blast against right-hander Mike Buddie in the fourth inning.

"What's interesting is that they wouldn't let him hit from the left side against us the other day," Torre said. "They pinch hit for him. And then to see him do this."

The Red Sox extended the lead to 9-0 with two runs in the top of the seventh. But for a team that has been cursed by the trade of Babe Ruth nearly 80 years ago, nothing comes easy, and the Yankees battled back.

Scott Brosius cut the lead to 9-3 with his 18th homer of the season off Wakefield in the seventh, and Bernie Williams added a solo shot in the eighth, his 25th of the season, to cut the lead to 9-4.

That's when the Boston manager got Gordon up in the bullpen. He couldn't let this one get away.

"Our team effort was good, and we're leaving with a split, which means that we're leaving with winning ways," Williams said.

The Yankees got a scare in the ninth inning when Torre brought closer Mariano Rivera in to get some work and watched him get drilled by a line drive off Varitek's bat.

> **"** It was just a matter of time before our hitting and pitching came together at the same time. **"**
>
> — *Jason Varitek*

"I'll give him the home runs, but he's playing with our postseason right there," a relieved Torre said after Rivera finished out the inning. "I was just glad to see Mo's smiling face when I got out there. And the next pitch he threw was 98 mph. He's fine."

And despite the score, there were bright spots for Torre, most notable the performances of Jeff Nelson and Darren Holmes out of the bullpen. Each came in to throw a perfect inning of relief.

"When I got hurt, I had no doubts that I would be back down the stretch," said Nelson, who still hasn't pitched back-to-back days. "It was just a question of how the back would feel after pitching two days in a row, and that will come. I think this tells my teammates that I'm back and ready to help them win games."

Wednesday, September 16, 1998
— at Tampa Bay Devil Rays

Devil Rays 7, Yankees 0

Torre stings Yanks after loss to Devil Rays

By KEN DAVIDOFF, Staff Writer

ST. PETERSBURG, Fla. — Yankees crossed the invisible line Wednesday night, the barrier that separates understandable drop-off from unacceptable sloppiness. And when they landed on the wrong side of that line, Joe Torre was there to issue a most unfriendly welcome.

"Tonight was sloppy. It stunk," the Bombers' manager said after his team suffered an ugly 7-0 defeat to Tampa Bay at Tropicana Field. "I let them know about it tonight. It stunk."

The Yankees now have lost two straight and 16 of their last 27, and their 104-46 record means that the 1906 Cubs can officially rest easy. Even if the Bombers won their remaining 12 games, they could only tie the record for most victories.

Andy Pettitte continued to struggle, allowing six runs (four earned) in six innings, making it six straight starts in which he has allowed five or more runs. But the southpaw wasn't at the top of Torre's hit list. For the first time since slowing down from their record pace, they acknowledged concern about their poor play.

"Everybody here knows it," Derek Jeter said. "We know we're not playing how we're capable of playing."

"It's embarrassing, the way we're playing," Joe Girardi added.

With Paul O'Neill, Tino Martinez, and Chuck Knoblauch on the bench, the Yanks stranded 11 baserunners against Devil Rays starter Tony Saunders (6-14) and a pair of relievers. They were charged with just one error, a first-inning misplay by Homer Bush that opened the floodgates for a two-run rally. Throw in a few fundamental mistakes like Chad Curtis throwing to the wrong base, and Torre held disdain for the entire package, as New York lost to the expansion team in George Steinbrenner's back yard for the first time after six straight wins.

"It didn't look like we played too motivated tonight," Pettitte said. "We need to get motivated. We don't want to go into the playoffs in this drought and think we can turn it on."

The lefty is trying to ward off similar anxiety about his own situation. In those last six starts, Pettitte (16-10) has surrendered 31 runs (29 earned) in 36 innings for a disturbing 7.25 ERA. His ERA for the season is 4.27, with just two more starts scheduled before the playoffs begin.

"We're concerned," Torre said. "I know he's there. I know he's healthy. We're running out of time. We're going to have to get it straightened out."

"I'm pretty positive," said Pettitte, usually his own toughest critic. "It's hard to say you're positive about it, but I thought I threw pretty decent tonight."

His fastball registered as high as 93 mph on the stadium's radar gun, which was probably faster than a Yankees' gun. He said he was happy with his change-up and his curveball. He issued just one walk after distributing five his last time out

Nevertheless, he continued to struggle finishing off innings and cleaning up messes. The latest explanation behind Pettitte's woes was that he was basically putting together strong performances, with the exception being one bad inning. On Tuesday, he allowed no more than two runs in any one inning, a step in the right direction. But the devil's advocate would note that the 26-year-old had three subpar innings on this night rather than just one.

"He's a very proud individual," said Torre, who said it was safe to assume that Pettitte would be in the postseason starting rotation.

Pettitte has either one or two regular-season starts remaining, and as he put it, "I almost wish [the play-offs] could just be here, and we could go ahead."

The Yankees had best shape up before they go ahead. "We've accomplished too many good things," Torre said. "They've spoiled me like they spoiled everybody else, and you set your standards higher."

Reporter's Notebook:

The Yankees wouldn't comment on a report Wednesday that talks between Steinbrenner and Cablevision were heating up regarding the sale of the team. One limited partner said that he hadn't been notified of any impending action. But one club source said he wouldn't be surprised if such a sale took place after the season. The Boss, in Milwaukee for an owners' meeting, didn't return phone calls.

Darryl Strawberry began serving his three-game

suspension (for his role in last Friday's brawl with Toronto) on Wednesday night.

Thursday, September 17, 1998
— at Tampa Bay Devil Rays

Yankees 4, Devil Rays 0

Back on the beam

Yanks respond to Torre's angry outburst

By KEN DAVIDOFF, Staff Writer

ST. PETERSBURG, Fla. — Derek Jeter nodded at Paul O'Neill on Thursday afternoon and made small talk. "You playing today?" the shortstop asked.

The right fielder flashed a wry smile. "We're all playing," he said.

This was no ordinary meaningless game Thursday night. The Yankees, as a team, had a point to make. The same went for Hideki Irabu as an individual. Ballclub and man succeeded, with Irabu tossing eight shutout innings in which he allowed two hits to thump the Devil Rays, 4-0.

"I think tonight, we played the way we've become used to playing," Joe Torre said. "Tonight we pitched, and that helps everything appear better. It's hard to look good when you lose, but you don't want to look ragged. I wasn't happy with how we played [Wednesday], and the players weren't either."

Wednesday night's embarrassing 7-0 defeat to expansion team Tampa Bay had earned the Yankees a tongue-lashing from Torre and put to rest the notion that everything was fine. This had to stop, the team said. No more lame explanations about experiencing a letdown after clinching the division. And, for one game, no night off to a starting position player.

Thursday night wasn't perfect; the Bombers (105-46) stranded 11 more runners, giving them 22 in two days at Tropicana Field. But as Bernie Williams put it, "Hopefully, this is the start of a good stretch. We'll get ourselves ready for a good performance in the playoffs. You've got to start somewhere."

For Irabu (12-9), it was more than a start. It was a rebirth after five consecutive brutal starts in which he lasted no longer than six innings and allowed no fewer than four runs. He notched his first victory since Aug. 10, fanning five, walking two, and needing just 102 pitches to cruise through his eight frames. The two hits he surrendered were infield singles to third.

The 29-year-old was en route to dropping off the postseason radar screen. Now, he has a fighting chance. "It's good information," Torre said. "Wherever we may use him [starting or relieving], we like tonight's game to help him confidence-wise."

"We want them to make it hard [to pick a playoff pitching staff]," pitching coach Mel Stottlemyre said. "We want games like this."

"I know I will have one or two more starts this season," Irabu said through his interpreter, George Rose. "Within the last part of September, I know the postseason will be decided. I know I've been pitching badly, and I wanted to get better as quickly as possible."

The key, Irabu said, was getting together with Stottlemyre and watching videotape of his recent outings. The coach showed the pitcher that he needed to drive his legs more for extra power. His fastball hovered around the mid-90s, his curveball had some bite, and his change-up was effective.

"Before, when I wasn't doing [the leg drives], the ball kind of looked like a watermelon for the hitters," Irabu said.

The Yanks looked like the ones hitting large fruit on this night. Williams took over the team lead with his 26th homer, and Jorge Posada knocked an opposite-field jack to left. O'Neill and Chili Davis, who looked so lost Wednesday, led the way with three hits each.

Reporter's Notebook:

The news continues to be good on Jeff Nelson, who said he felt fine after pitching on consecutive days for the first time since his Sept. 4 return from a bulging disk in his lower back. In six appearances totaling 3 2/3 innings, he has not allowed a hit or walked a batter.

"He had good stuff," Torre said. "It was probably better [Wednesday] than the day before." The next step will be to have Nelson throw for two innings.

The Yankees will announce shortly the signing of 20-year-old shortstop Alfonso Soriano, a native of the Dominican Republic who played most recently in Japan. Soriano, who will play in the highly regarded Arizona Fall League, will probably play at the Class AA level next season.

Friday, September 18, 1998
— at Baltimore Orioles

Yankees 15, Orioles 5

Wells wins, scowls
Torre upset by behavior

By KEN DAVIDOFF, Staff Writer

BALTIMORE — It was only the bottom of the sixth inning Friday night when Joe Torre called off the dogs at Camden Yards. Up by six runs, the Yankees manager reeled in his $19.05 million quartet of Bernie Williams, Paul O'Neill, Tino Martinez, and Tim Raines and told them to take the rest of the night off. After all, they had earned it.

As it turned out, Torre almost earned himself a tongue-lashing from George Steinbrenner that probably would have made the manager's Wednesday night diatribe to his players seem like a love song. The Orioles put together a frightening bottom of the sixth, only to fall short, and the Yankees rode a strong offense, and a strong bullpen to a 15-5 victory capped by Shane Spencer's first grand slam in the seven-run ninth inning.

David Wells (18-4) halted a personal two-game losing streak with an unimpressive 5 1/3 innings and incurred the wrath of Torre, not so much for yielding 11 hits, 10 of them singles, but for showing his frustration that many of those singles found holes.

"We've talked about it," Torre said, tersely.

"I'm showing my teammates up, and it's not fair to them," Wells said. "That was totally unprofessional on my part."

The play that seemed to annoy Wells the most was a pop fly by Danny Clyburn that fell among left fielder Ricky Ledee, center fielder Chad Curtis, and shortstop Derek Jeter in the bottom of the fifth. Torre felt Jeter should have run down the ball, but Wells gave all three a stare.

After the game, Wells apolgized to Curtis for his behavior (Jeter and Ledee already had left the park).

"I know Boomer," Curtis said. "I know his intentions aren't to show us up. From someone else, it might have been different."

Still, the Yanks (106-46) won their second straight by hitting the ball well for the second straight night. They have 10 games left in the regular season, needing to win five to set the team record and six for the

American League mark for wins in a season.

Orioles manager Ray Miller lifted starter Juan Guzman for Rocky Coppinger to start the sixth and that backfired when O'Neill drove a 1-2 change-up at the knees into the right field stands for a three-run home run and what appeared to be a safe 8-2 lead.

That's when Torre made his wholesale changes, pinch-running Curtis for Williams in the top of the sixth, inserting Curtis in center in the bottom of the inning, and flanking him with the rookies Spencer and Ledee in right and left, respectively. Luis Sojo came in at first.

And then the parade of Orioles hits began: A Lyle Mouton liner to left. Clyburn's pop to left-center which landed amid Ledee, Curtis, and Jeter. A Lenny Webster grounder through the hole into left, scoring Mouton. 8-3, Yanks.

A grounder to right by former Met Rich Becker, bringing Clyburn home. 8-4. A grounder to right by Roberto Alomar, loading the bases, bringing the tying run to the plate, and earning an angry Wells the hook. In came Ramiro Mendoza.

Pinch hitter Rafael Palmeiro drove in Webster with a sacrifice fly to left, making it 8-5, and Mendoza walked Eric Davis to load the bases and bring the lead run to the plate. Torre went for left-hander Mike Stanton to neutralize lefty pinch hitter B.J. Surhoff.

> **❝I know Boomer. I know his intentions aren't to show us up. From someone else, it might have been different.❞**
>
> *— Chad Curtis*

Surhoff knocked a bouncer to second that Chuck Knoblauch gloved. He reared back …and fired a horrible, low throw, the sort of toss that symbolized his first-half problems. Sojo, playing his weakest position, dove for the ball, held on, and jumped up. It took a few seconds before first base umpire Fieldin Culbreth made the out call to end the inning.

Reporter's Notebook:

Torre didn't rule out the possibility of omitting Andy Pettitte from the postseason starting rotation. If Hideki Irabu pitches well in his next start Tuesday and Pettitte struggles again, "There's always a chance" that Irabu could take Pettitte's spot, the manager said.

Saturday, September 19, 1998
— at Baltimore Orioles

Orioles 5, Yankees 3

Cone loses again
But triggers option clause

By KEN DAVIDOFF, Staff Writer

BALTIMORE — The ball crawled off Eric Davis' bat and rolled toward third base, and Scott Brosius made one of his patented bare-handed grabs to throw out the Orioles veteran. With that, there was one out in the seventh in Saturday afternoon's Yankees-O's game at Camden Yards.

But this wasn't your ordinary groundout. When first base umpire Greg Kosc called Davis out, he gave David Cone control of his own destiny this winter.

That the Yankees' right-hander dropped a 5-3 decision Saturday afternoon, failing in his second opportunity to get his 20th victory, didn't seem to bother anyone in the visiting clubhouse. Baltimore's fireballer Sidney Ponson shut down the Bombers for the second time this season with a lethal mix of high-90s fastballs and high-80s change-ups, and the Yanks showed some life by putting together a ninth-inning rally.

And Cone, whose remarkable comeback has ranked as one of his team's biggest surprises, hit the 200-inning mark with that Davis out in the seventh. According to a clause written into the contract he signed with the Yankees on Dec. 22, 1995, that milestone activates a $5.5 million player option for 1999. He could accept it or turn it down and become a free agent, or he and the Yankees could agree on a higher salary for next year.

"It's huge for any player," said Cone, who notched his 200th strikeout, as well, when he fanned Rafael Palmeiro following Davis' roller. "Every player would like, at some point in their career, to control where they play, to have a choice where they work. Right now, I have that leverage."

How he uses that leverage won't be known until after the season. At $5.5 million, he would be a huge bargain for the Yanks. Earlier this season, he said he admired teammate Paul O'Neill for accepting considerably less than market value to stick around.

He has also said he feels a sense of debt toward the Yanks because injuries kept him from performing at his best and landed him on the disabled list.

But he is also the American League representative for the players union, which always encourages its members to drive up the price for everyone else. And $5.5 million could be too low for a 167-game winner who has hit his highest win total in 10 years and has stayed healthy after two seasons of serious arm troubles.

His teammates can't see Cone, who admittedly enjoys New York, heading elsewhere. "Nah!" Darryl Strawberry said when asked that question. "I would think he'd want to come back here," Joe Girardi agreed.

"I haven't really given it a lot of thought," Cone said. "I'm content to let this play out. When you play for the Yankees, the postseason means a lot, and what you do in the postseason. I'm just concerned about that right now. I'm sure my performance in the postseason could have a bearing on what happens."

The forecasts for Cone's postseason are encouraging. That he has lost consecutive starts for the first time since May 1995 with Toronto (he made 96 starts in between the two back-to-backs) has no one discouraged.

That he has allowed nine runs in 12 2/3 innings over the last two starts has not sounded a single alarm. He has battled a case of the flu, and all of his pitches have been effective at times.

"You get to a point with David Cone, if he feels all right, that's all my concern with him," manager Joe Torre said. "I know you're going to turn the ball over to him and you're going to trust him."

Cone feels fine. A year ago he said, he couldn't lift his arm over his head because of tendinitis in his right shoulder. Two years ago, there was the aneurysm that torpedoed the bulk of his season. Now, he is back up to 200 innings, the mark of a healthy pitcher.

"I've been around David Cone a long time, and I have a great deal of respect for what he thinks of the game and his approach to the game," Strawberry said. "Any time I see a guy like him accomplish what he's accomplished this year, you have to feel good for him."

Cone will have one more chance to get his 20th victory. He will most likely start Saturday, and Torre said it will be a short start to keep Cone rested for the playoffs.

Sunday, September 20, 1998
— at Baltimore Orioles

Yankees 5, Orioles 4

El Duque sparks Yanks

By KEN DAVIDOFF, Staff Writer

BALTIMORE — Orlando Hernandez, Sunday night was just one more indelible memory in a year full of them. This time, though, El Duque was more observer than participant.

The Cuban right-hander spoiled the going-away party for Cal Ripken Jr.'s consecutive-games-played streak, throwing six quality innings to give the Yankees a 5-4 victory over the Orioles in front of 48,013 history observers at Camden Yards.

It was the second straight good showing for Hernandez (one run, five hits, four strikeouts, two walks), who raised his record to 11-4 and lowered his ERA to 3.18. The Yankees have to feel very good about their No. 4 starter, who could start Game 2 of the American League Division Series.

They can't feel very good about Graeme Lloyd, however. The left-handed reliever threw one pitch Sunday night, and it was smoked over the fence in right-center by B.J. Surhoff.

Even before the game, manager Joe Torre expressed concern about his lefty specialist. Mike Stanton also had a rough night, walking three batters in an inning of work.

Being the opposing pitcher on the night Ripken ended his streak at 2,632 might rank as small potatoes for Hernandez after surviving his escape from Cuba via raft in December.

But El Duque surely will store this one among the highlights of his brief professional career in the United States.

"I think when he gets through with this season, and hopefully it's going to be late October, he's going to be tired," Torre said. "You talk about living a life in a short period of time. The range of emotions he's had to go through, to think back, 'Where was I six months ago?' and start from there — it's pretty incredible what's transpired."

While Ripken made his way to the Orioles bullpen and shook the hands of numerous fans, the Yankees jumped to a 2-0 lead before Baltimore countered with one in the fifth. The Yanks escaped a bases-loaded, two-out jam in the seventh and scored two in the eighth, then Surhoff knocked his two-run shot in the bottom of the inning. The Yanks padded their lead in the ninth.

The Bombers won for the third time in four games and lifted their record to 107-47. They have eight games left and must go 4-4 to set the team record for wins — the 1927 Yanks were 110-44 — and 5-3 to break the American League mark of 111 by the 1954 Indians.

Monday, September 21, 1998
— Cleveland Indians

Indians 4, Yankees 1

Pettitte shaky once again

By KEVIN T. CZERWINSKI, Staff Writer

NEW YORK — Joe Torre can be a spin doctor as much as he likes, but the bottom line remains the same: Andy Pettitte lost again Monday.

The southpaw was on the losing end for the fifth time in seven outings and once again was the victim of a big inning as Cleveland upended the Yankees, 4-1, before 21,449 at The Stadium.

This time, Pettitte's Waterloo came in the fifth when he got in trouble and surrendered a grand slam to Cleveland's Enrique Wilson, a backup infielder who came into the game with just 69 at-bats. Wilson sent Pettitte's first offering just inside the right-field foul pole for his first major league slam, giving the Tribe all the offense they would need.

"I think it was a good outing," Torre said. "You hate to give up that one hit, but I liked his stuff. He was a bit calmer out there. I don't like the big inning, but you can't worry about the big inning when everything else was good. Andy is starting to trust himself more."

Pettitte (16-11) went seven innings and scattered eight hits while striking out five. Like Torre, he felt he had a good outing, but couldn't ignore the final score. And that Cleveland didn't start Brian Giles, David Justice, or Kenny Lofton can't be ignored, either.

"Obviously, I'm not happy with the fifth inning, but I felt like everything else was working," Pettitte said. "I only got one sinker up all night and it got hit. It's very frustrating when things are going like this. If that ball is over 30 yards, it's a routine fly ball."

Catcher Joe Girardi also liked what he saw in Pettitte.

"I haven't been discouraged by him at all," Girardi said. "I believe in Andy. People are tending to make a big deal out of this, but I'm not worried."

With Pettitte taking another loss, the question of whether he'll be in the Yankees' playoff rotation came up yet again. Torre dodged the issue.

"I don't want to answer any postseason questions," Torre said. "It's not that I don't have confidence in Andy, but when I start naming definite starters, the one man who is out of the rotation will know. Let's give it a couple of games."

Pettitte said he hasn't been thinking about the playoffs. Torre hasn't spoken to him about a spot in the rotation yet.

"I don't feel like I'm owed anything," Pettitte said. "Skip [Torre] hasn't said anything to me, but I'd be stunned if I wasn't one of the four in the playoffs. But, we'll just have to wait and see."

Torre also believes the New York offense won't be as lackluster as it was Monday. Based on the season the Bombers have put together, that's a safe assumption. But there are no guarantees.

"I'd like to believe we'll score more runs," Torre said. "If we score six runs, no one notices [Pettitte's performance]. We need to hit a little more. Normally if we give up three or four runs this year, we still win because of the way we've hit."

But the Yanks ran into a buzz saw in Charles Nagy (15-10), who collected his fifth win in his last six outings. Nagy scattered five hits over eight innings and kept the Yanks guessing all night. He struck out four and walked only two.

And, his performance also shoots a few holes in Torre's argument about scoring runs in the playoffs. The caliber of pitching the Yanks will face will be comparable to what they saw in Nagy.

Texas has Todd Stottlemyre and Rick Helling. Anaheim has Chuck Finley. And, if it comes down to it, the Red Sox have Tim Wakefield and Pedro Martinez.

Scoring runs in the playoffs is no guarantee, so with Pettitte continuing to suffer lapses like the one he had Monday should be cause for a few red flags.

Tuesday, September 22, 1998

— Cleveland Indians

Yankees 5, Indians 1

Sharp Irabu helps his playoff cause

By KEVIN T. CZERWINSKI, Staff Writer

NEW YORK — The uncertainty surrounding Hideki Irabu has disappeared.

The Yankee right-hander turned in his second impressive performance in less than a week, shutting down the Cleveland Indians, 5-1, Tuesday night to complete a sweep of a day-night doubleheader.

In the first game, rookie Shane Spencer hit two home runs as the Yankees defeated the Indians, 10-4.

Irabu went eight solid innings, scattering four hits, striking out seven, and walking only two. Coupled with his shutout effort last week against Tampa Bay, Irabu has not allowed an earned run in his last 16 innings. The run he surrendered Tuesday was unearned.

Yankee manager Joe Torre said that all five of his starters would likely be on the postseason roster. The starter who isn't in the rotation will come out of the bullpen. As of now, that will either be Irabu or Andy Pettitte, whose struggles over the last few weeks have been well-chronicled.

"Right now this is a nice problem to have," Torre said. "Over his last two starts, Irabu has been terrific. Anything is liable to happen, but I'm leaning toward taking 10 pitchers, and one starter will be in the bullpen. Everyone will be able to contribute.

"Either way, I'm picking from quality people. We pretty much have to make an evaluation on what we'll need. I talked to [pitching coach] Mel [Stottlemyre] about when he was with the Mets and Sid Fernandez came out of the bullpen. He was pretty effective and I think we could have that. Like I said, we're probably only going to take 10 pitchers and Irabu has pushed himself into that group."

Torre said that he wouldn't place whatever starter is in the bullpen in a position where he would have to come in in a tough situation. He would either start an inning or be a long reliever.

Based on what he has shown in his last two starts, Irabu could be effective in such a role. He threw 112 pitches, 72 for strikes, and was in command through-out. His fastball had pop and his off-speed pitches were sharp, erasing the memory of many of his struggles over the last month and a half.

Either way, in long relief or as a starter, Irabu would be pleased.

"I think just being able to throw in the most important part of the season is exciting," Irabu said. "It's a real responsibility and I want to be the pitcher that represents our team. I just want to keep my self-confidence going the way it is now.

"I just want to be given a chance to throw in the playoffs. I want to go out and do the best I can."

Irabu isn't the only player who made a push to get to the postseason Tuesday. Rookie slugger Shane Spencer had a huge day, starting both ends of the twinbill. He had five hits in seven at-bats, including a pair of home runs in the first game. He had three RBI on the day and impressed Torre.

"The thing about Spencer is that he gives you an ingredient you don't normally get on those split decision guys," Torre said. "He has power and that makes him intriguing. He's one of those guys that you look at maybe as a journeyman and then he hits 30 home runs."

> **"**It's a real responsibility and I want to be the pitcher that represents our team. I just want to keep my self - confidence going the way it is now.**"**
>
> *— Hideki Irabu*

For now, Spencer feels he finally may be getting the respect that he hasn't gotten all along.

"I've never been that [top] prospect," he said. "No matter how well I've done. I don't know what it is. Every team I've been on has won. Maybe I don't bring as much to the table, but in the clubhouse I think I do.

"I'm feeling pretty good right now, though. If I get the chance to go out and play in the playoffs, I just want to have fun. I'm not going to try and think about it."

Spencer and Irabu will have a little more time to hawk their wares. Spencer should get a few more starts during the final five games and Irabu is slated to start Sunday's season finale against Tampa Bay.

Wednesday, September 23, 1998
— Cleveland Indians

Yankees 8, Cleveland 4

Yanks on the verge of making club history

By KEVIN T. CZERWINSKI, Staff Writer

NEW YORK — There is no Babe or Iron Horse, no Murderer's Row in Yankee Stadium these days.

The 1927 Yankees were a team of which legends are made. A team larger than life, one that has cast a shadow over the history of the game.

Now, though, that great squad, the one considered by many to be the greatest ever, has some company.

The Yankees defeated Cleveland, 8-4, at the Stadium on Wednesday for its 110th victory of the season. The win equaled the franchise record for victories by the fabled '27 team. With the triumph, the Yanks moved to within one win of the American League record for victories in a season by the 1954 Cleveland Indians.

The Yanks are 62 games over .500 (110-48). It marks the first time any team since the '54 Indians has been that far above the .500 mark.

Yankees manager Joe Torre was visibly moved by his team's accomplishment. He paused after the game to look at the scoreboard message which told him and the 32,367 fans who were giving the team a standing ovation exactly what this bunch had just accomplished.

"The scoreboard was just amazing," Torre said. "This puts us in some pretty damn good company. The record of winning more games than any other Yankee team means more to me than winning more games than any other team in history.

"To me, this in and of itself, is very special. You can't look down your nose on any team that wins 110, 111, 112, or however many games it's going to be."

Torre has great respect for the history of this franchise. He has a statue in the bookcase that stands behind the desk in his office. It's a statue of the 1927 Yankees. He couldn't help but admire it after the game.

"It really is pretty incredible to match these guys back here," Torre said, pointing to the statue. "They are the standard all Yankee teams look to."

There still is the problem, though, that plagued the '54 Indians. They may have won 111 games, but were swept by Willie Mays and the Giants in the World Series. It's a fact that hasn't escaped Yankees general manager Brian Cashman.

"It's a heck of an accomplishment. These guys have a lot to be proud of. It certainly is breathtaking," Cashman said. "Right now, though, we rank as the 24th-best team in club history because the other 23 teams have World Series rings. We'll take a few more wins now and then 11 more in the postseason.

"In all our meetings, we never looked at win totals. All we ever talked about was whether we were good enough to win a World Series. Hopefully, we'll find out. If we want to be considered in the class with the other Yankee teams, we'll have to win one, too."

> **❝** The home runs are McGwire's game, not mine. I don't even have 100 at-bats yet. **❞**
>
> *— Shane Spencer*

If the Yanks want to win one, maybe Torre should make a point of putting Shane Spencer on the postseason roster. He'll never be confused with Babe Ruth or Lou Gehrig, but the rookie slugger is sure tearing the cover off the ball lately.

He collected three more hits Wednesday, including his third home run in as many games. He has 10 hits and a walk in his last 14 plate appearances to go with 10 RBI. He's hitting .415 in 53 at-bats. Oh, and if you're curious, he's averaging a home run every 7.6 at-bats. Those are very Mark McGwire-like numbers.

"The home runs are McGwire's game, not mine," Spencer said with a laugh. "I don't even have 100 at-bats yet. I'm just getting the chance to play and making the most of it. Timing like this only comes around once in a while when you're hot. It could go away the next day."

Spencer had a double and single to go along with the homer. He received a standing ovation after he blasted a three-run shot in the fourth inning and the crowd didn't stop until he came out for a curtain call.

He needed a triple in his last at-bat for a cycle, but the thought didn't cross his mind at first.

"I wasn't thinking about it until Mike Lowell came up to me and reminded me," Spencer said. "He said if you hit the ball in the gap, just keep running."

Thursday, September 24, 1998
— Tampa Bay Devil Rays

Yankees 5, Devil Rays 2

Shane's a smash hit

Slam helps Yankees tie AL win record

By GREGORY SCHUTTA, Staff Writer

NEW YORK — Joe Torre turned around behind his desk in the Yankees manager's office Thursday night, pointed to the first small round figure on his statue of Murderer's Row and said with a laugh, "This is Zimmer." Two figures stood over a large round figure with spindly legs and a tree trunk disguised as a bat.

At 5 feet 10, 210 pounds, Shane Spencer never will be mistaken for the legendary Babe Ruth. But 71 years after the 1927 Yankees wrote themselves into the Yankees record books with 110 wins, Spencer continued to write a legend of his own, blasting a grand slam in the bottom of the fifth inning to erase a 2-0 Tampa Bay lead and give the 1998 Bronx Bombers their club-record 111th win.

"I wanted to do it tonight," Torre said after the Yankees' 5-2 victory. "I didn't want to wait for tomorrow. We've made our place in history, especially Yankees history. The 1927 Yankees are the standard that most clubs are judged by."

"From the time I was a kid growing up, I've heard how great the '27 Yankees were," owner George Steinbrenner said in a statement from Tampa. "That's why it means so much. Joe Torre, his coaches, and the players deserve all the credit. You all know that winning is important to me, but it's not the most important. It's second. First is breathing."

As the Yankees piled up the wins this season and watched their lead in the American League grow to monumental proportions, a lot of talk turned to win records, especially the Major League record 116 wins by the 1906 Chicago Cubs and the American League record 111 by the 1951 Cleveland Indians. The Yankees tied Cleveland on Thursday, but what mattered more to Torre was being at the top of the Yankees record book.

"I don't think [breaking Cleveland's record] will mean as much as this one," said Torre, a New York native and student of Yankees history. "When you

have a storied franchise like the Yankees and a team like the 1927 Yankees that everybody talks about as being the best, to beat them is great. We've set ourselves up as the team to beat."

For a while, it looked as if the expansion Devil Rays were going to to spoil Torre's night. Wilson Alvarez handcuffed the Yankees for five innings. The left-hander didn't allow a hit until Scott Brosius doubled into left field with two out in the bottom of the fifth and the Devil Rays leading, 2-0.

Everything fell apart for Alvarez in the sixth as he gave up a walk to Chuck Knoblauch and back-to-back singles to Derek Jeter and Bernie Williams as the Yankees cut the lead to 2-1. Chili Davis walked to load the bases and bring up the red-hot Spencer, who had homered in his previous three games and had seven homers and 18 RBI in 55 at-bats to that point.

The 26-year-old rookie from California took a 1-1 change-up from Alvarez and banged it off the bleacher facade in right-center field for his second grand slam in a week. That was all five Yankees pitchers would need as Mike Buddie got his fourth win in relief of starter David Wells and Jeff Nelson notched his third save.

Wells, making his final tuneup before opening the American League Division Series on Tuesday at the Stadium, scattered five hits and two runs over five innings. The pinpoint control that lifted him to a career-high 18 wins this season, abandoned him in the second inning when he walked two batters in an inning for the first time since July and gave up two runs.

But as he has done for the past week, Spencer came to the rescue. It started with a grand slam in a victory over Baltimore last Friday and continued with three homers in three games against Cleveland on Tuesday and Wednesday.

"I was just hoping to get a chance to play some," said Spencer, who made four trips on the Columbus Shuttle before getting his last callup Aug. 31. "I'm seeing the ball real good right now, and when that happens everything seems to slow down and [the ball] looks bigger."

"He's certainly gotten our attention," Torre said when asked if Spencer was a lock for the postseason roster. "When you look at his numbers, they're pretty hard to ignore."

Reporter's Notebook:

Nelson gave Torre the game ball. "It will have a special place in my home," Torre said. ...Williams went 1-for-4, dropping him into a tie with Boston's Mo Vaughn (3-for-5) for the American League batting lead at .334. ... Jeter went 1-for-4, and is one hit short of becoming the first Yankee to have 200 hits since Steve Sax in 1989 and the first Yankees shortstop to do it since Hall of Famer Phil Rizzuto in 1950. ... Spencer's grand slam was the eighth of the season for the Yankees, second only to the 10 they hit in 1987.

Friday, September 25, 1998
— Tampa Bay Devil Rays

Yankees 6, Devil Rays 1

Yankees add another notch to proud history

By GREGORY SCHUTTA, Staff Writer

NEW YORK — After the Yankees won their 111th game of the season Thursday night, Jeff Nelson gave Joe Torre the game ball, and Torre went to the umpires room to retrieve the lineup cards. These mementos apparently weren't as meaningful from the 112th victory Friday night, and their whereabouts remain anyone's guess.

The night the Yankees set the American League record for most wins seemed almost anticlimactic for the team that made so much noise with its bats during the regular season.

The Bombers battered Tampa Bay pitching for five runs in the second inning and three pitchers made them stand up as they beat the Devil Rays, 6-1, before 32,447 at Yankee Stadium, thereby eclipsing the American League record of 111 wins in a season set by the 1954 Cleveland Indians.

Coming one day after toppling the record of the 1927 Yankees, a team many consider the best in major league history, and with the playoffs only four days away, the latest record did not seem as important.

"I went around and shook just about everybody's hand," Torre said. "It's something you can enjoy for a couple of days, but we're interested in higher goals."

"I'm glad to be a part of this team and a part of history," first baseman Tino Martinez said. "It means a lot. But our goal is to win the World Series and play

well in the postseason."

With Murderer's Row finally behind them, the Bombers set about preparing for the postseason as Orlando Hernandez and Andy Pettitte each made a pitch for the start in Game 2 of the Division Series on Wednesday at the Stadium.

El Duque got the start against Tampa Bay and allowed one run on four hits in five innings to pick up his 12th win. Pettitte made his first relief appearance since May 1996 and didn't allow a run, yielding two hits. Both struck out a pair of batters.

"I thought they were both great," said Torre, who got a scare when Hernandez took a shot off his foot in the fifth inning. "Andy pitched very well. You never know how a guy like that is going to come out of the bullpen, but he threw a little in the fourth inning and again in the fifth and he was OK."

"I'm definitely ready," said Pettitte, who has struggled for the past month. "I felt really good. It was a matter of going out and trying to get everything worked out [Friday night], and I think I did that."

El Duque, who hasn't lost since Aug. 23 (4-0, six starts), knew it was his last chance to impress Torre, but it was not the primary thought on his mind.

"That's a question for Joe Torre," he said through an interpreter when asked if he expects to start in the playoffs. "For me personally, it doesn't matter if I start or relieve as long as I contribute."

New York got a lot of contributions Friday night as it dismantled former Yankee Dave Eiland for six runs on six hits in less than three innings. Derek Jeter was the catalyst, banging a single and a double and scoring twice to join Phil Rizzuto as the only Yankee shortstops with 200 hits in a season.

Scott Brosius had a two-run single and Jorge Posada added an RBI double to highlight the Yankees five-run third inning. Bernie Williams regained the lead in the American League batting race from Boston's Mo Vaughn by going 2-for-2 to raise his average to .337. Vaughn went 2-for-4 against Baltimore and is now at .336.

"If it's going to happen, it's going to happen," Williams said about the batting title. "All I can do is take care of business on the field and make sure I get good at-bats. That's all I can control right now."

A batting title for Williams and 20 wins for David Cone, scheduled to make his third attempt at the milestone today against the Devil Rays, would apply the cappers to an incredible regular season for the Yankees. But Torre, ever a baseball historian, knows it's not the end. He remembers watching the Indians get swept by Willie Mays and the Giants in the 1954 World Series.

"I was happy they lost because I was a Giants fan," he said. "But that shows you what can happen in a short series when somebody comes in with a head of steam. But I don't have to tell these guys that. They've been around here long enough, and they'll be ready to play the first pitch."

Saturday, September 26, 1998
— Tampa Bay Devil Rays

Yankees 3, Devil Rays 1

Cone savors 20th win

Yanks vet repeats feat decade later

By GREGORY SCHUTTA, Staff Writer

NEW YORK — When David Cone failed in two attempts to win his 20th game of the season, he decided that if he didn't get it in his final start Saturday, he wouldn't let it affect him. Apparently his teammates had other ideas.

So when Scott Brosius' throw nipped Quinton McCracken at first base with the bases loaded in the ninth inning to seal the Yankees' 3-1 victory over the Tampa Bay Devil Rays, Tino Martinez, Paul O'Neill, Mike Stanton, and Chili Davis collectively leaped out of their chairs in the clubhouse and congratulated an emotional Cone on his first 20-win season since 1988.

"It was really quiet in here up until that time, and then everybody just let loose," Cone said. "I was fine until Joe [Girardi] gave me the game ball and a big hug. I think he wanted it more than I did."

Girardi was not alone. During a season in which the Yankees have accomplished everything a team could by this point, the only thing that remains until the playoffs start Tuesday is individual goals. And even though Bernie Williams is fighting for a batting title and Brosius is pushing for his first 100-RBI season, the milestone every Yankee wanted was 20 wins for Cone.

"It's been on my mind for the last three weeks,"

said Girardi, who took the ball from first baseman Luis Sojo's glove so he could deliver it to Cone. "We had a couple of chances and didn't do it, and I thought about it a lot. His reaction was just another way of him telling me how much he appreciates what I do back there."

Said manager Joe Torre: "I think it was so important that we get 20 wins for David, specifically because of where he came from and what he had to go through here physically over the last couple of years. In spring training, David was one of our biggest question marks on a questionable starting staff, because we didn't know what he could do."

That's because Cone missed the end of last season and underwent major shoulder surgery for the second time in three years in October. He was shaky early in the season despite a 7-1 record, allowing 16 runs and 18 hits in his first two outings. But things began to turn around in June, when he threw a two-hitter with 14 strikeouts in a 4-1 victory over the Florida Marlins.

Scheduled to go just five innings Saturday in his final tuneup for the playoffs, Cone threw seven shutout innings, allowing four hits and striking out eight to raise his record to 20-7 and break Yankees broadcaster Jim Kaat's record of seven years between 20-win seasons.

"It's probably my most gratifying season considering where it started and the disappointment of last year near the end," Cone said. "The only thing I can compare my reaction to is Game 3 of the World Series in 1996. Other than that, it's usually the losses that leave you crying."

Cone didn't do any crying as he set down the Devil Rays with machinelike efficiency. He threw 66 of his 101 pitches for strikes and allowed two batters to reach base in the same inning just once.

The only scare came in the third, when Rich Butler led off with a hard one-hopper that drilled Cone flush in the stomach. Cone, bent over at a right angle, managed to

> **❝** It's probably my most gratifying season considering where it started and the disappointment of last year near the end. **❞**
>
> *— David Cone*

throw out Butler at first but stayed that way for a minute or two.

"I took a pretty good shot off my ribs, and it knocked the wind out of me," Cone said. "I've got a good bruise on my ribs. It'll be sore tomorrow, but right now I'm feeling no pain."

Cone, who had a bottle of champagne compliments of George Steinbrenner waiting for him at his locker, meant that literally and figuratively. He has come a long way since he threw for the first time after last season during the Yankee Cruise in November with trainer Gene Monahan and coach Gary Tuck.

"If you could see me throw to Gary on the back of that ship," Cone said. "I never thought I'd be here talking about 20 wins right now. The last time I did it [for the Mets], I walked off the mound and [former] President [Richard] Nixon was in the dugout. But I was too young to understand the meaning of it. ... That's probably why it's so special now."

Sunday, September 27, 1998
— Tampa Bay Devil Rays

Yankees 8, Devil Rays 3

Spencer makes postseason list

By GREGORY SCHUTTA, Staff Writer

NEW YORK — It's rarely a good sign when a rookie is called into the manager's office. It's even worse when the owner is in the room. And it's downright deadly when the owner is George Steinbrenner.

So Shane Spencer didn't know what to expect Sunday when he was called into Joe Torre's office after his third grand slam in nine days helped give the Yankees their seventh straight win and 10th in the last 12, 8-3, over the Tampa Bay Devil Rays.

"Mr. Steinbrenner said, 'We've got some bad news for you,' but he had a smile on his face," Spencer said.

The "bad news" is that Spencer has been included on the Yankees' postseason roster. Also making the cut are Darryl Strawberry and Tim Raines, both of whom were on the bubble because of health questions.

"I've met Mr. Steinbrenner before," Spencer said. "I've been in the organization for eight years. We've had our run-ins."

But anything bad that might have happened in those eight years has been erased by Spencer's performance the past month. The rookie added to his legend Sunday with a grand slam to cap a five-run fifth inning, his third slam in four at-bats with the bases loaded.

"Just the right place at the right time," said Spencer, who in only a month leads the Yankees in curtain calls this season.

Reporter's Notebook:

Left-hander Graeme Lloyd won the bullpen sweepstakes, beating out right-hander Darren Holmes for the 10th and final spot on the postseason pitching staff.

"I'm very disappointed," Holmes said. "I'm not happy about it. I wanted to be a part of the playoff roster. I think I deserved to be a part of it. It was simply a numbers game."

And the number was two, as in the number of left-handers Torre feels he needs in the bullpen. With starter Hideki Irabu going to the pen for the playoffs, Mike Stanton would have been the only lefty reliever had Holmes been picked over Lloyd.

"You want to have a couple of left-handers in the bullpen," Torre said. "Lloyd has struggled this month, but he's come on in his last couple of outings. The pitching decision came down to we can't take 11, we have to take 10."

The 49,608 fans at the Stadium Sunday gave the Yankees a record attendance of 2,949,734 for the season, more than 300,000 over their previous record but less than the 3 million Steinbrenner said he wanted before he would discuss keeping the team in the Bronx. ...Spencer's home run gave the Yankees 10 players with at least 10 homers, tying the major league record set earlier this season by Baltimore ...The Yankees extended their club and AL records with their 114th win of the season and finished 62-19 at home, tying the 1932 team for second on the home-victory list behind the 1961 Yankees (65-16)

> **"** I'm not happy about it. I wanted to be a part of the playoff roster. I think I deserved to be a part of it. It was simply a numbers game. **"**
>
> *— David Holmes*

1998 Postseason

Tuesday, September 29, 1998

— Texas Rangers

ALDS Game 1: Yankees 2, Rangers 0

Wells-done!

Yanks ace handcuffs Rangers

By KEN DAVIDOFF, Staff Writer

NEW YORK — David Wells lived up to his high postseason standards Tuesday night,and so the Yankees lived up to their high 1998 standards.

With his eight innings of shutout baseball, the Boomer outdueled the Rangers' Todd Stottlemyre to give the Bombers a 2-0 victory in Game 1 of the American League Division Series. The virtuoso performance before 57,362 Yankee Stadium fans (the second-largest crowd in the 23 years since the ballpark's renovation) gave the Yanks the one-game-to-none cushion they so badly needed with the questionable Andy Pettitte taking the mound tonight.

"It was one of those nights where I felt very, very good," Wells said. "Two runs was all we needed."

"You don't want to take it for granted he's going to shut down a team like Texas, but he did that," teammate Paul O'Neill said. "He's got a lot of guts."

Chad Curtis, the surprise starter in left field, didn't play much of a factor defensively; he even misplayed a ball in the eighth inning that could have been crucial. But his second-inning double served as the night's key hit, as the two runs the home team tallied in that inning proved to be the only work the scoreboard operator would get all night. And Mariano Rivera, in his first postseason save chance since last year's infamous Sandy Alomar Jr. homer in Game 4 of the ALDS, did the job in the ninth.

Wells, who is 5-0 with a 2.06 ERA in playoff action, permitted just five hits, walked one, and set a career postseason high with nine strikeouts. He shut down the dangerous Juan Gonzalez, who didn't hit a ball more than two feet fair.

The tough-luck Stottlemyre held the Yanks to six

hits and tied his playoff best with eight strikeouts, but it wasn't good enough.

Wells, one of the game's best control pitchers, started the Yankees' postseason with a walk to Mark McLemore. Ball four was the second call to go against the pitcher, and Wells glared at home plate umpire Jim Joyce as he took the throw back from Jorge Posada.

Rather than let such a call throw him off, as happened to him a few weeks ago in Boston, The Boomer seemed to channel the energy to hisadvantage, handcuffing the next three batters to such a degree that none of them hit a fair ball past the mound. Roberto Kelly tapped a nubber that Wells grabbed and whipped to first; Rusty Greer struck out on a fastball that tailed away from him; and Gonzalez hit the ball less than a foot in front of the plate that Posada jumped on and threw to Tino Martinez.

He never really let up from there. He would retire the next seven batters before allowing his first hit, a Greer line drive that a diving Derek Jeter couldn't hold on to with one out in the fourth. A Rangers runner didn't reach second again until the seventh, when Will Clark and Todd Zeile put a pair of singles around an Ivan Rodriguez fielder's choice. With two outs, up stepped Mike Simms, who had already grounded a base hit in the fifth.

> **❝** You don't want to take it for granted he's going to shut down a team like Texas, but he did that. He's got a lot of guts. **❞**
>
> *— Paul O'Neill*
> *on pitcher David Wells*

Pitcher and hitter battled for nine pitches, with Simms fouling off three pitches after falling behind, 0-2. On pitch No. 9, Simms swung and missed at a change-up. End of inning, and the crowd erupted in appreciation.

"There, you want to go with a perfect pitch," Posada said. "He was throwing good change-ups all day. It was the right pitch at that time."

That was the 109th pitch of the night for Wells, and

when the eighth started, Jeff Nelson and Mike Stanton were warming up in the bullpen. With one out, McLemore knocked a liner to left. Curtis stood still, then backtracked too late, as the ball sailed over his head for a double.

Joe Torre dashed to the mound to check on Wells, who appeared frustrated. "He asked me, how do I feel?," Wells said. "I said, I feel OK. He said: 'really, how do I feel?' Then Jorge said: 'Joe, he's got it. He's got some left.'"

Wells proved it by catching Kelly looking at an inside fastball for strike three, and Jeter made an excellent run, grab, and throw on a Greer check-swing tapper to end the inning.

The bottom of the Bombers' lineup provided Wells with an early cushion. Posada walked with one out in the second, and Curtis knocked a Stottlemyre pitch to right field, where it avoided Gonzalez's glove and hit the wall on a bounce. Posada advanced to third.

Scott Brosius poked a 1-1 Stottlemyre offering between first and second base for a run-scoring single, with Curtis going to third. As Chuck Knoblauch struck out, the Yanks ran themselves into a somewhat successful double play.

Brosius took off for second, and when Rodriguez bit and threw across the diamond, Curtis broke for home. Brosius stopped in his tracks as McLemore, the second baseman, caught the ball and turned back toward first.

The subsequent rundown lasted long enough for Curtis to touch the plate before Brosius was tagged out, giving the home team a 2-0 edge.

It was good the Yanks cashed in their second-inning chances, for they had failed to do so in the first. Knoblauch took a pitch on the back to jump-start the Yankees' offense.

O'Neill laced a one-out double down the third base line, and Knoblauch was sent home by third base coach Willie Randolph. But Rodriguez was waiting, blocking the plate, and the relay from Greer in left field to shortstop Royce Clayton to Rodriguez was perfect. Knoblauch tried to run over Rodriguez; he probably would have had better luck running over the late Andre the Giant. He was out easily.

O'Neill went to third on a Rodriguez passed ball but couldn't score, as Martinez looked at a third strike after Bernie Williams walked.

If the Yanks win tonight, they might need to spend only one day in Texas.

"If we were going to make a statement tonight, we did," O'Neill said.

Wednesday, September 30, 1998
— Texas Rangers
ALDS Game 2: Yankees 3, Rangers 1

It's two, easy
Yankees in control of Rangers

By KEN DAVIDOFF, Staff Writer

NEW YORK — They arrived at work Wednesday and were served with troubling news: Darryl Strawberry, one of the Yankees' most popular players, would not be sticking around for Game 2 of this AL Division Series. With a CAT scan showing a spot on his colon, he needed to go home and prepare for further tests today.

Under the duress of that distressing bulletin, the Bombers responded with a sharp, focused effort at Yankee Stadium. And no one was more sharp or focused than Andy Pettitte, the man who looked only dull and distracted the past six weeks.

> **He's got a belly full of guts.**
> *— Joe Torre*
> *on Andy Pettitte*

Behind Pettitte's superb pitching and strong hitting from rookie sensation Shane Spencer and Scott Brosius, the Yanks pulled out another low-scoring contest, 3-1, to take a 2-0 lead over Texas in front of 57,360 fans. David Cone can complete the sweep Friday night – by which time the Yankees should know more about Strawberry's condition – at The Ballpark in Arlington.

"It's a big lift," Pettitte said of his performance. "That was a big game for me. So much negative stuff has been said about me. Just to come up with a big start feels great."

Said manager Joe Torre, "He's got a belly full of guts."

Before the game, Pettitte had a brief conversation with Strawberry, who delivered his news.

"He just let me know what was going on," said Pettitte, who admitted that he didn't fully absorb the news due to the fact that he was in his pregame zone.

He never left that zone. In his first victorious post-season start since a brilliant Game 5 effort in the 1996 World Series – when he threw 8 1/3 shutout innings – the left-hander went seven innings and allowed a run and three hits. His eight strikeouts are a career high for the playoffs, and he had no walks— just the second time this season that his control was so solid.

"That was the best stuff he's had all year," first baseman Tino Martinez said.

"That was better than [Tuesday] night's game," said David Wells, whose Game 1 brilliance prevented Pettitte from pitching down, 0-1. [Pettitte's performance] took a lot of pressure off of him. It earned a lot of respect from others."

Jeff Nelson pitched two-thirds of an inning, then Mariano Riveraworked the final 1 1/3 for his second save in two games to close the deal. Yankees pitchers have limited the Rangers offense — the same one that averaged almost seven runs a game against Bombers pitching in the regular season — to a run, 10 hits, and a walk in 18 innings.

"In my opinion, playoff baseball is much like what you've seen," Rangers manager Johnny Oates said. "We have the two most potent offensive teams in the American League, and we've scored six runs in two ballgames."

Consequently, once again, the Rangers' starting pitcher didn't really lose as much as not pitch well enough to win. Rick Helling, a 20-game winner, lasted six innings and permitted three runs and eight hits, walking one, and fanning nine. For the Rangers to get such stellar back-to-back outings from Todd Stottlemyre and Helling and lose both has to be frustrating for a club that routinely plays – and wins – slugfests.

And Pettitte seemed like just the candidate for the baseballequivalent of a quarterback sack. For all of the Yankees' hemming and hawing about how the 26-year-old would be just fine, the bottom line was this: In his final seven starts of the regular season, he had an ERA of 6.91 with 15 walks in 43 innings.

Torre said Game 5 in '96 gave him faith, and his loyalty was rewarded. Pettitte showed an excellent change-up and solid fastball, and his cut-fastball was effective in brief appearances. For his career, he is 3-3 in the postseason with a 6.23 ERA.

"Early in September, I was having trouble with everything," he said. "My mechanics were all out of sync. A lot of it had to do with my mechanics. Then you give up a couple of hits, and your confidence starts to go. I kept real focused tonight."

With two out in the second inning and the first six Yankees at-bats producing a Derek Jeter walk and five outs, Spencer stepped up for his first postseason plate appearance. He worked the count to 2-2, and then, unbelievably, it happened: The rookie connected on a low fastball and sent it over the left field fence, giving the Yanks a 1-0 lead.

When he rounded the bases and returned to the dugout, the crowd once again requested for a curtain call, his fourth in the past nine days. This time Spencer went with a Western theme, making a gun out of his thumb and index and pulling the trigger at the crowd.

Spencer singled with one out in the fourth, and Brosius followed by clubbing a high fastball the other way, well over the wall in right to make it 3-0.

After retiring the first 12 batters, Pettitte surrendered a Juan Gonzalez double down the third base line. Spencer's throw to second beat Gonzalez, but Chuck Knoblauch dropped the ball after applying the tag.

Ivan Rodriguez singled home Gonzalez one out later, and a call immediately went out to the bullpen: Warm up Ramiro Mendoza.

Perhaps the most troubling symptom of Pettitte's recent slump had been his inability to pitch out of trouble. On this night, though, withone run in and his margin for error small, he put out his own fire. Todd Zeile popped out to Jeter at shortstop, and Mike Simms grounded out to third.

As if for emphasis, Pettitte did it again in the sixth. Roberto Kelly knocked a two-out double to the base of the wall in right-center, and the dangerous Rusty Greer went down on a nasty cutter.

Friday, October 2, 1998 — at Texas Rangers

ALDS Game 3: Yankees 4, Rangers 0

Yankees win series, 3 - 0

Yanks send Rangers to showers

By KEN DAVIDOFF, Staff Writer

ARLINGTON, Texas — Neither rain, nor thunder and lightning, nor more rain could derail the Yankees from winning one for Darryl.

Onto the American League Championship Series. David Cone gave the Yankees a third straight night of excellent starting pitching, Shane Spencer provided yet another home run, and the Bombers completed their first-round sweep early this morning, blanking the Rangers, 4-0, in Game 3 of the AL Division Series at The Ballpark in Arlington. The two teams waited out a torrential rain storm that caused a 3-hour, 16-minute delay.

The victory meant that the Yankees could head home to be in town today as Darryl Strawberry undergoes surgery to remove the malignant, walnut-sized tumor that was found in his colon Thursday.

Cone, who has known Strawberry since their days with the Mets, put in 5 2/3 superb innings in out-dueling Texas' Aaron Sele, permitting just two hits, striking out six, and walking one.

And Spencer added to his already jumbo-sized legend by slamming a three-run homer off Rangers starter Aaron Sele. Paul O'Neill started the Bombers' four-run sixth with a solo blast, marking the first significant production from anyone – O'Neill, Bernie Williams, or Tino Martinez – in the heart of the Yankees' lineup.

> **❝** It's been a very emotional time for everybody. What I think Straw wants us to do is go out there on that emotion and finish them off. **❞**
>
> — *Mike Stanton*

The mighty Rangers' lineup, which punished the Yankees pitching staff like no other team during the regular season, finished the series with a lilliputian one run in three games. And now the Bombers will have three days off as they wait to see who their next opponent will be. Cleveland took a 2-1 lead over Boston in the other ALDS.

Before the game, manager Joe Torre made no speech to address his players. Instead, the Yankees watched a short video message from their teammate. Strawberry started off stoic, choked up at one juncture, then collected himself and pointed at the camera. "Go get them tonight, guys," he said, in a rallying tone. With a wry smile, and a deep, mock-serious voice, he added, "Get'em!"

That set off a chorus of laughter in the clubhouse, and Torre felt that was enough of the touchy-feely stuff. Said the manager before the game: "If I sense that we're straying, or if we're out there and don't look like we're paying attention, then we'll handle it as it goes. But I didn't think there was any reason to assume that these players aren't focused on what we have to do."

"It's been a very emotional time for everybody," Mike Stanton said. "What I think Straw wants us to do is go out there on that emotion and finish them off."

They did that, just with a major delay. At 9:08, with two outs in the bottom of the sixth and the Yanks holding their 4-0 advantage, the umpires summoned the grounds crew to put on the tarpaulin. Had they waited one more out, the game would have been official.

For the next 3 1/4 hours, the two teams huddled in their respective clubhouses while the rains came down by the gallon. The crowd of 49,950 slowly filtered out as a parade full of fans, several of them topless males, sneaked onto the field and did belly-flops on the infield. The Ballpark's lights went out momentarily, and a fire alarm, later declared to be false, went off.

Action finally resumed at 12:24, and Graeme Lloyd notched the final out of the seventh. Jeff Nelson and Mariano Rivera went the rest of the way for the Yanks.

It became very clear, very early, that it would again be a pitcher's night. After five innings, neither team had made it as far as third base. Cone struck out five Rangers, including Juan Gonzalez and Ivan Rodriguez in the same inning. Sele fanned three Yankees.

The Bombers received a scare in the top of the fifth when Scott Brosius knocked a one-out single to right, then stumbled and grabbed his right ankle as he was picked off by Rodriguez while Joe Girardi was at bat. Brosius was helped off the field by Torre and assistant trainer Steve Donohue, but he returned to play third base.

Derek Jeter started the sixth with a fly ball to right field that carried, carried — and was caught at the warning track by Gonzalez. That proved to be a harbinger of things to come: The next batter, Paul O'Neill, worked the count to 1-1. Sele offered a breaking ball that hung nicer than a new suit, and O'Neill, smacked it the other way, where it traveled over the fence in left-center for a 1-0 Yankees lead. The 408-foot shot was the sixth in O'Neill's ALDS career.

And right before the clouds opened, the floodgates opened. After Bernie Williams struck out looking,

Tino Martinez knocked an infield single to shortstop. Tim Raines lashed a double to left, moving Martinez to third. Spencer drove the first pitch he saw, another hanging breaking ball, over the left field fence. Martinez clapped as he jogged home, and Raines almost knocked third base coach Willie Randolph's hand off as he gave him a rock-hard high-five.

Tuesday, October 6, 1998

— Cleveland Indians

ALCS Game 1: Yankees 7, Indians 2

Yankees lead series, 1 - 0

Boomer, baby!

Yankees' Wells tops Indians

KEN DAVIDOFF, Staff Writer

NEW YORK — Van Halen thundered through Yankee Stadium as David Wells warmed up Tuesday night, and the ballpark's patrons did the same every time he got two strikes on a Cleveland batter. Darryl Strawberry made his presence felt courtesy of his family and some enterprising fans, and the Indians did their part by putting the detested Jaret Wright against Wells.

Raw energy. Anticipation. Sentiment. Rivalry. It all worked to Wells' advantage, because there has yet to be discovered something that doesn't work to the southpaw's advantage this time of year. Wells shined yet again, limiting the Indians to a pair of ninth-inning runs to record a 7-2 victory and deliver Game 1 of the American League Championship Series to the Bombers. David Cone will try to give the Yanks a 2-0 edge today.

"I was geared tonight," Wells said. "It's a situation where you want the first game because you can set the tone. You get one under your belt, and you try to do better the next game."

Consider the tone set. The Yankees have won 11 straight games, including seven in the regular season and three in the AL Division Series, and they seem to be getting better. After sweeping a trio of tightly played contests against the Rangers in the Division Series, they simply overmatched Wright and the Tribe in front of 57,138 chilly yet fired-up fans. Their team ERA for the playoffs is 0.75.

Wright, who played a gargantuan role in ending the 1997 Yankees' season earlier than planned, lasted just two-thirds of an inning, getting shelled for five runs and five hits (all singles), walking one, and fanning one. In two postseason games this year, he is 0-2 with a 19.80 ERA. The top of the Yankees' lineup, which did virtually nothing in the first round, created the five-run first.

"[The fans] hold grudges more than we hold grudges," Wells said. "To see Jaret go out in the first inning was very gratifying."

Wells, meanwhile, is 2-0 with a 1.08 ERA in these playoffs, and for his postseason career, he is 6-1.

"When I talked to him in spring training, I told him that he should be a 20-game winner every year with the stuff he has," said catcher Jorge Posada, who added a solo homer.

Against Texas last week, in Game 1 of the ALDS, the Boomer pitched under constant pressure, protecting a meek 2-0 lead. This time, he did his work in the top of the first with little difficulty, and the next time he came out to pitch, he was the proud owner of a 5-0 advantage – courtesy of the much-maligned top of the order.

> **"** The fans hold grudges more than we hold grudges. To see Jaret go out in the first inning was very gratifying. **"**
>
> *— David Wells*

Remember last year's Back-to-Back-to-Back in Game 1 of the ALDS against Cleveland, the consecutive homers by Tim Raines, Derek Jeter, and Paul O'Neill? This year's Game 1 featured a back-to-back-to-back-to-back, a more subtle but still significant four consecutive first-inning singles from Chuck Knoblauch, Jeter, O'Neill, and Bernie Williams.

And Wells took it from there, striking out seven (each one marked in the stands by a pinstriped 39, in honor of Strawberry, whose wife Charisse threw out the first pitch), walking one, and allowing five hits in 8 1/3 innings before Jeff Nelson finished the job. The celebrity-happy pitcher, performing to such owner's box guests as Billy Crystal and Donald Trump, once again used his change-up to complement his already dazzling fastball and curveball to render the Indians helpless.

The owner couldn't have appreciated the fact that Wells wore a virtually whole goatee — a direct violation of team rules on facial hair. But George Steinbrenner had to enjoy the rest of the evening.

The bottom of the first lasted 28 minutes, 10 batters, and 43 pitches. Wells wouldn't hit the 43-pitch mark until the fourth. The six singles in an inning and five runs in a first inning set ALCS records. Chad Ogea relieved Wright after eight batters.

Manager Joe Torre disputed the Wright-revenge theory, insisting, "The extra satisfaction is that he's a good pitcher and we were able to get to him in the first inning."

To his credit, Ogea kept the Yankees quiet and kept his team within semi-striking distance. Posada's leadoff homer in the sixth, the first of his career in the playoffs, made it a 6-0 ballgame.

O'Neill and Williams cranked back-to-back doubles to start the seventh, raising the lead to 7-0 and knocking out Ogea for southpaw Jim Poole.

Manny Ramirez ripped a two-run homer in the ninth, writing Wells' exit, and Nelson notched the last two outs.

Wednesday, October 7, 1998
— Cleveland Indians

ALCS Game 2: Indians 4, Yankees 1

Series tied, 1 - 1

Chucklehead
Knoblauch's mental lapse costs Yanks

By KEN DAVIDOFF, Staff Writer

NEW YORK — Time froze for a moment Wednesday evening at Yankee Stadium, and the Indians slipped through the hole to put the Yankees' pursuit of history on hold.

A long pitchers' duel turned in a bizarre fashion when Cleveland rookie Enrique Wilson capitalized on a Chuck Knoblauch mental error to snare victory for the visitors. The Indians wound up winning Game 2 of the American League Championship Series by a 4-1 score in 12 innings, but it was much closer than that.

In evening the series at a game apiece and grabbing the home-field advantage in this best-of-seven affair, the Tribe created a gigantic pair of goat horns for Knoblauch and had the Yankees, including George Steinbrenner, fuming at the game's umpires. All of which stemmed from a seemingly innocuous Travis Fryman bunt.

With Wilson on first base and none out, Fryman dropped a perfect bunt. After first baseman Tino Martinez's throw to first hit Fryman in the back, Knoblauch jawed with the ump while Wilson raced around the bases and scored the winning run.

"When you play four hours out there and go 12 innings, when it's decided like that, it's a shame," Knoblauch said.

The Yanks' first-year leadoff hitter, who cruised through his subpar season with nary a jeer from the hometown fans, was besieged with a massive stream of boos by what remained of the 57,128 fans when he came to bat in the bottom of the 12th inning. Said Knoblauch: "That's not a very nice feeling when you come to play. They're going to react the way they're going to react. That fired me up, actually."

But the Bombers' head of steam, energized by 11 straight victories extending from the regular season and including the first round of the playoffs, had already cooled off. They stranded 10 runners against Cleveland starter Charles Nagy and a sextet of relievers, thus wasting another superb New York pitching performance by David Cone and relievers Mariano Rivera and Mike Stanton.

"That's not the reason we lost," Martinez said of the bunt play. "We lost the game earlier. We had plenty of chances."

True, but clearly the game's turning point arrived the moment Fryman laid down his bunt. Jim Thome had started the 12th with a single off losing pitcher Jeff Nelson, and his pinch runner, Wilson, got a good jump off the bunt. Martinez didn't.

"I had to turn around and make a quick throw," Martinez said. "I didn't see Knobby there at all."

Fryman appeared to be inside the foul line, a violation of Official Baseball Rule 6.05 (k), and Martinez's throw hit Fryman in the back at about the time his front foot hit the bag. First base umpire John Shulock called him safe, and Knoblauch, blowing bubbles with his gum, began to argue. Manager Joe Torre joined him a moment later.

"He was on the grass," Torre said. "It was so blatant, you know, I don't know what to say. It was a terrible call."

"I expected him to be called out," Knoblauch said.

But umpire crew chief Jim Evans said Fryman was not declared out because the Indian had beaten the throw to first.

"The fact that he was literally on the base or half a step off the base when it hit him, he has a right to be in that position," Evans said.

As Knoblauch argued, the ball rolled slowly behind him. Wilson and Fryman kept running and running. Wilson tripped between third and home, he was so giddy, before beating Knoblauch's late throw and scoring to give Cleveland a 2-1 lead. Fryman made it to third.

"I'm saying, `Get the ball, get the ball, get the ball!'" Yankees catcher Jorge Posada said. "They called him safe, and the ball is just laying around."

"Once the ball dropped, you can't assume anything," Nelson said.

"The ball was just laying there. No one was getting it."

"It seemed like the game stopped for a second there," Martinez said.

"You have got to make the play, and then go back and argue with the umpire," Torre agreed. "But I think he [Knoblauch] was just shocked that they didn't make the call."

Knoblauch himself refused to shoulder the blame, saying: "I was kind of dumbfounded. I still thought there was a chance that they would call him out. . . . I didn't know where [the ball] was at."

"Knoblauch should have been looking for the ball," Steinbrenner said. "But he is a young man under fire. I understand."

Kenny Lofton's two-run single made it a 4-1 ballgame, and the Yankees went down meekly in the bottom of the 12th.

Cone brought a no-hitter with him into the fourth inning, and he caught Omar Vizquel looking at a third strike for the first out. He threw a first-pitch strike to

> **"**The sign of a good team is that we don't put the blame on anybody. We lost as a team. We'll go out there as a team and overcome this adversity. **"**
>
> *— Bernie Williams*

David Justice, then hung a curveball that the designated hitter sent to right field. Paul O'Neill pursued it, jumped against the wall — and couldn't reach it. The no-hitter was history, as was the shutout, and the Yankees trailed for the first time this postseason, 1-0.

Cleveland proceeded to load the bases with two outs, but Cone escaped when Sandy Alomar Jr. tapped one back to the mound.

Nagy, meanwhile, shut down the Bombers in a manner similar to the way he did Sept. 21, allowing just three baserunners in the first six innings and striking out four.

In the seventh, with so little room for error, Nagy fell. Bernie Williams led off with a line-drive single to center, and Martinez walked. Tim Raines whiffed, and Shane Spencer ripped a bullet to the edge of the warning track in center field that Lofton grabbed for the second out. Williams tagged up and went to third.

Nagy's first pitch to Scott Brosius proved to be his last of the night, as the third baseman pulled it into the left field corner.

Williams trotted home from third to knot the game at 1, and with Martinez just 90 feet away as the potential go-ahead run, Girardi grounded to the new pitcher Steve Reed.

That set up the crazy finish, and put the Yankees back at square one.

"The sign of a good team is that we don't put the blame on anybody," Williams said. "We lost as a team. We'll go out there as a team and overcome this adversity."

Friday, October 9, 1998 — at Cleveland Indians
ALCS Game 3: Indians 6, Yankees 1
Indians lead series, 2 - 1

Thome-hawked
Indians slugger leads assault on Yankees

By KEN DAVIDOFF, Staff Writer

CLEVELAND — The clickety-clack of forks and knives hitting plates was the only sound late Friday night in the Yankees clubhouse. Not a word was spoken. There was no grace under pressure.

And absolutely no sign of the fun that Joe Torre spoke of earlier in the day.

Their silence spoke volumes: Holy cow! This team is in trouble.

Andy Pettitte was shellacked, and Bartolo Colon shut down the Yankees for a 6-1 victory in Game 3 of the American League Championship Series at Jacobs Field. Orlando Hernandez makes his first career postseason start with his team facing a 2-1 deficit.

"We're in a dangerous situation," Paul O'Neill said. "[Today] is a huge game for us."

"Well, we just got our [butt] kicked tonight," Joe Torre said. "We were not scoring runs. I think everybody is a little frustrated with that fact alone."

Torre held a team meeting before the game to make sure everyone had put Wednesday's Game 2 and the infamous Chuck Knoblauch play behind them. "We'll make sure it's today we're thinking about," the Yankees manager said, "that we not be concerned over what's happened in the last 48 hours."

They showed signs of rebounding in the first inning, when Knoblauch started a rally and the Yanks scored a run. But Colon shut them down after that, and Pettitte couldn't hold the slim lead. He couldn't even keep the game close, for that matter.

> ❝Well, we just got our [butt] kicked tonight, ❞
>
> — *Joe Torre*

In his previous start in Game 2 of the AL Division Series, Pettitte lowered the volume on his critics when he delivered a 3-1 victory. But on this night, he looked more like the guy who had struggled so badly over the season's final six weeks. The killer inning, the four-run fifth, came with two outs — again, he wasn't able to get himself out of a jam. In all, Pettitte was pounded for six runs and eight hits in 4 1/3 innings. He allowed four homers for the first time in his career, two by Jim Thome, that tied an ALCS record for round-trippers by a team in one game.

"When you give a guy with that kind of stuff that big a lead, it's hard to come back," Pettitte said.

"Maybe Andy felt a little extra stress tonight because he knows we're not hitting," Torre said. "I thought he straightened out after the second inning. He left too many pitches out over the plate."

The Indians have now punished Pettitte for 17 runs and 23 hits over 16 1/3 innings spanning two post-seasons, a 9.37 ERA, and, most important, three losses. If there's a Game 7, Pettitte is slated to start it — a decision that Torre might have to reconsider.

He will definitely consider changes in his line-up. "You can focus on Andy, but the bottom line is, we didn't score runs," said Joe Girardi, who denied that he and Pettitte had a disagreement in the game-turning fifth inning. Pettitte retired the first two batters in that inning, making it eight straight, and all seemed calm in the Yankees universe. They needed just one run to tie, and it would be a brand-new contest.

But then it all unraveled. Manny Ramirez got hold of an 0-1 fastball and sent it the other way, over the fence in right field. 3-1, Indians. Travis Fryman walked, and that prompted the Yanks to warm up Ramiro Mendoza, with pitching coach Mel Stottlemyre dispatched to the mound to try to calm Pettitte.

Thome ripped the first pitch he saw well into the right field seats. 5-1, Indians. And finally, former Yankee Mark Whiten blasted a 416-foot dinger to left. To the tune of "Hit The Road, Jack," Pettitte was escorted to the dugout by Torre. The Indians' three homers in the inning tied an ALCS record.

Knoblauch received a huge applause during the pregame introductions, and again when he stepped to the plate to start the game.

In the stands, a fan carried a sign reading: "Thanks, Blauch Head." Knoblauch succeeded in quieting the cheers by grounding a single to left.

Derek Jeter sacrificed his teammate to second base, Knoblauch moved to third on O'Neill's grounder to short (there, the third baseman Fryman – who laid the bunt in Wednesday's infamous play – patted Knoblauch on the back), and Bernie Willliams' bullet to left dropped in to score Knoblauch for the 1-0 lead.

The Indians didn't score in the first, but they gave warning: After Pettitte walked the Tribe's second batter, Omar Vizquel, David Justice knocked a hard bouncer to third. It took a wicked bounce, but Scott Brosius gloved it and got the force at second. Fryman ended the inning by drilling a vicious line drive to left.

It didn't take long for the Indians to chip away at Pettitte. Thome ripped a homer to center field to knot the game at 1-1.

Whiten followed with a double, and that got Hideki Irabu up in the bullpen. Whiten went to third on Sandy Alomar Jr.'s grounder to second, and scored the lead run when Enrique Wilson bounced a single past a drawn-in Jeter.

That brought Stottlemyre to the mound, and Pettitte escaped without any further damage. He enjoyed two trouble-free innings before the sky fell in the fifth.

The sky will have virtually hit the floor if the Yankees lose tonight. But they voiced faith. Said Williams: "I think this series is far from over."

Saturday, October 10, 1998

ALCS Game 4: Yankees 4, Indians 0

Series tied 2 - 2

Duque no fluque

Hernandez comes up big to help Yanks get even

By KEN DAVIDOFF, Staff Writer

CLEVELAND — The Yankees' pendulum swung from panic to relief Saturday night, and they can thank Orlando Hernandez for making everything better.

El Duque showed no first-time playoff jitters, no two-week layoff rustiness, no cold-weather blues. He did show the Indians that the Bombers weren't ready to pack it in quite yet, as they tied the American League Championship Series at two games apiece with a 4-0 victory over Dwight Gooden at Jacobs Field. The series will return to Yankee Stadium, no matter today's result.

"This was the biggest game we've played all year," said Paul O'Neill, who homered and scored twice. "There's no doubt about it, we're playing for our lives, and he comes out and pitches out of trouble.

"It's great to see the way he goes about his business."

Said Hernandez, through interpreter Leo Astacio: "I knew we had a must-win situation. I had pressure, but I had no fear. I've been through many difficult moments in my life on the field and off the field, and I knew I could handle it."

Handle is a major understatement. In seven-plus innings, El Duque allowed three hits, walked two, hit a batter, and struck out six. His black stirrups high, his right hand constantly tugging at his cap, Hernandez merely recorded his most important victory as a major-leaguer. Mike Stanton and Mariano Rivera closed the deal.

"With everything he's been through, a playoff game is a playoff game," manager Joe Torre said. "It's like a walk in the park."

Earlier Saturday, the Yankees seemed as though they were on a walk in an unsupervised nuclear power plant. Though they tried to smile and laugh, their actions spoke of urgency.

> **❝** There's no doubt about it, we're playing for our lives, and he comes out and pitches out of trouble. **❞**
>
> *— Paul O'Neill*
> *on Orlando Hernandez*

Times were so desperate entering the workday that David Wells walked into Torre's office and volunteered to start on three days' rest.

Torre shot down that proposal, explaining that there was no way he could move David Cone up two days to start today's Game 5, nor could he push back Hernandez, who already had 14 days' rest.

Such a move could have set up Wells for a Game 7 Wednesday night on three days' rest, replacing the struggling Andy Pettitte. Wells will try to give the Yanks an edge today, and for now, Torre said, Pettitte is slated for Game 7.

In all, it was a busy day for the usually laid-back Yankees manager.

He tinkered with his struggling lineup, flip-flopping Tino Martinez and Chili Davis in the batting order's fifth and sixth spots and starting Chad Curtis in left field over the suddenly cooled rookie Shane Spencer.

Those moves hardly mattered. Davis, Martinez, and Curtis combined to go 2-for-9 with two RBI. In all, the still-slumping Yanks put together just four hits against Gooden and three relievers.

No, the move that mattered most was turning down the invitation from the rubber-armed Wells and showing faith in El Duque.

The Bombers' runs came in the first, via an O'Neill solo homer to right, and the fourth, with Davis' ground-rule double the key hit in a two-run frame, and one more came in the ninth.

El Duque, meanwhile, persevered through troubles early and late and cruised in the middle. An Omar Vizquel single and Manny Ramirez walk put runners on first and second with two out in the first inning, and up stepped Jim Thome, who homered off the Cuban right-hander in a July 13 game at Cleveland. The first baseman cranked a fly to right that looked gone as it left the bat. Yet it stayed in the park, and O'Neill snared it against the wall.

There was no real trouble again until the sixth. Hernandez faced a first-and-second, one-out jam with Ramirez and Thome coming up. He handcuffed Ramirez on a high fastball, and with a 1-2 count on Thome, Vizquel caught everyone off-guard and swiped third base before Hernandez began his wind-up.

Vizquel danced off third base, and El Duque successfully ignored him, finishing off Thome on a nasty off-speed pitch.

"That really turned the game around," Gooden said.

And maybe did the same to this competitive series.

Sunday, October 11, 1998

ALCS Game 5: Yankees 5, Indians 3

Yankees lead series, 3 - 2

In a Series mood
Yanks return to the Bronx a win away

By KEN DAVIDOFF, Staff Writer

CLEVELAND — Again Sunday, so many Yankees weren't themselves. The weak ground balls. The stranded runners. David Wells giving up some hard-hit balls.

The images accumulated rapidly, like flies gathering over a sandwich left out in the sun.

Yet the whole of the Bombers' performance was so much more attractive than its parts. And George Steinbrenner, for one, was every bit himself as he strutted through his team's Jacobs Field clubhouse after the Yanks topped the Indians, 5-3, in Game 5 of the American League Championship Series to take a 3-2 advantage. Friday night's awful feeling of being down 2-1 is but a distant memory.

"Now, we get to go to home and beat the [bleep] out of them," The Boss said. "We're not going to take any time."

A victory Tuesday or Wednesday at Yankee Stadium will put the Bombers in their second World Series in three years. And they have come this far, so far, with the bats slumping dramatically.

"It doesn't matter what cylinders we're on," second baseman Chuck Knoblauch said. "Winning games, that's the bottom line. We've got a three-games-to-two lead, and I don't care less if I get any hits anymore as long as I win games."

Knoblauch had no hits Sunday, but he got on base four times and scored twice. In all, the Yanks managed just six hits and stranded 11 runners. But they knocked out Cleveland starter Chad Ogea after 1 1/3 innings, collected 11 walks, and did enough to support the efforts of Wells.

> **❝ Now, we get to go to home and beat the [bleep] out of them… ❞**
>
> *— George Steinbrenner*

"I was thinking we were going to bust their [butts] early today," The Boss said. "We didn't have any hits after the fourth inning. [We had] gutty pitching. Wells was gutty."

Yes, Wells again. This time he didn't dominate from Pitch One as he did in his first two postseason starts this year. But he fought through some early difficulties and wound up going 7 1/3 innings, permitting three runs and seven hits (including two solo homers), and setting a career playoff high with 11 strikeouts.

The veteran left-hander is 3-0 with a 1.90 ERA in this postseason and 7-1, 2.41 all-time.

"This is what it's all about," he said, "fighting all year to get here, and it's been a lot of fun during the season, and now it's a lot of fun."

"He's a loose horse," Joe Torre said of his ace. "There's no question about it, he enjoys the game, and . . . it's catchy because [for] the rest of the club it seems to relieve some pressure."

It didn't take long for Ogea to dig a hole. The first batter, Knoblauch, was hit on the left elbow. One out later, Paul O'Neill bounced one up the middle that had "double play" written all over it.

But Ogea reached for it, and the ball glanced off his

glove and veered toward the hole between shortstop and third. Instead of the inning being over, the Yanks had first and third with one out.

O'Neill stole second, then Bernie Williams walked, jamming the bases. Chili Davis ripped a grounder off the glove of first baseman Richie Sexson into right field, scoring Knoblauch and O'Neill for the 2-0 lead and advancing Williams to third. Tino Martinez became the second player to take one for the team, receiving an Ogea pitch in his left ankle. Tim Raines' grounder to second brought Williams home, giving Wells a three-run advantage before he set foot on the mound.

"I think today we made Chad Ogea work a little harder than we had the last couple days with the other guys we faced," Davis said. "When we did so, he put himself in a bind, and we came off with some runs off of him."

It turned out that Wells needed that cushion. Kenny Lofton sent Wells' fifth pitch of the afternoon into the right field seats. Omar Vizquel singled up the middle, and Travis Fryman grounded a base hit out of a diving Derek Jeter's reach. Vizquel then stole third, and Fryman went to second on a Wells' wild pitch.

Vizquel cut the deficit to 3-2 when he tagged up and came home on a Manny Ramirez fly-out to right. Wells struck out Mark Whiten and Sexson in between a Jim Thome walk to hold on to the lead.

> **"**He's a loose horse. There's no question about it, he enjoys the game, and it's catchy because for the rest of the club it seems to relieve some pressure. **"**
>
> — *Joe Torre*
> *on pitcher David Wells*

O'Neill singled Knoblauch home in the second, knocking out Ogea and bringing in the Indians' deposed Game 1 starter, Jaret Wright. In the fourth, Davis' solo homer made it 5-2. Thome's 439-foot blast to right pulled the Tribe within 5-3.

And that would be all the scoring on this night. Jeff Nelson made the Yankees' blood pressure soar in the eighth when he put runners on first and second with one out. But Mariano Rivera saved the day when he got Whiten to hit into a 4-6-3 double play, and the ninth was a relative cruise.

So it's back to a cruiselike feeling in the Yankees clubhouse, even if the waters still are a bit choppy.

Tuesday, October 13, 1998

ALCS Game 6: Yankees 9, Cleveland 5

Yankees win series, 4 - 2

World Delirious!

Yankees return fall classic

By KEN DAVIDOFF, Staff Writer

NEW YORK — The Yankees weren't just battling the Indians on Tuesday night at Yankee Stadium. They were fighting against a terrifying future, a future so white-hot, it almost melted the Bombers in American League Championship Series Game 6: An ALCS Game 7.

But the Yanks steered away from it in time, and now we'll probably never know who would have started on the mound for the Bombers tonight. The Yankees are American League champions for a record 35th time, having defeated Cleveland, 9-5, in front of 57,142 rabid fans to win the series, four games to two.

"When you have a chance to close it out, you want to do that," said Scott Brosius, who slammed a three-run homer and made some key defensive plays at third base. "Obviously, a Game 7 would have been a little more stress-filled than winning tonight."

Game 7 would have meant the Indians gaining confidence by tying the series at three games apiece. The Bombers would have had to face Bartolo Colon, who shut them down in Game 3. Manager Joe Torre would have had to make a decision on his starting pitcher – the shaky Andy Pettitte, Orlando Hernandez on three days' rest, whoever.

Now it's all moot. What started out as a Yankees' blowout turned into a war of attrition. David Cone picked up the victory, but he barely made it through five innings and concerned Torre so much that the manager thought his right-hander might have been injured. Jim Thome, the Indians' behemoth first baseman, set an ALCS record with his fourth homer of the series, a grand slam, and sent the fear of Game 7 into everyone wearing navy blue and white, both Yankees employees and fans.

"That's not like Coney," Paul O'Neill said, "but who cares? It got us to the World Series."

Some clutch insurance hitting by Derek Jeter and Bernie Williams and some even more clutch relief by Ramiro Mendoza and Mariano Rivera staved off the scare. Williams finished the game with two RBI, Brosius added his three, and so the Yanks will play host to Game 1 of the World Series on Saturday night against the Braves-Padres winner.

It is their second pennant in three years and sixth of George Steinbrenner's regime.

"If we didn't win," said ALCS Most Valuable Player David Wells, "there would have been a lot of explanations and a lot of speculation because of the way we played [in the regular season]."

There still is, of course, the World Series to win if this history-making season is to be fully validated (the Bombers are now 121-50), and their clubhouse celebration reflected it.

It actually was the most mellow of the three champagne-fests they've had so far, including the clinching of the AL East and the sweep of the Rangers in the AL Division Series.

As players sprayed each other and conducted mass interviews, they took turns sneaking into the back of the room, where Darryl Strawberry waited on the phone.

When the Bombers emptied the dugout after Omar Vizquel hit a nubber that Rivera pounced on and whipped to first for the final out, a picture of their fallen teammate was shown on the giant scoreboard.

"He's pumped," Chili Davis said of Strawberry.

The Yanks were up, 6-0, after Brosius' homer in the fourth, and with Cone on the hill and the Stadium rocking so much it shook, this seemed to be a done deal.

The shaking proved to be premature.

While Dave Burba took over in the fourth and quieted the Yankees' bats, the Indians came alive in the fifth. Enrique Wilson and Kenny Lofton lined back-to-back singles, bringing Yanks pitching coach Mel Stottlemyre to the mound and getting up Ramiro Mendoza and Graeme Lloyd in the bullpen.

Vizquel sent a liner up the middle that hit second base umpire Ted Hendry, who was situated in front of the infielders; Hendry ruled it a dead-ball single and forced Wilson to stay at third.

Cone walked David Justice, sending Wilson home to ruin the shutout.

As Justice trotted to first base, Torre and assistant trainer Steve Donohue trotted toward the mound, with Torre instructing plate ump Jim McKean that he was making an injury inquiry (otherwise, it would have counted as a second mound visit and forced Cone out of the game).

Cone angrily dismissed the notion that he was hurting, and Torre and Donohue returned to the dugout.

"I sensed that he was tight," Torre explained later. The manager said he expected Cone to be fine for the World Series.

Cone managed to fan Manny Ramirez on a weak slider for the first out, but the first pitch he served up to Thome was absolutely crushed into the right field upper deck for a grand slam.

At 6-5, it was an entirely new ballgame.

Torre let Cone record the final two outs of the inning, making himself eligible for the victory, but Mendoza started the sixth for the Yankees.

And in the bottom of that inning, the Bombers opened things up a little when the Tribe's Ramirez misplayed Jeter's fly ball to right into a two-run triple, then Williams drilled a run-scoring single for the 9-5 lead.

That was how it ended.

"We're excited to be here," Tino Martinez said, "but we still have to win the World Series."

1998 World Championship

Saturday, October 17, 1998 — San Diego Padres

World Series Game 1: Yankees 9, Padres 6

Yankees lead series, 1 - 0

Grand opening

Tino's slam caps rally by Bombers

By KEN DAVIDOFF, Staff Writer

NEW YORK — Like a bird spotted out of season, a strange sound for this time of year emitted from Yankee Stadium on Saturday night:

"Tino! Tino! Tino!"

Finally, Tino Martinez converted his regular-season excellence into postseason heroism. After three years of October futility, the Yankees first baseman delivered the perfect hit at the perfect moment, cranking a seventh-inning grand slam to give David Wells and the Bombers a comeback 9-6 victory over the Padres in Game 1 of the World Series.

"I haven't done much, but we've been winning, and I knew eventually I'd come up in a a big situation and get a big hit to help the team win," Martinez said. "It's definitely a big relief to get the big hit to help the team win."

Said manager Joe Torre: "We felt we had something in the bank coming from Tino. It makes everybody feel good. It makes him able to turn the page and start again."

It was anything but a one-man show in the opening game of the 94th Fall Classic, though. The pitching battle between Wells and the Padres' Kevin Brown didn't come to be, yet that hardly bothered the 56,712 fans on hand. They were more than happy to see a seesaw affair highlighted by two homers from could-have-been-a-Yankee Greg Vaughn, a huge three-run bomb from Chuck Knoblauch, and terrible pitching from Padres middle relievers, the weak link between their impressive starters and elite closer Trevor Hoffman.

But only Martinez had suffered for three long years, constantly failing to do much of anything in his playoff at-bats, inspiring questions whether Torre would play Chili Davis at first base in Games 3, 4, and 5 at Qualcomm Stadium — where there will be no designated hitter — and sparking speculation that the Bombers would deal Martinez over the winter and pursue free agent Mo Vaughn.

In all, he entered the night with a career Yankees postseason average of .188 with one homer and five RBI. This year he was at .167 with no homers and one RBI.

And now he has a clean slate, putting an exclamation point on a seven-run seventh that had Padres manager Bruce Bochy on the defensive to explain his pitching changes and will test his players' tenacity.

Wells, meanwhile, lifted his postseason record this year to 4-0, although his ERA shot up from 1.90 to 2.93. Still, he earned the win by hanging in, lasting seven innings and giving up five runs and seven hits, three of them homers. Jeff Nelson struggled again, but Mariano Rivera came in to clean up the mess and earn his first Series save.

> **"**It's definitely a big relief to get the big hit to help the team win.**"**
>
> *— Tino Martinez*

The Bombers stranded two runners in the fifth, did nothing in the sixth, and a loss to Brown seemed inevitable. But Jorge Posada stroked a one-out single to right in the seventh, and when Ricky Ledee drew a walk, Bochy decided that Brown was done.

Donne Wall entered and fell into a 2-0 hole against Knoblauch. The diminutive second baseman pulled the next pitch down the left field line, and it carried as Vaughn dropped back. Would it be deep enough to go out? Knoblauch jogged toward first, carrying his bat, then tossed it about halfway down the line and nodded with satisfaction.

Gone. Tie score, 5-5. And Knoblauch, the scourge of the Bronx 10 days before, earned his first curtain call in pinstripes.

It hardly ended there. Derek Jeter knocked a single

up the middle. Left-hander Mark Langston replaced Wall and retired Paul O'Neill on a pop to right for the second out. But after his wild pitch allowed Jeter to move to second, he intentionally walked Bernie Williams to get to Davis, who walked to load the bases.

Up stepped Martinez, in the position of breaking the game open or sending it into the eighth tied. He took two balls, looked at a strike, fouled one behind, and took another ball — borderline at best — to put the count at 3-2.

"I was looking for a fastball again" Martinez said of the pitch that followed. "I figured he had to throw a strike. He got one up in the zone again."

All you needed to hear was the sound of Martinez's bat hitting Langston's offering down the middle to know that it was high, far, and gone into the upper deck in right. Martinez, doing his best Kirk Gibson imitation, pumped his fist as he rounded the bases. He looked like a man released from a death sentence as he bumped chests with his teammates, then raised both arms to the sky as he came out for his curtain call.

It was the 17th grand slam in Series history and the first since Atlanta's Lonnie Smith hit one in Game 5 of the 1992 Series against Toronto. Joe Pepitone was the previous Yankee to slam one, in Game 6 of the 1964 Series against St. Louis.

Sunday, October 18, 1998 — San Diego Padres

World Series Game 2: Yankees 9, Padres 3

Yankees lead series 2 - 0

Bronx bombing
Padres fall in Yanks' explosion

By KEN DAVIDOFF, Staff Writer

NEW YORK — If this were a 1,600-meter race, the Yankees would have lapped the Padres by now.

There are victories, and then there are displays of complete, utter dominance that humiliate an opponent. A Yankee Stadium crowd of 56,692 enjoyed the latter Sunday night, when the Bombers ran circles around the Padres, pounding them by a 9-3 score in Game 2 of the World Series.

"It's nice to have a game like this," Paul O'Neill said. "In the other games, every [one] has been close. This was textbook. It's not always that easy."

With a 2-0 lead in the 94th Fall Classic, these history-making 1998 Yankees might have played their last game at home. San Diego must win two of the next three at Qualcomm Stadium to bring this matchup back to the Bronx.

The question of whether the Yankees' thrilling comeback victory in Game 1 Saturday night would carry momentum into Game 2 was answered very early: Of course it would. With Orlando Hernandez picking up where he left off in Game 4 of the American League Championship Series, the Yanks exploded with 16 hits, their best output of the postseason. They hit the nine-run mark for the third straight game.

> **❝I am saving a Cuban one for when we win the title.❞**
>
> — *Orlando Hernandez*

Each of the nine starters recorded at least one hit, and everyone besides newest rookie sensation Ricky Ledee, who had two hits, scored. Six Yankees drove home at least one run, and Padres starter Andy Ashby lasted just 2 2/3 innings, getting bruised for seven runs – four earned – and 10 hits. Bernie Williams – who might have played his last game as a Yankee in the Bronx – and Jorge Posada each went deep, and former postseason goat Tino Martinez knocked three singles to raise his 1998 Series average to .500 (4-for-8).

And Hernandez, who has a career postseason record of 2-0 and ERA of 0.64, never gave the Padres much of a chance. The Cuban right-hander encountered his worst trouble in the first inning, and he was rescued when O'Neill made a superb, jumping, against-the-wall catch of a Wally Joyner missile with runners on first and second. After that, Hernandez cruised, retiring 10 straight at one point.

In all, he allowed one run and six hits in seven innings, walking three and striking out seven. Mike Stanton and Jeff Nelson closed up shop in shaky fashion, but it didn't really matter.

"He had a good plan today, and he followed it the whole way," Posada said.

After the game, El Duque smoked a cigar from Costa Rica, explaining, "I am saving a Cuban one for when we win the title."

The cigar police might want to get ready, because that title is looking pretty likely.

Chuck Knoblauch, coming off of his Saturday night power show, reverted to his leadoff mentality in the first inning Sunday night, and it paid off immediately: The second baseman worked the count full against Ashby after falling into an 0-2 hole, fouled off a few more pitches, and finally earned the walk. He stole second on the second pitch to Derek Jeter, who tapped one back to the mound.

O'Neill chopped a two-bouncer to third. Ken Caminiti grabbed it, planted, and threw to first – much too high. As the ball tipped off the glove of Joyner, Knoblauch scored for the 1-0 lead. Williams' hard liner back to the mound – which Ashby dropped but threw to first for the out – moved O'Neill to second, and Chili Davis singled O'Neill home. Martinez's hit down the right field line advanced Davis to third, and Scott Brosius' single to left scored Davis for a 3-0 lead.

The second inning provided much of the same for the Yanks. Jeter drove home Knoblauch from second on a single to center and Williams' blast to right-center made it 6-0.

When Ledee doubled home Martinez for a 7-0 advantage in the third, Padres manager Bruce Bochy finally decided that Ashby had suffered enough. Former Yankee Brian Boehringer took over lifeguard duty, although his team had already descended well beneath survival level on this night.

San Diego scored its first run in the fifth, courtesy of a Chris Gomez triple and Quilvio Veras double. But as if it were punishment for

> **❝**When you're struggling and you get a hit, it definitely gets you going.**❞**
>
> *— Tino Martinez*

ruining El Duque's bid for a shutout, Posada responded with a two-run blast to the right-center bleachers in the bottom of the inning to make it 9-1.

With the bats red-hot, all cylinders are running. "I felt great," Martinez said. "When you're struggling and you get a hit, it definitely gets you going."

As is their nature, the Bombers refused to concede that they are on the cusp of their 24th World Series crown.

"Not at all," Williams said. "We've got to go out there and stay intense. That's the only way we can win."

Tuesday, October 20, 1998
— at San Diego Padres

World Series Game 3: Yankees 5, Padres 4

Yankees lead series 3 - 0

Great Scott!
Brosius HRs put Yankees in command

By KEN DAVIDOFF, Staff Writer

SAN DIEGO — There are no more beasts remaining for these Yankees to slay, no more indomitable forces to neutralize. Just one more victory over these Padres in this World Series, and their elite place in baseball history will be secured with a flourish.

The Bombers solved San Diego closer Trevor Hoffman on Tuesday night at Qualcomm Stadium, with Scott Brosius' dramatic eighth-inning, three-run homer – his second of the game – giving the Yanks a thrilling, comeback 5-4 victory in Game 3 of this Fall Classic. With an overwhelming three games to none lead, an advantage that has never been — coughed up in 93 previous years of World Series, they go for the sweep tonight with Andy Pettitte on the hill. A team has jumped out to a 3-0 lead nine times since 1937; eight times, that team went on to win the fourth game.

An exciting pitcher's duel between David Cone, who no-hit the home team for five innings, and former Yankee Sterling Hitchcock was all but forgotten by the time the final out was made. No, this was all about Hoffman, who made himself a National League Cy Young Award candidate by recording 53 saves in 54 chances this regular season, proving all too human, like the rest of his teammates.

"There have been so many times this season that you would think there was no way they could win, and somebody steps up," George Steinbrenner said in a Yankees clubhouse where jubilation oozed out of the inclination to stay restrained.

"This is the type of thing that as a kid you dream about," Brosius said. "Something I've done in my back yard a hundred times. And you never know if you're going to get the opportunity to do it."

"This is it," rookie Ricky Ledee said. "This is the moment that everyone's waiting for."

Asked if Brosius' homer matched up with Jim Leyritz's famous shot in Game 4 of the 1996 World Series, The Boss responded, "This was even better. Even better. And Leyritz's was great. They're the same type of home run. One was off a great pitcher for Atlanta [Mark Wohlers], and this was off an equally great pitcher for them. When they played that [heavy metal], I think of that WCF, or whatever that is."

He meant the WWF, and he referred to the AC/DC song "Hell's Bells," which booms every time Hoffman, enters a game with a save on his plate.

In losing the first two games at Yankee Stadium, the Padres could at least console themselves with the hope that if they could bring a lead into the final inning, Hoffman would be there to close the door. But with his blown save that hope has been shattered, as has, it would seem, any hope for the NL's entry.

> **" This is the type of thing that as a kid you dream about. Something I've done ... a hundred times. "**
>
> — *Scott Brosius*

With the Padres holding a shaky 3-2 lead, former Met Randy Myers — couldn't do his job, walking Paul O'Neill to start the eighth.

That was it for him, as Hoffman entered the game to his usual sound and fury, volume that makes Yankee Stadium a library by comparison. This — would be the first time all season that he would be required to get six outs for a save.

"He was the guy we go to," Padres pitching coach Dave Stewart said. "We have to go to him."

Bernie Williams flied out to very deep right. Tino Martinez walked. And then, Brosius stepped up: Check-swing strike. Ball low. Ball low, prompting a mound visit from San Diego pitching coach Dave Stewart. Foul down the third-base line.

Hoffman delivered a fastball down the middle, and Brosius connected: It carried, carried, and over the 405-foot sign in center field it went. O'Neill and Martinez jumped in the air, their arms raised to the heavens, as they rounded the bases. It was just the third homer Hoffman had allowed all year. In Qualcomm, you could hear a season drop as

the Yanks took over, with a 5-3 lead.

"When you get a closer on the mound, my only thoughts were trying to pick the ball up and just see them as good as I could and put a good swing on the ball," Brosius said. "I hit it hard in the air on that one."

"He crushed that ball," Chili Davis said. Mariano Rivera allowed a San Diego run in the eighth, ran into some trouble in the ninth, but struck out Andy Sheets to leave Carlos Hernandez stranded at third. And the Bombers moved on the cusp of becoming the first Yankee team to sweep a World Series since the 1950 team took four straight from the Phillies.

Earlier, Brosius' solo homer in the seventh put the Yanks on the board after the Padres scored three runs in the sixth, thanks largely to a throwing error by O'Neill.

And now there's just one more to go. As his clubhouse entertained visitors ranging from Reggie Jackson to Charlie Sheen, Joe Torre preached calm. "We just want to win the fourth game," the manager explained, "not necessarily the fourth, but we want to win our fourth game and hopefully cap off a great year for us."

Wednesday, October 21, 1998
— at San Diego Padres

World Series Game 4: Yankees 3, Padres 0

Yankees win series

WORLD-CLASS
Yankees put Padres to sweep

By KEN DAVIDOFF, Staff Writer

SAN DIEGO — Destiny and reality reached their inevitable intersection Wednesday night at Qualcomm Stadium. The Yankees' fate became awesome truth.

When Scott Brosius fielded Mark Sweeney's bouncer and threw it to Tino Martinez at 11:24 p.m. EDT, baseball's best team of 1998 and one of its best clubs ever had completed its mission in style, blanking the San Diego Padres, 3-0, to complete a World Series sweep.

Champions. The Yankees, 125-50 for the season,

became professional sports' most accomplished team with their 24th title, breaking a tie with hockey's Montreal Canadiens. And with it they put the stamp of approval on their incredible campaign, putting to rest the ghosts of the 1906 Cubs and 1954 Indians, who failed to follow through on their remarkable regular seasons.

"There might be somebody better than us in another time, but we're just going to enjoy it for as long as we can," said David Wells, the team's top pitcher. "We're the greatest team now. Someone else might do it later, but you know what? We did it first."

"Obviously, we had the best record of all time — 125 and 50, you can't make it any better than that," manager Joe Torre said. "We may not be the best team of all time, but we had the best record, and a tough time getting to the World Series. The 1927 Yankees, they set the bar pretty high, but we leaped over it."

"This is the greatest team there's ever been," George Steinbrenner said. "If you want to pick the best team, as a group, this is it."

The Boss couldn't find a full bottle of champagne, dispensing Chili Davis to fetch one for him. Besides that, though, the postgame celebration went smoothly in the cramped visitors clubhouse.

Players shouted, "Straw Man! Straw Man!" in tribute to Darryl Strawberry, who missed the playoffs with colon cancer. When the media crush grew too tight, they headed to the serenity of the Qualcomm field, where they hugged families and friends and played to a small contingent of Yankees fans, who chanted, "Dar-ryl!" and "Best Team Ever!"

The final victory came, as so many did, via their pitching. Andy Pettitte, who fought through a season of personal and professional troubles, threw 7 1/3 shutout innings to outdo San Diego ace Kevin Brown and add another incredible Series start to his resume. Jeff Nelson and Mariano Rivera wrapped it up.

Bernie Williams, in what might have been his final game as a Yankee, drove in the winning run, even if it came via a bouncer back to the mound. Brosius, the Series MVP, added an RBI. Ricky Ledee, the star rookie, drove home the third run.

It was a team effort, as always, but Pettitte — who March 26 declared: "It's sickening how good we could be" — earned the gold star on this night. The left-hander matched the superb effort he gave in Game 5 of the 1996 World Series, when his 8 1/3 brilliant innings beat John Smoltz and the Braves, — 1-0.

All of the dedications – to Pettitte's father, recovering from a double bypass, to Brosius' father, dealing with colon cancer, to Strawberry, – were met thanks to Pettitte.

"Pettitte, what a courageous performance," Torre said. "Kevin Brown was wonderful. — . . . But Andy Pettitte, with everything that's been going on in his life, plus the struggles he's had in the second half in the year, it's remarkable."

Said Pettitte: "My father called me today, and he was able to go home. So I think it definitely helped my mind to be clear even more, when I found out that he was doing good and was able to leave the hospital today."

Williams' bouncer scored Derek Jeter in the sixth, and the Bombers increased the cushion in the eighth. Brown issued a leadoff walk to Jeter, and in the inning's key play, Paul O'Neill knocked a bouncer to first. Former Yankee Jim Leyritz — grabbed it, and instead of flipping it to the perfectlypositioned Brown, — took it himself, sliding into the bag.

> **"It's sickening how good we could be."**
>
> — *Andy Pettitte*

Firstbase umpire Tim Tschida — ruled O'Neill safe in what replays showed to be a close play. Brown, — Leyritz, and Padres manager Bruce Bochy argued vehemently, and when action resumed, Williams moved the runners over to second and third with a grounder to third.

Brown intentionally walked Martinez to get to Brosius, and with the infield drawn in, the Yankees third baseman punched a bloop single over shortstop Chris Gomez. Jeter scored for a 2-0 lead, and O'Neill came home on Ledee's sacrifice fly to left for a 3-0 advantage.

When Pettitte walked Quilvio Veras and allowed a Tony Gwynn single with one out in the eighth, he was done, lifted for Nelson. The righty struck out Greg Vaughn, then got the hook when he started Ken Caminiti with two balls.

Rivera gave up a single to Caminiti, loading the bases, and up stepped Leyritz, who had been so quiet throughout this series. On a 2-1 pitch, he ripped a bullet to center. Williams paused, stumbled, and regained control of himself to catch the third out.

The ninth was relatively painless, and then the celebrating began. And, finally, the contemplation of how special it is to be a part of this group.

Said general manager Brian Cashman, "I know I will never see anything like this again." *Tuesday,*

Postseason Commentary

September 29, 1998

Torre story no mystery

Success of Yankees manager anything but a fluke

By BOB KLAPISCH, Record Columnist

They are big and bad, cold and efficient — and, going into the postseason, the slickest, most well-oiled machine in American League history. Ask any AL official about the Yankees, and to a man they'll tell you this is a flawless team. In fact, A's general manager Billy Beane says the best way to conceptualize the talent gap the Yankees enjoy over the rest of the league is to "think of an army that's going to war with bows and arrows. Then you find out the other side has smart bombs."

This isn't hype or hyperbole. Everyone says the Yankees are the team to beat in October, which, if you think about it, means manager Joe Torre's burden will be enormous. If the Yankees win the World Series, it's only because they're supposed to.

But if David Wells falters in Game 1 of the Division Series, if Andy Pettitte can't find the inside corner with his cut-fastball, if we learn that Mariano Rivera is permanently scarred by the home run he gave up to Sandy Alomar in Game 4 of last year's Division Series upset by the Indians … What happens then?

Torre has no illusions about George Steinbrenner's loyalty quotient. He knows that an early-round loss likely will cost him his job and probably general manager Brian Cashman's, too. Still, Torre doesn't appear worried by the loaded gun that's pointed at his head. In fact, Torre merely smiles and says, "I've been through it before."

"All I ask for is a fair chance. Give me enough talent to be considered the favorite. I can live with that," he said the other day. "If that means my team has more expectations, that's fine. I prefer it that way."

He is calm and mature, as low-key as any manager in baseball, not to mention one of the game's most well-liked elders. Even umpires like Torre. Veteran National League ump Harry Wendelstedt said this summer that "when Joe comes out to argue, you listen. He never, ever tries to show you up, unlike some other managers who are out there just trying to make themselves look good."

Braves manager Bobby Cox calls Torre "one of the classiest people I've met in baseball." And even Mark Lamping, the Cardinals president who fired Torre in 1995, said that "everyone here in St. Louis feels Joe deserves this good thing that's happened to him in New York."

Lamping said that Torre's dismissal 47 games into the '95 season "really had less to do with Joe's ability as manager than the fact that we had to show our fans we were trying make some moves."

"It wasn't Joe's fault that we were losing, but it was my responsibility to take action," Mark Lamping said last week. "We all wonder if Joe had the same talent with the Cardinals in the early Nineties that he has with the Yankees now, would he have won for us? Our belief is that he would have."

Lamping's point, of course, is that a manager is only as good as his pitchers' fastballs and his hitters' ability to hit home runs to the planets. That's the irony that makes Torre laugh. With the Mets, Braves, and Cardinals he was a player's manager — which in those cases was an indictment against Torre.

A player's manager on a losing team is perceived as too easy-going, too reluctant to enforce clubhouse rules, too concerned about being friends with his players.

But on a winning team a player's manager has a different connotation. Or as Torre says, "Now it's something positive."

These days Torre is seen as wise and soft-spoken, experienced enough not to get in the way of his players. There are never any mood swings from the manager's office. Torre neither gloated when the Yankees were burying the AL East, nor did he panic when the Yankees flattened out this month, losing 16 of 28 during one stretch.

He knew better than that.

"Joe gives you the feeling that he's on your side, always," outfielder Paul O'Neill said. "There are managers who like you only when you're going good. Part of it is human nature, but with some [managers] it's more obvious. I've never seen Joe change from day to day on a player, because he was a player. Those are the things you respect."

But that's not to say Torre doesn't have a temper. In fact, his seasonlong calm was broken on two occasions. The first came in early April, after the Yankees had lost three of their first four games and there was open talk of the '98 Yankees turning into the '92 Mets, bloated and overrated, sunk by May.

Torre spoke to his players in an open, healthy way — but still letting them know he wouldn't permit the season to slip away. Said one Yankee: "The fact that he did that so early was really smart. It woke us up before the [losing] started to get out of control."

On Sept. 16, however, Torre's tone was far more aggressive. The Yankees had just been embarrassed, 7-0, by the expansion Devil Rays, prompting him to close the doors of the clubhouse and stand in the middle of the room. Looking each one of his players in the eye, Torre said, "We stunk. That was terrible tonight."

Players admit they were taken back by Torre's temper, although no one denied they deserved to flogged.

"We were all embarrassed," Joe Girardi said. The Yankees responded by winning seven of their next nine games and in the process set the franchise single-season win record.

In fact, in just three seasons Torre practically has rewritten his legacy, turning a mediocre managerial career into … well, don't be surprised if Torre becomes a strong candidate for a veterans' induction to the Hall of Fame now that he has piloted this Yankee golden era.

Think about it: When Torre replaced Buck Showalter in 1995, his managerial record was 109 games under .500, mostly because he was 134 under .500 in five seasons with the Mets. Going into the weekend, Torre had raised his record to six games over .500, a turnaround that Tony La Russa calls "just unbelievable, considering Joe did it in three years. No one does that."

Indeed, Torre might well go down in history as the Yankees' most beloved manager, especially if he wins the World Series for the second time in three years. He already has replaced Billy Martin as the public's Everyman, and he is as baseball savvy as Showalter but more personable. And he is a Brooklynite who is as working class as Billy Martin — minus the drinking and rage.

Despite all this, Torre could be in his last season, even though his contract extends through 2000. It's no secret that his wife, Ali, has asked him to spend more time at home, and Torre's agent has conducted exploratory talks with MSG Network about a broadcasting job in 1999.

Would Torre consider retiring as the reigning champ? He says the summer of '98 has been "the most fun I've ever had managing." That's easy to say now, after so much regular-season excellence. But October's road might not be so clear and unfettered.

After all, even smart bombs fail once in a while. To which Torre — patient to the end — says, "Let's just see what happens. But right now I'm feeling very good about this team."

Tuesday, September 29, 1998

Will their bubble burst?

Yanks wary of repeating '97 shocker

By BOB KLAPISCH, Record Columnist

No one's forgotten. No one dares. The Yankees spent the summer turning the American League East into their personal playground, and the whole time the Bombers were leaning on the pause button of Game 4 of last year's Division Series with Cleveland.

You haven't forgotten. Do you dare? The Yankees were four outs away from a 2-1 win over the Indians, and a quick leap to the AL Championship Series. But that was before Sandy Alomar took Mariano Rivera deep in the eighth inning — a stunning, opposite-field home run that tied a game the Indians went on to win, 3-2, in the ninth.

The series was tied at two games apiece, but any dime-store analyst could've sensed the Yankees were cooked. The next night the Tribe overran Andy Pettitte, 4-3, and just like that, the Yankees' 96-win season turned to mist. One year later, the question remains: How deep were those wounds?

Joe Torre insisted he metabolized the loss "overnight." The manager made his peace with Alomar's home run by telling himself: "It wasn't our year to win. We did everything right, and they still beat us." But Torre is in the minority on this issue. Several Yankees say Alomar's home run shook them from a quasi-complacency that was left over from the '96 World Series. The Yankees never realized they were so comfortable until the Indians shocked them in Game 4 and appeared to intimidate them in Game 5. In fact, Paul O'Neill said, "It made us realize even a world championship team can go home early. It can happen to anyone."

Tino Martinez agreed with O'Neill, saying the loss to Cleveland has, in some way, remained in the clubhouse all year — serving as a reminder to, "never, ever look past an opponent.

"I'm not saying we had the wrong attitude, but we're going to have a much better approach this year," the first baseman said. "The way we lost ... it left a bad taste in a lot of guys' mouths."

That's putting it gently. One Yankee said Monday that several players were reduced to tears after the final out of Game 5. The ones who didn't cry walked around the clubhouse looking as if they'd been punched in the face. On the charter flight home from Cleveland, a handful of Yankees — still in shock over the abrupt end — decided to keep their bond alive a few hours longer, and headed to an after-hours Manhattan bar.

Pictures of the late-night activities appeared on the front page of one New York tabloid, prompting George Steinbrenner to say he was "disappointed" in his players. The Boss wondered out loud how grief could turn into a party so quickly, although David Cone said, "Whatever it might've looked like, we were hurting inside. People find different ways to release that hurt."

Maybe that's why the Yankees never became obsessed with their winning percentage this year. They'd learned firsthand that one swing can flip the calendar to spring training. Of course, that axiom is two-sided: In 1996, the Bombers altered the course of the World Series on Jimmy Leyritz's Game 4 home run off Mark Wohlers. A year later, it was Alomar hitting a Rivera fastball that the reliever still swears "wasn't even a strike."

So the Yankees went home, the Indians eventually went to the World Series, and the baseball world was left to ponder which was the better team. The Yankees had more on-paper talent, but such is October's injustice. What does a summer of excellence mean if you run face-first into a one-week slump?

Even Johnny Oates, the Rangers' diplomatic man-

ager, said, "There's a certain pressure in winning 114 games and realizing that it can all end in three games. The Yankees can handle that, but I think they know there's pressure on them."

There has been some talk of extending the division series to a best-of-seven, but that doesn't change the equation much. It's still the hottest team that wins, not the best one. The only defense for the Yankees was to gather overwhelming firepower for 1998, which explains why Chuck Knoblauch, Orlando Hernandez, Chili Davis, and Scott Brosius were wearing pinstripes.

That was George Steinbrenner's way of ensuring that Alomar — or Juan Gonzalez or Mo Vaughn — couldn't break the Yankees' hearts this year. Even though there's no such thing as a sure thing, the Yankees have come close enough for general manager Brian Cashman to say, "We really don't have any weaknesses.

"I ask myself, `Where can we shore ourselves up?' And I realize there's not much for us to do," Cashman said. "We hit, we pitch well, we steal bases, we play good defense."

Still, Cashman knows better than to predict a Yankees victory against Texas. That arrogance disappeared with Alomar's home run. Now, the Yankees think of the '97 Indians and repeat a cold October mantra: Never again

Tuesday, September 29, 1998

Back in gear

Cone gets second wind at 'young' 35

By BOB KLAPISCH, Record Columnist

This was early April, which every Yankee remembers for the crisis that was threatening to swallow them. The Bombers had lost four of their first five, manager Joe Torre was answering questions about his job security, and rookie general manager Brian Cashman had that pale, no-sleep look that told you George Steinbrenner had been devouring him.

There was one other unraveling taking place, too. David Cone had allowed 16 earned runs in his first two starts, both against Oakland. That 15.65 ERA that suggested Cone still hadn't recovered from off-season shoulder surgery — and maybe never would.

In fact, Cone now concedes, "People were ready to write me off, and I can't say I blamed them." Here was a pitcher with more than 2,000 career innings, starting his 11th year, trying to explain why the weak-hitting A's made him look so vulnerable.

The fastball was barely in the upper 80s. The slider was flat, and all the splitter really did was bounce ineffectively in the dirt.

The vision was so ugly, it's hard to believe this was the same David Cone who'll start Game 3 of the American League Division Series against the Rangers on Friday night — a 20-game winner who's entering the second golden era of his careerCone can't specify when, but there was a time this summer when all his weapons finally returned.

He says, "It was just a matter of regaining my arm strength. Little by little, I found myself throwing the ball harder, being able to control hitters' bat speeds, gaining more and more confidence. And then suddenly, everything clicked in for me."

One AL scout goes as far as to say, "Cone is better now than at any time in his career," — an assessment that, if true, demonstrates how unique Cone really is. After all, how many pitchers get better at age 35?

Think of Cone's weapons — fastball, slider, splitter, sinker — and each one still qualifies as an out pitch. Dwight Gooden tells this story about the Indians, who after Cone had limited them to four hits and one run in eight innings on June 14, were close to being in awe. "Guys were coming back to the dugout saying, 'How the [bleep] does he still have so many good pitches?'" Gooden said. "I never really appreciated Coney until I was on the other side, in the other dugout, listening to the hitters talk about him. I mean, everyone has a way to attack a pitcher — our hitters know how to go after [Andy] Pettitte, or [David] Wells. But Jim Thome told me, 'There's nothing you can do against Cone except hope he makes a mistake. Otherwise, he's got you.'"

Indeed, hidden beneath Cone's 20 wins are numbers that demonstrate how effective he is under pressure. Cone kept opposing hitters to a .238 average with runners in scoring position, and a .195 average in the same situation with two men out.

Give Cone a one-strike advantage, and he'll smother you. Opponents batted .185 after he was 0-1 in the count, and just .156 when he was 0-2. No wonder Torre calls Cone "one of the gutsiest pitchers I've ever seen."

Cone succeeds with a unique ability to change his delivery, his release point, and his pitch pattern from inning to inning, even at-bat to at-bat. The AL scout, dispatched by a Central Division team, said, "I gave up a long time ago trying to figure Cone out. All I know is I'm glad I don't have to hit against him."

Perhaps the most remarkable aspect of Cone's resurgence this year is how hard he's throwing. He's at 90 mph again, and has even reached 92 mph on several occasions. Is there a secret to this seeming indestructibility?

Cone smiled and pointed to his locker — filled with protein powders, amino acid tablets, even creatine. Cone said he's "willing to try anything," in order to pretend he's 25 again. So far, it's worked. In fact, Cone lost 13 pounds this year, and is down to 192, which is practically the same weight as his Met days.

"I realized last year I was getting fat. I couldn't believe it, but it was happening," Cone said. "So I changed my diet, started sucking down protein shakes, and it came right off. I don't know if it helped me throw any harder, but I feel better."

That led Cone to experiment with other nutritional supplements. He heard about the amino acids from Paul O'Neill. By the next day, Cone had ordered a case.

According to the directions, the tablets were to be taken the day before he pitched and the day of. Of course, Cone took them every day.

Twice a day.

Which means Cone is either committed to winning. Or just crazy.

"Definitely crazy," is what Cone said, laughing so hard his eyes turned to slits.

Wednesday, September 30, 1998

Ardor of fans at stadium not a secret weapon

By BOB KLAPISCH, Record Columnist

The sound stretches beyond the definition of loud, and it can't always be called human. It's the noise that comes from the big Stadium every October, when the Yankees know their best weapon is the army of fans that will say anything —

anything — to intimidate opposing players.

Think athletes don't listen? They hear every word, although the best ones pretend to be deaf. Still, the hostility in the Bronx can be so real, many Yankees believe the Braves lost Game 6 of the 1996 World Series because they were scared.

"You could see it in their eyes, they didn't want to be here," said one Yankee veteran.

"All the confidence they had early in the Series, it was gone. It's like they were saying to each other, 'Let's play the game and get the hell out of here.'"

That's not just phony tough-guy talk. In fact, Braves manager Bobby Cox practically advertised his loathing for the Stadium when he waited until the last possible moment before Game 6 to bring the team bus from the Grand Hyatt hotel in Manhattan to the Stadium.

He didn't want his Braves exposed to Yankee fans any longer than they had to be, and the bus didn't arrive at 161st Street until almost 6 p.m. Was it fear? The Braves never would admit to that, obviously, but when Greg Maddux took the mound, he recalled he was showered with, "insults about my mother that I never thought were possible."

Maddux tried to dismiss the fans with a laugh, but the greatest pitcher of our generation suddenly became human in the third inning, allowing three runs.

Paul O'Neill, who led off with a double and scored on Joe Girardi's triple to right-center, said that upon crossing home plate, "it was so loud, I swear I could feel the ground shaking."

The point of all this, of course, is that in the two years since the Yankees beat the Braves in Game 6, they've became bigger and stronger. And likewise, the fans have become more formidable than ever. They have created an atmosphere that borders on danger for opposing players.

David Cone says, "The place has an edge to it that

> **"It's how you react to fear that makes all the difference. I've been booed here before, and I've managed to not let it affect me"**
>
> — *John Wetteland*

you don't see in the regular season. If I was a third baseman or first baseman for the other team, I'm sure it's not a pleasant experience reaching into the stands for a foul ball."

Dwight Gooden made the same observation in 1996, only his comparison was with the love-in crowds the Mets used to attract in the Eighties. He said, "Back then, Met fans were loud, but it wasn't the kind of football or hockey crowd that comes to big Yankee games. Even in batting practice, you've got guys screaming, 'Yeah, let's go.' It's three hours before the game and they're totally into it."

Maybe that's why the Rangers were speaking so openly about the thought of facing those fans. Right-hander Rick Helling, who starts Game 2 tonight, said, "The fans are going to be on me from the minute I throw a pitch. Even if the score is 0-0 in the ninth inning, I know they're going to play a role in this."

John Wetteland's assessment is even more candid, maybe because he has played to both sides of the Yankee public's loyalty.

He said an opposing player has to deal with, "fear" although he added, "that's not really the most important issue.

"It's how you react to fear that makes all the difference," Wetteland said. "I've been booed here before, and I've managed to not let it affect me."

But not every ballplayer is as mature or composed as Wetteland. Jeff Nelson recalled how in 1995, when he was playing for the Mariners, "A fan leaned over the railing and poured a full cup of beer on me when I was warming up in the bullpen.

"You try not to let it bother you, or at least you don't let the fans know it bothers you," Nelson said. "But the fact is, you're going into a game soaked in beer, smelling of beer. So whether you like it or not, the fans affect the way you pitch."

Nelson laughed and said, "The amazing thing is the fan knew he wouldn't get caught. There wasn't a single cop out there. I know a lot of pitchers won't go out to warm up in the [visitors] bullpen unless they specifically get the call from the dugout. They'd just as soon stay in the hut."

Of course, the Rangers know the best way to calm a riotous crowd is to hit and pitch well, which is exactly how Texas caught and passed the Angels in the last two weeks.

Hit and pitch. Sounds easy, doesn't it? In Yankee Stadium, though, the instruction manual calls for hitting, pitching, and being perfectly deaf to the $#${AT}# fans.

Wednesday, September 30, 1998

Rangers' best falls short against Bronx Bombers

By BOB KLAPISCH, Record Columnist

Mariano Rivera's last fastball thundered into Jorge Posada's glove, and for a moment, Ivan Rodriguez looked at his bat in disbelief. The Rangers catcher saw the ball perfectly, timed it, executed a textbook weight-shift, and... connected with nothing except the cool Bronx air.

At-bat. Inning. Game. Yankees.

"I'll tell you something, that is a very, very tough team in that other dugout," said Rangers manager Johnny Oates after the Yankees took Game 1 of the American League Division Series, 2-0. This was no concession from Oates, only a statement of fact from the Western Division champions.

Actually, you can create your own scouting report about the Bombers: David Wells' curveball was either too huge, or Derek Jeter — who devoured Juan Gonzalez's check-swing roller in the eighth inning with a runner on second — is too athletic. Or else the Yankees have a prearranged deal with the October gods, which no one, not even the Rangers, can void.

In a way, Rodriguez's ninth-inning strikeout was a microcosm of the frustration all the Rangers feel going up against the greatest American League team in regular-season history. Texas played flawless baseball in September, crushing the Angels in the past two weeks, and finished 1998 as the AL's top hitting team. Yet on Tuesday night, not even Texas' best weapons were a match for this Yankee monolith.

Think of the Rangers' shock: They started Todd Stottlemyre, who had a 2.10 ERA in September. They had Gonzalez, the Yankees-slayer, who was even more impressive than Stottlemyre this month, batting .381. There's Rodriguez, who throws harder than some Yankee pitchers and Will Clark, old, cynical, and still impossible to retire in late innings.

Yet none of them made the Yankees sweat. That's how mean and stingy Wells was for eight innings, breaking off neck-to-knees curveballs that Oates said are "as good as any I've ever seen. It drops right off the table."

Of course, Wells isn't embarrassed to accept that praise. In fact, he wants the attention, your attention. He wants the entire country to notice his pitching, his tattoos, his love of heavy metal music. He's a name-dropper, making a point of telling the press he chatted with guitarist Eddie Van Halen before the game, asking him to wear a Yankee T-shirt, "for the vibes." But above all, Wells is known among ballplayers as a gamer, the highest praise one athlete can bestow upon another. A gamer lives for big moments, thrives on them. Wells says, "I want the ball when it counts," which, if you think about it, is true about most of the Yankees.

Right now, the Bombers look invincible, even after just nine innings. In fact, the Bombers, drawing heavily from the soldout crowd's psychic energy, are already imagining Andy Pettitte's cut-fastball taking apart Gonzalez and Rodriguez, turning Game 2 into a bridge to a three-game sweep.

Joe Torre says, "There's going to be a lot of pressure on Andy, no matter what the situation is." But the manager knows the risk he took in naming Pettitte as his Game 2 starter, he was counting on Wells to win Game 1.

And part of the reason the Yankees leaned so heavily on the probability of Wells outpitching Todd Stottlemyre was the crowd — the army of loyalists who will say anything — anything — to intimidate opponents.

Oates was the first to admit Tuesday, "We're not immune to the noise. We hear it. But that's part of playing in New York. If you're going to be successful, you're just going to have to get used to it."

Before the game, David Cone was saying, "The [Stadium] has an edge to it that you don't see in the regular season. If I was a third baseman or first baseman for the other team, I'm sure it's not a pleasant experience reaching into the stands for a foul ball."

To this day, many Yankees believe the crowd played a role in the Braves defeat in Game 6 of the 1996 World Series — if not frightening them, at least making the National League champions uncomfortable.

One Yankee veteran said, "You could see it in their eyes, they didn't want to be here. All the confidence they had early in the Series, it was gone. It's like they were saying to each other, 'Let's play the game and get the hell out of here.'"

Of course, no one's saying the Rangers have surrendered, but Game 1 went exactly according to the Yankee blueprint: the crowd made a sound that was at times beyond the definition of loud and something other than human.

Wells kept Gonzalez from getting the ball out of the infield, and even though the Bombers didn't exactly punish Stottlemyre, they scored their second and most important run via a double steal.

Which should tell you something about the Bombers. It should tell you the October machine is only beginning to rev up the RPMs.

Thursday, October 1, 1998

Straw's last wait

By BOB KLAPISCH, Record Columnist

Darryl Strawberry's day began with a test that revealed a spot on his colon. It was either a spot or a shadow, but it didn't matter which description doctors chose. All Strawberry knows is that he's scared.

"Any time you've got something inside of you and the doctors can't tell you what it is, it's going to spook you," Strawberry said Wednesday, just before leaving the Stadium. He went home to prepare for a critical series of tests this morning, leaving the Yankees with the less important business of baseball.

By late today, Strawberry should know if he has cancer.

People around the Yankees were being careful with the language Wednesday, and understandably so. "Nothing has been ruled out," said general manager Brian Cashman, meaning Strawberry could simply have a bacterial infection or else he could be fighting a malignancy.

Strawberry tried to reassure his teammates that he's feeling upbeat and strong, and he showed up at the ballpark for that exact reason — to hang out in the clubhouse, speak to each Yankee individually, and to ask them to please not worry.

But Strawberry is too in tune with his body to lie about the pain in his stomach. It has cut through him for almost a month, which prompted him to call his childhood buddy, Eric Davis, on Monday. The Orioles outfielder told Strawberry that he, too, had a stomachache that wouldn't go away.

It wasn't long after that Davis was diagnosed with colon cancer.

Of course, our reflex is to say Strawberry waited too long to finally seek medical attention. He did. But there are other factors at work here: Strawberry has a contract that's heavily weighted with performance incentives, meaning the longer he played, and the more at-bats he accumulated, the fatter his salary.

He originally signed for a $750,000 base salary, but received an additional $25,000 for his first 100 plate appearances, got another $50,000 at his 250th plate appearance, and another $50,000 at the 300th.

Strawberry had climbed to 344 plate appearances, just six shy of another $50,000 check. Which probably explains why he suffered in silence. In fact, Strawberry admitted, "I was afraid they'd put me on the disabled list if I'd said anything."

Instead, Strawberry is staring at the greatest medical crisis of his life — a potentially more dangerous foe than alcohol or cocaine, or the Internal Revenue Service or the United States Attorney's office in White Plains, N.Y.

Strawberry has made his peace with all of them in the last three years, living a life that George Steinbrenner calls "something to be proud of." Not long ago, The Boss assured Strawberry that if he remained drug-free and committed to his family, he would receive Steinbrenner's financial assistance after he retired.

But not even the Boss can protect Strawberry from an illness this mysterious. Joe Torre, who has known tragedy in his life, met the issue squarely, telling reporters: "Anytime you take tests, obviously cancer is the one thing you fear. I'm sure by today we'll have a handle on what it is. You have to hope it's something they can handle real quick."

In the best-case scenario, Strawberry is treated with antibiotics and joins the Yankees in Texas for Game 3 of the Division Series. More realistically, Strawberry will remain at home for the rest of the week and wonder what he did — or ate or drank — in all these years that could make him hurt this badly.

Strawberry's friends have seen the change in recent weeks. He's been quiet and moody, playing without an edge, a metamorphosis backed up by his diminishing numbers. Strawberry batted only .207 after Aug. 1, and he didn't hit a home run in 35 at-bats in September.

But that doesn't mean the Yankees were losing interest in Darryl. Quite the contrary: Club officials say Steinbrenner was already leaning toward picking up Straw's $2.5 option for 1999. Those 24 home runs in only 295 at-bats are still a living, breathing endorsement of Darryl's muscles.

But that's a secondary issue now. "The only thing that we're worried about is Darryl's well-being," Torre said.

Torre had the same, grave tone in his voice when he

told the world David Cone had an aneurysm in his shoulder two years ago. Today, it's Strawberry and an illness he's not sure how to fight. Maybe that's why Straw showed up at the Stadium — not for his teammates' sake, but his own.

Maybe an afternoon in the clubhouse was Darryl's therapy, to which he's entitled. Anything to help this decent, reformed man fight his demons. Chili Davis spent time with Straw and said, later, "You don't want to go into any panic mode right now."

He's right, of course. But peace of mind doesn't come easily when you're waiting for a doctor to tell you why you're hurting all the time.

Friday, October 2, 1998

Yankees hit hard
Players united for Straw

By BOB KLAPISCH, Record Columnist

At 4:20 p.m. EST on Thursday, Joe Torre stood in the middle of the clubhouse, surrounded by the Yankees and their devastating silence. The manager cleared his throat, swallowed hard, and prayed he could remain composed long enough to relay the news about Darryl Strawberry.

Within seconds, Torre's stoicism crumbled and without embarrassment, he cried.

"Darryl has cancer. It's cancer," Torre said, his voice cracking. Around the room, the Yankees stared in disbelief, some of them sobbing before Torre had finished speaking. There was still a workout to complete, but as they filed out of the clubhouse onto the field, the Yankees were overcome with grief.

Paul O'Neill was bloodless white, mumbling to himself. Tino Martinez wore sunglasses, fooling no one. And David Cone simply stared at the ground, cursing the fates that threaten to bring down his friend.

Why? Why Darryl? Over and over the Yankees asked how this friendly, unpretentious man — so open about his past mistakes and now so proud of his new life — could be targeted by this deadly disease. Cone said that "it scares the hell out of me" to learn that doctors found a tumor the size of a walnut in Strawberry's colon and still don't know whether the cancer has spread to his lymph nodes or pancreas.

Torre made no pretense at minimizing the crisis.

"This is pretty tragic," he said. "Even to your worst enemy, you wouldn't want this to happen."

Somehow, in the next few hours, the Yankees have to find their equilibrium.

After all, there is still baseball in front of them, although Cone said, "It sure makes you look at things in a different way. One minute you're worried about how your slider will break to Juan Gonzalez, the next minute you're hearing Darryl has cancer."

Strawberry called the Yankees clubhouse to wish them well tonight against the Rangers, and in return the entire team gathered for a live, on-field shot for ESPN's "SportsCenter." It was a remarkable, touching scene, one that left Martinez's eyes moist and red even 30 minutes later.

"All I know is that if we'd had to play [Thursday], we probably would've gotten our butts kicked," the first baseman said. He tried to answer a few more questions, but after a while, the words just evaporated. Better to just get dressed, return to the team's hotel across the street from the stadium, and get on with the real business at hand, which was to pray.

It is all the Yankees can offer their friend now. Much of the players' suffering comes from their love for Strawberry and their respect for his new, humble lifestyle. He'd become a force in the clubhouse, a warehouse of experience and mistakes and lessons learned.

"See that boy over there?" Darryl said one day, nodding in Derek Jeter's direction. "He's smart. Smarter than I ever was at his age. He's never going to make the same mistakes I did because I told him, "Look what happened to me."

The list seemed to stretch into infinity: rehab stints at Smithers and Betty Ford; a felony tax conviction and with it, house arrest; domestic violence charges and too many wasted years at Shea — lost in a blur of cocaine and booze.

Incredibly, Strawberry hit more home runs in his first seven years as a Met than Mickey Mantle did during his same years as a Yankee. In fact, had Strawberry remained drug-free and continued to hit home runs at that pace, he would have more than 500 now, walking that straight, unfettered path to Cooperstown.

So much talent, so much of it thrown away. Yet Strawberry never regretted his life, because "It made me a better person today. I want people to remember me for the way I ended up, not the way I [messed] up. When my career is over, I want fans to say, 'Strawberry finished up strong.' That would make me proud."

"Every home run that Straw hit since he came back, that was his way of showing that he'd found a better life," Dwight Gooden said from Boston on Thursday, where his Indians will play Game 3 today against the Red Sox.

"It hurts me bad to hear that he's sick, because he was getting his life together," Doc said. "These last two years, Darryl really seemed happy."

Gooden called Straw on Thursday, the two of them speaking in a shorthand that had been learned over the years. There were no long speeches from Doc, only a from-the-heart promise to help.

"I told Darryl I loved him like a brother," Gooden said. "Hell, he is my brother."

Strawberry needs brothers everywhere now. The Yankees are doing their best, but forgive them for stumbling. They'd seen the face of tragedy Thursday, although their vision was blurred by tears.

Saturday, October 3, 1998

El Duque is feeling no fear

By BOB KLAPISCH, Record Columnist

Ernest Hemingway once wrote that a man is best measured under stress. The true hero, he believed, displays grace under pressure. Game 3 of the AL Division Series might not have been Hemingway's vision of pressure, but for the Yankees, it sure became a crossroads.

For David Cone, who had a chance Friday night to pitch the Yankees into the League Championship Series. For Darryl Strawberry, waging a war within his own body, seeking to reclaim it from cancer. And for Orlando "El Duque" Hernandez, who is on the verge of appearing in his first postseason game for the Bombers.

Is this pressure? Depends who you ask. Kenny Rogers was so overwhelmed pitching in Game 4 of the 1996 Division Series against the Rangers, one Yankee said he thought Rogers was hyperventilating on the mound.

But for El Duque, the possibility of facing the Rangers today, or the Indians or Red Sox in the ALCS, the prospect is dwarfed by his own history as a refugee. "Nothing scares me," Hernandez said recently, recalling the journey on the little raft that took him from Cuba.

Hernandez left because he'd been kicked off the Cuban National team — government officials suspected El Duque was about to defect — and forced to work for a few dollars a day in a hospital. Once he fled, after washing up on the shores of the Caribbean island of Anguilla Cay, he spent four days without food or water waiting for the U.S. Coast Guard's rescue.

We know this story. We know it by heart, having heard it every time Hernandez defeated another hitter with the freakish leg kick, and that sidearm delivery. The body language suggests Hernandez learned his pitching elsewhere, but he's quick to say he loves America and its brand of baseball.

> **❝I'm not tired emotionally or psychologically because I have a great will and a great want to live. I feel that I have a lot to battle, a great desire to live and succeed because I have people who are cheering for me to accomplish something. ❞**
>
> *— Orlando Hernandez*

Loves it, because … well, this is easy compared to the life he fled.

"You can tell he's been through some wars, just by the way he pitches to hitters," manager Joe Torre said the other day. "You look at him and you can tell nothing rattles him."

Watch Hernandez, and see how often and effectively he works the inside corner to a right-handed hitter. Doing so requires more than skill. It takes guts because a poorly thrown inner-half fastball either will drift over the heart of the plate — and be sent whistling toward the heavens — or it'll hit the batter in the ribs.

Hernandez won 12 games this summer more on his brains and his heart than his talent. An American League scout who spent the last six weeks of the season following the Yankees noted that Hideki Irabu "has a better arm." Meaning the Japanese right-hander is capable of throwing harder and making his splitter break more dramatically than any pitch in Hernandez' arsenal.

But the same scout also noted that Hernandez pitches with more charisma. He said, "The Yankees seem to be more alive when Hernandez pitches" because he throws so many strikes, is eager to confront hitters in a late-inning crisis, and, perhaps most simply, because the Yankees like him so much.

You'd be surprised how much that counts. As David Cone put it, "We found out in spring training what a good guy he really is. He made friends with us. He made a point of getting to know us, even though there was a language barrier."

The same is true of Irabu, but unlike the Japanese pitcher, Hernandez isn't afraid to piece together a few words in English, even if the grammar is fractured and the pronunciation makes you smile.

A less secure man wouldn't risk sounding so foolish, but Cone is right. Hernandez doesn't care. He wants to be heard. He wants to pitch, even though it's been a long and trying summer.

When someone asked Hernandez recently if he's fatigued — even emotionally — his eyes widened in a way that said: are you kidding? "I'm not tired emotionally or psychologically because I have a great will and a great want to live," he said. "I feel that I have a lot to battle, a great desire to live and succeed because I have people who are cheering for me to accomplish something."

All that's missing from Hernandez' new life in America is a reunion with his daughters. That will happen eventually as his agent, Joe Cubas, is working quietly with Cuban officials.

In the meantime, Hernandez is looking forward to his October debut.

Oh, he knows about the theater the Yankees can create in the postseason. He remembers Charlie Hayes catching the final out of the 1996 World Series, seeing it on a little TV while working in that hospital in Cuba.

Hernandez watched the riot of Yankees on the field, laughing, crying, thundering high-fives, and told himself he'd join them some day.

One raft trip and 10 months later, Hernandez has his wish.

He has thought about becoming part of a Yankee highlight film. Throwing the last pitch of the World Series, a fantasy for any pitcher, would, for Hernandez, be "one of those great moments where you feel total happiness."

Note the choice of words: happiness, not pressure. El Duque doesn't understand the pressure that baseball creates. Hemingway would love him.

Sunday, October 4, 1998

The biggest break of Straw's life

Avoiding jail term led to reform

By BOB KLAPISCH, Record Columnist

The date was April 25, 1995: Judgment Day for Darryl Strawberry, as he leaned forward in his seat in the Federal Courthouse in White Plains, N.Y., listening to Judge Barrington Parker. Strawberry's body was tense as a coil, his mind racing in fear. The U.S. Attorney's office had spent three years investigating Strawberry on charges of tax evasion, and the long ordeal was finally coming to a close.

On the advice of his lawyers, Strawberry had pleaded guilty to a felony. All that remained was the sentencing, and a minimum of six months in jail appeared to be a certainty.

In fact, only an hour earlier in Judge Parker's chambers, Strawberry's legal team had given up arguing against a prison sentence. They only asked that Strawberry be allowed to serve his time in California, so his wife Charisse, pregnant at the time, could be spared air travel when visiting him.

The room went silent as Judge Parker began to speak. Assistant U.S. Attorney Carol Sipperly, several months pregnant, just like Charisse Strawberry, looked confident, almost smug. Charisse dabbed a handkerchief to her moistened eyes, obviously expecting the worst.

Parker cleared his throat and began by noting Strawberry's "puzzling immaturity" in refusing to pay his taxes. Yet, Parker's next sentence left the courtroom so stunned, Sipperly's face tightened like a fist and Strawberry's eyes widened ever so slightly.

"We live in a society where the stigma of a felony is not easily erased," Parker said, "and barring an unlikely turn of events, it's likely you will carry that stigma with you to your grave."

Based on that logic, Parker sentenced Strawberry to a mere six months' house arrest. For all the government's efforts to put him away, not only did Strawberry beat a prison sentence, he wasn't even hit with court fines.

To this day, Strawberry points to Parker's stunning leniency as the crossroads in his life. Strawberry called it "a blessed day for me" and vowed to spend the rest of his personal and professional life "showing people that I've reformed."

For the past three years, Strawberry has kept his word: not one positive drug test, not one drink, not one dispute with teammates or his manager. Maybe that's why the baseball world is praying so intensely for his recovery from colon cancer — because his sobriety, indeed his love for his family, baseball, and God, are so real.

"Once in a while, someone on the team will come up to me and say, 'Come on, D, let's go out to a club,'" Strawberry said not long ago. "You know what I say? 'Why don't you come to church with me?' That's my club. Guys say, 'That's cool.' They respect that. They know I'm past all that other stuff now."

Strawberry isn't just a popular Yankee, he's one of the most well-liked figures in the game. Why else were Boston's Mo Vaughn and Cleveland's Bartolo Colon wearing No. 39 on their caps at Fenway Park on Saturday? Why else would John Wetteland have called Strawberry "one of the most decent people I've ever known."

Oh, there are still hints of the old Straw. Before his illness, he'd chain-smoke, show off his biceps — "check out these guns," he'd say — and brag that with him as their right fielder, the Mets would've never collapsed last month.

Still, that's a mild version of the old Strawberry. In fact, it's almost another lifetime since that fistfight with Keith Hernandez at the Mets' Picture Day in spring training, 1989. Who can forget it?

The dispute actually began the previous season, when Strawberry narrowly missed winning the National League's MVP award. Straw learned that Hernandez, his onetime mentor, had told several writers that Kevin McReynolds, and not Strawberry, deserved to win the award. Hernandez was once Strawberry's mentor, but after 1986 he had grown tired of Straw's mood swings and the frequency with which he showed up at Shea hung over.

Perhaps due to Hernandez's defection to McReynolds, the Dodgers' Kirk Gibson captured the award. Strawberry, looking for a chance for revenge, smoked Hernandez when a photographer suggested they sit together for the team photo.

"Remember that?" Strawberry said with a chuckle last month. "Mex didn't want any part of me. He knew better."

Even in his new, quieter life, Strawberry had a fighting man's temper. He was ready to take on Roger Clemens after the Blue Jays righty had hit Scott Brosius with a message-fastball. Strawberry comes from the hard streets of South Central L.A., but even as a born-again Christian, he still wasn't afraid of a fight.

But combine that temper with alcohol, as often occurred in the Eighties, and the potential for trouble was constant. As a Met, Strawberry would often badger teammates from the back of the bus or the plane, baiting them to see how far they could be pushed.

"I liked Darryl, but only when he wasn't drinking," Dave Magadan used to say. "When he got that way, it was best to just pretend you didn't hear him. He could be vicious."

One time, Strawberry accused Mackey Sasser of stealing his money from the valuables box. Sasser insisted, "I don't know what you're talking about." But Strawberry wouldn't listen. He punched Sasser in the face, a devastating blow, considering Straw was wearing his World Series ring.

On another occasion in 1988, Strawberry was ready to take on Gary Carter, for no other reason than he was in the mood for a fight. Even though Carter was a solid 6-foot-2, 220 pounds, the catcher chose not to fight. "Let's face it," Carter said, "Darryl was cut out of stone, and he could hurt someone really bad if he wanted to."

Ironically, the one Met who stood up to Strawberry was the mild-mannered Tim Teufel, who for weeks listened to ridicule over his inability to negotiate pop-ups in the no-man's land between second base and right field. Finally, Teufel wheeled on Strawberry and said, "I'm tired of listening to your [bleep]."

The two never exchanged blows; teammates wisely intercepted Strawberry before he could make his move. But as a result, Strawberry never again taunted Teufel. In fact, they became close friends.

"All Darryl ever wanted to do was see what you were made of, if you could take it," Dwight Gooden said. "Once he respected you, you were his friend for life."

It was an odd, indeed unfair, initiation. Looking back, Strawberry said he regretted his recklessness.

"I know I treated a lot of people very badly," Strawberry said. "But I've learned since then. I hope they can all forgive the mistakes I made."

The outpouring of love for Strawberry — and the prayers that come with them — say his wish has been granted.

Monday, October 5, 1998

Spencer heroics amaze Yankees

By BOB KLAPISCH, Record Columnist

The home runs keep coming in a ridiculous blur, fast enough to make you reach for the calculator and gasp. Here's what it tells you:

If Shane Spencer hit as many home runs in a full season as he did in his 67 September at-bats, he'd kick sand in Roger Maris' face, laugh at Sammy Sosa, and force Mark McGwire to use more andro.

If Spencer continued on a pace of hitting as many October homers as he did in six at-bats against the Rangers in the Division Series, he would … well, Major League Baseball would have to check his bats, his background, even his blood.

Repeat after the awed Yankees community: Is Shane for real? Is he even human?

"The guy's ridiculous. No one hits home runs like that," Derek Jeter said. "I'm telling you, man, it's ridiculous."

Jeter was smiling but not exactly joking. After all, Spencer hit a home run in his first-ever playoff at-bat in Game 2 against Texas, a solo blast to left off Rick Helling. Spencer then hit another homer in Game 3, a three-run monster off Aaron Sele that helped wipe out the Rangers, 4-0, and fast-forwarded the Yankees to the AL Championship Series against the Indians.

Sooner or later, Spencer, who hit 10 homers in September, or one every 6.7 at-bats, will go into a slump. Logic dictates it. The laws of baseball dictate it. The Yankees know it, although manager Joe Torre says, "I just hope Shane waits until next year to cool off. Right now he's so locked in, everything he's swinging at looks perfect."

That's a hitter's nirvana: fat fastballs and a bat that feels light and quick. The best hitters can last a week or two in this surreal state, but eventually they return to the race of men. So the real test of Spencer's major league ability is how he handles that inevitable drought when pitchers exploit the holes in his swing — assuming they exist.

Spencer looks almost perfect at the plate and, even more troubling to opponents, he's a mystery because of a lack of scouting report data. One National League bird dog said last week, "All I can tell you is that Spencer has a short swing — but with lift. In a way, it's a lot like McGwire's [swing]."

It might take an up-and-in fastball — way up and way in, close enough to create whisker friction — to let Spencer know this magic carpet ride won't last forever. Spencer's emergence as Mr. October is a wonderful Bronx tale, but only in the Bronx. The rest of the American League, and no doubt the National League, will find a way to smother him, even if it means pitching around him or even knocking him down.

But meanwhile, consider that Spencer is outproducing Paul O'Neill and Bernie Williams and Tino Martinez. All of them. He's gone from a 25th man to the starting left fielder to the Yankee who, in David Cone's words, "is carrying us."

"We're all in awe right now," Cone said. "It's like we're watching a cult hero. Shane gets a bigger ovation than any of us. We're at the point where we're expecting a home run every time. and that's pretty incredible."

The Yankees are equally as impressed with Spencer's demeanor. Unlike some rookies whose body language screams "Look at me," the Yankee neophyte has a particularly easygoing demeanor. Spencer went to dinner in Arlington, Texas, with Cone and David Wells and told both how much he enjoys being a home run hitting deity.

Loves it, but without feeling bitter about the nine years he has spent in the minor leagues. What's so touching about Spencer's story is that he is not J.D. Drew, the Cardinals' first-year player who demanded, and got, $7 million up front after sitting out an entire year because he couldn't exact enough cash from the Phillies.

Spencer is living proof that hard work pays, that there's hope for the diligent, that scouting directors aren't always right. You choose the lesson learned, but the Yankees are well aware that whatever last laugh Spencer is having on the system, he's inching the Yankees toward the World Series.

"Let's face it, the guy basically carried us against the Rangers," O'Neill said. "It's kind of nice to see someone who was told all these years that he wasn't good enough to finally get a chance to prove them wrong. Personally, I hope the kid hits 100 home runs."

One hundred? Did he say 100 home runs?

We reach for the calculator: six October at-bats, two homers. That ratio, over a 500 at-bat season, would translate to 166 home runs. One-Six-Six.

"Come on, man, be serious," Jeter said. "Guy hits that many home runs, you know what you say to that? It's ridiculous."

Tuesday, October 6, 1998

Torre possesses the Midas Touch

By BOB KLAPISCH, Record Columnist

The Yankees like to tell this little story about Joe Torre and how he proved early in 1996 that Buck Showalter's reign was over. It was April, and Torre had just pinch hit for Wade Boggs, sending a loud, forceful message: Torre would manage with his instincts and not from the safe embrace of his scouting reports and matchup data.

"Wade didn't like it very much, but Joe proved right from the start that he knew what he was doing,""Tino Martinez said. Indeed, it took guts to send a future Hall of Famer to the bench, even though a left-hander was on the mound. From that day forward, Torre has lived off a huge reservoir of respect from his Yankees.

Maybe that's why Torre is gliding through another perfect October, batting a clean 1.000. Think of it: He started Chad Curtis is Game 1 of the AL Division Series, ignoring what would have been an easy and popular alternative in Shane Spencer. Torre heard the masses begging for the rookie but wisely chose not to lean too heavily on such an inexperienced player.

The result? Curtis had two hits in a 2-0 win over Texas, including the successful back end of a delayed, first-and-third double steal in the second inning.

Torre also gambled heavily on Andy Pettitte in Game 2 against Texas, even though the left-hander had, to some observers, reached his meltdown point. The result? Pettitte allowed one run and three hits in seven innings en route to a 3-1 win.

And most recently Torre has acted as the emotional buffer between the Yankees and their grief over Darryl Strawberry's bout with cancer. Torre handled this tragedy with grace and sensitivity — he wasn't afraid to cry in front of his team in breaking the news Thursday — but the manager never once let the Yankees dissolve into self-pity.

These are the small, subtle ways that Torre has made the Yankees human this summer. To so many baseball people, the Yankees are about George Steinbrenner's mood swings or their unblemished pitching or the balanced offense that always finds a way to break opposing pitchers' hearts.

But Torre has made it fashionable to like the Yankees

— or, short of that, at least to respect their professionalism. Certainly he has been a billboard of modesty. When someone suggested that he was hot this month, Torre's eyelashes fluttered, and for a moment it looked as if he was embarrassed by the praise.

"Well, I don't know. It's tough to make a bad decision when you have quality players," he said. "When you have that much ability to draw on, it's more than just luck."

Indeed, a good manager doesn't just stumble into good decisions. His success depends on more than just deep scouting reports, too. If all it took were numbers, then why are some managers more successful than others?

It's like Gene Michael says, that to win — especially in New York — "you have to have a certain feel for your players. You have to be able to imagine how a certain guy is going to respond to a certain situation. Joe has that ability."

"He says he likes to get of the way of his players, which he does," Michael says. "But Joe also pays a lot of attention to what's going on around him. He knows his guys better than any manager around, because he's smart."

Maybe it's because Torre is a former player, and because of it has a formidable data base to draw upon. That's the reason Spencer didn't start Game 1 against Texas, because Torre knows exactly how overwhelming Yankee Stadium can seem to a rookie in October.

Torre was smart enough to let Spencer wait until Game 2, and now that he has hit two home runs in six at-bats, it's safe to start Spencer in Game 1 of the AL Championship Series against the Indians tonight.

That's called feel. That's called managing by feel. That's why Torre is slowly but surely climbing the ladder of past Yankee managers — already having passed Showalter, who was hard-working but unimaginative. And Torre has displayed Billy Martin's passion but has never been hounded by the devil of alcohol or the need to fight Steinbrenner.

Instead, Torre just moves along, crisis to crisis, somehow finding answers everywhere he looks. Torre made the Yankees feel safe during the Strawberry emergency, even though he isn't a doctor and had nothing to offer except his experience with tragedy.

But isn't that the point? The Yankees listened to Torre because — after losing his brother, Rocco, to a heart attack in 1996 and nearly losing his other brother, Frank — they know that he has cried, too.

"Obviously Joe is someone you can trust," coach Willie Randolph said.

With a 1.000 batting average, who wouldn't?

Tuesday, October 6, 1998

Gooden not bitter toward Yankees

Or at least that's what he says

By BOB KLAPISCH, Record Columnist

Dwight Gooden insists there's "nothing personal" about facing the Yankees in the AL Championship Series. At least those are the words he utters in public. But if Gooden pitches in Game 4 as Cleveland Indians manager Mike Hargrove plans, just watch: It will be the month's best theater.

That's because Gooden and the Yankees are complete on-field strangers, since none of Gooden's 134 innings in 1998 were thrown against the Bombers. That means the Yankees will be unfamiliar with Gooden's huge, bending curveball — the same way he has no real-life experience with the loop in Paul O'Neill's swing or the inside-out quality of Derek Jeter's power.

This is baseball's version of the blind date, which, in most cases, favors the pitcher. For this reunion to take place, though, Hargrove has to decide he wants to lean on Gooden. So far, the manager only says Gooden is "tentative" for Game 4, depending on whether he's used out of the bullpen early in the series.

If nothing else, Gooden's mere presence in the postseason roster is testimony to his rebirth this summer. After a brush with shoulder tendinitis this spring, Gooden spent almost two months on the disabled list — buried so deep at Class AAA Buffalo that he said, "There was a time where I said, "[Forget] it, I've had enough.

"I didn't think they were ever coming to get me," Gooden said at Yankee Stadium on Monday. "You get to a point in your career where you get tired of being injured, tired of pitching rehab in the minors. You think, 'Man, there's got to be more than this.' "

But Gooden rebounded after the All-Star break, going 5-0 after July 26.

"What Gooden did in the last half of the season, it was fabulous," Indians general manager John Hart said. "When we first signed him, we saw Gooden as a pitcher who could out-stuff you, but also someone who could win with finesse and change-ups, too. After his arm got strong, he gave us everything we could've hoped for."

Incredibly, Gooden still throws an angry heater, as the radar gun clocked him at 93 mph. And the curveball still breaks from the neck to the kneesfaster than a hitter can blink. If there's any sign of the 33-year-old Gooden's mortality, though, it's in how quickly he tires.

Opponents are hitting .328 against him after the seventh inning. More specifically, Gooden was at his worst in his 61st to 75th pitches, when opponents batted .324. That might explain why Hargrove is toying with the idea of starting Chad Ogea or Dave Burba in Game 4, depending on whether the Indians are about to upset the Yankees or are taking their final breath of 1998.

Still, Gooden knows a return to New York at least gives him an opportunity to visit former teammate Darryl Strawberry at Columbia Presbyterian Medical Center this afternoon. And even if Gooden goes the entire series without pitching, it still will be a form of revenge against the Yankees.

After all, they declined to pick up his option last year, choosing instead to fill his rotation spot with Hideki Irabu.

Remember the brief war of words Gooden had with Joe Torre after the 1997 season? When Gooden said the manager "let the team down" by passing him over so many times that summer?

The two have since made up, and Gooden says he has no grudge against Torre. In fact, he says he wants to beat the Yankees because "that's the team we have get through to get to the World Series."

There's more to Gooden's get-even plan, but he seals off the words with a thin smile.

"Really, it's nothing personal," Gooden said, convincing no one.

Wednesday, October 7, 1998

Pinstripes Wrights a wrong

By BOB KLAPISCH, Record Columnist

He has the face opposing players hate: young and arrogant, with just enough of a sneer to make it seem as if Jaret Wright is laughing at you. Don't believe the Yankees when they say Game 1 of the AL Championship Series wasn't personal. Don't be that naive, because it was all about repaying old debts.

"Believe me, Wright isn't nearly as good as he thinks he is," a veteran Yankee said this summer, still angry at the way Wright broke Luis Sojo's wrist with a spring training fastball and then nailed Paul O'Neill on the elbow June 19.

Revenge? You bet. Think of a bird being sucked into the turbine of a 727, and you have an idea what happened to Wright in the first inning — thrashed for five runs and five hits before he could register three outs.

In fact, even before Wright threw his first, doomed fastball, he was hurtling toward a black hole. Wright was booed the moment he stepped onto the field, jeered during his warm-up pitches and then, eight batters later, out of the game and openly taunted by fans delirious with get-even karma.

As Wright arrived at the top step of the third base dugout, a wise-guy Yankees loyalist leaned over and offered to shake Wright's hand — laughing, cruelly, as were hundreds of fans near the dugout. It was a good night to say "Take that," as the Yankees cruised to an easy, 7-2 win.

"It just wasn't my day," Wright said quietly. "I fell behind on them, and they did what good hitters do: They took advantage of my mistakes. It was not a good performance. But I'm still young, and, hopefully, it's something I can learn from."

Actually, Wright had what he considered "a really good fastball" warming up in the bullpen. But that was before he learned an old baseball lesson: Velocity is no match for a hitter with attitude.

To wit: Knoblauch single. Derek Jeter single. Paul O'Neill hit-and-run single. Bernie Williams single. Tino Martinez fielder's choice and a stolen base. There was a Tim Raines strikeout, but then a run-scoring hit from Jorge Posada.

By the time Indians manager Mike Hargrove began that long, slow, sad walk to the mound, the Indians were down, 4-0, and a dazed Wright could only stare at his feet as the call went to reliever Chad Ogea.

Why? How? Surely Wright was asking how the Yankees could have smoked him so thoroughly, so mercilessly. After all, he beat them twice in the League Championship Series in 1997, and defeated them two more times in 1998.

In all four victories, Wright threw that same, mean fastball, sprinkled in a few late-breaking sliders and made a point of working the inside corner. As Wright said before Game 1: "Pitching inside is part of my game, and I'm not trying to hurt anyone or hit anybody. That's just the way I was taught to pitch."

Not only did the Yankees disagree, but they said so on the record — a remarkable moment of candor from a team that's patented the safe quote. In a Monday news conference, David Wells flatly called Wright "a headhunter." To which Hargrove responded, "David Wells is a good pitcher, and he needs to stick to that."

Which was the manager's way of telling the Yankees pitcher: Get out of my face. Actually, for all their tough-guy talk, the Indians were concerned about Wright's performance against the Red Sox in Game 1 of the Division Series, when he allowed six earned runs in 4 1/3 innings, and an overall decline in the second half of the 1998 season.

Wright was 8-5 with a 4.09 ERA before the All-Star break, and opponents were batting a mere .260 against him . But after July 6, the American League came closer to devouring Wright. He went 4-5 with a 5.60 ERA, as the batting average against him soared to .299.

Somewhere, somehow, Wright lost the mystery on his fastball. Or was it that the American League was so eager to crush Wright, hitters simply tried harder against him? You'd be surprised how much those intangibles matter.

Like, how much hitters hate young, arrogant pitchers. How much they hate it when a pitcher stares at them after throwing up and in. And how they dream of hitting line drives right up the middle, right at that same pitcher's head.

The Yankees never got close to beaning Wright on Tuesday night, but their point was surely delivered. Four runs, five hits, one woozy pitcher — all in the space of 36 pitches.

The Yankees were too professional to smile or to gloat, at least in public. But any dime-store mind reader could see the Bombers sent Wright a two-word message. It wasn't "Take that."

Thursday, October 8, 1998

Bombers must live with this nightmare

By BOB KLAPISCH, Record Columnist

They spoke to reporters for almost an hour and still, after thousands of words and countless explanations, the Yankees hadn't digested that awful 12th inning. Dazed, confused, even panicked — you choose the description, they all fit — the Yankees realize they might live with the ghost of Travis Fryman's bunt for a long, long time.

Questions that linger: Was Fryman running in fair territory? Did he interfere with Tino Martinez's throw to Chuck Knoblauch, who was covering first? Should Fryman have been called out?

And most important, was there any defense for Knoblauch's paralysis after the throw hit Fryman and rolled on the dirt infield behind the bag?

It depended on whom you asked, or trusted, but that sequence doomed the Yankees in Game 2 of the AL Championship Series, and led to the Indians' 4-1 win in 12 innings. Suddenly, the Bombers are turning their gaze to Andy Pettitte for Friday night's Game 3, and if history means anything to you, remember Pettitte lost twice to the Tribe in the '97 Division Series.

Maybe that's why the Yankees were so unraveled by the thought of traveling to Jacobs Field, suddenly stripped of their October invincibility. The shock was so profound, there was even a hint of second-guessing among the Yankees, as Jeff Nelson, who was on the mound at the time of the meltdown, questioned Knoblauch for using up precious seconds before finding the ball that deflected off Fryman.

Let's work backward: With the score tied at 1, Jim Thome led off the 12th with a single to left off Nelson. Thome was promptly removed for pinch-runner Enrique Wilson. Then, with a 1-0 count, Fryman deposited a bunt halfway up the first base line.

Martinez made the pickup and, turning to throw to first, realized that Fryman was running a straight line toward Knoblauch. Since Knoblauch was standing on the base, which is in fair territory, he correctly concluded: "Fryman was in fair territory, too, and I think he should've been called out. I was standing there thinking, 'He should be out.'"

Martinez's throw hit Fryman on the back just as he

reached the base. Knoblauch, so completely eclipsed that he said, "I never saw the ball," stood helplessly at first base arguing with umpire John Shulock as the ball rolled 15 feet away, toward the the outfield grass. For several stunning moments, Knoblauch's inertia allowed Wilson to score all the way from first.

It happened for two reasons.

First, Knoblauch was arguing that Fryman had made an illegal sprint up the line. Therefore, Knoblauch said, "I was waiting for someone to call [Fryman] out."

And second, Knoblauch said, "I had no idea where the ball was, until Tino started yelling and pointing that it was behind me."

In both cases, Knoblauch miscalculated. Even the diplomatic Fryman said, "I was really surprised no one went after the ball. All I know is that it hit me, and when I saw everyone standing around like that, I thought I might as well keep on running."

Fryman's surprise was shared by Nelson, but the Yankee reliever's tone was considerably harsher.

"Once the ball dropped, you can't assume anything," Nelson said. "The ball was just laying there. No one was getting it."

Indeed, Joe Torre criticized Knoblauch as well, saying, "He was yelling at the umpire and you can't do that. You have to make the play and then go back and argue with the umpire."

Oh, the Yankees protested — heatedly, in fact, with Shulock and home plate umpire Ted Hendry, losing the argument on a judgment ruling. The rules state that a runner in entitled to be in fair territory at the moment he reaches the base, simply because the base is in fair territory.

Therefore, Fryman committed no infraction by running two feet inside the foul line, which TV replays showed he did all the way between home and first. In the words of crew chief Jim Evans, "As long as he didn't interfere with the throw — if it [the deflection] occurred right at the base — then [Fryman] had a right to be at that position."

Interestingly, though, neither Shulock nor Hendry appeared in the postgame press conference, leaving Evans — who was at third base all day — to explain the ruling. That may or may not indicate the umpires were less than certain about their decision, and when Evans was put on the spot, even he conceded, "It could've gone either way."

Torre, nodding, flatly said, "It was a terrible call,"and one league official agreed, saying, "The Yankees have a legitimate argument."

Actually, all the Yankees have is their first taste of mortality in. . . how long has it been since they really sweated? Months? Years?

Suddenly, the Championship Series is giving us real-life drama, which — by the unnerved, faraway look in their eyes — was obviously never in the Yankees' October blueprint. Stay tuned.

Friday, October 9, 1998

Pettitte puts on his game face

By BOB KLAPISCH, Record Columnist

Andy Pettitte listened to a question about the play — The Only Play — and his eyebrows turned to little arches. Did Chuck Knoblauch really plead for mercy? Pettitte was surprised the second baseman apologized so repeatedly, seven times in a 15-minute news conference, and said, "It wasn't necessary" for any Yankee to throw himself at the nation's feet.

The words were calm, the message unmistakable: Lean on me, Pettitte said on the eve of Game 3 of the AL Championship Series. Let my cut-fastball erase the awful memories of that 12th inning Wednesday, when Knoblauch didn't — or couldn't, or wouldn't — pick up the ball, that had deflected off Travis Fryman's back and led to the Indians' 4-1 win.

Suddenly, the Yankees need Pettitte to outpitch Bartolo Colon tonight. Actually, they're in a small state of desperation, since the series is tied at one game apiece, and another loss would force the Yankees to lean on Orlando Hernandez, who hasn't worked in 15 days and has never pitched in a major league playoff game.

But while the Yankees are asking Knoblauch to defeat his Game 2 ghosts, the question is: Can Pettitte outrun his own history with the Indians? It's not an insignificant question, since Pettitte was on the mound Oct. 6, 1997, the day the Tribe officially completed one of the most stunning comebacks in recent playoff history.

We've all memorized the step-by-step collapse of the '97 Yankees: First there was Sandy Alomar's game-tying homer in the eighth inning of Game 4, followed by Omar Vizquel's game-winning single. Then, the next night, the Tribe scored three runs off Pettitte in the third inning of Game 5 — thanks to Manny Ramirez's two-run blast off an 0-2 fastball.

That sent the Yankees to a 4-3 loss that left in doubt whether Pettitte can beat the Indians in October. You don't have to ask if he still lives with that failure. Pettitte wears it like his skin.

"The thing I remember the most was that 0-2 pitch to Manny, because I didn't do a very good job of expanding the strike zone," Pettitte said. "I should've wasted a pitch right there and I didn't."

Pettitte lost himself in the thought. He exhaled, long and slow, and said: "We had a chance to win that game. It was definitely a disappointment."

Actually, that's more than a recollection — it's a confession that the Yankees still live with '97 scar tissue. It's Pettitte's job to heal those wounds, but he knows there are eerie similarities between last year's Game 5 and the Game 3 faceoff with Colon tonight.

In both cases, the Indians are riding a tidal wave of perfect karma. In '97 it was Alomar's homer, and on Wednesday, of course, there was Knoblauch's failure to retrieve the bunted ball that Tino Martinez had thrown into Fryman's back.

Oh, there was plenty of day-after huffing and puffing. Joe Torre once again nuked the umpires, knowing he's on his way to a stiff fine by the American League. Knoblauch apologized — either on his own, or on the advice of a politically astute member of the front office. And the Yankees themselves vowed to use the Game 2 loss as a reintroduction to reality.

In fact, David Cone bluntly asked: "Where did anyone get the idea that we were going to win every single game? There's no shame in losing a game to the Indians. That's a great team over there."

Good enough to beat Pettitte? It depends on which Pettitte stands on the mound tonight. If he relies on his standard weaponry — cut-fastballs to right-handers, big looping curveballs to lefties — the Indians will almost certainly devour him as they did in 1997.

In fact, Torre was asked why he even bothered to position Pettitte to pitch Game 7, should the series go that far. After all, the manager could've easily thrown Pettitte in Game 2, saving Cone for Game 3 and a possible seventh game.

Torre nodded and said yes, that option was available to him. But the manager also noted that the pitcher for Games 2 and 6 would have five days' rest between starts, because of Monday's off-day, and said, "I wanted David to have that extra rest."

Firmly, emphatically, Torre said, "I have no problem with Andy Pettitte pitching in [Games] 3 and 7."

That's because Pettitte adopted an entirely different

philosophy in beating the Rangers, 3-1, in Game 2 of the AL Division Series. For the first time in two years, Pettitte relied on two-seam fastballs and change-ups to right-handed hitters, using the outside corner for most of the game.

The result was so startling, one American League scout said, "It's like Pettitte reinvented himself." The Indians noticed, too. Alomar watched the game on TV, and said, "it looks like [Pettitte's] changed from the way he used to pitch."

Of course, Pettitte wasn't giving away any secrets, but he knows the Indians know about his new love for pitching away to righties. That's the start of the mind war: will he or won't he?

Inside or outside? Closure on Knoblauch or more self-torture? Only Pettitte knows for sure.

Saturday, October 10, 1998

Torre calm before the storm

Manager makes an effort to soothe Bombers

By BOB KLAPISCH, Record Columnist

Joe Torre stood in the middle of the clubhouse Friday night a few hours before the Yankees' miniature Armageddon at Jacobs Field and reminded his players of the greatest medicine known to man and October goats alike: amnesia.

Forget about That Play, Torre said, forget about the umpires. No more apologies, no more indulging that unwinnable mind game called "What If." The manager invoked images of clean slates, blank pages, and an AL Championship Series against Cleveland that began anew with Game 3.

"I made up my mind to talk to them [Thursday], because we were so consumed with umpires, with Chuck Knoblauch, and you just can't do anything about that," Torre said. "Whatever the results were the other day, whoever messed up, it's over with and we can't do a damn thing about it."

Smart man, Torre. Even smarter manager. He spoke about the Yankees' 114 regular-season wins and how his players never once had melted in a crisis. The Yankees were facing a unique emergency

Friday — recovering from only one loss, but one so ugly Torre admitted he was compelled to close the doors to his clubhouse and, for the first time in a month, talk about matters other than signs or scouting reports.

Torre's words were directed at all the Yankees, but he wanted his message to be absorbed specifically by Knoblauch. That's one of Torre's charms — to be able to soothe a distressed player without singling him out. Certainly, Knoblauch was feeling the day-after effects of his apocalypse in the 12th inning in Game 2, being savaged by headlines and talk radio in New York.

Even the sold-out crowd at Jacobs Field couldn't help but devour Knoblauch, cheering him wildly during pregame introductions. Torre obviously knew his second baseman will encounter heavy turbulence the rest of the series — and very possibly the rest of his career in New York — should the Yankees lose to the Indians.

That's why the manager made a point of delivering that calm, lean-on-me message.

"It's a new day," Torre said to reporters. "We've won a lot of games during the course of the year, so we must've been able to bounce back from bad situations."

One of those black moments occurred Sept. 16, which was the last time Torre spoke to the Yankees with the clubhouse doors closed. That was after the Bombers had been humiliated, 7-0, by the expansion Devil Rays — a loss so embarrassing that Torre evicted his coaches, clubhouse attendants, even the public relations staff from the room and told the Bombers: "We stunk. That was terrible."

Even today, David Cone talks about the depth of Torre's anger.

"It took all of us by surprise," Cone said. "There's no question Joe was mad, more than we'd seen all season. We took it as a wake-up call. That shook us up."

The result was a seven-game winning streak and soon after the setting of the American League's single-season record for wins, along with a rebirth of "The World Is Ours" karma that made the summer so historic in the Bronx.

The Yankees might or might not still feel that way about themselves. So much depended on the outcome of Game 3. It could be argued that the winner of Friday's game was in a position to leapfrog right to the World Series because … well, think of it:

If the Yankees lost, they'd be leaning on Orlando

Hernandez to succeed after 16 days' inactivity, not to mention in his first-ever postseason appearance as a major-leaguer. But the Indians' position would be just as tenuous following a loss, since Dwight Gooden nearly will be as rusty as El Duque — Doc threw just 22 pitches in Game 2 of the Division Series against the Red Sox — and has never won a postseason game.

So pick your poison: Hernandez's invisibility or the enigma of Gooden's postseason appearances.

Of course, Torre still has the option to push David Wells ahead in the rotation and use him tonight on three days' rest. But there's no chance Torre would rob Wells of his best fastball, asking him to pitch on an accelerated schedule.

And besides, to alter the rotation this late in the season would be an open advertisement of panic, and if history has taught us anything about Torre, it's that his primary currency — what fuels his success in the Bronx — is pure, crystalline calm.

Maybe that's why Torre called Friday's meeting — not for the Yankees' therapy or the need to counsel Knoblauch. But so Torre could remind himself that the straightest path from the playoffs to the World Series is through strong, day-to-day amnesia.

"A lot of times, when a manager calls a meeting,'"Torre said, "let's face it: It's for the manager."

Sunday, October 11, 1998

Boss has faith in his ballclub

By BOB KLAPISCH, Record Columnist

The elevator doors opened and there he was, a billboard of optimism — even as his Yankees were in danger of becoming victims of the most stunning upset in modern baseball history.

"We're going to be fine. Just watch us, just fine,'"George Steinbrenner said as he descended to the lobby of the Marriott, a few hours before Game 4 of the AL Championship Series.

For the next 30 minutes — while strolling through the hotel and signing autographs for fans — The Boss expressed an unrelenting faith in the Yankees, despite their embarrassing 6-1 loss to the Indians in Game 3, one that left them leaning desperately on Orlando Hernandez.

If Steinbrenner was worried about the Yankees'

predicament, he didn't show it. Instead, the owner told anyone who would listen, "I've got a bunch of warriors in that clubhouse, and they're not about to give up because of that [Game 3] loss.

"If we win Game 4, we're going to be in good shape," The Boss continued. "I'll take my chances with [David] Wells and [David] Cone back to back, any time. This thing is far from over."

The words were like prophecy: the Yankees smothered the Tribe, 4-0, as Hernandez threw seven shutout innings. Afterward, Steinbrenner stood in the middle of the clubhouse and called El Duque's rescue mission "the best pressure performance I've seen in 25 years. That was outstanding."

Then The Boss lowered his voice to a conspiratorial whisper and added, "See, I told you we weren't dead. The fat lady hadn't even warmed up yet."

> ❝ That's me, but don't tell any one. I'm not a popular guy around here. This is Indians country. ❞
>
> — *George Steinbrenner*

Still, in retrospect, Steinbrenner was honest enough to admit he'd been nervous all night. That's how much he respects the Indians, the ferocity of their loyalists, and the credo they live by — which is, breathing is second on life's priority list to humiliating the Yankees.

"Everywhere we go, it's the same thing — get up for the Yankees, beat the Yankees," Steinbrenner said. "I guess we should take that in a positive way, because it means we're a great team. But there's no question this town is very, very enthusiastic about the Indians and you have to respect that. It's a great sports town."

Despite their pro-Indians passion, however, Clevelanders didn't mind having Steinbrenner in their midst Saturday afternoon. A small clutter stopped him outside the hotel, asking for autographs and pictures. The Boss graciously signed every piece of paper thrust in front of him, and posed for photographs with two sets of admirers.

The Boss even broke out in a rich, deep laugh when someone asked him to sign a golf ball.

"You expect me to fit 'Steinbrenner' on something that small?" he asked.

"It's all I have," the fan said, slightly embarrassed.

"Well, OK," The Boss said, and with the hotel's security people nervously looking on as the crowd by the curb grew, Steinbrenner slowly squeezed the 12 letters of his last name onto the golf ball.

Finally, Steinbrenner broke free and poured himself into a waiting taxi. The driver looked once, then twice, finally saying, "Hey, you're George Steinbrenner, aren't you?"

The Boss nodded. "That's me, but don't tell anyone," he said. "I'm not a popular guy around here. This is Indians country."

Indeed, moments later, the cab radio — already tuned to an all-sports station — blared out its happy pronouncement that "the Yankees are on the brink of elimination."

Steinbrenner shook his head in disbelief.

"Brink of elimination. Can you believe that?" Steinbrenner said. "I guess they don't realize we've still got a lot of baseball left. We're not done yet. It wouldn't be a series unless it was hard-fought."

But that prompted a question from the cab's other passenger: After so much struggle, had Steinbrenner finally grown weary? Was it true that he was poised to sell the Yankees, intending to ask the franchise's limited partners how they'd feel about selling their shares to Cablevision?

The Boss took a long moment before answering. Finally, cautiously, he said, "I'm getting older. It might be time to move on.

"I would miss the competitive nature of this team, being in baseball. There are other things I wouldn't miss. But we'll see what happens. I'm not sure how it's going to play out yet."

Clearly, a Steinbrenner-less franchise would be missing its most visible and charismatic personality. Who else would the fans cling to?

"Hey, George. . . George, over here!" a fan shouted as the cab pulled into Jacobs Field. The Boss turned his gaze towards a desperate-looking, twentysomething male who quite obviously needed a ticket for Game 4.

"George, I'm a big Yankee fan and they won't let me in here," the fan said.

Steinbrenner approached the man.

"Where are you from?" he asked.

"I'm from Manhattan," the fan said. "They're sticking it to me because I love the Yankees."

Steinbrenner, sympathizing with this fan, appeared ready to offer a ticket — but not before testing the fan's sincerity one last time.

"Let me see your driver's license," Steinbrenner said.

"My license?"

"Yup, let me see where you're from," Steinbrenner said.

The fan broke down, and with a smile, said, "All right, I'm from Cleveland. But I still love the Yankees."

Steinbrenner walked away laughing.

"Gets 'em every time," he said.

Monday, October 12, 1998

Tribe return to belly of the beast

By BOB KLAPISCH, Record Columnist

They already see you and hear you — and yes, they are wary of you. The Indians know exactly what awaits them Tuesday night at the Stadium. The decibel overload already fills the Indians' ears. They see a human monsoon in the stands.

The know the beast is ready to swallow them, whole.

"It's a crazy place to pitch, the ultimate stage," Charles Nagy said quietly. Someone asked about being nervous as the Indians' Game 6 pitcher, their last line of defense in 1998. Nagy considered the image for a moment and nodded.

"I'll be nervous out there," he said. "It's going to be an emotional scenario. There's a lot of things at that ballpark that can distract you."

Fans, noise, rage … an opposing pitcher can pick his poison in the Bronx, especially if the Yankees are on the verge of winning the AL Championship Series. After losing two of three to the Bombers over the weekend, the Tribe have the nearly impossible task of capturing the next two games in the Bronx.

Can they? The Indians used all the predictable, tough-guy words, but what else were they going to say? In actuality, the Cleveland clubhouse was filled with regret, because the players knew how close they had come to wiping the Yankees out after Game 3, when Andy Pettitte was pummeled beyond recognition in a 6-1 loss.

The Indians sensed the Yankees' vulnerability in Game 4, but, as Dwight Gooden put it, "We let them off the hook. I don't care what they say now, they had no idea what they were getting in [Orlando Hernandez].

"We had them on the ropes. Had them. Now, I'm

sure they've got all the confidence in the world. Two games at the Stadium, up 3-2? They have to be feeling really good right now."

Gooden knows the Yankees' history here: the last time they had an opponent pinned to the wall at the Stadium — just one game away from clinching — was in the '96 World Series. That's when the Braves were down, 3-2, having been swept three straight by the Yankees in Atlanta.

The National League champions showed up for Game 6 just two hours before the first pitch; that's how intimidated they were by the thought of facing the army of Yankee loyalists. Greg Maddux recalled stepping off the team bus, and hearing "things about my mother that I didn't think were possible."

By the time it had ended, Maddux had indeed blinked, allowing the Yankees three runs in the second inning. The Bombers went on to a 3-2 win, and to this day, they believe the Stadium's ugly karma cemented that victory.

Now it's the Indians' turn to enter this open-air asylum, and like the Braves in '96, the Tribe is wounded. True, they have their two best pitchers — Nagy and Bartolo Colon — lined up in a neat row, but one by one, the Indians came upon the realization the Yankees' October talent gap is overwhelming.

How else to explain Hernandez' 4-0 classic in Game 4, followed by David Wells' ability to shut down the Tribe in Game 5, even after fans near the visitors bullpen had taunted him about his deceased mother?

What other words are there to describe the Yankees' slow, methodical dissection of Chad Ogea and Jaret Wright?

What other reason, other than superior firepower, illustrates how the Yankees pretended Pettitte's embarrassment in Game 3 never occurred?

"You talk about momentum, but with the Yankees, there is no such thing as momentum," said Jim Thome. "That team is capable of winning three, four, five games in a row like it's nothing."

Mike Hargrove agreed, and although he obviously stopped short of a concession speech, the Indians manager admitted the window for an Indians' upset may have already closed.

"I've said it a thousand times — you don't win 114 games by being lucky," he said. "That team is good. They do so many things so well."

Oh, Hargrove and his players certainly could curse the fates. They could rationalize the weekend that way. After all, the Yankees' three-run, first-inning explosion would've never taken place had Ogea not deflected Paul O'Neill's one-bouncer up the middle.

Unmolested, that ball, in shortstop Omar Vizquel's words, "was definitely a double play." That would've ended the Yankee first, and who knows, maybe the Indians do even more damage against the wobbly Wells in the bottom of the inning.

Maybe the Indians would've pressured Wells more with David Justice and Sandy Alomar in the batting order. And perhaps Hargrove made a mistake not sending Justice to the plate as a pinch hitter in the eighth, when, with runners on first and second and one out, Hargrove allowed Mark Whiten to face Mariano Rivera.

Hargrove said Whiten was just as capable as Justice of hitting a fastball to the planets. "Maybe not as consistently as David," the manager said, "but he was capable."

Not on this night. Whiten bounced into a 4-6-3 double play that ended the inning — and deprived Thome of the one-on-one against Rivera that might've changed the game altogether.

But it didn't. Not on this night. Not in this series. All that's left now is the final breath the Indians are waiting to take. Thome said, "It's not going to be easy going there, but it's not impossible, either."

Maybe not, but Thome's eyes — glassy and far-away — seemed to be filled with images of the beast.

It is waiting.

Tuesday, October 13, 1998

Bombers can't afford to gamble on Pettitte

By BOB KLAPISCH, Record Columnist

It has been four days since Andy Pettitte threw his last fastball — a long, black weekend filled with images of that Game 3 flogging from the Indians. Pettitte has worn those mistakes like his skin, and although the left-hander still wants to start Game 7, he knows Joe Torre's once limitless reservoir of optimism about him is slowly turning to vapor.

The clues are all around Pettitte. Initially, Torre said Pettitte was his first choice for Game 7 — but qualified that by adding "for now." The manager downgraded Pettitte's status a day later, saying, "everyone" would be available to pitch the Series finale, and said any discussion about Game 7 would "hopefully be moot" after David Cone took the mound tonight in Game 6.

Finally, in a news conference Monday at the Stadium, Torre stopped answering "what if" questions about Game 7.

All the while, Pettitte has been listening — both to the words Torre chose and the ones he didn't. Not once, since the 6-1 loss to Cleveland, has the manager offered Pettitte an unconditional vote of confidence.

"He's the manager, it's his decision, it's his team," Pettitte said quietly. "Of course I would love to take the ball, but I'm not about to start any dissension over it. The only thing I want is to get to the World Series. I'm not a prideful man. I don't have to pitch Game 7 to feel good about winning the pennant."

No one questions Pettitte's loyalty to the Yankees, or his desire to win. He is, in Joe Girardi's words, "one of the most professional players in this clubhouse." And Cone added that Pettitte "deserves a chance" to redeem himself.

Still, the Yankees are understandably disturbed by Pettitte's inability to beat the Indians in the postseason. Dating back to 1997, he's 0-3, with an ERA over 9.00 against the Tribe in October, which is why it's likely Torre would start Orlando Hernandez in Game 7.

That would represent a huge about-face for Torre and the Yankees, who, for two years, have made Pettitte the architect of their postseason blueprints. But that was before Pettitte lost some of the mystery of his cut-fastball and precious velocity on his four-seamer.

While Pettitte is still able to defeat the mediocre and even better-than-average American League teams, the Yankees have to wonder if, come playoff time, Pettitte can smother the most heavily muscled lineups.

He says he can, pointing to an impressive 3-1 victory over the Rangers in Game 2 of the Division Series, in which Pettitte allowed just one run on three hits in seven innings, striking out eight. And Pettitte also is quick to remind you that he beat the Indians on July 14, 7-1, a six-hitter that represented the Yankees' first complete game in 1998.

But Pettitte isn't camouflaging how ugly Friday night's meltdown was, either. He admitted, "That's a great hitting team, and if I'm not on top of my game,

the Indians probably think they can get to me. In fact, I'm sure that's what they think."

That's Torre's dilemma: If the Tribe has invaded Pettitte's psychological exterior — indeed, if he's lost his self-confidence pitching to Jim Thome and Manny Ramirez — how can the manager start anyone except El Duque?

And if that's the scenario waiting to be played out, what future does Pettitte have in New York, if he no longer can be leaned on in October?

One far-fetched possibility would have the Yankees trading Pettitte this winter, and siphoning the $6 million he'll earn in 1999 toward an all-out, no-dollars-spared pursuit of free agent Al Leiter, or even Kevin Brown.

It's a long shot that Brown could ever be lured to New York, but there's no question he lives for October's sweatiest moments. And if enough dollars can sway Brown, who's represented by Scott Boras, it's not impossible to imagine Bernie Williams — another Boras disciple — returning to the Bronx, either.

The other option available to Torre is to skip Pettitte in Game 7, and if the Yankees win, use him in the World Series, perhaps in Game 4 at the back end of the rotation. Wait, and hope. Wait and let history cleanse Pettitte.

It might work, since the National League champions — especially if the Padres win the title — would be unfamiliar with the late, difficult break on Pettitte's cut-fastball.

Even the Braves would represent less of a threat than the Indians, since the last time Pettitte faced Atlanta, in Game 5 of the 1996 World Series, he outpitched John Smoltz, 1-0.

To this day, Pettitte lives on the emotional fuel from that win — slicing through the Braves lineup, inning after inning, smothering their right-handed hitters with that cutter, saving the Yankees in their most desperate hour.

Pettitte takes so much pride from that win, he said, "That's what makes me think I can go out there again and do the job, because I did it against Atlanta. Games like that give you confidence."

It's an athlete's best friend, selective memory. If Pettitte wants to forget about Game 3 Friday — and instead hit the replay button on a game two years old — who among us can argue? It's all about self-preservation, and right now, Pettitte could use a little help from his friends.

Even the ones in his memory bank.

Wednesday, October 14, 1998

From any angle, Cone's the man

By BOB KLAPISCH, Record Columnist

The date was June 14, the site was Yankee Stadium, and the mirage was taking place 60 feet, six inches from home plate. There, David Cone made the Indians believe he was 25, not 35, and that he didn't throw just four pitches, but that the mound was Cone's personal laboratory, where new pitches kept appearing out of this scientist's hand.

One by one, inning by inning, the Indians walked back to the dugout, wondering if their eyes were lying to them. Just how many arm angles did Cone have? How many different ways could a man dominate the strike zone, as he was against the Tribe?

The illusion was so profound, Jim Thome finally approached Dwight Gooden and, according to Doc, asked, "how does he do it?"

"Do what?" Gooden said with a knowing smile.

"Keep coming up with new pitches?" Thome said. "How many does he have, anyway?"

Gooden just shook his head and laughed, because, after so many years of being Cone's teammate, he understood Thome's frustration. But this was the first time Cone had been an opponent, and the first time Doc had seen, from the other dugout, what the Yankees right-hander did to a hitter's confidence.

Cone finished the day with a four-hit, 4-1 win over Cleveland, including 12 strikeouts — a performance so flawless, Gooden said afterward, "Coney made me appreciate how good he really is. It was kind of hard to watch because those were my teammates up there, but in a way, I couldn't help but think, 'he's an amazing pitcher.'"

Those weren't just the words of a friend; Gooden's endorsement of Cone echoed that of so many American League scouts, and why the Yankees thought they had an enormous advantage going into Game 6 of the AL Championship Series on Tuesday night at the Stadium. One more win, one more night of magic out of Cone's fingertips, and the Yankees would push even deeper into October. No wonder Joe Torre was saying before the game that he was, "putting all my eggs in one basket."

Logic said Torre was smart to lean on Cone, especially since, as a Yankee, he was 27-5 lifetime at the Stadium. For four innings, Cone was brilliant, elusive, throwing fastballs that were small and sliders that played "Here I Am, No I'm Not" with the Indians. In those four scoreless innings, Cone allowed just three hits and struck out seven.

But Cone was no match for Thome in the fifth, whose stunning grand slam erased almost all of the Yankees' early 6-0 lead over Charles Nagy. Gone, in one pitch, was the touch of perfection that proved Cone is aware of a simple, but irrefutable law about hitting.

It says hitting isn't really about bat speed.

As knowledgeable about hitting as Cone is, he also is aware that hitting is about seeing the ball out of the pitcher's hand, identifying the rotation, and knowing where and how it will break.

But the reason Cone has been so devastatingly effective, year after year, and even now at the age of 35, is because he rarely allows a hitter to be comfortable.

As one scout put it, "Cone hides the ball just well enough, and has enough different pitches that a hitter really had no idea what's coming next."

The reason that helps Cone is that most major leaguers are "guess" hitters. In other words, they'll try to predict what pitch is coming, and swing accordingly, even before a the ball has left the pitcher's hand.

Although that strategy requites a little luck, it often works because so many pitchers fall into familiar patterns, almost always throwing a first-pitch fastball, for instance, or using their curveball on 1-1, or returning to the fastball when behind in the count, at 2-1 or 3-1.

But that's not true about Cone, who has at least seven different pitches available. There are two types of fastballs — the power, four-seamer and the sinking two-seamer — a slider, curveball, and two types of splitters — one with the thumb tucked under the ball for greater velocity, the other with the thumb along side the index finger, for greater movement.

There's also the Laredo slider, a sidearm delivery of his slider which is particularly effective against right-handed hitters — breaking on a huge, flat plane like Jeff Nelson's, like a Frisbee, actually. But Cone has used the Laredo so often in the last few years, he was losing the element of surprise on that pitch, especially with two strikes.

That's why Cone was so intrigued by Orlando Hernandez's ability to change deliveries and arm angles, and the success he had with American League hitters this summer. Cone said, "I learned a lot watching El Duque," and indicated the most useful lesson was the way Hernandez used a sidearm fastball to perfection.

Cone embraced that pitch, too — although unlike El Duque, Cone used it to work the outside corner on righties, not the inside corner. But the addition fattened Cone's pitch total to eight.

Of course, having a warehouse of weapons doesn't mean much if the man throwing them has a confidence problem. But that never has been Cone's problem. In fact, the right-hander talked about his Game 6 start as if he was ready to rewrite history.

"This is my chance to make my mark on this franchise," Cone said. One more win. One night of illusions. The scientist walked to the mound, his laboratory open for business.

Wednesday, October 14, 1998

Each hit raises Bernie's value

By BOB KLAPISCH, Record Columnist

The collection of Yankees turned to a blur of human flesh — arms and legs in chaos, high-fives and bearhugs, and maybe even a tear or two. The crowd made a noise that filled the Bronx, as the American League champions exchanged looks that said: The world is ours.

Maybe it's the Yankees' destiny now, to keep rolling over what stands in their way. First the Rangers, then the Indians, and now the Braves or Padres — whoever's left standing after the NL Championship Series — all like coal being shoveled into a locomotive, fueling the most powerful engine in AL history.

Indians' manager Mike Hargrove could only lower his voice in respect and call the Yankees, "one of the best teams I've seen in a long time." His team had been beaten not by just one Yankee, but many of them — from Scott Brosius, to Derek Jeter, Ramiro Mendoza, and, of course, Bernie Williams.

The center fielder was at the epicenter of the miniature riot on the mound, hugging Jeter and Paul O'Neill and David Wells and anyone else he could find. Williams was entitled to the euphoria: He was 3-for-4 with two RBI, and finished the ALCS with a .400 average.

Not a bad metamorphosis for Williams, since he was 0-for-11 in the division series against Texas and had lost some of the magic from that regular-season batting title. Williams drove in the Yankees' first run in the first inning off Charlie Nagy, powering a single to center that said everything about the mugging Nagy was about to absorb.

But that base hit also said plenty about Williams, too, because he — more than any other Yankee — is living a day-to-day, at-bat to at-bat existence in pinstripes. With every base hit, we wonder: Will Williams be back in 1999?

With every Yankees postseason victory, the curiosity becomes more intense: Will the good feeling generated by this team be enough to convince Williams to re-sign? George Steinbrenner doesn't know, and the truth is, neither does Williams.

All he says about his future is, "I'll make my decision after the season." That's when agent Scott Boras will open the auction for what could make Williams the highest-paid player in baseball. Until then, Williams will ride this wave of perfect Yankees karma into the World Series, while the Yankees hope that Williams realizes there will be no such excellence in Arizona next summer.

No bridge to cross into October. No chance for a playoff spot. No way to avoid an 85-90 loss season. Just Buck Showalter and those softball-like uniforms the Diamondbacks wear. Will all these factors be enough to appeal to Williams' loyalty?

It depends on his agenda: If Williams merely wants to award himself to the highest bidder, then it's possible the Series will be his exit from the Bronx. But if Williams wants to finish his career in the place inhabited by DiMaggio and Mantle — if the Yankees can appeal to Williams' sense of history — then Steinbrenner might have a chance, after all.

Of course, The Boss will have to overpay to keep Williams, that already is a certainty. If Chuck Knoblauch is ready to sign a two-year, $18 million extension, then Williams has every right to ask for $13-14 million a year. And before you say he's not worth it, remember: Someone will pay it. Certainly Diamondbacks' owner Jerry Colangelo will. Colorado is lusting for him, too. The list will be long and sincere. Ask yourself: Without Williams, who plays center field next year? Chad Curtis?

The Yankees know they possess a precious gift in Williams, long and graceful, mature, and team-oriented, someone gifted enough — and sufficiently focused — to make a difference in these key October moments.

In fact, the most important run the Yankees scored Tuesday night might have come from Williams in the sixth, when the Indians realized their fantasy of returning from a 6-0 deficit was just that — a far-away dream turned to mist.

Friday, October 16, 1998

Yanks GM one step away from a perfect rookie year

By BOB KLAPISCH, Record Columnist

Brian Cashman may be a first-year general manager — and no doubt eager to impress George Steinbrenner — but when it came time to talk a little trash Thursday, Cashman proved his wisdom comes from the streets. In fact, the GM veered sharply from predicting a Yankee flogging of the Padres in the World Series, even though he heard from five Yankee scouts who believe the Bombers can solve Kevin Brown's monster sinker.

Still, to say the Padres are vulnerable means committing to it, and any Yankee historian knows there's an army of former Steinbrenner employees walking the streets today, victims of promises they couldn't keep.

That's why Cashman was remarkably low-key at the Stadium on Thursday, even though the Series euphoria is building toward a delicious crescendo. "The only thing I'm wishing for is that Saturday gets here," Cashman said with a laugh. "I'm not much for predictions. I just know the Padres are a good team."

Smart words, smart man. Cashman is letting the Yankees, and not his mouth, put the final touches on a perfect rookie season, in the hardest job in professional sports. Cashman is a candidate for Executive of the Year because of the remarkable restraint he showed this summer.

• Cashman refused to surrender to the temptation to acquire Randy Johnson, but nevertheless bluffed the Mariners into raising the price high enough to scare off the Indians. The Big Unit went cheaply to the Astros, and couldn't pitch Houston to the NL pennant.

• Cashman was patient enough to wait out Jeff Nelson's injury without making a panic trade in August.

• The GM never broke his promise to Bernie Williams and talked about a long-term contract once spring training ended. It's still fuzzy as to whether Cashman's integrity will have any effect on Williams' free agency decision, particularly since the center fielder continues to withdraw from his teammates.

Williams may be the first defection of Cashman's regime since he took a commercial flight after the Yankees defeated Cleveland in Game 5 instead of returning home on the team's charter. And Williams remained outside the clubhouse while the Yankees celebrated their Game 6, pennant-clinching victory Tuesday night.

Cashman believes Williams is resolving "personal" problems, and isn't expressing an anti-Yankee attitude. Still, the front office is convinced Williams and his agent, Scott Boras, have disregarded whatever feel-good sentiment the Yankees' prosperous October might bring.

That means Cashman's toughest work is still ahead. Does he let Williams leave this winter and pour that cash into the Mo Vaughn Courtship Fund? If so, do the Yankees trade Tino Martinez for the next center fielder? Does Cashman trade Andy Pettitte?

Regardless whether the Yankees hold off the Padres, they'll have Cashman's imprint by next spring — assuming that Steinbrennerextends the GM's contract. Cashman signed a one-year deal in February, when Bob Watson quit so abruptly, and he admits he has "no idea" about his standing with The Boss.

Cashman hasn't asked Steinbrenner for a vote of confidence, and won't. Not yet. First, because he knows a World Series victory would enhance his bargaining power greatly. And second, Cashman's attention has been divided between the office and his wife, Mary, who gave birth to the couple's first child, Grace Eva, during the 12th inning of Game 2 against the Indians.

"Talk about timing," Cashman said, chuckling. "They started delivering the baby in the 12th inning when we were still tied, 1-1. When we came out [of the delivery room], the anesthesiologist said, "The Yankees lost, 4-1." He had no idea who I was, so I asked him, "How did it happen?"

"He said,' On a really controversial play.' I said, 'Oh, that's just great.' "

Even though the Yankees survived that Game 2 crisis, it still wasn't an easy week for Cashman. Grace Eva came feet first, forcing doctors to perform a Caesarean section. Mary Cashman subsequently developed a fever that lasted three days, and although she's fine now, her temperature didn't return to normal until Orlando Hernandez beat Cleveland in Game 4.

Even now, with the Yankees American League champions, Cashman hasn't slept much lately, although he isn't complaining about the unfavorable exchange rate between rest and fatherhood. "Definitely, it's been a blessing for us," Cashman said. "In so many ways, this has been a dream season for me, personally and professionally. I think about all I've been through, and, honestly, I couldn't have asked for anything better."

There's only one piece missing from this portrait. It's a World Series triumph over the Padres, who are fresh from their slaying of Greg Maddux and Tom Glavine. That doesn't worry Cashman, though. He spent all summer believing the Yankees are bulletproof and, if he won't tell us he sees Brown being vanquished, at least Cashman will say, "We finally proved we're the best team in the American League.

"All summer we showed it, and then we went out and proved it. Now it's two great teams in the World Series." The rookie's unfinished business should be resolved by next weekend. Yankees in seven.

Saturday, October 17, 1998

Home sweet home

Leyritz back on the stage he once owned

By BOB KLAPISCH, Record Columnist

The day started with a ride on the No. 4 train, from Grand Central Station to 161st Street in the Bronx. Everywhere Jim Leyritz went Friday, nostalgia washed over him: the groaning of the subway, the cops who watched over him, the human wall of Yankees fans in each packed car, and then finally, the Stadium, which Leyritz is unashamed to call "a very special place."

Any dime-store therapist senses Leyritz still is a Yankee. He planned to give George Steinbrenner "a really big hug" when he saw him, and unlike so many departed Yankees, feels no bitterness at having been traded away.

With a .269 career average and 80 home runs, it's safe to say Leyritz has been a good but not great player. Talented for sure, but his skill has been turbocharged by a marvelous ego. Say this much, though: Leyritz is loyal to his friends, even the ones he's being paid to defeat.

At a Friday news conference at the Stadium, Leyritz made sure he wore a No. 39 on his cap — stitched prominently near his right ear. Leyritz knew his solidarity with Darryl Strawberry would flex a few eyebrows, especially now. But as he put it, "Some things are bigger than baseball."

"Darryl was a good friend of mine when I played here," Leyritz said. "I know his children. I know his wife. I just wanted him to know I was thinking about him. That was my way of saying, 'My prayers are with you.'"

It takes guts to honor an opponent — even one battling cancer — in the World Series, but Leyritz never has worried about the opinions of outsiders. As David Cone said the other day, "Jimmy loved himself, but not in a bad way."

That's why we loved Leyritz, too, the way he so shamelessly believed he was a 500 at-bat player.

Still, he managed to irritate both Buck Showalter and Joe Torre — stopping just short of becoming a clubhouse cancer but still making life difficult for his managers with a steady stream of "Play Me" sentiment usually voiced through the press. But is there any doubt Leyritz's self-esteem is the reason he hits so well in October?

Who among us can forget his stunning home run off Mark Wohlers in Game 4 of the 1996 Series, the one that devastated the Braves and effectively ended Wohlers' career? Leyritz's hitting skills never matched Wohlers' pitching talent, but Leyritz triumphed because he was fearless at the moment when fear ruins lesser men.

To this day, the Yankees still talk about Leyritz, huffing and puffing in the dugout, predicting he could "get" to Wohlers if only he had the chance. That was some boast, considering Wohlers' fastball was flirting with 100 mph on the radar gun, and as a pinch-hitter for Paul O'Neill in the eighth inning, Leyritz was coming off the bench cold.

Yet Wohlers was dropping little hints of his mortality. Starting the eighth, the Braves needed six outs for a 6-3 victory, but Wohlers gave up Charlie Hayes' swinging-bunt single up the third base line and then Strawberry's opposite-field single to left. Mariano Duncan's fielder's choice put runners on first and third, setting the stage for Leyritz and that massive, wonderful ego.

There he stood, poised in a batting stance that looks like a weight-lifter's pose, twirling his bat between pitches in the way that outrages opponents and makes teammates lower their heads in embarrassment.

As Dwight Gooden said afterward, "Not many guys would act the way Jimmy did, but at the same time, he knew he could back it up."

All he needed was a chance from Wohlers — just one mistake to crush. The count ran to 2-2 as Leyritz fouled off two of Wohlers' best fastballs.

"I was on them both," Leyritz explained later, which is why Wohlers made the worst possible choice in finally throwing a slider.

Not only did Leyritz see it, he timed it, met it perfectly on the barrel's sweet spot, and sent it screaming over the left field wall. In one swing Leyritz had tied the score at 6 in a game the Yankees eventually won, 8-6 in 10 innings, en route to a 4-2 Series victory.

Those are the moments that Leyritz draws upon in this Series. Now he intends to use that October karma against his old friends. Does it feel strange? You don't even have to ask, although Leyritz said, "I want another World Series ring that bad."

Somehow, it doesn't feel wrong for Yankees fans to root for him. That's because Leyritz comes from a different era at the Stadium — before the Yankees become so slick and corporate. Leyritz started working in the Bronx in 1990, when the Mets were the city's baseball proprietors. Back then it was OK for a Yankee to be a little unpolished, to say what he thought, and to max out with every swing.

Maybe that's why he still prefers to ride the 4-train to the Stadium.

"It beats getting stuck in traffic," Leyritz said with a laugh.

Sunday, October 18, 1998

Pressure? El Duque knows plenty about it

By BOB KLAPISCH, Record Columnist

For anyone looking to be inspired by the story of Orlando Hernandez's escape from Cuba — the tiny raft, the Caribbean's hostile waters, the foodless four-day wait for rescue by the U.S. Coast Guard — you're on your own. El Duque has hereby embargoed any further Q&A about his war with Fidel Castro.

That's not to say Hernandez doesn't still consider the Cuban dictator an enemy. He does. In fact, every time El Duque stands on the mound, he said, "I think about the fact that [Castro] is watching, and that makes me want to pitch better."

Hernandez will get his chance to tweak Castro one more time tonight, as he faces the Padres in Game 2 of the World Series. Unlike Game 4 of the AL Championship Series, when Hernandez was facing the Indians in a full Yankee crisis, it's the Padres who are desperate.

After their 9-6 loss Saturday night, the National League champions know El Duque has a chance to crush them. We'll see if the Padres ever recover from blowing a 5-2 lead with eight outs to go, and whether they'll be able to solve the chaos of El Duque's bizarre windup.

But even if Hernandez is too funky for Tony Gwynn and Greg Vaughn, don't expect him to lower the walls to his past. He's grown tired of repeating the details of his defection, and the fact that his daughters remain in Cuba with their mother. The pitcher also wonders if his audience can really appreciate what it means to be a refugee, especially in a country where people take freedom for granted.

As Hernandez said during lunch last Saturday, before pitching Game 4 of the AL Championship Series against the Indians: "People never miss an opportunity to ask about why I left Cuba. They all ask. But they cannot understand it, really. The reason is here."

Hernandez was tapping his chest, right over his heart. When the conversational road leads to Cuba and Castro and his defection, El Duque speaks with a fierceness that makes you understand the pressure of the World Series is nothing compared to the struggles of his past.

Baseball is one of Hernandez's priorities, but not the only one. He's not ashamed to live this way. On the Sunday before Game 1 of the ALCS against Cleveland, the Yankees had an early afternoon workout at the Stadium. Hernandez was five minutes late getting on the field. He was fined by manager Joe Torre, and the story made the rounds in the newspapers.

Hernandez never bothered to explain his tardiness, because, in his words: "When you are late, you are late. There is no excuse." But he then lowered his voice and said: "I was talking to my daughters in Cuba [on the telephone]. This was my only chance to speak to them. I was a father to my children in those five minutes. I was doing what a man must do. That's why I was late."

Hernandez never thought twice about the choice between baseball and parenting. That decision was made with his heart — which, if you think about, is Hernandez's best weapon on the mound. Oh, he's blessed with a terrific right arm and the ability to out-think hitters. But El Duque's inner strength is why Torre picked him — and not Andy Pettitte — to pitch Game 2 of the World Series tonight.

It's because Hernandez is not afraid of the Padres. Not of Tony Gwynn or Greg Vaughn or Jim Leyritz. To El Duque, they are just names. To El Duque, the World Series is just another important game in a life-time of big games — most of which he has won.

"I've pitched in three world championship games, and one Olympics. I've pitched in various national tournaments in Cuba," Hernandez said. He wasn't diminishing the enormity of the World Series, only reminding the Padres there isn't much he hasn't seen or heard on a baseball field.

Besides, Hernandez has already sampled Series pressure through his half-brother, Livan. Who among us can forget the sight of Livan Hernandez embrac-ing his mother before Game 7 at Pro Player Stadium last year, their first meeting since the Marlin pitcher's defection almost two years earlier?

The two hugged for almost 10 minutes without uttering a word. Like Orlando, Hernandez had pitched with his heart last October, winning the Most Valuable Player awards in the NL Championship Series against the Braves and the World Series against the Indians.

Orlando, who was still in Cuba at the time, heard about his half-brother's exploits through the newspa-per and Radio Marti. He said, "News gets around in Cuba," especially when it's about baseball.

All the while, Orlando was plotting his escape from Castro's clutches. He never imagined following Livan into the Series just 12 months later, but he did say, "I knew I'd be here some day."

Tonight, El Duque stands on the country's biggest sports stage. Before his first pitch, he'll take a deep breath, the kind that will stretch the lining of his lungs, and think of his life's long, strange journey. Of course, the Padres will see Hernandez's enormous, freakish leg kick and wonder how a man can deliver a baseball with such unorthodox mechanics. But Hernandez will.

In fact, El Duque will show the Padres an assort-ment of sliders, curveballs, two- and-four-seam fast-

balls, not to mention drop-down release points unlike any pitcher's repertoire in the National League. And this being their first look at Hernandez, it's likely the pitcher — and not the hitters — will have the advan-tage.

El Duque isn't guaranteeing he'll beat the Padres. He knows better than that. But Hernandez is certain of this much: He won't be afraid.

Monday, October 19, 1998
New York

Bombers never gave Ashby a chance

By BOB KLAPISCH, Record Columnist

The Padres arrived in New York last week as proud conquerors of the Braves, the National League's most glamorous franchise, and there was a minority opinion among baseball people that Bruce Bochy's team actually was capable of out-pitching the Yankees.

How wrong. How absurd to have fantasized like that. Today the Padres are home in small pieces, vic-tims of a talent gap that forced Bochy to lower his voice in awe.

"That's a very, very good team over there," he said after Sunday's 9-3 loss, one that has pushed the World Series that much closer to a Yankees sweep.

More and more, it appears the Padres' season was made complete with their stunning upset of the Braves, and all they want now is to save face. One win, maybe even one close game, anything to make the Yankees respect them. Anything but the disaster that swallowed up the Padres in Game 2.

The blame for the Padres' crisis belongs, in great part, with Bochy. That's because he left starter Andy Ashby in the game for 2 2/3 tortured innings. The right-hander surrendered seven runs, four earned, and 10 hits.

In all, Ashby faced 18 batters, 12 of whom reached base. By the time Bochy finally realized Ashby had melted, the Yankees had a 7-0 lead, turning the last six innings into an October spring training affair.

How could Bochy possible have allowed Ashby to be flogged so openly? How could the manager permit the Yankees to sprint so far ahead? Bochy cleared his throat and said something about "needing innings" from Ashby, that the bullpen had been stretched thin the night before and that "we were hoping that Andy would find it. I was hoping it would click in."

Pitching coach Dave Stewart added that Ashby was left to absorb that punishment because "we were playing in an American League park, and we're playing an American League game."

In other words, Bochy and Stewart were wishing their way through the first three innings — thinking that somehow they would be able to erase Ashby's mess with an ambush of their own against Orlando Hernandez.

But just as it was obvious that Ashby was naked, it was also clear that the Padres were baffled by El Duque's funky delivery. By the third inning, in fact — after Hernandez had blown away Ken Caminiti and Steve Finley and Quilvio Veras — Bochy had conceded.

Ashby was at least honest enough to admit his deficiency, saying, "I had no chance to get into any kind of a rhythm."

Of course, there's no shame getting blown out by the best team in American League history, but it sure raises an eyebrow when the opposing manager throws in the towel this early in the Series. It's still possible the Padres could be resurrected in Qualcomm Stadium this week, but with David Cone starting Game 3, it appears the Yankees' only vulnerability will be Andy Pettitte's appearance in Game 4.

It didn't have to be this way for the Padres. They at least could have made the Yankees sweat, the way the Indians did, by going to their bullpen early. Any half-trained eye could see that Ashby — who won only one regular-season game after Aug. 12 — was defenseless against the Yankees. The first batter Ashby faced, Chuck Knoblauch, battled through an eight-pitch at-bat. Ashby finally lost the mini-war by walking him.

To be fair, the three runs Ashby allowed in the first inning were unearned — thanks to Caminiti's throwing error on Paul O'Neill grounder behind third. And the Padres missed a chance in the first, when Wally Joyner's line drive to right with runners on first and second was caught by O'Neill in full sprint at the wall.

A few feet either way, Bochy said, and "we're looking at a three-run inning against Hernandez," And take away Caminiti's throwing error, the manager said, and "that's a six-run turnaround."

But that still doesn't explain why Bochy left Ashby in the second inning, when the righty made the inde-fensible mistake of grooving a 3-2 fastball to Bernie Williams with Derek Jeter on first base. Ashby threw what is known as a get-me-over fastball — the one used to avoid a walk as opposed to retiring a hitter.

The result? Williams crushed the fastball to center, a two-run home run that had the Padres flipping their calendar to Game 3 — and maybe even to next year's spring training. Ashby did bear down, finally, throwing a fastball past Chili Davis to end the inning, but by then the Padres were in ruins.

Broken into little pieces, looking like so many American League teams who learned a hard lesson this summer: The Yankees are baseball-killers. Without pity, they boarded a plane for San Diego on Sunday night, determined to finish their wounded enemy.

Monday, October 19, 1998
New York

Yanks know Gwynn is one of a kind

By BOB KLAPISCH, Record Columnist

There was a moment in Game 1 of the World Series when the Yankees realized the myth was, in fact, reality. That they should believe the hype, and that scouting reports aren't even worth the paper they're written on when it comes to coping with the best pure hitter of our generation.

The Yankees reached their crossroads with Tony Gwynn, eight-time National League batting champion, in the very first inning, after leadoff man Quilvio Veras drew a walk and was in the process of stealing second base against David Wells. Actually, the Padres were trying to hit-and-run against Wells, who, because of his slow delivery and mediocre pick-off move, is vulnerable to the play.

Still, Wells threw Gwynn one of his monstrous, neck-to-knees curveballs — the kind that devoured left-handed hitters all summer. Most swung right through the pitch; only the most talented even made contact.

But here is where Gwynn separated himself from the race of mere mortals: Not only did he stay with the enormous arc of Wells' curve, but he actually controlled where he hit the ball. Gwynn punched a single to left field, into the exact spot Derek Jeter had vacated as he broke to cover second base.

One swing. One perfectly executed hit-and-run play. One small moment of triumph on an otherwise dreary night for the Padres. But it was everything the Yankees needed to know about Gwynn, who quite simply is too tough to pitch to.

"As a pitcher, you see that kind of hitting, that kind of discipline at the plate, and you think, 'No one's supposed to be able to do that,' " David Cone said. "It makes you appreciate the guy. Tony is one of the all-time great ones."

Gwynn is Wade Boggs with power. He's Don Mattingly but with a longer golden era. He's Ken Griffey Jr. with a better attitude and more likable than even Mark McGwire. It's obvious that Gwynn still loves baseball in every one of his at-bats, even now, in his 16th major league season and at the age of 38.

There are some players who transcend team loyalty, who are appreciated everywhere they go. Gwynn is one of those special major-leaguers. When he was introduced to the Yankee Stadium crowd before Game 1, he was cheered wildly, almost lovingly.

The reception was so warm, Cone said, "That might've been the loudest ovation I've ever seen for a player who never spent any time in New York. It shows the fans here are intelligent, and it shows they have a heart."

It says Gwynn is appreciated for the many ways he has made baseball's landscape prettier. It's more than the eight batting titles and the .339 career average. Gwynn is loved because he's one of the few superstars who hasn't filled his checking account with free agency cash.

Think of the dollars he could have commanded in any off-season auction. Think of how well Gwynn would have done had he let George Steinbrenner or Peter Angelos court him. Gwynn could have named his price, his team, even what manager he wanted to play for.

Instead, Gwynn has played for only one team, the Padres, and most recently signed a deal that will keep him in San Diego through 2000. He's making only $4.2 million this season, but as he put it, "I've made enough money in my career that, at this point, what's another $1 million or $2 million if I'm not sure I would've been happy?

"I like where I am. I like this team. The reason I never left is because I couldn't have lived with myself if the Padres had gotten here, the World Series, and I hadn't been around for it."

Of course, the Padres might not last too long in this Series — not the way they were outhit and outpitched in Games 1 and 2. Not even Gwynn's two-run home run off Wells in the fifth inning Saturday night was enough to keep San Diego from melting.

But if the Padres go out quickly, at least the Yankees will have seen why the National League gave up years ago trying to solve Gwynn. Why Al Leiter said one day this summer, "The only way to pitch to Tony is throw the ball down the middle and hope he hits it at someone. And you just hope there's no one on base when he's at bat."

This one-week love affair is going both ways, too. This is Gwynn's first trip to the Series in 14 years, and a part of him is thankful for the chance to face the Yankees — even if means matching up with the greatest team in American League history.

Like Jim Leyritz, Gwynn rode the subways from the Padres midtown hotal to the Stadium for Friday's workout, taking a tour of the monuments as soon as he walked into the ballpark.

"Ruth, DiMaggio, Mantle, Gehrig, Ford — the baseball gods," Gwynn said, shaking his head. History means something to Gwynn. The Padres are in danger of being swallowed up by this history-making Yankees team, but after watching Gwynn defeat Wells in Game 1, even the Yankees know they're richer for the experience.

Tuesday, October 20, 1998

San Diego

Bombers rocking with glory knocking

By BOB KLAPISCH, Record Columnist

Al Leiter was standing near the coffee machine in Yankee Stadium's press room Sunday night, waiting for his turn on ESPN's World Series broadcast. When someone asked the Mets lefty if this constituted hard work, his smile was a billboard of embarrassment.

"This is easy," Leiter said. "I love it. There's about 10 of us [announcers], so I'm on for about one inning. I talk about what I'm watching. Easy."

Leiter was planning to make two points after the

Yankees' 9-3 undressing of the Padres in Game 2. The first was: throwing a scoreless first inning is Rule No. 1 for a starting pitcher, with San Diego's Andy Ashby being used to demonstrate what happens in the worst-case scenario.

Leiter's second lesson of the day was even more obvious. He intended to repeat the conclusion of a growing number of baseball executives, who believe the Yankees are the best team in major league history. One NL general manager — who initially believed the Padres were capable of upsetting the Yankees — said, "What the Yankees are doing is very, very impressive."

Leiter nodded in agreement. "They're unbelievable," he said. "They do everything right."

Not many baseball people believe the Padres can win even one game in this Series, let alone two, and thus force a return for a Game 6 at the Stadium. Ask yourself: can you really imagine David Cone struggling for the feel of his slider, in the circulation-friendly temperatures of Southern California?

After watching Kevin Brown vaporize in the seventh inning of Game 1, isn't it obvious his right shoulder is in desperate need of a winter's rest? Brown is close to 300 innings for the year, and won't do much better in Game 4 as he did in the opener — if he's healthy enough to pitch. In fact, one Yankees official correctly predicted before the Series, "Brown is going to look good for a little while, and then just run out of gas."

> **❝ All of us respect Tino because he's a very accountable guy. He doesn't run from his mistakes. ❞**
>
> *— David Cone*

If all this is true, the Yankees have played their final game of 1998 in the Bronx. All that'll remain this week are the TV images of hugging and high-five orgies, and champagne mixing freely with some tears.

Store these pictures in your memory bank, because we'll never again see a team so carefully woven. Joe Torre acknowledged a Yankee face-lift is coming, as he said Sunday, "The thing that's going to be sad is that some of the players here aren't going to be back. There's nothing you can do about that. That's baseball. But it's still sad to see."

So let's file away the best sights and sounds of this precious October. They're worth keeping.

• David Wells' eight-inning shutout of the Rangers in Game 1 of the Division Series: Juan Gonzalez, Will Clark, and Ivan Rodriguez were a combined 2-for-12 against Wells in his 2-0 victory, managing to get the ball out of the infield only twice.

What was so remarkable about Wells is that he so brazenly pitched inside to the Rangers' right-handed hitters. They knew what was coming. And he knew they knew. Yet, as Texas manager Johnny Oates put it, "There wasn't much we could do about it."

• Shane Spencer's home run in his first-ever postseason at-bat:

The rookie has become invisible lately, as the slump we knew was coming has swallowed him whole. But Spencer's blast in Game 2 was one more example of the dividend that patience can pay in baseball. Spencer waited eight years for his chance, and whether he emerges as a full-time outfielder next year, at least this cameo was thrilling.

• Chuck Knoblauch's mea culpa after his blank-out in Game 2 of the AL Championship Series against Cleveland:

Was he coached? Did someone tell the second baseman to apologize? Maybe not. David Cone said Knoblauch was stunned at Tino Martinez's full acceptance of his role in the botched 12th-inning play. As Cone put it, "Chuck heard Tino tell the press, 'I was slow getting to the ball. That was my fault,' and that made an impression on him. The next day, Chuck owned up to his mistake the same way.

"All of us respect Tino because he's a very accountable guy. He doesn't run from his mistakes. Hopefully Chuck learned from that."

• Padres manager Bruce Bochy standing frozen in the dugout during the second inning of Game 2, oblivious to the seven-run beating Andy Ashby was absorbing:

Any chance San Diego had of upsetting the Yankees vanished at that point, as Bochy made it clear he was conceding.

• The chorus of DAARRYLL drifting down from the upper deck, during Games 1 and 2 of the World Series.

Darryl Strawberry's presence is everywhere; in the stands, the dugout, in the clubhouse. The Yankees have dedicated this October to the good friend and teammate, and appears the Bombers will present Straw with a World Series ring next April.

The more difficult question, however, comes this winter. How can George Steinbrenner possibly decline to pick up Strawberry's option for 1999? No man is that black-hearted.

Wednesday, October 21, 1998

San Diego

Pettitte facing test of mind over matter

By BOB KLAPISCH, Record Columnist

Whenever Joe Torre looks at Andy Pettitte these days, he tries not to let his black, deep-set eyes give him away. But he's studying Pettitte. Watching him, probing him, wondering if Pettitte's mind is still in a Houston hospital, where his father, Tommy, underwent emergency, triple-bypass surgery last week.

If anyone knows the road map of family trauma, it's Torre. Two years ago, he went through an entire season helping his brother, Frank, search for a donor for a heart transplant — which the elder Torre received just hours before Game 6 against Atlanta.

It was an awful weight to carry, really. By October, Torre's days were reduced to the barest essentials: eating, sleeping, calling his brother, and then, finally, managing the Yankees.

But Torre also remembers his brother was healthy during the summerlong wait — that the ordeal was the wait. In a sense, the manager was luckier than Pettitte, whose father's life has been in jeopardy. The situation was so critical, Pettitte received an urgent, middle-of-the-night phone call from home last Wednesday, which put him on the first plane to Houston only 24 hours before the Series' first pitch.

Pettitte's father has survived the emergency, and, when asked, Pettitte says he'll be fine, too, pitching Game 4 against the Padres tonight. But Torre knows that's what Pettitte has to say to reporters. There's another universe Pettitte lives in, where he's alone with his thoughts and, understandably, his fears.

"I have a few more years experience than Andy does, learning to just hide out," Torre said before Game 3 Tuesday night. "Once he gets in uniform, I'm sure he's going to be thinking of his dad, but hopefully he can find a place to hide and get out there and pitch a good game."

Torre is talking about hiding in a figurative sense. He knows a clubhouse is the best place to seek refuge from worry because baseball is an island wholly separated from the real world. Pitching can be an especially wonderful medicine for a stressed-out athlete, because it requires so much mental energy.

In fact, when Dwight Gooden underwent a similar crisis — pitching when his father was awaiting bypass surgery in May 1996 — he said: "the only place I could relax was on the mound. That was the easy part."

Like Gooden two years ago, Pettitte has received assurances from his father that it was OK to return to the Yankees. That he could take the mound without guilt, and pour himself into the task of smothering the Padres.

Maybe that's what Pettitte needed to hear. The go-get-'em speech certainly worked for Gooden, who was so consumed with honoring his father, Dan, that he threw a no-hitter against the Mariners that May 14.

Actually, Pettitte may have a head start on the emergency, since not only does Tommy Pettitte have a repaired heart, but he underwent a blood transfusion Monday and, in the pitcher's words: "He feels about 100 percent better. I feel great about everything that's going on back home."

He says so bravely, his eyes lasering through you, delivering the words without pause. Maybe Pettitte has constructed a marvelous barrier between baseball and his father's illness. Then again, maybe not. He admitted that had he been asked to pitch Game 2 at the Stadium: "I don't know if I would've been able to, mentally. Maybe it was the best thing to wait."

The Yankees agree, because Pettitte's absence saved Torre from having to choose between his lefty and Orlando Hernandez. The result? El Duque threw a miniature classic against the Padres, a 9-3 win that many believe is the reason the Yankees will eventually win this Series.

But there were risks in waiting until Game 4 to use Pettitte, because he was a mere 7-7 on the road this year. By contrast, Pettitte was far more successful at Yankee Stadium, where he was 9-4.

Also, Pettitte is unique among left-handed pitchers, in that he's more successful against right-handed hitters. Primarily because of his cut-fastball, righties' average against Pettitte was 12 points lower than left-handed hitters'.

The Padres may pose problems for Pettitte because they bat six lefties in their lineup — although many scouts feel San Diego's potential advantage could be erased by their unfamiliarity with Pettitte and his big windup.

Of course, none of Pettitte's weapons will count for much if he's thinking about his father between innings or even between pitches. No one would blame Pettitte for letting his mind travel the long miles to Houston, but October isn't the month for mercy.

It's the time of year when the walls between baseball and the real world don't dare crack. Pettitte says his wall is strong enough for Game 4. We'll find out tonight.

Thursday, October 22, 1998

San Diego

Brosius in pinstripes a must for next year

By BOB KLAPISCH, Record Columnist

The final out of the greatest season for an American League team was a routine ground ball into Scott Brosius' glove — which, if you think of it, was the perfect way to end this perfect World Series.

Brosius, the poster boy of unpretentious, clutch baseball, calmly devoured pinch hitter Mark Sweeney's grounder and fired across the infield to Tino Martinez. There was no theater to this play, no flash, just a surreal moment when Brosius realized, in his words: "The season had just ended. It was incredible, the feeling of accomplishment. It's something I'll never, ever forget."

He shouldn't, not after hitting .471 in the Series and being voted its most valuable player. Is there any doubt the Yankees absolutely, unconditionally can't let Brosius slip away as a free agent?

Once again, Brosius was at the epicenter of the Yankees' 3-0 win over the Padres. With the bases loaded in the eighth inning against Kevin Brown, Brosius lifted a bloop single over the San Diego's drawn-in infield, somehow defeating Brown's two-seam fastball that registered 95 mph on the radar gun.

It wasn't quite the muscle shot that Brosius blasted off Trevor Hoffman in Game 3, but it was nearly as important. That RBI single gave the Yankees a 2-0 lead, more than enough breathing room for Andy Pettitte and Mariano Rivera. In fact, after Ricky Ledee's sacrifice fly, you could feel the air being sucked out of the Padres.

Padres manager Bruce Bochy admitted as much, telling reporters afterward: "That [Yankee] team just didn't have any weaknesses. They played baseball the whole series. You just have to give them credit for that."

When it was over, when Brosius' throw landed in Martinez's glove, the Yankees streamed out of their dugout, turning the infield at Qualcomm Stadium into a miniature, open-air riot. It lasted for nearly 45 minutes — this unembarrassed display of tears and hugging and high-fives and champagne.

The celebration was spontaneous and real — a combustion that was fueled with the realization that, in Joe Torre's words, "Not everyone is going to be back here next year."

He's right, of course. All season, the Yankees have obsessed over Bernie Williams' impending decision about a 1999 employer. Will he or won't he stay, the front office asks, trying to interpret every twitch on Williams' face, wondering why his quiet moods have turned into a darker moodiness.

The team is privately convinced that Williams will leave New York this winter, and, in fact, has already made up his mind to do so. The center fielder won't even say the Bombers are first in line among off-season suitors — "They're right up there" is as far as Williams would go Wednesday — which is why Brosius is now so much more important to the Bombers. It's true the organization is breathless over rookie third baseman Mike Lowell and his numbers at Class AAA Columbus this year — .304, 26 homers, and 99 RBI. But the reality is that without Williams and Brosius, the Yankees would have an instant 200-RBI deficit.

That's too much offense to re-create in one winter, even if George Steinbrenner is thinking of trading Martinez for another center fielder and luring Mo Vaughn to the Bronx. Lucky for Steinbrenner and general manager Brian Cashman that Brosius wants to return to the Yankees and, unlike Williams, isn't making the front office play 20 questions. Brosius has fallen in love with the Bombers' universe and is ready to accept a long-term deal. All Cashman has to do is pick up the phone and whisper the right dollar figure into Brosius' ear. What will it take? Brosius played cheaply this year, just $2.5 million as part of a convenient swap with the A's for Kenny Rogers. After hitting .300 with 19 homers and 98 RBI, Brosius is now easily worth $4 million, and if it weren't for the fact that he somehow finished second to Robin Ventura in the Gold Glove balloting, Brosius could claim he was the American League's best-fielding third baseman, too.

Still, even if Brosius did win the prestigious defensive award, it's his postseason work that's made him so valuable. He batted .395 with four homers and 15 RBI in the postseason, which is why one American League scout said before Game 4, "Brosius is [the Yankees'] most dangerous hitter right now," Derek

Jeter went one step further, saying the soft-spoken third baseman was "our most valuable player, period."

Brosius just blushes when he hears that praise. He's humble and polite and smiles a lot. His father, Maury, is battling colon cancer, just like Darryl Strawberry, and everyone would forgive Brosius if he were to merely withdraw from the world, even now, in October, when the Yankees need him most.

But Brosius showed in Game 3 why he's the Yankees' most devastating fastball hitter lately, and why that team-high .372 average with runners in scoring position this season was no freak accident. Brosius hit two home runs against the Padres in Game 3's 5-4 win, the second of which will be remembered as one of the most dramatic moments in recent October history.

> **"That [Yankee] team just didn't have any weaknesses. They played baseball the whole series. You just have to give them credit for that."**
>
> *— Bruce Bochy*
> *Padres manager on the Yankees*

Who will ever forget the setup to Brosius' one-on-one with Trevor Hoffman — the thundering sound of "Hell's Bells" pouring out of the PA system as the Padres closer walked from the bullpen to the mound?

If ever there was a time for a Yankee hitter to melt, it was then, in the eighth inning, with the Padres leading, 3-2, runners on first and second, and Hoffman — who was successful in 53 of 54 save opportunities this season — about to unleash his 94 mph fastball.

Brosius exhaled long and slow, then waited for a pitch "that I could drive somewhere," He swore he wasn't drawing images of home runs in his head, but Hoffman left a 2-2 fastball over the middle of the plate and … well, Brosius simply nuked it. In just one swing, Brosius made sure Lowell will wait another year. Or maybe, if Williams sulks his way into Buck Showalter's waiting arms in Arizona, Lowell becomes part of a mega-package to acquire a new center fielder.

Either way, Brosius isn't leaving. As Cashman put it, "He's sure opened our eyes," The Yankees sure love what they saw.

Friday, October 23, 1998
San Diego

Office goes back to work

By BOB KLAPISCH, Record Columnist

The postgame celebration had turned into a Yankees' personal frat party — music, cigars, alcohol, delirium — which might have explained why Brian Cashman's thin, pale face was slick with champagne. With rivulets dripping off his chin, the little general manager spent almost an hour after Game 4 hugging everyone in the clubhouse. Joe Torre offered him a fat cigar. David Wells thundered the executive's back with an open hand.

And George Steinbrenner gave Cashman the most meaningful of all votes of confidence — a simple thumbs up.

Cashman smiled and, under his breath said, "I'm enjoying all this while I can," He knows the World Series euphoria will began evaporating as soon as the final shred of confetti has fallen on Broadway, and the players fade into a long and marvelous off-season.

But while the Yankees themselves head home, members of the front office will assemble in Tampa, Fla., on Monday for the first in a series of organizational meetings. Steinbrenner has told his executives to be ready with a battle plan to keep the Bombers' World Series equation alive for another year.

One club official said Steinbrenner has made it clear "he wants answers," That won't be easy, since nearly every Yankees executive believes that Bernie Williams has decided to leave New York in his quest to earn at least $13 million a year. And if that's the case, the Yankees will have no choice but to pay Scott Brosius, another free-agent-to-be, whatever he asks for.

As is the case in most Yankees off-season strategy sessions, Steinbrenner and his lieutenants will convene in a Legends Field boardroom, and debate each player's status, one by one: Williams, Brosius, David Cone, who'll be eligible for free agency, and Chuck Knoblauch, who, because he was traded in the middle of a multiyear deal, has the contractual right to demand a trade. And then there's Darryl Strawberry, another potential free agent, but battling colon cancer.

Like every other team, the Yankees have a 15-day window to negotiate exclusively with their own players, which began Thursday, but one rival American League GM says that no matter how much cash the Yankees commit to keeping the '98 team intact, they're doomed to fail.

"It's just the nature of baseball today," the GM said. "People move on. They want more money. They want more playing time. Loyalties change. The question is how easily the Yankees accept that fact."

Actually, it seems the Yankees have been bracing for the day when Williams stands before a news conference in Arizona, a beaming Buck Showalter at his side, and announces that he's begun a second career with the Diamondbacks.

If the image hurts, at least the Yankees won't be shocked. JoeTorre went as far as to say, "If this was Bernie's last game with us, I'm glad we at least sent him away with a [World Series] ring."

Over and over Wednesday night, Williams answered questions about his impending decision — or, to be more precise, he skillfully avoided offering any real clues. Instead, he said he would go home to, "think abouteverything that's happened here this season."

Williams might just be telling the truth, torn between the overwhelming rush of goodwill the Yankees generated in 1998, and the stunning amount of money that awaits him in places like Arizona and Colorado. It doesn't help the Yankees' chances, either, that Williams is represented by baseball's most carnivorous agent, Scott Boras, and that the players association sees, in Williams, the chance to inflate baseball's out-of-control pay scale.

It's a win-win landscape for Williams; he cannot possibly take a wrong turn. Or can he? It'll be hard to forget the sight ofWilliams strolling in the outfield at Qualcomm Stadium with his wife, Waleska, at his side after Game 4, while the Yankees celebrated wildly on the field near their dugout.

Who knows if Williams was absorbing his final moments in a Yankee uniform? Or asking his wife if she wanted him to leave the Bronx? Who knows what Williams really knows?

"I think we're all wondering about that," said Cone. "None of us really knows what's in store for this team. It'd be nice to think of everyone coming back here next year, and just repeating the whole season. But it doesn't work that way."

There'll be no shame for the Yankees if they lose Williams. Or if Tino Martinez is traded for a replace-ment center fielder. Or if Mo Vaughn is lured to New York, and fashions that deep, dark stare in pinstripes in 1999.

The Yankees would have a different look next summer, but any baseball realist will embrace that evolution. Without change, David Wells would have never replaced Jimmy Key; Mariano Rivera could have never inherited John Wetteland's closer's role; Knoblauch could have never filled the void created by Mariano Duncan's departure.

And without the necessary need to change, to move on, to find happiness elsewhere, the Yankees could have never landed Scott Brosius from the A's. Instead, Kenny Rogers would still be in New York, wondering why his enormous talent shriveled in the big Stadium.

All of which is reason to take one last, long look at the 1998 Yankees. Memorize the images, all of them. They'll soon be vapor.

Tuesday, October 25, 1998

Yanks' feats far-reaching
What didn't they do well?

By BOB KLAPISCH, Record Columnist

The debate begins now and will rage as long as baseball is played on this earth: Are the 1998 Yankees the finest team the sport has ever created? Or just a very good version in an otherwise mediocre era?

Said Sparky Anderson, who managed Cincinnati's Big Red Machine in the mid-1970s — as well as the world champion 1984 Tigers: "There's no way to measure the great teams against each other, because they never went head to head. To me, though, you have to win three World Series before you can be considered part of history."

By Anderson's barometer, the Yankees are two-thirds of the way toward a dynasty after Series victories in 1996 and this year. But there's an overwhelming sentiment within the organization that this season's club — with a 125-50 overall record and 11-2 mark in the postseason — already belongs with powerhouses such as the 1927 and '61

Yankees, the '76 Reds, and even the '78 Bombers,

who won fewer games than the '98 edition but have a near-mythical reputation for October courage. But Joe Torre and Don Zimmer — who between them have nearly a century of baseball data in their memory banks — agree that none of those teams compare with the Yankees, who smoked the Rangers, Indians, and Padres in this postseason, and essentially competed against themselves after June.

"I know I've never seen a team as good as this one in my lifetime, and I won't ever again," Torre flatly said. "That's why I enjoyed every minute of this season, because I recognized early on it was a once-in-a-lifetime experience."

Zimmer — who managed the Red Sox to a regular-season tie against the '78 Yankees — agreed.

"No one in my 50 years in the game played like this," he said. "No one could stop us. Different teams tried different ways to do it, but we
    beat them all."

The Padres learned firsthand how impossible it was to contain the Yankees. Twice in the Series they had three-run leads going into the seventh inning — and lost both times. No World Series team ever had recovered from two deficits that deep, that late in the game.

Maybe that's why Padres manager Bruce Bochy finally admitted: "The Yankees had no weaknesses whatsoever. We had them on the ropes, and they came back against us. You come to a point where you have to just tip your cap and say they're one of the best of all time."

Not even Tony Gwynn could argue with that. Even before the Yankees completed their four-game sweep, the Padres outfielder pulled a reporter aside and, nodding in the direction of the Bombers, who were taking batting practice, asked, "Are they really this good?"

In some ways, yes, even better than the '61 Yankees — who unlike the '98 team — did not lead the American League in runs, despite their 240 home runs. And even better than the '76 Reds — who unlike the '98 Yankees, whose hurlers led the AL in ERA — were fifth in the National League in pitching. And even better than the '78 Yankees — who unlike the '98 Yankees — were forced into that one-game playoff against Boston just to get to the postseason. And since the '78 team didn't have to deal with the Division Series, and the League Championship Series still was a best-of-five, the '98 Yankees had to win more games in October to emerge as world champs. And certainly, it's hard to

remember the last time the World Series was so one-sided. When the Yankees beat San Diego, 9-6 and 9-3 in Games 1 and 2, it represented the first time all year any team scored nine runs or more against the Padres in back-to-back games.

The Padres never recovered. They hit three home runs off David Wells in Game 1 — and still lost. Then they handed the ball to Trevor Hoffman with a 3-2 lead with six outs to go in Game 3 — and still lost that game, too.

The Padres couldn't quite digest that one, since they were 57-0 in games when Hoffman had a chance to save them.

"We weren't used to losing games like that," Gwynn said. "When that happened, it made me realize the Yankees are as good as everyone said they were."

Finally, by Game 4, the Padres were broken psychologically. There was an inevitability to the innings as they rolled along. Sooner or later, the Yankees knew they'd win this one, just like all the others.

"I've seen many, many teams from all over the world, but this [Yankees team] is among the best, if not the best," Orlando Hernandez said. "I feel blessed to be here."

"Nothing was going to stop us," general manager Brian Cashman said. "It was an amazingly driven team, focused like you wouldn't believe. I'm proud to have been part of it, although Zim told me halfway through the summer: 'Don't get used to this, kid. You're never going to have it this good again, even you live to be 100.' "

Sunday, September 27, 1998

The laughter fades along with the hope

By ADRIAN WOJNAROWSKI, Record Columnist

There is a music to the Mets. There's laughing. There's teasing. There's chatter. There are players on the bench spitting sunflower seeds and timeless baseball cliches. Al Leiter missed hearing it Saturday. He counts on the cadence of these Mets. It makes him comfortable. It tells him everything is OK.

"This is the most emotional team I've ever been on, in terms of the kidding around, the kibitzing, talking, and jabbing," Leiter said. "There's a lot of emotion that comes with it."

Things aren't OK. This is a free fall. This is a collapse. Leiter wanted to believe his hitters could swing the bats, score a few runs and the Mets' mood made it impossible. Something is missing. Something is gone. Hope is turning to a vapor. Some players are pressing, some players are disappearing. It made every pitch the end of the world for Leiter. He had to be precise. Had to be perfect.

"I've got to be on," Leiter said. Then he said it again, slowly, so there was no mistaking his mind-set Saturday. "I've got to be on every pitch. Don't make a mistake. It's really mentally draining."

Even the Mets best pitcher couldn't save the season Saturday. He couldn't stop the bleeding. Awful tough to do it alone. He tossed scoreless ball into the sixth inning, but the Braves weren't going to stay down forever. Better believe they tried to crush the Mets. They threw Tom Gla vine, Denny Neagle, and Kevin Millwood in the 4-0 victory Saturday, three starters worth 52 wins to the starting rotation. Yes, Bobby Cox wants to play the Cubs or Giants. Yes, he wants to beat Bobby Valentine. Whatever. Want to be a playoff team, Mets? Show something. Show anything.

"We've hit a wall," Mike Piazza said.

The Mets are down a game, with one to play. The San Francisco Giants are on a dead sprint to the playoffs, the Cubs are hanging tough. Nobody expected the final days of the National League wild-card race to unfold this way for the Mets. One week, the Mets have a series for the ages with the Astros. The next, they collapse to the Expos and Marlins and Braves. All the emotion is gone, all the air is out of the balloon.

And today?

The Mets must beat Greg Maddux, the best living right-hander in the world.

The Astros must beat the Cubs, the Rockies must beat the Giants.

So this is how a dream dies, huh? Valentine issued the tired excuses inside the manager's office — line drives hit straight at outfielders, bloops unable to find green grass — and everyone is tired of hearing it. "There's something to it, but people don't care about that," Leiter said. And then he broke into the make-believe moaning of a whining player. " 'Oh boy, I gave up three runs but, gee, three of the guys hit broken-bat singles. I know I walked the one guy, but, gosh, they didn't hit the ball hard. . . .' "

His point was clear: The Mets had to stop searching for excuses and face the failure of this season's final week. This has turned into a total collapse. The Mets are trapped on 88 victories. One year ago, that total was considered a success. This time, it's a grave disappointment. Nobody told the Mets they had to win the wild card. Nobody wanted to call the season a failure for falling short. We wanted to see a fight to the end. We wanted to see the Mets go down swinging.

There's nothing left with these Mets. You can see it, you can feel it. You wouldn't like this team's chance against one of those kids the Expos and Marlins threw last week — never mind Maddux today. Once those teams embarrassed the Mets at Shea Stadium, it was hard to hear the things the Mets were telling you. Did they truly believe? Did they feel like a playoff team? What you heard were players discussing too much about the inevitable one-game playoff with the Cubs, and not enough about grabbing this final weekend around the throat and bringing back a wild-card playoff spot.

What else can Valentine tell his players?

"You don't have to close the door and have Oral Roberts deliver a message to the team," Valentine said. "Those messages have been given, if they were listening, and you can never tell if guys are listening or not."

Were they listening to themselves Saturday? There was no laughing, no teasing, no chatter. No life. Such a shame. The Mets used to live on emotion. Now, they were dying without it. The sounds of summer are gone. Can you hear it? The music of the Mets is dead.

Monday, September 28, 1998

Empty feeling for Valentine

By ADRIAN WOJNAROWSKI, Record Columnist

His belt unbuckled, his hair mussed, Bobby Valentine scribbled on a pink message pad inside his office at Turner Field. The Mets manager can show a thousand different faces. His words can be clear and cryptic. He can be thoughtful and introspective, sarcastic and smug. He's the smartest kid in the class. He wants people to remember it.

"I kept looking out there trying to figure out who it

was that could've stepped up more,"" Valentine said Sunday. He stopped short there. No list of names. He let those words settle into a room of reporters.

He wanted everyone to consider his words for a moment.

"There must have been something I could've done in the last week to win a game," Valentine said.

He had watched a season's work crumble into the coldest winter of his life. In his 1,541st game without a playoff appearance, in a September collapse, Valentine refused to deliver the blame to the feet of his players.

"The frustration is that I didn't do more," Valentine said. "Everything I tried didn't work. I should have tried something …"

Damn my players?

Damn me.

Anyone can guess about the sincerity of those statements. Even when he tries to take responsibility for an unforgivable finish, his words leave you guessing who exactly the manager considers most at fault. These five straight losses to end the season had nothing to do with the moves he made. It had to do with the state of mind of his Mets. How could they be so empty when the season was still so full of possibilities?

The Valentine resume stays incomplete. All these games managed, all the October baseball he has missed.

In eight seasons with the Rangers, the wild card didn't exist and the Oakland A's had a small dynasty. He has no excuse this time. The Mets had the pitching. They had a superstar, Mike Piazza. Sure, the lineup had holes. The Mets were imperfect. So are the Cubs and Giants, and they will play tonight at Wrigley Field in a one-game playoff to determine the wild-card winner.

Those teams don't have a starting pitcher with an ERA under 4.00. The Mets had four — Al Leiter, Armando Reynoso, Rick Reed, and Masato Yoshii. Consider the Cubs lost star rookie Kerry Wood for the final month of the season, the Giants are rickety old, and there was no mistaking the truth. The Mets were the favorite. This was the manager's time, the manager's season.

"They're still playing, so they're better," Valentine said.

It's doubtful he believes it deep down. And there's no shame there. Remember, Valentine was hired to tidy an unseemly mess. He helped give the Mets credibility again. General manager Steve Phillips has

work to do to make the Mets a true contender. It starts with signing Leiter and moves on to using the $13-14 million a year Piazza will turn down to bring more production to the Mets' lineup.

Even so, Valentine has to take his share of the blame. His teams don't finish seasons. Not with the Rangers, not with the Mets. It never reflected well on Valentine that his players refused to make him even the smallest subplot of the wild-card race. Never once did you hear one of his players say it would be nice to move him out of the record books for playoff futility and into October.

On the trail of the National League West championship a season ago, San Francisco's Rod Beck called the improbable season, "Dustiny," a tribute to manager Dusty Baker. His players lobbied hard for him to be voted Manager of the Year.

One Met — Brian McRae — suggested the disdain around the National League for Valentine was a reason why teams wanted so badly to end the Mets' wild-card dreams. As the race moved into the final weeks, one National League scout had an interesting take on the race. He believed the wild card of the wild-card race was the Giants' love for Baker. They'd play harder for him.

The Giants won nine of 11 to end the season. And the Mets, well, you watched the Mets. There was still an outside chance Sunday that they could force a playoff, and they played like they couldn't wait for school to get out. When the Mets were desperate to be crisp, they were clumsy.

Lenny Harris missed a cutoff man on a first-inning RBI double to right. Rey Ordonez didn't correctly time a leap for a bloop and fired a ridiculous throw over the reach of catcher Mike Piazza. Butch Huskey bobbled a ball in the right field corner and let Ozzie Guillen score the fifth run.

If Valentine delivered a message to his players that this season was worth fighting over one final day, they didn't listen.

Mostly, Leiter watched Valentine be Valentine throughout this slide. There was no brimstone. No desperate pleas. Whether they were winning or losing, nothing changed with Valentine. When traded to the Mets this winter, Leiter had his reservations about Valentine. On the pros and cons of re-signing with the Mets, Leiter throws Valentine into the plus column.

"I came into it very guarded because I didn't hear a whole lot of great things [about him]," Leiter said. "But I have to admit, he isn't a bad guy. He was very good to me. He's very good for the players. Half the time, you don't even know he's there."

This collapse can't be thrown to the feet of Valentine, because five losses to end the season can't override a spring and summer of smart thinking. Even so, his resume stays incomplete. All these games, all these empty Octobers. "I feel like there's something more I should have done," Valentine said. And yes, it would be something if he really believed it.

Tuesday, September 29, 1998

Rookie's sudden impact

Spencer wouldn't take shortcut to majors

By ADRIAN WOJNAROWSKI, Record Columnist

Who was Shane Spencer kidding, anyway? The Norwich Navigators used to score Yankees tickets for their off-days in the Eastern League. They hopped into cars for the easy drive down I-95 to the Stadium. Every time his teammates asked him to go, he refused. Why was he different?

Spencer plodded through six seasons of Class A ball. He had never made the 40-man roster. He never made much of an impression on management. And he refused to go on the players' trips to New York.

Someone should have told him: Take the tickets, kid. Stop dreaming.

"That was the only way for me to do it," Spencer said. "There was no way my first time was going to be sitting in the stands."

When he walked into the Stadium for the first time, he wanted to hear the clickety-clack of his spikes on the dugout steps.

There is a stubborn side to Spencer. This shouldn't surprise us. See, he isn't a kid. He's 26. He was a low-round pick out of high school, signed as an 18-year-old, and waited eight years to make the major leagues. When the Yankees finally gave him a chance, they couldn't get rid of him. When he hit his third grand slam within nine days Sunday — lifting his average to .481 with seven home runs and 19 RBI for his past 27 at-bats — his Yankee teammates

teased him on his return to the dugout. "It isn't this easy," they said.

He knows, he knows. Spencer isn't starting in left field tonight in Game 1 of the American League Division Series with the Texas Rangers at Yankee Stadium. Chad Curtis is the choice of manager Joe Torre. "He was right to go with the experience," Spencer said. "I'll be ready when they need me."

Torre had to consider Spencer, though. He's hitting .373 as a Yankee this year. He has 10 home runs and 27 RBI. All in 67 at-bats. Nobody is swinging a hotter bat for the Yankees. Here was the best team in American League history, with 114 victories, and out of nowhere, a career minor-leaguer — older than Derek Jeter, Ramiro Mendoza, and Andy Pettitte — makes New York stop cold for a few weeks.

On Sunday, Torre made him one of 25 players on the trail for a World Series championship.

On Monday, Torre said, "He can help us."

After the Yankees' workout at the Stadium, a wave of microphones and cameras rushed his locker Monday. They asked him about the possibility of playing, the pressure of the postseason. This made Spencer smile. "The pressure isn't playing here," he said. "The pressure is getting here. That's the hardest part."

A year ago, he had hit 30 home runs for Columbus and still couldn't get a September call-up to the Yankees. Two years ago, he hit 29 home runs for Norwich. There was Bernie Williams and Paul O'Neill and Darryl Strawberry and Tim Raines, and where could he find a crack to make the Yankees believe he could fit?

"He was so discouraged," his mother, Althea Olejniczak, said over the telephone Monday. "He wondered, 'What more do they want me to do?' "

Althea traveled to New York City for the first time this summer, witnessing her son go 5-for-5 for the Yankees. Seeing Shane standing on the steps of the dugout for the national anthem, she broke down. "You don't understand," Althea said to her son's girl-friend, Heidi. "These are the New York Yankees."

The mother lives in Shirley, Ark., a town of 387, not wired for cable television. She had a friend holding the telephone receiver to ESPN's "SportsCenter" on Sunday, so she could hear an interview with Shane.

"He's gone through so much to get there," Althea said. "I don't want to miss any of it."

Spencer could be an amazing story this fall. This could be the start to an improbable Yankees career.

Or it could be a cute footnote for the archives: the blond-haired, blue-eyed slugger who stole a slice of a September. That's for next year. Today, Spencer is the common man catching on late to a most extraordinary season. He's everyman chasing history with these Yankees.

The calls are flooding into his family now. Old teammates, old friends are on the line. They struggled with Spencer. They dreamed with him. "I think there are a lot of players living vicariously through me right now," he said. "I was one of those guys labeled at a young age: He can't do this, he can't do that. I should give a lot of guys hope. I know they're looking at me, 'If he can get there and do that, so can I.' I'll carry the flag for all of those guys. They're with me."

Maybe now they understand why he wouldn't make that ride down 95 to Yankee Stadium two years ago. Even when nobody believed, he had plans. He's still so stubborn.

Just this August, Torre wanted to see Spencer inside his office at Kansas City's Kauffman Stadium. The manager had bad news. Spencer had to catch a flight to Columbus. He had to go back to the minor leagues.

"Feel free to stay and take batting practice," Torre told him.

Nice of the manager to ask, but Spencer declined. He didn't belong to the team, he didn't belong on the field. He packed his belongings, left the clubhouse, and found a cab to the hotel. He never stepped foot in the stadium. "If I wasn't a part of the team," he said, "I wasn't going to take BP. When I actually see the inside of that stadium there, it'll be for the first time."

Got to do it on his own terms, got to do it his way.

Wednesday, September 30, 1998

Boomer's special season fits well in Yanks' history

By ADRIAN WOJNAROWSKI, Record Columnist

He's 20 years too late, a character belonging to the Bronx Zoo, to a clubhouse with characters and color lining the length of the room. David Wells could travel a time warp of two decades, to a different season, and fit into the fab-

ric of the insanity. Those were wild times. This is a wild pitcher.

Chris Chambliss considered the thought for a moment Tuesday and a smile slid across his face. Within two hours, Wells would be the Yankees starter for Game 1 of the American League Division Series against the Texas Rangers. The perfectly groomed, perfectly mannered Yankees give the ball to a slave of the sounds of AC-DC.

"In those days, we had a little of every personality," Chambliss said in the Yankee dugout. "We had guys like him. Yeah, Boomer loves to have fun. He'd fit in."

Walk into the clubhouse today and discover a cast considered a testament to clean living and All-American physiques. These Yankees — Derek Jeter and Bernie Williams and Tino Martinez — could pass for movie star idols, and who wouldn't want a daughter walking through the front door with one of them?

When this season is over and the Yankees are material for the time capsule, the left-hander with a belly hanging over his belt, the tattoos of family members on his arms, could be the player remembered as most responsible for a sweet summer and a magical fall. Where are the Yankees' World Series hopes without him? Andy Pettitte is a shaky No. 2 now. David Cone has the demons of '97 still lingering. Orlando Hernandez has never pitched a playoff game.

Wells is the absolute.

He is the irreplaceable pitcher for the Yankees.

Now, they believe Wells has the toughness to take his turn as the No. 1 starter for a most important postseason. For the postseason the Yankees aren't allowed to lose. For the trouble he has had in the past, nobody ever has flustered him in the postseason. This is his time. He's 3-0 with a 2.48 ERA in the Division Series. He's 1-0 with a 2.93 ERA in the American League Championship Series. When everything matters, Wells does his best work.

"I just want the ball," Wells said. "It's exciting to me. I want the opportunity to succeed or to fail if that were to happen. It makes an individual stronger being able to control the game. Some guys can't handle the pressure, but I want that opportunity."

This makes the developing lore around Wells perfectly ironic. How exactly did he thrust himself to the heart of this historic season, owner of an 18-4 record? For too long, he broke baseball hearts. Managers could see the talent, the arm, and were desperate to make a Cy Young Award candidate of Wells.

He sold himself short. This is a time ballplayers are cut of Creatine and Andro supplements. They pump iron pre- and postgame, adhere to regular regimens of running. Fitness is the new god of ballplayers, but always the devil to Wells.

Maybe it made him an enigmatic underachiever for those years with Toronto, Detroit, and Baltimore. He's toyed with his baseball life. Joe Torre hated to see it. There was a game when the Rangers destroyed him this May, hit him hard to every corner of The Ballpark at Arlington. Torre could live with Wells losing badly, but he couldn't watch him give up on the mound. Quit on the game, his team. Torre challenged him with a public and a private rip. This was long a symptom of his failures: Wells refused to show mettle, the focus to transcend good pitching into great pitching.

"You don't get irritated with someone if they get the most of their ability," Torre said. "I just felt the Boomer was cheating himself a little bit that night. He's become a pitcher this year."

Wells refuses to get deep into it, but the perfect game May 17 against the Twins transformed him. Suddenly, he had to be serious. He owed it to his talent. Owed it to his teammates. He studied for starts. He prepared. His burden was to be the Yankees stopper. It meant everything to him.

> **❝**I want the opportunity to succeed or to fail if that were to happen. It makes an individual stronger being able to control the game. Some guys can't handle the pressure, but I want that opportunity. **❞**
>
> — *David Wells*

"All of a sudden, he may have realized what he is," Torre said. "He's called a lot of attention to himself and he hasn't let anybody down."

Inside his locker the other day, Wells had a framed front of a daily newspaper, a full-color, bigger-than-life shot of him leaping into the air, his arms raised to the blue sky for the final out of the game. It is a frozen moment of summer, a frozen moment of Yankee history. One thing is for sure: He's a most unique man for an extraordinary season. Maybe Wells is right on time.

Wednesday, September 30, 1998

Boomer the type fighter needed in postseason ring

By ADRIAN WOJNAROWSKI, Record Columnist

Here David Wells used to unravel. Chad Curtis had blown a line drive to left field in the eighth inning Tuesday night, broke to the plate when he should have broken back. Wells watched Mark McLemore's shot fly to the fence for a double. His reaction was unforgiving: He scrunched his face. He waved his throwing hand to Curtis, as though to tell his teammate, "How could you?" These are the times Joe Torre understands he can lose his left-hander to his most destructive demons.

These are the times Wells used to melt down, lose his control, lose his focus. The manager made his move for the mound, his words reassuring, his question clear: Are you going to make it?

"How do you feel?" Torre asked.

"I feel OK," Wells assured him.

"Really," Torre pushed. "How do you feel?'"

The catcher, Jorge Posada, spoke up: "He's still got it."

Torre stayed with him. This isn't the season to stop believing in Wells. The manager stayed with him in the eighth. So did the Stadium fans. "LET'S GO BOOMER! ... LET'S GO BOOMER!" they screamed, desperate for him to get out of the inning, get out of trouble, get to 1-0 on the Rangers in the American League Division Series. He punched out Roberto Kelly with a fastball on the corner, his ninth strikeout. He shattered Rusty Greer's bat on a ground ball to Derek Jeter. Out of the inning, out of harm's way.

Wells watched Mariano Rivera set down the Rangers 1-2-3 in the ninth. Perfect ending to the perfect opener. Wells was magnificent — five hits, nine K's, one walk. This was his game, his time of the year. He had thrown 135 pitches. Near the end, he was tired. Near the end, he was running close to empty. Something pushes him beyond the exhaustion.

"This is crunch time," Wells said. "I thrive on it. I want to be the hero. I want to be the goat. I'm an all right pitcher, I think. But when it comes to playoff time, I get mean. I get hungry. if I don't get the ball, I get [ticked] off. I'm a fighter."

Wells fought to the end. He struck out hitters to end the second, fourth, fifth, and seventh innings. The Yankees needed to see him on top of his game. Game 1 of the Division Series was the one to deliver a statement to the Rangers, to the rest of the American League: We dominated the regular season, we're going to dominate October. The Rangers were desperate to find an opening with the Yankees, desperate for a hint of vulnerability. With Wells throwing, there was none.

The pressure was huge for him. In the back of his mind, he knew the Yankees couldn't afford to let the struggling Andy Pettitte walk to the mound for Game 2 down a game. This was the right order of things for the Yankees. Everything starts with him. Want to take a series on the Yankees, you've got to go through No. 33.

When this season is over and the Yankees are material for the time capsule, the left-hander with a belly hanging over his belt, the tattoos of family members on his arms, could be the player remembered as most responsible for a sweet summer and a magical fall. Where are the Yankees World Series hopes without him? Pettitte is a shaky No. 2 now. David Cone has the demons of a '97 still lingering. Orlando Hernandez has never pitched a playoff game.

Wells is the absolute.

He can't get enough of pitching these postseason games. He's 5-0 in the playoffs and absolutely lives for them. Here was his game day routine: Before he left for the ballpark, he listened to Metallica. On the ride, he punched AC-DC into his CD player. At the Stadium, he cranked Van Halen. Actually, he called Eddie Van Halen on Monday night. Wells told the guitarist to wear the Yankees jersey he gave him. "Send out those vibes, man."

Wells wore his Van Halen baseball cap to the news conference Tuesday night.

He shrugged and said, "Hey, I'm just a head-banger."

The vibes of the Stadium carried him, too. God, he loves this place. He loves the noise. He loves the action. He loves to be in the middle of it. Which is why the Stadium throws its arms around Wells, why it loves him back.

"They pumped me all night," he said of the capacity crowd.

Always, there's good David and bad David. You saw it in the eighth inning of Game 1, you saw it a couple of weeks ago against the Orioles. He embar-

rassed a few of his teammates — including Derek Jeter at Camden Yards, offering an incredulous stare to left field where a short pop had dropped amid three teammates. Jeter wasn't pleased. Torre was livid. He told Wells, too. Give Wells credit: Every ill-tempered episode ended with a vigorous apology and a resounding bounce back.

He swore to Curtis on Tuesday he wasn't mad at him. "If I'm out there screaming and yelling," Wells said, "it's not you guys. It's me."

The Yankees needed no apologies Tuesday night. In the end, Wells stayed cool. He stayed calm. You heard him, right? He's a fighter.

Thursday, October 1, 1998

Jeter's stature keeps growing with each hit, defensive

By ADRIAN WOJNAROWSKI, Record Columnist

Don Zimmer has watched 50 years of professional baseball, back to the spring of 1948 when Dodgertown was an old Army base in Vero Beach, Fla., and the young players slept four to a room in bunk beds. Fifty years ago, he fell for a shortstop named Pee Wee Reese. Fifty years later, he still gets goose bumps watching Derek Jeter.

Right away, when Jeter was a 22-year-old rookie in the World Series season of '96, Zimmer told manager Joe Torre: We've found a treasure. Jeter made the play of the game Tuesday night with a runner on second base, made it as easily as a man walks to the end of his driveway to gather the morning paper. He made a charging play on a slow roller in the eighth inning, reached across his body, and fired a furious throw to first for the final out.

Before Game 2 of the American League Division Series on Wednesday, Torre was still marveling over it. David Wells had run out of his good stuff, his pitch count was more than 130, but the manager preferred to make Mariano Rivera wait for the ninth inning. At his locker late that night, with ice packs wrapped around his shoulder, Wells flatly said: "[Jeter] saved the game."

"I think Derek makes that play as well as anybody," Torre said. "Maybe better than anybody.

We noticed that a couple of years ago — that was the one play he made very consistently. And [Tuesday night's play] was a lot tougher than the normal coming in on the ball because he had to go to his right first and throw across his body.

"He's got such body control for a big kid. You don't find many shortstops as tall as he is, as agile as he is."

You don't find many shortstops like him at all. Jeter is 24 going on 34. He is used to the red-white-and-blue bunting around the Stadium this time of year. He fought for a batting title to the final week of the season, hitting .324 for the year. He led the American League with 127 runs. He had 203 hits. Here's the most impressive part of his resume: Three full years as a Yankee, three trips to the playoffs. One World Series championship.

"I've been spoiled," he said.

He has played his best ball in the playoffs and World Series. It frightens people to think he isn't close to realizing his promise. Joe Morgan, the Hall of Fame second baseman, watched Jeter swinging inside the batting cage Wednesday.

"One of these days," Morgan said, "he's going to be the Yankee captain."

That would mean the world to Jeter. The history matters to him. Across sports, we get used to young players marching into the pros full of arrogance and swagger. Darryl Strawberry and Doc Gooden enjoyed similar baseball success in the Eighties, a couple of New York stars with World Series rings and appetites for destruction. Every step, Jeter has made people believe he can control the stardom, the celebrity. It hasn't controlled him. For goodness sake, he still calls his manager Mr. Torre.

Jeter is one of the centerpieces in a golden age of shortstops. This is an amazing generation of talent. At the top, there's Alex Rodriguez of Seattle, Nomar Garciaparra of Boston. And Jeter. They play the game with grace and dignity. They make people want to love the game again. They're matinee idols, out of a time when people used to learn about baseball stars on Saturday morning movie reels. The marketers trip over themselves to use these shortstops to sell the game.

"A lot of those young shortstops are hitting a lot of home runs," Morgan said. "Maybe right now, he's not going to get his due. I mean, there's Garciaparra hitting 30 home runs, there's Rodriguez going 40-40. Sometimes, people think that's better. And it really isn't. A shortstop's job is to play defense — and Jeter's better defensively than the other two. And to

hit the ball, too, to get on base."

Nobody around here is jealous of the Mariners and the Red Sox. They'll take Jeter. Before Game 2, Phil Rizzuto walked to the mound to throw out the ceremonial first pitch to Jeter. Rizzuto wore a Yankees jersey, wore No. 2. Old No. 10 for the Yankees wore Jeter's No. 2. Perfect. Just perfect.

Thursday, October 1, 1998

Another day, another believer that Spencer is 'The Natural'

By ADRIAN WOJNAROWSKI, Record Columnist

It was getting louder and louder now. Shane Spencer has heard these screams for a month. The Stadium wanted him. He couldn't think. He couldn't talk. Another home run, another curtain call. He is getting used to this noise, to these cheers. All Spencer, all the time at the Stadium now. Manager Joe Torre nodded to the dugout steps. Go get it, kid.

"Oh, gosh," Spencer thought. "Here we go."

Here we go again.

Another night, another chapter. Spencer crushed a fastball over the left-field wall in the second inning, a fastball he turned those meaty arms into and delivered 400 feet into the night. He makes a mockery of American League pitching. He makes a mockery of the pressure. He makes a mockery of 100 years of baseball logic. Career minor-leaguers don't rise out of the bushes in September to be October heroes.

"I'm just riding it," Spencer said. "I'm just trying to cherish every moment."

Now, Torre has to play Spencer. He has to play him. The Yankees are a runaway train, up 2-0 to the Rangers in the American League Division Series with the 3-1 victory Wednesday. Maybe Spencer is a vapor. Here this October, back to Columbus in April. That's an argument for the winter. Now, the Yankees need his pop. He climbed on late to this magical season, but maybe he climbed on just in time. Now, he goes to the wire with the Yankees.

They need Spencer. Darryl Strawberry has a colon infection. He needs tests to determine the extent of his illness. There are no assurances he can play in the playoffs. Tim Raines has a bum knee. Chad Curtis can't compare now.

Spencer hit the home run to make it 1-0 in the second inning. It set the Stadium on fire. Andy Pettitte owes him for it. Spencer had a hard single in the fourth inning and scored on Scott Brosius' home run. When he met a few reporters at his locker Wednesday night, a few minutes before he walked into the interview room, there was a glaze over his eyes.

Somebody asked him: What were you thinking running around the bases?

"I was a little pumped up," Spencer said.

Just a little. Sure. He has 70 at-bats as a Yankee. He has 11 home runs. It takes something to impress these Yankees. They won 114 games. They're marching into history. This is the most select fraternity in the game. And they stand there, incredulous, as Spencer walks to the plate and destroys pitchers.

"It's unbelievable to watch," Brosius said. "You've seen him do things that people who've played the games for 10 years don't do."

Suddenly, they're calling him "The Natural." People see the strapping frame, the blond hair, the booming home runs and it makes sense. This is curious to Spencer. They weren't watching the seasons — 1990 and 1991 — for Tampa and Oneonta of the Gulf Coast and New York-Penn Leagues. They weren't watching those seasons, when he didn't hit a single home run. They weren't listening when he called his mother, Althea, a year ago, with 30 home runs for Class AAA Columbus, to tell her the Yankees weren't impressed enough to make him a September call-up. The Natural never had to move mountains to get to the majors.

"That's a fun story," Paul O'Neill said. "The game has kind of slowed down when you're on that kind of roll. You need stories like this in baseball and he's living it right now."

Weeks ago, Spencer and Mike Buddie walked around the Yankees clubhouse asking each other, "Can you believe we're here?" He called his mother Sunday to tell her he made the postseason roster. He couldn't wait to tell her. News can be slow to travel to Shirley, Ark., where they can't get ESPN without a satellite dish on the roof. Even so, Althea Olejniczak found out. She had a function Sunday night at the Shirley Baptist Church and a friend found her with a telephone call.

"He was so mad I had already heard," Althea said with a laugh this week. "He really wanted to be the one to tell me."

Why not? He had shared so much frustration with her through parts of nine seasons in the minors. Just like his mother cried the first time she stepped into the Stadium this summer, it still awes Spencer. The ovations, the chants, all this September noise blows his mind.

"The people are crazy out there," Spencer said. "Thank God I'm doing good."

Thank God, all right. One year ago, his season was over and he had gone to Tampa for the Yankees fall prospect camp. He watched the Yankees Division series with the Cleveland Indians on television there. "You kind of have mixed emotions watching it," Spencer said. "You want the guys to do well on one hand, but then you're thinking too, maybe they could use me. Maybe I could help."

This time, he is sure of it. He can make a difference for these Yankees. Everybody can see it now. The calendar turns to October today. It's time to trust Shane Spencer with the most precious baseball month, with left field for the championship chase. It's time to start believing what we're seeing.

Friday, October 2, 1998

All Ledee wanted was a fair fight

By ADRIAN WOJNAROWSKI, Record Columnist

Ricky Ledee was 13 years old and vacationing in New York City for the summer. He had a couple of cousins living in Brooklyn, and they had tickets for a Mets-Astros game. Ledee was a sweet-swinging young left-hander, a star on the island of Puerto Rico, and it didn't matter to him that his Shea Stadium seats scraped the blue sky. He had come to see his hero. He had come to see Darryl Strawberry.

"He was New York baseball then," Ledee said. "In those years, he was hitting bombs and everybody was expecting him to hit a home run every pitch, of every at-bat. It was the most exciting thing."

And then Ledee shook his head with amazement and said, "Even when he'd strike out, they were cheering for the guy."

An official stopped Ledee at the Yankees' Tampa, Fla., complex Thursday morning. There was a 12:30 p.m. flight to Dallas-Fort Worth Airport and the young outfielder had to be on it. The Yankees needed him. Nobody could give Ledee a reason. What was happening? He had turned his television to Game 2 of the American League Division Series on Wednesday night, too late to hear Strawberry had left Yankee Stadium to prepare for a morning of medical tests.

He caught a cab to The Ballpark in Arlington and found his friend, Jorge Posada, in the Yankees clubhouse. Ledee asked him what was happening.

"Darryl is sick," Posada said.

So horribly sick.

Soon, the clubhouse doors slammed shut and manager Joe Torre told his players the terrible truth: Strawberry has colon cancer. The manager's voice cracked, players started to sob. This was the strangest trip for Ledee. All he ever wanted this season was to make the Yankees' playoff roster, all he wanted was to prove he belonged.

Now, he will have Strawberry's spot if the Yankees advance. The guilt washed over Ledee's face. He wanted to fight him for it. Fight him with his bat, his glove, his speed. Fight him fair.

"I really wanted to be here, but not like this," Ledee said.

God, no. Not like this. When the Yankees signed Strawberry for the first time in 1995, Ledee was a rising star in the system. The boyhood images Ledee had were gone, his icon reduced to rubble. Ledee had his doubts. Along with everyone else, he was disillusioned over Strawberry's collapse. He heard the stories of drugs and booze, the stories of domestic violence charges and felony convictions. He wondered how a man with everything could throw it away.

Before they met for the first time, Ledee braced. "I thought he was wild, that he wouldn't talk to me,""Ledee said. "It was just the opposite. He came right over to me. All of a sudden, we were catching fly balls together in the outfield."

Soon, Ledee found a comforting ear in Strawberry. He found a friend. Straw was there to offer advice, to listen, to be a friend. Strawberry had every reason to resent Ledee. Whenever the Yankees believed Ledee had developed into a major league outfielder, Strawberry would turn expendable. Ledee is one of the hot young prospects. He's a star of the system. He's the prospect general manager Brian Cashman refused to trade to Seattle for Randy Johnson. Those home runs Shane Spencer is hitting, well, it was supposed to be Ledee. He doesn't begrudge Spencer anything.

"I got my chances," Ledee said. "I can't complain."

Strawberry couldn't care less about Ledee's pedigree. Resent him? These were the kids he wanted to reach. Things were different this time. Few vices available to ballplayers had missed the darkest days of his life. So, yes, there were mistakes the kids in the clubhouse didn't have to make. It made Strawberry an inspiration to everyone surrounding the Yankees, the owner, the GM, the manager, the players. He didn't come preaching to people. He did his best work as a daily presence of perseverance.

The message was clear: It doesn't have to happen to you.

"He never used those words, but it seemed that's the thing he was trying to tell you," Ledee said. "You hear all these things about him and then you get to meet the guy. It's hard to believe he could've done all those things he did."

Around 6 o'clock Thursday, Ledee climbed the dugout steps and walked onto The Ballpark grass. Less than 24 hours away was Game 3 of the American League Division Series, everything Ledee ever wanted as a Yankee. There was the most empty expression on his face. Ricky Ledee wants Darryl Strawberry back. Wants him well. He wants to take his job all right. Always has. The kid just wanted it to be a fair fight.

Saturday, October 3, 1998

Torre adjusts to void of missing Strawberry

With the shocking news of Darryl Strawberry's colon cancer about 24 hours old, Joe Torre reverted to thinking about baseball Friday and how the absence of the powerful designated hitter-outfielder would affect the handling of the ballclub.

"You lose a weapon," Torre said before his team attempted to clinch the AL Division Series at The Ballpark in Arlington. "You don't have as much clout. But that's just the reality of this game. We started the season figuring out how we were going to [get enough playing time for all of the left fielders-designated hitters], and all of a sudden Chili Davis is out for four months. It's just something you don't dwell on, you deal with it."

Torre started Shane Spencer in left field, and the rookie responded with a home run before a rain delay. Tim Raines took Davis' designated hitter spot, a switch made because Raines entered the night 10-for-23 (.435) against Rangers starter Aaron Sele.

If the Yankees reach the Championship Series, rookie Ricky Ledee will take Strawberry's roster spot, but he doesn't figure to be in the mix for a starting spot. The 24-year-old probably would be used as a late-inning defensive substitute or possibly a pinch runner.

SO LONG, COWBOY: The death of Angels owner Gene Autry had special meaning for Torre, who spent five-plus years as a broadcaster for the team.

"He was a great man," Torre said. "When I took the [Cardinals managing job in 1990], I had to go to him to get permission, because I was under contract to the Angels. He gave me his blessing."

Torre recalled an instance in which he was sitting with Autry and Angels manager Gene Mauch before a game.

"[Autry] started saying, 'Catchers aren't the same. You don't have the Torres, the [Gabby] Hartnetts ...' And out of the corner of his eye, he was looking for my reaction."

> **"** Autry started saying, 'Catchers aren't the same. You don't have the Torres, the Hartnetts ...' And out of the corner of his eye, he was looking for my reaction. **"**
>
> — *Joe Torre*

THE WRONG KIND OF RECORDS: Entering Friday night's game, the Rangers had dropped five straight Division Series games — the last three of the 1996 series against the Yanks and the first two of this year's. That was one short of the mark held by the Dodgers, who were swept in 1995 and '96.

MOVES: Rangers manager Johnny Oates said he would consider bringing Game 1 starter Todd Stottlemyre back today, on three days' rest, if the Rangers beat the Yanks on Friday night. John Burkett has been listed as the Game 4 starter.

The Yankees will stick with Orlando Hernandez. Torre said that even if the team was in a 2-1 hole, he would have resisted the urge to bring back his Game 1 starter, David Wells, on three days' rest.

BIG DEAL? YOU BET: After winning 20 games for the first time since 1988, David Cone had time to reflect this week on a remarkable accomplishment. All along, he tried to tell himself it didn't matter if he finished with 19 or 20 victories. When No. 20 finally happened Sunday, he was a little surprised with the emotion surrounding it.

"You try to lie to yourself and say,' If you don't get to 20, you still had a great year,' "

Cone said this week. " 'You still rebounded from adverse situations.' I was going to tell myself not to let it bother me if I didn't get it. But when I did get it, it affected me much more profoundly than I thought. Part of that was just the reaction of my teammates.

"They wanted it as bad or more than I did. Especially [Joe] Girardi. You could just tell by the look on his face after the game that he wanted that one."

CASE OF THE BLUES: Umpire Chuck Meriwether was ill Friday and missed Game 3. The American League switched Joe Brinkman to the Yankees-Rangers series after the controversial ejections in Game 2 of manager Mike Hargrove and starting pitcher Doc Gooden in the Cleveland-Boston Division Series. Friday night the crew in Arlington called the game without an umpire down the right field line.

WHO TURNED OUT THE LIGHTS? A four-minute power outage wiped out scoreboards and interrupted a news conference by Torre about two hours before Game 3.

A spokesman for TU Electric said the power company wasn't sure what caused the outage that hit The Ballpark around 5:16 p.m. local time. Fierce storms hit the area all day, but it wasn't raining at the time.

Torre was in an underground interview room when the lights went out.

"I'm just kidding, Lord," he said.

With the room illuminated only by a spotlight from a television camera, Torre recalled a power outage that hit while he was in the batter's box in Montreal in the 1970s.

"The pitcher started winding up, and the lights went out," Torre said. "I took a quick backwards four steps."

PROUD PAPA: Ed Cone of Kansas City, Mo., was in attendance to watch son David pitch.

— By Ken Davidoff and Adrian Wojnarowski
The Associated Press also contributed to this report.

Saturday, October 3, 1998

Cone delivers his best when under duress

By ADRIAN WOJNAROWSKI , Record Columnist

David Cone has a capacity for closing everything out. He slips into the smallest spaces of solitude, loses mind and body in his work. He has made a memorable baseball life confounding hitters under the most extreme duress. It isn't that Cone craves a crisis. Just that he thrives within it.

Cone had the idea to embroider No. 39 on the back of his cap for his AL Division Series start on Friday. He wanted to honor Darryl Strawberry with symbolism, but did it with deed at The Ballpark. Strawberry's true presence was within Cone's heart. It was in the power of his performance.

Only the rains in the sixth inning which delayed Game 3 of the Division Series, with the Yankees leading 4-0, could stop the mastery of Cone. He pitched 5 2/3 innings and gave up two hits. He had five strikeouts. He had the Rangers off balance, guessing, closer to elimination with every pitch.

He and his teammates had watched a video in the clubhouse Friday, a message from Strawberry to the Yankees ending with Darryl pointing to the camera and imploring them: "Go get 'em." It had to ease Cone's mind to see Strawberry's smiling face in the minutes leading to Friday night's game.

"We grew up together in New York," Cone said the other day, his face flushed with fear in the visiting clubhouse. He had come out of a news conference concerning the revelation his friend had colon cancer. There was still a disbelieving distance to his blue eyes. The innocence of the old days were long gone.

He channeled his angst into a hardened resolve. Asked earlier Friday how he expected to marshal his emotions to pitch, Cone couldn't begin to tell people. His shock over Strawberry's diagnosis shook him to his core.

They hit New York together at a time when there were no limits to life in the city for a star of the Mets. David Cone was the Midwestern kid with a killer slider. Darryl Strawberry was the South Central Los Angeles kid with the sweetest stroke.

They found fame and fortune, success and sadness.

Most of all, they found a bond for life.

History was on his side Friday. Tough times, tougher Cone. Go back to the beginning, to his second year with the Mets a decade go. When a column ghost-written with Bob Klapisch during the NLCS sent the Dodgers into a furor, Cone forced a Game 7.

Go back to 1989, at Veterans Stadium, when a woman filed a bogus assault charge and Cone could see the Philadelphia police waiting for him in the runway to the dugout. He struck out 19.

Even this year, Game 3 of the Division Series wasn't the first time Cone had to pitch in The Ballpark with the specter of cancer hanging over a loved one. This spring, doctors found a mass on the lung of his mother, Joan. In May, as she waited to have it removed at Manhattan's Memorial Sloan-Kettering Cancer Center, Cone smoked the Rangers.

"It's not easy to shut out things, but sometimes [the field] is a place to hide to keep from thinking about them," Torre said.

Here was Cone again Friday, the emotions running through him like a live wire. Only 24 hours earlier, Cone was so visibly shaken. When he had to meet reporters two years ago to discuss the diagnosis of an aneurysm in his throwing shoulder, he held on to a brave face.

Somehow, it was different with his old friend. "I can identify with what Darryl is going through right now," he said. "I am sure that there are a lot of people with similar stories in their family's lives."

Across the years, Cone and Strawberry had come to consider themselves family. Perhaps nobody on the Yankees could truly appreciate the depth of change within Strawberry's life. Everyone else in the clubhouse had heard stories of the slugger's rise and fall. So much of it, Cone lived. It made the timing nothing short of insidious. Just when Strawberry had his life together, this bomb drops.

"He has always been a good person, in my mind," Cone said. "He has made mistakes, but we all have. He had come full circle. He had made a point to educate people about the problems he had, about the mistakes he made."

All winter, there were doubts Cone and Strawberry could be important players for the Yankees this season. Strawberry had 27 at-bats a season ago, and Cone's shoulder crashed in the opening round of the playoffs against the Indians. Each had a most remarkable season. Cone won 20 games, but the ending a season ago — the brutal Game 1 loss to Cleveland — chased him to Friday night. Twenty wins doesn't wash it away.

No matter how well things are going, there's a demon in the furthest reaches of his mind wondering when, exactly, his arm would break down this time. He beat back his own doubts with a magnificent performance. "Once you've got shoulder problems, you're never worry-free," Cone said. "You're always wondering the day after you pitch how you're going to feel."

David Cone had a lot to drag to the mound. He had doubt. He had fear. He had a touch of a sadness. He used everything. The Rangers were overmatched. Another time of crisis for Cone. Another night of throwing from the heart.

Sunday, October 4, 1998

Brosius no stranger to this pain

By ADRIAN WOJNAROWSKI, Record Columnist

Through the months of long talks on the telephone, the moments father and son shared at the All-Star Game and a September series at Yankee Stadium, nothing moved Maury Brosius as deeply as the images on his television Thursday. He considered the state of mind of the Yankees — the crying players, the sullen faces, the stunned sadness of New York — and realized the courage his son, Scott, the third baseman, has needed to manage this baseball season.

"You [saw] how devastated the team was, how David Cone and Joe Torre looked, how they talked about how they needed to keep going," Maury Brosius said Saturday from his home in McMinville, Ore. "And Darryl Strawberry is just a teammate. Scott lost his mother to cancer, too. I thought: 'If this affects the sports world, the city of New York, his teammates this way, what must Scott have had to face when he got that phone call from me?' "

Maury Brosius wanted to spare his son the agony in June, let him concentrate on a magical baseball season. This was the summer of his son's life. He had been traded out of last-place Oakland to the glorious Yankees, and he was in the middle of an All-Star season. The younger Brosius had worked so long, so hard to get to a year everything came together. Every step, his father dreamed with him. It made it so hard for Maury to make the call with news that doctors had diagnosed him with colon cancer.

"I wish I could've hid it from him until the season was over," Maury said. "But the truth was I needed his support."

The days and nights are brutal for Maury Brosius. The surgeons removed a softball-sized tumor from his colon, along with four feet of intestine. He is three months into a six-month cycle of experimental chemotherapy. He takes an oral dosage three times daily. He's nauseous. He's tired. He has diarrhea a dozen times a day. The prognosis for a full recovery is promising, but there are no assurances.

"He's been knocked down by the treatments," Scott said.

Every day the son goes to work with it on his mind. There was a telephone call nine years ago to Scott, to a 24-year-old in the minors in Huntsville, Ala., to tell him his mother had passed with cancer. How could his father's struggle ever be out of his mind? And yet every day, he's a professional. He sets his anguish aside and goes to work. As a No. 9 hitter he hit .300 in the regular season. He had 19 home runs and 98 RBI. He hit .400 in the Division Series sweep of the Texas Rangers, including the winning home run in Game 2.

Every day, Maury Brosius marvels.

"I know it had to affect him," he said. "I know he was scared for me. To see him continue to separate things — to see the strength for himself — it was amazing to me."

The ballgames turned into havens for Scott Brosius. Now the Yankees have a measure of understanding of his burden. When Torre told his players Thursday of Strawberry's condition, so much of Maury Brosius' phone call in June rushed back to Scott.

"There are times you're out on the field, and it's on your mind," he said. "That's natural. We live in a dream world as baseball players sometimes, outside of reality. Other people go through this, and they have to go to work every day, too."

Thank God for baseball this summer for the Brosiuses. Thank God for the game. Maury isn't so different from thousands of cancer patients. He finds solace in his love of baseball, love of his son. He watches Yankees games on a satellite. He gets on the Internet and devours statistics. When Scott made the American League All-Star team for the first time, he bought plane tickets for a couple of his college coaches, his grandfather, and Maury and brought everyone together for a weekend in Denver.

"It came at a good time for him to be able

to escape," Scott said. "For me, that's what I'll remember about the All-Star Game, the time we got to spend together."

Maury, 55, grew up in Oregon a Mickey Mantle fan, worshiping No. 7. He made his first trip East in September, watching the Yankees at Fenway Park and the Stadium. Hours before a game against the Blue Jays, with everything empty and silent, Scott and Maury walked to center field. They stood there, where Mantle used to stand, where Maury could see third base, where his Scott plays now, and he clicked his camera over and over to capture the blue-backed seats of the grandstand.

"A view most fans never get to see of the Stadium," Scott said.

They moved slowly across the green grass on that September day, just a father and son trying to hold on a little longer before the miles separated them again.

Tuesday, October 6, 1998

Revenge far from Yankees' minds

By ADRIAN WOJNAROWSKI, Record Columnist

We walk the Stadium clubhouse searching for pearls of resentment and bitterness, motivations real and imagined, searching for the Yankees to deliver diatribes on a desire to punish a punk pitcher and vanquish the memory of a Sandy Alomar Jr. home run disappearing over the Jacobs Field wall. It makes for compelling copy but a poor state of mind on the eve of the American League Championship Series. These Yankees don't need to lower themselves to the common cry of the scorned loser.

Let these pedestrian pursuits of redemption and rage belong to the October dreamers.

"We don't need anything on our bulletin boards," Tino Martinez said.

They are too professional, too driven, too locked on the true prize. They're right to be above the fuss. Nobody needs to feed motivation to them. You've been watching this season, haven't you? These Yankees have a chance to be remembered as one of the great teams of modern times. They don't need a headhunting pitcher, such as Jaret Wright, the memory of a lost October, to be the season's driving determination.

"I don't think you can create a motivation," Chili Davis said.

They aren't chasing the Cleveland Indians.

They aren't chasing Wright.

They're chasing history.

Yes, the Indians broke the Yankees' hearts a year ago. Yes, Wright broke Luis Sojo's left hand with a pitch in the spring. The magic of this season offered every reason for the Yankees to let it go. Demands it, really.

"I'm hearing so much about last year's series, and so many people in this locker room are tired of hearing about last year's series," Paul O'Neill said. "I don't think any team has an edge because we won last year or we because owe them this year. That's all a bunch of garbage."

Manager Joe Torre refuses to let his clubhouse get mired with playing this series in the newspapers. That's a distraction. The Yankees don't do distractions. Want sexy quotes on a loathing of the Indians? Stay out of his clubhouse. These Yankees are a reflection of Torre's calm and composed nature. As the Yankees moved into postseason play, the manager had a message for his players: Don't do anything different.

They're wise to heed his words. Cluttering minds with payback can manifest into counterproductivity. Better be careful to channel it or be doomed to let it devour you. Rage is perfect for a linebacker, useful for a rebounder, and perfectly worthless for a baseball player. A pitcher can throw the ball too hard, a hitter can grip the bat too tight. This is a game of control. All along, these Yankees have a been a vision of control.

"There are all sorts of methods for manufacturing motivations," David Cone said.

And all sorts of reasons why the Yankees are above it. Cone can tell one of the great modern tales of manufactured motivation. A decade ago in the National League Championship Series, Cone was the object scorn for the Dodgers. As much as the Yankees disdain Wright, manager Tommy Lasorda made sure the Dodgers disdained the Mets' Cone.

In a ghost-written column after Game 1, Cone referred to Dodgers' Jay Howell as a pitcher with a "high school curveball." Lasorda lived for exploiting those openings. He used the line to construct an "Us Against the World" mentality within the Dodgers clubhouse.

Those Dodgers weren't these Yankees. They won a World Series on the wings of emotion. They were short of talent but high on heart.

"Psychologically, any edge that you can manufacture can be useful," Cone said. "I think Tommy Lasorda probably understood that better than anybody. Nonetheless, it's still a manufactured edge. I don't know how that carries over to the game. It's tough to quantify. By the time I pitched Game 6, it was almost forgotten. And we won Game 3 after Game 2. It's hard to say."

Baseball is a game of texture. Every pitch connects to the next, every inning, every game, and every season. It makes for a rhythm. It makes for an unmistakable history. Mariano Rivera doesn't forget Alomar's home run. Cone doesn't forget his shoulder breaking down. O'Neill doesn't forget the season ending with him standing on second base. You take those moments, you move on.

"And those are things that we use to drive us through the winter to spring training," Cone said.

Cone was holding court outside his locker Monday, his usual cooperative self furthering the cause of writers reaching for story lines. Reporters were pushing him on the topic of motivation. Yes, the Yankees remembered losing to the Indians. Yes, the Yankees remembered Wright hitting Sojo. We asked him to feed the monster. So he fed it. The conviction of his words were hardly convincing.

So someone asked him about the Indians' motivation. The Yankees were four outs from the American League championship? What about Cleveland? They were winning Game 7 of the World Series in the bottom of the ninth inning. They were two outs away. Wouldn't that match the Yankees desire to destroy them?

This wasn't the argument Cone wanted.

He had to laugh.

"Look," he said, "I'm just trying to give you guys something to work with."

Tuesday, October 6, 1998

Bernie itching to snap out of skid

By ADRIAN WOJNAROWSKI, Record Columnist

Across the corridor a few nights ago, there was no champagne shower for Luis Gonzalez and Will Clark. They had done nothing in the American League Division Series, and now they had to fade into the winter. This wasn't lost on Bernie

Williams. He had gone hitless in the series. He hit the ball hard a few times, but the breaks were merciless for the AL batting champion.

As a teammate emptied a bottle over his head, Williams expressed relief. "I feel fortunate there's another series to be played," he said.

This is the privilege of playing for these Yankees. They'll cover for you. A year ago he hit .118 in the Division Series against the Cleveland Indians. He made the final out of Game 5 with the tying run on second base. This year he gets a break. This time Williams gets a chance to be an October hero.

He can forget 11 hitless at-bats against the Rangers. He gets a second chance.

"I feel like I'm close to getting my swing back," he said. "At least I'm hitting the ball hard. The only thing I can hope for is to hit the ball hard. [The slump] is not for a lack of trying."

It's crazy, isn't it? There were few lapses for Williams this season, especially across the final weeks of the season. The league batting race raged to the final day of the season, but Williams refused to let Boston's Mo Vaughn catch his .339 average. Williams had his mind locked on the ball. Everything went his way.

"I don't know [why this is happening]," Williams said. "I wish I knew. Baseball is funny. A week ago I won the batting title. I couldn't be swinging the bat better. I know I'm the same guy who got four hits the day before."

Beginning to end, he has been a marvelous model of consistency. People waited for him to get bogged down in the uncertainty of his future with the Yankees, the constant questions surrounding his impending free agent status. They waited for a lapse. Most remarkable was that it never came.

"Except for missing those few weeks with the injury," Chilli Davis said, "he stayed hot all season for us."

Now Williams gets his shot at Indians pitching. To believe they can keep him down over a long series borders on the ludicrous. He's had some unforgettable postseason series. He hit .429 with two homers against Seattle in '95, hit .467 with three homers against Texas in '96. In the five-game ALCS against Baltimore two years ago, he hit .474 with two homers and six RBI.

Nobody is more introspective when he's struggling. Sometimes Williams can think himself into trouble. And think himself out again. When the season ended a year ago, Torre was worried about Williams. The manager didn't want the final out of the Division Series against Cleveland to stay with his star center fielder through the long winter. About two weeks after the Yankees were eliminated, Torre called him.

"It meant a lot to me,"Williams said.

This season didn't have to end with Williams second-guessing his swing in Texas. The Yankees had his back in the Division Series.

"We have a tight unit working," he said. "Everyone pulls for each other. Everyone leans on each other."

The Yankees could survive early without the sweet swing of Williams, but it's sure hard to believe they'll thrive later if it's missing. Game 1 of the ALCS against Cleveland is at the Stadium tonight. Time for Bernie Williams to be Bernie Williams again.

Wednesday, October 7, 1998

Rock remains solid force on field, in clubhouse

By ADRIAN WOJNAROWSKI, Record Columnist

This was one of those seasons in the late 1980s and the Montreal Expos were struggling to stay alive in the race for the National League East championship. Every time they dropped a game in the standings, Rex Hudler found his nerves frayed. When he wanted to measure the climate of the clubhouse, he eased his ears toward the corner chair.

Hudler had to hear Tim Raines.

"We'd be on a downswing and I would come into that locker room and purposely listen for that laughter," Hudler, now a television reporter, said Tuesday near the Yankees' batting cage, "because I needed to hear it. You'd sit in your locker and listen to him cackling over in the corner, and I'd take a deep breath and say, 'OK, Hud, we're going to be all right.' "

These days the laugh resonates around Yankee Stadium, an unmistakably high-pitched cackle turned trademark for Raines. Walk into the room and guaranteed you won't miss it. There can be a corporate edge to the Yankee clubhouse, an air of professionalism befitting an IBM office. Which isn't bad. Still, this is the time of season when it doesn't hurt to hear Raines lost within a fit of laughter.

"It's a game for kids, but grown-ups are playing,"

Raines said. "It doesn't necessarily mean you're supposed to be manly all the time."

Darryl Strawberry leaves the Yankees for the rest of the season and there's a hole. The Yankees lose a little spirit, a little swing, a little toughness. Manager Joe Torre needs Raines these days. He doesn't have Straw. He can't count on Chili Davis. Where does he turn? To the man they call "Rock." Raines was the designated hitter Tuesday night for Game 1 of the American League Championship Series. Torre has had a run of hot hunches. He rolled No. 31 Tuesday.

"This seems to be his time of year," Torre said.

Raines doesn't play every day. He doesn't hit. .300 anymore, doesn't have seasons of 70 stolen bases. He's the oldest player on the Yankees, 39, and there are days he wakes up and his lower legs are killing him. Bad knees, bad hamstrings. His body is slowly breaking down. Raines is closing in on the end of his major league days. The rest of the names in the starting lineup for the Yankees are blazing the prime of their careers. His son, Tim Jr., was a draft pick of the Baltimore Orioles this spring. Raines is fighting time.

"If you watch him play, it doesn't get your attention," Torre said. "But he does a lot of things to help you win. To me, experience in a short series is important."

There's a resolute respect for Raines within the walls of the Yankee world. His teammates' love for Strawberry mirrors the love for Raines. People forget Raines had his trials, too. In the earliest days of his career with the Expos, he had to fight a drug addiction. That was a long time ago. Mostly, the Yankees see one of the great players of his generation, with 2,500 hits and 800 stolen bases, perfectly content to be a part-time player on a full-time champion.

"Your career doesn't have to end when you don't play every day," Raines said. "If you're able to get into a game when you haven't played in four or five days, and be able to contribute, I think it's special. There aren't too many players who played every day for 15 years who would be able to come to the ballpark and have to look at the lineup card to see if they're playing and be able to handle that."

Nobody's heard a complaint out of him. When the Yankees wanted to make a united stand for Strawberry on ESPN's "SportsCenter" on Thursday, they chose Raines to deliver the message on air. It was some sight. Twenty-five players standing in a sea of Yankee blue. Out front, speaking for everyone, was Tim Raines.

"I think it's good for the other players to see some-one who's been around for 18 years," Raines said. "I think a lot of these guys are amazed at the way I handle myself, what I do. I'd say I'm a leader in that guys look up to me. They look at me sometimes to give them a smile. They look at me sometimes to give encouragement, to have someone to lean on."

Some things don't change for Raines. His body aches, his speed is gone. Doesn't matter, really. He can still swing the bat, still play with the heart of a champion. All these years later, too, his manager notices something else. Something that has never changed. "When he isn't in the game," Torre said, "his giggle gives him away."

Wednesday, October 7, 1998

Bombers' Juggernaught leaves Indians cowering

By ADRIAN WOJNAROWSKI, Record Columnist

Those Yankee muscles rippled in the cold air Tuesday night, short sleeves and strong arms bashing balls to the reaches of the Stadium. Bell rings, the carnage commences. The Indians watched the smug smile of Jaret Wright disappear under an avalanche of Yankee fury. This was one of those messages the Yankees love to deliver to dreamers. Those doubts you feel festering deep down? They're justified. You aren't worthy of us.

How do you think the Indians feel this morning?

The Yankees reached for the Indians' heart in Game 1 of the American League Championship Series, several sucker punches to the punk pitcher of the Indians, leaving him battered and bewildered. Here's your ace, Cleveland. Go down and stay down. Yankees 7, Indians 2. Wright was dismissed with a humbling walk to the dugout and a couple of questions to ask himself: Will I get a chance to throw again in this AL Championship Series? And do I want one?

He can't be alone on the Indians.

All of them have to be asking themselves: What in the world is it going to take to beat the Yankees?

"We've got to keep going in that situation," Jorge Posada said. "We can't let him off the hook like we did last year. We scored three runs and then we

didn't score anymore. You've just got to go and get him out of the game."

How do you think the Indians feel this morning?

This is the relentless nature of these Yankees. Once they start coming hard, hope they'll have mercy. Chuck Knoblauch and Derek Jeter start the first inning with singles. Paul O'Neill and Bernie Williams get run-scoring hits. The Stadium is standing, it's screaming. The Yankees had the Indians cowering in the corner. Had them taking shots to the body, shots they couldn't answer. There were six hits, a walk, a wild pitch, and five runs.

"The message to the fans was unbelievable," David Wells said. "They deserved that. They hold grudges more than we hold grudges. I don't know how to say it. ... To see Jaret go out in the first inning was gratifying."

The Indians appeared aghast that the Yankees were considered such strong favorites for this series. They finished 25 games under them in the standings and still the Indians strutted into the Stadium with an unmistakable mantra: Don't belittle our chances. They'll be lucky to get out of New York with a shred of belief, let alone a victory to make the series 1-1.

This was one of those instances the Yankees tested the boundaries of reasonable belief. Whatever the questions, they answer them. Prior to Game 1 on Tuesday, there were two overriding issues for the Yankees: the slumber of the top of the order and the dominance of the young Indian pitcher. They struggled with the Rangers. Wright had four victories within 12 months over the Yankees.

What happens?

The top of the order — Knoblauch to Williams — had seven hits and two walks Tuesday.

Wright?

Before he gets three outs, he gets a shower.

The Indians watched the Rangers stumble 27 innings with a single run in the Division Series. Now, it's 36 innings. Just three runs. Wells was wonderful. Crushing the Indians wasn't enough for him. He had thrown eight shutout innings and Manny Ramirez hit a two-run, ninth-inning home run into the upper deck. It made him seethe. It wasn't enough for Wells to beat the Indians, he wanted to bury the Indians.

"My fault," Wells said. "I threw the damn ball."

His own standards are scraping the sky these days.

When the series with the Indians turned a season ago, there was an unmistakable feel to it: The Indians crushed the Yankees closer, Mariano Rivera, with a Sandy Alomar Jr. home run in Game 4. Break a closer, break a team's back. The momentum changed. The series belonged to Cleveland.

This time, it was the Indians starter, Jaret Wright. How do the Indians like their chances to beat the Yankees four times when the ace can't get three outs? Posada was right. The Yankees made a fateful mistake a year ago. The Yankees touched him for three runs in Game 2 of the Division Series, but let him stay in the game and fight for a victory. This time, there was no mercy.

The Indians couldn't score a run until the game was virtually over in the ninth inning.

How do you think the Indians feel this morning?

Maybe somebody needs to tell them they can come out from under their beds now.

Thursday, October 8, 1998

Knoblauch's reaction gums up works

By ADRIAN WOJNAROWSKI, Record Columnist

Chuck Knoblauch was a stunning and solitary figure of foolish defiance, his finger pointing to the baseline, his mouth screaming injustice. The throw to him at first base hit the Indians runner, Travis Fryman, and rolled away with Game 2 on Wednesday. "Get the ball!" his teammates screamed. "Get the ball!" He couldn't find the ball, Knoblauch said. He couldn't stop the winning run.

So he blew a bubble.

Huh?

He snapped his gum and blew a bubble.

"I didn't have any idea where [the ball] was," Knoblauch said.

Here was the problem in the 12th inning: Knoblauch wasn't looking for a baseball. He was looking for a fight. "He was yelling at the umpire," manager Joe Torre said. "You can't do that. You've got to make the play, then go argue with the umpire."

As Knoblauch refused to reach for the ball, insisted on pleading his case, the Indians' Enrique Wilson made the turn around third. He slipped. He stumbled. He was practically begging Knoblauch to get the ball and make a play. Begging him. When Knoblauch finally stopped his crying, he scrambled to the ball but his throw home was too late to get Wilson.

"I passed first base, saw the ball 30 feet away and

everybody with their hands in the air," Fryman said. "It surprised me that they were standing around looking for a call."

The best regular-season team in American League history doesn't do self-destruction. They don't go down screaming and yelling, with Knoblauch insisting on a different ruling with a runner rounding the bases, with Torre cursing the strike zone and the system used to assign umpires to the playoffs.

The Yankees faded into folly to end Game 2 of the American League Championship Series. The strapping, surging, rip-your-heart-out Yankees were reduced to an insufferable sea of excuses.

Suddenly, the Indians have life.

Suddenly, this is a series.

The Indians pushed the bully boy Yankees back. After the humiliating loss of Game 1, this was a monumental victory for Cleveland. When the Yankees were falling apart, the Indians made a move for home and a 4-1 victory.

Knoblauch walked to the plate in the 12th inning. The boos crashed around him. He deserved every one. This isn't hard. It isn't. These interpretations can be debated forever. Was the bunter, Travis Fryman, running out of the baseline? Should there have been interference? When the play was over, this was a fair argument for the Yankees to bring to home plate umpire Ted Hendry. When the play was over.

"That's fans," George Steinbrenner said in the clubhouse. "That's New York. I wish I had a nickel for every time I get booed."

He does, huh? Added together, maybe he could use it for the $9 million a season extension he's promised Knoblauch. The second baseman is considered one of the brightest players. Remember Game 7 of the '91 World Series between the Twins and Cardinals? When a ball was ripped into a gap on a hit-and-run play, Knoblauch confused the runner, Lonnie Smith, who had his head down, into thinking the ball was a routine grounder to second base. Knoblauch made a phantom scoop and throw to the base, making Smith slide.

The ball? It was rolling to the wall. Smith never scored the run. The Twins won the game. They won the Series.

This is the Knoblauch the owner of the Yankees believed he was getting with the off-season trade. In a season of triumphs, he's been a glaring disappointment. He ought to do himself a favor and think long and hard about signing his name to a contract to stay a Yankee. Bad enough he made that play Wednesday, bad enough he was 0-for-6, bad enough he's 2-for-21 in the playoffs. This postseason is a window into his mediocre season with the Yankees.

The Yankees have asked him to shorten his swing, stop shooting for the fences. They've asked him to be more aggressive on the bases, but his steals were cut in half to 31 this year. Look, he had a marvelous career for the Twins. This season had to make one thing clear about Knoblauch. He could be one of those players unfit to thrive in New York.

And, never once, could Knoblauch simply say: "My fault. I messed up." That's all. Don't stand there and tell the fans you couldn't find the ball when 57,000 at the Stadium could see you weren't even looking for it. Just say it. "I blew it."

A lot of us backed Steinbrenner this winter when he refused to give Bernie Williams an $11 million a year contract. That's a bargain now. Want to give Knoblauch $9 million a year for hitting .265, well, Williams has every right to set his starting price somewhere around $13 million. Imagine if the Yankees end up giving salary to Knoblauch they could've used to keep Williams? It would be unpardonable.

Seasons turn on these plays. Careers, too. Now, the ALCS turns to Cleveland for three games. The Indians stole one Wednesday. Absolutely stole one. Knoblauch needs to pray the Yankees get out of the series alive. Get out with a World Series berth.

Because they'll always remember the ball rolling away, always remember Chuck Knoblauch as a solitary figure of foolish defiance, smacking his gum and blowing a bubble. Blowing it big.

Friday, October 9, 1998

All isn't forgiven

Knoblauch's confession a day late

By ADRIAN WOJNAROWSKI, Record Columnist

Chuck Knoblauch walked out of the training room Wednesday night, turned the corner into the middle of the clubhouse, and locked his eyes on his locker. He found rows of reporters fighting for position. He stopped for a second and whispered, "You guys waiting for me?"

Knoblauch wanted to play the innocent. Who?

Me? Six months as a Yankee and he still didn't understand anything about New York. When fans wanted to hear an admission of responsibility — guilt isn't the word — for letting the winning run score in Game 2 of the AL Championship Series as he argued with an umpire, Knoblauch insulted everybody's intelligence. Couldn't find the ball. Wasn't my mistake. Wouldn't change a thing.

So Thursday, Knoblauch walked into the interview room at Jacobs Field with the appearance of the kid whose mother sent him back to the corner store to apologize for lifting that candy bar.

"I screwed up," Knoblauch said. "I screwed up the play, and I feel terrible about that."

His apology was entirely too neat — well-worded, well-timed. Maybe it came from the heart, but you had the idea it came with a little push, too. Even so, Knoblauch swears he made the decision to issue the mea culpa on his own. No pushing, no prodding. Long before the papers hit the streets and WFAN turned into hate radio, the Yankees charter had touched down in Cleveland, and Knoblauch and his wife, Lisa, retired to a downtown hotel room. When he had a chance to watch the replay, he says, the guilt washed over him.

Suddenly, the defiance was gone. Maybe it was a day too late, but make no mistake: Knoblauch had the appearance of a humbled man.

"He's been broken in," David Cone said. "He's no longer a virgin. He's a true Yankee now."

Even so, it doesn't end the ordeal. The scarlet letter goes on his chest now. These are the rules. He goes into a purgatory of baseball infamy. Does he end up Bill Buckner — branded for life with a Red Sox World Series loss? Or does he end up Brant Brown — paroled with a Cubs wild-card playoff berth? We'll find out fast. The Yankees and Indians are 1-1 moving into Game 3.

"People are going to remember that play for a long time, depending on what the outcome of the series is," Cone said. "If it so happens that if we lose the series and that play is looked to as a defining moment, he'll have to live with it."

When Brown dropped the fly ball to cost the Cubs a game in the final week of the season, Yankees manager Joe Torre felt for him. He hoped the Cubs made the playoffs to save Brown's good name. Now, Knoblauch needs the Yankees to cover for him — like they've done most of his disappointing season. If the Yankees lose the series, there's no salvaging Knoblauch's New York reputation. An All-Star talent goes into a perpetual state of shame.

"You don't want somebody labeled like that," Torre said. "Sure I'd like to win for reasons other than that, but that would be a great eraser for this whole thing. … Certain people like to put labels on people, and it's unfortunate when you've had a career like Bill Buckner. Brant hasn't had that career yet, and Chuck is still in the middle of it.

"I'd hate for someone to be remembered for something negative when his career has been good."

Knoblauch needs help. He needs the Yankees. He is wound so tightly, one of those players with the veins constantly popping out of his neck. He doesn't relax. He doesn't let down. After a monumental mistake, the culture of the clubhouse is to tease a player with an X-rated barrage of wisecracks.

Holding the ball and arguing with an umpire, Cone let two Atlanta runners cross the plate in a 1990 loss. He remembers his merciless Mets teammates roasting him on the flight home.

Things were different Wednesday night. Maybe the playoff loss was too raw. Maybe the players were deferring to good taste with wives and families on the charter flight.

Mostly, they left Knoblauch alone.

"He was a stand-up guy [Thursday]," Cone said. "And that opened the door for guys like [Tim] Raines to get on him a little bit, poke some fun at him, and keep him loose."

He could use the ribbing. He could use a laugh. Knoblauch has won a World Series. He has made All-Star teams. He doesn't need the organization to lecture him. People are tiptoeing like he had a death in the family, whispering words of encouragement into his ear. When he walked into the clubhouse after his news conference, Mariano Rivera told him, "I'm with you, bro," and tapped his fingers on Knoblauch's chest. "You've got a heart. This is what it's for."

Players have been arrested for beating wives and blowing paychecks up noses and never had to withstand the firestorm of fury surrounding Knoblauch.

He hasn't committed a crime. He let a ball roll on the ground, argued with an umpire, and caused a run to score in a baseball game.

He apologized Thursday. Right thing to do, wrong time to do it.

"When I go out [Thursday] and leave this room, there won't be any added pressure on me,"

Knoblauch said.

He wishes he could get off so easy.

Saturday, October 10, 1998

One man always sticks with Pettitte

By ADRIAN WOJNAROWSKI, Record Columnist

In a different season, nobody picks apart Andy Pettitte's performances this way, but the standard for the Yankees starting pitchers was a string of startling success stories. David Wells had the perfect game. David Cone had the comeback season. Orlando Hernandez had the magical debut. Hideki Irabu had a stirring redemption. When things were so smooth for the Yankees, the machine pumping victories on an assembly line, there were few instances the manager had to protect one of his pitchers.

Things were different for Pettitte. The doubt chased him out of the 1997 American League Division Series debacle against the Indians and right to this month. This was the season fans were searching for the sure thing with the Yankees, the guaranteed ticket to glory, and Pettitte couldn't be counted on for it. Always, Pettitte could count on Joe Torre to remain his strongest supporter.

"I've always appreciated people who've had faith in me, trust in me," Torre said. "Playing this game, I think the best way to look at it is to pick up the press guide and see what people do over the course of the season. For me to change my mind on Andy on account of what he's done in a half a year is not fair to him, especially with what he's given us. He's already proven that he's won big games."

When Torre gave Pettitte a Game 2 start in the Division Series against Texas, made him the starter for Game 3 of the AL Championship Series on Friday night — setting him up as the possible Game 7 starter — those telltale Pettitte victories were on Torre's mind. History counts for Torre. Pettitte made a world champion out of his manager two years ago.

Pettitte is his man. To the end.

"The first year I got there, in 1996, he beat Baltimore in a couple of games in a big series," Torre said. "Then he goes out there and wins Game 5 of the World Series. You can't win a bigger game than that. To do what he did in Game 5 will stay in my memory bank, and the only thing that will change that is if something changes dramatically with him."

There's a line Torre loves to use to describe Pettitte: "He has a bellyful of guts."

Part of the reason Torre believes so fervently in Pettitte is the passion for perfection he brings to his pitching. People mistake his easy Cajun twang for a dismissive, easygoing disposition. They're wrong. The way Paul O'Neill obsesses over his at-bats, Pettitte obsesses over his pitching. Nobody is harder on himself. Torre has made a point of never wavering with his support of Pettitte. When things were bleakest, Torre wanted the left-hander to understand he was going to give him the ball. Still send him to the mound.

For the final month of the season, as Pettitte struggled to a 16-11 record and 4.24 ERA, it seemed to him fewer and fewer were on his side. He needed to know his manager was on his side.

"He made me feel very comfortable with the situation going into the postseason, even though I was struggling," Pettitte said.

Said Torre: "I think the common thread is Andy's striving for perfect all the time. He's never satisfied with what he sees. We may be satisfied. And we have been satisfied over the last three or four appearances [of the regular season], the way he's thrown the ball. His stuff is as good [in that time] as it's ever been this season. He's never satisfied with himself.

"The perfect game would be the only thing."

Maybe that should have silenced the doubts over Pettitte, but they're surfacing again in Cleveland. This was a return to his darkest days of the '97 season, where Manny Ramirez crushed a two-run double in Game 5 of the Division Series to effectively end the Yankees season. Pettitte swore that wasn't on his mind for this series, but he is human. The Indians owned him a year ago.

> **"** I think the common thread is Andy's striving for perfect all the time. **"**
>
> *— Joe Torre*

"I just remember the 0-2 pitch to Manny," Pettitte said the other day. "I had him 0-2."

Pettitte was so cool for so long this season. He never gets defensive over his struggles. He is calm. He is polite. And yet something was simmering inside Pettitte after Game 2 of the Division Series. He had thrown seven innings of one-run, three-hit ball. For everybody doubting him, Pettitte offered a few veiled words of resentment. He wanted people to know the faith his manager had in him was justified.

Always, that was the one Pettitte could count on.

Sunday, October 11, 1998

No room for fear for this Bomber

By ADRIAN WOJNAROWSKI, Record Columnist

In a few hours, Orlando Hernandez had an appointment to rescue the Yankee season in the middle of a throbbing Jacobs Field, but here it was Saturday afternoon and he raised a glass of water for a toast to himself. "Buena Suerte," he said in the stillness of the Marriott restaurant. Good luck. The magnitude of Game 4 wasn't lost on him, but Hernandez insisted on staying true to his routine.

He disappeared into the kitchen for several minutes to select the thinnest strands of spaghetti. He planned a two-hour nap, a cup of espresso within 30 minutes of walking to the mound. Everything had to be right. Mostly, he talked and laughed free and easy, a most unruffled member of an increasingly edgy Yankee entourage. Just listening to his lunch guest tell the story, you got the idea Hernandez was a portrait of composure.

An assured Joe Torre happened to pass by the restaurant and noticed his rookie.

"He asked me how I was feeling," Torre said.

This was the Yankee season Saturday in Game 4 of the American League Championship Series. To go down 3-1 to the Indians had to be considered an act of self-mutilation. The threat of a Yankee collapse pushed David Wells to march into Torre's office and offer to pitch on three days' rest Saturday, and again Wednesday for a possible Game 7.

There was no need for Wells. Hernandez was perfectly fit for his shot to stop the Yankee bleeding. Hernandez saved the season Saturday, throwing seven innings, scattering three hits, and striking out six for the 4-0 victory over the Indians to even the series, 2-2.

"Hernandez," Torre said simply, "was spectacular."

Now, Hernandez hands the baton to Wells for Game 5 today. Now, the Yankees are back on course for destiny's World Series.

Near the end of lunch, his guest suggested to him he had to stay calm Saturday night. Hernandez offered an incredulous look, one that intimated, "Are you kidding me?"

He was right. Nothing confounded Hernandez. He doesn't have experience pitching in the cold, doesn't have experience pitching in the playoffs. Hernandez couldn't care less. Asked about the toughest game of his life before Saturday night's big challenge, El Duque said, "The biggest game I ever pitched was jumping on the boat and leaving Cuba."

Hollywood owns the rights to the story now. One year ago, he watched the playoffs on a small black and white television inside his Havana apartment. He watched his half-brother, Livan Hernandez of the Marlins, strike out 15 hitters in the National League Championship Series. He watched him raise the World Series MVP trophy to the sky. The tears streamed down his cheeks.

As he watched his half-brother, the one called El Duquito — Little Duke — mesmerize National League hitters, a most frightening realization washed over him: Would his immense talent rot on this decaying island?

Now, the world watched him in the middle of Jacobs Field. Now, they could see the magical El Duque. Even so, he had a few scares Saturday. Still he survived.

Jim Thome crushed a fly ball to the wall with two runners on in the first inning. In the sixth, the Indians had two runners on base with one out. He struck out Manny Ramirez with a sidearm fastball. And with Omar Vizquel dancing on third base, trying to fluster him, trying to make him make a mistake, Hernandez struck out Thome.

"We're playing for our lives out there tonight, and nothing affects him," Paul O'Neill said.

One of his childhood idols, Doc Gooden, whose exaggerated leg kick Hernandez emulates, lost for the Indians. As Hernandez befuddled with his body's confusing contortions and changing points of release and pitch location, the hitters were forever guessing. When the Yankees needed him the most, he was downright dazzling.

"I had pressure, but no fear," Hernandez said.

Be assured the beleaguered people of Cuba were following the game closely.

"Most [Cuban] people are Yankee fans," Livan said this summer on a visit to the Stadium. The pulls of Cuba are still strong for him. He had to leave two daughters with his ex-wife on the island, and it constantly eats away at him. He had been several minutes late to a Stadium workout Sunday and was upset that some reports portrayed it as an act of unexcused tardiness. He wished someone had asked him about it. There is a strict window of time he can call his daughters.

In one moment, Hernandez can speak with a measure of regret about his daughters. In another, he can speak about the endless possibilities as a major league pitcher. Emotions of adulation and despair are constantly running through him.

Over lunch Saturday, he told a story about the New York City police recently pulling him over in his 1998 vehicle for speeding, only to escort him to the Stadium upon discovering the driver was the indomitable El Duque. Amazing how fast a man's life changes.

Sometimes, Hernandez can't help the speeding. Freedom can do that to you. Suddenly, there are places to go. "In another two weeks, I could get rid of [the truck]," Hernandez said.

He was thinking of buying a '99 model.

"I believe 1999 is going to be a great year," Hernandez said.

Friday, October 16, 1998

First-year Yankees savoring the moment

By ADRIAN WOJNAROWSKI, Record Columnist

Every few seconds, Orlando Hernandez breathed smoke into his lungs and let a smile wash over his face. The look on his face asked, "Is this really happening to me?" A glance around the clubhouse Tuesday night confirmed it.

As he blew rings of smoke with a Cuban cigar that a friend sent him for his birthday, he stopped to consider the spraying champagne, the championship trophy, the live television shot across the world, and said no, he had never witnessed a thing to match the moment. He had won Olympic gold medals and amateur world championships, but El Duque had a look of amazement like a kid seeing snowflakes for the first time.

"We never celebrated like this," Hernandez said after the Yankees advanced to the World Series with a 9-5 victory over the Indians in Game 6 of the American League Championship Series. "We won many championships [in Cuba] but never partied like this. We celebrated, but not with any champagne. We had beer, rum … and a lot of happiness."

Just one year ago, there were several Yankees absolutely unaware they could be a part of an

American League championship and a chance to win a World Series. Scott Brosius was on a loser with Oakland. Chili Davis was going nowhere with Kansas City. Chuck Knoblauch couldn't wait to get out of Minnesota. Shane Spencer and Ricky Ledee were at Class AAA Columbus, and October plans called for an extended season at the Yankees' headquarters in Tampa, Fla.

Amazing how a year brings everyone together. How it changes everything.

Hernandez is the most improbable story. One year ago, he was forbidden to play for his national team, relegated to a job as a physical therapist. He watched on television and listened on radio as his half-brother, Livan Hernandez, helped pitch the Florida Marlins to the World Series championship. Months later, El Duque climbed into a small boat and risked his life for freedom. This postseason, he might just have saved the Yankees' season with a brilliant Game 4 victory over the Indians.

In the middle of the clubhouse celebration Tuesday, in the middle of the madness, he was asked: Could you ever have imagined, a year ago, standing here, seeing this? He took a long drag on his cigar. "Nooooo," he said, letting the word drag. "It was impossible."

It was different for Davis. He had his free agent status. He had the chance to play for a winner. Time was running out. He had won a World Series with the Minnesota Twins in '91, but hadn't been back to the postseason. "This was my last chance to get one," Davis said. "That's what this was all about for me. I had done all the individual things I wanted to do. But I wanted to win. I knew coming here, I was going to be part of a team able to do that."

Now, he goes into the World Series against the Padres as the Yankees' hot-hitting designated hitter. He missed most of the season with an injury, but finally it seems Davis is turning into the power threat the Yankees wanted when they signed him.

"It's nice," Davis said, "to finally get a chance to contribute."

Brosius hasn't wasted his opportunity this year. His trade to the Yankees was a starting over for him. He had the best year of his baseball life — hitting .300 with 19 home runs and 98 RBI as the ninth-place hitter in the order. He hit a three-run homer in Game 6 of the ALCS that pushed the Yankees to a clinching victory and a World Series berth.

"Last year in Oakland," Brosius said recently, "there were games at the end of the season where you could practically count the people in the stands. You could

hear everything they yelled at you. It gave you the feeling you were playing a Triple-A game. I've appreciated everything about this year, about being here."

And then there is Knoblauch, the former All-Star second baseman brought to the Yankees as a missing link to the World Series championship. He struggled this season. All across, his numbers were down. And then in Game 2 against the Indians, he made a mistake for the ages — arguing a call with an umpire as the go-head run scored in the 12th inning. The Yankees rescued his New York legacy with the ALCS victory, a fact Knoblauch could hardly miss in the aftermath of the Yankees' celebration Tuesday night.

"They picked me up," Knoblauch said. "This is what it's all about."

Friday, October 16, 1998

A lost Indians' summer

Rosen remembers epic collapse

Giants sweep in '54 Series made 111 moot

By ADRIAN WOJNAROWSKI, Record Columnist

The telephone calls have trickled into Al Rosen's California home this year, questioners asking him to remember a baseball season 44 years ago. How did it happen? How did it slip away so fast? Even now, he sometimes stops to consider it.

"You never get over it," Rosen said.

The 1954 Indians set an American League record with 111 regular-season victories, a mark that stood until these Yankees won 114. When the Indians strolled into October, most expected a World Series championship over the New York Giants. Then, suddenly, everything was over so fast: The Giants beat the Indians, four games to none.

"Even now," said Rosen, the third baseman on that team, "those four days are an absolute blur. It all happened so fast."

There was no Division Series, no League

Championship Series. The Indians, unchallenged for the American League pennant in September's final days, walked into an October massacre, a World Series loss most remembered for Willie Mays' over-the-shoulder catch on a Vic Wertz drive to deep center field at the Polo Grounds.

Rosen watched these Yankees this summer. He has his own ties — relationships with Chris Chambliss and Willie Randolph, to name a few — going back to the late 1970s, when he and Gabe Paul constructed the core of two world champions. Many of the '54 Indians admit to it: Bob Feller, Larry Doby, Herb Score. That AL record for victories mattered to them.

Those Indians are a good lesson for these Yankees. They're asked every day: How will history remember the Yankees if they fall short of a World Series championship?

Here's the answer, Rosen reports: People hardly will remember the successes.

"In '54, we had several Hall of Famers," Rosen said. "We had a terrific ballclub — great pitching — and yet the '54 Indians are remembered, in a lot of ways, for getting beat four straight by the Giants. And you can't feel very good about hearing that."

Maybe for Indians fans, with so little to cheer for so long, they hold '54 a little closer to the heart. Rosen knows New York enough to know things are different here. During the celebration over the League Championship Series on Tuesday night, Rosen listened to the words of Chili Davis, and it dawned on him one of the profound differences of Yankees expectations compared with other teams.

Davis, with the Yankees for the first time at 38 years old, was a little awed to see there are no banners for Division Series and League Championships hanging in the Stadium. Everywhere else he has played, every postseason success is commemorated with a visual reminder.

"And it struck me when Chili noticed: 'They only hang World Series championships here,' "Rosen said. "Getting to the World Series is one thing. But if you don't win, it's devastating. But I think it's entirely different circumstances between us and these Yankees. The Yankees stayed battled-hardened with the playoff series. I always felt that the teams who had to battle all the way through have the edge. I think they're in much better shape going into the Series than we were."

It's funny, this Yankees season. Maybe people would think those Indians of '54 might resent this team coming along with a 162-game schedule and banishing them from the top line in the AL history book. Except it isn't so. For so long, the '54 Indians were remembered for something they didn't do — win a World Series.

As the Yankees moved closer to the 111-victory record, it seemed, the Indians were celebrated again for what was a most amazing accomplishment. For what they did do.

"All of us fortunate enough to still be living reveled in this summer," Rosen said. "We talked now and again about it. We remembered doing something that hadn't been accomplished before [in the AL] — winning 111 games."

Before Rosen hangs up the telephone, he hesitates a moment and says to a reporter across the country, "Thanks for calling. It's always nice to be remembered."

1954 WORLD SERIES BREAKDOWN
Indians vs. Giants   Giants win Series, 4-0

GIANTS 5, INDIANS 2 (Sept. 29 at New York) — Tied at 2 in the eighth, the Indians put two men on for Vic Wertz, who sent a 440-foot rocket to center field. Willie Mays, with his his back to the plate, made a running catch and flung the ball back to the infield, preserving the deadlock. In the bottom of the ninth, pinch-hitter Dusty Rhodes cracked a three-run homer off Bob Lemon.

GIANTS 3, INDIANS 1 (Sept. 30 at New York) — Rhodes burned the Indians for the second time in two days, poking a pinch-hit single in the fifth to knot the score at 1. With the Giants clinging to a 2-1 margin in the seventh, Rhodes clubbed a solo home run to seal it. Johnny Antonelli scattered eight hits for the win.

GIANTS 6, INDIANS 2 (Oct. 1 at Cleveland) — Rhodes continued his assault with his third pinch hit of the Series, driving in two runs with the bases loaded in the third to make it 3-0. Trailing, 6-0, the Indians got a run in the seventh and the eighth before Hoyt Wilhelm retired the final five hitters, preserving the win for Ruben Gomez.

GIANTS 7, INDIANS 4 (Oct. 2 at Cleveland) — The Giants produced the National League's first World Series champion since 1946 by pounding Lemon, Hal Newhouser, and Don Narleski for seven runs in the first five innings. The Indians got three in the fifth and one in the seventh against against Don Liddle. Wilhelm and Antonelli closed out the final 2 1/3 innings.

Friday, October 16, 1998

Bombers skipper always a class act

It's hard to root against Torre

By ADRIAN WOJNAROWSKI, Record Columnist

There was a perfectly priceless moment, in the AL Division Series, when Frank Torre waited for his younger brother, Joe, inside the manager's office at Yankee Stadium. The Yankees had beaten the Rangers in Game 1, the march to the World Series was under way. Two years ago, the brothers visited in the hospital room where Frank was waiting for a heart transplant. Joe walked into the room, reached down, and hugged him.

This time, Joe found Frank waiting on the couch inside his office. Frank climbed to his feet and reached for his little brother. "This time," Frank said, "I'm going to hug you standing up."

This is Joe Torre. He isn't afraid to hug. He isn't afraid to feel. He isn't afraid to tell those stories and let everyone inside his world. He is still the Catholic school kid out of St. Francis Prep in Brooklyn, who behaves like the sisters are watching him. Everything about his job, his public life as the manager of the Yankees, he handles with the softest of touches.

Everybody knows Torre better this time around, as the Yankees bid for a second World Series title in three years. Tommy Lasorda cultivated a persona when the red light on the television camera was on. When the world was watching, Lasorda was glib and charismatic. Turn the light off, Lasorda could be a crude and vulgar bully. America had rare occasion to see the essence of the man.

After three division championships, two pennants, and a World Series title, we've taken a good long look into the window at Torre. Here's the amazing part: We like him even better.

Torre isn't afraid to take a playful jab at George Steinbrenner.

He inserts rookie Ricky Ledee into Game 6 of the AL Championship Series, when Ledee hasn't played an inning for the Yankees in weeks, and explains it this way: "Why not?"

When the Yankees clinch the AL East at Fenway Park, he whispers to David Cone to make sure the Yankees celebrate in the clubhouse — not on the field. He doesn't want to embarrass the Red Sox.

He breaks down and cries telling his players Darryl Strawberry has been diagnosed with colon cancer.

At one of his news conferences this week, a reporter asks why he hasn't played Tim Raines in left field. Except Torre had played Raines. It was a stupid question. Torre could've humiliated the man. Instead, he laughed. "You were watching football yesterday, right?"

Every day, there is a different vignette. Across the country, people are resentful of these Yankees. They used to disdain the arrogance, the swagger, and they almost get mad because there's nothing to get mad at anymore. Torre doesn't stand for it. The clubhouse is a reflection of his calm, reasoned disposition.

If Torre wins his second World Series in three years — and all of us agree these Yankees go down as one of the great teams in baseball history — how much closer has his resume inched to Hall of Fame status? As a player, he wasn't a Hall of Famer. A .297 career average, 252 home runs, and an MVP award isn't enough. Two World Series championships as a manager aren't enough.

All together, though, Torre delivers one of the most accomplished baseball lives of our time. Few others have transcended playing, managing, and broadcasting at the highest levels of accomplishment. Nobody would've dared consider this a decade ago, but the complete work of Torre could make him a candidate for the Hall of Fame.

There were whispers Torre had designs on marching out of New York as the conquering hero this month, slipping the second World Series ring onto his finger, and retiring to the broadcasting booth. The network television executives are desperate to get him on the air. He could make a cool $1 million a season as an analyst. When he worked in the booth for the Angels several years ago, he developed a reputation as one of the best in the game.

Yet Torre isn't done managing. Isn't even close. He has agreed in principle to a two-year contract extension. After all the years overseeing mediocre talent, he has his hands wrapped around some of the best talent ever assembled. He can't walk away now. This run isn't over. The Yankees still have a magnificent core — even if they lose Bernie Williams to free agency — and there is no reason to believe Torre has to be done managing championships.

And after all these years, all these managers, how could you get used to anybody else on the Yankee bench?

Saturday, October 17, 1998

Bernie may become leaver of the pack

By ADRIAN WOJNAROWSKI, Record Columnist

The Yankees walk the clubhouse carpet and wonder with everyone else. Who stays? Who goes? This was on the mind of Chad Curtis a month ago, so he tried to do his small part to hold the Yankee monolith together. He handed a small gift to Bernie Williams for his 30th birthday. He waited for the center fielder to open the box.

Williams had to take a moment to consider the gesture.

A pen?

"To sign with," Curtis said.

Even in the middle of the wild success of this season, the end of this Yankee run never strayed too far from the players' minds. Everybody could have a good time with the uncertainty surrounding Williams — dropping jokes to ease the tension — but suddenly his future is too raw a nerve to tweak.

He isn't alone. Who's staying? Who's going? The delicate chemistry in the clubhouse could dramatically change this winter. Most of the speculation centers around Williams, but there is a possibility Andy Pettitte and Tino Martinez could be playing for their Yankee lives in the World Series. Scott Brosius and David Cone are free agents. Assuming his recovery, the Yankees must make a decision on exercising the option year on Darryl Strawberry's contract.

This is the nature of the game today. Change is the true constant. Our nostalgia for teams used to cover decades, but now we measure championship runs with a core of talent in shorter doses. This is a golden age for the Yankees, a three-year sprint under manager Joe Torre. This World Series could be the victory lap.

And that fact isn't lost on these Yankees — even if they've been able to set it away in the deepest reaches of their minds. In a quiet moment recently, Cone took a long look around an empty clubhouse and said: "This could be the last one. This could be the last run. Who knows what our team is going to look like next year? Who will be back? Right here, right now, is what it's all about."

As the Yankees stand on the Stadium grass for the national anthem tonight, take a long look yourself:

There's no reason to believe the Yankees won't be standing here next October, but it's possible we'll hardly recognize them. Mo Vaughn could take Martinez' job. Al Leiter could take Pettitte's spot in the rotation. Anything is possible.

"The mission statement never changes," general manager Brian Cashman said. "The mission statement was the same in 1981 as it was in 1998, same it's going to be next year. If we win it, as soon as we take a shower to wash the champagne off of us, we'll be doing the things to chase it again next year."

As Williams slowly distances himself from his teammates in the playoffs — flying separate from the team charter, not taking part in the AL Championship Series champagne celebration — the doubt the Yankees can hold onto him grows with every passing day. He has turned moody and distant. Whatever is isolating Williams — a personal problem, organization officials say — it is making these possible final days as a Yankee sad to watch.

Everywhere else the Yankees could lose a player, they believe they can upgrade the talent. Williams is different. Who gets center field? Unless, they make a trade, it goes to Curtis, one of the players urging him to stay. Williams has been careful to keep his intentions to himself. The more the Yankees believe he is willing to walk, the more negotiating leverage he keeps. And nothing is so daunting to management as giving agent Scott Boras leverage.

"We want Bernie to stay," Cashman said, "but there is no mandate to do it."

What Cashman is saying is: There are limits to our love for Williams. If a bidding war is what Williams wants, he's likely done as a Yankee. People watched him grow up with the Yankees, watched him come of age. Williams has the corner locker for the Yankees, a symbolic space reserved across the years for Don Mattingly and Ron Guidry. The status of the stall carries clout in the clubhouse. People watch his every move.

"When I came up here it was incredibly different than it is now," Williams said. "Guys didn't seem to be as concerned with winning, or even losing, as they are now. They were worried about themselves, about what they were making, about whether they'd be here next year. Winning was a complete afterthought.

"Not everyone was like that, but enough were that it was a lot less fun coming to work then than it is now. Plus, as a young player, it was hard to get comfortable. I never wanted another young player to feel that way again."

These Yankees are human. They think about tomorrow, but they've never let go of the precious present. Williams won a batting title, his Yankees won 121 games and counting. Who's staying? Who's going? Slowly, it's pecking at the Yankees. No longer is it a laughing matter.

Williams talked for several minutes Friday at the corner locker, and finally, somebody asked him about the possibility of this World Series as his final lap with the Yankees. "I'm going to have fun," Williams said. "I'm going to let it all out." And with those words, he was done talking. Agitated and restless, he marched across the clubhouse carpet and disappeared through a door. Game 1 of the Series tonight at the Stadium. Just remember to take a long look at the Yankees. Here today, gone tomorrow.

Sunday, October 18, 1998

Knoblauch, Martinez get their redemption

By ADRIAN WOJNAROWSKI, Record Columnist

They delivered redemption with a most remarkable drama, Chuck Knoblauch and Tino Martinez chasing October demons with swings of sweet salvation. This is the magic of the World Series. One glorious swing and festering failures fade away. Knoblauch and Martinez on Saturday: One shot to break even, one shot to break out.

Here were the Padres preening over the undressing of David Wells in Game 1 of the World Series, hearing a stone-cold silence of Yankee Stadium and without notice, without a hint, Knoblauch and Martinez hit balls over the wall. Suddenly, there were 56,712 fans screaming, stomping, singing to the sky, and once again, the Yankees have delivered a shot to the heart. Once again, the machine rolls closer to destiny.

How did it turn so fast for the Yankees? And how did it turn with Knoblauch and Martinez? For these two beleaguered Yankees, a little luck and a lot of perseverance. They caught lightning in a bottle — a Knoblauch three-run homer to make it 5-5, a Martinez grand slam to make it 9-5 en route to a 9-6 victory — and they own a moment for the ages.

Does it matter Knoblauch refused to chase the ball in Game 2 of the League Championship Series? Does it matter Martinez was hitting .188 for the Yankees in

the postseason — one home run and five RBI in 96 at-bats — prior to Game 1 of the World Series?

All is forgotten, all is forgiven.

Yankees 1, Padres 0.

One shot to break even, one shot to break out.

"We got into the World Series, so once we get to the World Series the redemption is there," manager Joe Torre said. "There is nothing they can blame on him [Knoblauch] other than having a little blackout. If you try to make up for every time you strike out with the bases loaded, every time you make an error, you wouldn't be able to walk. Us getting to the World Series was a relief for everybody. We didn't want anybody to walk around with that burden."

Knoblauch and Martinez were hitting a combined .167 in the postseason. Once, Knoblauch was a World Series hero with the Twins. Things had changed with the Yankees. Things took a turn for the worst in the playoffs. All of us, we hit him hard. Knoblauch and Martinez have locked themselves in the practice cage the past few days, swinging bats and offering support. They worked together.

"Tino and I have been trying to pump each other up," Knoblauch said. "We've been in the cage the last couple days together, trying to help each other out. I was happier for him when he hit his home run. I was sitting on the bench, saying, 'C'mon Tino … Come on … This is it.'"

They were in the interview room Saturday now, sitting side by side, two Yankees with no more need for apologies. "When Chuck hit his, I ran out on the field as fast as I could," Martinez said.

The improbable seven-run seventh inning chased away the residue of Wells' absolute unraveling. He was downright dizzy. He watched the balls leave Yankee Stadium with a fury in the fifth — a Tony Gwynn shot to right, a Greg Vaughn shot to left — and suddenly the most invincible Yankee was stripped naked for the world to see. It was a merciless beating. The invincibility of the Yankees had been rendered a vapor. The World Series wasn't 90 minutes old and already the Yankees could feel the momentum rushing across the field to the Padres.

The Padres sucked the life out of the Stadium on Saturday night, a fifth inning that left Wells in a daze. He was a broken pitcher Saturday, and nobody seemed ready for it.

Suddenly, Saturday turned so silent. All the noise, all the rage, all the October energy, was vaporized. There was this sinking feeling that somebody shot the Stadium with a stun gun.

Finally, the Yankees made the Padres turn to the bullpen in the seventh. Kevin Brown had been tough, but he hadn't been untouchable. Jorge Posada singled to right. Ricky Ledee walked. Two on, one out. Padres manager Bruce Bochy made his move for Donne Wall. The whole Yankee bench breathed easier. The Yankees were between Brown and closer Trevor Hoffman, and against the Padres, this means there's a chance.

"Anytime you can get a starting pitcher out of the game it's a good thing, especially when it's Kevin Brown," Knoblauch said.

So Knoblauch wrapped a fly ball around the left field foul pole and a made a maddening sprint around the bases. The Stadium couldn't get louder, could it? We found out a few minutes later, when the bases were loaded, and Martinez crushed a fastball out of the park, that yes, it could get louder. It could get wilder. We found out this Yankee season never stops surprising you.

So there it was Saturday night, Chuck Knoblauch and Tino Martinez asked to the top of the dugout steps for curtain calls at the Stadium. How did this happen?

One shot to break even, one shot to break out.

Most of all, one down for the Yankees.

Sunday, October 18, 1998

Wells has gone soft next to Padres ace

By ADRIAN WOJNAROWSKI, Record Columnist

The rage used to consume David Wells. Always a nasty pitcher, he could be a nastier man. He could be a miserable teammate — swearing, stomping, once so angry at his Blue Jays manager for taking him out of a game that he fired the ball into left field. Where did he go soft? Where are the street fights outside bars in San Diego? Where are the threats to owner George Steinbrenner for a fistfight in the Yankee clubhouse? Why doesn't he invite Mark Fuhrman to the clubhouse anymore?

No longer does he get into trouble. What, a prediction on Howard Stern? Those are the lame headlines Wells makes now. He clings to movie stars and rock-and-rollers, embracing the establishment with his growing celebrity. Now and again, a Yankee will

make an error and Wells will shoot a nasty look his way. And then he'll practically call a news conference to apologize.

Wells is still wild. He still loves to stay out late and blast his Metallica in the clubhouse until his teammates scatter to the calm of the lounge and there's nobody left but him.

> **"**He did it in Houston the first game we won. He just gave the team a sense of confidence that, 'Hey, we can do this.' **"**
>
> — *Bruce Bochy*
> *on Padres pitcher*
> *Kevin Brown*

But nasty? Nobody can call him that anymore. He can't touch Kevin Brown. The Padres pitcher never cared to reform his renegade image. The beauty of Brown is unfettered: He is still sinister. He is one bad dude.

Brown walked to the mound with every drop of venom for a monumental Game 1 of the World Series on Saturday night at the Stadium. Kevin Brown vs. David Wells. The balance of the Series hangs on these power arms. Neither the Yanks nor the Padres wanted to be down a game this morning, without a chance for their ace to throw again until Game 5.

"This could be a more significant Game 1 than usual," David Cone said. "Especially with these two aces. If San Diego gets one with Brown, they'll say: Why not both?"

If the Yankees are going down, Brown will have much do with it. He struck out 16 hitters to beat the Astros and Randy Johnson, 2-1, in the National League Division Series. He threw a three-hit shutout at the Braves in the NL Championship Series. The Yankees can expect him for Game 5 in Qualcomm Stadium and available for relief in Game 7. All this with a 12-3 lifetime record against the Yankees.

Brown has a score to settle with the Series. You won't hear him say it, but he was 0-2 with an 8.18 ERA for the Marlins a season ago against the Indians. Brown has a vendetta with October. He didn't go to sunny San Diego, see the wispy waves, feel the warm breezes, and turn into a teddy bear. He goes to the mound to rip your heart out. So does Wells. Except when Brown isn't pitching, he still wants to rip your heart out.

"I guess I'm not much of a fun-loving guy on the day that I pitch," Brown said.

Padres pitching coach Dave Stewart had an unforgettable snarl on the mound for the Oakland A's. Just that look made hitters cower.

Here is Stewart on Brown: "Mine was intense. Kevin's look is crazy. Sometimes, he does look a little crazy out there. I wouldn't know what a serial killer looks like, but he has sort of a little smile on his face."

It isn't just game days. He stalks the clubhouse, his eyes as tight as slits. Nobody bothers him. Nobody gets in his way. "I don't talk to him," Stewart said.

There was the time at Padres training camp that he scared a rookie out of a seat on the bench without uttering a word. "Kevin just looked at the guy and he went — whoosh — moved right over," Tony Gwynn marveled.

Another time, the Padres bus was trapped behind a line of cones at the airport. The bus driver was stuck. He couldn't move. "Just run over them!" Brown barked. A security guard charged onto the bus. Brown exploded on the poor man and sent him away with a visceral diatribe. When the Padres bus was lost one night in Montreal, he paid a man $20 to call the beleaguered bus driver a nasty word.

"That one got him a standing O," Gwynn said.

Manager Bruce Bochy loves the toughness Brown has brought to the Padres clubhouse. He brings a belief that this team can do anything. "He sets the tone," Bochy said.

"He did it in Houston the first game we won. He just gave the team a sense of confidence that, 'Hey, we can do this.'"

Yes, David Wells used to be a little nasty. Now, he saves it for the mound. Part of it is the policing of the Yankee clubhouse. They won't stand for too much trouble.

After Wells pitched his perfect game this summer, he wanted the Yankees to have more than a memory of it. He had Balfour design a commemorative diamond-lined ring for the baseball personnel. General manager Brian Cashman has a Yankee World Series ring, but the one Wells designed for him is something else. "It's the most beautiful baseball ring I've ever seen," Cashman said.

Kevin Brown must think that's so nice. His teammates, they just need to remember to stay out of his seat in the dugout and everybody will get along fine.

Monday, October 19, 1998
New York

Ledee savors his moment in spotlight

By ADRIAN WOJNAROWSKI, Record Columnist

He had his baby boy bobbing on his lap for Game 1 of the Division Series, the TV flickering inside his apartment in Tampa, Fla. Ricky Ledee had gone to the minor league camp with an instruction to stay sharp. He considered it the cruelest tease. Deep down, Ledee didn't believe he was working out for the World Series. He believed he working out for spring training.

"I didn't think that I was going to be back," Ledee said Sunday.

His name on the lineup card for Game 1 of the World Series on Saturday night, Ledee approached manager Joe Torre and told him, "Thanks."

Thanks? Yes, thanks.

Ledee never expected to be with the Yankees in the World Series — never mind seeing his name in the starting lineup — and he wanted to express his gratitude. The kid doesn't pretend to be the toughest rookie in the room, doesn't believe this is owed him for eight years of minor league service.

He watched most of the Yankees season as a player for Columbus of the International League.

"Because of the season they were having," said Ledee, "we saw ourselves playing the whole year in Columbus."

Now, he gets to live the best part of the Yankees season. He gets to live the Series.

When Game 1 was over and Ledee had a two-run double and a hard single off the Padres' Kevin Brown, he was asked his state of mind stepping to the plate for the first time in the Series with one of baseball's nastiest pitchers staring him down.

Ledee couldn't lie.

"He scared me," Ledee said.

Nobody could tell. Maybe Ledee is playing with house money these days. Everything is happening so fast for him, there is no time to consider the magnitude of the moment. He made his second straight start in the Series on Sunday night, and had a single, an RBI, and a walk — on base seven straight times to start the Series — until the Padres finally retired him. He ripped a second-inning single into right field and an RBI double to chase Ashby in the third.

Once Shane Spencer started swinging the bat for the Yankees, Torre couldn't get him out of the lineup. Now there is no getting Ledee out of the lineup.

"We all have our chances," Ledee said Sunday. When it was Spencer, these were his words, too. Now, it's Ledee's turn.

He swallowed hard upon hearing the news of Darryl Strawberry's colon cancer. He hasn't stopped expressing regret over getting to the Series on Strawberry's bad fortune. This should be the time of his life, but Ledee is a sweet, sensitive 25, and the reason he's here — a tumor within Strawberry — is troubling to him.

He was asked Sunday: Do you still feel guilty sometimes?

"[I do] a little bit," Ledee said. "I really wish that Straw was here. But at the same time, I wish that I was here, too. Kind of mixed emotions."

He started these playoffs watching on TV in Florida and could end them with a parade through the Canyon of Heroes. Which is so amazing considering he was sure the power swing of Spencer made the postseason pass him by in September. It had to be troubling for Ledee. He had always been considered the better player, the better prospect. One month changed eight years.

"It bothered him," Torre said.

The Yankees refused to trade him for Hideki Irabu, Chuck Knoblauch, or Randy Johnson. Actually, the opportunity to leave should have been tempting for Ledee. Nobody would have blamed him. He signed with the Yankees as a 16-year-old outfielder, and he has s watched careers come to the Yankees system to die, bony skeletons lining the walls of the Columbus clubhouse.

"I didn't want to go," Ledee said. "I always said that. Even when they were going to trade for Knoblauch, I talked to my agent and I told him, 'I know I have no vote in this, but I don't want to go.^'I kind of knew I was going to be in the minor leagues [with the Yankees]. And if I was traded, I knew I'd have more chances to make the majors. But I wanted to stick with the Yankees."

Maybe it's harder here. He has discovered New York is worth the trouble. He rounded the bases after Knoblauch's home run in the seventh inning Saturday, and it seemed the noise rumbling down into the Stadium could carry him home.

"You could just feel all the people exploding," Ledee said. And again Sunday he had the Stadium

standing and screaming for him.

Yes, Ledee loves Strawberry. As a kid growing up, he was one of Ledee's idols. This didn't change as a Yankees prospect. Strawberry always had time for Ledee. Sometimes he offered advice. Sometimes he offered encouragement. Sometimes Strawberry offered something as simple as a reassuring smile in a strange and intimidating clubhouse.

When Ledee walked into the Yankee clubhouse at The Ballpark in Arlington two weeks ago, he plopped on a stool outside his locker and quietly said, "I wanted to be here, but not this way."

It was still on his mind this week. When Ledee thanked his manager for a chance to play in the Series, Torre made sure to remind him, "You've earned it."

If he didn't believe it then, Ledee believes it now. All the guilt ought to be gone. He belongs.

Tuesday, October 20, 1998
San Diego

Tough guys become San Diego chickens

By ADRIAN WOJNAROWSKI, Record Columnist

The Padres organized a rally in the parking lot of Qualcomm Stadium on Monday and the general manager, Larry Lucchino, stumbled on stage searching for a Padres cap. The organization's elder sounded meek and vulnerable, challenging a couple of thousand fans to "Kill the New Yorkers with kindness," and the people cheered his words, and this had to be the lamest October moment.

They're so nice. They're so sweet. They're lambs marching into the butcher's grinder. The fans danced into Qualcomm Stadium chanting "Keep the Faith … Keep the Faith …" and the Padres owner and general manager screamed into the cool, sun-splashed sky. Is this all they can do here? Is this all the humiliation they feel?

This wasn't supposed to be so easy for the Yankees. The Padres have to be willing to fight to the ends of the earth for the World Series, and they whimpered out of New York bruised and battered, a pitching staff with the flu bug and a general manager flustered and flailing in the Stadium stands. They're a sad and sorry sight staggering into Qualcomm Stadium for Game 3, down 2-0.The timing is perfect for the Yankees to roll into town and destroy them and lay claim on a sweep. San Diego is so rattled. Tony Gwynn walked into Yankee Stadium for Game 1 of the Series and marveled at the history and lore of the Yankees. It made him consider the miserable plight of the Padres. "Our history," Gwynn muttered, "is Kurt Bevacqua hitting a home run and blowing kisses," Two games into the Series, the disparities of these two towns, these two teams, are embarrassingly exposed.

Will the Padres ever make a stand? Has to happen tonight — or they're a mere footnote in the Yankees march into history. Let the Yankees come out with one of these endless first innings on Sterling Hitchcock — who has beaten Randy Johnson, Greg Maddux, and Tom Glavine this postseason — and the Padres could crumble. It isn't impossible to believe they can make a stand — not with Hitchcock and Kevin Brown throwing Games 3 and 4, and the shakiness of David Cone and Andy Pettitte in their

> **❝** Keep the Faith. Kill New Yorkers with kindness. **❞**
>
> — *Larry Luchino*
> *Padres general manager*

final starts of the Cleveland series. Man, it's doubtful. For somebody to stop these Yankees, they had to be a most merciless cast of players. It takes a toughness to beat the Yankees. Takes a will. The Yankees are so relentless, so deep. All we heard about these Padres was the toughness, the edge, the so un-SoCal ferocity of the Padres. Where are the Padres' tough guys? Where's Kevin Brown? And Ken Caminiti? And Jim Leyritz? All tough guys, all unafraid of the Yankees. Now, it's time to see it with the Padres. They've made toughness a baseball commodity in San Diego. Now, the Yankees have bullied the Padres to two Series losses at Yankee Stadium, and the world waits to see the Padres push back.

"We're going to have to go home and see if we can find a way to do what we want to do," Gwynn said in the quiet of the Padres clubhouse late Sunday night. "Right now, the Yankees are doing what they want to do. Right now, it doesn't look good from our standpoint. You give up nine runs in each of the first two

games of the World Series, it's hard to expect to win. We've really just got our butts kicked."

On the warm, breezy Saturday night of Game 1, Sammy Sosa lobbed a baseball to catcher Joe Girardi for the ceremonial first pitch.It seemed the pitch sailed across a summer of 70 home runs, 2,632 consecutive games played, sailed across the most magical baseball summer in memory, belonging to Sosa and McGwire and Ripken, and landed in the October destined to belonged to these Yankees. The script seems to be coming together.

All of us watching these Yankees, watching an unforgettable season, wanted teams and moments to measure them. The Rangers could do nothing. The Indians fought harder. Now, it's the Padres. They destroyed the Braves and swaggered into New York with a lot of big talk about big plans to take down the Yankees. So far, it's a big laugh.

Now the Series turns to San Diego, turns to a town still deciding whether it even wants major league baseball anymore. They stood in a parking lot Monday, chanting "Keep the Faith," listened to the Padres bosses tell them to "Kill New Yorkers with kindness," and all you could do was laugh and wait for the slaughter of a most unworthy opponent to end.

Wednesday, October 21, 1998
San Diego

Strong at the plate, stronger in the heart

By ADRIAN WOJNAROWSKI, Record Columnist

Scott Brosius had dreamed this a thousand times, in those backyard Wiffle ball games in McMinnville, Ore., one chance, one swing, one moment to make him a World Series hero. As the Yankees moved into October, those days were on his mind. How does this happen? How does this unfold? His old man, Maury, had watched the Yankees with reverence in the Fifties, one of the truest Mickey Mantle fans living in the Northwest. Amazing how dreams collide. Amazing how everything comes together.

Brosius had to smile Tuesday night, his arms folded on an interview room podium. "I'd done it a hundred times in my back yard," he said.

Maury used to be throwing the ball in the back yard

and Tuesday night in Game 3 of the World Series, he watched from the field level box seats. And in the eighth inning, he watched Scott hit his second home run of the game, a three-run shot to the deepest reaches of center at Qualcomm Stadium, to overtake the Padres. He watched his son pump his fists to the sky, a smile screaming across his face. Just like he used to see in the back yard, where all the dreams started for Maury and Scott.

The father has colon cancer. He is undergoing chemotherapy, in his third of six months of treatments. He was too weak to fly to New York for Games 1 and 2, but there was no way he was going to miss this 5-4 victory, moving the Yankees within a game of the World Series championship.

"It feels good having him see it," Brosius said. "It's good that he can stop thinking about real-life things for a little while and enjoy the dream."

The Yankees are going to win the World Series. They can thank themselves for it — the top of the roster, to the bottom — but isn't it something to imagine a .200 hitter for the miserable Oakland Athletics a year ago — a player Yankees scout Ron Brand urged the front office to take in a trade. All he's done is hit .538 in the World Series. All he's done is push this team closer to the brass ring.

They blared AC/DC over the public address system with one out in the eighth inning. Here came Trevor Hoffman. Here came the hammer. Manager Bruce Bochy had watched his bullpen do terrible damage to the Padres in Games 1 and 2, and this time, he was going to bring Hoffman into the game before it was too late. Hoffman saved 53 games for the Padres, and when he stands on the mound — 6 feet 5 inches of arms and legs — his is one of the most imposing figures in the game.

So "Hell's Bells" rocked Qualcomm, 64,667 moving to the music, towels waving into the night, everyone so sure the savior had come to slay the Yankees. Across three seasons, the Padres were 181-0 holding a lead into the ninth inning. Brosius wouldn't allow the Padres to take their lead into the ninth inning. He took the World Series MVP award and flipped it into his back pocket.

Tino Martinez had a magnificent at-bat setting the stage for Brosius. Before finally walking, he made Hoffman throw 10 tough pitches. You could see Hoffman getting tighter with Brosius. He bounced two balls to Brosius. Pitching coach Dave Stewart could see the invincible Hoffman suddenly so fragile. He walked to the mound to calm Hoffman. Tell him this was his stadium, his game, his time. Except this season belongs to the Yankees, except this Series belongs to Brosius.

This has been an unreal season. When he hears shortstop Derek Jeter calling him the most valuable player on these Yankees, Brosius blushes. Before the Yankees started to call him an MVP this season, before the rest of us grew to marvel at the acrobatic third base plays, the clutch hitting, he was someone else's MVP — the old Mantle fan, Maury Brosius.

He had to call his son 3,000 miles away and tell him he had colon cancer. He wanted to spare his son the pain, but Maury had to tell him. "But the truth was I needed his support," Brosius was a rock for his father this season. Through the diagnosis, the chemotherapy, they had some unforgettable times this summer. They visited the All-Star Game together, walked the outfield of Yankee Stadium, where Mantle used to roam, and finally Tuesday night, Brosius delivered the Yankees to the doorstop of the world championship. God, he was glad his father was here to see it.

> **"**It's good that he can stop thinking about real-life things for a little while and enjoy the dream. **"**
>
> — *Scott Brosius*

"He's amazed me all year long," Tino Martinez said. "Great clutch hitting. Whenever we've needed him to come through, he has."

When word hit the Yankee clubhouse that Darryl Strawberry had cancer, Brosius' father was across the country ever more impressed with his son. "You looked at how devastated the team was, how David Cone and Joe Torre looked, how they talked about how they needed to keep going," Maury Brosius said a couple of weeks ago. "And Darryl Strawberry is just a teammate. Scott lost his mother to cancer, too. And I thought, 'If this affects the sports world, the city of New York, his teammates this way, what must Scott have had to face when he got that phone call from me.' "

For one more night, anyway, Maury Brosius could forget he was a sick man. He watched his son run around the bases pumping his fists and laughing and smiling, for a moment they were in the back yard again in McMinnville, where they dreamed this dream all those years ago. Together.

Thursday, October 22, 1998

San Diego

The ultimate victory

By ADRIAN WOJNAROWSKI, Record Columnist

They scrambled to the mound and threw themselves into a confusing tangle of arms and legs, these Yankees ending a most amazing journey wrapped in the safe and sure embrace of history. One by one, the Yankees rushed to Mariano Rivera — from the outfield, the bench, the bullpen — and dissolved into laughs and screams and tears.

All for one, all for history.

And right in the middle was Andy Pettitte. Just days ago, he had rushed to the bedside of his father, Tom, in the intensive care unit of St. Luke's Hospital in Houston, where he had undergone a triple bypass. All Pettitte did was throw 7 1/3 innings of scoreless baseball Wednesday, beating the Padres, 3-0, for a sweep of the World Series.

Everything raced through his mind Wednesday night — the boy, Jared, he and his wife nearly lost at birth this summer, his father, his season of struggle on the mound and off it. "I tend to think of the bad things instead of the good things," Pettitte said.

When it was over, all the bad was washed away.

Everything ended right for Pettitte. Everything ended right for the Yankees. His father was released from the hospital Wednesday, able to watch Andy's brilliant performance on television. He was able to watch the game to eliminate the doubt over the Yankees standing in history. Greatest ever? Greatest ever. Beginning to end, the Yankees were a runaway locomotive, 125-50, and they ought to be remembered as the greatest team in history. They'll remember these Yankees as a fluid, seamless team, an assembly line of unending production.

"We have to take a back seat to no one in my lifetime," Joe Torre said.

Moments after Derek Jeter poured a bottle of champagne over George Steinbrenner, the owner declared: "There's never been a greater team. No team ever had to play under the pressure these fellas did."

Every loose end had been fastened for history with the Series sweep of the Padres. From Pettitte to Chuck Knoblauch to Tino Martinez, there wasn't a Yankee with a reason to believe he wasn't an intimate part of the World Series champions. Everyone. All year, this clubhouse had been a bastion of grace and dignity, of grown-ups going to work every day with a vision for victory. As the Yankees poured into the clubhouse, they let loose like school children out the door for summer vacation. The burden the Yankees had to make history was replaced with the euphoria of actually doing it.

Suddenly, David Wells screamed, "This one is for Straw," and soon there was a chorus of "DARRYL … DARRYL …" screamed wall to wall. And then they could see Scott Brosius gathering his MVP trophy on the stage across the room, and now the Yankees turned into the right field Bleacher Creatures at The Stadium, chanting "SCOT-TY BRO-SIUS … SCOT-TY BROSIUS …"

Across the room, he tipped his cap and bowed, and the Yankees roared again. Now, Torre was fighting his way through the crowd, stealing swigs from a bottle, soaked with a champagne shower.

Moments earlier, as Martinez gloved the final out, Torre reached for his trusted associates, Don Zimmer and Mel Stottlemyre, the coaches wrapping themselves in a long slow embrace before racing to middle of the field.

He loved these players. When he believed his baseball life was winding down, these Yankees delivered him a second World Series championship in three years. They moved him into the pantheon of New York coaches, Parcells to Holzman to Stengel. Now sits Torre on the mantle of champions, the manager, who Bernie Williams said Wednesday, "has really taken the trouble to know what makes everybody tick."

Something moved Torre to tears on the field. He had won the World Series. He had managed the greatest team in the history of baseball. This didn't do it. As his players rushed to hug him, one by one, they said, "Thank you, Skip," Paul O'Neill to Andy Pettitte and down the line. "Thank you."

"They said it before I said it," Torre marveled. "That knocked me off my stilts a little bit."

There is a touch of sadness to this unforgettable Series triumph. When everyone wakes up this morning, still drunk on the World Series championship, the most amazing Yankee season in history will be a mere memory. Where goes Bernie Williams? And Scott Brosius? Nobody could be sure. For a few fleeting moments, it no longer mattered.

For one night, anyway, they were still Yankees. They were World Champions. As the clock neared midnight, they retreated to the corner of the clubhouse, spraying champagne, hugging, laughing, crying, trying to hold onto a season, a night, a moment, they never wanted to end.

All for one, all for history.

Enjoy the kind of in-depth coverage in this book?

You can have it delivered to your door every day.

To subscribe, call (201) 646-4444

The Story of Life in Northern New Jersey